Canadian Perspectives on

MEN & MASCULINITIES

D1568090

Canadian Perspectives on

MEN & MASCULINITIES
AN INTERDISCIPLINARY READER

Edited by **Jason A. Laker**

OXFORD
UNIVERSITY PRESS

OXFORD
UNIVERSITY PRESS

Oxford University Press is a department of the University of Oxford.
It furthers the University's objective of excellence in research, scholarship, and education by publishing worldwide.
Oxford is a registered trade mark of Oxford University Press in the UK and in certain other countries.

Published in Canada by
Oxford University Press
8 Sampson Mews, Suite 204,
Don Mills, Ontario M3C 0H5 Canada

www.oupcanada.com

Library and Archives Canada Cataloguing in Publication

Canadian perspectives on men & masculinities : an interdisciplinary reader / edited by Jason A. Laker.

Includes index.

ISBN 978-0-19-543924-3

1. Masculinity—Canada. 2. Men—Canada—Identity.
I. Laker, Jason A. II. Title. III. Title: Men and masculinities.

HQ1090.7.C2C35 2011   305.310971   C2011-905407-8

Cover image credits: All photos ©iStockphoto.com
Brass Sign: Kevin Harrin, Barber Shop: Pgiam, Chess Piece: Uyen Le, Male Symbol Sketch: Prill Mediendesign & Fotografie,
Pedestrian Crossing: xyno, Digging: Laurent Nicod, Blue Male Symbols: Luliya Sunagatova, White Directional Sign: Robert van Beets,
Sportsmen Club: Perry Kroll, Men Working: Terry Wilson, Scratchy Sign: Gregory Olsen, Tie and Nametag: Jon Helgason, Blue Door:
diego cervo, Neon Sign: Jim Schemel, Worker Head Sign: sandramo, 'Gentlemen' Sign: Ian Francis, Application Form: Alex, Hiking Trail:
Julie Macpherson, Green Box Sign: Brandon Jennings, Figure with Flag: Jiri Kabele, Emergency Exit: Nick Free

Oxford University Press is committed to our environment.
The pages of this book have been printed on Forest Stewardship Council® certified paper.

Printed and bound in Canada.

1 2 3 4 — 15 14 13 12

Table of Contents

Acknowledgements

I would like to offer my most personal and sincere appreciation to a collection of friends and colleagues who provided immense goodwill and encouragement to me during the development of this text. First and foremost, thank you Leah, my best and smartest and most loving friend and someone who has inexplicably put up with me for my entire adult life. Thank you to our children for ruining my simple thinking about nature versus nurture, and for proving me a hypocrite every time it happens.

Thank you Canada and the city of Kingston, Ontario, for offering me a good and welcoming home as my family and I arrived and settled into a nice life, albeit only for four years. To the people I met in Lethbridge, St. John's, Saskatoon, and points around and in between, your sensibility and humour helped me to understand and explain what is reported in this book.

The Department of Women's Studies at Queen's University, which changed its name to Gender Studies during my time there, was a warm and supportive intellectual and professional home. One can always find a smile, listening ear, or deep conversation there. The Ban Righ Foundation and Centre at Queen's, whose mission is to serve women students of all ages, but most particularly those returning to education after time away, is a model of gracious inclusion and welcome. They exemplify that it is possible to make a space centric to a particular population while welcoming all. No one loses, everyone wins, many receive homemade soup. The hopeful inspiration of their idea is a cornerstone for this book project and what I hope readers will pursue having read it.

My students, both at Queen's and everywhere else, have been wonderful. Some are intensely driven, some wounded and healing, some strong and leading, some gifted, some struggling, some on an even keel and low-key, some dramatic and living out loud, some angry, some difficult, some easy, some wealthy, some poor, some in the middle. All have been absolutely worth the effort.

I would like to thank Kathleen Fletcher of Word Write for her detailed and thoughtful editorial assistance on this project.

I am extremely grateful to Oxford University Press, for suggesting that I develop a proposal, and for taking a chance with me by saying yes. I am particularly grateful to the developmental editors, Allison McDonald and later, Patricia Alexandra Simoes. Their patience, support, and thoughtful suggestions and reflections were grounding and provided a strong rudder for telling the story. When I started the project, I had barely settled in, and could not have imagined that I would be leaving and moving more than 4,500 kilometres away, and they hung in with me at every turn. Thank you so much for giving me this opportunity.

To Michele, Gilles, Pierre, Alex, Emily, Peter, Timothy, Walter, Jane, Karis, Michael, Pauline, Yves, Jane, William, Marty, Siphiwe, Danielle, Sam, James, and Gillian, thank you for being part of this little community and telling your truth. You have been so much fun, and so bright, fascinating, and lovely.

Jason A. Laker
March 2011

Contributors

Emily Bournival	University of Ottawa
William Bridel	Queen's University
Martyn Clark	Queen's University
Peter Cornish	Memorial University of Newfoundland
Gillian Creese	University of British Columbia
Walter S. DeKeseredy	University of Ontario Institute of Technology
Siphiwe I. Dube	Memorial University of Newfoundland
Alexandre Dumas	University of Ottawa
Pauline Greenhill	University of Winnipeg
Danielle Kwan-Lafond	York University
Yves Laberge	Sociologist and consultant based in Quebec City
Michele Landsberg	Activist and journalist based in Toronto
Pierre L'Heureux	University of Montreal
Jason Laker	San José State University
Jane McGaughey	Royal Military College of Canada
Sam McKegney	Queen's University
James McNinch	University of Regina
Timothy A.G. Osachuk	University of Manitoba
Michael A. Robidoux	University of Ottawa
Karis Shearer	McGill University
Jane Tolmie	Queen's University
Gilles Tremblay	Laval University

Introduction

Jason A. Laker

Welcome.

The purpose of this text is to serve as a primer on the topic of men's and masculinities studies. This subject is rarely covered overtly within university and college courses. Many have argued that this is rightly so, that the majority of subject areas privilege men, male voices, and ways of knowing. It was that premise, along with a great deal of struggle over a long period of time that gave rise to feminist theory and women's studies. Let me say from the outset that this book would not have been possible if not for the movements, epistemological and ontological questions, and theoretical models developed by women and by male allies in the form of feminist theory. Much work has been accomplished, at times with significant personal and professional costs, by women in particular who insisted upon and pursued the establishment of women's studies courses and departments, and who continue to study and teach it today. Much work has yet to be done. At the time of this writing, there are declining numbers of women's studies courses and departments, and students interested or perhaps willing to pursue studies in these areas. As such, the amount of metaphorical and perhaps literal real estate allocated to such study is declining. And there are people who would suggest rightly so, with the argument being that the core purpose of women's and feminist studies was to pursue equity, and that this has been achieved; and so now the continued presence of such discourse is actually counterproductive to women, hurtful to men, and thus unnecessarily polarizing.

And those who make that argument point to the significant gains made by girls and women in education, professions, and positions of leadership throughout society. In addition, the media have given a great deal of attention to what is described as a 'boy crisis', the declining levels of engagement and academic success of boys in schools as compared to their female counterparts. This dynamic plays out on college and university campuses, where the proportions of men on campus have shifted from the majority to the minority. The media also talk about a 'crisis of masculinity', citing statistics about men's rates of depression, suicide, health problems, mortality, and unemployment, insinuating or outright stating that men are now oppressed as a group. The two things are often connected in the argument: gains made by girls and women on the one hand, and deficiencies and losses faced by boys and men on the other, framed as cause and effect—women have displaced and emasculated men. For International Women's Day, Margaret Wente (2010) titled her op-ed piece in the *Globe and Mail*, 'For Women in the West, There's No Need to Gripe—The War Has Been Won'. She goes on to say we should '… spare the lamentations for the so-called decline of feminism. The war for women's rights is over. And we won.' Implicit in her framing is that feminism was and is for women, that it has nothing left to do, and presumably it should go sit demurely in the corner or leave altogether. While she reluctantly offers some acknowledgments of some accomplishments by women's movements and feminism, these are shared in her view with science and the Industrial Revolution. In using the term 'we', she collapses all women—at least those in the West—into one monolithic group, speaking on their collective behalf, and doesn't deal with questions of whether all women across intersecting identities of race, class, and sexual orientation, among others, have benefited from these movements. Although she mentions in passing that sexual harassment was common early in her career, she never mentions who was perpetrating it. In commenting on a recent sexual assault case in which the (male) judge questioned the clothing choices of the female victim, she calls him a 'blockhead', choosing a generic criticism without any mention of the implicitly gendered type of violence involved in sexual assaults, and the assumptions about female victims that serve to justify or minimize the violence.

This zero-sum game has the effect of pitting men and women, and their lot in life, against each other. These ways of articulating the issues and their relationships, and implicating or blaming intentions of the women's movement and feminist theory more generally are convenient, but overly simplistic and indulgent, playing fast and loose with assumptions, facts, and implications.

I would, and will, make quite a different argument. That is, the outcomes realized by gender-based reforms in laws, policies, education, health, and other realms is that gender matters, and that gender-informed applications work. In other words, girls' and women's gains are evidence of that, rather than of a war or its winning. It is an invitation and a roadmap for continuing the journey to support boys' and men's personal and academic development, to their benefit and, I believe, simultaneously for (not instead of) women. There is some 'ethical housekeeping' to do though, as well as some cautions and considerations to be incorporated into the work. There are also agendas at play that seek to preserve the either/or positioning of the issues and to situate feminism and its theoretical stances as passé and/or dangerous, and even as damaging to women and their interests. I have observed this many times.

As someone who has taught introductory courses in women's studies, I routinely ask students in the course whether they identify themselves as feminists. It continues to fascinate, though not surprise me that the vast majority of students taking these courses are women, and most of them answer 'no' to that question on the survey. When I share the results with them, I tend to ask what made them answer that way. It is common for these women students to say something to the effect that they like men, which they mean both romantically and more generally as peers—and/or that they are not angry. This tendency for at least some of the students to overtly claim heterosexual status along with providing assurances that they are not angry generally or at men particularly suggests to me that there is still a great deal more work to be done in and by women's and feminist studies, on campuses, and in Canadian society more generally. A number of them also say 'I like being a girl', and refer to purchasing and wearing clothes and makeup. What do all of these comments suggest about our understanding of the meaning and purpose of feminism, who does it, who can do it, and how it's done?

Moreover, what does it mean that these and other women routinely need a plan to safely move from the classroom to their residences? I see them waiting and calling for and offering escorts to each other. I have read their essays discussing experiences of anger, fear, frustration, abandonment, unfairness, violence, and pain, often in relation to men, and sometimes in relation to other women. To be sure, there are also stories of joy, hope, excitement, and humour. Are these not all valuable reasons for creating spaces—academic, social, and metaphorical—for feminist and women's studies? I have also had male students in my courses, some of whom arrived skeptically, others out of curiosity, or because they were searching for something. Some took it as a perceived easy way to fulfill an elective requirement. I welcomed them all, and almost invariably we had some complex, incredible, funny, and poignant moments together, and we all learned something with and from each other. So my position is that feminist and women's studies are critically important. They offer a vocabulary and spaces in which both hidden and overt elements of gender identities can be examined with a view toward understanding how they are constructed, in relation to what, with what costs and benefits, and how current and aspirant lived experiences and relationships may be realized. Women have benefited from this, and, I would argue, so have men. In the latter case, relatively few men have been in the conversation, but this is changing.

I could look no further than something I saw this very morning on a plane while working on this introduction. There was a couple—a man and a woman in this case—with a baby. The man was standing in the aisle rocking the baby to sleep, and kissing him on the head. We live in a time when this is unremarkable, and indeed common. I also watched some sitcoms on the small screen in front of my seat, and the men in those shows were depicted as lecherous predators, clueless buffoons, or aloof jerks, and in instances where they seemed expressive and authentic, they very often faced ridicule and questions about their masculinity and/or sexual orientation. I wonder whether that dad or the media will win the mind, heart, and life of that baby boy. What would it take to tip things one way or another? How will this affect women in his life, the mom, future sisters, friends and partners; and other men?

In my view, this raises an important ethical question. Is there a role for men, masculinities, men's studies, or studies of men or masculinities in women's studies? I will begin my answer by stating my conclusion, which is, 'probably, but only if they know their place'.

When talking or writing about identity issues, it's become customary to identify oneself in detail at the beginning in order to contextualize one's viewpoint transparently, and to make oneself accountable and honest about issues of power embedded in our subject. Fair enough. So, I will begin by disclosing that I identify myself as male, both in terms of my sex and my gender. I initially wrote *I am* male (*instead of I identify myself as male*), but quickly became self-conscious about it. It was a strange experience, because I believe the overwhelming majority of people would agree with me if I simply claimed male status. But, if I declare that I *am* male, am I not implicitly asserting a proprietary claim to a static location, and re-inscribing its position, invigorating its privilege, and strengthening my personal dividends? I wonder if this is exacerbated if I also identify as straight and white? If I told you I am married to a woman and that we have several children, would people wonder why I am in women's studies? Maybe I'm overthinking it. I could just try to be cute and simply say 'I'm a guy.' That usually buys me some slack on the technical details. Of course, if I do that I would be leaving out explicit racial, ethnic, or sexual orientational markings, among other intersections, and I have come to realize there are sometimes consequences for these which disproportionately affect people other than myself.

This is complicated further by the fact that I am a man who has been teaching in and about women's studies for a number of years, and this has resulted in my often being the only women's studies professor to receive kudos and interest from others for doing so. And not once has a student accused me of having a bias or agenda in the classroom—in fact, they have often said things to the effect that they are relieved or delighted to have a 'male perspective'. Once, a student told me that she took my Masculinities class because she had heard enough about feminism and wanted to hear the 'other perspective' (something I gently unpacked with her, revealing the binary framing and the assumption of 'sides' when studying gender). Not once has anyone scrawled the word 'bitch' on my teaching evaluations, as they have on those of some of my female colleagues. And . . . not once have any of my women colleagues ever expressed resentments toward me for any of this. In fact, I have without exception received incredible expressions of welcome and support from them, and expressions of gladness that I am in their department. I have tried really hard not to subject them to my self-consciousness or my internal and annoying liberal guilt about any of this, because I know that would be indulgent of the male privilege I enjoy in women's stud-ies, but I have found ways to let them know I know, and they have let me know they know I know.

Now I am beginning to feel self-conscious because I have been indulging in talk-ing about myself for quite a while. This is something guys, males, and men are often described as doing to a fault, especially by women who are expected and/or coerced to listen, generally at their expense.

I get myself tied into knots about this stuff sometimes. If I am going to be really honest, I need to say that it hurts or scares me sometimes, and it has at times also prevented me from calling out people from marginalized groups for inappropriate or diminishing behaviour directed at me or others because I couldn't come to a decision about the extent to which my privileged position mitigated my view of things, where *my* rights and dignity begin or end. This, I believe is one of the costs of binary fram-ing of identity. We don't create room for ambiguity, nuance, or simply not knowing altogether.

But, much more often this all has been and is a wonderful gift because it has opened me, and it has allowed me to have deeply meaningful and trusting relationships with women, with other men, and with queer and trans people . . . in other words, with people. I am sincerely and tremendously thankful for feminism and women's studies more generally for giving me the language to express myself honestly. My development as a man, as a husband, as a father, as a white person, as a straight person, as an able-bodied person, as a Jew, as a scholar, as a pro-feminist who won't presume to call him-self a feminist or to chime in on whether the department should be called something else, in order not to interfere with women's leadership and claim to defining it, and as a human being (all still in development). All of these parts of myself, separately and together, have been profoundly affected, challenged, and enriched by feminism's tools, permission, and insistence to make identities explicit—to excavate and name them, and to grapple with their meanings and implications. Feminism seems to have done a great deal for women, and I believe it has also done a great deal for men.

This story explains my main reason for coming to believe that masculinities, men's studies, and men's presence in women's studies spaces could be beneficial to women and those spaces. I don't view men's or masculinities studies as fundamentally different from feminist or women's studies, because we use the same lenses, have analogous debates, and are similarly criticized. Even as there are critics who declare feminism obsolete or cancerous, so too are there men's studies voices who believe men have been marginalized and unfairly blamed, to the benefit of women and detriment of men. You are encouraged to read the range of views and come to understand them and your take on the issues. I confess, however, that this particular text is a pro-feminist one. There is neither a demand nor apology in this point, just a transparent claim of stance. What I can say with certainty is that it's very hard to negotiate with a person or people without a shared language, and there is still a lot of negotiating to do.

I should add a point that a colleague made in an article we did on this topic some years ago, published in the journal *Feminist Teacher*. She is the chair of a women's studies department and identifies herself as queer and as someone who is read as very feminine. That is, an all-women's space is not assuredly a 'safe' space, particularly for queer women and women of colour. At the time that she wrote that and I read it, I confess I had been so wrapped up in my own desire to not take away or harm women's safe spaces that I hadn't reflected on the primary assumption that those spaces were, in the absence of men, safe. Even more profound was my coming to accept the notion that I had often been seen to offer women, queer people, and people of colour across genders safe space. That my non-participation in the lateral politics and lateral or internalized oppression gave invitation for people from marginalized identities to let their hair down, so to speak, when alone with me. And my willingness to talk about all these things in front of diverse groups, some of which were predominately male and/or white and/or straight, had also created safety by virtue of using my power in the position of teacher to articulate that expectation and to model a language for achieving it. My self-consciousness and ethical deliberations continue to challenge me regarding claiming this reality, but today at this moment I at least cognitively accept it to be true.

So, as for the implications of thinking and talking about men in women's studies spaces and more importantly the question, Is there a role for men, masculinities, men's studies, or studies of men and masculinities in women's studies? My conclusion: probably, but only if they know their place.

This book arises from these interests, and as such situates men's and masculinities' studies within feminist and gender studies. In other words, we are directing the conceptual and theoretical gaze of feminist theories toward questions of men's lives and gendered identities. This has been a growing subfield, particularly in the United States for several decades, though not as much in Canada.

A couple of years ago, I was visited by a sales representative from Oxford University Press, who hoped I would adopt something from their catalogue. We were discussing a course I was teaching at Queen's University in Kingston, Ontario, 'Masculinities in a Cross-Cultural Context'. I expressed my frustration over the difficulty of finding an appropriate text with a Canadian focus, and my self-consciousness as a newcomer to Canada that my students might not be served well if I didn't locate one. I think it's very important, and a lot more interesting and fun, to learn about a topic by connecting it with familiar and personal experiences. Although there are some Canadian books in the area of gender studies, and even some focusing specifically on some aspect of men and masculinities, none that I could find seemed to provide an introduction to the subject or an overview of perspectives about it.

Her answer was straightforward enough: 'Why don't you write one?' I laughed at first, but then I became quite interested in the idea. I didn't believe I could write one myself, but it seemed to me that I could assemble a collection of colleagues and we could do it together, so that is what I proposed to do. However, this proved to be more difficult than expected. The first problem was that I didn't know very many gender studies people in Canada, no less those who study masculinities. The second problem, which to some extent faces anyone interested in writing about identity, was the question of who and what to include in the hope of being comprehensive.

In terms of finding people to write the chapters, it turned out that I was not alone in believing such a text was needed. Each person approached either agreed to participate or referred me to someone who would. Scholars from several disciplines—history, literature, journalism, religious studies, sociology, psychology, kinesiology, education, and others—responded with enthusiasm and provided a richness to the enterprise for which I am very grateful.

With regard to a desire to be thorough, I conceded early. Readers will appreciate that identity issues are complex, and the prospect of achieving a truly inclusive and ample collection seemed impossible. To be honest, I believe it is impossible, and thus I would not suggest that this text could hope to represent the diversity of voices and debates about the subject.

Rather, I have found it helpful to think of identity research as capturing a series of still photos. Obviously, a snapshot is understood to be a picture of a moment in time as it appeared with the particular angle, light, and equipment, and which the observer found compelling for their own reasons. Similarly, it is important for identity researchers to be transparent about who they are, what they have observed, and why they find it important, and to exercise humility and care in their telling of a story, even more so if the story is not their own. As a reader, you add additional layers of meaning based on your personal history and worldview. Thus you are invited to interact with this text reflectively, not only taking in the material but also considering whether, how, and why it might resonate with or illuminate some element of your life.

As the editor, I am a curator of sorts for the collection. Even as the authors represent multiple disciplines and identities, they share an interest in offering ideas, questions, and understanding with you about how masculinities are developed and understood within a Canadian context. The term 'masculinities' is used in the plural because that more accurately describes the multitude of images, performances, and assumptions found in the world. For that matter, the term 'Canadian' is not a singular notion. To be sure, the text is discussing phenomena encountered within the geographic borders of the Canadian nation found on a world map at this point in time. Beyond that, the rules for what is or is not Canadian are still evolving, contested, and uncertain. Some of the people whose experiences are discussed may be thought of as Canadian by others but may not identify themselves with the term. Some may wish to be called Canadian but find that others do not consider them so. Thus, when we contemplate the question of whether there might be a 'Canadian masculinity' or perhaps several, things become muddled right away. As the editor, I am interested in developing a space for exploration of how these areas might intersect, along with additional identity dimensions, and invite you to participate.

Each chapter begins with a brief editorial introduction and ends with some discussion questions. I attempted to preserve the unique viewpoint of each author and their respective discipline. Given this, you will find that there are a number of different approaches to the subject. In order to offer some coherence and guidance, the text is divided into three sections.

Part I is titled 'Born and Becoming: On Growing Up Male in Canada' and contains chapters that consider how boys and men are taught who they should be, and what might be some positive, negative, or as yet unsure consequences of these mainly unwritten rules. In Chapter 1, activist and journalist Michele Landsberg reflects on her personal experiences and those of members of her family. In my view, we have language to name men's and masculinities' experiences because of women's struggles, movements, and the development of feminist theory and women's studies. Thus, it is apt that the first chapter is written by a woman, and that she approaches the subject in the first person. In Chapter 2, Québécois scholars Gilles Tremblay and Pierre L'Heureux provide an overview of the ways in which masculine identities are socially constructed. The chapter is translated from French to English—given the dominance of Anglophone voices in Canadian scholarship it is meaningful to have leadership in the text from Francophone voices. Since physicality and the body are centrally important elements of masculine role socialization, Dumas and Bournival connect these to men's health in Chapter 3. Cornish and Osachuk follow this by making sense of the tensions between masculine ideals of stoicism and control on the one hand with the human need for authenticity and vulnerability on the other. Finally, in Chapter 5, DeKeseredy takes on an issue that may hit close to home for the reader, which is the aspiration to end abuse and violence toward women on Canadian college and university campuses. Given that this is a course text, it is my hope that you and your peers will be galvanized to create a campus free of violence generally, and particularly a safe one for women.

Part II of the book is titled 'The Nation's Narratives: Men and Masculinity in the Canadian Imaginary'. Here we examine creative and cultural expressions of masculinities found in Canada historically and presently. Collectively, these offer a sense of what might be uniquely Canadian forms of masculinity, their origins and implications. This part begins with Chapter 6, in which Tolmie and Shearer analyze selections from Canadian English-language literature. Since gender is understood to be socially constructed, exploring the works of Canadian authors helps us to capture moments in the process and interrogate questions of power. In Chapter 7, Robidoux provides an analysis of men's hockey in which he introduces the distinctions and interrelationships between the systemic forms and individual experiences of masculinity and power. Television shows and commercials, films, music, and the like are rich locations for understanding how masculinities are reflected, reinforced, and produced in a society. So, in Chapter 8, Greenhill offers a guided tour of both familiar and obscure narratives, helping us to explore them in new ways or making them clearer for study. Following this, in Chapter 9 Laberge engages popular cultural ideas about masculinities in Quebec, arguing that the province is one of several distinct societies within Canada. Such an assertion troubles the question of whether there is a collective or singular Canadian masculinity to be found. In Chapter 10, McGaughey traces British and American influences on Canadian military culture that result in its implied and overt forms of masculinity. Bridel and Clark conclude Part II in Chapter 11 by questioning whether and how sport might act as a bond, tightly connecting men, masculinity, and Canadian identity.

To this point the text is about how and where masculinities are constructed. In Part III, 'Borders and Crossings: Canadian Intersectional Masculinities', the authors extend our understanding by considering how masculinities shape, or are shaped by, other dimensions of identity. Dube opens in Chapter 12 by comparing and contrasting representations of masculinity within several religious traditions found in Canada. Then, in Chapter 13, Kwan-Lafond reminds us that just as gender is socially constructed and contested, so are race and ethnicity. As such, it is important to contemplate how they influence each other, and how we might understand each of them in Canada as a nation that has instituted an official policy of multiculturalism. The complexity of these questions, their history and importance, are next examined by McKegney in Chapter 14 in relation to the diversity of indigenous communities and cultures found in Canada. After this, in Chapter 15 McNinch shares a personal account of growing up as a gay man in Canada, and the difficult and hopeful experiences along the way. For men who began their lives outside of Canada, the experience of entering and establishing one's life in Canada can be formidable and jarring. In Chapter 16, Creese discusses how deskilling, underemployment, and differences in expectations around parenting and spousal roles affect immigrant men, which also helps us to understand Canadian masculinity in new ways. I conclude with a reflection on what has been said by the diverse sets of voices represented in this text, my own experiences and observations as a newcomer to Canada, and an invitation to continue our journey together.

References

Wente, M. 2011. 'For Women in the West, There's No Need to Gripe—The War Has Been Won', *Globe and Mail*, 8 March, A1, A18.

PART I

Born and Becoming
On Growing Up Male in Canada

CHAPTER 1

Activist and journalist Michele Landsberg opens the text with a deeply personal reflection on the messages and experiences that shape masculine role socialization. Storytelling can be a powerful way to convey meaning and analysis of lived experience, and to invite critical analysis of ordinary day-to-day events and interactions that otherwise go unnoticed. Such experiences nonetheless cumulatively shape human perceptions and belief systems, and inform how we co-construct our reality.

In reading her account of being a mother, grandmother, and woman, consider the value of viewing masculinities through women's viewpoints, and how the role of 'other' in this regard offers insights into how we might celebrate, challenge, re-imagine, or incrementally shape our expectations and views on manhood and masculinity. By describing the joys, awkward moments, and challenges of partnering with her daughter in the raising of a baby boy, Landsberg illuminates the ways in which race, sexual orientation, generational differences, and others influence the construction of masculinities.

The narrative style of this essay is useful for comparison to the more technical discussions of later chapters. Although this is an essay rather than a research study, it illustrates how feminist research methods tend to feature human, often first-person, voice and use terms such as 'participants' rather than 'subjects', directly involving those being studied in the interpretation and reporting of results. Empirical research tends to require a strong boundary between researcher and subject, while feminist and other critical identity research tends to blur such boundaries and seeks to preserve the original voice and experience of people involved. Popular distinctions between masculine and feminine ways of knowing and behaving (e.g., dispassionate, rational, and objective vs. empathic, emotional, and attentive) arguably resonate with such methodological approaches. As you read this chapter, consider how you might analyze it if you were interviewing the author, and how that in turn might change the 'findings' of a study.

Cultivating the Human in the Boy

Michele Landsberg

In the late summer of 2002, my daughter and I, carrying her six-month-old son Zev, went shopping for a sun hat on a low-rise street of shops in central Toronto. The store racks, however, had already been picked clean. At length, we pounced on a navy blue round hat with a slightly ruffled brim; a small red bow perched on the crown. We put it on the baby—a perfect fit!—and headed for the checkout.

'Awww, isn't she adorable,' cooed the cashier.

'Thank you,' we smiled, 'he is, but he's a boy.'

A look of horror crossed her face. Snatching the hat from the baby's head, she snapped, 'He can't wear that, it's for a girl!'

We bought the hat anyway and, out on the street, giggled as we tried to parse the hat's innate girliness. The only possible explanation, we decided, was the red bow, red being a distinctive colour and not grimly inexpressive enough for a boy—even a six-month-old baby boy. This was the first distant early warning signal we were to receive about the gender swamp, policed by snapping alligators and poisonous serpents, that lay ahead of us.

I should explain my involvement. My daughter, a human rights lawyer and a lesbian, had decided to have a baby on her own. She left her terrific feminist job at the United Nations in New York and moved back to Toronto so that she could be close to family while raising her child. This was my first grandchild. I had been present at his birth and had been the first to hold him. My role hovered somewhere between *safta* (Hebrew for grandmother) and co-parent; I was shaken and astounded by the power of the love I felt for this magical little boy. After raising my own three—two girls with a boy in between—I did not imagine that I would ever again experience the same intensity of love, fascination, commitment, and sheer unreasoning joy in the existence of another human being. But when the doctor lifted Zev into the world, my heart leaped with wonder and rejoicing.

In many ways, my daughter's singlehood was a blessing in the months ahead. Her entire attention could be devoted to the baby. Family and friends, circling in support, never had to tiptoe warily around the ego needs of a privileged partner. (Ilana's married friends never ceased to complain about having to juggle the painfully conflicting demands of a hungry, tired husband and a hungry, tired baby. Sometimes it also seemed that grandparents and friends maintained a sacred zone of distance around the heterosexual couple, lest they infringe too much on the husband's 'primacy' needs.)

Ilana and I talked at length about the values and ideals that would guide the baby's upbringing. It's safe to say that masculinity never entered our minds as a valuable human trait that we must foster; if anything, we assumed that 'boyness' would emerge naturally enough, without our intervention. Indeed, it was the human, rather than the male, that engaged us most deeply.

Decades earlier, as a young mother, I had been an editor at *Chatelaine*, the national women's magazine then under the editorship of Doris Anderson, a beacon of early feminism to countless Canadian women. Among my duties was the writing of a parenting column, and I was once challenged to define the 'good father' for our readers. I remember sitting at my desk for hours, ploughing through reports, articles, and psychology texts, wrestling with the concepts and rejecting most of them. In the end, I couldn't write the article. I could only describe the 'good parent'; the qualities that made a good father, so far as I could puzzle them out, were exactly the same as those that made the good mother. Although gender distinctions were ironclad at that time, in the early '70s, none of the definitions stood up to scrutiny.[1] If the father, according to the popularized Freudianism of the time, was to bring the external world into the home, represent ethical standards, and stand for authority, how was that different from the mother? The gender distinctions began to crumble into dust the moment you examined them in the light of the changing role of women. Mothers earned money, embodied principled ways of being, and no longer exerted authority by threatening, 'Wait till your father gets home!' Fathers could be as nurturing and tender as mothers.

Now, contemplating the raising of a boy with no father, my daughter and I were confident that we did not need whatever an XY chromosomal presence could provide. In fact, we were both secretly relieved to think that an addiction to televised team sports, not to mention an implicit assumption of male hegemony, would not be present as corrupting role models for this child.

For the first several years, we found it fairly easy to avoid what we thought of as the negative style of masculinity. Zev, as a toddler, was as easily able as his mother had once been to sit peaceably for an hour drawing with markers or dunking his plastic animals into a bowl of water in lengthy make-believe scenarios. He was mesmerized by words and language, listening raptly to endless picture books. His favourite painting was *Starry Night* by van Gogh, and when he was carried outside to see the night sky, he breathed in awe: 'Starry night!' He loved to run in the garden, enjoyed rolling a ball or climbing on monkey bars at the park, and delighted in singing on the swings. By age four he had memorized the lyrics to at least one hundred songs; when his mother bought him a pair of blue, white, and grey budgies, he gazed at their colouring and named them 'Stormy Weather' and 'Cloudy Skies'. He had no guns or weapons of any kind, and had not been provided with Superman pyjamas or hockey player T-shirts. No one could have declared with confidence that he was either female or male. He had no effeminate gestures and no macho postures. He was affectionate, highly verbal, empathetic, exceptionally tender with infants, curious about the world, and eager to learn: a wonderful human being.

Until this point, we were living in the rainbow bubble of our family and my daughter's circle of lesbian friends, many of whom had equally non-stereotyped children. Even before Zev began nursery school, however, I knew that the mainstream world had intensified its gender straitjacketing. I knew this by the monomania of the toy and children's wear departments. It was literally impossible to buy a pair of boy's underpants or pyjamas that were not emblazoned with ferocious superheroes or snarling sports figures brandishing baseball bats or hockey sticks like weapons of aggression. (Did you ever see a cartoon of a sports figure smiling with enjoyment? Why do they always snarl?) Even plastic toddler tableware was strictly gender-segregated. No pink plastic tumbler went princess-less; no blue bowl was unadorned with gender-'appropriate' male cartoon figures. Among commercial icons beamed at children, only Dora the Explorer rose above the insanity. Beloved by preschool boys and girls alike, Dora had the energy, curiosity, boldness, and joy one would wish for any child. But she was alone as an emblem of gender-defying humanity.

In fact, when Zev began nursery school at three and a half, the other boys flinched back from his Dora backpack as though girl-germs might contaminate them. Not a single child in the class—except Zev—deviated from the strict gender guidelines. Every girl had princess tiaras and pink accessories; every boy had macho toys, especially Transformers—weird vehicles that 'transformed' into male killing machines.

It was at this same upper-crust nursery school, populated by a mixture of downtown intelligentsia and BMW-driving financier Masters of the Universe, that we were introduced to the ferocity with which small boys ages four, five, and six (the children in the class ranged from age three to age six) proselytized for maleness. Zev, a sunny, highly sociable child who had been raised to be collaborative, found himself isolated. The boys simply would not befriend a boy without a father and, equally damning, without any aggressive toys—or instincts. The girls, with whom he gladly would have played, were indignant that a boy wanted to join their games.

It was not until the school picnic that I began to understand what we were up against. The picnic was held at an elegant rural horse farm belonging to the parents of a classmate. I watched the children run races and compete at various games (apple-bobbing, sandbag tossing) and began to comprehend. These affluent fathers were exerting almost unbearable pressure on their four- and five-year-old sons to compete aggressively and to win, even to the point where some of them were calling their boys 'Wimps!' or 'Losers!' when they lost a foot race; red-faced with annoyance, they expressed their frustration at the child's lack of effort. The girls were happily playing their own games, while the boys looked anxious and ran wildly about.

Male conditioning begins very early, and the vehemence with which it must be enforced is a measure, to my mind, of how far from natural the 'masculine' is. At first I imagined that the children's insistence on strict gender conformity—amazingly, as strict as it was in my 1940s childhood—sprang from the culture's saturation in commercial stereotypes. Branding every item to be used by a child has become so much the norm that it seems invisible to most consumers. With the rise of Walmart-style offshore mass manufacturing and the gradual loss of diversity in the marketplace, overfamiliar icons and stereotypes are everywhere. ('Common' is the significant word in 'lowest common denominator'.) In turn, the branding has reinforced children's (and parents') perceptions of the vital importance of those gender boundaries. For a brief window of time in the 1970s, as new ideas seeped into the public mind, small boys could cheerfully wear pink T-shirts and long hair. That openness had completely vanished by the 1990s.

But the gender panic had to spring from deeper sources than the mass market. Not since the '60s had I seen so much parental shrugging at the 'inevitable' magnetic attraction between boys and violence, girls and Barbie. 'They're born that way,' even feminist mothers would ruefully confess as their boys died dramatically on the lawn, clutching their throats as they shot each other with toy guns.

Were they? Or was this a culturally induced backlash against the normalization of liberated women and same-sex marriage?

Whatever the motivation, it's clear that the pressure on boys to conform to masculinist stereotypes leads directly to the gender-policing of the schoolyard and the emotional deprivation imposed on boys by themselves and their peers.

If the supposedly universal masculine traits of strength, dominance, rationality, and impassivity were inborn, there would be little need to inculcate them with such hysterical insistence. At school, most of the small boys are passionately asserting their allegiance to one sports team or another long before they've seen these teams in action. Their loyalty to a sports brand is emblematic of their maleness, and their virulent maleness is the magic key to approval by their fathers, who teach them how to be sports fans.

The sociologist Raphaela Best observed long ago how strenuously the boys in a grade one

class denied themselves the affection freely offered by mothers and female teachers in order to prove their 'hardness' to one another.[2] The value of being accepted into the macho boys' inner circle was so superior to all other rewards that the boys in her study were willing to suffer emotional pain and loss to gain that status.

In Canada, the indoctrination into male dominance takes the form of an obligatory worship of ice hockey, the national religion. Although golf is the most popular participatory sport among adults, and soccer is the sport of first choice for schoolchildren, the game of hockey is constantly referred to as synonymous with being Canadian.[3] Sports writers, newscasters, and popular authors tiresomely reiterate their mantra that 'Canada is hockey' or 'Hockey is Canada'. I've always felt a kind of bullying insistence behind that battle cry. What few observers ever point out is that if Canada *is* hockey, females are not Canadian— or they are, at best, second-class citizens. No woman plays in the National Hockey League. No woman commentates on professional hockey on TV. Although there are now women's teams competing and winning at the Olympic level (and even scoring previously unthinkable front-page coverage for their victories), female participation is recent, rare, and underfunded. Even now, in 2011, girls' teams have been excluded from ice time at most Toronto hockey arenas and it took a concerted effort by elected politicians (over furious protest from adult male teams) to force a semblance of equal access.[4] Twenty years ago, when a gifted teenager, Justine Blainey, tried to play on a local boys' team that was more suited to her skill level than the available girls' teams, she was almost universally reviled by male players, coaches, and hockey officials. The Ontario Hockey Association fought her bitterly all the way to the Supreme Court of Canada, where she won her case under the Charter of Rights and Freedoms.[5]

The insistence of organized hockey on keeping women out is revealing. I do believe that hockey is the route to indoctrination in male domination and hegemony for Canadian boys. In asserting the sacred status of a thoroughly male game, and linking this male sport inextricably with bedrock Canadian identity, the exclusionary purpose becomes clear: men own Canada. Whatever progress or accomplishment women may attain in almost every other area of life, this core value, this central religious affiliation, will always belong to men.

The exaltation of hockey, in our increasingly urban, sophisticated, multicultural society, is inexplicable unless this almost desperate male chauvinism lies at the heart of it. Viewed solely on its own merits, the game itself is highly questionable. Violence is its primary aspect. The toothless grins of its uneducated participants are the evidence, as is the constant outbreak of fistfights—one of the most popular elements of the televised games, and a sure draw for the audience. Yet mothers of young boys are expected to rise before dawn, week in and week out in the bitter winter months, and ferry their children to the bleak chill of hockey arenas, where they will learn to play a game that leads a frightening number of them to concussions and potentially permanent brain injuries. An article in the *Canadian Medical Association Journal* brands hockey 'a collision sport', and cites the rising rates of concussions, with their very serious consequences.[6] (One study of players aged 5 to 17 concluded that they suffered 2.8 concussions per 1,000 player-hours of ice hockey, and as high as 6.6 among 'elite amateurs'. It has recently come to light that female players at university level have twice the rate of concussions as their male counterparts.) Neurosurgeons are now studying the brains of dead hockey players to look for signs of the same severe damage recently found in the brains of American football players.[7]

The tough-guy sentimentalists who report on the game insist on glorifying hockey injuries. Ken Dryden and Roy McGregor, muchhonoured player and scribe respectively, wrote in their book *Home Game* that a small-town player's chin 'oozes blood from a scuffle. The knuckles of his bare hands are as raw and swollen as those of the first pioneers who came to work this land.'[8]

The wounds, it seems, are testimony to the player's primal status as an alpha male of the country. The wounds are as noble as the scars borne by aristocratic swordsmen in nineteenth-century German duelling fraternities; they are equivalent to the masculinity-affirming scars of a primitive tribesman. Pain, suffered unflinchingly in pursuit of a puck, is the Canadian badge of manhood.

The revelations of sexual and/or verbal abuse by coaches, and the frequent bitterness of name-calling and racist insult between rival teams, cast a pall of unsavoury loutishness over the whole enterprise. Worse still are the documented patterns of sexual violence, both gang and individual, committed by junior-division hockey players, pampered and bathed as they are in entitlement.[9] In an atmosphere of misogyny, in which every weak or incompetent player is insulted as 'girly' and in which the most sexist terms for females are the common parlance of the locker room, young men are trained by their peers to forego loving relationships in favour of crude sexploitation and contempt. The most talented players are expected to sacrifice post-secondary education and in many cases to spend their adolescence far from families and community. A youth spent in hockey is a training steeped in violence, woman-hatred, callousness, and anti-intellectualism.

I think a case could be made that hockey is destructive to Canada in many and profound ways, spreading a disdain for intelligence and culture, inculcating misogyny and even, astoundingly, legitimizing a form of public racism that is tolerated in no other public pursuit. Don Cherry, the pre-eminent hockey commentator in Canada, is allowed to spout blatantly racist, xenophobic, and womanhating propaganda on CBC, the national public network. In him, hockey culture has spawned

Canada's Rush Limbaugh, and because of the compulsory loyalty of the masses to the game, the CBC is forced to promote and sanctify this semi-literate bombast whose views could surely otherwise land him in trouble with the Human Rights Commission.

Even hockey's adherents do not try to disguise the repugnant nature of the game. Colin Campbell, the NHL's executive vice-president and director of hockey operations (i.e., its disciplinarian) told *The Toronto Star* in 2007 that 'Players are competitive. We sell hate. Our game sells hate. You guys, the media, sell hate . . .'[10]

When pressed as to why organized hockey is seen as so valuable for young manhood, most Canadians will join in a chorus of 'team spirit, comradeship, sharing, sportsmanship, physical skills'. Especially since the gold medal victory of the men's hockey team at the 2010 Vancouver Winter Olympics, hockey has been re-sanctified as the ultimate expression of our national identity, validated now at the highest level as an unassailable good.

The evidence is so clearly contrary to the argument that one must seriously look elsewhere for a truthful explanation. What could lead loving parents to throw their sons to the lions this way? What, in general, is behind the overemphatic gender stereotyping, from colour coding of lunch boxes to the sports we inflict on children? Why do new fathers so often place birth announcements that hail the arrival of a 'new goalie for the Leafs!' or 'linebacker for the CFL!'? Suppose the newborn son, if left to his own devices, grew up to be a lover of ballet?

Sports are seen as the way the male can be made male enough. But science is beginning to show us how little difference is really innate, and brain science, above all, is swiftly erasing the gender certainties of just a few years ago. Most of what we think we know about male and female can be contested.

An interesting example of this involves the human voice. Accustomed as we are to the deeper, 'authoritative' pitch of the male voice, and even inured as we may be to hearing the female voice routinely denigrated as 'shrill', it comes as a shock to learn that these frequencies and pitches are, to some extent, learned—and shaped by cultural norms.[11] In more egalitarian countries, women tend to have voices pitched closer to the timbre of the so-called male voice. In Holland, according to author Anne Karpf, there is not much difference between the male and female voice; in countries of rigid gender hierarchies, like Japan, female voices are pitched very high. In fact, as women in North America have entered the workplace and fought for equality, their voices have deepened significantly in the last half-century.

Remarkably, the cultural conditioning of the voice begins in infancy. Karpf cites experiments in which a 10-month-old baby boy was recorded at 390 Hz when playing with his mother, but dropped to 340 Hz with his father. The same effect was found for a 13-month-old girl (390 Hz with the mother and 290 Hz with the father).

And yet, despite the clear evidence of how much an infant is affected by the voice, actions, gestures, style of play, and expectations of the caregivers, child 'experts' continue to dispense misguided nostrums about the 'hard-wiring' of boys and girls, as though they were small household appliances. I heard a female psychologist speaking on TVO (the public education network in Ontario) with two mothers who expressed their unease at noticing what they thought were 'innate' differences between their male and female children. 'But they're hard-wired!' exclaimed the psychologist in a merry voice. 'You look at your nine-month-old boy, with so much energy! He can't have learned anything by nine months. . . . It's hard-wired!'

As mothers observe their hyperenergetic little boys in the playground, they exchange rueful glances over the heads of the children, noting the male preference for balls, or anything with wheels—for the kinetic over the emotive. We'd like to believe these pronounced differences in play are ineluctable. It lets us off the hook for our own laziness in accepting the prevailing norms of consumerism and socialization. Studies do exist, however, to show that both boys and girls, in infancy, will choose dolls over trucks; it has been suggested that it may be that the preference for wheels kicks in when boys are over the age of two and their different physicality begins to develop. Or, just maybe, we have taught them by then what 'boys really like'.

Our influence over children—in what we glance at, the tone of our voice, our facial expressions, and our instinctive responses—is almost invisible to us. One revealing experiment comes to us from Sweden, where strenuous egalitarian efforts in 'gender pedagogy' have been made since the 1960s, particularly in selected preschools.[12] Researcher Emma Bayne reports that recent accounts of activity in Sweden in both primary and secondary schools reveal the familiar patterns: girls are self-deprecating and develop low self-esteem, while boys are boisterous, talk in class considerably more than girls do, elicit teacher attention more often than girls, engage in more offensive behaviour, dominate in play, and get away with more misbehaviour without reproach than do the girls. In textbooks, girls were expected to be pretty, caring, and compliant, while boys were to be mischievous, brave, and strong.

Yet teachers, especially in the 'gender pedagogy' preschools, were adamant that they treated boys and girls alike, and that any differences must be innate. Researchers then filmed the daily activities in these schools. Teachers were shocked and mortified to see, captured on film, how differently they behaved with boys and girls. Much more verbal communication was used with girls, while boys were given terse orders. Boys' needs were met with such urgency and priority that a term, 'boy panic', was coined to describe the pattern. Another clear pattern was the way in which preschool girls catered to the needs of the boys at lunchtime, serving them food and responding to the boys' grunted, monosyllabic expressions of need. Teachers were stunned to notice in the film how much they had colluded in this gender conditioning. In a class of physical exercise for five-year-olds, for example, one teacher singled out a boy for praise because he had stopped to help another boy. Only later did she realize that the girls had been helping each other all along; this went without notice because it was routinely expected of girls to be caring and helpful.

Some of these schools, awakened to their own biases, began a course of 'compensatory pedagogy', encouraging girls to become more autonomous and boys to develop emotional closeness with others. In one school, for example, teachers noticed that boys had a nickname for their private parts, 'snopp', whereas girls had none, leading to more shame and taboo around female sexuality. The teachers came up with a female equivalent nickname, 'snippa', which was so successfully implemented that it is now incorporated in the Swedish Academy word list.

Gender conditioning goes back to a child's earliest experience. We have seen ample evidence that male and female infants are responded to by their parents and caregivers in dramatically different ways, from birth on. The infant has most certainly learned an encyclopedia of responses and behaviours by the age of nine months, despite the TV psychologist's jolly assumptions—and gender-appropriate behaviour is surely one of the most significant lessons. Numerous studies describe how parents coo sweetly to baby girls, handle them gently, and surround them in soft pastel colours. With baby boys, parents tend to be more physical, tossing them in the air and speaking to them more loudly and less frequently. Their toys are different, the voices that speak to them are different, the physical handling, the clothing, and their surroundings are all dramatically different. One study showed how female infants, faced with a sloping ramp, were just as capable as and even slightly more adventurous in descending the ramp than the baby boys.[13] Their mothers, meanwhile, rated the boys' physical ability to negotiate the ramp within 1 per cent of accuracy—but underrated the girls as much as 9 per cent. We know from classroom experiments how drastically the teacher's expectations can affect the student's performance. How much more severe is the generally lower expectation of parents for their baby girls' physical capability?

Are gender differences hard-wired or acculturated? Can we really assume that infants up to nine months have learned nothing about their proper gender roles?

That a psychologist speaking on a public educational channel can be so oblivious to the accumulated science of infant conditioning is a shock. Apparently, however, such ignorance is as widespread and difficult to eradicate as crabgrass in an Ontario lawn. An entire industry has sprung up in the past 15 years, devoted to fostering the idea of the 'boy crisis'—the educational handicaps faced by boys because of their supposedly innate differences from girls, for whom the educational system is said to be favourably tailored. The boy crisis is deliciously useful to neoconservatives: it works its magic as a counterspell against the witchlike powers of feminism and also has the spectacular ability to make both race and poverty invisible. An alarmist statement about 'boys in crisis' is potent as a thinly veiled threat to the established order of male dominance because if boys are disadvantaged by girls in the education and job markets, the bedrock of the patriarchal family (i.e., male career and pay advantage) will tremble and fall. Ideologues of the right, in particular, have used the invented 'boy crisis' to spectacular effect, influencing entire school systems and effectively body-checking the feminist critique of girls' education.[14]

A common interpretation is that now we have fixed the girl problem, we must rush to ease the supposed suffering of the boys. The complaint about the 'feminization of boys' in the school system has been around for at least 40 years. Dr Daniel Cappon, an assistant professor of psychology at the University of Toronto,

worried early on, in 1970, that women's liberation would be confusing to boys: 'Boys are being led into homosexuality because they can't tell the *difference* between their mother and their father. . . . The modern woman makes both the home and the international markets tick. She is the consumer as well as the controller of personal wealth. . . . At home, the woman rules the roost.' To nail down his point, Dr Cappon quoted a divorced mother who supposedly told him, 'I started to worry when he wanted to shave his legs instead of his face.'[15]

By the late '70s, Dr Cappon had moved on to complaining about girls' accelerated progress in math and science scores: 'The boys have to be better at *something*,' he protested. Later commentators took more care to disguise this naked masculinist concern about 'beating the girls'.

His modern counterparts, popular authors like Leonard Sax and Michael Gurian, have made the various essentialist arguments that boys can't hear as well as girls, or that boys need more room to move around because they have 'less serotonin in their brains'. Lise Eliot, associate professor of neuroscience at Chicago Medical School, pours scorn on these 'Saxisms' as being based on minuscule physical differences that have no measurable or scientifically proven impact on learning styles or capacity. In fact, Eliot says, the argument that boys and girls need different educational experiences because their brains are different is 'patently absurd'.[16]

The Centre for Educational Research and Innovation at the Organization for Economic Co-operation and Development (OECD), which commissioned a thorough study on the latest brain science in 2007, echoed Eliot's conclusion.[17] The idea that different hemispheres of the brain are dominant in boys and girls, leading to learning differences, 'is based on scientific misinterpretation as the two halves of the brain cannot be so clearly separated'. As for other brain differences between males and females, the Centre cites other studies to demonstrate: 'Where differences can be shown to exist, they will be small and based on averages.

The much more important individual variations are such as to rule out being able to know if a young girl, taken at random, will be less capable of learning a particular subject than a young boy taken at random.'

So much for all the talk of hard-wired gender differences. The more astonishing and important truth about our brains is their intense plasticity, and the fact that the brain's abilities go on throughout our lives being shaped and influenced by our activities and environments. 'As you learn something new, the neurons in the brain actually change. They make new connections,' said neuroscientist Jonathan Sharples, of the Institute for Effective Education at England's University of York.[18] What an astonishingly encouraging insight this is, promising almost limitless progress toward true equity. As Lise Eliot stresses in her book *Pink Brain, Blue Brain*, 'the more similar boys' and girls' activities are, the more similar their brains will be.'

During the years of the so-called second wave of feminism, we overcame a widespread reluctance to acknowledge the limitations put on girls' learning. After twenty years of steady change in the educational realm, girls are surging ahead in math and science, an excellent demonstration that girls' supposed inborn limitations were anything but innate. The female inferiority in math and science was proven to be a matter of acculturation, of deliberate discrimination in learning expectations, opportunities, and environments. At this moment of high achievement, educational ideologues on the right are insisting that this is a zero-sum game. If the girls are winning, the boys must be losing. (Shades of Dr Cappon!) But in fact, boys are achieving at higher levels in reading and other subjects than they have in the past[19]—and the fact that they reach slightly lower levels than the girls in reading is likewise nothing new; they always did, no doubt because our culture incites them to and rewards them for excellence in sports but never in reading, a supposedly female pastime. (How

many boys see their fathers read for pleasure? How many boys see their fathers habitually slumped in front of TV sports?) In fact, boys in most schools actively and vocally despise and torment their classmate who is academically gifted.[20] The peer conditioning that, in nursery school, was aimed at excluding non-aggressive boys from the inner circle, intensifies at the secondary level to cast the studious or even intelligent boys to the outer realms of frozen darkness.

Even if girls did surpass boys academically in every subject, how much would it matter when males still earn more than females for the same jobs, and when men are still captains of industry, banks, media, unions, government, medicine, and every other field of human endeavour in which the prize can be rigged in their favour?

In all areas of empathy, of learning, of co-operation and cultural sophistication, it is acculturated boyness that is the problem with boyhood. The boyness that is described as essential and good is nothing more or less than a social construct developed over centuries to favour the ascendancy and supremacy of the male in a now-outmoded social structure. (Team sports, remember, were seen as a glorious tool of the British Empire, to impose the 'rules of civilization' on inferior peoples.)[21] In my family, the qualities we love and nurture in Zev and his little brother Yoav are imagination, curiosity, creativity, musicality, energy, kindness, and empathy. Not one of those is unique to maleness or femaleness.

How discouragingly ironic that the Toronto school system has just this year lent its enormous wealth and influence to a reactionary model of schooling designed to instil yet more boyness[22]—aggression, competitiveness, hardness—in the most disadvantaged boys. The board has been swayed by its new director of education—Chris Spence, an African-Canadian former professional football player—to establish an all-male 'leadership academy' where boys can be encouraged in all those counterproductive traits of male bonding and physical competition. Spence, of all people, ought to know that it is predominantly poor children, boys and girls alike, especially boys and girls of colour, whether black or Aboriginal, who are systemically disadvantaged in the school system. The last thing that boys who are failing educationally need is more boyness, because it is those masculinist traits that most curtail their ability to move forward.

I shudder when I see professional athletes brought in to be 'examples' for boys who are failing. They are role models for an unattainable wealth and privilege, with little experience themselves of literacy or love of learning, and less than average empathy and connection with females. Poor children need strengthened families through better shelter and food, more money and community support for single mothers, more access to the arts, updated and comfortable schools with smaller classes, and intense experiences of adult encouragement, kindness, and commitment. Being shouted at and humiliated by sports coaches may be the most counterintuitive and horrifying of all 'remedies' for boys who are failing.

There is a masculinity worth fostering in our children. It is the same as femininity, and it is called 'human' and humane. It means strength of character to follow one's inner light, a devotion to ethical principles, boldness in following those principles into social and political action, a readiness to be open to relationship and connection, and an embrace of difference and of possibility rather than capitulation to conformity and constraint.

Discussion Questions

1. How would you describe your definition of masculinity?
2. How might women perform and/or help to define masculinity?
3. Do expectations of certain clothing colours or toys being 'for boys' or 'for girls' have any consequences, either positive or negative? Explain your view.
4. In her essay, Landsberg says, 'Sometimes it also seemed that grandparents and friends maintained a sacred zone of distance around the heterosexual couple, lest they infringe too much on the husband's "primacy" needs.' What assumptions about men are implied in this description? How might those be supported or refuted?
5. Landsberg discusses the notion of bringing the world into the home. How does the distinction between domestic and external locations influence the definition of masculinity?
6. The essay makes a distinction between characteristics of being human versus those of being male. What is your view on whether and how such a distinction exists?
7. Do you believe there are 'natural' or preferable distinct roles for men and women? What are the benefits and costs associated with making such distinctions or not doing so?
8. How might being responsible for raising a boy or girl influence your definition of masculinity/ies?
9. Landsberg is critical of the establishment of an all-boys academy in Toronto. Describe your agreement or disagreement with her viewpoint.

Recommended Websites

Boys in education: http://boyseducation.ca

Ontario Ministry of Education: www.edu.gov.
on.ca/eng/curriculum/boysliteracy.html

Curriculum leaders: www.curriculum.edu.au/
leader/issues_in_boys%E2%80%99_
education:_encouraging_broader_
def,12017.html

Maclean's magazine: www.macleans.ca/
education/postsecondary/article.jsp?
content=20060626_129721_129721

Canadian Women's Studies Association: www.
yorku.ca/cwsaacef

Notes

1. 'The account of natural masculinity that has been built up in sociobiology is almost entirely fictional': R.W. Connell, *Maculinities*, 2d ed. (Berkeley, CA: University of California Press, 2005), 47.
2. Raphaela Best, *We've All Got Scars: What Boys and Girls Learn in Elementary School* (Bloomington: Indiana University Press, 1983).
3. 'Study: Participation in Sports', Statistics Canada, *The Daily*, 7 February 2008 (www.statcan.gc.ca).
4. Donovan Vincent, 'Female Teams Get Short Shrift, Survey Shows', *Toronto Star*, 18 November 2009. On 22 February 2010, Toronto City Council voted to centralize control over the allocation of ice time.
5. Hilary A. Findlay, 'From Blainey to Pasternak: Are We Making Progress?' Brock University, Centre for Sport and Law, speaking notes for a research conference, 20–2 May 2008, in which the Blainey Charter case is discussed in the light of the balance between formal and substantive equality analysis.
6. Anthony Marchie and Michael D. Cusimano, 'Bodychecking and Concussions in Ice Hockey: Should Our Youth Pay the Price?', *Canadian Medical Association Journal*, 22 July 2003: 169–80.
7. Anne McIlroy and Haley Mick, 'Toronto Doctor Proposes Brain Bank to Study Hockey Concussions', *Globe and Mail*, 4 December 2009.
8. 'Hockey Concussions Take a Toll'. I am indebted to Randy Starkman, sports reporter, for drawing attention to this example of the Canadian sports ethos in the *Toronto Star*, 23 December 2007.
9. Both Varda Burstyn, in *The Rites of Men: Manhood, Politics and the Culture of Sport* (Toronto: University of Toronto Press, 1999), and Laura Robinson, in *Crossing the Line: Violence and Sexual Assault in Canada's National Sport* (Toronto: McClelland & Stewart, 1998), have documented the link between male team sports and violent norms of male sexual practice.
10. Starkman, 'Hockey Concussions', *Toronto Star*, 23 December 2007.
11. Anne Karpf, *The Human Voice: The Story of a Remarkable Talent* (London: Bloomsbury, 2006).
12. Emma Bayne, 'Gender Pedagogy in Swedish Pre-Schools: An Overview', *Gender Issues*, 26, 2 (2009): .130–40.
13. Cited by Lise Eliot in *Pink Brain, Blue Brain* (Boston: Houghton Mifflin Harcourt, 2009), 66–7.
14. Michael Gurian and Kathy Stevens, 'What Is Happening with Boys in School?', *Teachers College Record*, 2 May 2005 (www.tcrecord.org). 'Boys' and girls' brains are wired differently for living and learning . . .' writes Gurian, claiming that schools are 'set up' to better fit the female brain.
15. Dr Daniel Cappon, 'The Freelance Star', 19 January 1971.
16. See Lise Eliot, *Pink Brain, Blue Brain* (Boston: Houghton Mifflin Harcourt, 2009).
17. *Understanding the Brain:The Birth of a Learning Science* (Paris: OECD, 2007).
18. Alanna Mitchell, 'The Three Rs and Neuroscience: A Love Story', *Toronto Star*, 1 November 2009.
19. Sara Mead, 'The Evidence Suggests Otherwise: The Truth About Boys and Girls' (Washington: Education Sector, June 2006, www.education sector.org).
20. Wayne Martino, 'Mucking Around in Class', *Canadian Journal of Education*, 25, 2 (2000): 102–12.
21. Dean Allen, 'South African Cricket, Imperial Cricketers and Imperial Expansion', *International Journal of the History of Sport*, 25, 4 (March 2008): 443–71.
22. *Toronto Star*, 'Boys-Only Grade School Proposed for Toronto', 21 October 2009.

CHAPTER 2

Tremblay and L'Heureux introduce theoretical and conceptual terms and frameworks that underpin identity research in general, and gender and masculinity research in particular. They especially draw upon psychoanalysis, social learning theory, and crisis of masculinity theory to explain the construction of masculinity and role socialization. This chapter lays the foundation for later chapters and for greater understanding of the scholarly study of men and masculinities more generally. Consider how developing a command of tools, language, and theories from multiple disciplines helps the reader to approach material with breadth and depth of interpretation, and build new ideas and research. As well, this methodological knowledge can help to more deeply interpret narratives such as the one Landsberg offered earlier, or a story from your own life or that of a friend. It allows us to name experiences more precisely—and in turn to draw new levels of insight into our own lives and life in general. This chapter may challenge you to think about your life, experiences, and relationships in new or perhaps more critical ways. This is common in the study of identity because, after all, it is the study of our lives as humans.

When reading or researching social identities, it is important to develop an ability to listen to and consider experiences in a person's own words even as you use academic skills to discern themes and to place what you are reading or observing within a context. In this chapter, the authors explain the development of masculine identity from several disciplinary perspectives, and they contemplate those most relevant to the Quebec context. After reading the chapter, it will be interesting to note whether you believe they have described masculine identity in a manner that is confined to one region, culture, or nation, or more globally. This point also offers a preview of the idea of intersecting identities (in this case, how masculinities and Québécois identities might interplay to form a hybrid identity or perhaps just a tightly coupled pair of identities), to be explored in more detail later in the text.

The Genesis of the Construction of the Male Identity

Gilles Tremblay and Pierre L'Heureux

This chapter focuses on the process of socialization and construction of identity from various theoretical perspectives, but primarily those of psychoanalysis, social learning theory, and crisis of masculinity theory.[1] It addresses the basic concepts regarding the difference between gender and sex, the main steps along the path of constructing the male identity (at key ages), gender role constraints and their effects, especially with regard to triple dissociation, and shame as the dominant emotion. It is based on the literature dealing with these issues that originates largely in the United States, Canada, Europe, and Australia. It also incorporates some data from research conducted in Quebec on men's physical and mental health.

So what does it mean to be a man? This question seems very simple and yet it remains difficult to find an answer when attempting to look beyond the obvious physical attributes. In his doctoral research among young male athletes, Lajeunesse (2007) reported that almost all participants had the same reaction when they were asked: 'According to you, what does it mean to be a man?' Most of the athletes looked around, devoid of any accurate description, seemingly perplexed. A similar response was encountered during the doctoral research of Roy (2008) on men exhibiting violent behaviour. What is it then that characterizes the social group known as 'men'? Judging by their reactions, to define a man in Quebec seems difficult to do in this day and age.

Moreover, not all men are identical. In fact, there are multiple ways to be a man just as there are multiple ways to be a woman. As such, this chapter does not aim to systematically revisit the many explanatory theories that exist; it proposes instead a synthesis, a singular understanding of the wide-ranging studies on the genesis of the construction of the male identity. So much has been written on the subject in fields as diverse as psychology, sociology, literature, history, anthropology, medicine, and many others that a truly comprehensive synthesis would be impossible. We will instead focus on material that seems most relevant to understanding the construction of boys and men in Quebec.

In sociology, masculinity is often discussed in terms of socialization and the power relations between men and women and among men themselves, especially in the writings of Connell (1995/2000), Hearn and Morgan (1990), and others. These texts are particularly useful for understanding the structural paradigms that influence the practice of masculinity but are somewhat lacking when it comes to understanding how people integrate, modify, or reject these social demands. Further, a very different body of literature is found in the field of psychology, often under the heading of identity formation. This perspective provides some very productive means of explaining what

takes place within the individual but often fails to integrate the individual into the social context or to a broader extent than only the immediate environment in which the individual or their family find themselves. This is particularly true of psychoanalysis. Some researchers have attempted to merge these two aspects, specifically by gaining an understanding of the process of male socialization, which gives the individual an active role, primarily found in the writings of Seidler (2006) and Kaufmann (2007). According to them, the social reformulates the identity, which in turn reformulates the social. Therefore, socialization (that which I am offered) and identity (that which I do) represent two sides of the same building block when it comes to the construction of identity. This chapter draws on this perspective.

We will first try to define what we mean by *identity*, a concept very often bypassed in many discussions. We will then discuss the process of identity formation. This is followed by a brief discussion of the concept of gender role stereotypes to explain how different theoretical perspectives agree that this process of identity formation is especially complex for boys. Subsequently, the major influences on the socialization experiences of boys and men will be identified, including what we call the triple dissociation and shame as being the dominant emotion; then the effects on men's help-seeking actions will be addressed. Finally, we conclude by detailing the positive aspects of traditional masculinity that can be mobilized during intervention practices.

What Is Identity?

But what is meant by identity? A great deal of writing has been devoted to the notion of identity. However, the definition of self or identity raises certain questions (Breakwell, 1983; L'Écuyer, 1978). Authors sometimes use the same term with different meanings or use different words when referring to what is effectively the same reality. The concept of identity is sometimes used synonymously with that of self, self-concept, self-image, self-awareness, etc. (Archer, 1992; Breakwell, 1983; Byrne, 1996; Waterman, 1988; Wylie, 1974; 1989). More often, the term 'self-concept' is used as the cognitive representation of self. On the contrary, the word 'identity' encompasses a broader vision of the self in a social context. It includes not only the cognitive representation of self, but also the ability to compare oneself as both similar and different to significant others, and make choices regarding the most important areas of one's life.

Erikson (1957/1972), in his conceptualization of identity, considered it to represent the basic personality that continues through time. Berry (1987) adds to this by claiming that it is the experience of oneself as being unique, the sense of cohesion. The identity would represent a construct (Kelly, 1955)—a synthesis of that which the individual has been, is (actual self), and will be or wishes to become (expected self). Such a combination would also correspond to this core personality's remaining the same in the face of the different roles played by the individual (Mead, 1934). Following up on the thoughts of Rogers, L'Écuyer (1978) considers that it is a configuration organized from perceptions of themselves brought out by the individuals' awareness of their personal characteristics. This configuration would lead to the selection of beliefs, values, and norms, and from that, to a profile of behaviours and attitudes that would be drawn up and then incorporated into their various dimensions of life. It would act as a self-regulating system whereby the individuals would select those behaviours that they would deem appropriate (Adams and Marshall, 1996).

The Components of Identity

It is generally accepted that identity contains different elements, all interconnected in a dialectical dynamism. We would find, among others, an objective aspect (ego) as well as a subjective one (self). Identity is perceived both as a structure, a process (Bourne, 1978; L'Écuyer, 1978) and as a form of behaviour (Marcia, 1993). Some authors also distinguish between social identity and personal identity, although others consider that the self is always social and that the distinction between the two appears only in conflicts of values and for control of behaviour (Breakwell, 1983). In fact, we cannot develop a personal identity without taking into account other people's perceptions of ourselves, of the interpretation that is made from this, and the image we want to project toward others. For his part, Mead (1934) speaks of the I and Me, with the I observing the Me and documenting his or her movements (Herman, Kempen, and Van Loon, 1992). These authors consider that one can also perceive the I as the writer and the Me as the actor, and thus consider the foundation of an internal dialogue that would be complemented by the many imaginary dialogues with the internalized social network that leaves its mark on personality. It is the self both as subject and object described by James (1890/1946), who becomes thereby knowing and known, evaluator and evaluated. Therefore, identity would be organized by and would organize future perceptions and bring itself to facing choices that confirm (Combs, Avila, and Purkey, 1979) and perhaps modify it. It is also seen as the product and producer of a personal history. There would be a dialectic exchange between the real self and the ideal self, wherein the construction of identity would aim for a balance between the two (Erikson, 1957/1972).

We must consider that the self would also include the physical, with the body thus representing the signifier and the signified (Birouste, 1980), a reality and a metaphor (Krueger, 1989). The self-concept would thus be a set of intrinsic and comparative properties that we apply to ourselves and in this way would differ from self-esteem—in other words, appreciation of the qualities that we see in ourselves (Kagan, 1989). We therefore begin to appreciate the importance that can be attributed to whether one is born with the body of a man or that of a woman.

Erikson (1957/1972) considers that the identity represents a synthesis and can be viewed from a developmental point of view as being in both accordance with and breaking away from previous identifications. It is also multidimensional in that it incorporates the main areas of life. In fact, whenever someone speaks of himself with the words 'I am . . .', he is defining a part of his identity. It thus includes

- the image of the body (I am tall or short, fat or thin, etc.);
- choices in ideological fields, including politics (I am a Liberal, Sovereignist, Conservative), lifestyle (I'm punk, nerd, hippie), career (I'm a doctor, worker, garbage man), religion (I'm agnostic, Catholic, Muslim);
- choices in interpersonal areas, including friendships (I am a member of gang X), love (I'm a big softy), recreation/sports (I am a hockey player, soccer player), gender role (I'm 'very masculine', a 'metrosexual', 'übersexual'), and sexuality (I define myself as 'straight', 'bi', 'gay');
- the ethno-cultural components (I am a Quebecer, Chinese);
- the behaviours (I'm an offender, a wise guy).

In short, the global identity represents a synthesis of this constellation of specific dimensions. Moreover, there may be a lag between different dimensions in the process of identity construction (Van der Werff, 1990). For example, a person may experience a major conflict between the definition of oneself as a member of a religious group and his or her sexual orientation. One could take as another example of an internal conflict in terms of identity that of a man with a collection of rigid gender roles who finds himself employed in a profession mainly pursued by women.

Identity as a Process

Identity formation is the process by which an individual responds to a fundamental question: Who am I and where am I going? (Martin, 1985). This process, according to proponents of Eriksonnian theory, involves engaging with and questioning those issues most vital to the attainment of a self-organized representation of oneself. It would imply a process that lasts a lifetime (Erikson, 1957/1972) within which, according to Kegan (1982), the boundaries between self and others become more structured, are lost, and reformed. It is a process that begins early in the life of a child. According to Winnicott (1974), an infant develops an image of himself in terms of his relationship with his environment. For Erikson, at times some issues become more important and must be resolved to move on to the next stage in the process. This then leads to an imbalance (Eccles, 1987) or crisis, the resolution of which brings about a balance or truce.

Specifically, there are two key moments that need to be considered in the construction of a male identity. A significant first step occurs around the age of two during toilet training (Roïphe and Galenson, 1981). Children learn to pee standing up like Dad or seated like Mom according to their gender. They develop a sense of belonging to one sex and being different from the other sex (Money and Ehrhardt, 1972; Nungesser, 1983; Shively and De Cecco, 1977; Tyson, 1986)—in the case that concerns us, that of being a boy and not a girl. This is called sexual identity (male/female). Then, later, he reorients his expectations, standards, and social values, both expressed and unspoken, to those associated with his sex, what is called gender and is usually interpreted as masculinity and femininity. Gender is that which is socially recognized as being feminine or masculine. More precisely, gender refers to the cultural demands of a society, which exaggerate the real and imaginary aspects of sex, coming to identify ways of being, acting, and thinking and feelings that are more appropriate for men or women (Blos, 1988; Mackie, 1991; Pleck, 1981; 1995). It is therefore understandable that a child is not born, but rather becomes, a girl or a boy (Chiland, 1988; De Beauvoir, 1949).

Gender differentiation begins to take shape very early on—in fact from the conception of the child. Parents from the outset are carriers of a range of expectations for their future baby based on his or her expected sex. These expectations and models are advocated by parents and relatives, then by society through the media, schools, etc., and influence the formation of the gender role identity. The individual is constructed from what others perceive him or her to be (Breakwell, 1983). Throughout life, these social representations of gender have a major impact on social relations of individuals and in different spheres of human activity (Tyson, 1986). It is at adolescence, considered by Erikson (1957/1972) as a pivotal period of identity formation, that this representation becomes more structured, more stereotyped even.

Stereotypes and Gender Role Construction

What is a stereotype? A stereotype is a general predetermined pattern, a sort of standard or ideal type. Specifically, it is 'a set of preconceived beliefs that are made by individuals or communities based not on factual observations, but rather on prejudice and community values' (Elbaz, 2001: 18). The stereotype is thus an oversimplification of our perception that gives rise to clichés by which we are able to categorize people. Note that to become a social stereotype, a belief must be shared by several people at the core of a social group. According to Elbaz, its social function is often to justify hierarchical relations. Thus, like all generalizations, gender stereotypes do not account for differences and individual characteristics. This form of stereotyping is a powerful social force which is difficult to break down. It participates at some level in the legitimization and perpetuation of power relationships between men and women as well as among men (Connell, 1995/2005).

Given the impact of gender stereotypes, it is important to spend time identifying those that are the most common. A study conducted in 25 countries in 1982 by Williams and Best (in Mackie, 1991) observed that some adjectives are attributed more to women, while others are assigned primarily to men. Figures 2.1 and 2.2 give some examples.

Within current social trends, some have invested in the idea that we should view and redefine masculinity and femininity as fundamentally distinct from one another (Bly, 1990; Lee 1993). Others support the notion that everyone bears a share of the female and male part within himself or herself (Corneau, 1989; Lacroix, 1983). From a humanistic and constructivist perspective, we can say that these classes take greater account of social conditioning than anything naturally inherent to either

Figure 2.1 Adjectives Attributed to Women

caring	charming
affectionate	curious
anxious	dependent
attractive	dreamy
emotional	fearful
submissive	sensitive
sexy	sweet
sentimental	chatty

Figure 2.2 Adjectives Attributed to Men

adventurous	aggressive
arrogant	ambitious
courageous	cruel
dominant	logical
nasty	rude
strong	lazy
opportunistic	pragmatic
independent	rational

men or women. Moreover, there are multiple ways to express one's masculinity just as there are thousands of ways to express one's femininity (Tremblay and L'Heureux, 2002; 2005).

In fact, not all men are alike, just as not all women are alike. Moreover, the male identity is not inherent to all male individuals and female identity is not restricted merely to females. These feminine and masculine identities are figments of social creation (Wilcox and Forrest, 1992) or even 'continuous fictions', as Weeks (1991) puts it. Masculinity and femininity remain the products of culture and history (Kelly, 1955). One has only to observe how social norms in Quebec on this matter have changed considerably over the past thirty years: without even mentioning the commercial aspects, one can point to the increased participation of women in the labour market, the emphasis on involving men in childcare, the proliferation of male cosmetic products, etc. Thus, it is important to take into account the fluidity of masculine and feminine representations in one person or a given group, highlighting the diversity of masculinities and femininities (Connell, 1995/2005), which are born out of the complex experiences of men and women.

The Complexity of Identity Formation in Boys

It seems very much the case that even with the advent of feminism and the questioning of traditional roles, the gender role identity seems more complex to define than before, particularly for men, so much so that several authors refer to a crisis of masculinity (Ethier, 1995; Goldberg 1979; 1981; 1990; Haddad, 1993; Hearn and Morgan, 1990; Pleck, 1981; Silver, 1981). Thus, psychoanalysts, social learning theorists, and proponents of the masculinity crisis theory all insist on the great vulnerability of boys during the process of identity formation. Let us then inspect the main arguments that demonstrate the high vulnerability of boys in this area.

Primarily Maternal Identifications, Attachment to the Father, and Male Gender Role Models

Chodorow (1978), a feminist and psychoanalyst, was probably one of the first to demonstrate that to be represented as male, the boy must cease identifying with his mother, to no longer resemble her, not only to separate himself from her (as a girl) but also to rid himself of any quality of his mother in him (Klein, 1984; Roïphe and Galenson, 1981; Stoller, 1980). This rejection of those primary maternal identifications would necessarily entail a process of mourning (Bégouin-Guignard, 1988) and rupture (Marcelli, 1989), something particularly emotionally difficult for the boy. This process would be facilitated, however, if the father is engaged in his paternal role. The boy, therefore, would turn to his father and identify with him. He would then experience a period of intense attachment to his father (Blos, 1988). However, when the father is emotionally or physically unavailable, the situation would become complicated. Osherson (1986) shows how mothers who are the sole caregivers of the child, in the absence of assistance from the father, can sometimes develop an emotional reaction to this in the presence of the child, unspoken yet all the while present in the emotional life of the family, referred to by Osherson as a 'silent internal anger'. Presumably this would be particularly true of separated families, especially those continuing to experience conflict between the former spouses. Thus, the boy finds himself in a predicament: how can he identify with this man, his father, who hurts the person he loves most in the world, his mother? This leaves him alone, without a male reference, to define himself only in the negative: not to be like his mother, in order to construct a masculine identity. This lack of a paternal role model is also exacerbated by the fact that we find very few men involved in primary childcare services (nurseries, kindergartens, and primary schools), where they could potentially serve as role models. We now understand that we can observe this tendency to 'avoid the feminine' even in more traditional adult males (McCreary, 1994; O'Neil and Egan, 1992; O'Neil et al., 1986). For many writers (Brannon, 1985; Chodorow, 1978; O'Neil, 1981), this principle of 'antifeminity' or 'avoiding the feminine in oneself' is the central guiding principle for construction of the male identity in the Western context as we know it (Kilmartin, 2007). With this in mind, to obtain recognition of their identity and to conform to the male gender role, men wishing to get closer to the dominant model should erase any behaviour perceived as being associated with the female gender, including the expression of emotions (Levant, 2001; O'Neil, Good, and Holmes, 1995). These men learn to restrain any tendency toward being gentle and to repress expression of their vulnerability (Levant and Pollack, 1995).

Moreover, according to several authors, boys and men would face a male model that would be devalued, fallen, wounded (Hurstel and Delaisi de Parseval, 1990). According to some psychoanalysts, male idols replace the father who is physically or emotionally unavailable (Esman, 1988; Gagey, 1988). The teenagers then would develop compensatory mechanisms to hide the longing for a father. Penot (1988), a French psychoanalyst, goes further by suggesting that boys who are unable to recapture and articulate enough fragments of events associated with their father figure come to call into question their very existence. They would then tend to exhibit masculine traits and exaggerated caricatures (Ullian, 1981) or to adopt destructive means (Erikson, 1957/1972) in order to find some sort of temporary comfort against the feeling of loss of identity, attempting to establish, in an exaggerated fashion, a clear and stable male gender identity.

Overvaluing Autonomy in the Socialization of Boys

Several authors (Klein, 1984; Pollack, 1998) show that the educational practices of fathers

and mothers tend to be different depending on whether they are dealing with a boy or girl. Generally, these practices promote greater attachment with girls and autonomy with boys. As a caricature, we could take the typical example of when a young child is injured and rushes to his parents; where parents would tend to hug a girl until she stops crying, with a boy the usual habit is merely to 'kiss it better' and return him to play. Yet we know from the attachment theory (Bowlby, 1988) that to develop basic security, at first a child needs a secure physical attachment that allows him subsequently to become independent and explore the world around him. This process of attachment-autonomy continues throughout life, the attachment being the central means to get security to become independent. This is particularly true during puberty when young people reconnect with their parents before distancing themselves during adolescence so that the group of peers becomes a new source of commitment (Cooper and Grotevant, 1987; Kamptner, 1988; Kroger, 1989; Lempers and Lempers-Clark, 1992; Willemsen and Waterman, 1991). However, these authors demonstrate that even at this stage of life, parents are detached with their sons and much less so with their daughters. To this end, Pollack (1998) demonstrates that by pushing boys too quickly toward autonomy, they develop what Winnicott (1974) labels a 'false self', wanting to do all by themselves, pretending to be independent but, in secret, retaining a great insecurity that will persist throughout their life as an ever-present latent anxiety.

Male Adolescents and Puberty

We cannot move on without saying a word about puberty, an important stage of development in terms of personal psychology. On average, for girls in Western countries, their first menstruation occurs at the age of 11.5 (Saucier and Marquette, 1985). After a year they have reached full physical maturity, including the onset of secondary sexual characteristics. This means that at only 12.5 years old, most girls have become fully fledged women, at least physiologically. In contrast, among boys, on average, puberty begins around a little before 12 years old with the enlargement of the testes and ends with the appearance of facial hair at around 15 (Anawi, 2007). This is to say, therefore, that very rapidly they experience a 'delay' of about two years compared to girls. In terms of maturity, that imbalance will not be redressed before the end of adolescence, at around 20 to 21 years of age. However, boys tend to experience significant hormonal surges, particularly between the ages of 12 and 14, with testosterone levels increasing from an average of between 0.5 and 1.04 nmol/L before puberty (until now similar to those in girls) and peaking to levels as high as 21.48 nmol/L at 13 to 14 years (Davis, 2008). These hormonal surges typically bring on frequent erections, sometimes for extended periods of minutes or even hours, at any time of the day or night, without the young person comprehending exactly what is happening to him. An American study (Stein and Whisnant Reiser, 1994) also noted that it is at about the age of 12.9 years that the first nocturnal ejaculation occurs in Caucasian middle-class boys. According to the authors, even if this event represents a very significant moment in the lives of teenagers, it remains socially invisible. Thus, few boys talk about it to others and most parents never discuss the matter with their sons (Frankel, 2002). The taboo surrounding this episode somehow confirms the fact that a boy must fend for himself despite the emotional upheavals he has to live through.

Conformity to Male Gender Role Models

Studies that examine the social messages put out by TV commercials show that male portrayals alternate between the silly, stupid, and foolhardy and the violent, domineering, and macho (Nathanson and Young, 2001). Thus, to mock the 'ordinary' man becomes a good way to promote the selling of a product, a negative image that Nathanson and Young have labelled

as 'misandry', or contempt of men. It is the same in films, especially when we watch action movies, the most popular type of film. To this end, the study Duret (1999) conducted in the late nineties in France, with young men and women's representations of masculinity, proved very revealing. Of all those surveyed—young adults, men, and women—most identified Bruce Willis as being the most representative of masculinity, especially in the movie *Die Hard*. In the film, he plays a 'battered and bruised hero' ready to fight at any time, in spite of numerous injuries. In short, the boys thus find themselves faced with a paradox: on the one hand, we criticize vehemently the traditional macho model (with good reasons) and on the other we suggest that they must identify with this if they do not want to feel silly, stupid, unable to properly put up a shelf or cook an egg. These problems of identity, associated with lack of clearly defined male-gender roles, would foster, according to Dulac (1990), a socialization in boys characterized by anxiety much more than for girls.

In addition, US studies suggest that changes in recent years ensure that Western societies are more open to breaking the stereotypes associated with female gender to include qualifiers previously more associated with men. However, these changes have not affected the social expectations (of men and women) with regard to masculinity, which still remains relatively stereotyped (Hort, Fagot, and Driver Leinbach, 1990). As a result, boys and men seem more bound by gender role stereotypes than girls and women (Klein, 1984; Maccoby, 1987; Nungesser, 1983) even though these stereotypes (especially that of a man being macho) have been broadly criticized over the past thirty years. Even in adulthood, violation of gender role stereotypes would lead, as Pleck (1981) portrayed, to a social condemnation and more severe psychological consequences for men than for women. It also seems that peer pressure is even greater among adolescents (Galambos, Almeida, and Patersen,

1990; Rust and McCraw, 1984), although flexibility concerning gender stereotypes can be modified by the social environment of the youth (Alfieri, Ruble, and Higgins, 1996; Katz and Ksansnak, 1994).

Gender Role Strain and Conflicts

Thus, the social construct of 'maleness' is considered more stereotyped in its form than that of 'femaleness' (Hort, Fagot, and Driver Leinbach, 1990) and is much less rooted in men than femininity is in women (Stoller, 1980). In fact, compared to that of girls, all the socialization of boys would be more restrictive and based on expectation formulated in negative terms (for example, 'Men do not cry') (Dulac, 1990). Moreover, tensions in gender roles (gender role strain) occur when individuals internalize social norms about gender ideals, even if they are contradictory, inaccessible, or incompatible with what they really think (O'Neil et al., 1986; 1995). According to several authors (Mahalik et al., 1998; O'Neil, 1990; O'Neil and Good, 1997), gender role conflicts may appear in situational contexts where the person deviates or violates the norms of gender roles; experiences differences between the concepts of their real and ideal self, based on gender role stereotypes; tries or fails to meet gender role standards of masculinity; puts himself down, restricts himself, or violates his own rights to live up to socially accepted gender roles; suffers the oppression, restriction, or violation of his own rights by others; or puts down, restricts, or violates the rights of others to fit in with gender role stereotypes. Those who do not meet these standards of 'masculinity' are encouraged to see themselves as inferior and feel devalued (Connell, 1995/2005; Pleck, 1995). The tensions of gender role, and the gender role conflicts that result, have significant consequences. Thus, every boy/man is pushed into having to come up with strategies in order to comply with, respond to, or oppose the social models conveyed.

The fragility of this process of identity formation in men would require daily attention

according to Brittan (1989). It is as if he has to make himself deserving of his title of man, and therefore, this title can be lost at any time (Kimmel and Messner, 1998). Not feeling accepted in their masculinity, some boys and men chronically doubt their masculinity and feel they must prove to others, and undoubtedly to themselves first of all, that they are 'real men'. Usually this means trying to stick as closely as possible to the dominant model of masculinity, one that depends heavily on gender role stereotype, what Connell (1995) refers to as 'hegemonic masculinity' and which dominates other forms of masculinities.

The Effects of Male-Gender Socialization

Among men, the success of gender socialization depends on the extent of affinity for or distancing from the constraints of the traditional model of masculinity. In fact, socialization among boys, because it is more stereotyped than among girls, may limit or slow their overall social adjustment; the socialization process has been shown to be most effective among boys and girls who are more androgynous, that is to say, displaying a high degree of both masculinity and femininity (Dusek, 1987; Glazer and Dusek, 1985). Research based on Bem's model (1974) showed that masculinity helps in the formation of an ideological identity while femininity contributes to the development of an interpersonal identity (Lamke and Peyton, 1988), and that men who purvey a more mature ego tend to attain a more appropriate balance between these two extremes of stereotypes (Block, 1984).

Thus, the principle of 'avoiding feminity', as has been well demonstrated empirically (McCreary, 1994; O'Neil and Egan, 1992; O'Neil et al., 1986), influences interactions with women. The more a man adheres to this principle, the more he tends to develop an attitude of seduction and domination toward women. Avoiding feminity involves also staying away from anything that might look like homosexuality and, in so doing, more easily demonstrating homophobia. As well as establishing a hierarchy among men, homophobia (Welzer-Lang, 1994) often leads to men avoiding being affectionate or intimate with one another and thereby reinforces the emotional isolation often present.[2] In the Quebec Social and Health Survey, twice as many men as women reported having no confidant (Tremblay et al., 2005) and when they did have one, more often than not that person was their female partner (Miller, 1984). We can appreciate the profound loneliness that many men experience after a separation or divorce.

Moreover, if the masculine identity can be earned, it can also be lost. This no longer involves just homophobia but also heterosexism[3] and ableism.[4] Overall, being gay, being vulnerable, being sick, and just being different from the male stereotype is to run the risk of being excluded from holding the title of man, to be considered a sub-human (Tremblay, 2000). Thus, some seek to prove their masculinity by working like crazy, overdoing sports, including extreme sports, overusing alcohol or drugs, or physical force, or worse, through violence, etc.

This socialization also has the effect of sustaining a deep sense of insecurity or anxiety. The more a man tries to cling to the constraints of traditional masculinity, the more he tends to hide his vulnerabilities and avoid compliant behaviour in an attempt to demonstrate his independence at all costs (Kilmartin, 2007; Pollack, 1998), including asking for help when he needs it (Dulac, 1997; 2001). It also means having troubles with intimacy. As shown by Erikson (1957/1972), genuine intimacy is possible only when one has developed a strong sense of personal identity. In this process in which men wrestle with their identity, intimacy, the next phase according to Erikson, becomes problematic.

One must consider also that, in adulthood, the integration of traditional male gender roles has had very negative physical and psychological impacts on men (Brooks-Harris, Heesacker, and Maji-Millan, 1996). The

empirical research undertaken since the 1990s indicates that these traditional men (those who endorse more stereotyped gender roles) perceive more pressure to succeed, to be powerful and competitive (Mintz and Mahalik, 1996). These studies indicate that they express their emotions very little and experience a high level of psychological distress (Good et al., 2004; Tremblay et al., 2007) and a higher level of suicide risk (Houle, 2005). Moreover, the level of stress linked to gender role constraints is linked to aggression and anger, behaviours that are risky to one's health (Eisler, Skidmore, and Ward, 1988), patterns of maladaptive coping (Eisler and Blalock, 1991), and the use of violence against women (O'Neil and Egan, 1992). Hayes and Mahalik (2000) cite several authors who found that male gender role conflicts are associated with behavioural problems, loss of sense of well-being, low self-esteem, difficulties in displaying intimacy, anxiety, depressive disorders, and alcohol abuse. Men with greater gender role conflicts are less likely to seek psychological help than other men. Among men who sought help, gender role conflicts would allow prediction of hostility, social discomfort, and obsessive-compulsive disorders. From their research and practice of psychotherapy, Good and Heppner (1995) concluded that the adoption of a traditional ideology of masculinity is the most reliable variable for enabling the foreseeing of beliefs and violent behaviours against women, including rape.

The Triple Dissociation

In fact, to build the sense of traditional masculinity, a man faces three types of dissociation. We refer first of all to a physiological dissociation by which a 'Steel Armour' is developed (Miller, 1984), this well-known stoic attitude toward pain and physical suffering. Thus, while men are more likely than women to suffer from diseases resulting in death (Robertson et al., 2009), when interviewed, they are less likely than women to point out that they are afflicted by those very same diseases (Tremblay et al., 2005), which reveals significant differences between objective data and the subjectivity of respondents.

Emotionally speaking, dissociation also occurs in Western societies at a very young age, when a boy learns that crying is feminine ('Boys do not cry!') and therefore suppresses emotions other than anger and aggression, which become the only vehicles of emotional expression available to him. Such vehicles of self-expression are valued, particularly in the media (Katz, 2006), and at the same time repressed through advocacy for zero tolerance toward violence. In terms of health data, it is also evident from the fact that studies report twice as many women than men suffer from depression, while three to five times more men commit suicide (Tremblay et al., 2007). Yet we know that depression was present in most people who committed suicide; this was the case in at least 70 per cent of subjects analyzed by Séguin and his team (2005). In men with less obvious symptoms of depression, this often remains invisible to professionals.

Finally, there exists a relational dissociation borne out by an attitude of domination or seduction toward women and homophobia among men. A relational approach, in general, according to Lynch and Kilmartin (1999) is adopted in the form of a 'neither too close nor too far' approach whereby men tend to maintain many social relationships but very few, if any, really intimate ones.

Shame

In fact, for various reasons and at different times in their lives, boys and men may find themselves in situations where they feel they have not reached the social standards that they believe others expect of them as males. Thus, when a problem or any difficulty arises, they have a tendency to self-assess as being either 'inadequate', 'incorrect', 'ugly', or 'sick'. The dominant emotion is thus one of shame.

Feminist interventions have identified that guilt is the main emotion that must be taken into account in intervention with women. Recognition of this element has greatly advanced work on the understanding of women. Many women very often have a tendency to rapidly develop feelings of guilt for even the slightest thing, even sometimes in the case of bruises received at the hands of a violent partner. Guilt raises the implicit assertion: 'I did something wrong.' It is a question that can present itself on several different levels. It places the woman directly in the relational field, a field in which female socialization has traditionally tended to reside.

In men, it is the neighbour or cousin emotion of guilt that tends to dominate: that of shame (Dulac and Groulx, 1999; Keefler and Rondeau, 2002; Krugman, 1998; Osherson and Krugman, 1990). The *Merriam-Webster Online Dictionary* ('Shame', 2010) defines shame as 'the painful emotion caused by consciousness of guilt, shortcoming, impropriety; a condition of humiliating disgrace or disrepute'. It represents a socially motivated emotion of feeling invalidated, of a negative self-image perceived from the reactions of those around us, a fear of being judged by others or of being a social outcast. Unlike guilt, it raises the implicit assertion 'I am not right' or 'I am pathetic.' It affects a person's fundamental right to exist within his own identity (De Gaulejac, 1989). In psychoanalysis, we also regard it as the emotion that generates the most defensive mechanisms.

The impacts of shame can be devastating. In everyday life, it brings out various defence mechanisms that may seem trivial but that may be harmful, particularly with respect to help-seeking practices, which we will deal with a little further on. And yet still the repercussions can be even more serious. For example, Garbarino (1999), an American psychologist and researcher whose specialization is in the study of young people who have committed acts of extreme violence, including school murders, noted that all these youths, besides all being boys, had one thing in common: all had a history of a strong sense of humiliation. The violence exacted was a form of revenge to escape the shame that they felt. Feeling 'less than nothing', 'sub-humans', or as 'failures', they somehow were trying to prove to others and to themselves that they were capable of 'grandiose achievements'—of being at the centre of everyone's attention when their actions take the front page of all the newspapers (Tremblay, 2007). Similarly, one can understand the suicidal gesture: 'I may have screwed up my life, but I will not screw up my death.' Ultimately, they can also say, 'if in life I was nothing, in death I can be somebody' (Tremblay, 2000). In short, the constraints of hegemonic masculinity are strong, so boys and men who have not learned to approach it from a more critical perspective may find themselves particularly vulnerable. A deep sense of shame may take hold in them as they realize their inability to achieve the masculine ideal.

Help-Seeking by Men

Several authors have shown that the constraints of traditional masculinity affect the help-seeking process at every turn (Brooks, 1998; Dulac, 1997; 2001; Kilmartin, 2007; Rondeau et al., 2004; Tremblay et al., 2005; Turcotte et al., 2002). The process of seeking assistance comprises three major steps: realizing, deciding, and acting. During the first stage, the person must become aware of the symptoms, identify that a real problem does exist, and realize that this problem can only be solved by seeking help (Dulac, 1997). However, the phenomena of physiological and emotional dissociation are such that men only begin to feel the negative effects later on down the line.

The mechanisms for detecting, weighing up, acting and selecting of behavioural avenues to take would depend specifically on the gender in hand. By analogy,

we could say that many men have 'health-fuses of 30 amps whilst their personal circuit breakers should really be cutting off at 20 amps' (Tremblay et al., 2005: 263; trans. author).

These constraints of the masculine gender also influence the way men handle the second stage, that of decision-making. Having been highly socialized to fend for themselves, the spontaneous tendency may persist to simply deny the problem, wait for the passage of time, or find an answer by searching on the Internet or elsewhere, all the time keeping the problem a secret, without talking to others. Finally, with the ineffectiveness of these methods laid bare for him to see (denial, delaying, sorting it out by himself), the next step is the third stage, that of taking action by seeking help. At this point relational dissociation once again risks influencing and inhibiting the help-seeking process. Moreover, while women on the whole have been made aware on many occasions of the health issues affecting them through the sheer volume of popular literature both in books/magazines and radio/television programs (including self-testing, information, resources, etc.), men are generally less well informed. The sports, car, four-wheels, and other such popular journals that men often consult do not bring to light these issues. Thus, they know little about the resources available to them and even less about how to use them. This often leads them to maintain distrust. It is therefore not surprising that often the search for help is initiated under pressure from someone close to them, often the spouse, the family, or the employer, once again in a moment of crisis (Dulac, 1997; 2001).

The Positive Aspects of Traditional Masculinity

In this chapter we have highlighted some aspects of male socialization that can be considered as constraints, a straitjacket, as Pollack wrote (1998), that hinders the full potential development of boys and men. We should not ignore other aspects of this socialization model that may be used as levers to initiate a change. Cochran and Rabinowitz (1996) and Dulac and Groulx (1999) have highlighted some of these aspects.

The emphasis on the role of provider fosters a sense of responsibility, including that of sacrifice for the welfare of the family. The old adage of 'women and children first' ensures that men often view their first priority as the protection of other family members before themselves. This is also seen more widely, particularly with respect to certain professions that have a strong male majority, such as firefighters, who learn to brave flames to save lives. For many men, family remains an important value that may be used in intervention. Most men are strongly attached to their children. Also, love and affection are perhaps not always conveyed through the words 'I love you' but rather by many gestures that can feel equally significant once one knows how to interpret them.

Similarly, the insistence on self-control is an important force during a tragedy or major disaster because one must sideline feelings of intense anxiety and fear in order to make decisions that have a critical impact on the outcome of events. Moreover, the emphasis on action can also represent an advantage in certain situations. For example, during a disaster, many men are uncomfortable with the expression of distress all around them, but often respond with practical support and assistance that promotes reconstruction after the tragic event.

The notion of 'sticking to your word', which is also valued by the male socialization model, can be used in various ways, including intervention. Many men get respect by honouring what they have promised.

This method of relying on the impulse to change more negative aspects represents an innovative avenue being developed at the level of intervention. In this respect, Quebec is leading the way—most notably with the campaign 'You are strong when you ask for help', developed in the Saguenay region as part of suicide prevention programs among men. Equally so, the social marketing campaign for the academic achievement of college boys undertaken at Cegep Limoilou (Tremblay et al., 2006) focused on the ability of boys (and not on their dropping out) as long as they made efforts to take full advantage of the help offered to them. This 'salutogenic' approach, in the words of Macdonald (2005), is gathering ever-increasing interest from all around the world.

Conclusion

Throughout this chapter we have attempted to summarize the wealth of understanding regarding the mechanisms of identity formation and socialization among boys and men. We have taken care to distinguish the concepts of sex from that of gender and then to focus on the construction of the male gender identity in all its complexity, taking into account the contradictions that boys and men face. Thus, every boy/man must define himself in terms of what he accepts and what he rejects from the constraints tied in to traditional masculinity. Among these can be found what we have come to refer to as a triple dissociation: on a physiological, emotional, and relational level. Subsequently, we have stressed shame as being the dominant emotion in the therapeutic work with men, and the difficulties that male socialization tends to create when it comes to help-seeking. Finally, we have concluded this paper on the construction of the male-gender identity by shedding valuable light on certain positive aspects of traditional masculinity from which interventionist practices can be cultivated to help men better contribute to the society.

Discussion Questions

1. What are the differences and relationships between sex and gender, and how do these manifest with regard to men and masculinity, and masculinities in the plural?
2. The authors provide a pair of charts listing adjectives most commonly associated with men or women. The list was developed in 1982. In what ways might these lists be different if they were prepared today? Given that the list was drawn from research in 25 countries, might there be a global definition of masculinity? How would your answer affect whether there is a Canadian definition of masculinity?
3. The authors indicate that they focus on material that seems 'most relevant to understanding the construction of boys and men in Quebec'. How would one determine such relevance? That is, what might be legitimate rather than stereotypically differentiating features of Québécois masculinity as opposed to some other form?
4. The chapter argues that 'feminine and masculine identities are figments of social creation' and 'products of culture and history'. Based on your personal observations, what examples support or challenge these ideas? In what ways might you be actively or passively participating in socially creating masculinities?
5. The authors refer to research suggesting that Western societies have fostered or allowed a broadening of female roles and social expectations, but have not particularly done so with men and masculinity. Discuss your level of agreement, and what you believe to be the positive or negative implications, as well as your recommendations for the future.
6. Emotions of guilt and shame are described as fundamental in the study of women and men respectively. In what ways do you agree or disagree with this argument?
7. Having read the chapter, what are your impressions about whether and how the authors have made a particularly Quebec-focused depiction of masculine identity and role socialization?

Recommended Websites

CBC Arts: www.cbc.ca/arts/tv/quebectv.html

Canadian Dimension: http://canadian dimension.com/blog/3598

Manvertised: http://manvertised.com/2009/ 09/20/canadian-manvertising

Notes

1. We want to thank *Masculinity and Society* for having funded the translation of this chapter.
2. Homophobia is generally defined as the fear of homosexuality. It is the product of fear of the 'other'. This form of discrimination encompasses all attitudes, all behaviours, and all the negative beliefs extended to homosexuals and bisexuals or those alleged to be. Thus, homophobia refers to all manifestations of rejection and hatred of people, practices, and representations with homosexual overtones. These events generally lead to physical (assault) and verbal (insults) violence, as well as

psychological and sexual abuse (rape) (Welzer-Lang, 1994).

3. Heterosexism refers to a form of oppression and discrimination that is based on a distinction concerning sexual orientation (Welzer-Lang, 1994). Health Canada (1998) defines heterosexism as promoting the superiority of heterosexuality by institutions, individuals, or groups making up society. It assumes that only heterosexuality is normal and acceptable and that all individuals are and should be heterosexual. Heterosexism also assumes that it is better and more moral to be a heterosexual person (SC 1998). This is manifested in the predominance of the heterosexual model in education, in religion, in social and political discourse. For example, textbooks show rarely, if ever, love between two men or between two women (Welzer-Lang, 1994).

4. This form of discrimination assumes that people without disabilities are 'normal' and others are 'abnormal'. Thus, generally, people with disabilities are regarded as incapable, incompetent, etc. These same rules apply to sick people, even if the disease does not always create a disability.

References

Adams, G.R., and S.K. Marshall. 1996. 'A Developmental Social Psychology of Identity: Understanding the Person-in-Context', *Journal of Adolescence*, 19, 5: 429–42.

Alfieri, T., D.N. Ruble, and E.T. Higgins. 1996. 'Gender Stereotypes during Adolescence: Developmental Changes and the Transition to Junior High School', *Developmental Psychology*, 32, 6: 1129–37.

Anawi, B.D. 2007. *Male Reproductive Endocrinology* [The Merck Manuals, Online Medical Library for Health Professionals], www.merck.com, accessed 11 Nov. 2009.

Archer, S. 1992. 'A Feminist's Approach to Identity Research', in G.R. Adams, T.P. Gulotta, and R. Montemayor, eds., *Advances in Adolescence Development*. Newbury Park, CA: Sage.

Bégouin-Guignard, F. 1988. 'Le rôle des identifications maternelles et féminines dans le devenir du masculin chez le garçon', *Adolescence*, 6, 1: 49–74.

Bem, S. 1974. 'The Measurement of Psychological Androgyny', *Journal of Consulting and Clinical Psychology*, 42: 165–74.

Berry, N. 1987. *Le sentiment d'identité*. Bégédis, France: Éditions universitaires.

Birouste, J. 1980. 'Comment l'identité ouvre des perspectives au corps', *Annales*, 16, 2: 52–67.

Block, J.H. 1984. *Sex-Role Identity and Ego Development*. San Francisco: Jossey-Bass.

Blos, P. 1988. 'L'insoumission au père ou l'effort adolescent pour être masculin', *Adolescence*, 6, 1: 19–31.

Bly, R. 1990. *Iron John: A Book about Men*. New York: Vintage.

Bourne, E. 1978. 'The State of Research on Ego Identity: A Review and Appraisal Part II', *Journal of Youth and Adolescence*, 7, 4: 371–91.

Bowlby, J. 1988. *A Secure Base: Parent-Child Attachment and Healthy Human Development*. New York: Basic Books.

Brannon, R. 1985. 'Dimensions of the Male Sex Role in America', in A.G. Sargent, ed., *Beyond Sex Roles*, 2d ed. New York: West.

Breakwell, G.M. 1983. *Threatened Identities*. Toronto: John Wiley.

Brittan, A. 1989. *Masculinity and Power*. New York: Basil Blackwell.

Brooks, G.R. 1998. *A New Psychotherapy for Traditional Men*. San Francisco: Jossey-Bass.

Brooks-Harris, J.E., M. Heesacker, and C. Majia-Millan. 1996. 'Changing Men's Male Gender-Role Attitudes by Applying the Elaboration Likelihood Model of Attitude Change,' *Sex Roles*, 35, 9/10: 563–80.

Byrne, B.M. 1996. *Measuring Self-Concept across the Life Span: Issues and Instrumentation*. Washington, DC: American Psychological Association.

Chiland, C. 1988. 'De l'essence du masculin: Réflexions à partir du transsexualisme', *Adolescence*, 6, 1: 75–87.

Chodorow, N. 1978. *The Reproduction of Mothering: Psychoanalysis and the Sociology of Gender*. Berkeley, CA: University of California Press.

Cochran, S.V., and F.E. Rabinowitz. 1996. 'Men, Loss, and Psychotherapy', *Psychotherapy: Theory, Research, Practice, and Training*, 33: 593–600.

Combs, A.W., D.L. Avila, and W.W. Purkey. 1979. 'Self-Concept: Product and Producer of Experience.' In D.P. Elkins, ed., *Self-Concept Sourcebook: Ideas and Activities for Building Self-esteem*. New York: Groth Associates.

Connell, R.W. 1995/2005. *Masculinities*. Cambridge, UK: Polity.

Cooper, C.R., and H.D. Grotevant. 1987. 'Gender Issues in Interface of Family Experience and Adolescents' Friendship and Dating Identity', *Journal of Youth and Adolescence*, 16, 3: 247–63.

Corneau, G. 1989. *Père manquant, fils manqué*. Montreal: Éditions de l'Homme.

Davis, B. 2008. *Healthwise Knowledgebase: Testosterone*. University of Michigan Health System, http://health.med.umich.edu, accessed 11 Nov. 2009.

de Beauvoir, S. 1949. *Le deuxième sexe*. Paris: Gallimard.

de Gaulejac, V. 1989. 'Honte et pauvreté,' *Santé mentale au Québec*, 14, 2: 128–37.

Dulac, G. 1990. *La configuration du pouvoir: Étude et analyse de la construction sociale et de la représenta-tion du masculin*. PhD thesis (Université du Québec à Montréal).

———. 1997. *Les demandes d'aide des hommes*. Montreal: Centre d'études appliquées sur la famille, École de service social, Université McGill.

———. 2001. *Aider les hommes . . . aussi*. Montreal: VLB.

——— and J. Groulx. 1999. *Intervenir auprès des clientèles masculines: Théories and pratiques québécoises*. Montreal: Centre d'études appliquées sur la famille, École de service social, Université McGill.

Duret, P. 1999. *Les jeunes et l'identité masculine*. Paris: Presses universitaires de France.

Dusek, J.B. 1987. 'Sex Roles and Adjustment', in D.B. Carter, ed., *Current Conceptions of Sex-Roles and Sex-Typing: Theory and Research*. New York: Praeger.

Eccles, J.S. 1987. 'Adolescence: Gateway to Gender-Role Transcendance', in D.B. Carter, ed., *Current Conceptions of Sex-Roles and Sex-Typing: Theory and Research*. New York: Praeger.

Eisler, R.M., and J.A. Blalock. 1991. 'Masculine Gender Role Stress: Implication for the Assessment of Men', *Clinical Psychology Review*, 11: 45–60.

———, J.R. Skidmore, and C.H. Ward. 1988. Masculine Gender-Role Stress: Predictor of Anger, Anxiety, and Health-Risk Behaviors', *Journal of Personality Assessment*, 52, 1: 133–41.

Elbaz, M. 2001. *Recueil de vocabulaire* ANT-13522, Recueil de textes. Département d'anthropologie, Université Laval.

Erikson, E.H. 1957/1972. *Adolescence et crise*. Paris: Flammarion.

Esman, A.H. 1988. 'Quelques allures masculines exa-gérées', *Adolescence*, 6, 1: 37–41.

Ethier, M.G. 1995. *La côte d'Adam: L'impuissance affective des hommes remonte-t-elle au paradis terrestre?* Montreal: Éditions de l'homme.

Frankel, L. 2002. '"I've Never Thought About It": Contradictions and Taboos Surrounding American Males' Experiences of First Ejaculation (Semen-arche)', *Journal of Men's Studies*, 11, 1: 37–54.

Gagey, J. 1988. 'Nostalgie du père, sentiment religieux et pratiques rituelles', *Adolescence*, 6, 1: 117–29.

Galambos, N.L., D.M. Almeida, and A.C. Patersen. 1990. 'Masculinity, Femininity, and Sex Role Attitudes in Early Adolescence: Exploring Gender Intensifica-tion', *Child Development*, 61: 1905–14.

Garbarino, J. 1999. *Lost Boys: Why Our Sons Turn Violent and How We Can Save Them*. New York: Free Press.

Glazer, C.A., and J.B. Dusek. 1985. 'The Relationship between Sex-role Orientation and Resolution of Eriksonian Developmental Crises', *Sex Roles*, 13, 11/12: 653–61.

Goldberg, H. 1979. *The New Male: From the Macho to Sensitive but Still All Male*. New York: Signet.

———. 1981. *Être homme: Se réaliser sans se détruire*. Montreal: Le jour/Actualisation.

———. 1990. *L'homme sans masque: Comment surmonter la crainte de l'intimité*. Montreal: Le jour/Actualisation.

Good, G.E., and M.J. Heppner. 1995. 'Sexual and Psychological Violence: An Exploratory Study of Predictors in College Men', *Journal of Men's Studies*, 4, 1: 59–72.

Good, G.E., P.P. Heppner, K.A. DeBord, and A.R. Fischer. 2004. 'Understanding Men's Psychological Distress: Contributions of Problem-Solving Appraisal and Masculine Role Conflict', *Psychology of Men and Masculinity*, 5, 2: 168–77.

Haddad, T., ed. 1993. *Men and Masculinities: A Critical Anthology*. Toronto: Canadian Scholars' Press.

Hayes, J.A., and J.R. Mahalik. 2000. 'Gender Role Conflict and Psychological Distress in Male Counselling Center Clients', *Psychology of Men and Masculinities*, 1, 2: 116–25.

Health Canada. 1998. *À la recherche de son identité sex-uelle: Faire les premiers pas*. Ottawa: Gouvernement du Canada.

Hearn, J., and D. Morgan., eds. 1990. *Men, Masculini-ties and Social Theory (Critical Studies on Men and Masculinities 2)*. London: Unwin Hyman.

Herman, H.J.M, H.J.G. Kempen, and R.J.P. Van Loon. 1992. 'The Dialogical Self: Beyond Individualism and Rationalism', *American Psychologist*, 47: 23–33.

Hort, B.E., B.I. Fagot, and M. Driver Leinbach. 1990. 'Are People's Notions of Maleness More Stereotypi-cally Framed Than Their Notions of Femaleness?', *Sex Roles*, 23, 3/4: 197–212.

Houle, J. 2005. *La demande d'aide, le soutien social et le rôle masculin chez les hommes qui ont fait une tenta-tive de suicide*. PhD thesis (Université du Québec à Montréal).

Hurstel, F., and G. Delaisi de Parseval. 1990. 'Le pardessus du soupçon', in J. Delumeau and D. Roche, eds., *Histoire des pères et de la paternité*. Paris: Larousse.

James, W. 1890/1946. *Précis de psychologie*. Paris: Librai-rie Marcel Rivière.

Kagan, J. 1989. *Unstable Ideas: Temperament, Cognition and Self*. Cambridge, MA: Harvard University Press.

Kamptner, L. 1988. 'Identity Development in Late Ado-lescence: Causal Modeling of Social and Familial Influences', *Journal of Youth and Adolescence*, 17, 6: 493–514.

Katz, J. 2006. *The Macho Paradox*. Napierville, IL: Sourcebooks.

Katz, P.A., and K.R. Ksansnak. 1994. 'Developmental Aspects of Gender Role Flexibility and Traditional-ity in Middle Childhood and Adolescence', *Develop-mental Psychology*, 30, 2: 272–82.

Kaufmann, J.-C. 2007. *L'invention de soi*. Paris: Hachette Littératures.

Keefler, J., and G. Rondeau. 2002. 'Men and Shame', *Intervention*, 116: 26–36.

Kegan, R. 1982. *The Evolving Self: Problem and Process*

in Human Development. Cambridge, MA: Harvard University Press.

Kelly, G.A. 1955. *The Psychology of Personal Constructs*, vol. 1. New York: Norton.

Kilmartin, C.T. 2007. *The Masculine Self*. Cornwall-on-Hudson, NY: Sloan.

Kimmel, M.S., and M.A. Messner., eds. 1988. *Men's Lives*. Boston: Allyn & Bacon.

Klein, C. 1984. *Mères et fils*. Paris: Robert Laffont.

Kroger, J. 1989. *Identity in Adolescence: The Balance between Self and Other*. London: Routledge.

Krueger, D.W. 1989. *Body Self, Psychological Self: A Developmental and Clinical Integration of Disorders of the Self*. New York: Brunner/Mazel.

Krugman, S. 1998. 'Men's Shame and Trauma in Therapy', in W.S. Pollack and R.F. Levant, eds., *New Psychotherapy for Men*. New York: John Wiley and Sons.

Lacroix, A. 1983. *L'homme nouveau au masculin-féminin*. Quebec: Marie-Claire.

Lajeunesse, S.-L. 2007. *La masculinité mise au jeu: Construction de l'identité de genre chez des jeunes hommes sportifs*. PhD thesis (Université Laval).

Lamke, L.K., and K.G. Peyton. 1988. 'Adolescent Sex-Role Orientation and Ego Identity.' *Journal of Adolescence*, 11: 205–15.

L'Écuyer, R. 1978. *Le concept de soi*. Paris: Presses universitaires de France.

Lee, J. 1993. *Je tuerais mon père . . . mais il n'est pas là*. Montreal: Stanké.

Lempers, J.D., and D.S. Clark-Lempers. 1992. 'Young, Middle, and Late Adolescents' Comparisons of Functional Importance of Five Significant Relationships', *Journal of Youth and Adolescence*, 21, 1: 53–96.

Levant, R.F. 2001. 'Desperately Seeking Language: Understanding, Assessing, and Treating Normative Male Alexithymia', in G.R. Brooks and G.E. Good, eds., *The New Handbook of Psychotherapy and Counseling with Men: A Comprehensive Guide to Settings, Problems, and Treatment Approaches*. San Francisco: Jossey-Bass.

———and W.S. Pollack. 1995. *A New Psychology of Men*. New York: Basic Books.

Lynch, J., and C. Kilmartin. 1999. *The Pain behind the Mask: Overcoming Masculine Depression*. New York: Haworth Press.

Maccoby, E.E. 1987. 'The Varied Meanings of "Machism" and Femininity', in J. Machover-Reinish, L.A. Rosenblum, and S.A. Sanders, eds., *Masculinity/Femininity: Basic Perspectives*. New York: Oxford University Press.

Macdonald, J. 2005. *Environments for Health*. London and Sterling, VA: Earthscan.

Mackie, M. 1991. *Gender Relations in Canada: Further Explorations*. Toronto: Hartcourt Brace.

Mahalik, J.R., R.J. Cournoyer, W. De Franc, M. Cherry, and J.M. Napolitano. 1998. 'Men's Gender Role Conflict and Use of Psychological Defenses', *Journal of Counseling Psychology*, 45, 3: 247–55.

Marcelli, D. 1989. 'Imitation + représentation = identification? Quelques hypothèses sur le processus d'imitation précoce et d'identification secondaire entre le fils et le père', *Adolescence*, 7, 2: 35–52.

Marcia, J.E. 1993. 'The Ego Identity Status Approach to Ego Identity', in J.E. Marcia, A.S. Waterman, D.R. Matteson, S.L. Archer, and J.L. Orlofsky, eds., *Ego Identity: A Handbook for Psychosocial Research*. New York: Springer-Verlag.

Martin, D.H. 1985. 'Fathers and Adolescents', in S.H. Hanson and F.W. Bozett, eds., *Dimensions of Fatherhood*. London: Sage.

McCreary, D.R. 1994. 'The Male Role and Avoiding Femininity', *Sex Roles*, 31, 9/10: 517–31.

Mead, G.H. 1934. *Mind, Self and Society*. Chicago: University of Chicago Press.

Miller, S. 1984. *Les hommes et l'amitié*. Paris: Robert Laffont (Réponses).

Mintz, R.D., and J.R. Mahalik. 1996. 'Gender Role Orientation and Conflict as Predictors of Family Roles for Men', *Sex Roles*, 34, 11/12: 805–21.

Money, J., and A. Ehrhardt. 1972. *Man and Woman, Boy and Girl: Gender Identity from Conception to Maturity*. Baltimore, MD: Johns Hopkins University Press.

Nathanson, P., and K. Young. 2001. *Spreading Misandry: The Teaching of Contempt for Men in Popular Culture*. Montreal: McGill-Queen's University Press.

Nungesser, L.G. 1983. *Homosexual Acts, Actors, and Identities*. New York: Praeger.

O'Neil, J.M. 1981. 'Male Sex Role Conflicts, Sexism, and Masculinity: Psychological Implications for Men, Women, and the Counseling Psychologist', *The Counseling Psychologist*, 9, 2: 61–80.

———. 1990. 'Assessing Men's Gender Role Conflict', in D. Moore and F. Leafgren, eds., *Men in Conflict: Problem Solving Strategies and Interventions*. Alexandria, VA: American Counseling Association Press.

———and J. Egan. 1992. 'Abuses of Power against Women: Sexism, Gender Role Conflict, and Psychological Violence', in E. Piel Cook, ed., *Women, Relationships, and Power: Implications for Counselling*. Alexandria, VA: American Counseling Association Press.

———and G.E. Good. 1997. 'Men's Gender Role Conflict: Personal Reflections and Overview of Recent Research (1994–1997)', *Society for the Psychological Study of Men and Masculinity Bulletin*, 3, 1: 10–15.

———, B. Helms, R. Gable, L. David, and L. Wrightman. 1986. 'Gender Role Conflict Scale: College Men's Fear of Femininity', *Sex Roles*, 14: 335–50.

———and S. Holmes. 1995. 'Fifteen Years of Theory and Research on Men's Gender Role Conflict: New Paradigms for Empirical Research', in R.F. Levant and W.S. Pollack, eds., *A New Psychology of Men*. New York: Basic Books.

Osherson, S. 1986. *Finding Our Fathers: The Unfinished Business of Manhood*. New York: Free Press.

———and S. Krugman. 1990. 'Men, Shame, and Psychotherapy', *Psychotherapy*, 27, 3: 327–39.

Penot, B. 1988. 'Lorsqu'il y a quelque chose de pourri chez le père', *Adolescence*, 6, 1: 161–72.

Pleck, J.H. 1981. *The Myth of Masculinity*. Cambridge, MA: MIT Press.

———. 1995. 'The Gender Role Strain Paradigm: An Update', in R.F. Levant and W.S. Pollack, eds., *The New Psychology of Men*. New York: Basic Books.

Pollack, W.S. 1998. *Real Boys: Rescuing Our Sons from the Myths of Boyhood*. New York: Random House.

Robertson, S., B. Frank, D.R. McCreary, J.L. Oliffe, G. Tremblay, T. Naylor, and M. Phillips. 2009. 'The Current State of Men's Health in Canada', in D. Wilkins and E. Savoye, eds., *Men's Health around the World: A Review of Policy and Progress in 11 Countries*. Brussels: European Men's Health Forum.

Roïphe, H., and E. Galenson. 1981. *La naissance de l'identité sexuelle*. Paris: Presses universitaires de France.

Rondeau, G., (ed.), et al. 2004. *Les hommes: S'ouvrir à leur réalités et répondre à leurs besoins. Rapport du comité de travail en matière de prévention et d'aide aux hommes*. Quebec: Ministère de la santé et des services sociaux.

Roy, V. 2008. *L'expérience de socialisation aux rôles d'homme et de femme vécue par les conjoints aux comportements violents dans le cadre de leur participation à un groupe de thérapie animé par un homme et une femme*. PhD thesis (Université Laval).

Rust, J.O., and A. McCraw. 1984. 'Influence of Masculinity-Femininity on Adolescent Self-Esteem and Peer Acceptance', *Adolescence*, 19, 74: 359–66.

Saucier, J.F., and C. Marquette. 1985. 'Cycle de l'adolescence, processus sociaux et santé mentale', *Sociologie et société*, 27, 1: 7–32.

Séguin, M., A. Lesage, G. Turecki, F. Daigle, A. Guay, M.-N Bayle, and R. Landry. 2005. *Projet de recherché sur les décès par suicide au Nouveau-Brunswick entre avril 2002 et mai 2003*. Montreal: Centre de recherche Hôpital Douglas.

Seidler, V.J. 2006. *Young Men and Masculinities: Global Cultures and Intimate Lives*. London: Zed Books.

'Shame.' 2010. *Merriam-Webster Online Dictionary*, www.merriam-webster.com/dictionary/shame, accessed 5 March 2010.

Shively, M.G., and J.P. De Cecco. 1977. 'Components of Sexual Identity', *Journal of Homosexuality*, 3, 1: 41–8.

Silver, S.J. 1981. *The Male from Infancy to Old Age*. New York: Charles Scribner's Sons.

Stein, J.H., and L. Whisnant Reiser. 1994. 'A Study of White Middle-Class Adolescent Boys' Responses to "Semenarche"', *Journal of Youth and Adolescence*, 23, 3: 373–84.

Stoller, R. 1980. *L'identification: L'autre c'est moi*. Paris: Robert Laffont.

Tremblay, G. 1989. 'L'intervention sociale auprès des hommes: Quelques pistes en vue de préciser un modèle d'intervention'. MA thesis (Université de Sherbrooke).

———. 2000. 'La détresse des hommes: Comprendre pour mieux intervenir', in *Actes du Congrès international de la francophonie en prévention du suicide*.

———. 2007. 'Le complexe John Wayne ou donner un sens à sa vie par la violence'. Conférences de la Faculté des sciences sociales, Université Laval. Rediffusée au Canal Savoir.

———H. Bonnelli, S. Larose, S. Audet, C. Voyer, M. Bergeron, M. Massuard, M. Samson, M. Lavallée, J-P. Lacasse, B. Rivière, and D. Lessard. 2006. *Recherche-action pour développer un modèle d'intervention favorisant l'intégration, la persévérance et la réussite des garçons aux études collégiales*. Fonds de recerche sur la société et la culture (FQRSC), www.criviff.qc.ca.

———R. Cloutier, T. Antil, M-E. Bergeron, and R. Lapointe-Goupil. 2005. *La santé des hommes au Québec*. Quebec: Publications du Québec and Ministère de la santé et des services sociaux.

———and P. L'Heureux. 2002. 'L'intervention psychosociale auprès des hommes: Un modèle émergeant d'intervention clinique', *Intervention*, 116: 13–25.

———M.-A. Morin, V. Desbiens, and P. Bouchard. 2007. *Conflits de rôle de genre et dépression chez les hommes* (Études et analyses 36). Quebec: CRI-VIFF.

———. 2005. 'Psychosocial Intervention with Men', *International Journal of Men's Health*, 4, 1: 55–72.

———Y. Thibault, F. Fonséca, and R. Lapointe-Goupil. 2004. 'La santé mentale et les hommes: État de situation et pistes d'intervention', *Intervention*, 121: 6–16.

Turcotte, D., G. Dulac, J. Lindsay, G. Rondeau, and S. Dufour. 2002. 'La demande d'aide des hommes en difficulté: Trois profils de trajectoire', *Intervention*, 116: 37–51.

Tyson, P. 1986. 'Male Gender Role Identity: Early Developmental Roots', *Psychoanalytic Review*, 73, 3/4: 405–25.

Ullian, D.Z. 1981. 'Why Boys Will Be Boys: A Structural Perspective', *American Journal of Orthopsychiatry*, 51, 3: 493–501.

Van der Werff, J. 1990. 'The Problem of Self-conceiving', in H. Bosma and S. Jackson, eds., *Coping and Self-concept in Adolescence*. Berlin: Springer-Verlag.

Waterman, A.S. 1988. 'Identity Status Theory and Erikson's Theory: Communalities and Differences', *Developmental Review*, 8: 185–208.

Weeks, J. 1991. *Against Nature: Essays on History, Sexuality and Identity*. London: Rivers Oram Press.

Welzer-Lang, D. 1994. 'L'homophobie: La face cachée du masculin', in D. Welzer-Lang, P. Dutey, and M.

Dorais, eds., *La peur de l'autre en soi: Du sexisme à l'homophobie*. Montreal: VLB.

West, C., and D. Zimmerman. 1987. 'Doing Gender', *Gender and Society*, 1: 125–51.

Wilcox, D.W., and L. Forrest. 1992. 'The Problems of Men and Counseling: Gender Bias or Gender Truth?', Special issue: Mental Health Counseling for Men, *Journal of Mental Health Counseling*, 14, 3: 291–304.

Willemsen, E.W., and K.K. Waterman. 1991. 'Ego Identity Status and Family Environment: A Correlational Study', *Psychological Reports*, 69: 1203–12.

Winnicott, D.W. 1974. *Processus de maturation chez l'enfant*. Paris: Payot.

Wylie, R.C. 1974. *The Self-Concept: A Review of Methodological Considerations and Measuring Instruments*. Lincoln, NE: Buenos Institute of Mental Measurements.

———. 1989. *Measures of Self-Concept*. Lincoln, NE: Buenos Institute of Mental Measurements.

CHAPTER 3

So much about identity is connected to our bodies. Whether in terms of physical appearance, development and use of strength, self-care, or social conventions around touching and physical space, identity and body are tightly bound. The physicality associated with masculine performance also mitigates how men attend to their health or may be consciously attuned to their body's natural processes and needs. In general, men take more physical risks, face more life-threatening health risks, seek medical and psychological assistance less often, and live shorter lives than women.

In this chapter, Dumas and Bournival explore sociological perspectives on these phenomena and their consequences. They argue that biological differences between men and women do not explain the significant differences in health outcomes. As such, it becomes even more important to understand the social and cultural influences discussed in other chapters, because they undoubtedly would help to improve health. For example, the previous chapter talked about men putting on metaphorical steel armour, keeping others at a distance. It would not be difficult to see how this would relate to how men consider and treat their bodies.

Interestingly, noting that men experience higher mortality rates or more incidents of life-threatening disease than women can stimulate debates about privilege and oppression. People interested in issues of social inequality could understandably be concerned about whether these statistics might be used to dismiss the impact of other issues, such as gender violence or sexism (e.g., that we all have problems and as such no one's problems are more or less important or worthy of consideration). While these debates can be divisive, they can also lead to valuable insights and especially an opportunity to replace 'either/or' or 'zero-sum' thinking with more nuanced understanding of the layers and subtleties associated with identity issues. Arguably, masculine gender role socialization is implicated in both arenas, in men's personal and collective experiences of health, and in women's personal and collective experiences of violence and sexism. As such, we have an opportunity to attend to all of these through our learning about gender identities.

As you read this chapter, consider how other factors, such as socioeconomic class, affect men's health. This is another important example of intersectionality (e.g., of gender with class). It can be socially awkward to speak about how different identities impact lived experience, yet this chapter offers support for the value of doing it anyway. Namely, we can explore the development and impact of identities with enough sensitivity to avoid perpetuating stereotypes, while contributing to considerations of value to relationships and health.

Men, Masculinities, and Health: Theory and Application

Alexandre Dumas and Emily Bournival

The issue of men's health is gaining interest in Canada as national statistics clearly indicate that men have a lower life expectancy than women, have higher mortality rates for most leading causes of death, are associated with more risk factors of illness, and more often adopt unhealthier lifestyles. As it stands, however, men's health is underresearched and more information is needed on the underlying causes and the appropriate perspectives to be used to understand this issue. In Canadian university curricula, the study of men's health through a gender perspective remains sporadic and irregular, and only recently have national public health accounts, such as the *Report on the State of Public Health in Canada* (PHAC, 2008) or the *Social Determinants of Health: The Canadian Facts* (Mikkonen and Raphael, 2010) begun to address men's poor health and related health promotion strategies.[1]

Will Courtenay (2000: 1387) wrote a key article on men's poor health in the United States, and as one of the most cited articles on men's health, it discusses the unquestioned and unproblematized factual evidence of men's health problems in comparison with women's. The men's health movement and social studies in masculinity are exploring men's health issues by revealing relevant factors of men's experiences of health and illness that will contribute to the larger project of making the consequences of masculinity more visible (Kimmel, Connell, and Hearn, 2005).

This chapter focuses on gendered inequalities in health that relate to men and masculinities. It aims to identify key issues about men's health and to highlight the value of a sociological approach that studies men's bodies in order to prevent the continuance of damaging health patterns. It focuses more precisely on the social representations of masculinity and how they translate into men's lifestyles

and experiences of health and illness. The final section of the chapter features a case study that offers an application of a class-based approach to masculinities and health in relation to underprivileged men suffering from heart disease in the context of social inequality. The theoretical and empirical components of this chapter emphasize the idea that men's health can be better understood when both their social class and their gendered positions in society are considered.

The universality of Canada's health care system and its associated provincial legislation have sparked international interest while displaying Canadians' political sensitivity to equitable access to quality health care. Notwithstanding the social benefits of universality, health inequalities remain very present in Canada, suggesting that other determinants of health are at play (PHAC, 2008). Public health experts have warned political leaders not to confuse the role of health care systems (the provision of health care) with other broader social systems (e.g., social services, social rights, income redistribution) that improve people's living conditions and, as a consequence, their health (Raphael, 2002), especially as there is a well-documented and strong connection between social structure and health (Marmot and Wilkinson, 2006). Because gender has been identified as one of the major health determinants, patterns of health and illness in society can testify to wider issues pertaining to social inequalities. If Canadians politically choose to value health, then reducing gendered health inequalities should be prioritized in their health policy.

Gendered Health

Historical accounts show that life expectancy of social groups varies across time depending on many factors, such as sociopolitical contingencies, biomedical knowledge, public health policies, and quality of living standards. Such variations are unevenly translated in society as changes in gender differences in mortality and morbidity have also been noted (Annandale and Hunt, 2000). In Canada, data on life-expectancy trends tend to show that women outlive men and that gender differences have fluctuated significantly over the past several decades: for example, whereas in 1920–22 there was a two-year difference in age at mortality, during the 1970s and early 1980s, it reached a peak of seven years; it has now decreased to four and a half years (Statistics Canada, 2010a). For Waldron (2000), these differences can be explained by the considerable increase in women's health that occurred because of the decrease in maternal morbidity and gender-specific illnesses, such as uterine cancer. However, although there is now no single explanation for all causes of death linked to this gender gap, traditional gender roles continue to play a major influence.

Biological differences between the sexes have been associated with women's greater longevity, and while this is a plausible explanation for specific illnesses, they do not appear to be a major factor in comparison to other socio-cultural and psychological factors that come into play in global gender inequalities in health (Aïach, 2001; Cockerham, 1995; Sabo, 2005). According to Bonhomme, overly biological conceptions of health determinants can have negative policy implications:

> at present, a deterministic view has dominated our thinking, holding that the observed gender differences in longevity are due exclusively to unchangeable biological factors. This assumption has prevented us from searching for and examining specific cultural, environmental, and behavioural factors that might be amenable to modification through targeted preventive health care efforts (2009: 154).

Broadly speaking, there are two social mechanisms that explain the relationship between society and health inequalities (see Evans et al., 1994; Marmot and Wilkinson, 2006). The first can be related to the somatization of one's place in society. Several studies have confirmed the negative physical and mental health consequences for men who are socially stigmatized or situated at the bottom of the socioeconomic hierarchy. For example, the often cited Whitehall Studies in the United Kingdom have demonstrated the harmful effects of stress on cardiovascular health of male civil servants at the lower end of the organizational hierarchy. The second mechanism relates to the impact of social structure on health-damaging lifestyles. We can refer here to the socially produced lifestyles associated with masculinity, such as higher risk-taking or lower use of health care services.

In Canada, as elsewhere, statistical evidence supports the view that men's health is doubly determined by gender (masculinity) and socio-economic status (social class). First, national trends show that men's age-adjusted death rates surpass women's for most non-gender-specific causes of death. According to Canadian official statistics on the causes of mortality between males and females (Statistics Canada, 2010b),[2] men die 1.4 times more than women from cancer (malignant neoplasms), 1.7 times more from lung cancer (malignant neoplasms of trachea, bronchus, and lung), 1.5 times more from diabetes (diabetes mellitus), 1.8 times more from diseases of the heart, 2.4 times more from motor vehicle accidents, and 3.3 times more from suicide.[3] Second, the class–gender nexus also accounts for explaining the diversity of men's experiences of health (Connell, 2005). Statistics on the social gradient for health in urban Canada show strong social inequalities between the populations living in the highest- and lowest-income urban neighbourhoods, and similar data that focus on men and women show that this gradient is much steeper for men—in Canada the life expectancy at birth of the men in the highest income bracket is more than four years higher than for those in the lowest (PHAC, 2008). A statistical report on Quebec residents living in the National Capital Region (Gatineau, Quebec) revealed a 10-year difference in life expectancy between extreme income quintiles of low-income men and high-income women (Courteau and Finès, 2004).

There are thus two different but related questions that should be asked if we are concerned with understanding men's health: why are men not as healthy as women and why are some groups of men healthier than others? The first part of the question can be answered primarily through a strict gender analysis and the second through intersectional analysis combining gender and social class. These questions are being debated within the men's health movement, which appears to be gaining interest across Canada, the United States, Australia, and the United Kingdom.

Men's Health Initiatives in Canada

On 31 March 2010, every member of the Canadian Parliament wore a blue tie or scarf to support NDP leader Jack Layton's fight against prostate cancer and to sensitize Canadians to the fact that one in six men in Canada will be diagnosed with this illness (Prostate Cancer Canada, 2010). Given the extent of men's poor health status, it is surprising that health organizations and national health policy have not been more proactive in promoting men's health concerns in Canada. Robertson and his colleagues exposed the poor state of research on men's health promotion in Canada, especially the lack of health promotion efforts and absence of a men's health network: 'To date, there is no Canadian network, or single point of contact, for gathering research evidence, collating examples of good practice, or examining policy in order to . . . explore how best to promote the health of men' (2009: 267).

There are signs, however, that men's health is a growing political concern in Canada. For instance, the creation of the National Research Institute of Gender and Health in 2000 and the establishment of local organizations dedicated to the health of males of various ages, sexual orientation, and socioeconomic status are promising ventures. In Quebec, this concern has been publicly voiced (perhaps more intensely than in the rest of Canada).[4] The Quebec Ministry of Health and Social Services commissioned a report entitled *Men: Opening Up to Their Realities and Answering Their Needs (Les hommes: S'ouvrir à leurs réalités et répondre à leurs besoins)*, aiming to assess the needs and outline the priorities on men's health (Gagnon, Rondeau, and Mercier, 2004). In the words of the then Quebec minister of health, Philippe Couillard, this was the first time the government had established men's health as a formalized priority. The report presented 16 recommendations that were aimed at improving the quality of health care services, health promotion initiatives, community resources, and professional development. Internationally, this initiative is not isolated, as most industrialized countries are building the foundations of a systemically organized men's health movement (Robertson et al., 2009).

As most earlier work on gender and health has focused on women (Sabo, 2005), a change to include more studies on men comes with the risks of presenting an uncritical view of men's health problems and of avoiding a wider discussion on male dominance over women (Annandale and Clark, 1996). Similarly, the risk of undermining women's health issues by emphasizing men's is a concern in the promotion of a men's health movement. As recognized in the Quebec report on men's health, institutional concerns for promoting men's health touch a sensitive issue:

> Without calling into question the legitimate claims and social benefits which were gained through the struggles of the women's movement . . . it is more than time that Quebec unequivocally begins

and seriously considers the multiple difficulties that many men face (Gagnon, Rondeau, and Mercier: 38–9) (trans. author).[5]

Sociology, Masculinity, and Health

Frequently, Canadian media report health-related issues that remind us that our bodies are more than biological organisms, and that the way we treat them, and the experiences we have through them, are constructed by social norms and values of the particular society in which we reside. Media often expose how young men take unnecessary risks by conforming to social expectations of masculinity, how men refuse to talk or consult with a health professional when facing an illness, or how some boys suffer from their body appearance. Social research on men's bodies has shown that forms of masculinity are contingent on time and place, and that the body of a man bears symbolic value, and that its social construction shapes health and lifestyle experiences (Robertson, 2007). In its simplest form, masculinity encompasses the characteristics of and appropriate to the male sex (Scott and Marshall, 2005). This definition, however, can become more intricate if it encompasses its relational and positional features that involve the social and personal spheres of life. For Connell, masculinity is 'simultaneously a place in gender relations, the practices through which men and women engage that place in gender, and the effects of these practices in bodily experience, personality and culture' (2005: 71). This latter approach is a valuable means of exposing the commonalities and pluralities that characterize men, and the socializing agents and cultural producers that participate in reinforcing dominant forms of masculinity.

There are two distinctive approaches to the human body in the social sciences that are relevant to understanding the study of the body in relation to men's health.[6] The first perspective treats the body as a system of cultural signification

that can be read as a representation of the structure of power (body-as-representation). It focuses on the values and norms that shape social representations of masculinity. Here, the gendered body is understood as a product of culture and society, and it can become the object of political control, policy, and rationalization (Detrez, 2002). Because masculinity is socially constructed, this perspective aims at understanding what images of masculinity are produced within a specific society.

The second perspective considers the body as the basis of experience and action, and focuses on the 'lived body' and on the forms of embodied experiences of masculinity in the everyday world, thereby putting emphasis on feelings, emotions, and social practices. This focus on practice also allows for an analysis of the transformative power of social structure on the material aspects of the body. Such a perspective helps to identify what type of gendered experiences, bodily practices, and lifestyles are produced by a specific society. Therefore, both generic perspectives support the understanding of the social mechanisms that govern gendering processes related to the body and ultimately to health.

Social Representations of Masculinity and Health

Social representations of masculinity refer to dominant images of men that are disseminated through culture. They are often shaped by institutional structures that participate in constructing gendered norms and behaviours that can encourage unhealthy practices of men (Courtenay, 2000). For instance, a critical analysis of *Men's Health Magazine* revealed how its content reproduced a form of masculinity linked to unhealthy practices (emphasizing muscle size, alcohol tolerance, eating red meat, and violence) while denigrating healthier ones (cooking, eating vegetables, safe sex) (Stibbe, 2004). Representations of masculinity are not necessarily undesirable because we can celebrate multiple forms. However, some may have adverse effects on health when they stigmatize, when they provoke shame and humiliation, or when dominant forms of masculinity incline men to neglect their health, to adopt risky behaviours, or to avoid access to health-enhancing resources. According to Schofield and colleagues (2000), traditional characteristics of masculinity can undermine men's health by discouraging the adoption of health-promoting behaviours. For the authors, these characteristics may include the denial of weakness or vulnerability, the desire to appear strong and robust, the reluctance to seek help, the need to display emotional and physical control, the ceaseless interest in sex, and the display of aggressive behaviour and physical dominance. In short, such representations can be translated into emotions, feelings, and actions that negatively affect health (Robertson, 2007).

Although gendered representations may appear to be somewhat removed from the field of health, they participate in the production of hierarchies of masculinity that have consequences on men's social value and their health. Because masculinity involves body, action, and character, nonconformity to its dominant forms can have harmful effects on the health of men through social isolation. Theories of social capital have explained health status through the size and the quality of social networks, as well as through the social support provided by friends and family. This approach to health has convincingly revealed high mortality rates of socially isolated older adults. For example, Erik Klinenberg's (2003) case study on the social production of isolation reported an excess of death rates in Chicago due to hyperthermia during the 1995 heat waves. Male death rates were twice as prevalent as those of females, and 80 per cent of unclaimed bodies at the city morgue were men. Klinenberg argues that modern societies have brought profound social transformations that have increased the vulnerability of this group. This relationship between social isolation and mortality was partly

attributed to the gendered condition of older men who had lost their social networks after retirement, who valued conventional forms of masculinity that encourage toughness and independence, and who experienced shame and humiliation on moving in with their children, all factors that undermine valuable social ties that could have provided them with help in periods of distress.

The inability to conform to the work and income standards of masculinity is also of concern for men's health. Whereas social representation of masculinity can be relatively stable over time, the dynamically volatile fluctuations of the current economy have rendered it more difficult for men to conform to these expectations. Sociology has identified employment and work as a central feature of men's social status, and a key variable in explaining men's health in modern societies (Bartley, Ferrie, and Montgomery, 2006). In Canadian families, although husbands are more often the primary breadwinners in a proportion of 70 per cent (Sussman and Bonnell, 2006), their general decline in this position and increasing job insecurity have had repercussions on their health; this strongly contrasts with traditional forms of masculinity characterized by authority and control. As argued by Morgan, 'the idea of the man as "provider" remains remarkably persistent in a wide range of modern cultures . . . [and this] idea of the provider is a major element in the construction of masculine identity. . . . Hence, the devastating personal effects of unemployment' (2005: 169).

Moreover, adverse labour-market experiences negatively affect physical and mental health by the exposure to long-term stress, adoption of health-damaging behaviours, and loss of social support (Bartley, Ferrie, and Montgomery, 2006; Kasl, Rodriguez, and Lasch, 1998). The working-class men who are ill-equipped to face the pressures of modern life and difficulties of work expectations that are thrust upon them can be subjected to various degrees of social suffering. One of the major studies on work-related health patterns of men dealt with the early mortality of 4 million people, mostly men, in the former Soviet Union following the economic and political turmoil after the fall of the Iron Curtain (Marmot, 2004). These men died mostly from stress-related diseases and lifestyles (heart disease, alcohol consumption, non-accidental death) that were directly linked with mass unemployment, social inequality, and masculinity. Their increased social isolation, sense of insecurity, and high rates of divorce were consequences of the loss of the protective effects of employment.

This connection between social representations and health is also a promising avenue for understanding men's personal anxieties about their bodies. Nonconformity to dominant representations of bodies may have deleterious effects on boys and men who become devalued, socially excluded, and stigmatized. Gill and colleagues (2005) argue that the social changes that gave rise to the visibility of men's bodies in popular culture have also raised concerns about health, self-esteem, negative body image, and eating disorders. Thus, males may increasingly be defining themselves through their bodies in ways that are different from women and that concur with dominant ideals of masculinity. For example, the health risks associated with unsupervised use of muscle-enhancing drugs, such as steroids and growth hormones, have been noted as having consequences on men's health (Kayser, Mauron, and Miah, 2007). Furthermore, social psychologists have indicated that body dysmorphic disorder in boys is a rising health preoccupation as it has nearly tripled in 25 years (Pope, Phillips, and Olivardia, 2000). It was also found that boys too suffer from obesity stigmatization that can have serious psychological, social, and health-related consequences later in life (Puhl and Latner, 2007). In a study of the records of 5,749 Canadian young teenagers, Janssen et al. (2004) have shown that overweight and obese school-aged children are more likely to be the victims of bullying and to suffer from loss of

friendship, rumours or lies, overt name-calling, teasing, and physical abuse.[7] Social integration is identified as a significant health resource for youth (Dumas and Laforest, 2009) and, conversely, as shown in Janssen and colleagues, marginalization and stigmatization hinder a child's social and psychological development for the future.

In the same vein, men's representations of sexuality and their erectile performance have been other sources of anxiety in the context of aging and later life. Shame associated with the decline of erectile function is fuelled by the medicalization of men's sexuality that has transformed 'normal aging' into a social and biomedical problem, most currently identified as erectile disorders. The pharmaceutical industry reinforces the idea that normal aging constitutes a threat to masculinity (Calasanti and King, 2005; 2007). As demonstrated by Katz (1996), geriatric sciences and medicine have been important forces in this problematization of the male body. The global men's health industry constitutes a $17-billion (US) pharmaceutical market opportunity (Marshall, 2006), and the commercial successes of Viagra and Cialis testify to the internalization of these male insecurities; they have become cultural signifiers of virility and bio-perfection (Marshall and Katz, 2002). Western societies have developed a contemptuous attitude toward the aging body because it fails to meet current societal standards of performance and reliability that are anchored in dominant representations of the body (Le Breton, 2003). Calasanti and King reveal the inevitable fate of permanent dissatisfaction and loss of self-worth if men embody dominant forms of representations of male sexuality in the context of bodily decline tied to aging: 'The promise that men can control their masculinity and thus their aging offers empowerment but can condemn them to the trials of Sisyphus, hauling the rock-hard ideals of manhood in vain as their aging bodies grow less able to live up to them' (2007: 67–8).

Masculinity and Lifestyles

Although gender is one of the most important predictors of healthy behaviours, few explanations have been offered to account for men's unhealthy lifestyles (Courtenay, 2000: 1386–7). As mentioned earlier, there is a strong relationship between men and poor health-related lifestyles, and, according to national statistics, the likelihood of men developing an illness because of their lifestyle clearly surpasses women's. Understanding gender lifestyle differences may also help to explain the health paradox whereby dominant positions in society held by men, relative to women, 'should have a positive effect on health', but instead translate into higher mortality and morbidity rates—why are men disadvantaged by their social domination with regard to gender (Aïach, 2001)?

Many key social theorists have demonstrated the complex and dynamic relationships linking social representations of gender, embodiment, and lifestyles (e.g., Bourdieu, 2001; Connell, 2005). The lifestyles adopted by men and women contribute to a process of gender distinction, and because they are symbolically charged with gendered connotations, they are made public through performances that reproduce gender differences. The fact that popular culture is conveying more importance to socially valued forms of men's bodies may explain why men are increasingly policing themselves to ensure conformity to accepted forms of masculinity (Gill, Henwood, and McLean, 2005).

Aïach (2001) argues that the mechanisms that produce gendered inequalities in health derive from a gendered socialization where men acquire a specific relationship to the body that is less preventive, more competitive, risk-oriented, and ultimately more harmful to their health than that of women to their bodies. This concurs with a number of studies that have drawn on Pierre Bourdieu's (1984) sociocultural theory in order to understand the social variation of bodily practices between

social groups. Although Bourdieu's approach has mostly dealt with social class, it has more recently been applied to gender and women (Bourdieu, 2001; Fowler, 2003) and masculinity (Lee, Macdonald, and Wright, 2009; Wacquant, 2004). In order to understand the logic according to which social agents feel more or less inclined to adopt a given bodily practice, Bourdieu argues that one must delve into a person's deeper dimension, that is, one's bodily habitus or the particular relation one has to the body (Laberge and Kay, 2002). Distinctive gender types of bodily habitus are the result of ongoing socialization processes fashioned by the conditions of existence (material, family, and social) characteristic of a given milieu (Bourdieu, 2001). From an early age, the conditioning linked to social position tends to inscribe one's relationship to the social world in a lasting, generalized relationship to one's own body (Bourdieu, 1984). In the case of gender, masculinity participates in fashioning both a vision of the world and a relationship to the body that is inscribed in power relations through ways of treating the body, caring for it, feeding it, and otherwise maintaining it.

This approach conceives people's lifestyles in terms of socially acquired sets of priorities and tastes within particular groups of society, rather than the sole product of rational calculation (Wacquant, 1992) or the sole prerogative of people's personal attributes (Morgan, 2005). It has been extensively used to compare attitudinal and behavioural patterns relative to health (e.g., Boltanski, 1971; Poland et al., 2006; Williams, 1995) and shown to be particularly relevant in the study of gendered health inequalities as it connects gender, social representations, and the multiple health practices that compose lifestyles (Aïach, 2001; Lee, Macdonald, and Wright, 2009). Thus, gendered variations in health-related lifestyles are explained by a wide array of socially learned behaviours and attitudes. Social practices (e.g., healthy eating, low utilization of medical services, lower adoption of preventive practices, risk-taking, adoption of health risks) and attitudes (e.g., refusal to seek help, nonconformity to a healthy regimen, fatalist assumptions about improving health, lower receptiveness to health promotion messages, weaker responses to symptoms of illness) have been identified by research as two of the primary barriers to men's maintenance or improvement of their health.

For instance, masculinity is tied to men's medical consumption patterns and lower use of health care services (Smith, Braunack-Mayer, and Wittert, 2006). The proportion of Canadian males (25.3 per cent) over the age of 12 years who reported not having had contact with a medical doctor in the previous 12 months is almost double the proportion of females (13.6 per cent) (Statistics Canada, 2003). Men's reluctance to seek medical help in the context of illness, especially for younger or working-class men, has been explained sociologically: they respond weakly to the symptoms of illness (Aïach, 2001; Boltanski, 1971; Saltonstall, 1993) and they are reluctant to consult health services (Moser et al., 2004; O'Brien, Hunt, and Hart, 2005). Studies on men's perceptions of health show that they are less willing to consult medical professionals because they minimize health problems, have less knowledge of the signs, symptoms, and treatments of illness, and associate overt attention to body pains as weakness. Similarly, in a study of Australian and Canadian men, Oliffe and Thorne (2007) argued that certain types of masculinity threaten the quality of patient–physician communication that is necessary for adequate health care; this lack of communication will, in all probability, be exacerbated by our current economically challenged health care system.

Men's embodied identities and their attempts to conform to expectations of masculinity are associated with health risks, injury, and death. In the US, 11 of the 14 leading recognized health risks are more common amongst men (Courtnay, 2000). This also appears to be the case in Canada where, for example,

smoking, excessive alcohol consumption, illicit drug use, and suicide all have a higher degree of association with males (Lefebvre, 2004; PHAC, 2008). In a review by Sabo (2005), men's risk-taking has been tied to male bravado, fighting, physical injuries, drinking, and auto accidents. In Canada between 2000 and 2004 the average annual rate of death from motor vehicle accidents was consistently higher for males across every age group: males had a mortality rate 2.6 times higher than females (Ramage-Morin, 2008). Furthermore, drinking patterns and bouts of heavy drinking among depressed men have also been tied to accidental or violent deaths or associated diseases (Marmot, 2004). High alcohol consumption is also apparent in Canada, where death rates attributed to cirrhosis of the liver are 2.9 times higher for males (Statistics Canada, 2010b). Finally, more men die from violent deaths (car accidents and homicides) because they adopt a lifestyle that exposes them to risks and dangerous situations (Gagnon, Rondeau, and Mercier, 2004: 114).

Nonconformity to formal health recommendations has also been tied to masculinity (Courtnay, 2000; Schofield et al., 2000). In the case of diet, Gough and Conner (2006) found that both practical constraints tied to men's work (time and income) and conventionally masculine virtues such as autonomy and control prompted men to resist adopting diet regimens. In their study, the participants valued traits such as independence and individual agency, which were maintained by reclaiming their personal eating tastes, resisting strict dietary lifestyles proposed by health lobbies and government initiatives or advertising campaigns. Similarly, Gill and colleagues found that individualism, libertarianism, and self-respect were dominant traits of masculinity that characterized men's relationship with their bodies; individualism refers to autonomy and independence in relation to all body and lifestyle decisions; libertarianism stresses the importance of one's right to make decisions about one's own body; and self-respect relates to the ability to take responsibility for, and to self-discipline, the body. In relation to this latter point, the authors noted that 'it does not seem as though the same moral reprobation is attached to health choices, with many men reporting various kinds of harmful bodily practices without criticism' (2005: 55).

Both epidemiological and sociological studies show that income and educational attainment are significant factors shaping the quality of men's health and their health practices (Marmot, 2004). Taken together, these variables support a class-based analysis of health by focusing on how living conditions provide access to resources and shape people's view of the world, as well as exposing them to culturally specific repertoires of practice (Messner, 1996). In fact, the vulnerability of socioeconomically deprived men has regularly been highlighted in public health reports. Although men have often been stereotypically perceived as holding dominant positions in society, R.W. Connell argues that the 'dividend that accrues to men from patriarchal privilege is very unevenly distributed' (2007: 57) and that this loss of 'patriarchal dividend' is strongly influenced by social class (2005: 116). Therefore, a research focus on masculinity and health cannot exclude the relationships or intersections with other similar conventional social categories such as social class, ethnicity, and sexual orientation (Schrock and Schwalbe, 2009). The following case study will stress the importance of the class and gender intersection in order to better make clear the lifestyles of underprivileged men in the context of heart disease.

Class-Based Masculinities and Lifestyle: A Case Study on Cardiac Rehabilitation in Quebec

In the province of Quebec, Canada, of all the people who die prematurely, underprivileged men are more than 3.4 times more likely to die from heart disease than those of privileged groups, and 2.9 times more likely to die

from this condition than women of the same socioeconomic status (Pampalon, Hamel, and Gamache, 2008). Although social class and gender have been identified as major determinants of heart disease and unhealthy lifestyles, few studies have provided an in-depth account of class-based masculinities and cardiac rehabilitation practices. This case study was situated in the Outaouais region, a French-speaking area of Quebec bordering Ottawa, the capital city of Canada; with a population of 359,000, it possesses one of the highest overall living standards in Quebec (high average income, low unemployment), though significant socioeconomic inequalities exist. This region was selected because of its high socioeconomic inequalities, the low life expectancy of the male population (approximately two years less than the neighbouring population of Ottawa), and the high social inequalities in health; it has the second highest level of urban health inequality in Canada (Courteau and Finès, 2004). According to a government report, cardiovascular diseases were the main explanation for the excessive premature mortality recorded amongst underprivileged groups in the region.

Self-responsibility is a core assumption of health promotion in liberal societies. In the context of heart disease, individuals are strongly expected to pursue a rehabilitative regimen after receiving heart surgery. However, underprivileged groups, and particularly men, have been identified as being less receptive to such measures (Cooper et al., 2002; Taylor, Victory, and Angelini, 2001). While much valuable research has been undertaken to promote heart-healthy behaviours, the sociocultural mechanisms that influence bodily practices of vulnerable populations are often neglected. This case study aimed to understand the post-trauma lifestyles and commitments toward bodily care of materially and socially disadvantaged men suffering from cardiovascular disease and experiencing social inequality.

Sixty Francophone men aged between 25 and 79 years (mean age of 53.6) participated in the study between 2007 and 2010.[8] All lived either in the most underprivileged or wealthiest areas of the region, and all had undergone a medical intervention related to heart disease. Qualitative data were collected through semi-structured interviews of an average duration of 90 minutes. A content analysis was performed based on participants' perceptions, dispositions, and appreciation of cardiac rehabilitation programs and heart-healthy lifestyles.[9] The results presented here focus exclusively on the 30 most underprivileged men in the sample. They highlighted three key reasons to explain men's non-compliance to adequate cardiac rehabilitation norms: (a) incompatibility of life priorities, (b) maintaining status through hypermasculinity, and (c) resistance to an imposed lifestyle.

Focusing on the Priorities

The sample comprised men who were underprivileged at multiple levels, i.e., financially, materially, and socially. Clear indicators attest to their deprivation, such as histories of crime, child abuse, unhealthy behaviours (alcohol, tobacco, and drug addictions), and unhealthy diet. Most of them were in their fifties and sixties; therefore, they had sufficient life experience to establish a hierarchy of priorities for themselves that enhanced their general well-being. Their proximity to economic necessity was a significant structuring factor that governed the priority attributed to health. These men's incomes were well below poverty thresholds and they were not inclined to engage in preventive care related to their heart condition. Achieving rudimentary financial stability and psychological well-being, focusing on daily emergencies, and simply keeping busy in order to combat boredom held more priority than their cardiovascular health issues.

Studies have shown that time conflicts between health activities and occupational demands often undermine men's health concerns (e.g., Devine, 2005; Saltonstall, 1993). Since many participants in this study had worked

as manual labourers (construction industry, unspecialized factory work) or in the transportation industry (mover, tow-truck driver, taxi driver, public and commercial transportation, food delivery), lack of time, incompatible schedules, and lack of energy were mentioned as reasons for not taking the time to adopt healthier lifestyles or consult health care services. Decisions to allocate time and efforts were usually made in favour of their work rather than health-enhancing activities. Consequently, their motivations to improve their health lay chiefly in restoring their functional abilities to work: a day away from work also signified a smaller paycheque.

Immediate financial urgencies linked to being the sole or main breadwinner of the household were a significant burden, especially for those still employed, because most men were hired on part-time shifts or outside the formal system, for cash, that offered little or no employment security.

> *Frank, 53, unemployed builder:* The stress was go, go, go, production, production, production. Pay the bills; make sure that all bills are paid on time. Production was constant. . . . I lived day to day, for cash. It was more important to have those around me living. . . . It was not for me.[10]

Adding to this are the pressures to increase general economic well-being in order to have what eighteenth-century moral philosopher Adam Smith called the 'necessaries', that is, 'not only the commodities which are indispensably necessary for the support of life, but whatever the custom of the country renders it indecent for creditable people, even of the lowest order, to be without' (1863: 393).[11]

> *Max, 44, unemployed tow-truck driver:* [After my first heart attack] I went right back to towing, after two hours. Yep. The doctors told me 'we'll keep you until the evening.' No, no, no! Let's go. Do your

tests and things, and at noon, ciao, I'm gone . . . life goes on. . . . Work, work, work. They said I was like the Energizer bunny. . . . My wife tried to stop me but forget it. . . . I told my boss I had a little pain and that all was fine. I worked and worked as if nothing ever happened. . . . I didn't need to see a doctor, and I didn't have time to waste in a clinic. . . . My well-being is my biggest frustration! It's not my heart! It's my life, it's my money. . . . Now, I say to myself, look, I am tired of fighting against life. Life is not that great. . . . It wouldn't be the same if I had a big house, and a big bank account, a limo, big car, truck and all. Maybe then, life would be nice, but when you fall on social support, pfff, you don't have a life anymore my friend.

Conditions of necessity fashion working-class men's time horizons by prioritizing short-term over long-term concerns (Boltanski, 1971; Bourdieu, 2000). Many conditions, such as marital, family, legal, or substance addictions, were frequently mentioned as being lasting and pressing problems that needed to be urgently dealt with. After hospitalization, immediate concern over chest pain declined and more pressing psychological satisfactions became the priority, and for those whose lives had been particularly harsh, physical and cardiovascular health and prevention are clearly of secondary importance once the primary pain is alleviated.

Claude, 52, unemployed: Seriously, physically I am OK; I can't complain about anything. It's hurting in my head, not in my heart.
Jean-Charles, 53, unemployed delivery-man: I have so many problems, it's insane! . . . that's why I have become a spontaneous person. . . . All I do is react, react, react. . . . I have enough of all of this! In my opinion, my heart is healed.

Maintaining Status through Hypermasculinity

Characteristics that have traditionally been used to describe masculinity have been found to undermine men's health by discouraging them from adopting certain health behaviours linked to cardiovascular health (Courtenay, 2000; O'Brien, Hunt, and Hart, 2005; Schofield et al., 2000). The stories of these men tend to show that risk-taking is a hypermasculine response to class inequality to maintain social status and personal dignity. Their apprehension about losing social status was expressed as concern about losing their autonomy, exposing their vulnerability, becoming a burden for others, and fearing a loss of income.

Efforts to maintain masculinity had consequences on the subject's medical supervision and on adherence to a beneficial health regimen. Many participants mentioned they were conscious of the risks of their unwillingness to consult health care professionals or to pursue post–cardiac trauma follow-up examinations. *Lionel, 55, food bank volunteer:* 'I'm too pig-headed. I have always been pig-headed. I am not a complainer. My mother always said, you never complain, one day you'll die.' Other interviewees were forthright about their reluctance to seek medical help in the presence of clear symptoms of illness. Leo, 55, a retired amateur boxer, mentioned being a 'tough man', evidenced by enduring his chest pain for more than two months before finally going to the hospital. 'Shit, did my chest hurt! I had trouble breathing, walking, I was soaked through, and I was coughing, eeeehhh. . . . I had headaches, sweating all the time. I was like this for two months . . . two months my man. I'm a tough man.' One participant expressed his notions of masculinity through his desire to preserve his autonomy. *Fern, 63, unemployed:* 'As I told you, if I've got a flu or if I cut my finger or whatever, I try to fix it myself, or whatever, just like, here, I chopped off my fingertip, and I never went to the hospital. Fixed it myself, you know.'

Help-seeking was more readily accepted when spouses or friends facilitated the contact with health care providers, or when such aid could help preserve masculinity (O'Brien, Hunt, and Hart, 2005):

> *Albert, 72, retired salesman:* The tip of my penis began to hurt like crazy [because of my diabetes]. . . . At the time, I said: 'What the heck is going on.' Wash, wash, wash and no change. So then I said: 'I'm going to the doctor. . . . I don't want to loose that body part' (laugh). . . . After my heart attack, I waited one week before going to the hospital . . . I didn't feel I needed it. No, I don't go there for nothing. I am tough, too tough . . . that could have been the end for me that day. I am not a complainer. . . . I wasn't afraid. . . . but on that Sunday. . . . I was pretty dizzy and I was afraid of falling down on the floor. . . . I told my wife to help me down and to phone 911.

As argued by Charlesworth (2000), underprivileged and unemployed men suffer from a deficit of symbolic capital because of their position in society. Under these conditions, people find prestige where they can (Bourdieu, 1984), and it comes as no surprise that poor men find power, honour, and dignity through values that they associate with masculinity. In specific cases, illness posed a particular threat when social status came from the quality of their manual labour. For movers, truck drivers, and construction workers, health risks and pain tolerance were taken to high levels in order to maintain their work status, a key aspect of their identity:

> *Paul, 48, unemployed mover:* I am what you could call a workaholic. . . . I need to work. I won prizes as the most productive mover. They used to call me Paul-the-Machine. I have always taken my body to the limit. . . . After my

second heart attack, the doctors gave me strict instructions that I couldn't lift more than 15 kilos . . . that I needed to get a lot of rest, that I had to change my eating habits, stop smoking, and to completely change my lifestyle. . . . But I am a mover, so, I went back to moving furniture. . . . I know it's stubbornness, I know it's pride. I can't accept the fact that my body can't follow through with the work anymore. . . . I don't think I am an overly proud person, but I have pride when it comes to being a man. I am a man, and a man is made to work and we're made to be strong . . . but I know it's stubbornness. . . . My boss told me: 'Listen, you're going to have to be careful.' . . . I said, 'I am not going back into the office.' So I stayed on the truck up until I had my fourth and fifth heart attacks. . . . That was my last job.

Resisting a Health Regimen

Despite the fact that all the men of this sample had suffered from one or more heart complications, and that their basic knowledge of health practices was sufficient, they did not conform strongly to recommended post-trauma health advice. The participants' low adherence to a health regimen is explained by their relation to normative lifestyles and to health professionals they encountered during their stay at the hospital. In order to grasp their view, we need to consider the structuring effect of living at the margins of society, of being the focus of constant surveillance measures by public systems (education, law, employment, social services), and of often being the object of criticism, either subtle or straightforward. Similarly to the study of Gill and colleagues (2005), lives of hardship have inclined them, on the one hand, to make a virtue out of their independence, personal judgment, and life choices, and on the other, to distrust others, to be cautious of 'helpful advice', and to resist the imposition of normative standards.

As middle-aged and older men, many are coming to terms with their social position and the possibility of reaching socially valued lifestyles and conventions. Although they appreciated the health advice offered by medical staff, they did not feel obliged to follow it. For instance, only a few had agreed to participate in a free workshop offered by their local cardiac rehabilitation centre after their heart intervention. Generally speaking, they held a uninterested attitude toward health messages while maintaining a polite and respectful relation with health professionals. As seen earlier, health advice often did not correspond to their living conditions and social reality. Their lifestyles, whether healthy or not, were their own; they provided well-being, familiarity, and enjoyment.

> *Lionel, 55, food bank volunteer:* I do what I want . . . and [healthy living] is not for me. . . . I am not the type to bother you, it's your life! I won't say 'do this' and 'do that' even though it's for your own good. I could give you advice, get you in touch with a contact. . . . I can respect your opinion but I am not required to accept it, even if I am aware that what you're saying is good, and even if it's for my own good. . . . Listen, I will never have the body I had before.

A profound sense of disbelief in the personal gains of improving one's health was also at stake. The health benefits proposed by public health experts are perceived as being not worth the benefit of lifestyle changes. The fatalist attitudes of many participants toward health improvement, their weak belief in self-realization, and the appreciation of their lifestyles constitute some of the main factors that limit their propensity to change their ways of life.

In the context of social inequality, this gap between what people know about health and their actual lifestyles could be explained by Sayer's (2005) approach to anti-normative

lifestyles. For Sayer, experiences affect the reception of norms, and people who negatively experience social inequality can develop ethical positions that lead to anti-normative lifestyles. Emotional responses to experiences of inequality, such as resentment, shame, humiliation, or envy, are tied to symbolic domination. They fashion people's lifestyles, even if sometimes these reactions go against normative behaviours, and go against one's self-interests (a process akin to R.W. Connell's idea of protest masculinity in reaction to class frustration). In this sense, there is a parallel to be made between the hypermasculinity of the underclass and attitudes to rehabilitative practices.

Conclusion

Two premises underlie this chapter: health is a valued social good that is influenced by social structure, and multiple perspectives are needed to understand social inequalities in health. First, this chapter joins the voice of other health observers that expose the limits of the Canadian universal health care system in its goal to reduce health inequalities. Using health as a *social accountant* (Marmot, 2004), it argues that men's health is doubly determined by gender and power. Second, this chapter privileges sociological (Pierre Bourdieu's approach was privileged and was extended in order to include masculinity studies, particularly the works of Raewyn W. Connell) and epidemiological explanations of health. This combined approach enabled the productive marriage of health statistics and the complex sociological theory of embodiment. The connections made between social representations of masculinity and the 'lived body' help to clarify the effect of social status, experience, and performance on health. This separation between body-as-representation and the lived body is a heuristic device to understand human embodiment. In this sense, masculinity is multifaceted and stands at the core of any understanding of men's health. Finally, intersectional approaches that combine significant elements of social structure, such as masculinity and social class, can provide a fruitful framework for understanding the diversity of men's experiences of health. Further analysis of how gender and class act and interact in men's lives is needed in order to understand health inequalities.

The study of embodiment also sheds light on the problem of agency in the context of male vulnerability. Contra forethought, the domination of men in wider society does not always have expected outcomes (Aïach, 2001). Although control and autonomy are valued characteristics of masculinity, they have ambiguous consequences for men's health. On the one hand, they are associated with risk-oriented behaviours and anti-normative lifestyles (Courtenay, 2000) and, to a certain extent, self-harm, but paradoxically, as shown in the case study, they are linked to empowerment, self-respect, and agency.

These tensions between agency and health in the context of masculinity are linked to the foundational argument that human beings, whether male or female, are characterized by their vulnerability, and by the precarious character of their social and political arrangements (Turner, 2001: 206). With continuous threats to the welfare state, employment, income security, and the collective provision of care, it is likely that the most dependent groups of men will suffer hardship from lack of control over their futures.

The question of human embodiment is central to health concerns. Bryan S. Turner (1992) has coined the term 'somatic society' to represent a society where dominant political concerns and social anxieties tend to be translated and embodied in the body. In this sense, embodiment can be a call to transcend the nature–culture divide, and for the use of a more holistic approach to understanding men's and women's health. Because the body is constituted by material and sociopsychological dimensions, the way we perceive our bodies has consequences on efforts to promote health. Do we act and feel like men or women because of our genes or because of socialization? As socially constructed and biologically experienced consequences, stress, body dissatisfaction, or risk-related injuries can be perceived as reactions to embodied masculinity or femininity. Although it is clear that society plays a major role in our health, the increasing popularity of deterministic theses proposed by geneticists and sociobiologists is forcing a wider discussion on agency, embodiment, and gender.

Such barriers to men's health are not insurmountable. A number of sociological studies have shown that in specific conditions, men adopt a reflexive or re-skilling process in order to improve their health and well-being (Wheatley, 2006). However, the results of the case study presented here highlight how gendered representations, socioeconomic inequality, and poor social and material living conditions shape a view of the world that is at odds with the lifestyle promoted by standard health guidelines. As proposed by Denis Raphael (2002), this chapter supports the claim that health promotion efforts aimed toward men focusing solely on lifestyle modification are insufficient and must consider the wider sociopolitical and gendered characters of health enhancement strategies.

Discussion Questions

1. Identify some reasons why men have poorer health than women in Canada.
2. How do social representations of masculinity affect the health of boys and men?
3. In what way is 'embodiment' useful in understanding gendered health patterns?
4. Identify some links among work, masculinity, and health.
5. In your opinion, why is the term 'masculinity' generally written in its plural form in the social sciences?
6. In your opinion, why do men take more risks concerning their health?
7. How can we explain the health inequalities amongst men from a sociological perspective?
8. Given the authors' argument that caring for one's health is essentially breaking the rules of masculinity, what strategies would you recommend to improve the health of Canadian boys and men?
9. The authors discuss how culture facilitates dominant images of men and masculinity, particularly through institutions (e.g., schools, religion, families, government, media). What are some examples of images that have shaped your own perceptions of masculinities, and what institutions have been sources of these ideas?
10. The chapter discusses connections between sexual performance and masculinity. In a university setting, how do these connections play out in social life and discourse amongst your peers? Consider using a particular example of an observation or event, and analyze it in light of the theoretical material and terms in this text.

Recommended Websites

Boyhood studies: www.boyhoodstudies.com

Health Canada, Just for You: Men: www.hc-sc.gc.ca/hl-vs/jfy-spv/men-hommes-eng.php

Statistics Canada: www.statcan.gc.ca/start-debut-eng.html

Men's Studies Press: www.mensstudies.com/home/main.mpx

Men's health resources: www.menshealth.org

Movember Foundation: http://ca.movember foundation.com/fr/mens-health/mens-health-resources

The Chief Public Health Officer's Report on the State of Public Health in Canada 2008: www.phac-aspc.gc.ca/cphorsphc-respcacsp/2008/fr-rc/pdf/CPHO-Report-e.pdf

The Men's Bibliography: http://mensbiblio.xyonline.net

Notes

1. No significant amount of attention has been afforded to the connections among Canadian men, masculinity, and health in three major Canadian sociological textbooks that cover the topic of gender and health: see Clarke (2008), Bolaria and Dickinson (2009), and Lacourse and Émond (2006).
2. These data refer to age-standardized mortality rates. According to Statistics Canada, 'Age-standardization removes the effects of differences in the age structure of populations among areas and over time. Age-standardized death rates show the number of deaths per 100,000 population that would have occurred in a given area if the age structure of the population of that area was the same as the age structure of a specified standard population' (Statistics Canada, 2009: 113).
3. In other words, in the case of total deaths by motor vehicle accidents, men have a death rate of 13.1/100,000 in comparison to women at 5.1/100,000.
4. For additional information see the works of Tremblay et al. (2005), Gagnon, Rondeau, and Mercier (2004), and Lefebvre (2004).
5. Original text: *Sans remettre en question les revendications et les acquis légitimes obtenus de haute lutte par le mouvement des femmes il est plus que temps que le Québec s'engage sans équivoque et prenne réellement en compte les multiples difficultés auxquelles sont confrontés bon nombre d'hommes.*
6. This analysis has previously been applied to the aging body in Dumas and Turner (2006).
7. There was no significant association between obesity and stigmatization for boys between 15 and 16 years old, who instead were more prone to bully perpetrating behaviour.
8. The sample included three groups of men based on their socioeconomic circumstances. Thirty-one came from socially and materially deprived neighbourhoods, 18 from the lower-middle-class neighbourhoods (unspecialized and blue-collar workers), and 11 from the privileged neighbourhoods (white-collar workers). Participants were recruited through public advertisements and with the help of non-profit organizations and the regional hospitals.
9. This study applied a class-based analysis that drew on Pierre Bourdieu's later work on social suffering, on Andrew Sayer's work on the moral significance of class, and on theories of embodied masculinities (e.g., Connell, 2005, and Sabo, 2005).
10. All quotes give a pseudonym and the age and work status/occupation of the participant.
11. Michael Marmot (2004) presents a thought-provoking case on the links between men's social participation and their health by drawing on Adam Smith's concept of 'necessaries' and Anthony Giddens' concept of 'ontological security'.

References

Aïach, P. 2001. 'Femmes et hommes face à la mort et à la maladie: Des différences paradoxales', in P. Aïach, D. Cèbe, G. Cresson, and C. Philippe, eds., *Femmes et hommes dans le champ de la santé: Approches sociologiques*. Rennes, FR: Éditions de l'ENSP.

Annandale, E., and J. Clark. 1996. 'What Is Gender? Feminist Theory and the Sociology of Human Reproduction', *Sociology of Health and Illness*, 18: 17–44.

Annandale, E., and K. Hunt. 2000. *Gender Inequalities in Health*. Buckingham, UK: Open University Press.

Bartley, M., J. Ferrie, and S.M. Montgomery. 2006. 'Health and Labor Market Disadvantage: Unemployment, Non-Employment, and Job Insecurity', in M. Marmot and R.G. Wilkinson, eds., *Social Determinants of Health*, 2d ed. Oxford: Oxford University Press.

Bolaria, S.B., and H.D. Dickinson. 2009. *Health, Illness and Health Care in Canada*, 4th ed. Toronto: Nelson Education.

Boltanski, L. 1971. 'Les usages sociaux du corps', *Annales: Économie, société, civilisation*, 1: 205–33.

Bonhomme, J.J. 2009. 'The Gender Longevity Gap: Is It Really Biology?', *Journal of Men's Health*, 6, 3: 151–4.

Bourdieu, P. 1984. *Distinction: A Social Critique of the Judgment of Taste*. Cambridge, MA: Harvard University Press.

———. 2000. *Pascalian Meditations*. Cambridge, UK: Polity.

———. 2001. *Masculine Domination*. Cambridge, UK: Polity.

Calasanti, T., and N. King. 2005. 'Firming the Floppy Penis: Age, Class, and Gender Relations in the Lives of Old Men', *Men and Masculinities*, 8, 1: 3–23.

———. 2007. '"Beware of the Estrogen Assault": Ideal of Old Manhood in Anti-aging Advertisements', *Journal of Aging Studies*, 21: 357–68.

Charlesworth, S.J. 2000. 'Bourdieu, Social Suffering and Working-Class Life', in B. Fowler, ed., *Reading Bourdieu on Society and Culture*. Oxford: Blackwell.

Clarke, J.N. 2008. *Health, Illness, and Medicine in Canada*, 5th ed. Don Mills, ON: Oxford University Press.

Cockerham, W.C. 1995. *Medical Sociology*, 6th ed. Englewood Cliffs, NJ: Prentice-Hall.

Connell, R.W. 2005. *Masculinities*, 2d ed. Cambridge, UK: Polity.

———. 2007. 'Men, Masculinity Research and Gender Justice', in I. Lenz, C. Ulrich, and B. Fersch, eds., *Gender Orders Unbound: Globalisation, Restructuring and Reciprocity*. Farmington Hills, MI: Verlag Barbara Budrich.

Cooper, A.F., G. Jackson, J. Weinman, and R. Horne. 2002. 'Factors Associated with Cardiac Rehabilitation Attendance: A Systematic Review of the Literature', *Clinical Rehabilitation*, 16, 5: 541–52.

Courteau, J-P., and P. Finès. 2004. *Évolution de 1986 à 1996 de la relation entre le revenu et la mortalité en Outaouais urbain, dans l'ensemble des grandes villes du Québec et au sein de l'agglomération d'Ottawa-Gatineau*. Agence de développement de réseaux locaux de services de santé et de services sociaux du Québec, Direction de la santé publique.

Courtenay, W.H. 2000. 'Constructions of Masculinity and Their Influence on Men's Well-being: A Theory of Gender and Health.' *Social Science and Medicine*, 50, 10: 1385–1401.

Detrez, C.. 2002. *La construction sociale du corps*. Paris: Édition du Seuil.

Devine, C.M. 2005. 'A Life Course Perspective: Understanding Food Choices in Time, Social Location, and History', *Journal of Nutrition Education & Behavior*, 37, 3: 121–8.

Dumas A., and S. Laforest. 2009. 'Skateparks as a Health-Resource: Are They as Dangerous as They Look?', *Leisure Studies*, 28, 1: 19–34.

Dumas, A., and B.S. Turner. 2006. 'Age and Ageing: The Social World of Foucault and Bourdieu', in J.L. Powell and A. Wahidin, eds., *Foucault and Ageing*. New York: Nova Science Publishers.

Evans, R., G. Morris, L. Barer, and T.R. Marmor. 1994. *Why Are Some People Healthy and Others Not? The Determinants of Health of Populations*. New York: Aldine de Gruyter.

Fowler, B. 2003. 'Reading Pierre Bourdieu's *Masculine Domination*: Notes Towards an Intersectional Analysis of Gender, Culture and Class', *Cultural Studies*, 17, 3/4: 468–94.

Gagnon, L., G. Rondeau, and G. Mercier. 2004. Comité de travail en matière de prévention et d'aide aux hommes, *Les hommes: S'ouvrir à leurs réalités et répondre à leurs besoins*. Quebec: Ministère de la santé et des services sociaux.

Gill, R., K. Henwood, and C. McLean. 2005. 'Body Projects and the Regulation of Normative Masculinity', *Body & Society*, 11, 1: 37–62.

Gough, B., and M.T. Conner. 2006. 'Barriers in Healthy Eating amongst Men: A Qualitative Analysis', *Social Science & Medicine*, 62, 2: 387–95.

Grundy, E., and A. Sloggett. 2003. 'Health Inequalities in the Older Population: The Role of Personal Capital, Social Resources and Socio-economic Circumstances', *Social Science and Medicine*, 56, 5: 935–47.

Janssen, I., W. Craig, M. Boyce, F. William, and W. Pickett. 2004. 'Associations between Overweight and Obesity with Bullying Behaviors in School-aged Children', *Pediatrics*, 113, 5: 1187–94.

Kasl, S.V., E. Rodriguez, and K.E. Lasch. 1998. 'The Impact of Unemployment on Health and Well-being', in B.P. Dohrenwend, ed., *Adversity, Stress, and Psychopathology*. New York: Oxford University Press.

Katz, S. 1996. *Disciplining Old Age: The Formation of Gerontological Knowledge*. Charlottesville: University of Virginia Press.

Kayser, B., A. Mauron, and A. Miah. 2007. 'Current Anti-doping Policy: A Critical Appraisal', *BMC Medical Ethics*, 8, 2. doi:10.1186/1472-6939-8-2.

Kimmel, M.S., R.W. Connell, and J. Hearn. 2005. *Handbook of Studies on Men and Masculinities*. Thousand Oaks, CA: Sage.

Klinenberg, E. 2003. *Heat Wave: A Social Autopsy of a Disaster in Chicago*. Chicago: University of Chicago Press.

Laberge, S., and J. Kay. 2002. 'Bourdieu's Sociocultural Theory and Sport Practice', in J.A. Maguire and K. Young, eds., *Theory, Sport and Society*. London: Elsevier.

Lacourse, M-T., and M. Émond. 2006. *Sociologie de la santé*, 2d ed. Montreal: Chenelière Éducation.

Le Breton, D. 2003. *Anthropologie du corps et modernité*, 3d ed. Paris: Quadrige/Presses universitaires de France.

Lee, J., D. Macdonald, and J. Wright. 2009. 'Young Men's Physical Activity Choices: The Impact of Capital, Masculinities, and Location', *Journal of Sport & Social Issues*, 33, 1: 59–77.

Lefebvre, C. 2004. 'Un portrait de la santé des hommes québécois de 30 à 64 ans (2004)', Institut national de santé publique du Québec, Ministère de la santé et des Services Sociaux, www.inspq.qc.ca/pdf/publications/285-PortraitSanteHommes30-64ans.pdf.

Marmot, M. 2004. *The Status Syndrome*. New York: Henry Holt.

——— and R.G. Wilkinson. 2006. *Social Determinants of Health*, 2d ed. Oxford: Oxford University Press.

Marshall, B.L. 2006. 'The New Virility: Viagra, Male Aging and Sexual Function', *Sexualities*, 9, 3: 345–62.

——— and S. Katz. 2002. 'Forever Functional: Sexual Fitness and the Ageing Male Body', *Body & Society*, 8, 4: 43–70.

Messner, M. 1996. 'Studying Up on Sex', *Sociology of Sport Journal*, 13: 221–37.

Mikkonen, J., and D. Raphael. 2010. *Social Determinants of Health: The Canadian Facts*. Toronto: York University School of Health Policy and Management.

Morgan, D. 2005. 'Class and Masculinity', in M.S. Kimmel, J. Hearn, and R.W. Connell, eds., *Handbook of Studies on Men and Masculinities*. Thousand Oaks, CA: Sage.

Moser, D.K., S. McKinley, K. Dracup, and M. Chung. 2004. 'Gender Differences in Reasons Patients Delay in Seeking Treatment for Acute Myocardial Infarction Symptoms', *Patient Education and Counseling*, 56: 45–54.

O'Brien, R., K. Hunt, and G. Hart. 2005. '"It's Caveman Stuff, But That Is to a Certain Extent How Guys Still Operate": Men's Accounts of Masculinity and Help Seeking', *Social Science & Medicine*, 61, 3: 503–16.

Oliffe, J., and S. Thorne. 2007. 'Men, Masculinities, and Prostate Cancer: Australian and Canadian Patient Perspectives of Communication with Male Physicians', *Qualitative Health Research*, 17, 2: 149–61.

Pampalon, R., D. Hamel, and P. Gamache. 2008. 'Évolution récente de la mortalité prématurée au Québec selon la défavorisation matérielle et sociale', in K.L. Frolich, M. De Koninck, P. Bernard, and A. Demers, eds., *Les inégalités sociales de santé au Québec*. Montreal: Presses de l'Université de Montréal.

PHAC–Public Health Agency of Canada. 2008. *The Chief Public Health Officer's Report on the State of Public Health in Canada 2008*, Catalogue no. HP2-10/2008E. Ottawa: Minister of Health.

Poland, B., K.L. Frohlich, R.J. Haines, R.J. Eric Mykhalovskiy, M. Rock, and R. Sparks. 2006. 'The Social Context of Smoking: The Next Frontier in Tobacco Control?', *Tobacco Control*, 15, 1: 59–63.

Pope, H.G., K.A. Phillips, and R. Olivardia. 2000. *The Adonis Complex: The Secret Crisis of Male Body Obsession*. Sydney: Free Press.

Prostate Cancer Canada. 2010. 'Members of Parliament Show Support for Layton's Battle', www.prostate cancer.ca.

Puhl, R.M., and J.D. Latner. 2007. 'Stigma, Obesity, and the Health of the Nation's Children', *Psychological Bulletin*, 133: 557–80.

Ramage-Morin, P.L. 2008. 'Motor Vehicle Accident Deaths, 1979 to 2004', Health Reports–Component of Statistics Canada, Catalogue no. 82-003-X 19, 3: 1–8.

Raphael, D. 2002. *Social Justice Is Good for Our Hearts: Why Societal Factors—and Not Lifestyle—Are Major Causes of Heart Disease in Canada and Elsewhere*. Toronto: CSJ Foundation for Research and Education.

Robertson, S. 2007. *Understanding Men and Health: Masculinities, Identity, and Well-being*. Berkshire, UK: Open University Press.

———. P. Galdas, D.R. McCreary, J.L. Oliffe, and G. Tremblay. 2009. 'Men's Health Promotion in Canada: Current Context and Future Direction', *Health Education Journal*, 68, 4: 266–72.

Sabo, D. 2005. 'The Study of Masculinities and Men's Health', in M.S. Kimmel, R.W. Connell, and J. Hearn, eds., *Handbook of Studies on Men and Masculinities*. Thousand Oaks, CA: Sage.

Saltonstall, R. 1993. 'Healthy Bodies, Social Bodies: Men's and Women's Concepts and Practices of Health in Everyday Life', *Social Science and Medicine*, 36, 1: 7–14.

Sayer, A. 2005. *The Moral Significance of Class*. Cambridge, UK: Cambridge University Press.

Schofield, T., R.W. Connell, L. Walker, J.F. Wood, and D.L. Butland. 2000. 'Understanding Men's Health and Illness: A Gender-Relations Approach to Policy, Research and Practice', *Journal of American College Health*, 48, 6: 247–56.

Schrock, D., and M. Schwalbe. 2009. 'Men, Masculinity, and Manhood Acts', *Annual Review of Sociology*, 35: 277–95.

Scott, J., and G. Marshall. 2005. *Oxford Dictionary of Sociology*. Oxford: Oxford University Press.

Smith, A. 1863. *An Inquiry into the Nature and Causes of the Wealth of Nations*. Edinburgh: Adam and Charles Black.

Smith, J.A., A. Braunack-Mayer, and G. Wittert. 2006. 'What Do We Know about Men's Help-Seeking and Health Service Use?', *Medical Journal of Australia*, 184, 2: 81–3.

Statistics Canada. 2003. 'Contact with Medical Doctors in the Past 12 Months, by Age Group and Sex, Household Population Aged 12 and Over, Canada, Provinces, Territories, Health Regions', Table 105-0461, CANSIM, www.statcan.gc.ca/pub/82-221- x/2005002/t/html/4063590-eng.htm.

———. 2009. *Mortality, Summary List of Causes, 2005*. Catalogue no. 84F0209X, www.statcan.gc.ca/pub/84f0209x/84f0209x2005000-eng.pdf

———. 2010a. 'Life Expectancy at Birth, by Sex, by Province,' Table 102-0512, CANSIM, www40.statcan.gc.ca/l01/cst01/health26-eng.htm

———. 2010b. *Age-Standardized Mortality Rates by Selected Causes, by Sex (Both Sexes)*. Catalogue no. 84F0209X, www40.statcan.ca/l01/cst01/health30a-eng.htm.

Stibbe, A. 2004. 'Health and the Social Construction of Masculinity in *Men's Health Magazine*', *Men and Masculinities*, 7, 1: 31–51.

Sussman, D., and S. Bonnell. 2006. 'Wives as Primary Breadwinners', *Perspectives on Labour and Income*, 7, 8: 10–17; Statistics Canada, Catalogue no. 75-001-XIE.

Taylor, F.C., J.J. Victory, and G.D. Angelini. 2001. 'Use of Cardiac Rehabilitation among Patients Following Coronary Artery Bypass Surgery', *Heart*, 86: 92–3.

Tremblay, G., R. Cloutier, T. Antil, M-È. Bergeron, and R. Lapointe-Goupil. 2005. *La santé des hommes au Québec*. Sainte-Foy, QC: Les publications du Québec.

Turner, B.S. 1992. *Regulating Bodies: Essays in Medical Sociology*. London: Routledge.

————. 2001. 'The Erosion of Citizenship', *British Journal of Sociology*, 2, 52: 189–209.

Wacquant, L. 1992. 'Toward a Social Praxeology: The Structure and Logic of Bourdieu's Sociology', in P. Bourdieu and L. Wacquant, eds., *An Invitation to Reflexive Sociology*. Chicago: University of Chicago Press.

————. 2004. *Body and Soul: Ethnographic Notebooks of an Apprentice Boxer*. New York: Oxford University Press.

Waldron, I. 2000. 'Trends in Gender Differences in Mortality: Relationships to Changing Gender Differences in Behaviour and Other Causal Factors', in E. Annadale and K. Hunt, eds., *Gender Inequalities in Health*. Buckingham, UK: Open University Press.

Wheatley, E.E. 2006. *Bodies at Risk: An Ethnography of Heart Disease*. Burlington, VT: Ashgate.

Williams, S.J. 1995. 'Theorising Class, Health and Lifestyles: Can Bourdieu Help Us?' *Sociology of Health and Illness*, 17, 5: 577–604.

CHAPTER 4

Earlier chapters have discussed dominant images of masculinity and how they form a pervasive dynamic of pressure to conform to a singular ideal. In this chapter, Cornish and Osachuk introduce the argument that the significant diversity of identities across Canada offers alternative and multiple forms of masculine ideals. As psychologists, they offer valuable perspectives on whether and how men may be changing in their self-awareness and willingness to pursue assistance with healing and/or personal growth. As well, the concept that men are stoic and do not make themselves vulnerable is considered in view of cultural and generational differences that are changing the way men make sense of themselves over time. The authors also point to the fragility of the stereotypic masculine ideal. That is, the model is frankly unattainable and subject to intense conflict personally and interpersonally. As such, there is vulnerability in men's lives associated with the pursuit of eminence and strength that will never be fully realized. This is exacerbated by the constant expectation to prove one's masculinity to oneself and to others. This realization offers potential for people across gender identities to find points of common ground, since we are all subject to impossible ideals in one or more forms.

The authors certainly believe that long-standing implicit and overt rules of masculinity are alive and well, but they offer hopeful optimism about the prospect that rigid models are changing. This affirms other authors' remarks about the negotiable nature of gender and identity, as well as the choices we can make to be purposeful in shaping our own approaches in life. That said, it is difficult to depart from collective ideas about what constitutes 'normal' or desirable role performance. The authors use the term 'hegemony', which has a number of definitions worth researching. Essentially, hegemony is the cumulative and myriad ideas and images that are so pervasive as to become invisible and thus considered natural. Describing something as natural gives it a great deal of power, because it is thus regarded as inevitable and, more importantly, right and good. Many of the authors in this text discuss hegemony, and hegemonic forms of masculinity, and their consequences and alternatives.

Like Landsberg and others, these authors affirm the value of stories and personal accounts of lived experiences, and how these promote insights and personal growth as well as the therapeutic value of claiming one's voice. The accounts of particular personal stories in this chapter connect well with the broader discussion in the second section about Canadian folklore, media, and culture. As you read this chapter, consider how the individual stories resonate with the broader and collective ideas about what it means to be a man in Canada.

Canadian Men's Relationships and Help-Seeking over the Lifespan: The Role of Public Narratives

Peter Cornish and Timothy A.G. Osachuk

Contrary to stereotypes about male stoicism, there is anecdotal evidence suggesting men are more emotionally prepared for help-seeking than they used to be. In turn, when these men do present for help, they appear more comfortable expressing vulnerability and more willing to take responsibility for self-reflection and psychological adaptation. Has the research to date determined whether contemporary Canadian men are more prepared than their predecessors to lead active emotional lives? Does this vary by region, culture, or other factors? The present chapter explores influences on, and characteristics of, contemporary Canadian men's relationships and help-seeking.

Canadian Demographic Diversity

Canada is the second largest country in the world, smaller only than Russia, with a total land area of 9,976,140 square kilometres (Advameg, 2009), a relatively small population for its size of 31,612,897 people (Statistics Canada, 2006), and the majority of inhabitants living in the southern regions of the country. Estimates of the adult sex ratio (the number of males to females in a population) range from 1.02 (Kaiser Family Foundation, 2009) to 1.06 to 1 (About.com, 2008). This ratio, however, varies by age and geographical location across Canada's 10 provinces and 3 northern territories (Statistics Canada, 2006). The overall diversity of people across the nation is vast. For example, as of the 2006 census, Canadians reported more than 200 languages as their mother tongue (Statistics Canada, 2007a). This diversity is a product of the first inhabitants/ indigenous people (Arthur and Collins, 2005; Guisepi, 2002), early historical settlement, and waves of immigrants who have contributed

to the Canadian Cultural Mosaic over time (Dominion Institute, 2008). We argue that there is not just one but many cultures of men in Canada that vary by region, urban versus rural status, race, social class, socioeconomic status, sex-role orientation, age, period of immigration, and cultural origins. Understanding how Canadian men define themselves, their relationships, and their help-seeking requires an appreciation of the cultures of *being male* and the construction of multiple masculinities throughout Canada.

Men's Help-Seeking

As is the case in many countries, Canadian men are less likely than women to seek help for health and mental health concerns (Statistics Canada, 2005). This is despite the fact that life expectancy is lower for Canadian men, they are more likely to be obese or suffer from diabetes, are less physically active, and eat less healthy food than women (Statistics Canada, 2007b).

For every two women now attending university, only one male attends. The gap has been increasing since the early 1980s (Statistics Canada, 2009). Given both the direct and indirect relationships between education or literacy and health outcomes (Rootman and Rhonson, 2005), it would appear that men's health outcomes will deteriorate in relationship to those of women.

There is some reason for cautious optimism. Although men are still seeking help less than women, both men and women are seeking help from physicians and mental health professionals more than they did 20 years ago. And while the gender gap in mental health contacts remains stable, the gap between men's and women's visits to physicians is slowly closing.

The gap in life expectancy is also closing (CBC, 2008; Statistics Canada, 2010). The percentage of males attending university counselling centres in Canada and throughout North America has stabilized despite declining male university enrolments (AUCCCD, 2010). Counselling centre directors report anecdotally that males seem more comfortable and more prepared to engage in psychological change processes than a decade ago (Sam Cochran, personal communication, 20 January 2010).

Theory

Several theories have been proposed to explain the differences in men's help-seeking behaviour.

Sociocultural Construction

The social construction view of men's gender role holds that . . . the important fact of men's lives is not that they are biological males, but that they become men. Our sex may be male, but our identity as men is developed through a complex process of interaction with the culture in which we both learn the gender scripts appropriate to our culture and attempt to modify those scripts to make them more palatable (Kimmel and Messner, 1992: xv).

In a sense, being male is an endless performance (West and Zimmerman, 1987), which begins for young boys (Way and Chu, 2004) as they act out gender role scripts prescribed through the popular media culture of the day (Harris, 1995). Over the decades, Canadian masculinities have been portrayed with humour and self-deprecation on television. In the 1970s, hockey, a snow-covered Canadian map, and cases of beer defined the masculinity of the McKenzie brothers (Thomas and Moranis, 1976–81; 2009). Considerable ambivalence about male sexual identities was central to the *Kids in the Hall* series of the 1990s (Foley et al., 1988–94). A fundamentally flawed masculinity

was characterized by unsuccessful fishing expeditions and bumbling, ill-fated handiwork in the *Red Green Show* (Green and Smith, 1991–2005).

A wide range of symbols or archetypes of Canadian identity were on display during the opening and closing ceremonies of the 2010 Winter Olympic Games in Vancouver. Slam poet Shane Koyczan brought the house down with his nationalistic performance 'We Are More' (Koyczan, 2010). With an inspiring rap rhythm, he proclaimed that Canada is more than hockey or 'please and thank you'. There was something refreshing about a standing ovation for a Caucasian man reading slam *poetry* at a sporting event. Like the Canada portrayed in the opening ceremonies, Canadian masculinities are increasingly informed by an expanse of rich and varied influences that shape and colour the Canadian Mosaic (Mackie, 1983).

While broadening scripts suggest opportunities for healthier ways of being male, it is probably too soon to detect significant impact on health outcomes. The enactment of traditional scripts for male masculinity (toughness, competitiveness, emotional inexpressiveness) remains a barrier to men's help-seeking (Addis and Mahalik, 2003; Mahalik, Good, and Englar-Carlson, 2003). Dominant, culture-specific norms for suppressing vulnerable emotions have led to underreporting of mental health concerns and missed diagnoses of depression among men (Cochran and Rabinowitz, 2000). Though men still may not seek help as easily or as frequently as women, attempts are being made to further understand those who do seek help. Attention is now turning to alternative formats of delivering help that might further encourage men's help-seeking behaviour (McKelley and Rochlen, 2007).

In the pages that follow, we review the influences impacting the social construction of masculinity, how these influences affect the experiences of being male, and how these experiences in turn influence men's relationships and help-seeking behaviour. We begin this complex task by describing the journey taken by one of our clients as he struggles to relate as a male in Canadian society.

Aabid[1] was born in Canada and lives at home with his family, who are Arabic in ethnicity and practising Muslims. Originally, his parents worked in professional careers in their native North African/Mediterranean country. Like many professionals immigrating to Canada, their credentials were not recognized upon arrival and they were required to retrain.

When Aabid first presented for counselling at age 19 during his second year at university, approximately three years ago, he was angry and lonely. He reported problems with organization and study skills. He also reported experiencing an unusually high level of test anxiety. Compounding this, he was having difficulty getting along with others. Although he was bullied as a child, he did have one close friend growing up. However, since that boy moved away years ago, he has remained friendless. Aabid's mother first suggested he seek help after she learned about autism in a psychology class she had taken. She suspected his restricted social functioning was attributable to an undiagnosed case of the high-functioning autism spectrum disorder Asperger's syndrome (APA, 2000). Typically, individuals with autism spectrum disorders do not easily understand subtle social cues guiding appropriate same- or opposite-sex interactions.

Aabid attended 27 individual counselling sessions and many counselling groups to address social deficits in his interactions with both men and women. A strong sense of not belonging represented a core theme in his counselling work. He identified very much as a Canadian male, but one struggling to integrate aspects of his parents' culture, including the teachings of Islam. Despite his challenges in understanding social cues and relating with others, Aabid was lonely and desperately wanted emotionally intimate relationships with others. In addition to the social deficits associated with Asperger's syndrome, it seems the dominant scripts for

'being male' in Canada deprived Aabid of affectionate male relationships more typical of Middle Eastern cultures. In fact he was puzzled by the homophobic reluctance to express affection among heterosexual Canadian males. And although Aabid recognized that heterosexual displays of affection are permitted in Canada, he insists that his Muslim identity prohibits dating or interactions with women prior to marriage.

Ways of being male in Canada are a function of the varying and complex histories, rules, or scripts associated with cultures represented in the Canadian Mosaic. Being male differs across rural and urban boundaries, by province and region, and through language and culture. This is a dynamic process. Male identities are fluid, in constant flux within a rapidly evolving multicultural context. This flux leads to increasing confusion and apprehension about how to be male given current uncertain economic conditions, the deteriorating industrial sector, and an expanded, female-dominated service economy (Levant and Pollack, 1995).

Gender Role Conflict Theory

Gender role conflict or stress has been observed in many cultures throughout the world (Levant and Richmond, 2007; van Well, Kolk, and Arrindell, 2005). Gender role conflict is defined by O'Neil and colleagues as a 'psychological state in which socialized gender roles have negative consequences on the person or others' (O'Neil, Good, and Holmes, 1995: 166). According to gender role conflict theory, stress arises from a discrepancy between one's perceived gender role identity and societal expectations regarding gender. Given that traditional tenets of masculinity make such impossible demands as 'be a sturdy oak, take a give 'em hell stance, become a big wheel and make sure there is no sissy stuff' (David and Brannon, 1976), an experience of stress upon failing to meet these demands is inevitable. After all, there is only room for one 'big wheel' at the top of an organization. Confusion arises with the contemporary conflicting expectations that men be simultaneously emotionally sensitive, courageous, and competitive. While this confusion could otherwise motivate help-seeking, the sturdy oak imperative deters it, thereby isolating men. The give 'em hell stance reinforces acting out and externalizing of conflict, thereby incriminating men.

Men who have elevated scores on measures of gender role conflict have an unrealistic drive for success, power, and competition, demonstrate restrictive emotionality and affectionate behaviour between men, and experience conflict between work and family responsibilities. For traditionally socialized men, stress results from the failure to satisfy the four impossible tenets of masculinity noted earlier. This stress has been exacerbated over the past 25 years by new, more flexible gender role expectations demanded by socioeconomic changes, including the emergence of dual-income families, employment equity, and respectful workplace policies.

Men with high gender role conflict engage in greater health-risky behaviour and express more negative attitudes to mental health help-seeking (Levant et al., 2009). Specifically, seeking psychological help is inversely related to the drive for success, power, and competition, restrictive emotionality, and restrictive affectionate behaviour among men (Blazina and Watkins, 1996). In other words, men who are driven to succeed and feel compelled to restrict expressions of vulnerability or emotional needs are less likely to seek psychological help. Levant and his colleagues suggest that psychological services need to be reoriented to fit with values of traditionally socialized men. For example, instead of providing therapy that is emotionally focused, providers are more likely to succeed with cognitive approaches, Internet-based services, or therapy provided by women.

Although more women present with depression to health professionals, men are not necessarily less depressed. Some researchers suggest that men's depression is masked by more gender-appropriate forms of emotional expression, such as anger, aggression, increased addictive or sexualized behaviour (Cochran and Rabinowitz, 2000; Lynch and Kilmartin, 1999). These observations are consistent with research on help-seeking and attachment theory. High levels of anger among depressed males appear related to insecure attachment styles (Alfonso and D'Argenio, 2004). Men with secure attachment styles have significantly less restrictive emotionality when compared with men with preoccupied, dismissive, or fearful attachment styles. In addition, men with a secure attachment style have significantly less conflict among success, power, and competition when compared with men with fearful attachment styles (Schwartz, Waldo, and Higgins, 2004).

Attachment Theory

According to attachment theory, forming relationships, including help-seeking relationships, is a function of the security of attachment bonds formed early in life with parents or guardians. Research indicates that appropriate help-seeking behaviour is more common for those with secure attachment styles than for people with anxious or avoidant attachment styles (Mallinckrodt, Gantt, and Coble, 1995; Morran, 2007). Insecure attachment ranges from *anxious*, with a negative view of self and worries about relating to others, to *avoidance*, with negative views of others, difficulty trusting others, and avoidance of relationships altogether (Shaver and Fraley, 2004).

In the context of interpersonal conflict, a person with an avoidant attachment style would be likely to withdraw and repress feelings. In contrast, a person with an anxious attachment style would be likely to approach the conflict with excessive affect. Anxiously attached people are more likely to express vulnerability and seek connection, whereas avoidantly attached people are more likely to repress affect and avoid connection. Those with avoidant attachment styles tend to report more physical symptoms on visits to physicians, whereas those with anxious styles present with more emotional issues (Zech, de Ree, Berenschot, and Stroebe, 2006). Avoidant attachments are more typical for men, whereas anxious attachments are more common for women (Bakermans-Kranenburg and van Jzendoorn, 2009; del Guidice, 2009). There is emerging evidence suggesting that men's tendency toward avoidant interpersonal conflict management in adulthood has origins in early childhood socialization pressures that discourage male bonding with maternal attachment figures (Land, Rochlen, and Vaughn, 2011).

Avoidant attachment styles appear to be contributors to poor relationship outcomes for both men and women. Withdrawal in the face of conflict is typical for a person with an avoidant attachment style. Attachment theory proposes that when traditionally socialized men experience high stress, they are more likely to withdraw from relationships, whereas traditionally socialized women under stress are more likely to approach others with complaints or requests. A person who withdraws from a relationship may be perceived to be abandoning the relationship and this could activate pursuit in a partner with an anxious attachment style (Rogers, Bidwell, and Wilson, 2005). Canadian couples therapist Susan Johnson's emotion-focused therapy (Johnson and Whiffen, 1999) is founded on observations that avoidant withdrawal is typical of males in heterosexual relationships, as is the consequent pursuit by female partners (Christensen and Heavy, 1990). Females are less satisfied in relationships with men who have avoidant attachment styles, whereas men are less satisfied in relationships with women who have anxious attachment styles (Kane, Jaremka, and Guichard, 2007). Women typically enter counselling or therapy wanting change, whereas men more often have the agenda of preserving the status quo (Jacobson, 1989).

Although anxiously insecure women are vulnerable to unsuccessful relationships, there is some evidence that both secure and anxiously insecure men (those with anxious attachment styles) have successful relationships (Collins et al., 2002; Simpson, 1990). Whereas only secure attachment styles predict successful relationships for women, men with both anxiously insecure and secure attachment styles are likely to have successful relationships. Some vulnerability in men may be important for the development of intimacy

Psychoanalytic Theory

While many writers in the field of men and masculinity have lamented the caricature of the male buffoon, humour and irony are literary devices for exposing and accepting the vulnerability inherent in male hegemony. Humour softens the defences of the powerful, opening the door to self-reflection and humility. Vulnerability is essential for connection, as well as the development of trust and intimacy. Vulnerability is disarming and it allows the powerful to save face while demonstrating humility. It says, 'I am flawed, open to criticism and likeable, but don't take me seriously because I'm only joking!'

Psychoanalytic theory considers humour to be a mature defence against anxiety (Vaillant, 1992). According to gender strain theory, men have much to be anxious about but must not reveal fear openly. Humour is a device for releasing anxiety in the face of conflict. It is a non-intimate way to accept conflict and vulnerability. Self-deprecating humour is at once humbling and protective. It reveals the vulnerability necessary for connection (e.g., compassion, caring) but creates distance by way of levity.

Stages of Change Theory

The transtheoretical model of intentional behavior change was developed in the 1980s to understand the processes involved with successful addictions treatment (Prochaska and Diclemente, 1982). Since then, this model, otherwise known as the Stages of Change model, has been expanded and successfully applied to virtually all aspects of behavioural change, ranging from programs designed to increase condom use by textile workers in India (Reza-Paul, Grimley, and Kristensen, 2004) to diabetes management (Andres, Gomez, and Saldana, 2008), exercise (Marshall and Biddle, 2001), treatment of eating disorders (Hasler et al., 2004) and many other health and mental health concerns (Prochaska et al., 1994).

Stages of Change theory may help explain men's reluctance to seek help relative to women's. With respect to making a behavioural or lifestyle change, the theory proposes that people fall into one of five stages: precontemplative, contemplative, preparation, action, or maintenance. In the precontemplation stage there is neither recognition that there is a problem nor any interest in making a change. In the contemplation stage, there is both consideration and ambivalence about making a change. In the preparation stage, preparatory action (like making an appointment to see a professional helper) is taken to enable change. In the action phase, concrete changes are made, and in the maintenance stage, ongoing efforts are expended to preserve the change. For a variety of behavioural change goals, including dieting, weight loss, exercise, stress reduction, and help-seeking, men are typically in earlier stages than women in terms of readiness to take action (Garber et al., 2004; Paddison and Flett, 2005). Stages of Change theory suggests that men are either unaware of the need to make changes or are in denial about the negative health consequences associated with taking no action.

Feminist Sociopolitical Theory

Since the late 1980s, profeminist scholars have applied feminist theory to deconstruct hegemonic masculinity (Clatterbaugh, 1990; Kaufman, 1987; Kimmel and Messner, 1992) and, in some cases, propose alternative models for being masculine (Cornish, 1999). Feminist theory posits that society, males included, would benefit from both personal and

social transformations aimed at dismantling hegemonic masculinity. For men, this means intrapsychic, interpersonal, and community/sociopolitical transformations that enable flexible gender roles and a more even distribution of power at all three levels. It means preserving healthy aspects of masculinity (e.g, assertiveness, decisiveness, action orientation) while integrating creative and flexible ways of connecting with others and participating collaboratively in community and wider sociopolitical and cultural contexts. Although there was a brief popular movement to reclaim and celebrate traditional hegemonic masculinities in the early 1990s (Bly, 1990; Keene, 1991), it was for the most part conservative and short-lived. While it may have offered men some opportunities to attend to both emotional and spiritual growth, it did so often in isolation from and opposition to women's interests (Newton, 2005).

Socioeconomic factors have motivated positive changes in men's parenting behaviour and domestic labour practices (Rochlen, McKelley, and Scaringi, 2008; Rochlen, Suizzo, and Scaringi, 2008). Feminist theory encourages the consideration of power (both vertical/hegemonic and horizontal/collaborative) within interpersonal, sociopolitical, and cultural contexts. Over the past 40 years, traumatic political events (e.g., school massacres, wars, national security events) have heightened an awareness of the need for educational and counselling programs aimed at both prevention and postvention of post-traumatic stress disorders among men. Although events such as these affect policies and programs for those in immediate need, they do not seem to have broad appeal. Furthermore, negative events are not likely to motivate positive or healthy changes. Instead, positive, inspirational messages are needed to instill hope and enthusiasm for healing change. As such, it is important to identify positive male role models that encourage help-seeking, particularly during times of confusion, change, or redefinition of men's roles (Levant and Pollack, 1995).

There are increasing numbers of high-profile men who exhibit healthy help-seeking behaviour. Their stories have been told but not with much emphasis on the changing masculine roles inherent in their experiences. The remainder of this chapter identifies theoretically relevant elements of evolving masculinities that promise to inspire help-seeking or emotional growth among Canadian men.

Canadian Men's Stories

Narratives are powerful educational tools. Storytellers often captivate large audiences in their delivery of complex messages that are personally relevant, authentic, and entertaining. Sometimes academic writing in the social sciences appears dry and removed from the subject matter, perhaps due to neglect of narratives. Given that men are more likely to resist prescriptions for health or behavioural change, inspirational narratives delivered by gifted, high-profile, and influential men may have more potential for promoting healthy masculinities.

Storytelling is as old as humankind. The first written record of an account of storytelling appears in the Egyptian papyrus known as the Westcar Papyrus, produced sometime between 2000 and 1300 BC (Pellowski, 1991). The oral tradition of storytelling in Newfoundland, while not nearly as old, has been much better preserved, due in part to the fact that it persisted much longer than in many other places in the world. A typical Newfoundland folktale begins as follows: 'Well there was three fellers, you know, three fellers sold theirselves to the Devil for three year. One of 'em was a shoemaker, an' the other one was a tailor. Well Jack, of course, he was a sailor. Of course he *would* be' (Widdowson, 2002: 152). This is a typical beginning to a 'Newfoundland Jack tale', a colourful adaptation of Jack tales such as Jack and the Beanstalk or Jack and the Three Giants that originated in England and Ireland and were transplanted to the colonies. These Newfoundland versions have outlived their continental counterparts in their nuanced oral tradition because of relative isolation and a less industrialized economy. The Newfoundland tradition of storytelling by men continues today, as evident in the rants of Rick Mercer and the playful intellectual wanderings of Rex Murphy.

According to folklorists, Newfoundland 'Jack tales' have conveyed wisdom to young men about 'how to be' in the world, especially the working world (Lovelace, 2001). They often represent the 'master and man' employment relationship and 'they are lessons in life as seen from the perspective of a subordinated social class'. According to Lovelace, Newfoundland has until recently been 'a hard luck place'. It has one of the highest unemployment rates in North America. Work is scarce and seasonal, and never constant. As such, Newfoundland men have identified with a central feature of the magic tale, that of the search by the 'poor hero' for work. According to Ortutay, heroes have 'a rebellious desire for the re-creation of the world and for heroic adventure, combined with the serf's fear and religious humility in the face of the realm of secrets and powers' (1972: 253).

Fishing has dominated the economy of Newfoundland for hundreds of years. It is a challenging livelihood that provides opportunities to be one's own boss and to work independently and outdoors. While it has long been the cultural ideal for Newfoundland men, it is one of the most hazardous of occupations (Power, 2008). As such, it is intricately connected to larger narratives of hardship and survival in one of the most inhospitable, dreary climates in North America. It is no surprise, then, that wit, colour, and caustic humour are trademarks of the Newfoundland folktale that creates and recreates cultural meanings for a most difficult environment.

British folklorist J. Widdowson describes the character of Jack in detail. Consider Newfoundland characters in Canadian television.

They seem to have many of the characteristics of Jack:

[H]e is usually presented as good-natured and prepared to take life as it comes, although he can also be offhand, truculent, and cheeky or, as the storytellers themselves sometimes refer to him, 'a devil-may-care' fellow. His behaviour in the face of whatever unkind treatment he receives is quiet, resigned, and stoical. However, once he is in a position to outwit his enemies he becomes aggressive, decisive, and ruthless. . . . In these respects he is seen as the champion of the underdog, fearless and invulnerable in fighting against oppression. He is also mischievous, something of a trickster, agile both physically and mentally, as well as being witty and alert to what is going on around him. . . . In many ways, he represents 'the common man'—ordinary, apparently unpromising, not easily provoked, but also resourceful, optimistic, and someone whose perseverance wins through against the odds. Jack engages our attention, arouses and sustains our interest in what he will do next, and in particular how he will outwit his adversaries. Whereas in most published texts the plot is paramount, and Jack seems merely to be manipulated by circumstances and events over which he has little or no control, in the oral storytelling it is his character that drives the plot (Widdowson, 2009: 25).

Rick Mercer

Rick Mercer is a lot like Jack. He was born in St. John's on 17 October 1969. He is famous in Canada for his satirical television news shows, *This Hour Has 22 Minutes* and *The Mercer Report*. Mercer is perhaps most famous for his rants. Like Jack, Rick is mischievous, cheeky, challenging of authority. He often outwits his targets—politicians or other prominent Canadians,

but he does so with humility. Whether it be bungee-cord jumping with wheelchair-bound Rick Hansen or skinny dipping with a former premier of Ontario, Rick Mercer is not afraid to look the fool, albeit a fool with a social conscience. Although he rants at the establishment, he does not preach. Instead he reveals ironies and gives us pause to think about complex problems in a serious yet lighthearted manner. He helps us to see humanity and humility in public figures. He is assertive yet disarming. These are some of the positive characteristics of the Newfoundland male.

Rick was 'outed' as a gay man by the *Globe and Mail* newspaper, but like most people he keeps his sexuality private. Like Jack, Rick 'is circumspect about whatever he reveals of himself to figures of authority' (Lovelace, 2001: 154). Rick is a public figure, but unlike the political figures whom he skewers, he is not on display (Gatehouse, 2004). As Gatehouse writes, '[with Rick] you will never read the type of confessional, misspent youth, tears-of-a-clown profile that we have come to expect' from Hollywood celebrities. Gatehouse continues that Mercer may well be the bright, articulate, fun guy with the sly sense of humour that we see in his TV personality, but 'for a man who has built a successful career out of putting famous people on the spot, he politely, resolutely, refuses to be paid in kind. Want to know what makes Rick tick? Fine. Good luck to you. Oh dear, look at the time.' Sly and circumspect, just like Jack.

In a rant from a 2007 episode of *The Mercer Report*, Mercer alludes to the high risks associated with bullying male teens, given their vulnerability around questions of identity and sexual orientation. Bullying, Mercer says, is a serious social problem with devastating consequences—the number of results returned by an Internet search for the terms 'bully', 'Canada', and 'suicide', he informs, is distressingly high. 'And', he adds, 'we're not talking about just one or two stories here—we're talking about hundreds.' For the kids who are being bullied, attending school is not much different to being in a penitentiary. For twelve years they are incessantly subjected to emotional harassment, verbal derision, and physical abuse. It is not surprising, then, that these children become hopeless, lose perspective, and forget that this is a short period of their lives. After all, murderers in Canada, Mercer quips, do less time in jail.

In this same rant, Mercer reminds us that public awareness campaigns against bullying are lumped with countless other causes and ignored, and those of us who endured and overcame the abuses of bullying quickly forget how difficult this time can be for others. Using his trademark sardonic humour, Mercer subtlety rallies his audience to take an interest in these children—to remind them that things do get better, that they will be successful, they will have friends, and that they can be geeky, or openly gay, and happy. And, to those students who are different, Mercer offers this advice: '. . . if you're being bullied in school because you're different, please, tell someone about it and remember, even in a real prison, eventually, everyone gets parole'(Mercer, 2010).

In all of his rants, Mercer challenges the sociopolitical status quo using humour to soften the blow and enable those he is skewering to engage with him. In one episode, he is filmed diving off a cottage dock naked with a former provincial premier who was at the time a member of the federal Opposition. This irreverence and willingness to show humility while delivering poignant calls to action, as he does in the rant just quoted, allows for thought-provoking yet friendly debate. That Rick Mercer is an assertive, private, successful celebrity who champions the underdog with wit and humility and who happens also to be gay is an inspiration to male teens, who may now see that being male is much more about confidence, engagement, social conscience, and self-expression than sexual identity.

Feminist, gender role strain, attachment, and psychoanalytic theories are evident in Mercer's work. Men respond well to bids for connection when humour lowers defences. Men may be more receptive to challenges and open to more flexible gender roles when these are explored within a playful context. And within a playful context, a sermon of sorts can be delivered, as Mercer does through his rants, without sounding either preachy or self-indulgent.

Romeo Dallaire

Unlike Rick Mercer, who grew up the left-leaning son of a Newfoundland fisherman, Romeo Dallaire was raised in a much more conservative Quebec military family. His autobiographical account of his command in Rwanda prior to and during the genocide in 1993 and 1994 is written in the clipped, mechanical detail typical of a military mind. It is difficult to get a sense of who the man is at his core from this book. Despite the masking effect of his writing style, his disclosures are open and revealing of vulnerability. And perhaps because of the style there is an ironic element of confidence in his accounts of personal failure. This struggle between the traditional masculine imperative to be the strong, sturdy oak and the attachment need to elicit compassion, connection, and healing through the expression and acceptance of vulnerability and ambiguity mirrors the healing struggle inherent in psychoanalysis. Gender role conflict is evident in this passage describing his mixed allegiances in his role in quelling the Quebec sovereignist terror threat during the 1970 October Crisis:

> I have often been criticized for being an 'emotional' leader, for not being macho enough, but even during this early stage in my career, I believed that the magic of command lies in openness, in being both sympathetic to the troops and apart, in always projecting supreme confidence in my own ability to accomplish whatever task is set for us (Dallaire, 2003: 26).

Like Mercer, Dallaire challenges the socio-political status quo. Unlike Mercer, the political was and still is personal for Dallaire. By virtue of his extremely limited UN poltical mandate, Daillaire was under strict instructions not to intervene even when a murder was occurring in front of him during his command of the skeleton peacekeeping force in Rwanda. White, middle-class guilt associated with neutrality in the context of ethnic brutality was overwhelming for Dallaire. It became tragically personal with his descent into suicidal depression. His depression reflected the utter helplessness he experienced while witnessing a genocide that could have been prevented. But in keeping with the feminist 'personal is political' slogan, Daillaire's political writings, grounded as they are in his own failings, proclaim a powerful message on sociopolitical and ethnic imbalances throughout the world. Daillaire remains wounded and in conflict, and as psychoanalytic theory suggests, there is a fundamental existential truth in facing and accepting one's humility:

I am not healed. I don't go into the grocery stores because the opulence of the food, the aroma and color, literally paralyzes me. I see people dying of starvation killing each other at food distribution points. Women and children dead, trampled to death. I live with these scenes because I've built a sort of prosthesis that keeps the pain under wraps. The prosthesis is the result of therapy and having friends to talk to. I had to negotiate with the devil. I talked to him, laughed, and maneuvered with him. One night in particular comes to mind. Extremist battalions were coming up the flank of a hill toward the headquarters. The few troops I had with me had been ordered by their commanding nations not to fight to protect Rwandans. I looked out the window knowing that we were going to be attacked and that we would be

wiped out. And then I heard the sound of the wind carrying the voices and screams of women and children from far off and at that moment I knew we were going to stay and fight and protect, even if we saved one Rwandan, we'd do that. I believe that sound was the presence of a stronger entity. I know there's a God because I negotiated with his enemy (Dallaire et al., 2006: 61–2).

Before his command in Rwanda, Dallaire was known to be a hard-working leader on the one hand and a fun-loving, life-of-the-party extravert on the other. Afterwards, he was unable to relax or socialize. He was confused and easily distracted as he descended into deep, self-loathing depression (Off, 2000). In her interview with Dallaire in the late 1990s, Canadian journalist Carol Off observes:

I . . . met a man anxious and grey, intense and sad. He paused during conversations to deal with searing head pains. A flood of emotions crossed his face every minute. He talked freely about his condition, how easy it is to lapse back into thoughts of suicide. He was open and often eloquent but extremely unhappy (118).

Dallaire appears to be a broken man at the time of the interview. Although it is clear from his writing and his political work that Dallaire (now a Canadian senator) is productive, his emotional and intimate interpersonal health states are less obvious. Dallaire continues to dedicate himself to public (now political) service, as men often can (Garcia et al., 2011), but is he personally grounded in or intimately attached to significant and meaningful interpersonal relationships? Has he found the balance he lost? PTSD likely continues to affect his emotional quality of life.

As Razak cautions, there is a risk that psychoanalyzing or personalizing war and trauma divorces us from the structural historical political conditions underlying injustice (Razak, 2003). By keeping his analysis firmly political in his own writings and grounding it only minimally with brief references to his own personal struggle, Dallaire avoids co-opting legitimate oppression in the form of white middle-class, male victimization. Dallaire is not the victim. He is not the hero. He is human.

Craig Kielburger

Given the relative importance of secure attachment to facilitate help-seeking, and research which suggests that less secure individuals are at higher risk for mental illness, it follows that children with less secure attachments are less likely to have family support figures that can facilitate access to services. The classroom is therefore an important venue for promoting healthy male development and access to health-related resources. Teachers often become the 'professionals of choice' among adolescents needing emotional or interpersonal support (Morran, 2007).

Philip Zimbardo (1971), creator of the infamous Stanford prison experiment in the early 1970s, recognizes that good people do bad things under certain conditions. More recently, Zimbardo (2007) suggests that we deal with this reality by setting the conditions for the creation of heroes. The classroom is an ideal place for setting those conditions.

On 19 April 1995, Toronto-area resident Craig Kielburger was about to read the comics while eating breakfast when a news story caught his eye (Kielburger and Major, 1999). The headline read 'Battled Child Labour, Boy, 12, Murdered'. Craig was 12 at the time and this proximity engaged his attention and filled him with questions and bewilderment. The article reported that a Pakistani boy, Iqbal Masih, had been sold into slavery by his parents when he was four years old. He escaped enslavement as a carpet weaver after six years and participated in an international campaign against child labour. Iqbal was riding his bicycle alongside a friend when he was shot dead.

Craig went to his public library in search of answers, but instead he discovered how extensive the problem was and was angered by how little attention seemed to be devoted to resolving the issue. Craig was emotionally activated by an event on the other side of the world, across economic and cultural divides. His anger quickly transformed into political activism, beginning with an impromptu speech to his grade six classmates. His older brother, Marc, had been engaged in activism for some time, and served as a role model to Craig. Craig learned about the power, energy, and idealism that youth can bring to social causes. Along with 18 of his classmates he launched the 'Free the Children' campaign, which over the next decade expanded to involve one million participants in 35 countries. In part through Craig's initiative, child labour is being reduced throughout the world.

Craig's capacity to transform shock, bewilderment, and anger into action for the public good represents a core value of traditional hegemonic masculinity. However, his approach, as described in his second book, co-authored with his brother, Marc, is consistent with a collective profeminist process that orients away from the power-over dynamic characteristic of the narcissistic hero to a power-with community-building approach. This philosophy is obvious from the title of the book: *Me to We: Finding Meaning in a Material World* (Kielburger and Kielburger, 2006). In their book, Marc and Craig provide practical suggestions for promoting healthy social change and nurturing young heroes who will eschew egocentricism in favour of a collectivist, synergistic, and sustainable process of sociopolitical change—change that is far greater than the sum of the individual participant contributions could ever be (Cornish, 1991; 1999). Not only is Craig's story inspirational to youth, it demonstrates how everyday heroes can easily become reality in the context of our community classrooms.

Conclusion

Being male or masculine in Canada is largely contextual and influenced by multiple factors: the history of Canada as a country along with its geography, socioeconomic status, age, race, sexual orientation, culture, country of origin, number of generations in Canada, level of assimilation, degree of cultural retention, and level of exposure to various male mentors. There are many cultures of men in Canada. As such, understanding a particular male, his masculinity, and the nature of relationships with others within the Canadian Mosaic is best accomplished from a transtheoretical, multicultural competency framework (Arthur and Collins, 2005). Understanding a particular male in Canada requires an understanding of the many influences contributing to his socialization— the *how and where* he learned to be male (Pleck, 1981; 1995), along with the ways he expresses his identity through the Canadian Mosaic. We recognize the importance of varied, multiple male role models (or heroes) for guiding healthy male development. Inspirational figures are particularly important given current conflicting gender role expectations and the resulting confusion men experience (Levant and Pollack, 1995). New role models are advancing alongside old ones (Kimmel, 1987). Identification and appreciation of emerging diverse male role models promises the development of varied alternative constructions of healthy, respectful, and adaptive Canadian masculinities.

Discussion Questions

1. Who were important role models/male mentors in your life, and what did you learn from them?
2. What is gender role strain/conflict?
3. How can attachment theory explain help-seeking behaviour in men?
4. Although Canadian men's help-seeking behaviour is less frequent than women's, it remains stable and there are some signs that it is increasing. Discuss how this can be encouraged.
5. Discuss the role of Canadian masculinities (considering geographic, demographic, and cultural diversity) on men's help-seeking.
6. From your reading of the chapter, and your own experience, what are some of the influences that inform Canadian scripts about how to be male?
7. Discuss the role of vulnerability in help-seeking as portrayed in the stories of men in the chapter.
8. How might Stages of Change theory explain the lower rate of help-seeking among men compared to women?
9. What is hegemonic masculinity?

Recommended Websites

American Psychological Association: www.apa.
org/divisions/div51

Monitor on Psychology: www.apa.org/
monitor/jun05/helping.aspx

National Organization for Men Against
Sexism: www.nomas.org

Centre for Mental Health and Addiction: www.
camh.net

Canadian Psychological Association: www.cpa.
ca/public

Canadian Mental Health Association: www.
cmha.ca/bins/index.asp?lang=1

Note

1. We have changed this client's name and not pro-
    vided all the details about him in order to afford
    him some anonymity.

References

About.com. 2008. 'Sex Ratio Represents the Number of
Males to Females in a Population', *Geography*, 1 July
2009.

Addis, M.E., and J.R. Mahalik. 2003. 'Men, Masculinity,
and the Contexts of Help Seeking', *American
Psychologist*, 58, 1: 5–14.

Advameg. 2009. 'Canada—Location, Size, and Content',
Encyclopedia of the Nations, accessed 15 Jan. 2009.

Alfonso, T., and A. D'Argenio. 2004. 'The Relationship
between Anger and Depression in a Clinical Sample of
Young Men: The Role of Insecure Attachment', *Journal
of Affective Disorders*, 79: 269–72.

Andres, J., J. Gomez, and C. Saldana. 2008. 'Challenges
and Applications of the Transtheoretical Model in
Patients with Diabetes Mellitus', *Disease Management
and Health Outcomes*, 16: 31–46.

APA. 2000. *Diagnostic and Statistical Manual of Mental
Disorders (DSM-IV-TR)*. Washington, DC: American
Psychiatric Association.

Arthur, N., and S. Collins, eds. 2005. *Culture-Infused
Counseling: Celebrating the Canadian Mosaic*. Calgary:
Counselling Concepts.

AUCCCD. 2010. *Director Surveys*, www.aucccd.org,
accessed 1 Oct. 2010.

Bakermans-Kranenburg, M.J., and M.H. van IJzendoorn.
2009. 'The First 10,000 Adult Attachment Interviews:
Distributions of Adult Attachment Representations
in Clinical and Non-clinical Groups', *Attachment and
Human Development*, 11: 223–63.

Blazina, C., and C.E. Watkins, Jr. 1996. 'Masculine

Gender Role Conflict: Effect on Men's Psychological
Well-being, Chemical Substance Use, and Attitudes
toward Help Seeking', *Journal of Counseling Psychology*,
43: 461–5.

Bly, R. 1990. *Iron John: A Book about Men*. Reading, MA:
Addison-Wesley.

CBC. 2008. 'Life Expectancy Hits 80.4 Years: Statistics
Canada', www.cbc.ca/canada/story/2008/01/14/death-
stats.html, accessed 14 Feb. 2010.

Christensen, A., and C.L. Heavy. 1990. 'Gender and Social
Structure in the Demand/Withdraw Pattern of Marital
Conflict', *Journal of Personality and Social Psychology*,
59: 73–81.

Clatterbaugh, K. 1990. *Contemporary Perspectives on
Masculinity: Men, Women, and Politics in Modern
Society*. Boulder, CO: Westview.

Cochran, S.V., and F.E. Rabinowitz. 2000. *Men and
Depression: Clinical and Empirical Perspectives: Practical
Resources for the Mental Health Professional*. San Diego,
CA: Academic Press.

Collins, N.L., M.L. Cooper, A. Albino, and L. Allard.
2002. 'Psychosocial Vulnerability from Adolescence to
Adulthood: A Prospective Study of Attachment Style
Differences in Relationship Functioning and Partner
Choice', *Journal of Personality and Social Psychology*,
70: 965–1008.

Cornish, P. 1991. 'Defining Empowerment: Towards the
Development of Phenomenologically-Based Theory
and Research Methods'. MA thesis (University of
Saskatchewan).

———. 1999. 'Men Engaging Feminism: A Model of Personal Change and Social Transformation', *Journal of Men's Studies*, 7: 173–99.

Dallaire, R. 2003. *Shake Hands with the Devil: The Failure of Humanity in Rwanda*. New York: Carroll and Graff.

———, T. Moore, M. Woodman, S. Lewis, and M. Rutte. 2006. *Seeking the Sacred: Leading a Spiritual Life in a Secular World*. Toronto: ECW Press.

David, D.S., and R. Brannon. 1976. *The Forty-Nine Percent Majority: The Male Sex Role*. Reading, MA: Addison-Wesley.

del Guidice, M. 2009. 'Sex, Attachment, and the Development of Reproductive Strategies', *Behavioral and Brain Sciences*, 32: 1–21.

Dominion Institute. 2008. 'Black Settlement in Early Canada', *Black History Canada*, http://blackhistory canada.ca/theme.php?id=2, accessed 15 Jan. 2009.

Foley, D., B. McCulloch, K. McDonald, M. McKinney, and S. Thomson (Writers) and J. Blanchard, K. Makin, S. Surjik, R. Boyd, and J. Budgell (Directors). 1988–94 [Television]. In L. Michaels (Producer), *The Kids in the Hall*. Canada.

Garber, C.E., J. Allsworth, B. Marcus, J. Hesser, and K.L. Lapane. 2004. 'Correlates of Stages of Change in a Population Survey', *Medicine and Science in Sports and Exercise*, 36: S48.

Garcia, H.A., E.P. Finley, W. Lorber, and M. Jakupcak. 2011. 'A Preliminary Study of the Association between Traditional Masculine Behavioral Norms in Iraq and Afghanistan Veterans', *Psychology of Men and Masculinity*, 12, 1: 53–63.

Gatehouse, J. 2004, Feb. 'Rick's Shtick: Canada's Hottest TV Comic Can't Resist That Blood Sport, Politics', *Maclean's*.

Green, R., and S. Smith (Writers) and R. Green (Director). 1991–2005 [Television]. In S. Smith and R. Green (Producers), *The Red Green Show*. Canada.

Guisepi, R. 2002. 'Prehistory to Early European Contact', *Canada, An Early History*, http://history-world.org/ canada.htm, accessed 1 Oct. 2009.

Harris, I.M. 1995. *Messages Men Hear: Constructing Masculinities*. Bristol, PA: Taylor and Francis.

Hasler, G., A. Delsignore, G. Milos, C. Buddeberg, and U. Schnyder. 2004. 'Application of Prochaska's Transtheoretical Model of Change to Patients with Eating Disorders', *Journal of Psychosomatic Research*, 57: 67–72.

Jacobson, N.S. 1989. 'The Politics of Intimacy', *The Behavior Therapist*, 12: 29–32.

Johnson, S.M., and V.E. Whiffen. 1999. 'Made to Measure: Adapting Emotionally Focused Couple Therapy to Partner's Attachment Styles', *Clinical Psychology: Science and Practice*, 6: 336–81.

Kaiser Family Foundation. 2009. 'Adult Sex Ratio (Proportion of Males to Females, Aged 15 to 64) 2009', www.globalhealthfacts.org/topic.jsp?i=80, accessed 1 July 2009.

Kane, H.S., L.M. Jaremka, and A.C. Guichard. 2007. 'Feeling Supported and Feeling Satisfied: How One Partner's Attachment Style Predicts the Other Partner's Relationship Experiences', *Journal of Social and Personal Relationships*, 24: 535–55.

Kaufman, M. 1987. *Beyond Patriarchy: Essays by Men on Pleasure, Power and Change*. Don Mills, ON: Oxford University Press.

Keene, S. 1991. *Fire in the Belly: On Being a Man*. New York: Bantam.

Kielburger, C., and M. Kielburger. 2006. *Me to We: Finding Meaning in the Material World*. Toronto, ON: Wiley.

Kielburger, C., and K. Major. 1999. *Free the Children: A Young Man Fights against Child Labor and Proves That Children Can Change the World*. Toronto: Turtleback Books.

Kimmel, M.S. 1987. 'Rethinking "Masculinity": New Directions in Research', in M.S. Kimmel, ed., *Changing Men: New Directions in Research on Men and Masculinity*. Newbury Park, CA: Sage.

———and M.A. Messner. 1992. *Men's Lives*, 5th ed. Needham Heights, MA: Allyn & Bacon.

Koyczan, S. 2010. 'We Are More', www.youtube.com/ watch?v=Hg-jeGpwq0c&NR=1, accessed 21 March 2010.

Land, L.N., A.B. Rochlen, and B.K.Vaughn. 2011. 'Correlates of Adult Attachment Avoidance: Men's Avoidance of Intimacy in Romantic Relationships', *Psychology of Men and Masculinity*, 12, 1: 64–76.

Levant, R.F., D.J. Wimer, C.M. Williams, K.B. Smalley, and D. Noronha. 2009. 'The Relationships between Masculinity Variables, Health Risk Behaviors and Attitudes toward Seeking Psychological Help', *International Journal of Men's Health*, 8: 3–21.

Levant, R.F., and W.S. Pollack. 1995. *A New Psychology of Men*. New York: Basic Books.

Levant, R.F., and K. Richmond. 2007. 'A Review of Research on Masculinity Ideologies Using the Male Role Norms Inventory', *Journal of Men's Studies*, 15: 130–46.

Lovelace, M. 2001. 'Jack and His Masters: Real Worlds and Tale Worlds in Newfoundland Folktales', *Journal of Folklore Research*, 38: 149–70.

Lynch, J., and C. Kilmartin. 1999. *The Pain behind the Mask: Overcoming Masculine Depression*. New York: Haworth Press.

Mackie, M. 1983. *Exploring Gender Relations: A Canadian Perspective*. Toronto: Butterworths.

Mahalik, J.R., G.E. Good, and M. Englar-Carlson. 2003. 'Masculinity Scripts, Presenting Concerns, and Help Seeking: Implications for Practice and Training',

Professional Psychology Research and Practice, 34, 2: 123–31.

Mallinckrodt, B., D.L. Gantt, and H.M. Coble. 1995. 'Attachment Patterns in the Psychotherapy Relationship: Development of the Client Attachment to Therapist Scale', *Journal of Counseling Psychology*, 42: 307–17.

Marshall, S.J., and J.H. Biddle. 2001. 'The Transtheoretical Model of Behavior Change: A Meta-analysis of Applications to Physical Activity and Exercise', *Annals of Behavioral Science*, 23: 229–46.

McKelley, R.A., and A.B. Rochlen. 2007. 'The Practice of Coaching: Exploring Alternatives to Therapy for Counseling-Resistant Men', *Psychology of Men and Masculinity*, 8, 1: 53–65.

Mercer, R. 2010. 'It Does Get Better', www.rickmercer.com/Rick-s-Rant/Blog/November-2007/It-Does-Get-Better.aspx, accessed 7 March 2010.

Morran, P. 2007. 'Attachment Style, Ethnicity and Help-seeking Attitudes among Adolescent Pupils', *British Journal of Guidance and Counselling*, 35: 205–18.

Newton, J. 2005. *From Panthers to Promise Keepers: Rethinking the Men's Movement*. New York: Rowman & Littlefield.

Off, C. 2000. *The Lion, the Fox and the Eagle: A Story of Generals and Justice in Yugoslavia and Rwanda*. Toronto: Random House.

O'Neil, J.M., G.E. Good, and S. Holmes. 1995. 'Fifteen Years of Theory and Research on Men's Gender Role Conflict: New Paradigms for Empirical Research', in R.F. Levant and W.S. Pollack, eds., *A New Psychology of Men*. New York: Basic Books.

Ortutay, G. 1972. *Hungarian Folklore: Essays*. Budapest: Akademiai Kiado.

Paddison, J., and R. Flett. 2005. 'Age and Gender Differences in the Stages of Change for Six Health-related Behaviours: A Pilot Study in New Zealand', *Health Education Journal*, 64: 372–81.

Pellowski, A. 1991. *The World of Storytelling*. New York: W.H. Wilson.

Pleck, J.H. 1981. *The Myth of Masculinity*. Cambridge, MA: MIT Press.

———. 1995. 'The Gender Role Strain Paradigm: An Update', in R.F. Levant and W.S. Pollack, eds., *A New Psychology of Men*. New York: Basic Books.

Power, N.G. 2008. 'Occupational Risks, Safety and Masculinity: Newfoundland Fish Harvesters' Experiences and Understandings of Fishery Risks', *Health, Risk and Society*, 10, 6: 565–83.

Prochaska, J.O., and C.C. Diclemente. 1982. 'Transtheoretical Therapy: Toward a More Integrative Model of Change', *Psychotherapy: Theory, Research and Practice*, 19: 276–88.

Prochaska, J.O., W.F. Velicer, J.S. Rossi, M.G. Goldstein, B.H. Marcus, W. Rakowski, and S.R. Rossi. 1994.

'Stages of Change and Decisional Balance for 12 Problem Behaviors', *Health Psychology*, 13: 39–46.

Razak, S. 2003. 'Those Who "Witness the Evil"', *Hypatia*, 18: 204–11.

Reza-Paul, S., D. Grimley, and S. Kristensen. 2004. 'Application of Transtheoretical Model of Change for Measuring Condom Use among Textile Factory Workers in India', Paper presented at the Fifteenth International Conference on AIDS, Bangkok, Thailand.

Rochlen, A.B., M.-A. Suizzo, and V. Scaringi. 2008. 'Predictors of Relationship Satisfaction, Psychological Well-being, and Life Satisfaction among Stay-at-Home Fathers', *Psychology of Men and Masculinity*, 9, 1: 17–28.

Rochlen, A.B., R.A. McKelley, and V. Scaringi. 2008. '"I'm Just Providing for My Family": A Qualitative Study of Stay-at-Home Fathers', *Psychology of Men and Masculinity*, 9, 4: 193–206.

Rogers, W.S., J. Bidwell, and L. Wilson. 2005. 'Perception of and Satisfaction with Relationship, Power, Sex and Attachment Styles: A Couples Level Analysis', *Journal of Family Violence*, 20: 241–51.

Rootman, I., and B. Rhonson. 2005. 'Literacy and Health Research in Canada: Where Have We Been and Where Should We Go?', *Canadian Journal of Public Health*, 96 (S): 62–77.

Schwartz, J.P., M. Waldo, and A. Higgins. 2004. 'Attachment Styles: Relationship to Masculine Gender Role Conflict in College Men', *Psychology of Men and Masculinity*, 5: 143–6.

Shaver, P.R., and R.C. Fraley. 2004. 'Self-report Measures of Adult Attachment', www.psych.uiuc.edu/~rcfraley/measures/measures.html, accessed 17 March 2010.

Simpson, J.A. 1990. 'Influence of Attachment Styles on Romantic Relationships', *Journal of Personality and Social Psychology*, 59: 971–80.

Statistics Canada. 2005. 'Contact with Health Professionals about Mental Health in the Past 12 Months, by Age Group and Sex, Household Population Aged 12 and Over, Selected Provinces and Health Regions (June 2005 Boundaries), Every 2 Years', Table 105-0463, CANSIM, http://cansim2.statcan.gc.ca/cgi-win/cnsmcgi.exe?Lang=E&CNSM-Fi=CII/CII_1-eng.htm, accessed 22 Jan. 2010.

———. 2006. 'Portrait of the Canadian Population in 2006, 2006 Census', http://dsp-psd.pwgsc.gc.ca/collection_2007/statcan/97-551-X/97-551-XIE2006001.pdf, accessed 1 July 2009.

———. 2007a. 'The Evolving Linguistic Portait, 2006 Census', http://dsp-psd.pwgsc.gc.ca/collection_2007/statcan/97-555-X/97-555-XIE2006001.pdf, accessed 1 July 2009.

———. 2007b. 'Canadian Community Health Survey (CCHS 1.1) Urban-Rural Profile, by Sex, Canada, Provinces and Territories, Occasional', Table

105-0114, CANSIM, http://cansim2.statcan.gc.ca/cgi-win/cnsmcgi.exe?Lang=E&CNSM-Fi=CII/CII_1-eng.htm, accessed 28 Feb. 2010.

———. 2009. 'University Enrolments, by Registration Status, Program Level, Classification of Instructional Programs, Primary Grouping (CIP_PG) and Sex, Annual (Number)', Table 477-0013, CANSIM, Using E-STAT (distributor). estat.statcan.gc.ca/cgi-win/cnsmcgi.exe?Lang=E&EST-Fi=EStat/English/CII_1-eng.htm, accessed 1 Feb. 2010.

———. 2010, 21 June. 'Life Expectancy at Birth, by Sex, by Province', www40.statcan.ca/l01/cst01/health26-eng.htm, accessed 1 Oct. 2010.

Thomas, D., and R. Moranis (Writers) and G. Bloomfield, M. Bessada, and J. Blanchard (Directors). 1976–81. 'The Great White North', *SCTV*. Toronto: Old Firehall Productions.

——— (Writers). 2009 [Television]. In D. Thomas and R.Moranis (Producers), *Bob and Doug*: Animax Entertainment.

Vaillant, G.E. 1992. *Ego Mechanisms of Defense: A Guide for Clinicians and Researchers*. Washington, DC: American Psychiatric Publishing.

van Well, S., A.M. Kolk, and W.A. Arrindell. 2005. 'Cross-cultural Validity of the Masculine and Feminine Gender Role Stress Scales', *Journal of Personality Assessment*, 84: 271–8.

Way, N., and J.Y. Chu. 2004. *Adolescent Boys: Exploring Diverse Cultures of Boyhood*. New York: New York University Press.

West, C., and D. Zimmerman. 1987. 'Doing Gender', *Gender and Society*, 1, 2: 140.

Widdowson, J.D.A. 2002. *Little Jack and Other Newfoundland Folktales*. St. John's: Memorial University of Newfoundland Folklore and Language Publications.

———. 2009. 'Folktales in Newfoundland Oral Tradition: Structure, Style, and Performance', *Folklore*, 120: 19–35.

Zech, E., F. de Ree, F. Berenschot, and M. Stroebe. 2006. 'Depressive Affect among Health Care Seekers: How It Is Related to Attachment Style, Emotional Disclosure, and Health Complaints', *Psychology, Health and Medicine*, 11: 7–19.

Zimbardo, P. 1971. *The Stanford Prison Experiment: A Simulation of the Psychology of Imprisonment Conducted August 1971 at Stanford University*. Stanford, CA: P. Zimbardo.

———. 2007. *The Lucifer Effect: Understanding How Good People Turn Evil*. New York: Random House.

CHAPTER 5

When developing a text about men and masculinity, it is unfortunately necessary—both ethically and intellectually—to discuss manifestations of violence. Although it is true that not every man exhibits violence, it is also true that the overwhelming majority of violent acts are committed by men. As well, this reality has a profound impact on women, even those who do not personally experience acts of violence. For instance, women must contend with the threat of violence each day. Consider, for instance, that when class ends after dark, women must have a plan to navigate safely to their homes, transportation, or to their next appointment. Men rarely have to give overt consideration to such details. The need to manage one's safety in such detail, or the absence of such need, arguably has consequences for well-being and sense of agency. As discussed in earlier chapters, raising this topic can cause discomfort, defensiveness, anger, sadness, or guilt. However exciting and interesting college and university campuses may be, they are also particularly challenging environments in terms of these topics, with their densely populated peer groups and disarming sense of familiarity and safety. They also often have a sexually charged atmosphere and the presence of alcohol and other drugs, which present additional risks.

DeKeseredy analyzes the complex variables that shape these phenomena, and offers an alternative by calling upon men who are interested in gender equity and a socially just society. There are opportunities to work toward solutions and to foster strong and trusting relationships through actively taking responsibility to interrupt and prevent violence and its precursors. Men have an important role to play in this regard. It is notable that those men who do threaten and harm women and other men have a disproportionately large impact on men's reputations. That is, even if most men would not act out violently, the fact that most also do not actively and overtly demand an end to violence is itself part of the problem. As university students, readers of this text are in an especially valuable position to stake claim to a campus and community free of violence, and to continue that practice when entering a profession and establishing homes and families over time.

Ending Woman Abuse on Canadian University and Community College Campuses: The Role of Feminist Men

Walter S. DeKeseredy

Nearly 20 years ago, the results of the Canadian National Survey (CNS) on Woman Abuse in university/college dating were released to the media, the academic community, government agencies, and the Canadian general public. Data distributed then revealed:

- Of the female participants, 28 per cent stated that they were sexually abused in the past year, while 11 per cent of the males reported having sexually victimized a female dating partner during the same time period.
- Approximately 45 per cent of the women in the sample stated that they had been sexually abused by a boyfriend or male dating partner since leaving high school and 19.5 per cent of the men reported committing at least one sexual assault in the same time period.
- Nearly 14 per cent of the men reported physically abusing a girlfriend or female dating partner in the past year, while 22.3 per cent of the women were targets of such victimization.
- Of the women, 35 per cent reported having been physically abused, and 17.8 per cent of the men stated that they had been violent since leaving high school (DeKeseredy and Kelly, 1993).

Woman abuse on and near campuses plagued the entire nation in the early 1990s and arguably still does today. For example, Schwartz and DeKeseredy's (2000) analysis of the CNS dataset found no Canadian regional variations in physical and sexual abuse. This provides evidence that there is a culture that supports male violence against women across Canada. Schwartz and DeKeseredy uncovered that men report being sexual or physical abusers at a fairly constant rate from the Atlantic to the Pacific Oceans, whether in two-year community colleges or major research universities, and whether they are Anglophone or Francophone. Further, one of the most powerful determinants of woman abuse in all types of intimate heterosexual relationships—male peer support—was a constant within Canadian post-secondary institutions. Male peer support refers to attachments to male peers and the resources these men provide that perpetuate and legitimate male-to-female violence (DeKeseredy, 1990).

Like corporations and other formal organizations, universities and community colleges are institutions that, under some circumstances, legitimate race, ethnic, class, and gender inequality (Wagner, Acker, and Mayuzumi, 2008). Some university organizations, such as fraternities, may even take an active role in legitimating these inequalities, which help to develop a social bond that fosters and justifies woman abuse in an atmosphere that, unfortunately, is conforming rather than deviant. It is not an accident that so many university campuses have very low rates of other serious or violent crime but at the same time have alarming rates of woman abuse, with more than 25 per cent of university/college women reporting sexual assault or attempted sexual assault in most surveys (DeKeseredy and Flack, 2007; Godenzi, Schwartz, and DeKeseredy, 2001). Moreover, differing studies have found that, depending on the survey question, between 25 and 60 per cent of male undergraduate students reported some likelihood that they would rape a woman if they could get away with it (Briere and Malamuth, 1983; Russell, 1998). Thus, in the context of post-secondary school education, rather than being a rare event committed by a few deviant men, 'the experience of violent intrusion—or the threat of such intrusion—is a common thread in the fabric of women's everyday lives' (Renzetti, 1995: 3).

At the time of writing this chapter there had been no recent replication of the CNS. Therefore, whether or not the abuse of women on university/college campuses is still constant across Canada is an empirical question that can only be answered empirically. Doing so will be a major challenge in the current political economic climate. For example, Statistics Canada no longer conducts surveys that focus primarily on violence against women and instead produces sexually symmetrical findings generated by the problematic and highly controversial Conflict Tactics Scale (e.g., equal rates of male and female violence).[1] In fact, Statistics Canada is currently being influenced by political forces guided by right-wing fathers' rights groups and others intent on minimizing the pain and suffering caused by male-to-female abuse (DeKeseredy, forthcoming; DeKeseredy and Dragiewicz, 2007).[2] Furthermore, on 3 October 2006, Bev Oda, former federal minister for Status of Women Canada (SWC), announced that women's organizations would no longer be eligible for funding for advocacy, government lobbying, or research projects. Moreover, SWC was required to delete the word 'equality' from its list of goals (Carastathis, 2006).

In early September 2007, the Harper federal Canadian government added more fuel to an ongoing fire by eliminating funding to the National Association of Women and the Law (NAWL), which is a non-profit women's group that struggles to help end violence against women and other forms of female victimization. Thus, some researchers assert that Canadians are going to see more cases on campuses and elsewhere where many women are 'twice victimized' (DeKeseredy, 2009a): first by

violence and the men who abused them and then by the lack of social support provided by the federal government (DeKeseredy, 2009b; Elias, 1993).

Although it is highly unlikely that another rendition of the CNS will soon be conducted, there are strong indictors that rates of violence against women on Canadian campuses are not decreasing. Consider the results of DeKeseredy, Perry, and Schwartz's (2007) representative sample survey of hate-motivated sexual assaults on female undergraduates at two Ontario institutions of higher learning (one university and one community college). These researchers found that slightly less than 11 per cent of the 384 women in their sample stated that they had experienced one or more of the five variants of hate-motivated sexual assault presented in Table 5.1 in the past seven months.[3] DeKeseredy and colleagues also found a significant positive correlation between women who publicly identify themselves as feminists and the likelihood of experiencing a hate-motivated sexual assault since they were 16 years old.[4] Together, these findings suggest that many female undergraduates, especially those who are feminists or who are perceived as such, may be more likely to be perceived as belonging to 'target groups', and their experiences are 'part and parcel of a larger hate crime problem' in Canada, the United States, and other countries (Jenness, 2004: 189).

Ironically, while Canadian universities and colleges contribute to the advancement of learning and broadening young minds, DeKeseredy and colleagues' (2007) data support Ehrlich's (1999) claim that these schools are showing dramatic trends toward intolerance, as evidenced by ongoing rates of racial, ethnic, and gender harassment.[5] Some US studies have uncovered similar problems on post-secondary school campuses (Southern Poverty Law Center, 2003; Van Dyke and Tester, 2008). Thus, while the 'multicultural women's movement has utterly transformed the cultural landscape' on Canadian university/

Table 5.1 Hate-Motivated Sexual Violence Incidence Rate

Type of Sexual Assault	n	Percentage
Been threatened with unwanted sexual behaviours	14	3.7
Been sexually harassed	8	2.1
Been verbally sexually harassed	29	7.7
Been touched sexually when you didn't want to be touched (e.g., your breasts, rear end, or genitals	14	3.7
Had sexual relations when you didn't want to because someone threatened or used some degree of physical force (e.g., twisting your arm, holding you down) to make you	1	0.3

college campuses (Katz, 2006: 1), there is now evidence that on top of having to worry about 'intimate intrusions' such as abusive acts committed by male intimates and random acts of male 'stranger danger' that 'come out of the blue' (Stanko, 1985; 1990), many women live in fear of being attacked by their peers because of a perception that they have overstepped their boundaries. Consequently, Canadian female undergraduates must be 'hyper-vigilant—sometimes 24/7' about the likelihood of being sexually assaulted from many different directions (DeKeseredy, Perry, and Schwartz, 2007; Katz, 2006).

More recent support for this claim is found in survey data provided by a sample of 1,174 university and college students in southwestern Ontario (72.9 per cent were women). Tremblay et al. (2008) discovered that 64.9 per cent of the female participants reported at least one of what these researchers refer to as 'negative social experiences', ranging from insults to sexual assault. Although most of their experiences were verbal (e.g., gossip/jokes, intimidation, and threats of harm), they should not be

deemed 'mild' or 'minor'. For example, a large literature reveals that many women find psychological or emotional abuse to be more painful than physical and sexual violence (DeKeseredy and Schwartz, 2011). Moreover, being objects of discomfiting sexual remarks reaffirms women's vulnerability in public places. Such remarks are constant reminders of 'the relevance of their gender' (Gardner, 1995: 9).

The behaviour which induces a fearful state in wide numbers of women is often not rape itself but leers, suggestive comments, being followed for blocks down the street, being yelled at from cars, phone calls, 'being hit on' in restaurants and bars, and other forms of harassment (DeKeseredy et al., 2003; Radford, 1987). These behaviours are either not against the law or else viewed as so 'minor' that virtually any police force will ignore them. Yet what Kelly and Radford (1987: 242) stated more than 20 years ago still holds true today: '[A]t the time women are being followed/flashed at/harassed they do not know how the event will end. It is only in retrospect that such events can be defined as "minor".'

What is to be done about gendered violence on Canadian campuses and their immediate surroundings? One frequent answer to this question is to involve men in the struggle to enhance women's health and safety in institutions of higher learning and elsewhere. After all, as is often pointed out, since men are the primary abusers of women, it should be men who change their behaviours, attitudes, and beliefs (Funk, 2006). Certainly, starting shortly after Marc Lepine killed 14 female engineering students at the University of Montreal on 6 December 1989, we have seen more progressive male students, faculty, administrators, and other men on university/college campuses individually and collectively take steps to end all variants of woman abuse. Although these men constitute a relatively small group, they have experienced some successes and salient obstacles. The main objective of this chapter is to describe some of the 'highs and lows' of the male feminist movement on Canadian campuses. New strategies for change will also be suggested, including those that target the 'dark side' of new electronic technologies, such as Internet pornography. First, however, it is necessary to outline the main elements of the feminist men's movement on campus.

Major Elements of the Campus-Based Feminist Men's Movement

Many major progressive social, political, and cultural transitions that have occurred at Canadian institutions of higher learning over the past 30 years, such as the creation of sexual harassment policies and procedures, but most men on campus still neither embrace feminism nor see woman abuse as a significant social problem. Worse, many male university administrators, security personnel, and students indirectly and/or directly support the abuse of women (DeKeseredy, Schwartz, and Alvi, 2000). Consider what happened to a part-time instructor while she was teaching at an urban Ontario university in March 2006. Her name is

not revealed here for legal and ethical reasons, but her experiences reflect an ongoing and ever-changing pattern of misogyny among Canada's undergraduate student body. She received horrifying e-mail messages from male students, including ones that threatened to rape her with a baseball bat 'sooner or later'. Added to some of the violent messages were pornographic pictures of women and racist statements equating people of colour with monkeys. Fearing for her life, she left her house to stay temporarily with another professor and never returned to teach her classes. Further, a high-ranking member of the school's security department responded to her in a tardy, insensitive fashion until I demanded that he show up at her host's house. Shortly after he arrived, I insisted that he and a senior administrator go to her class and talk about this crime to all of the students, including a few females in the classroom who were also targeted by some of the perpetrator's violent e-mail messages. The female instructor, albeit a survivor of cybersexual assaults and other forms of woman abuse, will probably never return to this school, and the perpetrator was never caught. Nevertheless, she did not react passively and did not let the atrocities described here drag her down. She now has an exciting career with the Ontario provincial government, but she will be dearly missed by her former university colleagues and friends (DeKeseredy, 2011b).

This virtual attack needs to be placed in a broader social context. For example, the school mentioned above and another institution of higher learning located near it had, up until September 2007, a 10-year history of allowing a 'sex pub' to function on campus once a year. Described by its organizers as an event designed 'to promote awareness' and 'safe sex', the 'sex pub' actually objectified women for the sake of profit and involved displays of pornographic pictures. According to one student who helped cancel this pub night, 'What you're doing is commodifying sex, so in other words we can relate that to prostitution. So what are we saying to students? What are we saying about ourselves? What perception do we want to give out to students?' Further, on 27 September 2007, a woman walking to her car in the campus parking lot was repeatedly punched in the face by a male stranger, but school officials neglected to inform all the faculty, staff, and students about this attack. Rather, a few members of the campus community, including me, learned about it by reading an e-mail sent by a campus clerk to her son that included a release issued by the local police with accurate details about the beating. So much for the notion that university campuses are safe havens divorced from the hard realities of what is commonly defined as 'the real world'. And, by the way, 'no arrests were made' (DeKeseredy, 2011b).

For the thousands of students and hundreds of teachers across Ontario and other parts of Canada, the new school year generates much excitement, hope, and optimism. It is also a time of year for reconnecting with old friends and for making new ones. However, on Tuesday, 2 September 2008, the start of the school year turned out to be a horrific nightmare for an 18-year-old Fanshawe College student. Two men entered a common area in a student residence at this London, Ontario, school and sexually assaulted her. Although the majority of perpetrators of sexual assault are never arrested or charged, two men were charged for committing this crime. Nevertheless, Fanshawe College spokesperson Emily Marcoccia did not seem to see their behaviour symptomatic of a systemic problem. Rather, she was quoted as calling the attack 'a very brutal, but isolated incident' (cited in DeKeseredy, 2011b). Unfortunately, sometimes women also contribute to creating and maintaining 'chilly climates' on Canadian campuses.

It is not surprising, then, that many feminists believe that all men are potential abusers and that women routinely report to survey researchers alarmingly high levels of fear of crime (Katz, 2006; Schechter, 1982). It is also not surprising that many feminists are hesitant to work with men to make women's lives safer. One reason for such hesitancy is the fear of collaborating with potentially abusive men (DeKeseredy, Schwartz, and Alvi, 2000). For instance, Catharine, a female undergraduate interviewed by Schwartz and DeKeseredy (1997) was raped by a male friend who worked with her giving anti-rape lectures to men's groups on campus. Many feminist women also do not want to work with men because of a well-founded fear that men will live up to their patriarchal socialization and end up taking over their work (Funk, 1993). Still, feminist women do have honest, dedicated male allies on campus and elsewhere, and they are feminist men.

There are variations in the feminist men's movement, but a general point of agreement is that men must take an active role in stopping woman abuse and eliminating other forms of patriarchal control and domination throughout society (DeKeseredy, Schwartz, and Alvi, 2000). Furthermore, feminist men place the responsibility for woman abuse squarely on abusive men. A widely cited statement is that 'since it is men who are the offenders, it should be men—not women—who change their behaviour' (Thorne-Finch, 1992: 236).

Feminist men are involved in an ongoing process of changing themselves, self-examination, and self-discovery (Funk, 1993), with the ultimate objective being the shedding of their 'patriarchal baggage' (Thorne-Finch, 1992). This is what Katz (2006: 260) refers to as 'similar to the sort of introspection required of anti-racist whites'. Moreover, every day, these men take great strides to escape entirely from the 'man box', and they have definitely moved from being 'well-meaning men' to becoming feminist men. The 'man box' is a term created by Tony Porter (2006a) and in this box are the elements of hegemonic masculinity (Connell, 1995). The basic components of this type of masculinity are to avoid all things feminine, restrict one's emotions severely, show toughness and aggression, strive for achievement and status, exhibit non-relational attitudes toward sexuality, 'measure up to the school view of the ideal masculine body', and actively engage in homophobia (DeKeseredy, 2007; Levant, 1994; Messerschmidt, 2000: 93).

According to Porter (2006b: 1), a well-meaning man is

> A man who believes women should be respected. A well-meaning man would not assault a woman. A well-meaning man, on the surface, at least, believes in equality for women; a well-meaning man believes in women's rights. A well-meaning man honours the women in his life. A well-meaning man, for all practical purposes, is a nice guy, a good guy.

However, well-meaning men also directly or indirectly collude with abusive men by remaining silent. As Ted Bunch correctly points out, 'When we remain bystanders we are making a choice to support the abuse. The abusive behaviour by any man reflects and therefore reinforces the established status and privileges of all men' (2006: 1).

Feminist men, on the other hand, are very vocal about ending male privilege, woman abuse, and other highly injurious symptoms of patriarchy. They also work collectively and individually to change men by criticizing and challenging through other means the broader social and economic structure and institutions like the pornography industry, the military, the mainstream media (e.g., television shows), professional sports, and the justice system (Funk, 2006; Kimmel and Mosmiller, 1992; Thorne-Finch, 1992). Still, feminist men accept that, having been socialized in a patriarchal, racist, and class-based society, their re-education process will not end or die.

Many progressive scholars, teachers, practitioners, activists, and policymakers often state that one cannot eliminate one form of inequality by promoting another. This is true, and often woman abuse on campus and elsewhere is simultaneously a function of economic, racial, and class inequality (DeKeseredy, 2007). Thus, feminist men consistently call for a higher minimum wage, state-sponsored childcare, and an anti-racist curriculum, among other initiatives. Further, they pressure politicians with letters, e-mail messages, Facebook protests, and telephone calls that strongly encourage them to address these concerns. Voicing their thoughts and views in the mainstream mass media (e.g., newspapers) is another technique feminist men use, which is what critical criminologist Gregg Barak (1988) defines as 'newsmaking criminology'.[6]

These strategies constitute just the tip of the iceberg. As others have repeatedly discussed (e.g., Katz, 2006), feminist men take many more individual and collective steps to end woman abuse and other oppressive practices. They are 'part of a long tradition of people who have dared to make a difference—to look at things as they are, to imagine something better, and to plant seeds of change in themselves, in others, and in the world' (Johnson, 1997: 253).

The 'Highs and Lows' of the Male Feminist Movement on Campus

While feminism has gained more ground on the Canadian academic landscape and there is more scholarly, media, and political attention given to woman abuse (Freedman, 2002), progressive members of campus communities continue to come across many males (mostly students) who publicly express great disdain for those who attempt to sensitize them to the pain and suffering caused by patriarchal discourses and practices such as woman abuse.[7] This reaction is partially the function of a rabid anti-feminist backlash fuelled by fathers' rights groups, neo-conservative journalists, and academics (e.g., Dutton, 2006) hostile to feminism (DeKeseredy, 2003).

Another key element of the current political climate also fosters many students' negative response. For example, at the time of writing this chapter, Canadian troops were participating in a war in Afghanistan, a violent event that spawned a 'hypersensitized milieu of male camaraderie', 'heightened militarism', and 'blinding patriotism' (Sever, 2002: 205). Consequently, course material and public presentations on how the political economic status quo contributes to women's suffering at the hands of their male partners is seen by many students as 'unpatriotic', especially if they are exposed to statements such as this one made by journalist Brian Vallee (2007: 28–9) about the dangers many Canadian women face in their own country behind closed doors:

> There is another war—largely overlooked but even more deadly—with far more victims killed by 'hostiles'. But these dead are not labelled heroes, nor are they honoured in the national media or in formal ceremonies. From time to time they may attract a spate of publicity as the result of a high-profile trial, or an inquest that will likely conclude that society let them down once again and recommend changes to prevent future deaths, though these recommendations will be mostly ignored. This war is the War on Women.

Others on campus oppose hearing about woman abuse because the subject matter challenges the popular notion of intimate relationships as safe and loving, as well as the myth of equal opportunities and rights for women (DeKeseredy, 2003; Freedman, 2002). There are obviously other facts that promote the resistance and hostility identified here and it is beyond the scope of this chapter to describe them all. A more important point to note is that, together with their female friends and colleagues, feminist men have developed some effective ways of minimizing opposition, enhancing the campus community's understanding of woman abuse, and mobilizing critical masses of people to take progressive action.

As stated earlier, many men first got involved in the campus feminist men's movement shortly after the 6 December 1989 Montreal Massacre. This mass murder spawned the development of the White Ribbon Campaign, a movement initiated in October 1991 by the Men's Network for Change (MNC) in Toronto, Ottawa, London, Kingston, and Montreal (Luxton, 1993). MNC drafted a document stating that violence against women is a major social problem, male silence about violence against women is complicity, and that men can be part of the solution (Sluser and Kaufman, 1992).

The Campaign is still alive and strong, and its goals are to get men involved in the struggle to end woman abuse, to raise public awareness of this problem, and to support organizations (e.g., campus women's centres) that strive to advance women's rights. Furthermore, approximately one week prior to the annual anniversary of the Montreal Massacre, men are encouraged to wear a white ribbon symbolizing a call to all men to lay down their arms in the war against our sisters (cited in Luxton, 1993: 362). The idea caught on and attracted much attention throughout Canada, the United States, and elsewhere (DeKeseredy, Schwartz, and Alvi, 2000).

One recent activity organized by the White Ribbon Campaign in Toronto is the 'Walk a Mile in Her Shoes' march. This event is informed by the adage that understanding someone's life and experiences involves walking a mile in their shoes. Based heavily on research showing that empathy-based strategies are effective (Foubert and Perry, 2007), the march requires men to walk one mile wearing women's high-heeled shoes to raise awareness and opposition to women abuse. Another goal is to secure donations from march sponsors (Bridges, 2010). 'Walk a Mile in Her Shoes' marches are also organized by male university and college students across Canada without the leadership of the White Ribbon Campaign, and some men wear stereotypical women's clothes in addition to high heels.

For some people, the march is seen as a positive event, one that sensitizes men to violence against women and other injurious symptoms of inequality. For others, including me, this event is highly problematic. For example, Bridges' (2010: 5) case study of five marches reveals that the performance of drag at marches 'symbolically reproduces gender and sexual inequality despite good intentions'. This point is well taken, given that cross-cultural research shows that gender inequality is the most robust correlate of sexual violence and that high heels are symbolic of societies that promote patriarchal relations (Bridges, 2010; Sanday, 1981). According to feminist scholar Susan Brownmiller (1984: 184), 'An artificial feminine walk seems to gratify many psychological and cultural needs. The female foot and leg are turned into ornamental objects and the impractical shoe, which offers little protection . . . induces helplessness and dependence.'

It is also wrong to assume that all women wear high heels. As one woman stated at a march observed by Bridges (2010: 15), 'If all they have to do is walk a mile in women's shoes, why did they all pick high heels?' Bridges also discovered that homophobia is a key element of each march. Thus, for Bridges and many other female critics, 'Walk a Mile in Her Shoes' marches confirm 'our worst fears about acknowledging men doing feminism' (2010: 20). To make matters worse, Bridges observed, such marches do little, if anything, to achieve empathy. Is this the case for all marches or only those observed by Bridges? This question can be effectively answered only with sound research. Nevertheless, the one march I observed at a university located in the Greater Toronto Area (GTA) did not include a critical mass of male students who publicly identify themselves as feminist. Further, it is fair to assume that many of them are unfamiliar with the day-to-day efforts of the White Ribbon Campaign.

Simply wearing a white ribbon for a week and/or participating in a drag performance does not 'undo the patriarchal knot' (Johnson,

1997) that contributes to violence against women. Similarly, despite the best intentions, inviting prominent feminist male educators for one campus presentation or several workshops has not proven to do much to increase awareness about violence against women or to lower the rates of this problem on campus. The difficulty is that while any single educator or activist may do an excellent job, it is very difficult to counteract the broad variety of influences that students encounter. If only a small number of students, faculty, or staff are engaged in programming against woman abuse, then the influence of students in other classes, when combined with peers, the mass media, and other broader societal influences, will no doubt make presentations and workshops a very doubtful enterprise. It is essential to achieve a critical mass of commitments amongst instructors, counsellors, and administrators, supported by parents and broader community members, to make necessary progress toward reducing or ending violence by men against women. Indeed, creating an environment that is anti-sexist requires a collective effort (Kimmel, 2008).

Nearly 10 years ago, in an article we co-authored for the journal *Violence Against Women* on the role of feminist men in dealing with woman abuse on campus (see DeKeseredy, Schwartz, and Alvi, 2000), my colleagues and I stated that most Canadian feminist male students, faculty, administrators, and support staff either 'go it alone' or get involved in small, loosely connected groups. The same can be said today. Even so, feminism continues to enhance some men's critical consciousness, helps people come together to engage in collective problem-solving, creates some conditions for the reduction of future male-to-female abuse, and continues to influence some men to shed their sexist, homophobic, and racist baggage.

Sometimes, too, a progressive cohort effect occurs. For example, in the fall of 2005, I taught a senior undergraduate class on woman abuse. I expected low attendance and low enrollment because this class met twice a week and one of the classes was on Friday at 3:40 p.m. The total class size was 45, and nearly 17 men were enrolled, which also surprised me because many male students repeatedly state that they 'don't want to hear this stuff' and hence go out of their way to avoid classes that involve a feminist understanding of gender issues (cited in DeKeseredy, 1999: 30). Fortunately, and perhaps luckily, I was granted a number of 'teachable moments' (Kimmel, 2008).

At first, most if not all the men in the class seemed taken aback that a man would study and struggle to end a major social problem deemed by thousands, if not millions, of North Americans to be primarily a woman's issue. As Jackson Katz (2006: 5) puts it,

> Most people think violence against women is a women's issue. And why wouldn't they? Just about every woman in this society thinks about it every day. If they are not getting harassed on the street, living in an abusive relationship, recovering from rape, or in therapy to deal with the sexual abuse they suffered as children, they are ordering their daily lives around the threat of male violence.

As is often said, 'to make a long story short', the students and I developed a very close pedagogical relationship, and most of the men publicly and routinely expressed how the course made them reflect on their own lives and rethink their relationships with women. Additionally, most of the men actively participated in a fall campus-based violence against women awareness week, and a few who have since graduated continue to send me electronic messages. This outcome is rare and I have not experienced it since. Nevertheless, it is an indication that change is possible despite many obstacles.

Other examples of progressive change fostered in part by feminist men on campus are the creation of graduate and undergraduate courses on masculinities studies, men participating in 'Take Back the Night' marches, and men participating in activities sponsored by women's centres. So, all is not lost. The more men who become feminist, the more likely that changes will occur. Still, since woman abuse on campus and its immediate surroundings 'is a never ending and constantly evolving issue' (Ledwitz-Rigby, 1993: 93), those currently involved in the feminist men's movement and those who will soon join it need to consider new strategies.

New Strategies for Change

One of the biggest challenges feminist men on campus face is recruiting new male allies. For instance, although I was deeply moved by the aforementioned men in my woman abuse class, I also knew that they would soon graduate and that it would be extremely difficult to find new replacements like them. Thus, a formal campus-based organization or club needs to be established and could be done with the assistance of the White Ribbon Campaign and progressive members of the campus community. Another method is to make contacts with feminist male organizations at other campuses to obtain information on how to create and sustain an anti-sexist men's group. Regardless of how such a group is created, it is always necessary for members to actively recruit new students, faculty, support staff, administrators, and other members of the campus community.

Volunteers can help organize feminist men's activities, including recruitment. Still, it is absolutely essential to have at least one full-time paid employee to coordinate peer volunteers and to coordinate campus-wide efforts (DeKeseredy and Schwartz, 1998). This will also help avoid 'burnout, which typically happens when members of the campus community take on too much work, and it addresses the serious problem of time demands' (DeKeseredy, Schwartz, and Alvi, 2000). For example, during exam periods or when essays are due, it is extremely difficult, if not impossible, for students to devote much time and energy to organizing feminist men's initiatives.

Canada is becoming more ethnically diverse, especially in metropolitan areas. For example, by 2031, close to 28 per cent of the population could be foreign-born. Moreover, more than 71 per cent of the entire visible minority population will likely live in Toronto, Vancouver, and Montreal (Statistics Canada, 2010). Universities and colleges, too, will become more diverse in the near future. Note that in March 2010, Ontario premier Dalton McGuinty publicly stated that his province's goal is to increase the number of foreign students by 50 per cent over the next five years to 55,000. The McGuinty government's intent is not to promote progressive change but rather to generate an 'income stream' for schools, given that foreign students pay much more for tuition than do Canadian residents (Cohn, 2010). Regardless of the reasons for the increase in ethnic diversity on campus, the fact remains that men from historically marginalized ethnic/cultural backgrounds will be prominent members of the post-secondary school community, and their insights should be taken into account. So should those of lower-class men, men who are disabled, gay men, and men from other minority groups, as well as the insights of minority women, including lesbians. Unfortunately, most feminist men's groups mainly consist of males who are white, middle class, and heterosexual (DeKeseredy, Schwartz, and Alvi, 2000; Thorne-Finch, 1992). There may be several other groups that can offer feminist men guidance, and thus, at every group meeting, 'we should always be conscious of who is not there and that we are not hearing those perspectives' (Gilfus et al., 1999: 1207).

Taylor, Walton, and Young's *The New Criminology* (1973) raised questions about the role that progressive scholars should play in the broader arena of political activism (Walton, 1998). Certainly there are many innovative political actions feminist men can take on campus

and elsewhere that do not require much time, effort, and money. One example is using new computer technologies such as Facebook. For example, as of 20 January 2010 nearly 200,000 Canadians had signed a Facebook petition protesting Prime Minister Harper's prorogation of Parliament on 30 December 2009. The Canadian legislature was originally set to reconvene on 25 January 2010 but Harper delayed the return until 3 March. This prorogation eliminated bills tabled at the previous parliamentary session, including some related to important environmental and pension issues (Werbowski, 2010). Prorogation also shut down a public inquiry about the Harper government's knowledge of the torture of detainees handed over to Afghan forces by the Canadian military.

Social networking websites make a difference. Two weeks after the creation of the above petition, the Harper government's lead over the Liberal Party fell to only 1 per cent (Hebert, 2010). This is strong evidence that new technologies are effectively being used to mobilize large numbers of people to demand government accountability and to challenge attempts to cover up state crime and other government wrongdoings. Further, progressive Facebook initiatives are examples of reinvigorated civic engagement that are also being employed to digitally protest white supremacy online (Daniels, 2009). Contrary to what many people claim, social networking sites are now key arenas of political struggle. As University of Bergen scholar Jill Walker Rettberg (2009: 1) observes,

> Obviously people find it easier to join a Facebook group to make a political point than to march the streets. Perhaps it's actually more effective, too. Right now, it's entirely possible that you get more press and thus more national notice for a Facebook group with 2000 members than a demonstration of 500 people. And it's a *lot* easier to get 2000

people to join a Facebook group than to get 500 people to show up at a particular time and place with banners.

Using Facebook to help achieve social justice is a contemporary initiative that attracts more and more people each day. So are blogging and other new means of exchanging information. Communication is vital, and if Facebook, Twitter, etc., enable more people to become aware of various injustices, more people will voice their discontent with the prevailing inequitable status quo by electing politicians committed to a more progressive way of dealing with social problems such as violence against women. At the very least, such political work makes the issues addressed by feminist men and other progressives very visible to the public, in the same way that the Canadian Facebook petition mentioned earlier in this chapter raised considerable public awareness about the problems related to the prorogation of Parliament.

As communications scholar Joseph Walther and his colleagues (2001: 105) stated nearly 10 years ago, 'With the expansion of the Internet and new communication technologies, we are witnessing the diffusion of high-end, high-bandwidth multimedia technology for a wide range of people. It is common for many computer-mediated communication (CMC) users to create multi-media World Wide Web sites with graphics and pictures.' This statement is still relevant today. Many such sites are beneficial to corporate executives, small business owners, educators, students, and a myriad of other people eager to enhance their understanding of social, political, cultural, and economic factors that directly or indirectly influence their lives. However, there are also numerous highly injurious features of new information technologies, and adult Internet pornography is one major example.

While many women consume adult pornography, it is created primarily for generating sexual arousal in heterosexual men (Jensen, 2007).

From the standpoint of many feminist scholars (e.g., DeKeseredy, 2009c; Dworkin, 1994), pornography, regardless of whether it appears on the Internet, in stores, on television, in literature, or in other media, is also a variant of hate-motivated violence and has become 'normalized' or 'mainstreamed' in North America and elsewhere (Jensen and Dines, 1998), despite becoming increasingly more violent and racist (DeKeseredy and Olsson, 2011).

Whereas it is beyond the objectives of this chapter to describe graphically what appears on contemporary pornographic Internet sites, some brief examples of violence and racism are necessary. For instance, Doghouse Digital is a company that produced the film *Black Bros and White Ho's*, which offers stereotypical images of 'the sexually primitive black male stud' (Jensen, 2007: 66). Another example is the interracial film *Blacks on Blondes*, which features a white man in a cage watching black men have sex with his wife (Dines, 2006). An additional common feature of new pornographic films that exist online and elsewhere is painful anal penetration, as well as men slapping women and/or pulling their hair while they penetrate them orally, vaginally, and/or anally (Dines and Jensen, 2008a).

'Normalized' is an understatement. Pornography is a giant industry, and it is estimated that there are more than a million pornography sites on the Internet, with as many as 10,000 added every week (Funk, 2006). Note, too, that worldwide pornography revenues from a variety of sources (e.g., Internet, hotel rooms, etc.) recently topped US$97 billion. This is more than the revenues of these world-renowned technology companies combined: Microsoft, Google, Amazon, eBay, Yahoo!, Apple, Netflix, and Earthlink (Zerbisias, 2008). Keep in mind, too, that rare are men who have not been exposed to pornographic images and narratives on the Internet (DeKeseredy and Olsson, 2011). Even if people go out of their way to avoid pornography, it frequently 'pops up' on people's monitors while they are working or 'surfing the Web' for information that has nothing to do with sex (Dines and Jensen, 2008b).

To make matters worse, as stated earlier, what men and boys watch on adult pornographic Internet sites are not simply 'dirty pictures that have little impact on anyone'. Rather, the images typically endorse 'women as second-class citizens' and 'require that women be seen as second-class citizens' (Funk, 2006: 165). Another challenge to the assertion that 'pornography is just fantasy' are quantitative and qualitative data showing that pornography is strongly associated with various types of violence against women (DeKeseredy, 2011b; Jensen, 2007), especially sexual assault. In addition, some studies found that the contribution of pornography to woman abuse in university/college dating, marriage, and during or after separation/divorce is related to male peer support discussed at the start of this chapter (DeKeseredy and Schwartz, 2009). For example, many violent, patriarchal men often view pornography in all-male groups and share videos and other media electronically with a 'wider circle of friends' via the Internet (DeKeseredy et al., 2006; Giordano, 1995).

Such 'strengthening' of male 'misogynist bonds' is not a recent phenomenon (Lehman, 2006). As film scholars have documented, cinematic pornography originated in 16 mm silent films, which were

> usually shown in private all-male 'smokers' in such contexts as bachelor parties and the like. Within such a context, the men laughed and joked and talked among themselves while watching the sexually explicit films about women, who though absent from the audience, were the likely butt of the jokes, laughing, and rude remarks (Lehman, 2006: 4).

Similarly, a study done about 20 years ago uncovered that university fraternity 'brothers' also generally went to pornographic theatres in groups. For example, some of the brothers interviewed by Sanday (1990: 129) stated that

> seeing pornography is something to do before their parties start. They want to learn what it's like to 'have a two foot dick' and to have a good time together. They never go alone, always together. They go together in order to have a good time, laugh, and make jokes during the movie. They dissociate themselves from the men who go alone to porno movies downtown and sit in seats 'with coats and newspapers spread out over their laps' and 'jerk off' during the movie. They believe that this is sick, but they don't think 'getting off' while reading *Playboy* privately or enacting a porno fantasy in their house is necessarily sick.

We live in a 'post-*Playboy* world' (Jensen, 2007), and increasingly, pornography has moved from theatres to people's homes (Jordan, 2006), including those owned by university/college students. For example, in 2000, a man referred to by DePauw University fraternity brothers as 'The Smut Peddler' reported that he used to sell about 100 pornographic VHS tapes to the fraternities per year, but after 15 years in the 'business', he witnessed a dramatic decline in sales due to Internet viewing (Claus, 2000). Almost 10 years later, it is logical to assume that this man has probably pursued another 'career', thanks, for the most part, to Internet technology, which provides students easy and constant accessibility that cannot be offered by 'The Smut Peddler' (Dines and Jensen, 2008b).

Male students' consumption of pornography hurts and requires immediate attention from feminist men. For example, of the 1,638 women who participated in the Canadian National Survey on Woman Abuse in University/College Dating (CNS), 137 (8.4 per cent) stated that they were upset by their dating partners trying to get them to do what they had seen in pornographic media (DeKeseredy and Schwartz, 1998). This is comparable to the 10 percent figure that Russell (1990) uncovered from asking a random sample of 930 women in the San Francisco area a similar question. It should be pointed out that, for the most part, Russell interviewed women significantly older than the females who participated in the CNS.

What is more important here is that the CNS found a significant relationship between being upset by men's attempts to imitate pornographic scenes and sexual victimization. Of those who were sexually abused, 22.3 per cent had also been upset by attempts to get them to imitate pornographic scenarios. Only 5.8 per cent of the women who were not victimized reported not being upset by pornography. The relationship also holds for physical violence. Of the female CNS respondents who reported being physically abused in a dating relationship, 15.4 per cent also reported being upset by pornography. Only 4.5 percent of those who were not physically victimized reported being upset. CNS data, then, help us to conclude that pornography plays a major role in the sexual and physical abuse of Canadian women in college and university dating relationships. These findings mirror the abuse reported in surveys by married and formerly married women (Bergen, 1996; Bergen and Bogle, 2000; Harmon and Check, 1989).

Student consumption of pornography is a widespread problem that is only likely to get worse due to easy access offered by the Internet. For example, one US study of undergraduate and graduate students aged 18 to 26 around the country uncovered that 69 per cent of the male and 10 per cent of the female participants viewed pornography at least once a month (Carroll et al., 2008). Although hardly a reliable estimate, also note that at least 50 out of about 65 students in my 2009 violence against women class estimated that between 75 and 80 per cent of male students enrolled at my school view Internet pornography. While it is unlikely that the actual percentage is that high, students' perceptions of social norms influence their own sense of what is normal and acceptable, and whether it is safe to challenge those perceived norms. What, then, is to be done by feminist men on campus?

One answer to this question is to give workshops and presentations that encourage critical thinking and that begin by asking questions such as the following graphic ones suggested by feminist male educator Rus Funk (2006: 168). These questions are designed to humanize women in the pornography industry.

- Does the woman in pornography really like that?
- Does she like the names that men in pornography call her?
- Does she really like being ejaculated upon, probably several times? Does she really like double or triple penetration?
- Would she want her sister or daughter doing the same things?
- Would they (the male audience members) want their sister, mother, daughter, or girlfriend to be in the pornography they watch?

A cautionary note, however, is required here. As Funk correctly points out, many men in the audience are likely to answer these questions with a resounding 'yes'. Even when feminist male educators attempt to generate 'honest talk and careful hearing' (Jensen, 1995: 52), there is a chance that such events can turn into celebrations of male sexual and patriarchal power (DeKeseredy and Schwartz, 1998; Sanday, 1996). Thus, Funk recommends that educators engage men in the audience who oppose pornography and facilitate a conversation and debate amongst men who disagree with each other. Again, the goal is promote critical thinking and perhaps a number of men will leave the workshop or presentation with a different way of thinking about pornography.

One more cautionary note is necessary. Educators and activists must be very careful when attempting to use pornographic images to make points about the harm they cause. Some instructors show such images in some courses (e.g., a course on woman abuse sponsored by a women's studies program) and understand its use as an educational tool in the right environment. Still, many women have not been exposed to pornography and are unaware of the level of anti-woman hatred embedded in many Internet sites and other pornographic media (Gronau, 1985). Showing pornographic media, then, may cause some women much discomfort or trigger painful memories, and therefore educators need to work closely with counsellors on campus to prepare for possible traumatic outcomes.

Feminist men in and outside academic circles respond to pornography in other ways that warrant more attention and support. For example, some feminist men's groups, such as the Minnesota Men's Action Network: Alliance to Prevent Sexual and Domestic Violence, participate in variations of the Clean Hotel Initiative.[8] This involves encouraging businesses, government agencies, private companies, and so on to hold conferences and meetings only in hotels that do not offer in-room adult pay-per-view pornography. Further, new groups of men and women are joining hands to collectively expose and criticize injurious media coverage of woman abuse (e.g., wife beating) and to boycott companies that profit from pornography. Robert Jensen (2007: 182) is right to state that 'it's not enough for us to change our personal behaviour. That's a bare minimum. Such change must be followed by participation in movements to change the unjust structure and the underlying ideology that supports them.'

Such efforts make a difference because of their financial impact, but they are also accused of promoting censorship. So, in efforts to formally and informally sensitize people to the harmful nature of pornography, such as boycotts, some feminist male academics suggest that anti-pornography educators and activists should respond to claims of censorship by stating that there are many types of harmful films that cannot be found in hotels, video stores, and other places, mostly because they do not exist (DeKeseredy, 2011b; DeKeseredy and Schwartz, 1998). Rather than constituting outright censorship, citizens of many countries manage to express their disgust and dismay at even a slight hint of harm to animals in motion pictures. Where the plotline requires an animal to be fictionally hurt (e.g., a great white shark eating a swimming dog),[9] Hollywood producers find it essential to report in the credits that their set was inspected and monitored by animal rights organizations. Even then, however, there are virtually no movies that show animals being burned, dismembered, stabbed or shot to death, electrocuted, beaten or kicked, or raped. These images are saved for stories about men and women.

Similarly, it is important to mention to those making claims about censorship that there are no movies available showing in an approving manner the mass execution of Jews, gypsies, and the mentally ill by the German Nazis in World War II. There are also no pro-slavery movies showing approvingly how white people need to beat, starve, and torture African slaves to get them to behave 'properly'. This is because people show a very high intolerance for movies of this nature being publicly available. Why is it that there are very firm reactions against seeing a dog raped but find it appropriate, or at least a free speech issue, to allow films approvingly showing women being beaten and gang-raped by a group of men? Thus, there is a major point to be made to those who accuse opponents of pornography to be 'pro-censorship': rather than calling for censorship, anti-porn activists argue that in a better society, it would be considered morally reprehensible to show or attend certain types of films, just as it is now for non-documentary films about animal torture, pro-slavery violence, or Nazi killings (DeKeseredy, 2011b; DeKeseredy and Schwartz, 1998).

Conclusion

The feminist men's strategies described in this chapter are by no means exhaustive, and there are numerous other innovative ones, many of which may already be in use in a variety of social settings and formal organizations. Regardless of what feminist men do, though, as Thorne-Finch (1992: 258) correctly points out, 'Battling the status quo to bring about change is not easy work.' Arguably, this work seems to be getting harder in a country like Canada, under the leadership of a conservative government opposed to progressive change. Note, too, that the anti-feminist backlash in this country and in other nations is gaining strength and is highly injurious (DeKeseredy, 2007). All, though, is not lost. Fortunately, on university campuses and elsewhere, more men are quietly considering becoming part of the ongoing movement to end violence against women. Katz (2006: 255) is another progressive man who sees the same transition:

> I am convinced that millions of men in our society are deeply concerned about the abuse, harassment and violence we see—and fear—in the lives of our daughters, mothers, sisters, and lovers. In fact, a recent poll conducted for Lifetime Television found that 57 percent of men aged sixteen to twenty-four believe that gender violence is an 'extremely serious' problem. A 2000 poll conducted by the Family Violence Prevention Fund found that one-quarter of men would do more about the issue if they were asked. And some compelling social norms research on college campuses suggests that one of the most significant factors in a man's decision to intervene in an incident is his perception of how other men would act in a similar situation. Clearly, a lot of men are uncomfortable with other men's abusive behaviours.

If what Katz claims is true, then why are so few men publicly participating in the struggle to end woman abuse on campus and in other parts of Canada? Funk (1993: 81) offers the following reasons:

- They don't know how to respond.
- They don't feel there is a place for them in the movement to stop woman abuse.
- They experience feelings of guilt and shame.
- They don't know other men who are working to end woman abuse and thus they feel fearful, isolated, and afraid of doing the wrong thing.

Obviously, much more work needs to be done to recruit men to join the feminist men's movement. Retaining them is another challenge, especially since university/college students eventually leave institutions of higher learning unless they go on to become university/college employees. Other factors related to the problem of retention are feelings of burnout, frustration, marginalization, and anger (Gilfus et al., 1999). Thus, it is essential for feminist men to make contacts with feminist men at other campuses to broaden their social support network. Personal experiences and emotions can be shared, which helps alleviate stress and other problems associated with doing feminist work. As Stanko (1997: 84) puts it, 'building alliances for social support and social change is one way to combat the feelings of isolation and frustration many of us working in the field . . . inevitably feel.' Additionally, sharing experiences and emotions helps men reject hegemonic masculinity, which dictates, among other things, that men should severely restrict their emotions and exhibit self-reliance (DeKeseredy, Schwartz, and Alvi, 2000; Levant, 1994). Recognizing and making explicit to others that one needs affirmation, nurturing, and support symbolizes strength and is an important step toward creating an oppositional masculinity (Connell, 1995; Thorne-Finch, 1992).

Creating an oppositional masculinity also entails developing strong, egalitarian, and meaningful alliances with women from a wide range of socioeconomic backgrounds. Being allies with women is as much about 'liberating men from the constraints of masculinity' as it is about helping to save women's lives and supporting their inherent right to live in peace (Funk, 2006: 207). As has been repeatedly stated, the time has come for making men's involvement in the progressive struggle to end woman abuse a 'usual, rather than unusual part of public policy' (Hearn, 1996: 113).

Discussion Questions

1. According to the author, how do universities and community colleges legitimate race, ethnic, class, and gender inequality?
2. In what ways does DeKeseredy argue that Internet pornography harms women?
3. Why are many feminists hesitant to work with men to make women's lives safer?
4. What are the key elements of hegemonic masculinity?
5. What is a 'well-meaning man' and how do 'well-meaning men' contribute to woman abuse?
6. Identify some key individual and collective strategies used by feminist men to help reduce woman abuse on campus.
7. What are some of the 'highs' and 'lows' of the male feminist movement on campus?
8. Discuss and respond to DeKeseredy's arguments that 'Walk a Mile in Her Shoes' marches are problematic.

Recommended Websites

White Ribbon Campaign: www.whiteribbon.ca

Centre for Research and Education on Violence Against Women and Children: www.crvawc.ca

A Call to Men Committed to Ending Violence Against Women: www.acalltomen.com

Notes

1. Developed in the 1970s by University of New Hampshire sociologist Murray Straus (1979), the original or modified rendition of this measure is often used to solicit information from both men and women about ways of handling interpersonal conflict in their relationships with intimate partners. See DeKeseredy (2011a) for an in-depth critique of the Conflict Tactics Scale.

2. Statistics Canada's 1993 national Violence Against Women Survey was heavily influenced by feminist scholarship. See Johnson (1996) for more information on this study and the data gleaned by it.

3. These five items were introduced with this preamble: 'Since the school year started, have any of the following incidents happened to you on campus because of your (real or perceived) race/ethnicity,

national origin, religion, sex, sexual orientation, physical or mental disability, or political orientation? Please answer each item.'
4. One hundred and four female respondents said they identified themselves publicly as feminists (12.9 per cent of the sample).
5. For more recent information on racist discourses and practices on Canadian campuses, see the Canadian Federation of Students *Final Report of the Task Force on Campus Racism* (Toronto: Canadian Federation of Students, 2010).
6. Here, critical criminology is defined as a perspec-

tive that views the major sources of crime as the unequal class, race/ethnic, and gender relations that control our society (DeKeseredy, 2011a; Young, 1988).
7. This section includes modified selections from work published previously by DeKeseredy (2011a), DeKeseredy, Schwartz, and Alvi (2000), and DeKeseredy and Olsson (2011).
8. For more information on the Clean Hotel Initiative, go to www.menaspeacemakers.org/programs/mnman/hotels.
9. See, for example, the 1975 Hollywood movie *Jaws*.

References

Barak, G. 1988. 'Newsmaking Criminology: Reflections on the Media, Intellectuals, and Crime', *Justice Quarterly*, 5, 4: 565–8.

Bergen, R.K. 1996. *Wife Rape*. Thousand Oaks, CA: Sage.

——— and K.A. Bogle. 2000. 'Exploring the Connection Between Pornography and Sexual Violence', *Violence and Victims*, 15, 3: 227–34.

Bridges, T.S. 2010. 'Men Were Just Not Made to Do This: Performances of Drag at Walk a Mile in Her Shoes Marches', *Violence Against Women*, 24, 1: 5–30.

Briere, J., and N. Malamuth. 1983. 'Self-Reported Likelihood of Sexually Aggressive Behavior: Attitudinal versus Sexual Explanations', *Journal of Research in Personality*, 17, 3: 315–23.

Brownmiller, S. 1984. *Femininity*. New York: Linden Press.

Bunch, T. 2006. *Ending Men's Violence Against Women*. Charlotte, NC: A Call to Men: National Association of Men and Women Committed to Ending Violence Against Women.

Canadian Federation of Students. 2010. *The Final Report of the Task Force on Campus Racism*. Toronto: Canadian Federation of Students.

Carastathis, A. 2006. 'New Cuts and Conditions for Status of Women Canada', *Toronto Star*, www.dominionpaper.ca/canadian_news/2006/10/11new_cuts_a.html, accessed 11 Oct. 2006.

Carroll, J.S., L.M. Padilla-Walker, L.J. Nelson, C.D. Olson, C.M. Barry, and S.D. Madsen. 2008. 'Generation XXX: Pornography Acceptance and Use among Emerging Adults', *Journal of Adolescent Research*, 23, 1: 6–30.

Claus, M. 2000. 'Internet Changes Porn Scene at DePauw U', *High Beam Research*, 12 Dec., www.highbeam.com/doc/1P1-37925753.html, accessed 26 Aug. 2009.

Cohn, M.G. 2010. 'Paying a Price for Selling Our Schools', *Toronto Star*, 30 March: A17.

Connell, R.W. 1995. *Masculinities*. Berkeley, CA: University of California Press.

Daniels, J. 2009. *Cyber Racism: White Supremacy Online and the New Attack on Civil Rights*. Lanham, MD: Rowman & Littlefield.

DeKeseredy, W.S. 1990. 'Male Peer Support and Woman Abuse: The Current State of Knowledge', *Sociological Focus*, 23, 2: 129–39.

———. 1999. '"I Don't Want to Hear This Stuff": Teaching Woman Abuse in Sociology of Deviance Classes', in M.D. Schwartz and M.O. Maume, eds., *Teaching the Sociology of Deviance*. Washington, DC: American Sociological Association.

———. 2003. 'The Challenge of Teaching Woman Abuse in Deviance Courses', in M.D. Schwartz and M.O. Maume, eds., *Teaching the Sociology of Deviance*, 5th ed. Washington, DC: American Sociological Association.

———. 2007. 'Changing My Life, among Others: Reflections on the Life and Work of a Feminist Man', in S.L. Miller, ed., *Criminal Justice Research and Practice: Diverse Voices from the Field*. Boston: Northeastern University Press.

———. 2009a. 'Girls and Women as Victims of Crime', in J. Barker, ed., *Women and the Criminal Justice System: A Canadian Perspective*. Toronto: Emond Montgomery.

———. 2009b. 'Canadian Crime Control in the New Millennium: The Influence of Neo-conservative Policies and Practices', *Police Practice and Research*, 10, 4: 305–16.

———. 2009c. 'Male Violence Against Women in North America as Hate Crime', in B. Perry, ed., *Hate Crimes*, vol. 3: *The Victims of Hate Crime*. Santa Barbara, CA: Praeger.

———. 2011a. *Contemporary Critical Criminology*. London: Routledge

———. 2011b. *Violence Against Women in Canada*. Toronto: University of Toronto Press.

———and S. Alvi. 2000. 'The Role of Profeminist Men in

Dealing With Woman Abuse on the Canadian College Campus', *Violence Against Women*, 6, 9: 918–35.

———, S. Alvi, M.D. Schwartz, and E.A. Tomaszewski. 2003. *Under Siege: Poverty and Crime in a Public Housing Community*. Lanham, MD: Lexington Books.

——— and M. Dragiewicz. 2007. 'Understanding the Complexities of Feminist Perspectives on Woman Abuse: A Commentary on Donald G. Dutton's *Rethinking Domestic Violence*', *Violence Against Women*, 13, 8: 874–84.

———, D. Fagen, and M. Hall. 2006. 'Separation/Divorce Sexual Assault: The Contribution of Male Peer Support', *Feminist Criminology*, 1, 3: 228–50.

———, and W.F. Flack, Jr. 2007. 'Sexual Assault in Colleges and Universities', in G. Barak, ed., *Battleground Criminal Justice*. Westport, CT: Greenwood.

——— and K. Kelly. 1993. 'The Incidence and Prevalence of Woman Abuse in Canadian University and College Dating Relationships', *Canadian Journal of Sociology*, 18, 2: 137–59.

——— and P. Olsson. 2011. 'Adult Pornography, Male Peer Support, and Violence Against Women: The Contribution of the "Dark Side" of the Internet', in M. Vargas Martin, M.A. Garcia Ruiz, and A. Edwards, eds., *Technology for Facilitating Humanity and Combating Social Deviations: Interdisciplinary Perspectives*. Hershey, PA: IGI Global.

———, B. Perry, and M.D. Schwartz. 2007. 'Hate-Motivated Sexual Assault on the College Campus: Results from a Canadian Representative sample', Paper presented at the annual meetings of the American Society of Criminology, Atlanta.

——— and M.D. Schwartz. 1998. *Woman Abuse on Campus: Results From the Canadian National Survey*. Thousand Oaks, CA: Sage.

———. 2009. *Dangerous Exits: Escaping Abusive Relationships in Rural America*. New Brunswick, NJ: Rutgers University Press.

———. 2011. 'Theoretical and Definitional Issues in Violence Against Women', in C.M. Renzetti, J.L. Edleson, and R.K. Bergen, eds., *Sourcebook on Violence Against Women*, 2d ed. Thousand Oaks, CA: Sage.

Dines, G. 2006. 'The White Man's Burden: Gonzo Pornography and the Construction of Black Masculinity', *Yale Journal of Law and Feminism*, 18, 1: 296–7.

——— and R. Jensen. 2008a. 'Pornography', in C.M. Renzetti and J.L. Edleson, eds., *Encyclopedia of Interpersonal Violence*. Thousand Oaks, CA: Sage.

———. 2008b. 'Internet, Pornography', in C.M. Renzetti and J.L. Edleson, eds., *Encyclopedia of Interpersonal Violence*. Thousand Oaks, CA: Sage.

Dutton, D.G. 2006. *Rethinking Domestic Violence*. Vancouver, BC: University of British Columbia Press.

Dworkin, A. 1994. 'Pornography Happens to Women',

www.nostatusquo.com/ACLU/dworkin/PornHappens.html, accessed 15 Aug. 2009.

Ehrlich, H.J. 1999. 'Campus Ethnoviolence', in F. Pincus and H.J. Ehrlich, eds., *Ethnic Conflict*. Boulder, CO: Westview.

Elias, R. 1993. *Victims Still: The Political Manipulation of Crime Victims*. Newbury Park, CA: Sage.

Foubert, J., and B. Perry. 2007. 'Creating Lasting Attitude and Behavior Change in Fraternity Members and Male Student Athletes', *Violence Against Women*, 13, 1: 1–17.

Freedman, E.B. 2002. *No Turning Back: The History of Feminism and the Future of Women*. New York: Ballentine Books.

Funk, R.E. 1993. *Stopping Rape: A Challenge for Men*. Philadelphia: New Society Publishers.

———. 2006. *Reaching Men: Strategies for Preventing Sexist Attitudes, Behaviors, and Violence*. Indianapolis, IN: Jist Life.

Gardner, C.B. 1995. *Passing By: Gender and Public Harassment*. Berkeley: University of California Press.

Gilfus, M.E., S. Fineran, D.J. Cohan, S.A. Jensen, L. Hartwick, and R. Spath. 1999. 'Research on Violence Against Women: Creating Survivor-Informed Collaborations', *Violence Against Women*, 5, 10: 1194–1212.

Giordano, P.C. 1995. 'The Wider Circle of Friends in Adolescence', *American Journal of Sociology*, 101, 3: 661–97.

Godenzi, A., M.D. Schwartz, and W.S. DeKeseredy. 2001. 'Toward a Gendered Social Bond/Male Peer Support Theory of University Woman Abuse', *Critical Criminology*, 10, 1: 1–16.

Gronau, A. 1985. 'Women and Images: Feminist Analysis of Pornography', in C. Vance and V. Burstyn, eds., *Women Against Censorship*. Toronto: Douglas and McIntyre.

Harmon, P.A., and J.V.P. Check. 1989. *The Role of Pornography in Woman Abuse*. Toronto: LaMarsh Research Program on Violence and Conflict Resolution, York University.

Hearn, J. 1998. *The Violence of Men*. Thousand Oaks, CA: Sage.

Hebert, C. 2010. 'Court of Public Opinion Turns on Tories', *Toronto Star*, 15 Jan., www.thestar.com/news/canada/article/751087--hebert-court-of-public-opinion-turns-on-tories, accessed 20 Jan. 2010.

Jenness, V. 2004. 'The Dilemma of Difference: Gender and Hate Crime Policy', in A.L. Ferber, ed., *Home-Grown Hate: Gender and Organized Racism*. New York: Routledge.

Jensen, R. 1995. 'Pornographic Lives', *Violence Against Women*, 1, 1: 32–54.

———. 2007. *Getting Off: Pornography and the End of Masculinity*. Cambridge, MA: South End Press.

————and G. Dines. 1998. 'The Content of Mass-Marketed Pornography', in G. Dines, R. Jensen, and A. Russo, eds., *Pornography: The Production and Consumption of Inequality*. New York: Routledge.

Johnson, A.G. 1997. *The Gender Knot: Unraveling Our Patriarchal Legacy*. Philadelphia: Temple University Press.

Johnson, H. 1996. *Dangerous Domains: Violence Against Women in Canada*. Toronto: Nelson.

Jordan, Z. 2006. 'A View at Cyberporn and Its Influence on Aggression Against Women', unpublished ms. (Iowa State University).

Katz, J. 2006. *The Macho Paradox: Why Some Men Hurt Women and How All Men Can Help*. Naperville, IL: Sourcebooks.

Kelly, L., and J. Radford. 1987. 'The Problem of Men: Feminist Perspectives on Sexual Violence', in P. Scraton, ed., *Law, Order and the Authoritarian State*. Philadelphia: Open University Press.

Kimmel, M.S. 2008. *Guyland: The Perilous World Where Boys Become Men*. New York: HarperCollins.

————and T.E. Mosmiller. 1992. 'Introduction', in M.S. Kimmel and T.E. Mosmiller, eds., *Against the Tide: Profeminist Men in the United States, 1776–1999*. Boston: Beacon Press.

Ledwitz-Rigby, F. 1993. 'An Administrative Approach to Personal Safety on Campus: The Role of a President's Advisory Committee on Women's Safety on Campus', *Journal of Human Justice*, 4, 2: 85–94.

Lehman, P. 2006. 'Introduction: "A Dirty Little Secret"—Why Teach and Study Pornography?', in P. Lehman, ed. *Pornography: Film and Culture*. New Brunswick, NJ: Rutgers University Press.

Levant, R. 1994. 'Male Violence Against Female Partners: Roots in Male Socialization and Development', paper presented at the annual meetings of the American Psychological Association, Los Angeles.

Luxton, M. 1993. 'Dreams and Dilemmas: Feminist Musing on the Man Question', in T. Haddad, ed., *Men and Masculinities*. Toronto: Canadian Scholars' Press.

Messerschmidt, J. 2000. *Nine Lives: Adolescent Masculinities, the Body and Violence*. Boulder, CO: Westview.

Porter, T. 2006a. *Well Meaning Men: Breaking Out of the Man Box*. Charlotte, NC: A Call to Men: National Association of Men and Women Committed to Ending Violence Against Women.

————. 2006b. *Becoming Part of the Solution*. Charlotte, NC: A Call to Men: National Association of Men and Women Committed to Ending Violence Against Women.

Radford, J. 1987. 'Policing Male Violence—Policing Women', in J. Hanmer and M. Maynard, eds., *Women, Violence and Social Control*. Atlantic Highlands, NJ: Humanities Press International.

Renzetti, C.M. 1995. 'Editor's Introduction', *Violence Against Women*, 1: 3–5.

Russell, D.E.H. 1990. *Rape in Marriage*. Bloomington: Indiana University Press.

————. 1998. *Dangerous Relationships: Pornography, Misogyny, and Rape*. Thousand Oaks, CA: Sage.

Sanday, P.R. 1981. 'The Socio-Cultural Context of Rape', *Journal of Social Issues*, 37, 4: 5–27.

————. 1990. *Fraternity Gang Rape*. New York: New York University Press.

————. 1996. *A Woman Scorned: Acquaintance Rape on Trial*. New York: Doubleday.

Schechter, S. 1982. *Women and Male Violence: The Visions and Struggles of the Battered Women's Movement*. Boston: South End Press.

Schwartz, M.D., and W.S. DeKeseredy. 1997. *Sexual Assault on the College Campus: The Role of Male Peer Support*. Thousand Oaks, CA: Sage.

————. 2000. 'Aggregation Bias and Woman Abuse: Variations by Male Peer Support, Region, Language, and School Type', *Journal of Interpersonal Violence*, 15, 6: 555–65.

Sever, A. 2002. *Fleeing the House of Horrors: Women Who Have Left Abusive Partners*. Toronto: University of Toronto Press.

Sluser, R., and M. Kaufman. 1992. 'The White Ribbon Campaign: Mobilizing Men to Take Action', paper presented at the 17th National Conference on Men and Masculinity, Chicago, IL.

Southern Poverty Law Center. 2003. *10 Ways to Fight Hate on Campus: A Response Guide for College Activists*. Montgomery, AL: Southern Poverty Law Center.

Stanko, E.A. 1985. *Intimate Intrusions: Women's Experiences of Male Violence*. London: Routledge.

————. 1990. *Everyday Violence: How Women and Men Experience Sexual and Physical Danger*. London: Pandora.

————. 1997. 'I Second that Emotion: Reflections on Feminism, Emotionality, and Research on Sexual Violence', in M.D. Schwartz, ed., *Researching Sexual Violence: Methodological and Personal Perspectives*. Thousand Oaks, CA: Sage.

Statistics Canada. 2010. 'Study: Projections of the Diversity of the Canadian Population', *The Daily*, March 9: 1–4.

Straus, M.A. 1979. 'Measuring Intrafamily Conflict and Violence: The Conflict Tactics (CT) Scales', *Journal of Marriage and the Family*, 41, 1: 75–88.

Taylor, I., P. Walton, and J. Young. 1973. *The New Criminology: For a Social Theory of Deviance*. London: Routledge and Kegan Paul.

Thorne-Finch, R. 1992. *Ending the Silence: The Origins and Treatment of Male Violence Against Women*. Toronto: University of Toronto Press.

Tremblay, P.F., R. Harris, H. Berman, B. MacQuarrie, G.E. Hutchinson, M.A. Smith, S. Braley, J. Jelly, and K. Dearlove. 2008. 'Negative Social Experiences of University and College Students', *Canadian Journal of Higher Education*, 38, 3: 57–75.

Vallee, B. 2007. *The War on Women: Elly Armour, Jane Hurshman, and Criminal Violence in Canadian Homes*. Toronto: Key Porter Books.

Van Dyke, N., and G. Tester. 2008. *The College Campus as Defended Territory: Factors Influencing Variation in Racist Hate Crime*. Pullman, WA: Department of Sociology, Washington State University.

Wagner, A., S. Acker, and K. Mayuzumi. 2008. 'Introduction', in A. Wagner, S. Acker, and K. Mayuzumi, eds., *Whose University Is It, Anyway?: Power and Privilege on Gendered Terrain*. Toronto: Sumach Press.

Walker Rettberg, J. 2009. 'Joining a Facebook Group as Political Action', http://jilltxt.net/?p=2367, accessed 20 Jan. 2010.

Walther, J.B., C.L. Slovacek, and L.C. Tidwell. 2001. 'Is a Picture Worth a Thousand Words: Photographic Images in Long-Term and Short-Term Computer-Mediated Communication', *Communication Research*, 28, 1: 105–34.

Walton, P. 1998. 'Big Science: Dystopia and Utopia—Establishment and New Criminology Revisited', in P. Walton and J. Young, eds., *The New Criminology Revisited*. London: St. Martin's Press.

Werbowski, M. 2010. 'Prorogation Nation in Crisis: Is Canada Sliding Towards Dictatorial Rule?', *OhmyNews*, 18 Jan., http://english.ohmynews.com, accessed 20 Jan. 2010.

Young, J. 1988. 'Radical Criminology in Britain: The Emergence of a Competing Paradigm', *British Journal of Criminology*, 28, 2: 159–83.

Zerbisias, A. 2008. 'Packaging Abuse of Women as Entertainment for Adults: Cruel, Degrading Scenes "Normalized" for Generation Brought Up in Dot-Com World', *Toronto Star*, 26 Jan., L3.

PART II

The Nation's Narratives
Men and Masculinity in the Canadian Imaginary

In Part I of this text, the authors considered how images and ideals influence the construction of masculinities and some of the implications for individuals and communities. By definition, the use of the term 'construction' suggests that elements are being produced and assembled with other elements to generate something. This process happens through individual and collective effort, whether actively, passively, or inadvertently. Because there are seemingly unlimited variables that come together to shape masculinities, it can be difficult to point to particular ones or to assert that any are themselves consequential. Yet there are recurring themes that can be found across many actual or metaphorical locations. By identifying and studying them, we can better understand their origins and impacts.

Canadian society (like any other) has particular institutions, traditions, and stories that cumulatively define and transmit its values and beliefs—and that are continually affirmed, contested, and refined over time. Part II considers some of these, beginning with an examination of Canadian literature. It is important to acknowledge that this chapter focuses on Anglophone writings, and for that matter, this text is produced in English. In the context of an officially bilingual nation, this presents opportunities and challenges to the authors and to you as the reader. As you read this and other chapters in the text, you are encouraged to compare and contrast their Anglophone and Francophone dimensions, and to decide whether these further nuance the construction of masculinities in Canada.

Tolmie and Shearer, as literary scholars, approach their topic differently from the social scientists and journalist who authored earlier chapters. Their expertise in cultural studies helps us to unpack the intricate strands of meaning in the Canadian literary canon and sets the stage for later chapters in their attention to intersections with race, ethnicity, sexual orientation, and other identities.

Masculinities in Canadian Literature

Jane Tolmie and Karis Shearer

This chapter integrates considerations arising from recent scholarship on masculinity into the analysis of a range of Canadian literary texts in English, both canonical and lesser known. In our analyses we understand men and masculinities as socially produced, and as R.W. Connell, Jeff Hearn, and Michael S. Kimmel phrase it, we 'recogniz[e] men and masculinities as *explicitly gendered* rather than nongendered' and 'emphasiz[e] men's relations, albeit differentially, to *gendered power*' (2005: 3). We take a theme-based approach in order to highlight dialogues that can be opened up by locating men and masculinity as primary subjects of study in a selection of Canadian poems, plays, and novels from the colonial period to the present day. The Canadian literary-critical scene is as busy and hybrid as our national literature itself, and obviously this piece cannot provide any sort of thorough survey of the enormous topic of *masculinities in Canadian literature*, though we try to be attentive to different genres and historical periods, as well as to recent criticism sensitive to issues of sexuality, gender, and race. One goal of this chapter is to demonstrate that masculinity studies and literary criticism can work together in ways that complement rather than efface feminist critical activities of the last decades, an endeavour that, as Bryce Traister observes, requires 'an especially energetic rhetorical and critical insistence' to avoid further entrenchment of the masculine as 'transcendental anchor' (2000: 281). Rachel Adams and David Savran express anxiety that '[given] the limited resources in universities to support teaching and research on gender, it seems an unfortunate inevitability that masculinity studies, if it were to gain any institutional status, would enter into a competitive relationship with other fields' (2002: 7). However, this piece emphasizes non-competitive models for the relationships among women's studies, gender studies, queer studies, feminist literary criticism, and masculinity studies. The article has four main thematic strands, which are not mutually exclusionary (any given text can almost always be discussed in more than one analytic context): masculinity and nation; masculinity and race; queer and trans masculinities, including female masculinities; and masculinity and didacticism/role models.

Masculinity studies is increasingly important in the academic study of Canadian literature, and we begin our chapter with brief suggestions for building a critical bibliography; each thematic section also includes further suggestions for critical reading, and occasional suggestions about further major themes that must go unexplored in this limited space. When Peter Cumming wrote his PhD dissertation, *Some 'Male' from Canada 'Post': Heterosexual Masculinities in Contemporary Canadian Writing*, he found that although there had recently been much written on men and masculinities, there was, in fact, very little criticism on men and masculinities in literature specifically, with this being especially the case for Canadian literature (2002: 13). Cumming's work seeks to address

this gap by providing a study of the heterosexual male in such Canadian texts as Leonard Cohen's *Beautiful Losers*, Thomas King's *Medicine River*, and Michael Ondaatje's *Running in the Family*. Yet points of intersection between masculinity studies and Canadian literary studies are evident at least as early as the beginning of the 1990s. In 1993, Daniel Coleman, one of the leading scholars of masculinity studies in Canada, published his article 'Masculinity's Severed Self: Gender and Orientalism in *Out of Egypt* and *Running in the Family*' in *Studies in Canadian Literature*, which was followed by the essay 'Hustling Status, Scamming Manhood: Race, Performance, and Masculinity in Austin Clarke's Fiction' in a 1995 issue of *masculinities*.

Shortly thereafter, the journal *Textual Studies in Canada* devoted a special issue to 'Politics, Pedagogy, and Masculinities', which, as Coleman notes in his foreword, marked 'a growing importance in Canada of a concerted, careful analysis of masculine performances and practices' (1996: 40) and signalled the need 'at this early stage in the project of masculine reassessment for critics and writers to attend carefully to the paradoxes and double-binds of the process of reassessment itself. In the interests of getting material on masculinities "out there", we need critics—female and male, gay and straight, marginalized and privileged—to observe, to reflect upon, and to critique the reassessment even as it unfolds' (1996: 41–2). To this end, Coleman's book-length study on the perspectives of immigrant writers of South Asian and Caribbean descent, *Masculine Migrations: Reading the Postcolonial Male in 'New Canadian' Narratives*, is a highly self-reflexive study, conscious of its own process, that examines 'masculinities in moments when their usually assumed ideologies and structures become exposed to conscious reconsideration in the encounter with a new cultural environment or medium' (1998: 3).

Still other studies emphasize how social, historical, and/or cultural issues intersect in important ways with masculinities. Coleman's

White Civility: The Literary Project of English Canada, for instance, explores four tropes that emerged in nineteenth- and early-twentieth-century fiction: 'the Loyalist fratricide, the enterprising Scottish orphan, the muscular Christian, and the maturing colonial son', which Coleman argues, 'enable us to trace the ways in which these regularly repeated literary personifications for the Canadian nation mediated and gradually reified the privileged, normative status of British whiteness in English Canada' (2006: 6). Coleman's work is especially important to masculinity studies in Canada for its attention to the shifting intersections of race and masculinity. D.M.R. Bentley's historical study *The Confederation Group of Canadian Poets, 1880–1897* provides due attention to the ways in which the coterie of the Confederation poets constructed their collective identity using specific discourses of masculinity and fraternity to establish themselves, highlighting some of the 'masculinist assumptions that permeated the writing and context of the Confederation group' (2004: 31), including 'the supposedly masculine values of intellectual clarity, moral seriousness, disinterested inquiry, and social responsibility for which "high Victorian" still seems the most adequate term' (2004: 20). Michael P. Buma's doctoral dissertation 'Refereeing Identity: The Cultural Work of the Canadian Hockey Novel' makes the incisive argument that '[b]y hearkening back to an imagined state of national coherence and masculine stability, hockey novels attempt to reassure readers that these "threatened" identities remain benignly in place in at least one area of culture, the hockey rink' (2008: iii). Buma's chapters 'National Manhood', 'Myths of Masculinity', and 'The Homosocial Dressing Room' offer sophisticated readings of sport, gender, and nationalism in Canadian literature.

Terry Goldie's volume *Pink Snow: Homotextual Possibilities in Canadian Fiction* breaks important ground in the area by providing new readings of '"classic Canadian texts"

[that] have seldom been, at least in print, treated as in any sense "gay fiction"' (2003: 3). His chapters that parse homosocial relationships in John Richardson's *Wacousta* and the 'closeted homosexual character as artist manqué' (2003: 76) in Ernest Buckler's *The Mountain and the Valley* are especially rigorous in their examination of what Goldie calls 'homotextual possibilities'. More recently, Paul Nonnekes's *Northern Love: An Exploration of Canadian Masculinity* offers a theoretical framework for 'the distinctiveness of a maternal and a paternal northern love . . . in relation to the specific experience of Canadian men and the influence of masculine ideals on their lives' (2008: 2). Strongly influenced by Sherrill Grace's book *Canada and the Idea of North* (2002), Nonnekes's work uses material from G.W.F. Hegel, Jacques Lacan, and Slavoj Žižek to unpack the 'importance of the North for Canadian men and Canadian masculinity' in Rudy Wiebe's *A Discovery of Strangers* and Robert Kroetsch's *The Man from the Creeks*, leading ultimately to the assertion that 'Canadian masculinity can look to the imaginary father as the ideal figure of northern love' (2008: 130). Though the book has many strong individual readings of gendered scenes, it is limited in scope and thus is perhaps most valuable for its contributions to the large body of critical reflections on Canada's cultural status as a northern nation. However, Nonnekes's book, like the other critical texts included in this brief introductory section, clearly signals the growing importance of the analysis of literary constructions of men and masculinities in Canadian literary texts.

Masculinity and Nation

Works of early Canadian literature frequently emphasize the transformation of 'unruly' young men into community or national leaders through self-discipline as well as literary and spiritual education. Isabella Valancy Crawford's *Malcolm's Katie: A Love Story* (1884) and Ralph Connor's *The Man from Glengarry* (1901) both feature protagonists who undergo a series of trials during which they must learn to temper their robust strength and achieve spiritual balance before emerging as ideal representatives of their respective communities. This transformation involves the male protagonists channelling their strength into productive and profitable *physical* labour, and thereby conforming to a traditional masculinity that emphasizes familial leadership, protection, and provision. One interesting, if slight, variation to this paradigm is Archibald Lampman's *The Story of an Affinity* (1900), in which the hero's transformation takes place in the city, through intellectual or academic labour. The result is an Arnoldian man of letters rather than a pioneering man of the land—a shift of value Bentley suggests may be located in Canada's changing economy and urban development at the turn of the century, when 'pioneering and farming were no longer reliable or expanding avenues to prosperity' (1993: 552). Regardless of whether the labour is physical or intellectual, '[b]y fulfilling the expectations of the wage-earner role', Buma argues, 'men, specifically white men, have often been encouraged to see themselves as contributing productively to the national well-being and greater public good' (2008: 168).

In Crawford's and Connor's texts, the narratives of masculine toughness move toward and conclude with idealized heterosexual unions that promise to further the nation through the establishment of the traditional family. As Anne McClintock explains in *Imperial Leather: Race, Gender, and Sexuality in the Colonial Contest*, '[t]he family trope is important for nationalism' because 'it offers a "natural" figure for sanctioning the national *hierarchy* within a putative organic *unity* of interests' (1995: 357). McClintock notes that in spite of 'many nationalists' ideological investment in the idea of popular *unity*, nations have historically amounted to the sanctioned institutionalization of gender *difference*' (ibid.; original italics). This difference can be found in exploration poems that use figurative language to feminize a

landscape that will be conquered and exploited by male colonizers. In this section, however, we focus on two Confederation-period texts by white writers that present hierarchies of gender difference as natural ones and class hierarchies as ones to be transcended by (some) men. We then turn to the work of African-Canadian writer-critic George Elliott Clarke, whose long poem *Whylah Falls* offers a narrative of belonging that both recognizes and celebrates Black identity, often in nationalist terms.

Crawford's long poem, *Malcolm's Katie*, features a Herculean protagonist (Bentley 1994: 274), the 'full-muscled and large-statured' Max Gordon, who courts the title character, Malcolm Graem's daughter Katie (II, 174). The poem, as its subtitle suggests, is 'A Love Story', but before the two lovers can marry, Max is determined to clear a remote homestead, thereby advancing his social status and putting him in a better position to convince Katie's father to allow them to marry. The poem continually stresses the importance of male labour; Max's role as 'the labourer and the lover' (II, 149) is a dual one through which he must become the main provider for his future wife and family in order to secure the continuation of the nation. Two important hierarchies emerge from the courtship ritual: gender and class. Both the poem's title and its opening line ('Max plac'd a ring on little Katie's hand') signal that male–female relationships in the poem will be predominantly possessive ones. Katie, whose diminutive stature the poem repeatedly emphasizes (she is often referred to as 'little Katie' [II, 17]), is described as a 'rich man's chiefest treasure' (III, 216) who, Bentley notes, 'passes from Malcolm Graeme [sic] to Max Gordon (two men with the same initials, note) as the key item of exchange in a patriarchal economic system' (1993: 508). That the poem ends with a scene 'in the home of Max' (VII, 3), rather than in the home of 'Max and Katie', further emphasizes male agency. It is Max's position as an able-bodied white male that allows him to transcend the second hierarchy—socioeconomic class—in the role of the land-clearing pioneer. These two hierarchies are not unrelated; Bentley observes that '[t]he social ideal advanced by *Malcolm's Katie* is . . . the pyramidal family with a self-made man at its apex' (1994: 278).

As a nation-builder, Max must first use his axe to clear a piece of farmland 'part of a world away' (II, 71) from Katie's home, and his work is framed as male-to-male combat with the 'King of Desolation', a tree. Max asks: '"And have I slain a King? / "Above his ashes will I build my house— / "No slave beneath its pillars, but—a King!"' (II, 160–4). Max's triumph over the tree allows him to emerge as 'King' in its place. His love-inspired labour becomes an essential rite of passage that transforms him from a 'young soul' into a man: 'Max, the lover, found / The labourer's arms grow mightier day by day— / More iron-welded as he slew the trees; / And with the constant yearning of his heart / Towards little Kate, part of a world away / His young soul grew and shew'd a virile front, / Full muscl'd and large statur'd, like his flesh' (II, 167–73). That this work is directly connected to nation-building is made clear by Max's own description of his work: '"My axe and I—we do immortal tasks— / "We build up nations— this my axe and I!"' (IV, 55–6). But Crawford complicates any straightforward reading of Max's transformation into the manly nation-builder by inserting an intelligent rival, Alfred, who points out that 'Nations are not immortal!' and asks: '"Is there now / "One nation thrown'd upon the sphere of the earth, / "That walk'd with the first Gods and saw / "The budding world unfold its slow-unleav'd flow'r?"' (IV, 58–61). Of course, there is no such nation, a fact that creates some ambivalence around the ideal of the axe-wielding, nation-building hero and opens up other spaces of interrogation, inviting readings that employ eco-criticism and critical race theory to examine Max's destruction of the forest and question settler characters' relationship to indigenous peoples; note, for example, that Max 'wrought alone, but for a half-breed lad' who is mentioned only in passing but is obviously a factor in Max's success (II, 165).

Like Max Gordon, Connor's protagonist in *The Man from Glengarry*, Ranald Macdonald, must labour physically before securing his love interest and his status as a nation-building hero. For Ranald, however, this change is as much a spiritual one as it is a physical one, though the two are strongly tied under the doctrine of muscular Christianity. Coleman describes how in the imagination of British settler-subjects in late-nineteenth- and early-twentieth-century Canada, '[t]he figure of the muscular Christian, with his untiring and virile physical body balanced by his spiritually sensitive heart, made a perfect representation of the ideal Canadian who could carry out the hard physical work of territorial expansion, as well as the equally important social work of building a new civil society' (2006: 190). Ranald's journey from disreputable boy from Glengarry to the 'noble man' from Glengarry of the novel's title involves training his body through work. In a scene remarkably reminiscent of Max's axe-wielding activity, Ranald joins his male Macdonald relatives in the woods the winter after the death of his father and, 'taking his father's axe', joins in their labour as an equal for the first time. As with Max, the physical transformation that results is dramatic: 'those months in the woods made a man out of the long, lanky boy, so that, on the first Sabbath after the shanty-men came home, not many in the church that day would have recognized the dark-faced, stalwart youth had it not been that he sat in the pew beside [his uncle] Macdonald Bhain' (2006: 163). At one point Ranald's physical development draws the admiration of a visiting city boy: '"Well, that's the finest chap I ever saw. . . . And what a body he has!"' (2006: 144). Yet, in keeping with the codes of muscular Christianity, Ranald's transformation is not complete without the more difficult spiritual transformation. Under the guidance of the Presbyterian minister's wife, Mrs Murray, Ranald also learns to embrace the values of self-restraint and forgiveness such that his spiritual interior matches his hypermasculine exterior.

Together, these changes see Ranald move toward material wealth and class-transition, something Connor's narrative suggests, in theory, is available to anyone willing to commit to physical conditioning and spiritual grace. This is a position Crawford also adopted in the final lines of the volume in which *Malcolm's Katie* was originally collected: '[A]ll men may have the same / That owns an axe! an' has a strong right arm!' (*Old Spookses' Pass, Malcolm's Katie, and Other Poems*, 1884: 224). This universal membership to the nation is a myth, of course. While, in theory, both authors would seem to advocate this position, their texts simultaneously offer examples in which this is simply not the case. We need only think back to the 'half-breed lad' who labours unrewarded alongside Max, and for whom the possibility of becoming a nation-builder in his own right is never entertained. So too with *The Man from Glengarry*, in which Ranald's role as a nation-builder is strongly tied to his Scottish heritage, his Glengarry origin, and his whiteness. As Coleman argues, Ranald's upward mobility has much to do not only with his gender but also with the way ethnicity and gender intersect in this story. 'At the most basic level', Coleman explains,

> [Ranald's] whiteness and his Presbyterian Britishness enable him to emerge as a national figure in a way that is simply not available in Connor's imagination to any of the French or Irish Catholic loggers with whom the Glengarry Scots compete for Ottawa Valley timber. Nor does it seem possible for Connor to imagine such a leading role for any of the St. Regis Mohawks, who never appear in the novel but whose lease of land to the Highlanders haunts the narrative (2006: 121).

By offering white, able-bodied men as 'universal' examples of self-fashioned nation-builders, Connor's and Crawford's narratives work to naturalize very specific and exclusive examples of such a figure in the name of a mythic national unity.

The work of African-Canadian writer, critic, and anthologist George Elliott Clarke disrupts such myths of national unity. By uncovering and promoting the work of African-Canadian writers—particularly those he calls 'Africadians' from his native Nova Scotia, Clarke's cultural work has sought to contest literary-nationalist narratives that normalize whiteness through the exclusion, erasure, and effacement of Black literature in Canada. Introducing his anthology *Fire on the Water*, Clarke has said: 'If there is a subtle reason for its existence, it is to ensure that Africadians will never again be barred from anthologies of African-Canadian, Atlantic, and Canadian writing in general' (1991: 9). Clarke's creative work also explores narratives of national belonging. In *Whylah Falls*, Clarke constructs the imagined Africadian community of Whylah Falls, to which the hero, Xavier Zachary, or 'X', returns after spending a 'five-winter exile' away at college (1990: 17). This return allows Clarke to explore notions of belonging through the exiled hero who has been indoctrinated with a presumably white education, resulting in his alienation from his community. 'X' courts Selah and Shelley, who 'vows she'll not be tricked' by his 'words that she will know have been pilfered from literature' (1990: 4). Shelley, speaking on behalf of the community, expresses a deep suspicion toward the poet's language: '"You bust in our door, / talkin' April and snow and rain, / litterin' the table / with poems—/ as if we could trust them!"' (1990: 24). The tension between 'X' and Shelley, between 'literary' English and the Black English of Africadia persists until the poet admits he '"[has] no use for measured, cadenced verse / If [she] won't read"' (1990: 23). 'X's' 'college speech' becomes what the poem calls 'Negro-natural' upon his return to Whylah Falls, where the 'green, soiled words / Whose roots mingle with turnip, carrot, and squash, [Keep] philology fresh and tasty' (1990: 57). In

Whylah Falls 'X's' connection to his community is contingent upon his ability to express himself as a heterosexual lover and as a citizen in a language 'authentic' to the Black community. Participation in a common language is, according to Benedict Anderson, strongly connected to the emergence of nationalism: 'there is a special kind of contemporaneous community which language alone suggests—above all in the form of poetry and songs' (1991: 145). At the same time, however, that Clarke's work disrupts a Canadian literary nationalism that has excluded Black literary production and erased Black subjects, Clarke's *Whylah Falls* also replicates some troubling aspects of nationalism. As David Chariandy observes, '*Whylah Falls* evokes the familiar poetics of nationalism: the emphasis on martyrdom, the casting of women as faithful representatives of national consciousness, and even (though in a relatively critical manner) the addressing and downplaying of class tensions and contradictions within national communities' (2002: 79). Nevertheless, *Whylah Falls* shows that men's relationship with nation is never inextricable from race and provides a strong critique of the idealized relationship between men and nation depicted in the earlier texts in this section, in which (white) men achieve comfortable middle-class status by working in the interest of the state.

Masculinity and Race

R.W. Connell's influential work *Masculinities* emphasizes that 'masculinities are not only shaped by the process of imperial expansion, they are active in that process and help to shape it' (1995: 185). It is impossible to separate the concerns of this section from those of other sections such as that on masculinity and nation, as this brief martial quotation from 'The Anglo-Saxon' by nineteenth-century poet Alexander McLachlan makes clear:

> The Anglo-Saxon leads the van,
> And never lags behind,

> For was he not ordain'd to be
> The leader of mankind?
> (McLachlan, 1900/1974: 33).

Canadian/British Ismaili Muslim poet Ian Iqbal Rashid similarly highlights the inextricability of discourses of race, sex, and nation in his poem 'An/other Country' (1991), in which his 'humble penis' is 'cheated by the imperial wealth of yours', leading to the poet's final climactic pose: 'I must close my eyes and think of England' (2006: 265–6). As noted in the nation section earlier in this chapter, McClintock's *Imperial Leather* draws our attention to the 'gendered discourse[s] of nationalism; she laments that feminist 'analyses of nationalism have been few and far between' and is especially critical of white feminists who have been 'slow to recognize nationalism as a feminist issue' (1995: 356–7).

Rather than reproducing material from the nation-building section, then, this section draws on materials from two sets of resources that now enable the feminist study of racialization and masculinity in Canadian literary culture. These are: Canada's—in particular, British Columbia's—vibrant contemporary theatre culture with its powerful focus on race relations; and the Canadian Poetry Press at the University of Western Ontario, which makes early Canadian texts available to the public in electronic format (2010: online). Unfortunately this chapter lacks space for a contextualizing discussion of multiculturalism (itself a contested term) in Canadian literature, but we present here some suggestions about primary resources—especially creative texts by non-white authors—with the reminder to turn to Coleman's work in *Masculine Migrations* for crucial critical context on masculinities and race in Canada (1998). Readers should be aware of the Centre for the Study of Black Cultures at York University, which maintains African Canadian Online (2010). Of great value are Lisette Boily's working bibliography of First Nations writers and writers of colour, and several texts/anthologies compiled/edited by Clarke (Boily, 1994; Clarke, 1991; 1992; 1996; 1997). These are arbitrary selections and overlook, as only one of many examples of inadequacy, the rich resources available on Asian-Canadian writing; see criticism, anthologies, and primary sources by Roy Miki, Gerry Shikatani, David Aylward, and Fred Wah (e.g., in *Diamond Grill* and his 'Elite' poems, Wah explores the effect of the nationally endorsed systemic racism of the Chinese Exclusion Act on a father-son relationship); see also the Ryerson University Library and Archives website on Asian Heritage in Canada (RULA, 2010). Finally, Winifred Siemerling's entry 'Cultural Plurality and Canadian Literature' in the *Encyclopedia of Literature in Canada* offers a strong compilation of primary sources for further study of racialized masculinities in Canada (2002: 265–71).

Let us begin with two plays, both offering feminist critiques of race and masculinity set in the Vancouver area—Sharon Pollock's *The Komagata Maru Incident* (2005) and Marie Clements' *The Unnatural and Accidental Women* (2005). Pollock's play offers an account of an incident in 1914 in which anxiety about Asian immigration led to the refusal to admit passengers on the *Komagata Maru*, a Japanese steamship, to Canada. The ship sailed from Hong Kong to Shanghai to Yokohama, and then to Vancouver, carrying 376 passengers from Punjab, India. The passengers were refused permission to enter Canada despite their being British subjects. The premise(s) for exclusion included financial restrictions and the requirement for a continuous journey—a requirement designed to keep out immigrants from India, as that voyage usually required a stop in Hawaii or Japan. The passengers consisted of 340 Sikhs, 24 Muslims, and 12 Hindus. Only 24 passengers were admitted to Canada and the ship was forced to return to Asia, where the remaining passengers, having already been subjected to six months of incarceration and deprivation on board the ship, were placed under guard by the British government of India; 20 passengers were killed during an attempt to arrest so-called agitators in what has become known as the Budge Budge (Baj Baj) Riot, and while there were some escapees, the majority of the remaining passengers were kept under some form of arrest—village arrest or actual imprisonment—for the duration of World War I. In 2008, both the legislative assembly of BC and the federal government issued apologies, though public reactions have been mixed, especially among Canadian Sikhs. Pollock's play, first presented in 1976, was the first on the subject. Sherrill Grace and Gabriele Helms describe Pollock as exposing 'the mechanisms through which race and gender support the construction of a white, masculinist construction of Canada' (2006: 90).

The play is an effective vehicle for critique of biased immigration policy and makes it clear that public policy is tied to an anxious model of assailable white manhood—a model that, by needing to defend itself, reveals its own weakness. Immigration officer William Hopkinson is a man with a dubious professional past and a complex bi-racial masculinity that exerts itself to suppress and expel the racialized *other* as part of his performance of the role of privileged white government employee. In a sense Pollock offers a feminist critique of racism and white masculinity because she gives her main critiques through the voices of women, but her approach is problematic. Both of her main female characters are flat and stereotypical, one being a hooker with a heart of gold, Evy, and the other a nameless Sikh woman called simply 'Woman' who may get the final word in the play but who nevertheless fails as a compelling voice. In the former case, Evy's insights into Hopkinson's personal anxieties about having a (secret, repressed, hidden) brown mother offer a reductive approach to his particular racism, one sourced in self-loathing and internalized racism (Evy also continues to love and support Hopkinson, despite being assigned many lines that deplore racism); in the latter case the stage direction designating Woman's voice as 'hard, not sentimental' when describing herself as 'not a thing' and as 'strong' is simply not sufficient to overcome her namelessness and abjection throughout the text (2005: 133). Grace and Helms observe of Woman that her 'position as woman of Colour and single mother turned away from the Canadian door is never explored because she remains, within the presentational mode of the play, the object of our gaze and the objective reminder of *Hopkinson's* identity and history: she is the return of his repressed [past]' (2006: 97).

Métis playwright Clements' piece, *The Unnatural and Accidental Woman*, moves away from the historiographic, docudramatic approach adopted by Pollock to offer a surrealist take on a series of murders of Native Canadian women in the Vancouver area between 1965 and 1987, described by the coroner as unnatural and accidental, though in fact Clements succeeds in reminding us that the abuse of racialized women has a place in Canadian everyday real life; in fact, more than five hundred Aboriginal women have gone missing across the country in the past two decades (Native Women's Association of Canada, 2010: online). Framed as a mother-daughter story, the play traces Rebecca's search for her mother, Aunt Shadie, who turns out to have been one of the victims of Gordon Paul Jordan, a barber who fed at least seven middle-aged Native women alcohol until they died (for details, see the Missing Native Women website, 2010: online). The play is a strong critique of gendered and racial violence and is successful in giving its victimized women character, depth, and voice. Clements' play shows Canada's Aboriginal women as assailed by white masculinity and unsupported by Native masculinity. A passage in which two Native women joke about Mounties' and cops' dicks highlights ways in which (mainly white, male) policing often fails indigenous populations, and indeed the primary interactions these Native women have with white men is with their dicks/being dicked around. Rebecca's cop lover, Ron,

takes her for Italian rather than Indian, saying, 'It's just that you don't seem Indian,' leading Rebecca to say, sharply: 'That begs the question—what does an Indian seem like?' (2005: 97). Ron is unable even to perceive her cultural and racial difference, and Aunt Shadie offers a key to the hermeneutics of the entire play when she says, that 'White is a blindness—it has nothing to do with the colour of your skin' (2005: 82). 'Feminist critique' as terminology may present problems for the analysis of Clements' piece, however, much as other Eurocentric terminologies present problems for analysis of indigenous cultural products; as Reid Gilbert observes, though 'the categories "feminist writing" and "Métis story-telling", may be present in Clements's work, these separate "genres" are not linked, nor are they necessarily mutually supportive' (2003: online). Yet the revenge fantasy of the final scene, in which the barber is barbered, bloodily, remains satisfying both as feminist fantasy—Eurocentric sense intact—and as storytelling, offering as it does both an imagined end to male abuse and an imagined reunion between mother and daughter.

This brings us to the point that feminist analysis (like queer analysis, like analysis of race) need not inhere in or depend on the intent of the author; that is merely one way of approaching a text, and often a flawed one. For the final reading of this section, our feminist critique aims to highlight opportunities for productive collaboration between feminist literary criticism and masculinity studies, as brought to bear on material without explicit feminist aims. Thus we turn now to a brief analysis of an incident described in Samuel Hearne's *A Journey from Prince of Wales's Fort, in Hudson's Bay, to the Northern Ocean . . . in the Years 1769, 1770, 1771 & 1772* (accessible through the Canadian Poetry Press online), a text that offers rich resources for examination of the social construction of men and masculinities in the Hudson's Bay Company years, a final reminder, as this section draws to a close, that masculinities are historically specific rather than stable across time.

Just as the *Komagata Maru* incident must be understood in the context of early-twentieth-century immigration, just as the murders of Native women in Clements' play must be understood in the context of late-twentieth-century Aboriginal disenfranchisement on the West Coast, Hearne's writing must be unpacked in the context of the establishment of fur-trading posts within the vast expanses of Rupert's Land (named in honour of Prince Rupert, cousin of Charles II of England and first governor of the Hudson's Bay Company). The figure of Chipewyan guide Matonabbee is one obvious starting point for this analysis within Hearne's journals. Matonabbee twice acted as Hearne's guide on arduous expeditions for the Company and was key to Hearne's success as an explorer in the early 1770s. Matonabbee is a major figure in Canadian literary history and criticism, as a key middleman in relations between the Cree and the HBC and also for the dubious distinction of being a famous suicide, having hanged himself after the destruction of the Churchill Factory. In many moments in Hearne's journals, his stature is larger than life and he attracts Hearne's admiration; however, Matonabbee himself is not the focus of our analysis. Instead we choose to focus on Hearne's responses to the Bloody Falls massacre of 20 Inuit by Matonabbee and his tribe.

During the massacre, Hearne's gaze is particularly drawn to the mutilated body of an adolescent Inuit woman:

> my horror was much increased at seeing a young girl, seemingly about eighteen years of age, killed so near me, that when the first spear was stuck into her side she fell down at my feet, and twisted round my legs, so that it was with difficulty that I could disengage myself from her dying grasps. As two Indian men pursued this unfortunate victim, I solicited very hard for her life; but the murderers made no reply till they had stuck both their spears through her body, and transfixed her to the ground (Hearne, 1795: 78, online).

Hearne's pleas have no effect, and the woman is killed by the 'Yellowknife Indians', described here as 'savages' and 'barbarians' by Hearne. Matonabbee and his men then examine all the dead bodies of the Inuit in a fascinating scene in which their pseudoscientific approach to racial difference seems to provide an eerie parallel to European scientific racism(s) deployed to support imperialist projects; see Strother Roberts on 'cross-tribal' senses of belonging in the eighteenth century for an extended treatment of this incident (2008: online). Hearne describes the scene making precisely this analogy, in fact:

> The brutish manner in which these savages used the bodies they had so cruelly bereaved of life was so shocking, that it would be indecent to describe it; particularly their curiosity in examining, and the remarks they made, on the formation of the women; which, they pretended to say, differed materially from that of their own. For my own part I must acknowledge, that however favourable the opportunity for determining that point might have been, yet my thoughts at the time were too much agitated to admit of any such remarks; and I firmly believe, that had there actually been as much difference between them as there is said to be between the Hottentots and those of Europe, it would not have been in my power to have marked the distinction. I have reason to think, however, that there is no ground for the assertion; and really believe that the declaration of the Indians on this occasion, was utterly void of truth, and proceeded only from the implacable hatred they bore to the whole tribe of people of whom I am speaking (Hearne, 1975: 79, online).

With due credit to Hearne for his insights into this parallelism, the real interest of the scene lies in Hearne's attention to and sympathy for the massacred female body *in particular*. Hearne's sympathy, however genuine, does not give moral stature or neutrality to an observing posture; nor does his particular focus on the rescue of the female serve to ennoble European masculinity. He is there, he is participating (he ties his hair back like Matonabbee and his men and readies for the battle, though he does not strike a blow himself), and in fact his presence, arguably, is the motivating factor that brings everyone together. Hearne's self-positioning in this scene is profoundly troubling. Here we might want to turn to Gayatri Chakravorty Spivak's influential piece 'Can the Subaltern Speak?' in which she observes that imperialism's self-promotion as pro-woman all over the world presents white men as 'saving brown women from brown men' (1994: 93). And yet it is not a simple matter to transfer the discourses built up around a particular cultural context of Third World–First World tension—the 'rescue' paradigm as applied to South Asian women— to a discussion of the so-called Fourth World. As is so often the case, theory here appears to leave behind the genocide of Native North American peoples, perhaps especially women. Readers may find Andrea Lee Smith's *Conquest: Sexual Violence and American Indian Genocide* (2005) useful on this topic.

Queer and Trans Masculinities

From studies of Sinclair Ross, Timothy Findley, and Tomson Highway that examine their works in light of their homosexuality, to studies by critics such as Goldie pursuing homotextual possibilities in texts without 'overt homosexual elements' (see, e.g., Bonnie Kathleen Hughes' reading of Ernest Buckler's *The Mountain and the Valley*, 2005), Canadian literature offers rich resources for the queer theorist/critic. In 2008 the Mark S. Bonham Centre for Sexual Diversity Studies at the University of Toronto held an exhibition titled 'Queer CanLit: Canadian Lesbian, Gay, Bisexual, and Transgender (LGBT) Literature in English' accompanied by a valuable descriptive catalogue covering a wide range of novels, poetry, anthologies, zines, drama, and periodicals (Goldie, 2003: 3; Rayter, McLeod, and Fitzgerald, 2008). From this wealth of material, we have organized this small section around a group of texts that use the queer or trans body to critique hegemonic power structures, given masculinity studies' consistent questioning of masculine hegemonies (a questioning sourced in both feminist and gay studies); we have also selected texts with a particular emphasis on the performative. Two such texts, coming from very different places in the cultural spectrum, are Timothy Findley's *Not Wanted on the Voyage* and Lyndell Montgomery's 'Border Crossings: On the Edge' from *Boys Like Her: Transfictions*, written by the collaborative performance troupe Taste This (Anna Camilleri, Ivan E. Coyote, Zoë Eakle, and Lyndell Montgomery).

Described by W.J. Keith as a 'brilliantly imaginative moral fable about the biblical Noah and the abuse of human power over the animal kingdom', Findley's *Not Wanted on the Voyage* offers a strong starting point for precisely the sort of politicized literary-critical intervention that Keith denounces as 'against the preservation of traditional values' (2006: 103, 131). While the book is, indeed, a brilliant moral fable, its brilliance lies in the exposure of a destructive religious patriarchy, not 'human power' but masculine self-delusion in true Lacanian Name-of-the Father style, complete with a scene in which Noah is paralyzed by the knowledge that 'there [are] no fathers' while taking part in the 'Ritual Ceremony of the Holy Phallus' (Findley, 1984: 261–2; masculinity and faith is obviously another major unexplored thematic strand, e.g., in Margaret Atwood's *The Handmaid's Tale*, Sinclair Ross's *As for Me and My House*, John Marlyn's *Under the Ribs of Death*, Michael Ondaatje's *The English Patient*, to make only a few suggestions). Findley depicts a sickly, violent regime plagued by horror that it cannot reproduce or sustain itself autonomously, thus resulting in an endless cycle of abuse of women and animals. Goldie observes rightly that 'Findley finds the ultimate expression of life in animals because they lack the monstrous mis-shapen motives of men—not "adults", but pre-cisely "men"' (2003: 158). The book ends with its primary sympathetic character, Mrs Noyes, praying—to the 'absent clouds' rather than the 'absent God'—for rain so that the overloaded ark may never land (Findley, 1984: 339). Her horror of the voyage's ending springs from her recognition of the destructive potential the boat carries within it from place to place, symbol-ized through monstrous births, endless conflict, and the dark, cramped quarters of the animals. She understands that without radical paradigm shifts, a new world must merely be a repeat of the old, saying to herself: 'And now, Noah want-ed another world and more cats to blind' (ibid.).

Against this backdrop, the one possibility for a brighter future, and indeed, for thoughtful critique of the entire allegorical infected vessel, emerges as the ageless, sexually indetermin-ate figure of Lucy, at once male martial figure, married woman, and sexless angel. Like Mrs Noyes, Lucy sees clearly that the current regime has no healthy generative potential, saying bit-terly, 'they will go on throwing all the apes and all the demons and all the Unicorns overboard for as long as this voyage lasts' (1984: 335). Having questioned the boundaries of heaven, having lived as angel and human, Lucy alone has the capacity, at the book's end, to wonder 'What for—the human race? And why?' and to imagine the possibility of 'another world' with-out immediately assuming that it must be a re-peat of the old (1984: 325). From earlier in the text we know that the question why? may have been at the heart of Lucy's—Lucifer's—expul-sion from heaven, as Michael Archangelis re-veals when he rages: 'Why? All you ever said was why? Why this and why that and why every-thing' (1984: 103). Michael Archangelis, him-self described by Japheth as offering 'the most

dazzling images of manhood', insists to Lucy 'you *are* male' while she counters merely, 'I like dressing up' (1984: 71, 102). This dressing-up is real enough that she is able to marry and live as a woman with Ham, even have sex with him; before the wedding, she says of their sexual rela-tions, 'I'll make it up as I go along' (1984: 103). This gender performance, the freedom to make up one's body and role as one goes along, is the only freedom that shows itself able to survive the cataclysmic events of the text, and is the bodily and social counterpart of the freedom to ask *why*. *Not Wanted on the Voyage* is only one of many Findley works in which gender is of central concern; while *The Wars* attracts the lion's share of critical attention in terms of queerness, *Not Wanted on the Voyage* offers an extremely positive reading of the in-between queer body; as Judith Butler puts it in *Undoing Gender*, there are 'advantages to remaining less than intelligible, if intelligibility is understood as that which is produced as a consequence of recognition according to prevailing social norms' (Butler, 2004: 3). Heterosexual men and women in Findley's text are alike complicit in propping up the normative phallic regime. Goldie observes that: 'The women, if engaged in heterosexuality, seem in one sense the true inverts, the dangerous obverse of male sexual-ity. The evil embodied in male heterosexuals is most evil because of the female heterosexual' (a position occupied most clearly by Hannah, who sells out her own sex and the human race with it) but Lucy, neither man nor woman but some-how both, offers a way forward past the limita-tions of phallocentrism (Goldie, 2003: 158).

Moving from a Canadian classic to a lesser-known text, let us turn now to Montgomery's chapter 'Border Crossings: On the Edge'. In Margaret Atwood's similarly titled essay 'Border Crossings: The Beetle and the Teacup', she says that people constantly ask her, 'Is there a na-tional literature?' and she answers, 'Sort of [...] But the boundaries are stretchy' (2009: 52). The boundaries crossed in Montgomery's text are at once national and sexual. Montgomery's piece, one of several in the book covering the same episode (Ivan Coyote describes it as 'four queers crossing the border in a borrowed car, four smiling and self-satisfied queers' [Coyote, 1998: 18]), offers a brief reading of the physical act of crossing between the United States and Canada in which the groping hands and penetrative aggression of the border guards signal other coercive identifications between state and sexual bodily policing. The bodies of the members of Taste This—queer, ambiguous, non-normative—attract the negative attention of the guards, in particular Montgomery's close-cropped, male-attired female masculinity. Montgomery wonders aloud: 'Are border guards specifically trained to be as fucking rude as these guys? Are they so threatened by people like us that the only way they can gain any sense of worth is by trying to make us feel like shit?' but is told to shut up by Anna because she has 'a kilt on with no underwear' (Montgomery, 1998: 78–9). The implications are obvious and the short piece leaves the reader in no doubt that the 'fucking border' is literally just that (1998: 78). This brief episode reminds the reader that female masculinities can offer profound reinventions of masculine subjectivity, including lesbian masculine subjectivities (transman, drag queen, butch, stone butch) as well as heterosexual female masculine subjectivities (tomboy, transvestite/crossdresser). *Boys Like Her: Transfictions* highlights ways in which, as Judith Halberstam points out, masculinity 'has finally been recognized as, at least in part, a construction by female- as well as male-born people' (2002: 361).

In moving on now to an examination of Cree playwright Tomson Highway's *Dry Lips Oughta Move to Kapuskasing,* we again signal our awareness that non-Native criticism of Native texts runs a series of risks of cultural appropriation, oversimplification, and stereotyping. Susan Billingham's study of the play warns that the 'complicated interplay among colonization, political disenfranchisement, shifting gender roles, and same-sex desire' must be considered

'in light of both the Cree/Ojibway context and Euro-American theoretical paradigms'—hence phrases such as *two-spirited* must be considered alongside *queer, gay,* and *gender-ambiguous* (2003: 359; see also Sam McKegney's essay, Chapter 14 in this volume). Goldie describes his critical approach to this problem as considering 'the sociocultural implications of the text as aesthetic construct' rather than making any assumption that the 'Native text in some way documents Native culture', and that approach is largely echoed here (2003: 204). Highway organizes *Dry Lips* around seven men from the Wasaychigan Hill Indian reserve (also the location of his earlier play *The Rez Sisters;* in many ways *Dry Lips* serves as a masculine counterpart or foil to *The Rez Sisters*) who face grim realizations about the relationships between colonialism, fetal alcohol syndrome, sexual violence, female power, and hockey. Organized around two 'iconic moments: the re-enactment of the birth of Dicky Bird Halked seventeen years earlier, in 1973—the same year as the stand-off at Wounded Knee—to a mother drunk nearly senseless in a bar; and the rape, with a crucifix, of Patsy Pegahmagahbow/Nanabush by Dicky Bird,' the play draws audience attention again and again to 'homosocial relationships' and ways in which same-sex desire subverts conventional gender roles (Billingham, 2003: 358). Framed at both start and end by close-ups of naked male asses and containing one male character's awkward confession of love for another, the play abounds with homosocial/sexual tensions; role reversals such as men baking and women playing hockey are also common. These non-normative gender performances, however, are not necessarily given a positive spin, as the tone is often one of nostalgia for active, meaningful masculinity that is not destructive of other and/or self; several scenes display a sense of emasculation, as when Simon Starblanket says to his male friends: 'You guys have given up, haven't you? You and your generation. You gave up a long time ago. Scared shitless to face up to the fact it's finally happening, that women are taking power back into their hands, that it was always them—not you, not men—who had the power, the power to give life, the power to keep it. Now you'd rather turn your back on the whole thing and pretend to laugh, wouldn't you' (Highway, 1989: 95).

Nanabush himself/herself—the Trickster figure—shifts between genders throughout the play, with much spirited discussion about whether s/he has a cunt or not, which functions to add elements of grim humour to the post-rape scenes. While this may remind readers of Findley's Lucy, now is the time to consider that, as Peter Dickinson points out, much of the most common academic vocabulary about sexuality was 'formulated in Anglo-American and Eurocentric contexts'—here he mentions Eve Sedgwick, Butler, and Michel Foucault—and 'the First World/Third World binary inherent in many academic discussions of race and nationality cannot be adapted to the so-called Fourth World entirely unproblematically' (Dickinson, 1999: 176; recall this same problem of cultural context with the Hearne reading). Other vocabularies are available, however. Simon Starblanket babbles to himself, 'Fucking goddamn crucifix yesssss . . . God! You're a man. You're a woman. You're a man? You're a woman? You see, nineethoowan poogoo neetha ("I speak only Cree")' (Highway, 1989: 112). This passage is a riff on an extended theme in which English, the colonizers' language, fails to be expressive of the shifting gender realities of Native lived experience, *weetha* in Cree meaning him/her without gender specificity. In several ways, of course, the scene also reminds us that both Native men and women have been screwed by colonialism, by the Catholic Church, by the residential schooling system—all things made explicit in Highway's semi-autobiographical novel on the subject of sex abuse by priests in the state-sanctioned residential school system, *Kiss of the Fur Queen* (1998; see Goldie, 2003: 204–17). However, violence, and especially male violence, in *Dry Lips* is examined *within* the reserve rather than depicted as a force imposed

from without. Highway himself describes *Dry Lips* as an attempt to 'expose the poison' of misogyny, inspired (as with the rape motif in *The Rez Sisters*) in part by the Helen Betty Osborne case, saying that:

When you want healing you have to talk about men talking about women. Most heterosexual men, most straight men do talk about tits and ass, and that's what I was portraying. What is the real source of misogyny? How do we explain the origin? To me, I see [misogyny] as directly related to the origin of God as a man. That's where misogyny comes from. I remember hearing about the fourteen women who were killed in Montréal. December 6th, that's my birthday, I'll never be able to forget it. All my plays are about that in some way, the terrible way misogyny has split the world . . . why are women treated like this? God is a man, Jesus was a man. Until we conceive of God as female, women will not have that power to be treated with respect. And that's why . . . [in *Dry Lips Oughta Move to Kapuskasing*] you see the birth of the goddess as a little girl. The difference between Indian people and white people is that one is patriarchal in structure. . . . In the Cree language, there's no gender. The world isn't divided into that kind of gendered hierarchy. But along the road in history, God as man met God as woman and raped her. And that's where that line comes from [in *Dry Lips Oughta Move to Kapuskasing*], the one that so many people reacted so strongly against, that they couldn't stomach: 'Because I hate them, them fucking bitches. They took the power the ones with the power.' That's Big Joey's line. He can't stand being impotent in the face of women, and he blames women. But people don't want to hear what's true all the time (Highway and Schmidt, 1998: online).

The ending of *Dry Lips* is not entirely bleak, despite pervasive doubts about the state of Native masculinity. The final scene of the play offers redemptive and even transformative potential: 'And the last thing we see is this beautiful naked Indian man lifting this naked baby Indian girl up in the air, his wife sitting beside them watching and laughing. . . . Finally, in the darkness, the last sound we hear is the baby's laughing voice, magnified on tape to fill the entire theatre' (Highway, 1989: 130). Whatever hope the play offers for renewal inheres in this scene, though audience members will respond differently depending on their reactions to the play's ugly gender politics.

Masculinity and Role Models

Throughout this chapter we emphasize that masculinities are historically and culturally specific, and yet one of the most interesting things about masculinity is that it is so powerfully conceptualized as an unproblematic universal, often through the didactic invocation of the idea of 'being a man'. David Cohen recalls with some pain in the introduction to *Being a Man* that 'When I was a little boy I was often told to be a man,' adding that it was never clearly specified what this might mean; every invocation had to be figured out in context (1990: 1). While the nostalgic tone of Cohen's chapter 'The Hobbled Hero' is not compelling, the very idea of a 'stable hero'—a form of fantasy, in fact—is clearly compelling and is invoked as such across a wide range of literary texts (1990: 25). Prolific and popular author Farley Mowat, known for his engagement with conservationism and the natural world, frequently uses the concept of being a man as a form of the highest praise in his fiction and non-fiction alike, as in this scene from his memoir *The Boat Who Wouldn't Float* (1969), which, as it is typical of a number of such invocations across his works, is worth considering in some detail. The setting is a fishing boat off the coast of Newfoundland. The net is full of cod. One unfortunate young

sailor is caught in a swell, breaks his arm badly, drops the net, and clearly needs urgent attention. But rather than have the skipper free the fish and attend to his injuries, Mowat recalls, 'he would not let us leave the trap until every last cod had been dip-netted out of it . . . he sat on the engine hatch watching us and grinning, as the blood soaked the sleeve of his heavy sweater and ran down his oilskin trousers' (1969: 36). The injured sailor later apologizes and worries that he spoiled the morning, and Mowat makes clear that he cannot in fact articulate his praise: 'how was I to find words to tell him what kind of a man I knew him to be?' (1969: 37). In this scene as elsewhere, there is a sense that being a man is a universally understood quality that does not need to be defined, and perhaps should not be—it is best invoked elliptically rather than pinned down. There is a mystique that frequently attends the phrase, to the point that the possible specific meaning(s) of the phrase in individual context(s) become almost less interesting than the persistence of the rhetorical turn itself. It is this mystique that makes the concept so powerfully flexible; while masquerading as universal, the very lack of specificity of the phrase 'being a man' enables it to express a wide range of meanings.

Let us examine a number of these meanings. In the section on nation-building, we refer to the didactic tone of several early works of Canadian literature, including Lampman's *The Story of an Affinity* (1900) and Connor's *The Man from Glengarry* (1901). The notion that literature and citizenship are strongly related is one that is most often associated with Matthew Arnold, and it is well articulated by the Reverend's wife, Mrs Murray, in *The Man from Glengarry*. To the novel's young protagonist, Ranald Macdonald, she gives books by Sir Walter Scott, later explaining: 'I want you to love good books and good men and noble deeds. . . . Then some day you will be a good and great man yourself . . . and you will do some noble work' (1901: 61), as though there were a causal connection between loving 'good' books and being a 'good and great man'. Yet there is perhaps a stronger argument to be made for the role institutions play in shaping individuals, and, in particular, for the way in which literary education has played a role in constructing and normalizing certain forms of masculinity. Terry Eagleton puts it this way: 'From the infant school to the University faculty, literature is a vital instrument for the insertion of individuals into the perceptual and symbolic forms of the dominant ideological formation, able to accomplish this function with a "naturalness," spontaneity, and experiential immediacy possible in no other ideological practice' (1976: 56). Instead of being merely didactic in tone, Connor's *Glengarry School Days* (1902) concerns itself with the teacher as role model, with specific attention to his or her ability (or inability) to mould 'real men' out of boys, as teacher Archibald Munro does here:

> The school never forgot the day when big Bob Fraser 'answered back' in class. For, before the words were well out of his lips, the master, with a single stride, was in front of him, and laying two swift, stinging cuts from the rawhide over big Bob's back, commanded, 'Hold out your hand!' in a voice so terrible, and with eyes of such blazing light, that before Bob was aware, he shot out his hand and stood waiting the blow. The school never, in all its history, received such a thrill as the next moments brought; for while Bob stood waiting, the master's words fell clear-cut upon the dead silence, 'No, Robert, you are too big to thrash. You are a man. No man should strike you—and I apologize.' And then big Bob forgot his wonted sheepishness and spoke with a man's voice, 'I am sorry I spoke back, sir.' And then all the girls began to cry and wipe their eyes with their aprons, while the master and Bob shook hands silently (Connor, 1902: 15).

In this passage of high melodrama in the classroom, the teacher appears to possess near-superhuman powers as he traverses the room to lash the student. It is only through the noble teacher's transgression of them, however, that the implied ideal codes of manly behaviour become clear: as he thrashes 'big Bob Fraser', a student who—mid-punishment—Munro recognizes to be not a child but a man, he realizes that he is breaking the implicit code of adult male–male behaviour by physically humiliating a social equal. The logic of this code is conveyed through the chiasmic 'You are a man. No man should strike you.' But it is also notably followed by an apology, by way of which Munro illustrates another of Connor's ideal masculine traits: humility. The teacher's correction of his own actions and his apology offer Bob a model for adult male behaviour and Bob's subsequent apology restores balance to the scene. As Clarence Karr notes, Connor's novels reflect the 'prevalence of violence in nineteenth-century society *and* the fervent desire of the middle class to repress it' (2000: 83; italics added).

Munro is, in fact, full of subtle and not-so-subtle lessons about what it means to 'be a man', and, indeed, in his chapter 'National Manhood', Michael P. Buma reads *Glengarry School Days* as a 'respon[se] to the late-nineteenth-century crisis of masculinity and to the cultural preoccupation with developing Canadian society and identity' (2008: 198). When one of Munro's pupils, Thomas, sulks openly after losing a spelling bee, Munro proclaims: '"There is just one thing better than winning and that is, taking defeat like a man." His voice was grave, and with just a touch of sadness' (Connor, 1902: 21). This scene is a typical one in Connor's novels, which advocate self-control, stoicism, and restraint on the part of men, as well as the qualities of Christian forgiveness and humility. Munro is presented as one of two ideal teachers in the novel whose 'struggle for self-mastery that made him the man he was, and taught him the secrets of nobleness that he taught his pupils with their three "R's"' (1902: 25).

It is not long, however, before Munro is replaced by a series of female teachers whose femaleness, it is suggested, makes them inherently worse teachers. The following passage deploys the language of nation-building (dynasty or 'ages', good and evil), as well as remarkably explicit misogyny, to summarize the succession of teachers:

> After the expulsion of the master, the Twentieth School fell upon evil days, for the trustees decided that it would be better to try 'gurl' teachers, as Hughie contemptuously called them; and this policy prevailed for two or three years, with the result that the big boys left the school, and with their departure the old heroic age passed away (1902: 151).

The use of nation-building discourse to describe the school, the 'reigns' of its 'leaders', and the different phases of romantic national growth ('evil days' and 'old heroic age'), characteristic as it may seem of the language of schoolboys, actually reminds us that one of the primary functions of schools—from primary to university—has been to produce model citizens and future community leaders. It is more than clear from this passage that a 'gurl' teacher is, for Connor, as inadequate a figure to 'lead' the nation as to teach the local schoolchildren. The nostalgic tone here, in which the passing of an heroic age is mourned, is not totally disconnected from the Mowat mystique in which to name the object of desire is to lose it; nor is it fully separable from the nostalgia expressed by David Cohen, who mourns the 'lack of a clear hero' for modern man, and asserts that '[o]ur forefathers had a more set and settled agenda' (1990: 25).

It must be acknowledged that a nostalgic mode in which a golden age of masculinity is mourned—much like a model in which *everybody knows* what it means to *be a man*—can easily be self-indulgent in terms of both whiteness and privilege. In many texts by non-white writers (as just one analytic category—texts written from various positions of alterity/disenfranchisement must be considered here), a lack of strong male role models is not a matter for nostalgia but a destructive reality that affects every aspect of quotidian life. In the section on masculinity and race, we mention the destructive gender relations of Highway's *Dry Lips*; in a similar vein, Métis novelist Beatrice Culleton Mosionier's *In Search of April Raintree* tracks the breakdown of practically all positive male role models in April's experience. The scene in which April's father fails to speak up to keep his children out of foster care at the start of the novel sets up the ensuing tragedies of the text, from April's experience of brutal rape to the alcoholism, prostitution, and suicide of her sister Cheryl. 'I was hoping Dad would walk in, and he would make them all go away,' recalls April, describing her forced separation from mother and father by Children's Aid, adding: 'He would make everything right' (Mosionier, 1999: 18). But he, like the mother, does nothing, and indeed *can* do nothing—he is totally disempowered in this scene, hampered by alcohol abuse, poverty, self-hatred, internalized racism, and grief. Although the novel, like Highway's *Dry Lips*, ends with a potentially redemptive scene of rebirth and renewal figured through a child, readers must wonder what does eventually happen to little Henry Lee, and may not feel entirely confident about his future. *In Search of April Raintree* may be loosely termed semi-autobiographical, and the suicides of Mosionier's own two sisters and nephew in 'real life' hang over the text. We conclude this section with a scene from her non-fiction personal essay, 'The Special Time', describing a meeting between her biological father and her foster father, Mr Roy:

> Framed pictures of relatives—children, grandchildren, brothers, sisters, nieces, and nephews—cover their walls and they show that the people who live here have long-term stability in their lives with close family ties. As Mr Roy was showing us albums of yet more pictures

. . . I caught a look on my Dad's face. He had been quietly listening, quietly looking about, and it occurred to me that perhaps he saw in this place what he could have had in his life had he been a white man. I think I saw that in my Dad's eyes. And I don't think he wanted it for himself. I think he wanted it for his children (1999: 247).

This passage reminds us of our responsibility to make and understand connections between text and life, art and politics.

Conclusion

There is no single or stable literary definition of Canadian masculinity that emerges from this study, just as, appropriately enough, there is no simple paradigm available to define the boundaries of Canada's national literature. Border crossing, to return to the language of both Atwood and Montgomery, is the name of the game, and in fact the desire for a simple answer once again runs the risk of self-indulgent nostalgia. There are, however, some conclusions to be drawn about the value of treating men and masculinities as explicit subjects of literary analysis. We end this chapter with brief remarks about that quintessential and dearly beloved girls' book, L.M. Montgomery's *Anne of Green Gables*, to highlight what we hope is now clear: that the consideration of men's relations to gendered power opens up textual possibilities and enables critical engagements, even when it does not seem obvious that the book is about men or masculinities. As with feminist and queer analysis, masculinity studies need not depend on or inhere in the intent of the author. With this in mind, let us take a look at the terms of Miss Marilla Cuthbert's initial discussion with Mrs Rachel Lynde about the decision to adopt a child at Green Gables:

We thought we'd get a boy. Matthew is getting up in years, you know—he's sixty—and he isn't so spry as he once was. His heart troubles him a good deal. And you know how desperate hard it is to get hired help. There's never anybody to be had but those stupid, half-grown French boys; and as soon as you do get one broke into your ways and taught something he's up and off to the lobster canneries or the States. At first Matthew suggested getting a Barnado [sic] boy. But I said 'no' flat to that. 'They may be all right—I'm not saying they're not— but no London street Arabs for me,' I said. 'Give me a native born at least. There'll be a risk, no matter who we get. But I'll feel easier in my mind and sleep sounder at nights if we get a born Canadian (Montgomery, 1908: 6).

Readers will be immediately aware that this passage signals a whole series of complicated discourses about masculinity and labour; masculinity and nation; masculinity and race; masculinity and economics; masculinity and faith; masculinity and class; masculinity and migration. In fact this single passage could kickstart an immense research project into masculinity in Montgomery's work. Dr Thomas John Barnardo was arguably one of the most important figures in late-nineteenth-century child migration, and was responsible for setting up an evangelical organization that organized, among other things, the export of poor and orphaned children from Britain into countries such as Canada. As we all know, Marilla does not get a boy, and yet the framing of her decision to adopt opens up fascinating areas for discussion, far beyond the scope of this brief chapter. If this one passage can compress so much into so small a space, it must be clear how much exciting work remains to be done in the literary analysis of subjects such as masculinity and embodiment theory, masculinity and the fantastic, masculinity and post-colonialism, masculinity and aboriginality, masculinity and parenting . . . the list is as long as the reader's imagination can make it.

Discussion Questions

1. The authors make connections between Canadian nationalism and the concepts of settler masculinity and whiteness. In this regard, how do they describe the difficulty of attempting to outline a national literature for a nation they argue is founded in part on the abjection of non-white peoples? What other literary texts make you aware of these connections and how?

2. This chapter acknowledges anxiety about a competitive relationship between masculinity studies and feminist studies. Why does this anxiety exist? What forms does it take? Using outside sources (Internet and print), search for articles discussing integration of masculinity studies into the academic curriculum and consider the various opposing perspectives offered.

3. What does it mean to say that men and masculinities are explicitly gendered? Why say 'masculinities' rather than 'masculinity'?

4. This chapter works from the premise that masculinities are socially constructed. What roles do literature and education play in constructing and/or challenging received notions of masculinity?

5. Authors of early Canadian literature created texts that were often fairly explicit about what they believed it meant to 'be a man'. Have those ideas changed in contemporary texts or can we find these same ideas implicitly or more subtly expressed?

6. This chapter argues that literary masculinities must be considered in context (time and place), and that there is no stable, universal 'masculinity'. Select two texts and consider how representations of masculinity in Canadian literature have changed in different contexts.

7. Consider Judith Halberstam's term 'female masculinity'. How do female characters perform masculinity in Canadian novels?

8. Heteropatriarchy: what is it? Using any one of a range of classic Canadian texts to be determined by the instructor, discuss how heterosexual men and women are alike complicit in propping up a rigid gender regime that discards non-normative bodies and identities.

9. Consider the chapter's closing remarks about *Anne of Green Gables*. Which classic children's/young adult book does this chapter make you want to reread, and why?

Recommended Websites

African Canadian Online: www.yorku.ca/aconline/about.html

Asian Canadian Literature Bibliography: www.asian.ca/books/booklist.htm

Canadian Literature (major reference): www.library.ubc.ca/jones/canlit.html

Canadian Literature: A Quarterly of Criticism and Review: www.canlit.ca

Canadian Literature Encyclopedia: www.thecanadianencyclopedia.com

Canadian Poetry Online. University of Toronto Libraries: www.library.utoronto.ca/canpoetry

Canadian Poetry Press. 2010. University of
Western Ontario: www.uwo.ca/english/
canadianpoetry/abtcanpo.htm

History in Focus. Gender: www.history.ac.uk/
ihr/Focus/Gender/websites.html

LibraryThing. Masculinity in Literature:
www.librarything.com/subject/
Masculinity+in+literature

Literary History.com. Masculinity in Literature:
www.literaryhistory.com/20thC/
masculinity_in_literature.htm

Native Women's Association of Canada: www.
nwac-hq.org/

RULA (Ryerson University Library & Archives).
Asian Heritage in Canada: www.ryerson.ca/
library/events/asian_heritage/anthologies.
html

References

African Canadian Online. 2010. www.yorku.ca/aconline/
about.html, accessed 19 May 2010.

Anderson, B. 1991. *Imagined Communities: Reflections on
the Origin and Spread of Nationalism*. London: Verso.

Atwood, M. 2009. 'Border Crossings: The Beetle and the
Teacup', *The Atlantic: Fiction 2009* Special issue, 52–3.

Adams, R., and D. Savran. 2002. 'Introduction', in R.
Adams and D. Savran, eds., *The Masculinity Studies
Reader*. Malden, MA: Blackwell.

Bentley, D.M.R. 1993. *Early Long Poems on Canada*.
London, ON: Canadian Poetry Press.

———. 1994. *Mimic Fires: Accounts of Early Long Poems on
Canada*. Montreal: McGill-Queen's University Press.

———. 2004. *The Confederation Group of Canadian Poets,
1880–1897*. Toronto: University of Toronto Press.

Billingham, S. 2003. 'The Configuration of Gender
in Tomson Highway's *Dry Lips Oughta Move to
Kapukasing*', *Modern Drama*, 46, 3: 358–80.

Boily, L. 1994. 'Contemporary Canadian First Nations
Writers and Writers of Colour: A Working
Bibliography', *West Coast Line*, 13/14: 303–18.

Buma, M.P. 2008. *Refereeing Identity: The Cultural Work
of Canadian Hockey Novels*. PhD thesis (University of
Western Ontario).

Butler, J. 2004. *Undoing Gender*. New York and London:
Routledge.

Canadian Poetry Press. 2010. University of Western
Ontario, www.uwo.ca/english/canadianpoetry,
accessed 24 May 2010.

Chariandy, D.J. 2002. *Land to Light On: Black Canadian
Literature and the Language of Belonging*. PhD thesis
(York University).

Clarke, G.E., ed. 1990. *Whylah Falls*. Vancouver: Polestar,
2000.

———. 1991. *Fire on the Water: An Anthology of Black Nova
Scotian Writing*, vol. 1. Lawrencetown Beach, NS:
Pottersfield.

———. 1992. *Fire on the Water: An Anthology of Black Nova

Scotian Writing*, vol. 2. Lawrencetown Beach, NS:
Pottersfield.

———. 1996. 'African Canadiana: A Primary Bibliography
of Literature by African-Canadian Authors', *Canadian
Ethnic Studies/Études ethniques au Canada*, 28, 3:
120–209.

———. 1997. *Eyeing the North Star: Directions in African-
Canadian Literature*. Toronto: McClelland & Stewart.

Clements, M. 2005. *The Unnatural and Accidental Women*.
Vancouver: Talon Books.

Cohen, D. 1990. *Being a Man*. London: Routledge.

Coleman, D. 1993. 'Masculinity's Severed Self: Gender
and Orientalism in *Out of Egypt* and *Running in the
Family*', *Studies in Canadian Literature/Études en
Littérature Canadienne*, 18, 2: 62–80.

———. 1995. 'Hustling Status, Scamming Manhood:
Race, Performance, and Masculinity in Austin Clarke's
Fiction', *masculinities*, 3, 1: 74–88.

———. 1996. 'Politics, Pedagogy, and Masculinities',
Special issue, *Textual Studies in Canada*, 8: 39–42.

———. 1998. *Masculine Migrations: Reading the Postcolonial
Male in 'New Canadian' Narratives*. Toronto: University
of Toronto Press.

———. 2006. *White Civility: The Literary Project of English
Canada*. Toronto: University of Toronto Press.

———, C. Bullock, G. Burger, and A. McTavish, eds.
1996. 'Politics, Pedagogy, and Masculinities', Special
issue, *Textual Studies in Canada*, 8.

Connell, R.W. 1995. *Masculinities*. Cambridge, UK: Polity
Press.

———, J. Hearn, and M. Kimmel. 2005. 'Introduction',
in M.S. Kimmel, J. Hearn, and R.W. Connell, eds.,
Handbook of Studies on Men & Masculinities. Thousand
Oaks, CA: Sage.

Connor, R. 1901/1967. *The Man from Glengarry*. Toronto:
McClelland & Stewart.

———. 1902. *Glengarry School Days*. New York: Grosset
& Dunlap.

Coyote, I. 1998. 'Border Crossing: No Proof', in *Boys Like Her: Transfictions by Taste This*. Vancouver: Press Gang.

Crawford, I. Valancy. 1884/1993. *Malcolm's Katie*, in D.M.R. Bentley, ed., *Early Long Poems on Canada*. London, ON: Canadian Poetry Press.

———. 1866/1888. *Old Spookses' Pass, Malcolm's Katie and Other Poems*. Toronto: James Bain and Son.

Cumming, P. 2002. *Some 'Male' from Canada 'Post': Heterosexual Masculinities in Contemporary Canadian Writing*. PhD thesis (University of Western Ontario).

Davies, B. 1989. '"We Hold a Vaster Empire Than Has Been": Canadian Literature and the Canadian Empire', *Studies in Canadian Literature*, 14, 1, www.lib.unb.ca/Texts/SCL/bin/get.cgi?directory=vol14_1/&filename=Davies.htm, accessed 19 May 2010.

Dickinson, P. 1999. *Here Is Queer: Nationalisms, Sexualities, and the Literatures of Canada*. Toronto: University of Toronto Press.

Eagleton, T. 1976. *Criticism and Ideology: A Study in Marxist Literary Theory*. London: Verso.

Findley, T. 1984. *Not Wanted on the Voyage*. Toronto: Penguin.

Gilbert, R. 2003. 'Marie Clements's *The Unnatural and Accidental Women*: "Denaturalizing" Genre', *Theatre Research in Canada*, 24, 1–2, www.lib.unb.ca/Texts/TRIC/bin/get9.cgi?directory=vol24_1_2/&filename=gilbert.htm, accessed 20 May 2010.

Goldie, T. 2003. *Pink Snow: Homotextual Possibilities in Canadian Fiction*. Peterborough, ON: Broadview Press.

Grace, S.E. 2002. *Canada and the Idea of North*. Kingston, ON: McGill-Queen's University Press.

——— and G. Helms. 2006. 'Documenting Racism: Sharon Pollock's *The Komagata Maru Incident*', in G. Ratsoy, ed., *Theatre in British Columbia: Critical Perspectives on Canadian Theatre in English*, vol. 6. Toronto: Playwrights Press.

Halberstam, J. 2002. 'An Introduction to Female Masculinity', in R. Adams and D. Savran, eds., *The Masculinity Studies Reader*. Malden, MA: Blackwell.

Hearne, S. 1795. *A Journey from Prince of Wales's Fort, in Hudson's Bay, to the Northern Ocean...in the Years 1769, 1770, 1771 & 1772*. London: Strahan and Cadell. Available online through the Canadian Poetry Project: www.canadianpoetry.ca/eng%20274e/pdf/hearne.pdf, accessed 20 May 2010.

Highway, T. 1989. *Dry Lips Oughta Move to Kapukasing*. Calgary: Fifth House.

——— and P. Schmidt. May 1998. 'Interview with Tomson Highway', www.playwrights.ca/portfolios/tomsonint.html, accessed 10 May 2010.

Hughes, B.K. 2005. 'Ernest Buckler's *The Mountain and the Valley* and Sinclair Ross's *As for Me and My House*: Two Cases of Canadian Canon Making', MA thesis (University of Saskatchewan).

Karr, C. 2000. *Authors and Audiences: Popular Canadian Fiction in the Early Twentieth Century*. Montreal and Kingston: McGill-Queen's University Press.

Lampman, A. 1900/1993. 'The Story of an Affinity', in D.M.R. Bentley, ed., *Early Long Poems on Canada*. London, ON: Canadian Poetry Press.

Keith, W.J. 2006. *Canadian Literature in English*. Erin, ON: Porcupine's Quill.

McClintock, A. 1995. *Imperial Leather: Race, Gender and Sexuality in the Colonial Contest*. London: Routledge.

McLachlan, A. 1974. *The Poetical Works of Alexander McLachlan*. Toronto: University of Toronto Press (originally published in 1900 by William Briggs, Toronto).

Missing Native Women website. 2010. www.missingnativewomen.ca, accessed 21 May 2010.

Montgomery, L. 1998. 'Border Crossings: On the Edge', in *Boys Like Her: Transfictions by Taste This*. Vancouver: Press Gang.

Montgomery, L.M. 1908/1935. *Anne of Green Gables*. London: Seal Books.

Mosionier, B. Culleton. 1999. 'The Special Time', in C. Suzack, ed., *In Search of April Raintree: Critical Edition*. Winnipeg: Portage & Main.

Mowat, F. 1969. *The Boat Who Wouldn't Float*. New York: Random House.

Native Women's Association of Canada website. 2010. www.nwac-hq.org, accessed 21 May 2010.

Nonnekes, P. 2008. *Northern Love: An Exploration of Canadian Masculinity*. Edmonton: AU Press, Athabasca University.

Pollock, S. 2005. 'The *Komagata Maru* Incident', in C. Zimmerman, ed., *Sharon Pollock: Collected Works*, vol. 1. Toronto: Playwrights Press.

Rashid, I.I. 2006. 'An/other country', in R. Cavell and P. Dickinson, eds., *Sexing the Maple: A Canadian Sourcebook*. Peterborough, ON: Broadview Press.

Rayter, S., D.W. McLeod, and M. Fitzgerald. 2008. *Queer CanLit: Canadian Lesbian, Gay, Bisexual, and Transgender (LGBT) Literature in English*. Toronto: University of Toronto, Mark S. Bonham Centre for Sexual Diversity Studies.

Roberts, S. 2008. 'Indians, "Esquimaux," and Race: Identity and Community in the Lands West of Hudson's Bay in the Eighteenth Century', *Online Proceedings of the History Department's James A. Rawley Graduate Conference in the Humanities*. Lincoln: University of Nebraska, http://digitalcommons.unl.edu/cgi/viewcontent.cgi?article=1024&context=historyrawleyconference, accessed 20 May 2010.

RULA (Ryerson University Library & Archives). 2010. Asian Heritage in Canada website, www.ryerson.ca/library/events/asian_heritage/anthologies.html, accessed 19 May 2010.

Siemerling, W. 2002. 'Canadian Literature and Cultural Plurality', in W.H. New, ed., *Encyclopedia of*

Literature in Canada. Toronto: University of Toronto Press.

Smith, A.L. 2005. *Conquest: Sexual Violence and American Indian Genocide*. Boston: South End Press.

Spivak, G.C. 1994. 'Can the Subaltern Speak?', in P. Williams and L. Chrisman, eds., *Colonial Discourse and Postcolonial Theory: A Reader*. New York: Columbia University Press.

Traister, B. 2000. 'Academic Viagra: The Rise of American Masculinity Studies', *American Quarterly*, 52, 2: 247–304.

Wah, F. 1985. 'Elite', in *Waiting for Saskatchewan*. Winnipeg: Turnstone Press.

———. 1996. *Diamond Grill*. Edmonton: NeWest Press.

CHAPTER 7

In this chapter, Robidoux offers an historical perspective of Canada's development as a nation, particularly through an exploration of stories about English and French colonialists, the coureurs de bois—early fur traders in what was then New France—and their interactions with indigenous peoples, on to the present day, making several links to the construction of masculinities within Canadian contexts. He builds on earlier discussion about the connections among masculinity, body, and physicality more generally. He also challenges some of the viewpoints represented in this text and elsewhere on the concept of hegemony.

This is also the first instance in the text when Canada's relationship with hockey is substantively explored. Obviously, this sport is pervasively represented across Canadian popular culture and is stereotypically associated with many notions of its national identity. Sport is an important conveyance of masculine socialization and identification, and hockey is particularly so in Canada. Robidoux's interviews with male hockey players are especially useful in the context of this book, given the importance of personal accounts in understanding human identity. The excerpts from several interviews powerfully depict the issues and tensions associated with manhood and masculinities, and their relationships with power.

One of the most striking aspects of the interviews is the recurring theme of being kid-like, not 'growing up', and perpetual adolescence amongst the men. A survey of masculine stereotypes reveals interesting paradoxes in this regard. On the one hand, we encounter ideas about being responsible and in charge, while simultaneously themes of aloofness and entitlement arise. As you read this chapter, consider the ways in which these seemingly incompatible ideas are woven through ideas about manhood and what implications this paradox may have.

Male Hegemony or Male Mythology? Uncovering Distinctions through Some of Canada's Leading Men: The Coureurs de Bois and Professional Hockey Players

Michael A. Robidoux

It almost seems passé in today's academic climate to state that masculinity is not a monolith—something natural that has remained historically intact and culturally consistent. Yet as gender scholars readily admit, efforts to correct the 'purposefully ignored chronicling' of women and their history has produced 'an unintended result', which was for 'men's gendered behaviour to be treated as "natural" and therefore left invisible' (McPherson, Morgan, and Forestell, 1999: 5). This result has meant that hegemonic masculinity is taken for granted (Phillips, 1995: 605) and the processes by which masculine identities are produced, and the identities themselves, are neglected. Only within the past ten years, however, have there been serious efforts to critically address hegemonic masculinity by making it 'visible' and recognizable as a construct, one with deliberate and specific designs (Connell and Messerschmidt, 2005; Demetrakis, 2001; Jefferson, 2002). Critical here is that these efforts have been to confront and challenge hegemonic masculinity, which has been useful in many ways for studying men and constructs of masculinity, but in terms of specific constructs of masculinity in Canada, simultaneously problematic. The problems involve assumptions consistently made about what constitutes hegemonic masculinity and how this hegemonic ideal is maintained.

In researching the homosocial environment of professional hockey, I have attempted to come to terms with the paradoxical situation of privileged male athletes who are seemingly powerful yet susceptible to exploitation, by using Foucault's (1977) ideas about the ubiquitous potential of power, most usefully explicated through his theories of the docile body (Robidoux, 2001: 135). By recognizing the temporal and fluid nature of power, I have not been comfortable with labelling hockey players as hegemonic, or part of male hegemony, despite powerful images or rhetoric assigned to the male athlete as representative of masculine hegemony. Scholars have repeatedly argued that male athletes demonstrate certain qualities that are identifiably masculine and hegemonic; yet these qualities appear to have little bearing on what constitutes power in contemporary Western society, or throughout much of Western history. Because of these inconsistencies, which I will address momentarily, research on male professional sport is riddled with contradictions that poorly represent how masculinity is experienced and expressed by male athletes—in this case hockey players. Therefore, the intention of this chapter is to reconsider issues of hegemonic masculinity in order to appreciate more fully expressions of gender in professional hockey and the enabling/disabling paradox of power this gendered identity entails.

Masculine Power Relations

In *Which Way Is Up?* R.W. Connell warns against certain social science trends that attempt to hierarchize gender structures and create a power grid where identities are rated on a scale—for example, from high 'bearded Marlboro advertising executives' to low 'pregnant teenage lesbians' (1983: 42). The point is well made, because gender categories are neither static nor stable and therefore unable to support such classifications. However, Connell does assign levels of power to particular identities (for our purposes, masculine). This is unavoidable for someone attempting, as Connell does, to expose and dismantle masculine hegemony:

> There is a hegemonic form of masculinity . . . but which is by no means evenly spread among men. The celebration and enforcement of this hegemonic form creates a complex penumbra of repression and subordination. It defines by exclusion groups of men who are systematically oppressed: gays and effeminates, notably (1983: 41).

In so doing, Connell describes not necessarily a gradation of male power but qualities of masculinity that have greater capital in specific social and historical contexts. In Demetrakis's (2001: 341) critique of Connell, he remains sympathetic to this notion of dominance of specific constructs of masculinity over other more marginalized constructions of gender, male or female. Although not wanting to naturalize these relations of power by emphasizing their cultural and historical inconsistencies, scholars continue to identify expressions of gender that are seen as either subordinated or subordinating.

The difficulty here is not the obvious imbalance of power of gender identities, but rather the unified power construct that Connell, as well as many gender scholars, categorizes as

hegemonic. The definition of masculine hegemony is repeatedly associated with physical
force and dominance. The idea of male power
being understood through the physical is correct in a Foucauldian sense: in that all subjects,
relatively speaking, are in positions of power.
Yet associating physical power with masculine hegemony is problematic for two reasons.
First, it locates an expression of male power
that has limited currency within male relations; second, it poorly reflects the exclusivity
of male hegemony and those who contribute to
it. In other words, this definition does not acknowledge the most enduring and oppressive
form of male dominance, which is maintained
by a privileged minority and done so through
the mind, not the body. The consequences of
this definitional shortcoming are real; it diverts
attention from those wishing to contest and
dismantle hegemonic masculinity, creates illusions of power where power is limited, and reduces any inclination to challenge this hegemonic position from within—as is the case with
professional hockey players.

Canadian Masculinities

It is important to consider how this physically
dominant construct of masculinity has come to
be associated with male power. To do so from a
Canadian perspective, historical context needs
to be provided, most notably Canada's colonial
heritage and its struggle for national identity.
Early Canadian colonialists were influenced
by European traditions of masculinity but also
reacted against them. In pre-Confederation
Canada, European constructs of masculinity,
which emphasized rationalism and restraint,
remained dominant indicators of male worth
and privilege, yet they were largely inaccessible
and irrelevant to those making a life in northern North America. European gentlemen (most
notably English and French) derided emergent
constructs of masculinity in Canada (and in the
United States) that were increasingly based on
industriousness and entrepreneurial success.

In 1820, Edward Talbot, visiting Canada from
Ireland, writes to a British audience about
Canadian bourgeois delusions of superiority because of their new-found wealth: 'Most
of these persons . . . who have made fortunes
in Montreal . . . were originally mechanics of
low origin and scanty acquirements', and he
describes these men who attempt to associate
their fortunes with 'airs of nobility' as having
mistaken 'wealth to be the statesmen of distinction, instead of the means by which . . .
distinction may be procured' (1963: 282, 285).
The airs of nobility that Talbot disqualifies were
attempts by this new Canadian bourgeoisie to
seek legitimacy in the existing (male) power
structure—traditionally one was born into it,
and did not enter through one's deeds. Attempts
to buy one's way into traditional lines of power
'were common ways that the bourgeoisie could
associate themselves with nobility and aspire
to gentry' (Podruchny, 2000: 61); yet most remained outside of this powerful elite. As a result, Canada's emergent bourgeoisie began to
establish a sense of identity and legitimacy that
was distinct from European gentlemen, but
without ridding themselves entirely of the ac-
coutrements of the European nobility.[1]

This new forged identity employs aspects
of a romanticized physical identity that were
rhetorically useful in depicting a specific
sense of masculinity in Canada. Interestingly,
these qualities were almost as irrelevant to the
emergent males as they were to the European
gentlemen from whom they were attempting
to disassociate. Nevertheless, bourgeois males
wished to express themselves as Canadian *men*,
and thus deliberately turned to an unmistakably
Canadian source for their newfound identity,
the fur trade. First, the fur trade was the source
of tremendous wealth for this burgeoning class
of men (and Canada as a whole), and second, it
was associated with a type of man whose status
was legendary not only in Canada but also in
Europe. These men were the coureurs de bois,
'runners of the woods', the physical labourers who, along with the First Nations peoples,

made the fur trade possible. Bruce Trigger explains that the 'traders quickly adopted items of native dress, accustomed themselves to use canoes and snowshoes, hunted alongside Indian men, and joined them in their ritual steam baths' (1985: 195). Their ability to adapt to this unforgiving lifestyle made fur traders a source of romantic narrative, celebrating their ordeals as part of the local folklore. One such account comes from a Jesuit Father who claims that a Frenchman 'who lived with them [First Nations] last winter, told us that during two days he ate nothing but a small piece of candle, that he had accidentally carried in his pocket' (le Jeune, 1959: 171). These tales of surviving the Canadian wilderness, however bleak in reality, 'stirred the imaginations of every habitant and seigneur in the colony' (Clark, 1962: 25), elevating the coureurs de bois to heroic figures.

The fur trader was seen in Canadian folklore as invincible, able to overcome the unforgiving conditions of the Canadian wilderness but also the restrictive lifestyle dictated by English and French colonial authorities. Fur traders were the first of a long list of renegade heroes who helped shape a larger masculinist tradition that 'continued as a characteristic part of sexual ideology in former colonies of settlement such as the United States, South Africa, and Australia' (Connell, 1993: 612). Like other frontier heroes, these men 'lived recklessly, heedless of what the future held in store for them. Danger was cheerfully faced, and privation grimly accepted' (Clark, 1962: 26). With this recklessness came a disdain for authority; they were perceived as outlaws, thwarting the laws of the land. In *Jesuit Relations*, Thwaites provides an editorial note that describes the role of the coureurs de bois in Canadian history:

> For many years—since at least 1660—the fur trade had been illegally carried on by wandering Canadian trappers and voyageurs, who were commonly termed coureurs de bois, 'wood-rangers.' Laws

against this illicit traffic were enacted by the French government, but they were seldom effective; and it was openly charged that the Canadian governors and other officials were in collusion with the coureurs de bois, and sharers in their profits (1959: 272).

In reality these men were more often sharers in First Nations culture and traditions, not the exploitative villains described here (Schmalz, 1991: 36). However, qualities associated with conquest had greater political value within a newly developing capitalist economy that was dictating colonial interests and development throughout French and later British expansion. Therefore, much of the heroic status grafted on those who traded and trapped alongside First Nations peoples was based on their perceived ability to conquer their environment, and also to conquer the indigenous population to produce even greater economic gain. These qualities of conquest became useful symbols of emergent masculine hegemony in Canada, which spoke to emergent capitalist ideologies that were fuelling the colonialist imperative.

Likely the greatest evidence of appropriation of fur trader identity is seen in a nineteenth-century bourgeois men's club, the Beaver Club in Montreal. The club was an exclusively English male association that enabled upward-striving businessmen in urban Canada to foster relationships with other businessmen and celebrate their new-found status as wealthy entrepreneurs. Unlike other fraternal organizations, the Beaver Club was made up of entrepreneurs who had made their fortunes via the fur trade as merchants and who would have wintered in Canada's hinterland, sharing first-hand experience with the romanticized fur traders/trappers and First Nations peoples. Beaver Club activities and rituals were celebrations of the exotic and dangerous lifestyle of the fur trader, providing members with a distinctly Canadian homosocial experience. Carolyn Podruchny explains: 'Men who had braved the unknown, encountering what they thought were strange, exotic, and potentially menacing natives, and surviving the rigors and dangers of travel by canoe, came together in Montreal to remember and honour their rugged adventures in the North American interior' (2000: 54).

The evenings became a means for the men to celebrate the 'bush masculinity' that became so distinctively associated with Canadian traders and fodder for romantic narrative. This bush masculinity, involving 'displays of physical performance, such as feats of labour, fights, races, and contests of strength' (Wamsley, 1999: 27), was an excuse for the men to do exclusively 'men things' in styles only someone with such a rugged sense of manliness could enjoy. These behaviours would include excessive drinking and swearing, but also ritualized behaviours that would have been specific to fur-trading life, originally derived from First Nations culture. First Nations–inspired behaviours were of special significance because of their exoticism and perceived danger, and they offered the perfect counterdiscourse to masculinity within the British European gentry. It is noted that 'Indian manners, customs, and language, especially war whoops, were closely imitated at club dinners' and that peace pipes were passed around to connote some rich ritualistic history and significance (Podruchny, 2000: 68). Yet the profound irony here is that Beaver Club members, fur trade merchants, had never actually experienced the behaviour appropriated through their ceremonies. Moreover, those people on which Beaver Club members were basing their newfound masculine identity, the actual labourers themselves, were not permitted membership or access to Beaver Club society.

Beaver Club members associated themselves with the fur trade because they would spend significant periods of time at trading outposts, where they had contact with the traders and trappers who were responsible for providing product for the merchant. The remote locations of these outposts, coupled with the seclusion and desolation of the winter months, were not easily endured, but these men did not participate in the fur trade and did not experience the adventures that, although romanticized, were arduous, dangerous ordeals. Podruchny explains how Beaver Club members would regale each other with tales of overtly physical, and generally risky, labour practices that were symbolically gratifying but literally quite beneath them:

> [B]ourgeois men . . . reminisced about paddling canoes and running through rapids, even though this was the work of the voyageurs. The bourgeois did not risk their lives in rapids and portages, carry backbreaking packs, paddle at outrageous speeds, nor survive on minimal food, as did the voyageurs. Both the distancing from and the imitation of voyageurs reflected a code of ethics that applauded rugged behaviour of the bourgeois in the right settings (2000: 61).

The paradox here is that specific qualities based in the physical are celebrated, yet it is precisely the physicality of the labourer that prevents him from entering the privileged society of the Beaver Club.

By attaching themselves to this heroic tradition, bourgeois males were at once symbolically celebrating masculine privilege and also sustaining a consumable male construct that was being further popularized in fiction of the time, most notably in Robert Michael Ballantyne's *The Young Fur Traders* (Phillips, 1995). In typical adventure-story fashion, the text tells of the adventures of two adolescent boys, in this case in northern Canada. Richard Phillips describes the story as a tale about a land where the rules of 'civilized' society (Britain) do not apply and where it is required that boys live 'rough', developing 'body and spirit' in ways that 'an easy life' would not permit (1995: 598). Present in the story, among others, are a French voyageur and a First Nations male who embody the necessary qualities for survival in the Canadian

North. These qualities are specifically male qualities that presented in this literary form become 'metaphorical journeys from boyhood to manhood', where 'manhood is constructed, naturalized, and normalized' (ibid.). Interestingly, these identical qualities are celebrated in Beaver Club rituals, and are consumed primarily by an audience even further removed from northern adventure than Beaver Club members themselves. Physicality then became the means by which Canadian bourgeois gentlemen could dissociate themselves from gentry masculinity yet embrace physicality in a purely symbolic form, in order to uphold principles of mind–body dualism that are critical in maintaining class and gender divisions. Those who depend on their bodies for their livelihood are subordinated by their corporal reality, in contrast to aristocratic and later capitalist elites, whose existence and power are enabled by the bodies of others. These relations are maintained throughout Western history, yet it is the paradox of Canadian masculinity that it symbolically subverts this relationship but literally supports it.

The Myth of Man

As we consider the unfolding of this masculine construct in a more modern Canadian sport context, an important acknowledgement must be made. Bruce Woodcock provides a starting point: 'We can talk of "male mythologies" in the sense that mythologies are the myths of ideology at work within history for the perpetuation of power by a dominant social group', but the 'usefulness of the term lies in its suggestion that such definitions are themselves "fictional" constructions with a remarkable power to shape the social imagination, but capable of deconstruction' (1984: 10–11). The myth of hegemonic masculinity is very much an ideological construct based in the historical processes alluded to earlier in this chapter, yet it is, precisely as Woodcock indicates, a fiction requiring deconstruction. This is perhaps where the

confusion lies regarding hegemonic masculinity, in that as myth it is construed and conceived as 'natural' and subsequently difficult to challenge, let alone deconstruct. This is the enduring and penetrable nature of myth that Roland Barthes warned against almost 50 years ago. In *Mythologies*, Barthes demonstrates the naturalizing effect of myth, which he locates within bourgeois social practices. He states that 'everything, in everyday life, is dependent on the representation which the bourgeoisie *has and makes us have* of the relations between man and the world' (1957: 140). Such is the case with the myth of masculinity in that it is understood as a 'normalized' form without origin; it is part of a 'natural order' that becomes more naturalized 'the further the bourgeois class propagates its representations' (ibid.). In this way, masculinity is a product of hegemonic relations but is not hegemonic (Featherstone, 1991).

The basis of masculine mythology in Canada is a bourgeois ideal that promotes qualities of physicality and ruggedness that have little bearing on bourgeois patriarchal relations. This corporal construction, however, served—and continues to serve, as will be discussed later in this chapter—deliberate ideological and class designs that typify hegemonic practices, which Raymond Williams articulates as follows: 'laws, constitutions, theories, ideologies, which are so often claimed as natural, or as having universal validity or significance, simply have to be seen as expressing and ratifying the domination of a particular class' (1989: 382). Like Barthes, Williams sees this naturalization of power as made possible through the manipulation of history, whereby selective historical details are highlighted while others are discarded to construct a 'selective tradition' passed off by dominant culture as '*the* tradition' (ibid.). *The tradition is the culture's mythology*, the way in which people perceive themselves and their current order of existence, yet may have little to do with actual experience. This is the basis of traditional masculinity, whereby selections of Canadian history have been celebrated and naturalized yet do not necessarily correspond to the actual lives of Canadian men.

The relationship between myth and hegemony is important in that mythologies are the tools of hegemony but should not be confused with one another. In Mike Donaldson's 'What Is Hegemonic Masculinity?' he correctly identifies the designs of masculine hegemony but confuses these designs with what is truly hegemonic. He argues that hegemonic masculinity is not 'what powerful men are, but is what sustains their power, and is what large numbers of men are motivated to support because it benefits them' (1993: 646). The statement reads true if Donaldson is referring to the *mythology* of masculinity, not hegemony, in that the dominant (in terms of popularity) construct of masculinity does sustain power, and is supported by most men because it is beneficial. The problem, however, lies in the fact that as most men enact this mythological construct, they subordinate themselves to the organizing 'intellectuals' who have construed this mythology (Gramsci, 1994: 67) and thus make up *hegemonic* masculinity. In true hegemonic form, most men willingly assume the hegemonic construct of masculinity, but by assuming the hegemonic construct, they are outside of the existing hegemony. In other words, the romanticized corporal construct of masculinity is endorsed and enacted upon by most men, which provides them with societal rewards. But as we see actual manifestations of the myth, we see these rewards quickly dissipate as they cater to and perpetuate the imbalance of power in male gender relations.

Mythological Men in Sport

There are many public domains in which masculinities are played out, but none probably as profound as the sporting arena. Modern sport is a ready-made construct for males to express and demonstrate qualities that intellectual organizers have construed as emblematic of manliness. The performances themselves 'create value-bearing

mythologies around particular kinds of heroic figures: large strong, often violent, record-setting champions' (Burstyn, 1999: 22). In a Canadian context, hockey players dominate this mythological landscape, assuming the heroic status once held by the coureur de bois. It is more an extension of coureur de bois mythology than a replacement, as the hockey player embodies virtually the same qualities romanticized in the physical culture of the fur trade. The hockey player is celebrated for his ability to physically dominate and endure on a frozen terrain. Occupational tasks are riddled with danger and demand incredible physical fortitude. They are men of action, not words, and their working-class backgrounds foster hope that dreams are realizable if one works hard enough to achieve them. They exist in a place where only the strong and the brave survive, and their feats make up the folklore of the nation. These are the *new bearers of tradition*, a tradition wonderfully construed by the bodiless entities that enable their mythology to unfold: National Hockey League executives and owners.

The heroic status grafted upon professional hockey players for their physical feats places them in a privileged position in Canadian society, summed up nicely by Ken Dryden in *The Game*:

> [T]his kind of special treatment we have grown accustomed to, and enjoy. We have been *special* for most of our lives. It began with hockey, with names and faces in local papers as teenagers, with hockey jackets that only the best players on the best teams wore, with parents who competed not so quietly on the side. . . . On the street, in restaurants and theatres, you are pointed out, pointed at, talked about like the weather (1983: 158).

This privileged position is slightly misleading, as it pales next to the lifestyle of those who control virtually every aspect of the players' lives. In fact when collisions between bodies (players) and minds (NHL executives/owners) occur, we see how superficial physical power actually is.

Relations of power in professional hockey were made known to me while studying professional hockey players over a three-year period, from 1995 to 1998. The research I conducted (which eventually culminated in the book *Men at Play* [2001]) afforded me the opportunity to witness the paradoxical labour relationship of pro hockey. Early into the research it was apparent that players revelled in their special status as professional hockey players in Canada, yet they simultaneously described to me their powerlessness within the professional hockey industry. Through their daily occupational tasks the players prove their worth as men, yet through these tasks the players willingly subordinate themselves to those who present these tasks to them. With alarming consistency, all players with whom I spoke regarding the job of hockey understood their situation as being almost entirely beyond them. The only recourse they had was to play their very best to help dictate their positions in the league; but even playing well could not provide career stability, as was openly acknowledged in an interview I conducted with a veteran defenceman toward the end of the season. He claimed that 'you knew which way the game was going when Wayne Gretzky got traded. I mean there's the greatest hockey player ever, and a guy can look at him and say, still with great years left in him, we're going to trade him' (Player A).[2] He continued by saying, 'if he can get traded, anybody in the league can get traded', concluding that 'they look at you as a commodity or as a piece of meat' (Player A). The Wayne Gretzky trade (or sale, to be more precise) is another example of the hegemonic construct of male power being publicly defrauded, and, while it was an important point of realization for many hockey players, the brief dismantling of male mythology has only made players more apt to cling to the somewhat desperate illusions of power the existing hegemony provides them.

To explain, in my dealings with the players, they were cognizant of their relative powerlessness within professional hockey but defended this as part of the tradeoff for being in the enviable position of being hockey players. If we consider the following passage, where a player describes his predicament of being moved around throughout his career, it becomes evident how necessary this paradoxical disposition is.

Player B: I went—well actually I went down back to junior. I played in [City 1] and then I finished the year in [City 2]. And then the next season, I played a little bit in the minors in [City 3]. And I finished the second half of the season up in [City 4]. And the following season I played about twenty or so games and then I was traded to [City 5]. I was there—I played there for two and a half years. And in fact I was traded in the summer just for the expansion draft to [City 6]. I played about a year and three-quarters there. And then I was traded just before the playoffs before the lock-out year to [City 7]. And I played last season in [same city], and a little bit in [City 8]. And I signed a deal with [City 4] this past summer.
Researcher: How do you deal with all the instability?
Player B: Well, it's part of the business of hockey . . . and uh, you know, if I was running a team, that's what I would do with the players too. Because it's the business side. You don't want your people sitting around when they can be getting better or, improving their skills by playing elsewhere. And that's pretty much how the teams deal with them nowadays. And as players it's our job to accept that.

Players such as this are forced to accept each new playing situation as an opportunity to succeed as players, not as being discarded by an organization that no longer finds their services useful. In fact, as this player later explained, his only thought was to 'get back in the line-up, hopefully this weekend . . . and contribute' (Player B). He did come back, but his contribution was minimal and he was traded the following year, never making it back to the NHL. This player was originally a first-round pick, sixth overall, in the NHL's entry draft.

With such limited control over their situations, players end up dissociating themselves from the external forces that ultimately control their fate. In fact they discuss the business of hockey as an unfortunate inevitability rather than the very source of their livelihood. One player explains to me that he has, as do most players, 'other' people to worry about the business of hockey so he can simply play the game. He explains that 'they [agents, managers] take care of all of that kind of stuff. So that's something I don't have to worry about. . . . I just like to have someone deal with that and I just deal with my hockey' (Player C). Another player sees himself and other players as 'a bunch of kids . . . playing a game' and that 'if anybody out there is not having fun at what they're doing, then they should move on, because life is too short to be worrying in misery over a job' (Player A). In withdrawing from the more 'serious' matters of hockey the players are ultimately withdrawing not only from hegemonic masculinity but also male adulthood, entering into a perpetual world of male adolescence.

> *Head Coach:* It's a man's game, but you gotta be a boy at heart. And if you get too mature, and you don't have fun with it—that's where the boy comes out.
> *Player D:* I mean, we're away from home, and we're still, a lot of us are young kids. And, uh you know, we stick together. . . . And you're always acting like kids too. So, you know, you have to be grown up and you have to be mature and, at certain levels. But other times, you know, you're mostly having fun. And you're

mostly still being a kid.
> *Player E:* You're playing a game for a living: you're never serious and you're with a bunch of guys who think exactly the same as you. So you never really have to grow up.

When players concern themselves only with *playing*, in the larger game of the business of hockey, they become emasculated by an industry that intentionally uses this artificial division between the world of work and the world of play to its advantage. Players are led to believe that their success depends on them focusing on hockey, and that to worry about anything else will only distract them from their true purpose: 'if I start worrying about that now, it's going to take away from my game and my focus. If I can work on how I can improve myself and how I can get better, and how I can just play as hard as I can, I think that later on in life, that will just take care of itself' (Player C). Thus, in being celebrated for their physicality, players inadvertently position themselves outside of male power relations.

The result is a highly paternalistic labour relationship in which players are treated as children incapable of making decisions. As one player states, 'you have no responsibilities at all when you're playing. Everything is—you're told when to get up, when to go to bed. Your travel plans are always made for you. You never have to make any decisions' (Player E). In this regard the hockey player becomes the antithesis of hegemonic masculinity, and in playing hockey he merely plays at being a man. He is an actor in a larger dramatization of masculinity of which in real life he has no part. Through playing, he symbolically demonstrates power, control, and dominance, but as former NHL player Eric Nesterenko so eloquently puts it in Studs Terkel's *Working*, he is highly conscious that as a hockey player, he is none of these things:

> You realize owners don't really care for you. You're a piece of property. They try

to get as much out of you as they can. . . . You know they're making an awful lot of money off you. You know you're just a piece of property. . . . But you just get fed up with the whole business. It becomes a job, just a shitty job (1972: 383).

Pro hockey players are celebrated bodies in a bodiless age, as Nesterenko states earlier in his interview with Terkel, and for this their relevance is symbolic and highly temporal: 'You're the boy of the moment or nothing. What we show is energy and young bodies' (Terkel, 1972: 382). When these boys become men no longer playing hockey, their symbolic worth disappears, a fact not lost on one player who explained to me that 'I think people forget about you pretty quick, you know. . . . I think people forget about you big-time' (Player F). This is the predicament of the majority of professional hockey players and thus it is misguided to connect them to hegemonic masculinity.

Conclusion

The argument that hegemonic masculinity is an ideological construct is not new. Nor is the realization that male athletes are largely disempowered by the nature of their occupations, as Donaldson points out in 'What Is Hegemonic Masculinity?': 'But how powerful is a man who mutilates his body, almost as a matter of course, merely because of a job' (1993: 647). Why then is masculine hegemony consistently discussed in terms of male physicality and dominance, most visibly demonstrated through specific male sports, when, as Donaldson states clearly, 'This is *not* power' (ibid.; emphasis added)? The answer to this is that scholars, and the public in general, too often associate hegemony with the ideological configurations of power and not power itself. It is certain that power is a construct and, as Gramsci argued, a process, yet this does not deny what is meant by hegemony and what then is constitutive of hegemonic, in this case

hegemonic masculinity. Simply put, hegemony is power, and thus hegemonic masculinity is 'a question of how particular groups of men inhabit positions of power and wealth, and how they legitimate and reproduce the social relationships that generate their dominance' (Carrigan, Connell, and Lee, 1987). Critical here is that hegemonic masculinity cannot be understood merely as dominance over women, because hegemony implies power over other men as well: 'the crucial difference between hegemonic masculinity and other masculinities is not the control of women, but the control of men and the representation of this as "universal social advancement"' (1993: 655). Moreover, falsely assigning hegemonic status to particular categories of men has real consequences because it falsely depicts them as powerful, and thus makes individuals/groups more vulnerable to male hegemonic interests.

In the case of professional hockey, the prestige and status that hockey players receive in Canada confuses the fact that professional hockey players are symbolic representations of masculine hegemony, not hegemony itself. In perceived positions of power, players strive desperately to maintain professional status and are willing to forsake much to achieve this end. In so doing they make themselves vulnerable to labour demands dictated by bodiless entities who profit from unlimited compliance. The enormous monetary rewards that are increasingly negotiated in professional hockey do little to offset the levels of exploitation that players face in terms of unbounded obligation, commitment to the game, and career brevity. Yet hockey players in Canada continue to be central figures in the mythologies of masculinity, where the physical becomes the means by which men prove their worth and enter into traditions of power. In this way physical labour is romanticized and situated as a clear demonstration of male worth, and the hockey player, who has mastered physical execution, becomes the ideal emblem of masculinity without actually receiving the advantages associated with being part of the hegemonic structure, that is, power, self-esteem, control, and even satisfaction. In other words, hockey players find themselves being responsible for displaying qualities of masculinity that are ideologically posited as hegemonic, and are critical for maintaining patriarchy in contemporary North America. Yet as players they are merely actors in the larger mythology of high capitalist patriarchy. Only as players' careers erode do they realize the disconnect between playing with power and power itself.

Discussion Questions

1. What is the author's perspective on the idea that there are multiple masculinities?
2. Why has hegemonic masculinity often been associated with physical prowess?
3. How does the author support his argument that, despite living within contemporary capitalist society, corporal power has little to do with masculine power relations?
4. Why was the Beaver Club in Montreal an important site for the expression of masculinity?
5. What were the qualities that men in the Beaver Club publicly displayed versus the actual qualities the men had to possess in order to be permitted access to the Club?
6. According to the author, what do professional hockey players in Canada have in common with the coureurs de bois?
7. Explain and respond to Robidoux's argument that playing professional hockey may undermine one's hegemonic position in contemporary Canadian society.
8. Why might playing professional hockey in Canada be associated with hegemonic masculinity?

Recommended Websites

Canadian Museum of Civilization. Virtual Museum of New France: www.civilization.ca/cmc/explore/virtual-museum-of-new-france/people/les-coureurs-des-bois/les-coureurs-des-bois-intro

North American Society for the Sociology of Sport: www.nasss.org

Society for International Hockey Research: www.sihrhockey.org/main.cfm

Notes

1. Carolyn Podruchny explains that certain bourgeois males would procure 'their own crest and motto, which were important signifiers of membership in the gentry' (2000: 61).

2. Names of the team and players are being withheld to ensure anonymity.

References

Barthes, R. *Mythologies*. 1957. Trans. Annette Lavers. New York: Hill and Wang.

Burstyn, V. 1999. *The Rites of Men: Manhood, Politics, and the Culture of Sport*. Toronto: University of Toronto Press.

Carrigan, T., B. Connell, and J. Lee. 1987. 'Toward a New Sociology of Masculinity', in Harry Brod, ed., *The Making of Masculinities*. Boston : Allen & Unwin.

Clark, S.D. 1962. *The Developing Canadian Community*, 2d ed. Toronto: University of Toronto Press.

Connell, R.W. 1983. *Which Way Is Up? Essays on Sex, Class and Culture*. London: Allen & Unwin.

———. 1993. 'The Big Picture: Masculinities in Recent World History', *Theory and Society*, 22, 5: 597–623.

——— and J.W. Messerschmidt. 2005. 'Hegemonic Masculinity: Rethinking the Concept', *Gender and Society*, 19, 6: 829–59.

Demetrakis, D.Z. 2001. 'Connell's Concept of Hegemonic Masculinity: A Critque', *Theory and Society*, 30: 337–61.

Donaldson, M. 1993. 'What Is Hegemonic Masculinity?', *Theory and Society*, 22, 5: 643–57.

Dryden, K. 1983. *The Game: A Thoughtful and Provocative Look at a Life in Hockey*. Toronto: Totem Books.

Featherstone, M. 1991. *Consumer Culture and Post-modernism*. London: Sage.

Foucault, M. 1977. *Discipline and Punish: The Birth of the Prison*. Trans. A. Sheridan. New York: Pantheon Books.

Gramsci, A. 1994. *Letters from Prison*. Ed. Frank Rosengarten. Trans. Ray Rosenthal. New York: Columbia University Press.

'Head Coach'. Interview by author. Tape Recording. 12 December 1996.

Jefferson, T. 2002. 'Subordinating Hegemonic Masculinity', *Theoretical Criminology*, 6, 1: 63–88.

le Jeune, Paul. 1959. 'Relation of What Occurred in New France in the Year 1633'. *The Jesuit Relations and Allied Documents: Travels and Explorations of the Jesuit Missionaries in New France, 1610–1791*, vol. 5. Ed. R.G. Thwaites. New York: Pageant Book Company, 71 vols.

McPherson, K., C. Morgan, and N.M. Forestell. 1999. *Gendered Pasts: Historical Essays in Femininity and Masculinity in Canada*. Don Mills, ON: Oxford University Press,

Phillips, R.S. 1995. 'Spaces of Adventure and Cultural Politics of Masculinity: R.M. Ballantyne and *The Young Fur Traders*', *Environment and Planning*, 13: 591–608.

Player A. Interview by author. Tape Recording. 21 March 1997.

Player B. Interview by author. Tape recording. 14 November 1996.

Player C. Interview by author. Tape Recording. 20 January 1997.

Player D. Interview by author. Tape Recording. 11 November 1996.

Player E. Interview by author. Tape recording. 28 April 1996.

Player F. Interview by author. Tape Recording. 5 March 1997.

Podruchny, C. 2000. 'Festivities, Fortitude, and Fraternalism: Fur Trade Masculinity and the Beaver Club, 1785–1827', in J. Noel, ed., *Race and Gender in the Northern Colonies*. Toronto: Canadian Scholars' Press.

Robidoux, M.A. 2001. *Men at Play: A Working Understanding of Professional Hockey*. Montreal and Kingston: McGill-Queen's University Press.

Schmalz, P.S. 1991. *The Ojibwa of Southern Ontario*. Toronto: University of Toronto Press.

Talbot, E.A. 1825/1963. *Five Years' Residence in the Canadas: Including a Tour through Part of the United States of America, in the Year 1823*. New York: Johnson.

Terkel, S. 1972. *Working: People Talk about What They Do All Day and How They Feel about What They Do*. New York: New Press.

Thwaites, R.G., ed. 1959. 'Bibliographical Data: Vol. LXV', *The Jesuit Relations and Allied Documents: Travels and Explorations of the Jesuit Missionaries in New France, 1610–1791*, vol. 65. New York: Pageant Book Company.

Trigger, B.G. 1985. *Natives and Newcomers: Canada's 'Heroic Age' Reconsidered*. Montreal and Kingston: McGill-Queen's University Press.

Wamsley, K.B. 1999. 'The Public Importance of Men and the Importance of Public Men: Sport and Masculinities in Nineteenth-Century Canada', in P. White and K. Young, eds., *Sport and Gender in Canada*. Don Mills, ON: Oxford University Press.

Williams, R. 1989. 'Base and Superstructure in Marxist Cultural Theory', in R.C. Davis, ed., *Contemporary Literary Criticism*. New York: Longman.

Woodcock, B. 1984. *Male Mythologies: John Fowles and Masculinity*. Brighton, UK: Harvester Press.

CHAPTER 8

O ne of the important features of studying gender and other identity dimensions is the opportunity to examine even the most common everyday experiences in order to call out the intricate strands of meaning to be found. For instance, when a baby is born, the new parents are often asked, 'What did you have?' or 'What is it?' The questioner may be expecting one of two answers: boy or girl, and the answer to this question can activate a number of assumptions and expectations to be imposed on the baby. When we put it this way, it sounds like quite an onerous set-up for the baby, and yet it continues to happen as a central organizing principle in society.

Of course, the particular ways this may happen will vary by family, community, culture, and other factors, and in some cases it may not happen this way at all. For that matter, there are many who would argue either the merits or that we are making too big a fuss over it. You may recall the first chapter of this text, in which Landsberg described simply trying to buy a hat for her grandchild, and how that became a case study in hegemonic masculine role socialization. In any case, moments like these have significance and impact and incorporate subtle and overt means of enforcing the reproduction of particular societal arrangements, the benefits and costs of which can be debated.

One of the most interesting and rich locations for coming to understand a country's collective thinking about identity is its media. In this chapter, Greenhill does two important things. First, she offers an accessible re-introduction to several key concepts important to understanding and conducting identity research, especially with regard to sex and gender. Second, she presents examples of particular popular media and some lesser-known material with a view to examining how these shape, challenge, and/or rigidify ideas about sex and gender in Canada.

Men, Masculinities, and the Male in English-Canadian Traditional and Popular Cultures

Pauline Greenhill

From the very moment of birth, people begin to experience both gender[1] and culture.[2] When friends and family hear of a child's delivery, their first question inevitably follows: 'Is it a boy or a girl?' Even the query itself has already been culturally inflected. First, it identifies only two options, though those binary oppositions do not comprise the sole possibilities.[3] That is, as this chapter shows, neither male/female (biological sex) nor masculine/feminine (cultural gender) incorporates the totality of actual practice or expression of sex/gender. In fact, even the male (sex), masculinity (cultural), and men (those who instantiate the male and/or masculinity)—too often misrecognized as entirely overlapping identifications—demonstrate an extensive range of possibilities, some of which merge with aspects of the female, femininity, and women. Second, 'Boy or girl?' has a cultured order. The male, as the primary, the standard, comes first; the female, as secondary, rarely gets priority. Thus, 'husband

and wife'—and even 'masculine and feminine' and 'male and female'—becomes the expected arrangement. The sequence's reversal usually marks a special politeness, as in 'ladies and gentlemen' (see King, 1991).

Once a child has been identified—in Euro–North American society, as either male or female—a great variety of processes deploy to enforce a differentiation of boys from girls—to make them masculine, rather than feminine. Culture and gender become inextricably linked. Traditions dictate that children dress in coded colours, and parents or caregivers who choose to avoid the expected blue for boys and pink for girls predictably encounter considerable resistance. Family, friends, and even strangers may find it difficult to interact with a child without knowing her/his gender. But though Euro–North Americans often believe the differences between women and men are innate, other sociocultural groups organize the genders in varying ways. Anthropologist Margaret Mead (1950) famously argued that some societies understand women as aggressive and men as nurturing—quite the opposite of how Euro–North Americans see the inherent qualities of females and males. Yet even outside Euro–North American cultures, value judgments invariably align the male with the positive and the female with the negative. Thus, being rational (understood by Euro–North Americans as a male trait) is better than being emotional (a female trait); the public sphere (where men are presumed to be most active) predominates over the domestic sphere (the place for women); and technology (seen as men's creation) controls nature (associated with women).

Arguably, even sex is cultured.[4] Boys are identified from the presence of penis and testicles (and presumed to have an XY chromosomal structure); girls are identified from the presence of a vulva and vagina (and presumed to have an XX chromosomal structure). But as many as 4 per cent of births are 'anomalous' (Fausto-Sterling, 1993: 21), including those

now termed 'intersex'. That is, children can be born—including some with XX or XY chromosomal structures—with what physicians call 'ambiguous' genitalia—not readily identified as either male or female. Doctors invariably react by conducting invasive genital surgeries to enforce one or the other option (Kessler, 1998). Further, XX and XY are only two among a variety of possible chromosomal structures; others include XXX, YYY, XYY, XXY, and XO (Ward and Edelstein, 2006: 171).[5]

But intersex folks are not the only people whose identities and embodiments demonstrate the culturing of sex. What may commonly be understood as biological heritage, from physical strength to breast development, can be influenced by traditions and social expectations, and by culturally inflected behaviours from sports involvement to diet choices to plastic surgery. For example, when parents encourage boys to go out and play sports and girls to stay in and play with dolls, they create conditions for their sons to develop greater physical strength than their daughters. And when transgender and transsex are included in the mix of culture and sex, Euro–North Americans need to understand that people who appear unambiguously biologically female may feel male, neither female nor male, or both.[6] The material I discuss in this chapter, then, will always pertain to men, masculinities, and males. But that does not mean it will have no implications for women, femininities, and females.

Indeed, a current theory about the formation of sex/gender posits that its construction takes place in the context of performance, not biology. Judith Butler (1990; 1993; 2004) argues that human beings become gendered not in terms of who they are but rather through what they do. Sex/gender's performative quality means that it operates primarily through its creation and recreation in a myriad of everyday acts, like clothing choice, but also in specially marked ones, like wedding ceremonies. Sex, rather than offering a pre-existing state onto which gender is mapped, also develops as an *effect* of all kinds of discourses. Thus culture, and particularly its traditional and popular forms, becomes central to understanding sex/gender, and by extension to understanding males and masculinities. Traditional and popular culture not only offer models for how to be sexed and gendered (which can be accepted, resisted, or both), but they also recreate sex and gender in every act and performance.

Unlike sex and gender, traditional and popular culture are not usually seen as binary oppositions, but instead as varying aspects of culture, broadly defined. Both traditional and popular culture are vernacular[7] forms—that is, they are associated with everyday lives and experiences. Popular and traditional culture—everyday texts[8] of all kinds encountered through various media from feature films to word of mouth—can be places where dominant culture ideas find expression, but also where resistance can form. Beliefs and values are created and recreated in various types of traditional and popular culture, but the relationship is dynamic. That is, the vernacular neither simply reflects culture nor does it always directly form it; instead, a combination of creation and re-creation of culture develops in a constant back-and-forth process. That means that someone who played with Barbies as a child, or collects them now, does not necessarily buy into Mattel's apparent vision of conical-breasted, material-goods-obsessed women who must always wear high heels. Similarly, an interest in rough contact sports will not necessarily foster (male) aggressiveness in other aspects of life.

Most popular culture comes from mass culture forms like the mainstream media of film, television, and the Internet, whereas most traditional culture (or folklore) comes from more direct interactions among people. But the relations between the two can be close and even intertwined. For example, 'You Are My Sunshine' began life as a popular American song, but when sung in Canada and/or by Canadians at a camp or by a group of friends around a bonfire, it is shared in a traditional

cultural interaction. The traditional and popular also become relevant as locations in which distinctions and commonalities between Canadian and other cultures develop and flourish—or wither and fade. Thus, just as traditional and popular cultures link, similar interactions and overlaps happen between Canadian and American vernacular cultural forms. Further, popular cultural forms disseminated across borders can morph into modes nearly unrecognizable to their originators. For example, reality television has many international precursors and interrelations (see, e.g., Murray and Ouellette, 2009). Yet a program like the 2005 Global Television production *My Fabulous Gay Wedding*, hosted by Scott Thompson, the flamboyantly out gay actor from *The Kids in the Hall*, seems directly linked to its Canadian time and place. The show, in which Thompson and a wedding planner accompany lesbian and gay couples as they prepare for their nuptials, was first aired during the year in which same-sex marriage was legalized in Canada (Pearson, 2006; see also Greenhill and Armstrong, 2006).

Some forms of popular media—particularly mainstream film, television, magazines, and advertising—have become scapegoats for explaining the persistence of sexism and misandry alike,[9] while some other forms—such as the Internet and social media—have been lauded as humanist and democratizing. Indeed, it sometimes appears that the news media, with their continual search for divergent perspectives, find feminism and gender difference easy targets for generating controversy, and thus newsworthy material (see, e.g., Leff, 1997). The range of popular media available, combined with their often skewed perspective on gender, means that sometimes men (and women) face difficulties in dealing with the vast differences between ideals and their everyday experience. Their confusion at the paradoxes they face is understandable. As men's studies theorist Michael Kaufman puts it, 'There is, in the lives of men, a strange combination of power and powerlessness, privilege and pain' (1994: 142).

All these interactions lead to the conclusion that even when people can recognize geographical or analytical contrasts between traditional and popular, male and female, Canadian and non-Canadian, in practice it can be hard to sunder them. That difficulty in turn complicates a chapter like this that links them. What, then, is Canadian masculine/male traditional and popular culture? The answer is never as easy and satisfying as anyone might like, and sometimes raises further questions instead of suggesting responses! I will posit, however, that English-Canadian masculinities are constructed—sometimes explicitly and sometimes silently—in a dialogue between presumptions of what men are or should be primarily in terms of race, ethnicity, sex, class, and sexuality, and presumptions of what Canadians are or should be primarily in terms of distinguishing them from Americans. (Though Canadians can be compared to other groups and nationalities, Canada's nearest neighbour, the United States, is its most frequent comparator for English speakers.) Traditional and popular culture offer a location in which such interactions can be expressed, performed, contextualized, and often contested.

In working through these ideas, I draw primarily on research conducted by Canadian scholars and/or about Canada and published in English that offers implications for men, males, and masculinity and its relationship to traditional and popular culture. I've chosen examples to illustrate the taken-for-grantedness of some aspects of masculinities and Canadian culture and the marking of some other aspects.[10] My examples also complicate that process (as the texts themselves sometimes do). My treatment of this material primarily involves deconstruction, a rigorous academic practice of approaching meaning by identifying and then questioning the premises underlying an idea or text. Deconstruction shows that what may be taken for granted, and/or appear very simple in everyday understanding, is invariably rather more complex, troubled, and unstable than it might initially seem. For readers who may wish to delve further, I offer more possible readings in a separate section at the end of the article.

Masculinity Presumed; Canadian Elaborated

Some cultural forms work to clarify what makes individuals Canadian but do so without making explicit underlying gendered presumptions around nationality and nationhood. For example, in 2000, during the National Hockey League playoffs, the Molson brewery company introduced a new series of advertisements, which immediately became immensely popular in Canada (Seiler, 2002: 45). Usually called 'I am Canadian', one in particular and its text, commonly referred to as 'the rant', appeared (among other locations) on websites, in informal discussions, and in parodies. The text itself seems to refer primarily to male-identified symbols and ideas without being explicit about gender. Reference to Canada's distinctiveness—ways of pronouncing the last letter of the alphabet, different forms of government, and more—make the comparator, the United States, very obvious to most Canadians who encounter it:

> Hey,
>> I am not a lumberjack, or a fur trader.
>> I don't live in an igloo,
>> or eat blubber, or own a dogsled,
>> and I don't know Jimmy, Suzy, or
> Sally from Canada,
>> although I am certain they are really, really nice.
>> I am Canadian.
>> I have a Prime Minister, not a President.
>> I speak English and French, not American.
>> I pronounce it 'about' not 'a boot'.
>> I can proudly sew my country's flag on my backpack.

I believe in peacekeeping, not policing;
diversity, not assimilation;
and that the beaver is a proud and
noble animal.
   The toque is a hat,
   A chesterfield is a couch,
   and 'Z' is pronounced 'Zed' not 'Zee',
'ZED'.
   Canada is the second largest land
mass,
   the first nation of hockey, and
   the best part of North America.
   My name is Joe, and
   I am Canadian.

(adapted from www.craigmarlatt.com/canada/
symbols_facts&lists/i_am_canadian.html)

This ad seeks to distinguish Canadians from Americans by asserting what it means to be 'Canadian'. But while the speaker does not say 'My name is Joe and I am a Canadian *man*', much less 'a Canadian, white, young, heterosexually identified, middle-class, able man', most of what he talks about concerns matters relevant to more Canadian males than females. The first identifier offers a clear example—Canadian women are rarely presumed to be lumberjacks or fur traders; the two are male-associated occupations. The allusion to Canadians as being 'really, really nice' may distance them from the stereotyped American brash forthrightness, but even that quality can distinguish men better than women—Euro–North American women are always supposed to be nice! Though Canada has had a female prime minister (Kim Campbell in 1993), she has only male American presidential and Canadian federal prime ministerial counterparts. Both the military and (professional) hockey sectors are male-dominated, and Joe is a male-identified name. The apparently white, young, able man who delivers the speech in the commercial also implicitly represents hegemonic masculinity.[11]

   Yet the text also shows some problems with offering analysis that simplistically enumerates characteristics and assigns them locations on a power hierarchy and/or uncomplicated identification with maleness and hegemony. Joe wears a T-shirt and jeans, with an open plaid shirt; his youth and casual working clothing do not suggest he is an upper-class professional in a powerful elite occupation. Allusion to historicized practices of the indigenous peoples of Canada's North could be an assertion of white ethno-racial identity (as Joe's appearance suggests). Currently, however, many Inuit do not live in igloos, eat blubber, or travel by dogsled; but those who do are as such clearly dislodged and de-legitimized as (mainstream) Canadians, and their identity is foreclosed in favour of entitling white settler subjectivity. Or these allusions could indicate that Canadians have a modernized lifestyle, less dissimilar to that of Americans than many may suspect. References to French and English obscure the fact that most Canadians do not speak both official languages.[12] Indeed, even the apparently male elements of Joe's speech are by no means inherently or invariably masculine. Women, like men, can play hockey and aspire to high political office. And as feminist theorists have argued, focus upon occupations like lumbering and fur trading as exclusively male has obscured the manifest presence of women as integral to both industries (see, e.g., Van Kirk, 1999).[13] Thus, analyzing this text underlines problems with the idea of hegemonic masculinity as an inventory of characteristics, the notion of men as profoundly different from women, and even the idea of Canadian distinctiveness.

   It's important to recognize how slippery and illusory, then, this kind of popular text can be. Though it seems to list a series of qualities that mark and distinguish Canadians, the individual items break down upon further investigation. It's not only Canadians but also those from the United Kingdom who pronounce 'zed'; folks from Japan are stereotyped as even more polite than Canadians; and so on. Even the grouping of characteristics identified refers neither to *all* Canadians nor to Canadians *only*. Further, just as not all Canadians are male or masculine (though the characteristics addressed in the rant are primarily associated with them), not all male Canadians are hockey-obsessed, wear lumberjack shirts, and so on. Though these features are primarily male-associated, they do not include all men, nor do they include men only.

Whiteness is often integral to presumptions of Canadian identity, but racial issues have gendered dimensions that are sometimes not considered as such. Overall, as Anthony Stewart argues, 'to live in Canada is to pretend that race is not a problem. . . . [W]e live in a state of dishonesty that is at times offensive when it comes up against the reality, obvious to some who live here, that Canada has not transcended questions of race. . . . [T]o say such things is to risk one's acceptance, one's membership, as a Canadian' (2004: 37). Note that Stewart himself presumes that the Canadians he justifiably criticizes are white-identified; few citizens or residents of colour would be blind to institutionalized or personalized racism in Canada! Just as using male-identified symbols and ideas to represent the entire country exposes a fundamentally sexist idea, the underlying (and patently false) assumption that Canadians are white operates as a racist construction. Analyses of racism uncover self-satisfied stereotypes that Canadians, unlike Americans, are not prejudiced, and indeed welcome peoples of all other nations. Yet racism, too, is gendered. The male rap performers that Rinaldo Walcott (2002) discusses address Black Canadian urban men's experiences, including police shootings, yet they and Walcott both generalize those to the entire Black community. Of course, neither Black women nor women of colour in general are immune to police violence in Canada or elsewhere. But avoiding that violence's gendered tendencies, as well as the gendered understandings of its consequences, does not adequately nuance the situation.

As the shameful and too often repeated case of Helen Betty Osborne shows, the simultaneous sexualization of and indifference to First Nations women leads to extensive violence against them (see www.amnesty.ca/campaigns/sisters_overview.php). But racial profiling and overpolicing affect men and women of colour differently (see Nelson and Nelson, 2004: 15–18). For example, public exposés suggest that police take Aboriginal men, not women, on 'starlight tours' to the outskirts of prairie cities and towns to dump them there without transportation, often injured and inadequately clothed, in the middle of winter. Probably the most famous such case is that of Neil Stonechild, left on the outskirts of Saskatoon to die in 1990 (see Figure 8.1). As in his case, 'Aboriginal people (especially young males) are an easily identifiable, targetable group. They are routinely harassed, detained, abused . . . and sometimes worse' (O'Neal and Larue, 2008). Starlight tours exemplify how the gendered and gendering culture of Canadians does not always simply express a positive identity, but can lead to atrocities of discrimination.

Masculinity Presumed; Canadian Presumed

At times both masculinity and Canadian identity can be taken for granted; however, deconstructing them can demonstrate some of their constituent elements and historical enactments. Reconceptualizing the generic in male and Canadian terms can be useful in deconstructing and exploring English-Canadian films such as *Goin' Down the Road* (directed by Don Shebib in 1970). Though this movie focuses on experiences that primarily applied to men, most viewers at the time saw it as simply Canadian. But Shebib's film about migrants leaving Nova Scotia for Toronto in search of work concerned an exodus that mainly involved younger men. Paying attention to this gendered, generational aspect allows for recognition that its narrated experiences, though historically specific, nevertheless resemble recurrent social phenomena in Canada. By 2010, in difficult economic times,

Figure 8.1
Starlight Tour. A representation of the police practice of removing Aboriginal men from prairie cities. David Garneau.

from Atlantic Canada particularly, but from working-class families across Canada, men move to Alberta for work in the oil industry. A document from that province's government notes that 77 per cent of those employed in its mining and oil and gas extraction industry are men (http://employment.alberta.ca/documents/LMI/LMI-IP_mining.pdf).

Several studies have focused on women's positions in such male-dominated locations, and the effects upon their culture (e.g., McLeod and Hovorka, 2008). For example, Gloria Miller discusses the Alberta oil industry in terms of

'everyday actions . . . characterized by informalism and paternalism based on shared masculine interests that exclude women from power; individualistic competition . . . combined with a dominant engineering occupational culture effectively to reinforce the division of work by gender; and gendered interactions and occupations . . . embedded

in a consciousness derived from the powerful symbols of the frontier myth and romanticized cowboy hero' (emphases in original removed, 2004: 48).

Yet her work attends primarily to women's strategies for survival in these circumstances. Taking feminist approaches to address the problems for women in these contexts is entirely appropriate. Yet few studies have taken up the opportunity to explore a literally male-dominated culture, except in negative terms that presume heterosexuality and implicitly see women as a necessary yet missing or marginalized civilizing force. Gender, as already stated, means more than just women. Research should be conducted to examine implications these contexts have for maleness and masculinities (including female masculinities) and traditional and popular cultures.[14] Further, rather than taking this practice's geographical location for granted, researchers could explore the construction of this masculine culture in the context of Canada's relation to global capitalism.

Figure 8.2 Illustration by Walter Crane from Jeanne-Marie LePrince de Beaumont's *Beauty and the Beast*. © Metropolitan Museum of Art / Art Resource, NY

Not Necessarily Canadian, But Definitely Male

Part of what comprises masculinity for Canadian men can, as already indicated, come from a culture that's neither exclusively Canadian nor exclusively male. Traditional cultural forms like fairy tales are a cross-cultural human heritage, not the property of particular individuals or groups. Traditional culture has been extensively criticized for both misogyny and misandry. For example, in *Spreading Misandry: The Teaching of Contempt for Men in Popular Culture*, Canadian researchers Paul Nathanson and Katherine K. Young discuss Disney's film *Beauty and the Beast* (directed by Gary Trousdale and Kirk Wise in 1991) as an exemplar of contemporary popular culture's vilification of men. They point out many changes from the traditionally inspired version written by Jeanne-Marie LePrince de Beaumont in 1756 (see Figure 8.2). For example, Disney absents the

two selfish and less beautiful stepsisters who conspire against Beauty, and the new character of 'Gaston, the village bully and braggart' (Nathanson and Young, 2001: 163) takes some of their functions. The main Disney male protagonist's enchantment by a good fairy, who punishes him for his metaphorically beastly behaviour by making him a literal Beast, contrasts with the Beaumont tale's good man enchanted by an evil fairy. Suggesting that the original tale 'adds up to a balanced picture of both sexes' (ibid.), these writers contend that in the Disney version, 'The major male characters, representing men in general, are evil in either the bestial or sexist sense' (2001: 164).

Analyzing Disney's fairy-tale films as exemplars of problematic gender relations owes a great deal to feminist analyses (see, e.g., Haase, 2004). Even before Canadian folklorist Kay Stone began exposing 'Things Walt Disney Never Told Us' (1975), feminists criticized Disney's narrow view of gender relations, and indeed the corporation's generally sexist, racist, imperialist cultural pedagogy (see, e.g., Bell, Haas, and Sells, 1995). The Disney view of women is no more progressive and feminist than its perspective on men that Nathanson and Young justifiably find dubious and fundamentally negative. However, their blaming of feminism not only for misrepresentation of men (as they see in Disney), but also for what they understand as a broader contempt and hatred for men in Euro–North American society, would not be shared by most who identify as feminists, nor by many who would not so term themselves.

The men's movement, to which Nathanson and Young's work contributes, has been called 'patriarchy with a New Age face' (Kimmel and Kaufman, 1994: 260). Much of Robert Bly's *Iron John: A Book about Men* (1990), a programmatic text for that movement, exemplifies both its historically founded and newer aspects. Bly draws upon traditional folk culture. The 'Iron John' of his title is 'Iron Hans', tale number 136 in the Grimm brothers' famous collection of *Kinder- und Hausmärchen (Children's and Household Tales)*.[15] Bly posits that during the Industrial Revolution, fathers going to work outside the home and farm lost the fundamental relationship with their sons that included initiating the boys into manhood. He argues that mothers cannot make their sons into (real) men, and that women must relinquish their hold upon their sons and male partners alike. He also seeks rituals to re-establish men's mythopoetic—archetypal and symbolic—connections with their fundamental masculinity. Like the young prince in the Grimm story, men must go to the woods to seek the wild man within. Focusing on the alleged feminization of men, the need for maintaining homosocial connections, blaming absent fathers and alleged feminist-inspired male bashing, Bly's work tends to foster essentialist Euro–North American notions of masculinity.[16] Theorists Michael S. Kimmel and Michael Kaufman call Bly's decontextualized references

to anthropological literature 'historical hokum' (1994: 276). While the work's dichotomous constructions of male and female do not adequately reflect experiences of masculinities and maleness, the attention to homosocial groupings is a valuable insight from that work.

Definitely Canadian; Definitely Male

Particularly in recent traditional and popular texts and analysis, both maleness and Canadianness have been elaborated. Currently, perhaps English-Canadian popular culture's most quintessential homosocial grouping is the *Trailer Park Boys*. Beginning as a short film in 1998 and then becoming a 'no-budget' feature-length film in 1999 (www.trailerpark-boys.com/site_story.php), the television series spawned two additional movies, *Trailer Park Boys: The Movie* (directed by Mike Clattenberg in 2006) and *Trailer Park Boys: Countdown to Liquor Day* (directed by Mike Clattenberg in 2009). These mockumentaries (fictitious, often humorous, works taking the structure of films documenting real life; see Hughes-Fuller, 2009) follow three primary characters, Ricky (Robb Wells), Julian (John Paul Tremblay), and Bubbles (Mike Smith), who live in a trailer park in Dartmouth, Nova Scotia.

They spend their days and nights in various nefarious, sometimes illegal activities, frequently resulting in their incarceration. Zoë Druick refers to their characters' constructions as 'hyperbolic hoser masculinity' (2010: 172; following Waugh, 2006: 203). She notes that '[t]he working class, backwoods, white masculinity both mocked and celebrated . . . harkens back to the phenomenon of Bob and Doug McKenzie, awakening the nation to its true hoser spirit' (2010: 171–2). In the films,

> [t]he shaky hand-held style becomes a low budget aesthetic to match the low rent lifestyles of the main characters . . . and the other side of the story of a reality show like *COPS* that follows the police

into trailer park settings. However . . . [*Trailer Park Boys*] emphasizes the humour of white trash, where poverty and slum living are the source of laughs precisely because the characters are white but not upwardly mobile. . . . [T]he hoser masculinity of the main characters is the butt of the jokes, but simultaneously, it is precisely what enables them to assert their subjectivities and their bond at the expense of the meddling filmmakers (2010: 175).

Druick also links these masculinities to '*Wayne's World*, *The Red Green Show*, and some of the CODCO and *Royal Canadian Air Farce* sketches' (2010: 172). She argues that they serve 'as a site of the formation of Canadian publics', that 'the formation of national identity occurs in part through the public sphere', and that 'important aspects of citizenship occur in and through such textual interactions' (2010: 162; see also McCullough, 2009). The texts Druick identifies are primarily white-identified, thus their construction's terms remain hegemonic with respect to race.

A more nuanced view of racialization can be found in Clément Virgo's film *Poor Boy's Game* (2007), about racism, its consequences, and its transcendence in a working-class Halifax, Nova Scotia, community. The film is Virgo's sixth and 'the first dramatic feature film in Canadian history to take the Black community of Halifax as its focus' (Medovarski, 2009: 119). Unlike the *Trailer Park Boys'* carnivalesque and humorous but ultimately dismissive celebration of obscenity, the abject, the degraded, and the disorderly, *Poor Boy's Game* takes the same qualities seriously. It uses the sport of boxing that '[f]or the last two centuries . . . has been an athletic forum in which North American racial and political tensions have been manifest' (ibid.: 122). The *Trailer Park Boys* 'trash aesthetic' with its 'grotesquely hilarious, upside-down world' (Hughes-Fuller, 2009: 106) is replaced with a story of the

consequences of the brutal beating of a Black youth by a White youth and his older brother. Released from prison, the younger perpetrator, Donnie Rose (Rossif Sutherland) wants to make amends. Alluding to recent historical incidents, including a riot protesting a Halifax bar's exclusion of Black patrons and the arson and bombing of Nova Scotian Black cultural centres, the film seeks a complex resolution to too-often submerged Canadian racism and racist discourses. It focuses on Donnie's search for forgiveness from George Carvery (Danny Glover), whose son was the beating victim. George represents mercy when he trains Donnie for a boxing match against Ossie Paris (Flex Alexander), who intends to exact family and community revenge by killing or maiming him in the ring. Andrea Medovarski argues that '[t]he final boxing match between Donnie and Ossie represents the culmination of the film's desire to think beyond racial boundaries and ethnic absolutism' by writing 'a counter-narrative of athleticism which . . . envisions a . . . political paradigm that might enable alternate forms of reconciliation and justice' (2009: 127). Substantially enabled by George and his son Charlie (K.C. Collins)—Donnie's and his brother's brain-damaged victim—Donnie and Ossie forge a temporary alliance that acknowledges harm on each side but moves 'away from the punitive and the carceral and towards the ethical' (2009: 129). This guarded, realistic intervention offers a possible model for reconciliation in other contexts.

Notably, as Medovarski underlines, 'this discursive shift is enacted by two characters who are . . . marginal figures within the Canadian nation, only ever provisionally admitted as social citizens, when at all' (2009: 130)—Donnie because he is bisexual, Ossie because he is Black, and both because of their poor, working-class origins. Both homosocial cultures—in *Trailer Park Boys* and *Poor Boy's Game*—arguably 'affirm the validity of life on the margins, and assert the spirit of community embodied in those who, while ill-equipped to handle the legal niceties and social proprieties of the cultural mainstream, still manage to survive, together' (Hughes-Fuller, 2009: 107). Such works go well beyond a simple identification of ideology in the representation of men toward indicating the subtle intersectional implications of masculinity and nation.

Nuancing Canadian Masculinities

Vernacular culture can trace the difficult path of being, becoming, and remaining a man. But it also—perhaps inherently—problematizes its own texts, as do the examples I discuss in this section. Even works that ostensibly establish the hegemonic man in firm control contain the seeds of ideas that offer possibilities for understanding maleness and masculinity in divergent and sometimes revolutionary terms. The most self-consciously realist genres—formal types—of popular culture, film documentaries, for example, work and play with choice, selection, and intervention. Thus it becomes impossible to avoid invention and creativity, opening toward alternative inventions and other creative elements. The almost immediate popular, vernacular, traditional reactions and responses to some texts offer excellent examples of the fundamental interpretability of texts of all kinds. Take, for example, the 'I am Canadian' advertisement discussed earlier. A plethora of parodies and celebrations followed, representing Torontonians, Newfoundlanders, Muslims, and more. Molson riffed further on the theme, this time depicting well-dressed men in an office. One Internet site posted a more critical view of the same text, including:

> I do not like Céline Dion or Shania Twain but I am glad they are getting rich.
>
> I do know Richy and Sally from Canada, but they aren't as nice as you think.
>
> I am ruled by a rich white Prime Minister not a rich white President.

> I don't know French but I can converse fluently in American . . .
>
> When I am at home I realize I had better not protest deforestation or sexist dictators
>
> Without risking a face full of pepper spray and a criminal record . . .
>
> I believe in turning back boatloads of Chinese immigrants, a failing health care system, and late night cable porn disguised as art . . .
>
> My name is Joe,
> And until we are added by the States,
> I am Canadian

(adapted from www.indefual.net/canada/jokes/rant-cnd.html)

The simultaneous irony and critique in this text is less gender-exclusive than the original, noting successful female performers and sardonically denouncing racism along with the fiction of Canadian openness to political protest. It deconstructs both the original text and orthodoxies of Canadian nationalism.

In the spirit of deconstructing ideas of Canadian masculinities is Helen Holmes and Helen Allison's discussion of the male leads in the Canadian 1980s–90s television series *Street Legal* as 'new Canadian heroes'. They begin with the first season, in which primary character Leon is 'neither handsome nor tall, but . . . not overweight, bald, or a klutz. And he is endowed with traditionally heroic qualities of a thirst for knowledge and the courage to stand up for his principles. He has a Canadian respect for the law and, as a lawyer, he uses legitimate avenues in his quest for social justice' (1992: 312). Though he epitomizes what Holmes and Allison see as a distinctively Canadian character type, they note that Leon was 'too eccentric' to be the most popular character in the series. That the 'relatively tall and handsome' Chuck was 'initially more popular than Leon was, likely the result of his appearance' (1992: 313). However, in the second season, 'Leon's appearance was more conventional' and he arguably became the pivotal character. Indeed, '[d]espite a sexual peccadillo in the 1991 season, Leon has remained a boon bringer, a strong, effective, idealistic hero who embodies and upholds and brings about those values of social justice that Canadians hold dear, such as adequate housing, human rights, and environmental concerns' (1992: 314). In contrast, Chuck 'developed as all too humanly frail to fit the heroic mould'; while police officer Nick emerged as 'CBC's first "heroic hunk of manhood"'. Holmes and Allison see Leon and Nick as 'a recognizably Canadian heroic team' (1992: 319). The two men's romances with pivotal female leads on the show mean that their homosocial linkages never raise suspicions of homosexuality.

Similarly, Julie Rak's look at CBC's *The Greatest Canadian* (see www.cbc.ca/greatest/top_ten/) alludes to qualities of the hegemonic Canadian man. The top 10 nominees were Frederick Banting (discoverer of insulin);

Alexander Graham Bell (inventor of the telephone); Don Cherry (sports broadcaster); Tommy Douglas (the eventual winner; head of the first socialist government in North America in the province of Saskatchewan, and social policy innovator) (see Figure 8.3); Terry Fox (cancer victim and fundraiser; see Greenhill, 1989: 159–210); Wayne Gretzky (hockey player); John A. Macdonald (first Canadian prime minister); Lester B. Pearson (Liberal politician, Nobel Peace Prize winner, and prime minister); David Suzuki (environmental activist); and Pierre Elliott Trudeau (Liberal politician and prime minister). Rak summarizes: 'There were no women included in the top 10 and . . . the highest-ranked woman was . . . Shania Twain. . . . [There were] only nineteen francophones in the top fifty. . . . Only one, Pierre Trudeau, made the top ten. The only person of colour in the top ten was David Suzuki, and no Aboriginal people were represented at

Figure 8.3 Tommy Douglas, CBC's Greatest Canadian. © Frank Lennon/GetStock.com

all' (2008: 54). No out gay or lesbian person made the top 100, though the top 10 had one disabled person (Fox). Of course, the selection process was by no means scientific, and indeed complaints surfaced in the popular media about the nomination of Don Cherry and about 'a radio host from Winnipeg who had sponsored a mass voting campaign to get himself included' (2008: 55).

However, as an inventory of Canadian hegemonic masculinity, the top 10 offer a compelling group. Three (Banting, Fox, Gretzky) became famous for their activities when young; two are inventors (Banting, Bell); three are associated with sports (Cherry, Fox, Gretzky); four, including the winner, are politicians (Douglas, Macdonald, Pearson, Trudeau); two are activists (Fox, Suzuki). Only three were alive during the contest in 2004. All are associated with communitarian activities, teamwork, and labouring for the benefit of many, with the distinct exception of Don Cherry—known mainly for repulsively ugly suits, arguing with his co-host, championing difficult-to-defend issues such as violence and not using visors in hockey, and disparaging players from Quebec and Europe. Rak argues that the case for Cherry, offered by 'advocate' wrestler Bret 'Hit Man' Hart, 'comes closest to disregarding the merit discourse in celebrity history and to making an appeal for Don Cherry as a populist ideologue who embodies the contradictions of celebrity without resolving them' (2008: 64; see www.cbc.ca/greatest/advocates/bret-hart.html). In eleventh place, and the top-ranking Aboriginal (Métis) person, is Louis Riel. Canadian history has alternated between seeing him as a rebellious, possibly insane, religious prophet and as a statesperson (see Figure 8.4). Artist David Garneau alludes to all these qualities, depicting a heroic figure and modelling his work on Jacques Louis David's 1801 painting *Napoleon Crossing the Alps*. Simultaneously ironic and glorifying, Garneau paints Riel in Métis garb and in a stereotypically Canadian context— is that Niagara Falls in the background?—but develops a potentially contrasting comparison to Napoleon as triumphant military leader and French imperialist figure. Using Riel's chosen name, 'David', invokes his role as religious visionary prophet, sometimes termed insanity (see Reid, 2008: 12–13). Indeed, the visual representation of Riel has been intensely controversial, primarily because of the fundamental lack of congruence in the views of Riel that Garneau merges.

The historic Riel was born in 1844 in St. Boniface, Red River Settlement (now Manitoba), and was executed by the Canadian government in 1885 for treason because of his pivotal role in the North-West Rebellion (see ibid.). Arguably the founder of Manitoba, he was initially recognized at the province's legislature with a statue created by Marcien Lemay and Étienne Gaboury (unveiled in 1971). The naked representation of Riel as a tortured figure, 'between two towering pillars of concrete, drew immediate censure from politicians as well as the Manitoba Métis Federation', who deemed it '"undignified"' and '"an incongruous monstrosity"' (2008: 4). It was frequently subjected to vandalism (see Figure 8.5). In 1994, the statue was taken to the Collège universitaire de Saint-Boniface and replaced with another sculpture, by Miguel Joyal, unveiled in 1996, depicting Riel as a gentleman, incongruously wearing a bowtie and formal coat with a *ceinture fléchée*/Assomption sash (see Barbeau, 1937) and moccasins (see Figure 8.6). Winnipeg artist Michael Olito noted that 'depicting [Riel] as a staid bureaucrat rather than a tortured rebel is an insult not only to the Métis of Canada but to all rebels. . . . History cannot be made right simply by making Riel larger than Queen Victoria' (quoted in Greenhill, 2001a: 115). Notably, the statue of Victoria is located at the front of the Legislature; Riel's is at the back. Olito's group, the Zapatistas del Norte, expressed their disdain for the new statue shortly after its erection by placing a willow-stick sombrero on its head and serenading it with mariachi music. These divergent representations and the reactions to them demonstrate how vernacular and popular

Figure 8.4 David Garneau's *Louis 'David' Riel (after Jacques Louis David),* 2009. David Garneau.

culture can alternatively interpret the identical figure as avatar of hegemonic masculinity (Riel as statesperson and politician) and of non-hegemonic masculinity (Riel as tortured, possibly insane, Métis rebel).

In another traditional genre, the 'English male dance tradition' of Morris as practised in Ontario further complicates Canadian masculinity. Originally collected by folklorist Cecil Sharp in the English Midlands at the turn of the twentieth century, Morris has had its Englishness fostered in performance by almost all white-identified participants, who wear white clothes and gesture with white hankies. Though England is not now and never has been exclusively white, various hegemonic discourses encourage the viewpoint that non-white Britons are immigrants, incomers without historical connections to the nation. Similarly, viewing Morris as dance selects but one aspect from a ritual complex including socializing and multiple levels of performance. Morris's construction as tradition focuses on its allegedly stable practice over time, obscuring the many

Figure 8.5 Vandalized Louis Riel statue by architect Étienne Gaboury and sculptor Marcien Lemay. © University of Manitoba/ Archives and Special Collections

Figure 8.6 Bronze statue of Louis Riel outside Manitoba Legislative Building by sculptor Miguel Joyal. © Government of Manitoba

changes that Euro–North Americans have fostered. Finally, throughout history women participated in Morris, including the actual dance. An essential part of Morris's construction as male has been its circular definition as a male practice. That is, when women enacted the same movements in similar contexts, it was excluded from Morris, because Morris was defined as a *male* tradition (see Greenhill, 2001b). Morris as Canadian, gender-free or female, ritual event, and newfangled raises questions about the taken-for-granted in obscure minority practice as well as better-known ones—and, by extension, of Canadian masculinity.

To take an equally fraught but better-known topic, Michele Byers and Rebecca J. Haines discuss interracial heterosexual dating and marriage as represented in the *Degrassi* franchise, a series of television shows. They detail one plot line which centres on the reaction of a white girl's parents to her romance with a boy of colour. In quintessentially liberal discourse, they explain to their daughter that their concern is for the problems she will encounter, rather than coming from fundamental racism or prejudice against people of colour. The show's narrative exposes the often obscured modes in which Canadian racism operates, and presents a positive relationship, but problematically excludes the views of the Black boy's parents. Haines, who acted in the series, recalls reaction from Black viewers that reinforced stereotypes about Black males preferring White females. *Degrassi* also addressed 'issues of race and ethnicity outside the romantic-sexual relationship or the Black-white [sic] dyad' (Byers and Haines, 2005: 176), in exploring the friendship between two boys, 'Yick, an Asian-Canadian refugee and Arthur, a middle class Jewish kid' (2005: 175). The authors point out that *Degrassi* highlighted class issues between them, rather than race (or, I might add, gender), yet it 'continually challenged the notions about what were the "appropriate" topics to address on a program aimed at youth (i.e., AIDS, abortion, dating violence)' and did so 'through

presenting these issues exclusively from an adolescent's point of view' (2005: 178).

Degrassi eventually began to present beautiful people, including conventionally attractive kids, from adult points of view. Similarly, it began to shy away from the difficult issues that initially had made the show famous. Indeed, both the British Broadcasting Corporation and the American Public Broadcasting Service airings censored some of the show's material, and the American cable channel The N never aired a 2003 abortion-focused episode of *Degrassi: The Next Generation* (Byers, 2008: 196).[17]

Work on minority men's cultures and intersectionality has been relatively rare in Canadian cultural studies.[18] Wesley Crichlow's study of 'buller men and batty bwoys'—sometimes derogatory terms describing Caribbean men in same-sex relationships—in Toronto and Halifax offers an exception. Gathering life stories from these men, Crichlow discusses them as 'invisible' but also as 'unspeakable', noting the inapplicability of 'North American, Western, or European homosexual concepts' (2001: 75) to this group. He notes the homophobia in Black communities that identify 'same-sex practices . . . as part of the external, a white man's disease' (2001: 80). Nevertheless, Crichlow and the men he talked with hold out hope for 'dissenting same sex and anti-heterosexist' work. Crichlow speaks from his own position as 'a buller man who affirms a Black, same-sex, nationalistic politic attempting to make sense of how Black men experience domination through Black nationalistic discourse' (2001: 81). Thus, his work offers a place to begin to understand how traditional and popular culture are (re)created in Canadian selves.

Michael Robidoux (2002) offers gender-sensitive, male-focused work on various aspects of Canadian identity and male sport (see Chapter 7 in this text). As Robidoux's work shows, Canadian men's traditional culture sometimes resists mainstream ideas through expressions that might cause bourgeois discomfort. For example, a Manitoba Mennonite

New Year's ritual involves young men who go from house to house playing a traditional noisemaker called a *brommtopp*, constructed like a drum. Men pull on a horsehair rope attached to the drum skin to produce a throbbing noise in time with their song, offering wishes for luck and prosperity. Their behaviour can range from the subdued to the rowdy, and their costumes also vary from community to community. However, most involve some kind of disguise, incorporating cross-dressing, white-face, blackface, and ethnic drag[19] (see Figure 8.7). Similar practices by homosocial or mixed groups continue in various parts of the Atlantic Provinces (see Bauman, 1972; Best, 2008; Halpert and Story, 1969).

Canadian Perhaps; Male Perhaps

As should be clear by now, masculinity is not 'a synonym for men and maleness' (Halberstam, 1998: 234); historically, female masculinity has been obscured because of its fundamental challenge to the fiction that male masculinity as normative is non-performative. However, traditional culture has been a rich source for representations of female masculinity. Even before drag king performances became (relatively!) popular (see Troka, Lebesco, and Noble, 2002) (see Figure 8.8), women dressed as men to seek a wider variety of social, occupational, and sexual opportunities. These women became the subjects of traditional broadside ballads that narrated their lives and adventures. These songs, which have been recorded from oral tradition in Atlantic Canada, include 'The Soldier Maid', about a woman who runs away, joins the army, and becomes a drummer who is so valuable that s/he is guarded by her general. In 'The Handsome Cabin Boy', the title character's female sex is discovered when she gives birth to the ship captain's child—but the song suggests that s/he has also been sexually active with the captain's wife (see Greenhill, 1995).

This chapter has been able to offer only a small sampling of the vast range of Canadian traditional and popular culture pertaining to men, masculinities, and the male. As suggested

Figure 8.7 Brommtopp Group, 31 December 1930, Plum Coulee, Manitoba. Courtesy Tammy Sutherland and Dave Dyck, Winnipeg, Manitoba

Figure 8.8 Image from the documentary *Drag Kings on Tour*. © Aubin Pictures

at the outset, more questions than answers remain. However, whether exploring the *brommtopp* tradition or Morris, considering a historical figure like Louis Riel or a fictitious character like Donnie Rose, the emergence of men, masculinity, and males in Canadian traditional and popular culture reveals the multiplicity of ideologies constructed, rather than a series of invariant characteristics. The intersectional need to consider race, ethnicity, ability, and language (among many other social groupings), and the difficulty of pinning down sex/gender as much as nationality, makes representations of Canadian masculinities in traditional and popular culture particularly compelling—if not always entirely satisfying. That these kinds of texts become part of the cultural raw materials from which individuals construct masculinity renders Canadian men and their masculinities a truly fascinating, if ever-changing, conundrum.[20]

A Few Suggestions for Further Reading

A special issue of the journal *Canadian Folklore canadien* addresses masculinities—mostly Cana-dian, and mostly traditionally based (Tye and Taft, 1997; see also Bronner, 2005 on American male folklore).

The Beaver Bites Back? American Popular Culture in Canada (Flaherty and Manning, 1993) examines intersections between Canadian and American football, baseball, and other popular cultural forms. Though it addresses such male-identified figures as Mounties, televangelists, and priests, like much other work of its time, it generally does not make explicit their gendered aspects (with the exception of Poirier, 1993).

Essays in *Slippery Pastimes: Reading the Popular in Canadian Culture* (Nicks and Sloniowski, 2002) consider performers such as Stompin' Tom Connors (Echard, 2002) and Ian Tyson (Cox, 2002). Andrew Wernick (2002) riffs on the choice of a muscle-bound white man to represent the Canadian Olympics and Ray-Ban sunglasses. Neil Earle (2002) examines the 1972 Canada-Soviet hockey series.

Most of the studies in *Programming Reality: Perspectives on English-Canadian Television* (Druick and Kotsopoulos, 2008) have implications for masculinity. An explicit link to hockey's masculinity in Canadian culture is Derek Foster's forthright discussion of the sport's 'gender exclusion' (2008: 94). He also considers the classic exception, that of female Olympic goalie Manon Rhéaume, the only woman ever to play in a National Hockey League (exhibition) game. Foster also explores intersectionality, in the greater ethnic diversity of hockey recently than would have been expected a decade or more ago. Lyle Dick shows how TV history focuses on the nation-state but ignores 'other struggles . . . such as the status and right of First Peoples, racial minorities, women, people with disabilities, lesbian, gay, transgendered, and bisexual people, the homeless, the unemployed, and others' (2008: 40). Glen Lowry's work on *Da Vinci's Inquest* and *Da Vinci's City Hall* notes that: 'in the later seasons . . . Da Vinci's personal weaknesses, which initially place him among those he seeks to help, have more or less disappeared. His drinking and his sexual proclivities are firmly under control, and . . . he has learned to use sex to further his career' (2008: 265). Lowry links the changes in Da Vinci's character to the show's demise in Canada: 'Contrary to his earlier edgy defiance, Da Vinci has become a shinier, safer commodity for export' (ibid.). *How Canadians Communicate: Contexts of Canadian Popular Culture* (Beaty, Briton, Filax, and Sullivan, 2010) also offers an extensive range of generally gender-sensitive work.

Terry Goldie's *In a Queer Country* (2001) includes Elaine Pigeon's consideration of Michel Tremblay's play *Hosanna!* Though it 'deals with the anguish of two aging homosexuals caught in the trap of identifying with heterosexually defined gender roles as a means of sustaining their relationship' (2001: 31), Pigeon outlines its complex relation to Quebec language, culture, and nationalism. Gordon Brent Ingram's discussion of male homoerotic culture on Wreck Beach in British Columbia explores the problems and possibilities of queer spaces as contested sites. He notes that 'such "spontaneous" landscapes . . . challenge compartmentalized notions of culture, architecture, nature, sexuality, body, and landscape' (2001: 202). Gary Kinsman's exploration of Canadian and queer nationalisms exposes the idea, extensively developed in the 1960s, that gay men and lesbians were natural security risks. He also traces queer national histories into the twenty-first century of queer resistance, and argues that continued struggle is necessary against oppression 'directed against our communities, our bodies, our genders, and our sexualities' (2001: 226; see also Kinsman, 2010).

Work on queer Canadian cinema includes James Allen's article on the 'bewildering array of Canadian filmmakers', straight as well as gay, male and not, who are 'famously intrigued by unusual, atypical sexual practices and identities' (2001: 138), as well as studies by Thomas Waugh (2006). Lee Parpart (2001) looks at representations of the nude male body in Canadian cinema as a manifestation of colonial experience.

Discussion Questions

1. Contrast, compare, and/or relate the author's explanation of sex and gender to your own ideas of sex and gender.
2. What is hegemonic masculinity, and what does it mean for Canadian traditional and popular culture?
3. What alternative models of masculinity have you encountered in Canadian traditional and popular culture?

4. What does intersectionality mean for gender, and specifically, masculinity? How is intersectionality expressed in Canadian traditional and popular culture?
5. Explain the challenges for feminist research methodologies in researching masculinity and Canadian traditional and popular culture.
6. Describe the differences between homosociality and homosexuality. Explain what each term means in the context of Canadian hegemonic masculinity. Use examples from traditional and popular culture.
7. Describe the relationship between popular culture and traditional culture, and how the two forms relate to the construction of sex and gender in Canada.
8. Think of some texts from Canadian traditional/popular culture that highlight how some aspects of masculinity are taken for granted while others are marked. Explain how they deconstruct and complicate the process of making masculinity seem natural rather than cultural.
9. How would you evaluate the following website's representation of traditional and popular culture as explained in this chapter: www.savethemales.ca?
10. Relate the idea of female masculinity to the idea of binary oppositions and give some examples from traditional and popular culture.

Recommended Websites

Canadian traditional and popular culture:

Folklore Studies Association of Canada: www.acef.ulaval.ca

Places to study traditional and popular culture, from east to west:

Department of Folklore, Memorial University of Newfoundland: www.mun.ca/folklore

Department of Folklore and Ethnomusicology, Cape Breton University: http://culture.capebretonu.ca

CÉLAT, Université Laval: www.celat.ulaval.ca

Département de folklore et ethnologie, Université de Sudbury: www.usudbury.ca/content/folklore-et-ethnologie-fr

Peter and Doris Kule Centre for Ukrainian and Canadian Folklore, University of Alberta: www.arts.ualberta.ca/~ukrfolk

Notes

1. Most social scientists understand *gender* as the cultural elaboration of a male/female duality. That is, Euro–North Americans generally presume that despite the myriad similarities between all humans, male people have profoundly different qualities and characteristics than female people. Those presumptions too often become prescriptions: statements that describe not only how men and women often *are* but also how they *should be*. Further, ideas about gender and the cultural mix uncomfortably with understandings of what might be biological and inherent (see *sex*, note 4, later in this chapter). For example, most Canadians understand men as naturally aggressive and violent but women as fundamentally warm and nurturing. Thus, though killing people rarely serves as a marker of biological masculinity, a male murderer acts within his sex/gender expectations but a female murderer becomes anomalous. Similarly, the biological ability of most women to

become pregnant and give birth links to the idea that a woman serving as primary caregiver to her children fulfills sexed/gendered expectations. But a male in the same role can become either a hero for going beyond the norm or subject to suspicion as deficient in masculinity, or even as having ulterior, usually sexual, pedophilic motives.

2. I use *culture* in its anthropological and sociological senses. Culture here connotes not the elite tastes and manners of the wealthy and educated, but instead the full range of knowledge, values, attitudes, images, perspectives, and behaviours within a particular group, such as those who share a language or ethnicity.

3. *Binary oppositions* offer theoretically contrasted elements which people usually understand as mutually exclusive. Thus, within a binary sex/gender system, a person cannot be both male and female, or neither male nor female, but must be one or the other only. However, as I discuss here, such oppositions reflect neither the actual manifestations of biology (sex) nor those of culture (gender).

4. '"*Sex*" can mean sex-as-biology (the physiology of male or female), it can mean sex-as-gender (the learned processes through which females enact femininity and males enact masculinity), and it can mean sex-as-sexuality (the complex terrain of the erotic)' (Prentice, 1994: 9). In this chapter, I will use *sex* to refer to primarily biological distinctions, *gender* to primarily cultural ones, and *sexuality* to the erotic.

5. In a now classic article, biologist Anne Fausto-Sterling argued for no fewer than five sexes (1993; see also Preves, 2001).

6. *Transgender* is an umbrella term to cover all those whose sex and gender do not align simply as uncomplicatedly male or female. *Transsex* usually refers to those who see their gender as contradicting what appears to be their biological sex. These folks may opt to use hormones and/or surgery to alter their bodies to better fit what they understand to be their fundamental sex/gender identity. However, medical intervention can never be definitional for transsexuals, since many cannot fit the strictures used by medical gatekeepers to allow or disallow medical intervention; many cannot afford the treatments even if they could pass institutional medical scrutiny (most provinces do not include all aspects of sex reassignment under their funded medical services); and many simply opt to live the contradictions of their bodies. For further reading on transgender and transsex, see Stryker and Whittle (2006).

7. *Vernacular* cultural forms are organized, constructed, and/or reconstructed by people for themselves, their families, and their communities. Participation in vernacular culture can be voluntary or involuntary, but it is rarely paid. Despite these informal elements, though, it may involve mass-produced items, texts, and ideas.

8. Just about any cultural form can be understood as a *text*, when it is analyzed in terms of its constituent parts and their relations. Thus, text means not only oral and/or written verbal forms but also material, visual, musical, sensory, and even ideological ones.

9. *Sexist* attitudes and practices relegate one sex/gender, usually women, to an inferior status. Many gender scholars dispute the value of calling 'sexist' beliefs and actions that render men inferior, such as the idea that they do not make good primary caregivers for children. Just as *racism* refers to a dominant group's dealings with a subordinate group (subordinate groups can discriminate but cannot be racist), *sexism* applies to the generally dominant group, men, dealing with the generally subordinate group, women. For this reason, the more specific terms *misogyny*, or hatred of women, and *misandry*, hatred of men, have replaced the apparent generic of *sexism*.

10. *Markedness*, an idea from linguistics, offers a useful distinction for sorting out particular kinds of relations between concepts. The unmarked element is that which is generally taken for granted as the norm, and the marked element is usually seen as a development or change from unmarked norm. For example, 'man' can often be used as a generic to talk about people or humans in general; whereas 'woman'—a specific kind of man—rarely is so used. 'Man' is unmarked, and 'woman' is marked.

11. *Hegemonic masculinity* is normative, in that few individuals clearly manifest all its aspects, while it nevertheless conceptualizes what most people think men *should* be. It is constructed in relation to subaltern or non-hegemonic masculinities, which are suspect in some way as to their relationship to instantiating real manhood. The concept has been contested, with most recent formulations understanding masculinities, including hegemonic forms, as multiple and intersectional (see *intersectionality*, note 18, later in this chapter) rather than offering a simple hierarchy; contextually nuanced; sometimes internally contradictory; and despite their relation to privilege and power, changeable and open toward more equitable social relations (see, e.g., Connell and Messerschmidt, 2005).

12. Dated September 2005 and based on the 2001 Census, Canada's Office of the Commissioner of Official Languages states that only 17.7 per cent of the Canadian population reported that they knew both official languages—43.4 per cent whose first language was French and only 9 per cent whose first language was English (see www.ocol-clo.gc.ca/html/biling_e.php).

13. *Feminism* and feminists hold multiple ideological and theoretical positions. An excellent intro-

duction to and summary of recent forms and positions in feminism is bell hooks's aptly titled *Feminism Is for Everybody* (2000). Second-wave feminism is usually dated from the early 1960s to the early 1990s. It involved consciousness-raising, recognition of women's legal rights, and analysis of men's violence against women as a mode of patriarchal control. See Natasha Pinterics (2001) for an elaboration and critique of the 'waves' distinction.

14. *Female masculinity*, as conceptualized by Judith Halberstam (1998), is the performance/expression of male-identified traits and qualities by individuals not considered biologically male. Halberstam understands female masculinity as one constituent element in defining hegemonic masculinity in the negative; its use of the qualifier 'female' expresses that women-identified persons are not and cannot be uncomplicated male or masculine.

15. The Grimm brothers published three editions of the fairy tales they collected, mainly from family, friends, and servants, in 1812–15, 1819, and 1856 (see Zipes, 2003: xix; for 'Iron Hans', see 443–9).

16. The term 'homosocial' came into common use in gender studies beginning with Eve Kosofsky Sedgwick's *Between Men: English Literature and Male Homosocial Desire*, examining 'social bonds between persons of the same sex' expressed in fiction (1985: 1). Sedgwick notes that the idea is formed in relation to but also distinct from that of homosexuality. In fact, it applies to 'such activities as "male bonding," which may . . . in our society, be characterised by extreme homophobia, fear and hatred of homosexuality' (ibid.).

17. Jennifer MacLennan offers more information on English Canadian identity and the show's discussion of issues not found on American TV shows allegedly portraying the same age group and aiming at an adolescent audience—'teen pregnancy, abortion, AIDS, homosexuality, drug use, family violence, cancer and the death of a parent' (2005: 151), to which I would add pedophilia and rape.

18. *Intersectionality* is a term originally coined by Kimberlé Crenshaw to work with the idea that forms of discrimination and oppression do not take simplistically additive forms. For example, the idea that a Black woman would be doubly oppressed because she was female and Black incorporates a variety of dubious presuppositions, such as that the modal woman is White, able, upper-middle-class, and heterosexual, lives in the United States, and so on, and that the modal Black person is male. In contrast, the idea of intersectionality explores 'interrelationships of gender, class, race and ethnicity and other social divisions' (Yuval-Davis, 2006: 194). Nira Yuval-Davis points out that 'each social division has a different ontological basis, which is irreducible to other social divisions' (ibid.: 195), discusses how human rights discourses have problematically applied the concept of intersectionality, and offers methodological alternatives (ibid.).

19. *Ethnic drag*, the physical and often stereotypical representation and self-manifestation as a member of an ethnoracial group with which a person is not identified, includes both whiteface and blackface, but also dressing up and cosmetic representation as a member of another ethnic group (e.g., an English Canadian dressing as a *Rom*, or gypsy, or a White French Canadian as a First Nations person) (see Sieg, 2005).

20. Thanks to Marcie Fehr and Kendra Magnusson for their assistance in preparing questions and searching for websites.

References

Allen, J. 2001. 'Imagining an Intercultural Nation: A Moment in Canadian Queer Cinema', in T. Goldie, ed., *In a Queer Country: Gay and Lesbian Studies in the Canadian Context*. Vancouver: Arsenal Pulp Press.

Barbeau, C.M. 1937. *Assomption Sash*. Ottawa: Department of Mines and Resources.

Bauman, R. 1972. 'Belsnickling in a Nova Scotia Island Community', *Western Folklore*, 3, 4: 229–43.

Beaty, B., D. Briton, G. Filax, and R. Sullivan, eds. 2010. *How Canadians Communicate: Contexts of Canadian Popular Culture*. Edmonton: Athabasca University Press.

Bell, E., L. Haas, and L. Sells, eds. 1995. *From Mouse to Mermaid: The Politics of Film, Gender and Culture*. Bloomington: Indiana University Press.

Best, K. 2008. '"Making Cool Things Hot Again":

Blackface and Newfoundland Mummering', *Ethnologies*, 30, 2: 215–48.

Bly, R. 1990. *Iron John: A Book about Men*. Reading, MA: Addison-Wesley.

Butler, J. 1990. *Gender Trouble: Feminism and the Subversion of Identity*. New York: Routledge.

———. 1993. *Bodies That Matter: On the Discursive Limits of 'Sex'*. New York: Routledge.

———. 2004. *Undoing Gender*. New York: Routledge.

Bronner, S.J., ed. 2005. *Manly Traditions: The Folk Roots of American Masculinities*. Bloomington: Indiana University Press.

Byers, M. 2008. 'Education and Entertainment: The Many Reals of *Degrassi*', in Z. Druick and A. Kotsopoulos, eds., *Programming Reality: Perspectives on English-Canadian Television*. Waterloo, ON: Wilfrid Laurier University Press.

———— and R.J. Haines. 2005. '"That White Girl from That Show": Race and Ethnicity within Canadian Youth Cultures', in M. Byers, ed. *Growing Up Degrassi: Television, Identity and Youth Cultures*. Toronto: Sumach Press.

Connell, R.W., and J.W. Messerschmidt. 2005. 'Hegemonic Masculinity: Rethinking the Concept,' *Gender & Society*, 19, 6: 829–59.

Cox, T. 2002. '"Coyboyography": Matter and Manner in the Songs of Ian Tyson', in J. Nicks and J. Sloniowski, eds., *Slippery Pastimes: Reading the Popular in Canadian Culture*. Waterloo, ON: Wilfrid Laurier University Press.

Crichlow, W. 2001. 'Buller Men and Batty Bwoys: Hidden Men in Toronto and Halifax Black Communities', in T. Goldie, ed., *In a Queer Country: Gay and Lesbian Studies in the Canadian Context*. Vancouver: Arsenal Pulp Press.

Dick, L. 2008. 'Representing National History on Television: The Case of *Canada: A People's History*', in Z. Druick and A. Kotsopoulos, eds., *Programming Reality: Perspectives on English-Canadian Television*. Waterloo, ON: Wilfrid Laurier University Press.

Druick, Z. 2010. 'Cosmopolitans and Hosers: Notes on Recent Developments in English-Canadian Cinema', in B. Beaty, D. Briton, G. Filax, and R. Sullivan, eds., *How Canadians Communicate: Contexts of Canadian Popular Culture*. Edmonton: Athabasca University Press.

———— and A. Kotsopoulos, eds. 2008. *Programming Reality: Perspectives on English-Canadian Television*. Waterloo, ON: Wilfrid Laurier University Press.

Earle, N. 2002. 'Hockey as Canadian Popular Culture: Team Canada 1972, Television and the Canadian Identity', in J. Nicks and J. Sloniowski, eds., *Slippery Pastimes: Reading the Popular in Canadian Culture*. Waterloo, ON: Wilfrid Laurier University Press.

Echard, W. 2002. 'Forceful Nuance and Stompin' Tom', in J. Nicks and J. Sloniowski, eds., *Slippery Pastimes: Reading the Popular in Canadian Culture*. Waterloo, ON: Wilfrid Laurier University Press.

Fausto-Sterling, A. 1993. 'The Five Sexes: Why Male and Female Are Not Enough', *The Sciences*, 33, 3: 20–4.

Flaherty, D.H., and F.E. Manning, eds. 1993. *The Beaver Bites Back? American Popular Culture in Canada*. Montreal and Kingston: McGill-Queen's University Press.

Foster, D. 2008. 'Hockey Dreams: *Making the Cut*', in Z. Druick and A. Kotsopoulos, eds., *Programming Reality: Perspectives on English-Canadian Television*. Waterloo, ON: Wilfrid Laurier University Press.

Greenhill, P. 1989. *True Poetry: Traditional and Popular Verse in Ontario*. Montreal and Kingston: McGill-Queen's University Press.

————. 1995. '"Neither a Man nor a Maid": Sexualities and Gendered Meanings in Cross-Dressing Ballads', *Journal of American Folklore*, 108, 428: 156–77.

————. 2001a. 'Can You See the Difference?: Queerying the Nation, Ethnicity, Festival, and Culture in Winnipeg', in T. Goldie, ed., *In a Queer Country: Gay and Lesbian Studies in the Canadian Context*. Vancouver: Arsenal Pulp Press.

————. 2001b. 'Folk and Academic Racism: Concepts from Morris and Folklore', *Journal of American Folklore*, 115, 456: 226–42.

———— and A. Armstrong. 2006. 'Traditional Ambivalence and Heterosexual Marriage in Canada', *Ethnologies*, 28, 2: 157–84.

Haase, D., ed. 2004. *Fairy Tales and Feminism: New Approaches*. Detroit: Wayne State University Press.

Halberstam, J. 1998. *Female Masculinity*. Durham, NC: Duke University Press.

Halpert, H., and G. Story, eds. 1969. *Christmas Mumming in Newfoundland: Essays in Anthropology, Folklore, and History*. Toronto: University of Toronto Press.

Holmes, H., and H. Allison. 1992. 'Where Are the Hunks? "Street Legal" and the Canadian Concept of Heroism', in H. Holmes and D. Taras, eds., *Seeing Ourselves: Media Power and Policy in Canada*. Toronto: Harcourt Brace Jovanovitch Canada.

hooks, b. 2000. *Feminism Is for Everybody: Passionate Politics*. Cambridge, MA: South End Press.

Hughes-Fuller, P. 2009. 'Wild Bodies and True Lies: Carnival Spectacle and the Curious Case of *Trailer Park Boys*', *Canadian Journal of Communication*, 34, 1: 95–109.

Ingram, G.B. 2001. 'Redesigning Wreck: Beach Meets Forest as Location of Male Homoerotic Culture and Placemaking in Pacific Canada', in T. Goldie, ed., *In a Queer Country: Gay and Lesbian Studies in the Canadian Context*. Vancouver: Arsenal Pulp Press.

Kaufman, M. 1994. 'Men, Feminism, and Men's Contradictory Experiences of Power', in H. Brod and M. Kaufman, eds., *Theorizing Masculinities*. Thousand Oaks, CA: Sage.

Kessler, S.J. 1998. *Lessons from the Intersexed*. Piscataway, NJ: Rutgers University Press.

Kimmel, M.S., and M. Kaufman. 1994. 'Weekend Warriors: The New Men's Movement', in H. Brod and M. Kaufman, eds., *Theorizing Masculinities*. Thousand Oaks, CA: Sage.

King, R. 1991. *Talking Gender: A Guide to Nonsexist Communication*. Toronto: Copp Clark Pitman.

Kinsman, G. 2001. 'Challenging Canadian and Queer Nationalisms', in T. Goldie, ed., *In a Queer Country: Gay and Lesbian Studies in the Canadian Context*. Vancouver: Arsenal Pulp Press.

———. 2010. *The Canadian War on Queers: National Security as Sexual Regulation*. Vancouver: University of British Columbia Press.

Leff, L. 1997. 'The Making of a "Quota Queen": News Media and the Bias of Objectivity', in M.A. Fineman and M.T. McCluskey, eds., *Feminism, Media and the Law*. New York: Oxford University Press.

Lowry, G. 2008. '*Da Vinci's Inquest*: Postmortem', in Z. Druick and A. Kotsopoulos, eds., *Programming Reality: Perspectives on English-Canadian Television*. Waterloo, ON: Wilfrid Laurier University Press.

MacLennan, J. 2005. 'Only in Canada, You Say? The Dynamics of Identity on *Degrassi Junior High*', in M. Byers, ed., *Growing Up Degrassi: Television, Identity and Youth Cultures*. Toronto: Sumach Press.

McCullough, J. 2009. 'Imperialism, Regionalism, Humanism: *Gullage's*, *Trailer Park Boys*, and Representations of Canadian Space in Global Hollywood', in D. Varga, ed., *Rain/Drizzle/Fog: Film and Television in Atlantic Canada*. Calgary: University of Calgary Press.

McLeod, C., and A. Hovorka. 2008. 'Women in a Transitioning Canadian Resource Town', *Journal of Rural and Community Development*, 3: 78–92.

Mead, M. 1950/1962. *Male and Female: A Study of the Sexes in a Changing World*. Harmondsworth, UK: Penguin.

Medovarski, A. 2009. '"Boxing Ain't No Game": Clement Virgo's *Poor Boy's Game* as Canadian Racial Counter-narrative', *Topia*, 22: 117–37.

Miller, G. 2004. 'Frontier Masculinity in the Oil Industry: The Experience of Women Engineers', *Gender, Work and Organization*, 11, 1: 47–73.

Murray, S., and L. Ouellette, eds. 2009. *Reality TV: Remaking Television Culture*, 2d ed. New York: New York University Press.

Nathanson, P., and K.K. Young. 2001. *Spreading Misandry: The Teaching of Contempt for Men in Popular Culture*. Montreal and Kingston: McGill-Queen's University Press.

Nelson, C.A., and C.A. Nelson. 2004. 'Introduction', in C.A. Nelson and C.A. Nelson, eds., *Racism, Eh? A Critical Inter-disciplinary Anthology of Race and Racism in Canada*. Concord, ON: Captus Press.

Nicks, J., and J. Sloniowski, eds. 2002. *Slippery Pastimes: Reading the Popular in Canadian Culture*. Waterloo, ON: Wilfrid Laurier University Press.

O'Neal, M., and F. Larue. 2008. 'Dark Legacy: Neil Stonechild and the Saskatchewan Police Force', *First Nations Drum*, 18, 6 (June), www.firstnationsdrum.com/2008/june/dark_legacy.html.

Parpart, L. 2001. 'The Nation and the Nude: Colonial Masculinity and the Spectacle of the Male Body in Recent Canadian Cinema(s)', in P. Lehman, ed., *Masculinity: Bodies, Movies, Culture*. New York: Routledge.

Pearson, W.G. 2006. 'Not in the Hardware Aisle, Please: Same-Sex Marriage, Anti-Gay Activism and *My Fabulous Gay Wedding*', *Ethnologies*, 28, 1: 185–212.

Pigeon, E. 2001. '*Hosanna!* Michel Tremblay's Queering of National Identity', in T. Goldie, ed., *In a Queer Country: Gay and Lesbian Studies in the Canadian Context*. Vancouver: Arsenal Pulp Press.

Pinterics, N. 2001. 'Riding the Feminist Waves: In with the Third?' *Canadian Woman Studies*, 20/21, 4/1: 15–21.

Poirier, C. 1993. 'Wives, Whores, and Priests: Gender Relations and Narrative Voices in Two Quebecois Traditions', in D.H. Flaherty and F.E. Manning, eds., *The Beaver Bites Back? American Popular Culture in Canada*. Montreal and Kingston: McGill-Queen's University Press.

Prentice, S. 1994. 'Introduction. Sex in Schools: Canadian Education and Sexual Regulation', in S. Prentice, ed., *Sex in Schools: Canadian Education and Sexual Regulation*. Toronto: Our Schools/Our Selves.

Preves, S.E. 2001. 'Sexing the Intersexed: An Analysis of Sociocultural Responses to Intersexuality', *Signs: Journal of Women in Culture and Society*, 27, 2: 523–56.

Rak, J. 2008. 'Canadian Idols? CBC's *The Greatest Canadian* as Celebrity History', in Z. Druick and A. Kotsopoulos, eds., *Programming Reality: Perspectives on English-Canadian Television*. Waterloo, ON: Wilfrid Laurier University Press.

Reid, J. 2008. *Louis Riel and the Creation of Modern Canada: Mythic Discourse and the Postcolonial State*. Albuquerque: University of New Mexico Press.

Robidoux, M. 2002. 'Imagining Canadian Identity through Sport: A Historical Interpretation of Lacrosse and Hockey', *Journal of American Folklore*, 115, 456: 209–25.

Sedgwick, E.K. 1985. *Between Men: English Literature and Male Homosocial Desire*. New York: Columbia University Press.

Seiler, R.M. 2002. 'Selling Patriotism/Selling Beer: The Case of the "I AM CANADIAN!" Commercial', *American Review of Canadian Studies* (Spring): 45–66.

Sieg, K. 2005. *Ethnic Drag: Performing Race, Nation, Sexuality in West Germany*. Ann Arbor: University of Michigan Press.

Stewart, A. 2004. 'Penn and Teller Magic: Self, Racial Devaluation and the Canadian Academy', in C.A. Nelson and C.A. Nelson, eds., *Racism, Eh? A Critical Inter-disciplinary Anthology of Race and Racism in Canada*. Concord, ON: Captus Press.

Stone, K.F. 1975. 'Things Walt Disney Never Told Us', *Journal of American Folklore*, 88, 347: 42–50.

Stryker, S., and S. Whittle, eds. 2006. *The Transgender Studies Reader*. New York: Routledge.

Troka, D.J., K. LeBesco, and J.B. Noble, eds. 2002. *The Drag King Anthology*. Binghamton, NY: Harrington Park Press.

Tye, D., and M. Taft, eds. 1997. 'Masculinities/ Masculinités, Special Issue', *Canadian Folklore canadien*, 19, 1.

Van Kirk, S. 1999. *Many Tender Ties: Women in Fur Trade Society, 1670–1870*. Winnipeg: Watson and Dwyer.

Walcott, R. 2002. '"It's My Nature": The Discourse of Black Experience and Black Canadian Music', in J. Nicks and J. Sloniowski, *Slippery Pastimes: Reading the Popular in Canadian Culture*. Waterloo, ON: Wilfrid Laurier University Press.

Ward, M., and M. Edelstein. 2006. *A World Full of Women*, 4th ed. Boston: Pearson.

Waugh, T. 2006. *The Romance of Transgression in Canada: Queering Sexualities, Nations, Cinemas*. Montreal and Kingston: McGill-Queen's University Press.

Wernick, A. 2002. 'Canada, the Olympics and the Ray-Ban Man', in J. Nicks and J. Sloniowski, eds., *Slippery Pastimes: Reading the Popular in Canadian Culture*. Waterloo, ON: Wilfrid Laurier University Press.

Yuval-Davis, N. 2006. 'Intersectionality and Feminist Politics', *European Journal of Women's Studies*, 13, 3: 193–209.

Zipes, J., trans. 2003. *The Complete Fairy Tales of the Brothers Grimm*, 3d ed. New York: Bantam Books.

CHAPTER 9

One of the most significant challenges in preparing a text like this is attempting to include and/or represent the many perspectives that are present within a diverse nation. The title of this book begins with the words 'Canadian Perspectives'. But, whose perspectives do we mean when using that title? One of the complexities in answering this question is that not every person in Canada—even amongst those who hold technical citizenship—would use the word 'Canadian' to describe themselves. For many people who do so, or aspire to do so, this could be regarded as confusing or even offensive. To make matters even more complicated, it is not uncommon for people to claim Canadian identity while simultaneously claiming another nationality, either culturally or in terms of legal citizenship. One location for such nuances and tensions is the case of Quebec. Obviously, these tensions have included overt referenda on whether Quebec should be part of Canada, and this question pervades many personal and community stories. This text takes the view that many of these stories are gendered, and as such it is important to consider some of the many ways these contribute to and/or are affected by the construction of masculinities.

In this chapter, Laberge is interested in considering Quebec as a distinct society and giving space and voice to a review of the masculinities represented within it. These are alternative representations to those in Anglophone Canada, and as such can offer unique insights about masculinities useful to understanding Quebec, certainly, but Canada and notions of 'Canadian' as well. This idea will also be useful when Part III of the text takes up the idea of intersections in more depth, particularly with regard to masculinities within indigenous cultures. French and English and other Western European influences on masculinities in Canada have differences, but they do share a patriarchal structure in common. Indigenous ideas about gender and masculinities offer additional perspectives that often do not map onto that arrangement.

Social Representations of Men and Local Heroes in Québec's Public Sphere and Culture: Another Case of a 'Distinct Society'?

Yves Laberge

The aim of this chapter is to demonstrate that the ways in which men are pictured in the specific Québécois culture reconfirm Québec's status as a 'distinct society'. This chapter is divided into three parts. First, the theoretical framework situates men's studies within gender studies. It also presents arguments that advocate the Québécois nation as a distinct society, despite the historical resistances to that idea which occurred in English Canada during recent decades. This overview includes as well the significant role of feminism and women's studies in Québec, when compared to Canada and other countries. Second, some elements from the Québécois popular culture will be analyzed, in order to show how masculine identities are constructed and represented in selected popular movies and on some classic television programs produced in Québec. Then, a few concluding remarks will question the existence of a typical masculine identity in Québec, that is, in some points similar to the mainstream global culture, but generally different from what can be observed in English Canada.

The Men in Québec, Within and Without Canada

During the past century in Québec, the actual situations and representations of men, boys, fathers, and local heroes have evolved, as for everywhere else in Canada, but perhaps not always in the same ways or at the same moment. Cultural references and foreign influences in Québec and English Canada were at times similar (for instance, Hollywood movies were shown in all provinces), but in some cases, European influences—e.g., French cinema, French songs, and Francophone culture in general—appeared exclusively in Québec and nowhere else in Canada

Being French or Francophone always implies a collective identity that does not ignore or reject other cultures and languages; but most Francophones would feel that other cultures and languages are different from theirs or foreign and, more importantly, from abroad. In other words, Francophones would think that other cultures, such as the English-speaking cultures, are not 'theirs'. This distant attitude is confirmed by Christopher Forth and Bertrand Taithe in the introduction to their edited book *French Masculinities: History, Culture and Politics* (2007). Both professors argue that in France, the French men have adopted but also rejected various elements from foreign cultures; they constructed their own set of influences by selecting and refusing different aspects of these

cultures and images from abroad: 'Inspired and challenged by British and German modes of being men, the French state and society have pursued contradictory paths of emulation and repulsion in relation to foreign gender models' (2007: 3). This same selecting attitude can be observed in Québec, since the linguistic barrier between France and most of its neighbours can be compared with the actual experience of French Canadians, who are concentrated mainly in Québec.

As a consequence, many people in Québec will have in mind male heroes who are neither Canadian nor Québécois, who are almost unknown in English Canada. One example for a whole generation was French actor Jean Marais, who was an unusual type of man. In his lesser-known book of personal memories related to the films of his youth, titled *Les vues animées (Moving Pictures)* (1990), author Michel Tremblay recalls the fascination of his mother with French actor Jean Marais in the Jean Cocteau films they watched on late-night television in Montréal during the 1950s and 1960s. Marais's perfect diction and typical European French pronunciation contrasted sharply with their own Québécois accent. The numerous characters played by Jean Marais in movies from the 1940s and 1950s were quite different from other masculine models at the same time in Hollywood or anywhere else: Marais talked like a poet, behaved like a gentleman, and often played the role of a charming prince. But where did the Québécois get their other masculine models and heroes? Jean Marais was just one example of a popular actor, and audiences in Québec were not unanimous in their admiration of him; many preferred the more brutal Humphrey Bogart. But who were the main inspirations for heroes and models in twentieth-century Québec? In the field of sociology of culture, issues relating to the external influences are fundamental if we question our collective identity and some of the construction of our masculine identities: 'That masculinities are socially constructed is now a truism of gender scholarship' (Forth and Taithe, 2007: 3). And in order to understand how individuals construct their individual and collective identities, one has to investigate the sources of art, popular culture, and media they have access to, and similarly, what they do not have access to, that is, cultural products in a language that they cannot understand or products that are not available to them.

My hypothesis for this chapter is that the culture in Québec is based on other influences and specific social practices which are quite different from those in English Canada; therefore, because of that set of influences, the representation of men might not be the same as elsewhere. Even though this question is still debated and somehow controversial, many scholars acknowledge the fact that 'Québec has a distinct and rich intellectual tradition', as argued by Gail Faurschou, Souraya Mookerjea, and Imre Szeman in the introduction to their 2009 anthology *Between Empires: A Canadian Cultural Studies Reader*.

I do not see Québec as just 'one of the regions of Canada' or 'one of the 10 Canadian provinces', but as a different and unique culture; in other words, I believe there are more differences between Québec and any other province than, say, between any two distant provinces in Canada, for example, British Columbia and Newfoundland. For those who might be unaware, the much-debated concept of 'distinct society' that emerged during the 1980s can be misleading, at least in the English language, whenever one refers to Québec: in French, the expression *société distincte* implies only a difference between two equivalent societies, while in English, some people often understand implicitly that the distinct one is perhaps more 'sophisticated, special, distinctive, exceptional, or *distinguée*'; in other words, 'better'. Most people just don't like to call or represent their neighbour citizens as being 'better than themselves' or simply 'better than you', especially if this other group is seen as a minority.

But still, I think a 'distinct society' label can encapsulate the Québécois culture and specificity within Canada, not only because the majority/minority relationship between Anglophones and Francophones is reversed only in Québec, the only Francophone province in Canada, but mainly because there is in Québec a hybrid Francophone culture that cannot be found anywhere else in Canada: it is the result of four centuries of Francophone presence and traditions linked with the French language. Compared to the other Canadian provinces, the 'cultural recipe' (if I may say so) of foreign influences is mixed differently in Québec. Mainstream culture in Québec is broadly made of works by a variety of creators from Québec, plus various influences from Francophone countries (mainly France) and of course, as anywhere else, from the United States. Knowledge of the English-Canadian culture in Québec is often minimal, especially with Francophones. This lack of knowledge of 'the other Canada' and their differences, either by Francophones about Anglophones in Canada or vice versa is sometimes called 'the two solitudes', an expression taken from Hugh MacLennan's classic novel *Two Solitudes* (1945) but often borrowed and transposed in various contexts ever since (Gaudreault-DesBiens, 2007). Nevertheless, for obvious reasons (mainly the linguistic barrier), most English Canadians are not exposed to the same amount of French culture (music, literature, movies), either from Québec or from France. It is clear that in Canada, because most Francophones live and concentrate in 'la Belle Province', Québec is the place *par excellence* where French culture flows and blossoms, if compared to other Canadian provinces. It does not mean that French minorities do not exist elsewhere in Canada; but in Québec, most Francophones do not have the feeling that they are a linguistic minority.

This imbalance of knowledge about 'the other nation' in Canada is obviously amplified by the lack of bilingualism of many Canadians; the main consequences were described in many places, including David Cameron and Richard Simeon's book *Language Matters: How Canadian Voluntary Associations Manage French and English* (2009). The presence of English culture and media in Québec is much stronger that the opposite in the English-speaking provinces in Canada. The case of the Canadian television and cable networks speaks for itself: half of the TV channels most Québécois have access to are in English, while cable television in western Canadian provinces offers access to only one or two stations in French (both from the national network, Radio-Canada). In most English-speaking provinces, it is easier to watch a sports channel or even a porn television network in English than a station in French!

Even if most Québécois have access to channels in English and French, surveys have often confirmed that many Québécois watch their local programs and their 'téléromans' (television series made in Québec) on television more than all other Canadian viewers would select Canadian-made programs (Baillargeon, 1986). Unlike many English Canadians, most of the Québécois often watch and appreciate their own television series, that is, the ones produced in Québec, made with their familiar stars from Montréal. As Professor Marc Raboy (1990) once said, if one wants to see a distinct society in Canada, just watch the television in Québec. The typical Québécois like and consume their own culture and media, in which they recognize themselves as a nation and can see the world through their own lenses and shared values (Sauvageau, 1999). But if there is an 'official' Québécois nation, is there as well a 'Québécois identity'? Moreover, can the masculine models that are typical and exclusive to Québec be identified and compared?

In this chapter, I would like to redefine in an operational fashion a typical Québécois masculinity within the Québécois identity. In this context, men's studies should be understood as the analysis and understanding of how men are represented in various social discourses, art, culture, and the media. Obviously, men's studies are not against women or against feminism; as a part of gender studies that include other aspects and women's studies, men's studies investigate the identities of men and how their social position and representations are lived, negotiated, and symbolized in a given place, at a certain time. As Michael Kimmel and Amy Aronson put it in their extensive encyclopedia *Men and Masculinities*, 'studies of men' is a new discipline that focuses on men as 'corporeal beings', while masculinities concentrate on 'the ideologies and attitudes', and I would add the images and representations 'that are associated with those corporeal beings' (2004: xvi). Also men's studies should not be confused with homosexuality, and they are not conducted exclusively by men; included in this domain's topics are women and children.

A Culture Linked with the French Language

Anthropologists have demonstrated for centuries that masculinity cannot be conceived as universal or monolithic. As we know, cultures, traditions, trades, ethnicity, stereotypes, religions, and fashions have framed the ways people see men and also how men define and perceive themselves. Studying nations, nationalities, collective identities, and social representations can confirm, for instance, that teenage boys can recognize themselves and situate the images they see in a variety of models, roles, and identities, according to where they live and to whom they feel they belong. Many sociologists would argue that 'male masculinity is fragmented; it can, for example, be hegemonic, subordinated, marginalized, and complicit in form' (Annandale, 2010: 108).

These reflections about individual identity and group identity have echoes when we consider the collective national identity of a country. Whenever one considers its colonial past, Canada seems to have an elusive identity. Its national identity is difficult to describe, even for Canadians themselves; it is challenging to distinguish what makes Canada different from the United States or England, or what makes Canadians different from other Anglophones living in, say, New York City, Oxford, or Melbourne. Even the Canadian accent seems to have more or less disappeared in the recent decades when compared to the fellows living south of the forty-ninth parallel. Moreover, multiculturalism complicates matters, since all multiculturalisms in the English-speaking nations seem to be alike from one country to another. But for the Québécois, their own collective identity is not a problem; their presence as Francophones surrounded by Anglophones make them distinctive, that is, different from the others; they are not a visible minority but a cultural group that constitutes a minority within Canada.

In order to complete this conceptual framework that shall be used as prerequisites in the following demonstration, three primary observations should be made. First, despite their cultural differences, the Québécois collective identity is not completely different from the Canadian identity as such; there are many similitudes as well. Second, it is clear that US culture and media play an important role and influence in Canada, including Québec; however, there are other elements that differ in the way that culture and ideologies are constructed. One example is the characters of heroes, which are just about everywhere in US culture, television, and feature films; in Canadian culture, heroes are rare, and most of the time we see 'ordinary people' and 'losers' as the main characters of our fiction stories. Even 'our' celebrities, from William Shatner to John Candy, are difficult to identify as Canadians, but not the Francophone Céline Dion (Laberge, 2010). Third, the characters in Canadian culture, despite the fact they are not heroes, are often complex characters who are evolving, changing, but are not heroic. They sometimes do something good or positive, but not always. There is no 'Superman' in Canadian culture.

These three postulates could be discussed and even contested whenever considering the Québécois culture. For example, in traditional tales and songs from nineteenth-century Québec, heroes are numerous and emblematic: popular characters like 'Tit-Jean' and Joe Monferrand (a giant who became the hero of the first song composed in 1959 by poet Gilles Vigneault), plus a few authentic characters like the 'Géant Beaupré' (a famous giant), were bigger than nature. A wonderful song by the group Beau Dommage could have celebrated the 'Géant Beaupré'; but instead, the lyrics refer only to his skeleton. On the big screen, our Québécois heroes were sometimes heroic, smart, and good talkers, but at the same time they were often broken souls, as in *Tit-Coq* (1952), a famous play adapted as a feature film, in which the central character is a soldier and an orphan who 'loses' his fiancée while he is abroad during World War II.

But before exploring masculinities in a few works 'made in Québec', one more remark is necessary. During the mid-1970s, feminism acquired an astonishing place and power in many Western societies, including Canada and the United States. This historical shift has been studied elsewhere. However, my point is that the *'Mouvement féministe'* as a social movement was much stronger in Québec than anywhere else in Canada and arguably in the world in the late 1970s. The feminist movement came during the same years as the rise of the separatist movement, which culminated with the election of the Parti Québécois (PQ) in 1976. These two ideas co-existed, but more importantly, they were shared and advocated by the same persons, political parties, and groups, including unions. Three illustrations of this feminist power 'made in Québec' could be given. First is the creation by the newly elected Parti Québécois of a never-before-seen 'ministry of state for the status of women' in Québec, as early as 1976. Second is the provincial law from 1981 that made Québécois women retain their birth name forever (instead of adopting their husband's last name). Third is linguistic changes in the French language, unique in Québec, which imposed, against the rules of French dictionaries and grammars, a '*féminisation*' of some terms that had been exclusively masculine, with words like *auteur*, which could be changed to *auteure*, *écrivain*, which became *écrivaine*, or *ingénieur*, transformed into *ingénieure* whenever referring to a woman. These gender adjustments were not only linguistic, however. For instance, the consecrated expression '*droits de l'homme*', referring to human rights, was common until it was changed during the 1980s, but only in Québec, to '*droits de la personne*', in order to reflect a more neutral form. Political correctness in the 1990s brought speakers on the public scene, such as politicians, to adopt a repetitive way of referring to 'everyone and everybody': instead of saying in French *tous*, which implicitly implied 'all the people', they adopted the *tous et toutes*, which means 'all the people and all women'. These changes in the ways people would 'feminize' their discourses and speeches in public were exclusive to Québec and did not occur anywhere else in Canada and nowhere else in the Francophonie; they are only mentioned here as tangible proofs in order to illustrate the strength of the feminist movement in Québec, more than everywhere else, and sometimes in subtle ways, a few years before the advent of affirmative action in the workplace. As for the inevitable consequences of this relatively powerful position are the social representations of men during these two decades. If women were to be given more power, it was of course to bring equality, balance, and fairness. However, this long fight led by Québécoise women was not an attack against men but rather a challenge against the inflexible institutions and traditions that were out of date or inappropriate. Some men resisted; others agreed to see change happen in women's access to power, especially in the workplace.

Before entering into the second part of my demonstration, some of the main elements and ideas from the theoretical framework must be wrapped up. First, since the Québec culture is Francophone, its inspiration and influences are not the same as those in English Canada. Second, the culture in Québec is not much influenced by the Canadian culture; like anywhere else, the culture, art, and media in Québec are confronted by US and global culture, but because of the linguistic barrier, most Québécois see it as different, foreign, and to a certain point transposed into other terms, with other cultural references. Finally, one should not overlook that fact that within just a decade, women in Quebec got a boost in the public perceptions of their social status and gained respect, power, visibility, and access to the media as artists, critics, and leaders. These three elements will help us understand how the gender relationships have evolved in Québec, and why it was uniquely different in Québec and is nowhere else in Canada or in the world.

There are enormous cultural barriers between Québec and the rest of Canada. There are countless valuable works—books, songs, movies—which are revered by most Québécois and totally ignored by many English Canadians. Some people living in France have a better knowledge of the Québécois culture than many Anglophones living in Canada. In the following demonstration, I will highlight the portrayal of men in a few films and TV programs, in order to demonstrate the specific ways in which men are seen and represented.

Probably the most interesting example of the Québécois culture is the téléroman *Les belles histoires des pays d'en haut*, which can be seen as the most enduring fiction story of the twentieth century. It was originally created by Claude-Henri Grignon as a novel, *Un homme et son péché* (1933); then it became a radio show (as a play for radio) during the 1930s; it was later adapted for the big screen for two movies (*Un homme et son péché* and *Séraphin*), and then almost 500 weekly episodes on national television from 1956 to 1970. There were later reruns on television, plus versions on videocassettes and DVD, another feature film from the original novel, directed by Charles Binamé in 2002, and finally on the Internet through YouTube. All these different versions were huge successes. No television series has had such durable success in Québec, even if we include American weekly series programs such as *Star Trek* or *Dallas*. Everybody living in Québec has seen at least one episode of *Un homme et son péché*; it tells the story of a village north of Montréal, around 1889. The main character is the powerful mayor Séraphin Poudrier, who is known to be avaricious, miserly, and greedy. In each episode, every citizen is broke, spending more than what they actually earn, except Séraphin, who is rich although he rarely spends a dollar. Married but childless, Séraphin lives with his wife like a poor man, on his farm outside the village. In many households in Québec, Séraphin was the epitome of the covetous, the opposite of the generous. He remains the rich character who looks like a poor man, a man whom everyone in the audience loves to hate; in other words, the opposite of the hero. Nevertheless, Séraphin Poudrier was the best-known character in Québec television for many generations of Québécois.

The theme of 'becoming a man' has been part of some of the most important feature films in Canada, as it was in *Mon Oncle Antoine* (1971), directed by Claude Jutra from an autobiographical script written by Clément Perron. Often considered 'the best Canadian movie of all time' by critics and academics such as Peter Harcourt, this masterpiece illustrates the coming of age of a teenage boy who lives in a village in Québec (Black Lake) during the 1940s. Benoît, the teenager, who does not seem to have parents (only his uncle Antoine), observes 'the world of adults' who are in fact often immature; he encounters femininity, treason, and the death of another boy from the same region. Here, the main character is young, not very strong, and not really handsome; but he becomes the 'hero of the day' when he successfully throws snowballs at the rich owner of the mine, a man who is hated by the whole population.

One important landmark in the evolution of feminism and representation of men in movies was the movie *Mourir à tue-tête* (1979), directed by Anne-Claire Poirier and produced by the National Film Board of Canada. Its French title literally means 'dying loudly'; its official English title is *A Scream of Silence*. This film mixes documentary and fiction; it is based on a true story and was shot in Montréal. A full-time, skilled director and experienced scriptwriter at the NFB, Anne-Claire Poirier wanted to show the ugliest crime—rape: before, during, and after the event, as lived by the victim. The film is very powerful. It begins with a devastating scene: we see an ordinary crowd in a public place like a station, with men walking randomly; then a female voice identifies the man who has raped her. This scene is repeated twice in various contexts, and the rapist seems to be almost the same character in every situation. This opening scene is very challenging for most individual men because it implies that anybody, that is, any man, could be a rapist. This situation brings a strong identification between the audience and the main characters; it has an echo when the rape actually occurs, very early in the movie: the rapist tells his victim, 'I chose you randomly'. The scene of the rape is very long, with elements of *distantiation* that exclude erotism and avoid voyeurism. The second half of the film demonstrates that rape in itself is a crime and a trauma, but to make things worse, it is a never-ending event that continues in the police station, when the victim has to retell her story, repeating it to various persons (policemen, doctors, etc.). Furthermore, rape takes on a universal dimension in other continents, with examples of forced unions in which teenage girls cannot choose their husband, or the case of the genital mutilations of African women in many countries.

This movie, *Mourir à tue-tête*, was a huge hit in Québec: it was aired on the national television network (Radio-Canada) and presented in movie theatres, schools, and universities. The best of the Québec filmmakers and actors participated in it: director Michel Brault served as a cinematographer, Julie Vincent starred as the nurse who is the victim, and actor Germain Houde was tattooed with his character of the rapist for the rest of his career. It was a much-needed shock treatment against machismo and harassment. However, men were collectively represented as the perpetrators of this crime and as being responsible for the inequalities lived by women. In front of these women who are the victims of rape, men are always the bad guys: not only the rapist but also the policemen, gynecologists, reporters, and the media, who reproduce the humiliation felt by victims. This does not mean that all men actually commit a rape crime, but they are portrayed in the film as accomplices, as those who perpetuate the trauma because of their desire for women. And as one woman declares in the film, '[T]his is a justice, but it is made by and for men.'

In my view, *Mourir à tue-tête* was the ultimate feminist movie, one that could only have been done in Québec and produced by the NFB. Its non-commercial approach of documentary and fiction mixed together, its use of indifference, its lack of a happy ending, its strong feminist message were too unusual in the late 1970s to interest private producers (Laberge and Smith, 2004). However, given its numerous qualities, it was a well-deserved success. The man–woman relationship in this film is quite different than in other movies of that era that challenged the male–female relationship, such as Robert Altman's *Three Women* (1978) or Nicolas Roeg's *Bad Timing* (1980). In a radical way, *Mourir à tue-tête* antagonizes the male–female relationship in an approach that makes other movies look rather innocent. However, *Mourir à tue-tête* dangerously generalizes in its prologue the cliché of every man's being a potential rapist or an unpunished rapist. Nevertheless, this film was uncontested, unchallenged, and celebrated; it was presented at the Cannes Film Festival in 1979 and its director later received the Ordre national du Québec.

In its script and storyline, *Mourir à tue-tête* offered a sharp contrast with previous movies made in Québec, especially those made by Gilles Carle, who remains a celebrated filmmaker, sometimes considered a genius by many film critics. But some of Carle's early movies could be seen as an apology for rape and bad attitudes of men towards women, such as *Le viol d'une jeune fille douce* (*The Rape of a Sweet Young Girl*, 1968) and *Les Mâles* (1970). In the first movie, the rape of a girl is presented almost as a light comedy scene which is not directly shown on the screen. Even in his film *La vraie nature de Bernadette* (1972), the woman is portrayed as a person who can offer her body and charms as a service to the frustrated old men who live in the village. As Anthony Synnott puts it on the first page of his book, men are too often seen in a Manichean fashion, as either 'heroes or pigs', 'villains or victims' (2010: 1).

During the feminist era in Québec, mainly during the 1980s, many masculine characters became like the prisoners of some female scriptwriters, under their imaginary torture experiencing humiliating situations under the control of some powerful women perhaps seeking a kind of collective revenge. Those men who were the 'villains' were transformed into feeble, inoffensive characters. In many Québec plays, television series, and movies written by women, the 1980s was the era of the feeble man, or the man who cries. Cheating husbands were frequent in the téléromans, the epitome of this type of seducer being Jean-Paul Belleau in *Des dames de cœur*, written by Lise Payette with her daughter Sylvie Payette, and from 1989 in their follow-up series, titled *Un signe de feu*. On the theatre scene, one of the first and foremost playwrights in Québec (and, I would add, one of the best), Janette Bertrand, wrote in 1981 a famous play titled *Moi Tarzan, toi Jane*, in which she inverted the common stereotypes about heroes and strong men: the main character, a typical 'feeble man', admits he is a virgin, shy with potential girlfriends, and sometimes tempted by homosexuality.

In an interview with Martial Dassylva following the huge success of her play in theatres in Montréal, Bertrand admitted that she wanted to show that 'a man could cry and a woman can have a strong will' (Bertrand, quoted by Dassylva, in *La Presse*, 1981).

Another case would be a 'feminist' movie directed by Micheline Lanctôt, *L'Homme à tout faire* (1980), in which the main two male characters are either dumb or macho. In this film, it is the women who know better and have the positive roles. It contrasted with two other Québécois films from that era, made without female characters, which depict men in their more conventional activities such as hunting and fishing, for example, in *Le temps d'une chasse* (1974), directed by François Manckiewicz, and *La bête lumineuse* (1983), by Pierre Perrault. Both films depict as well the competition between men in their quest for wild animals and the control of their symbolic territory.

On the other hand, the non-hero character was even comic in at least one case in Québec. In the comedy program *Samedi de rire*, aired on Canadian television (Radio-Canada) during the late 1980s, actor Normand Chouinard played the character of Ben Béland, the enthusiastic ambassador of Québec, wearing a big fur coat like the old coureurs de bois and always advocating for an invention made in Québec or by a Québécois that could really save some desperate situation. This improbable character was so unusual that people could only mock these plots.

Nevertheless, the inequalities between sexes could not be resolved in just one decade of feminism, and films acknowledged that. The same unfair patterns that existed before the 1980s between men and women were represented again in the most praised feature film made in Canada, Denys Arcand's *Le déclin de l'empire américain* (1987), but this time, these institutionalized distortions were highlighted and criticized in many scenes. This film tells the story of a group of friends, many of whom work at a university in Montréal, who gather during a weekend to cook a meal while remembering their sexual encounters and affairs. Some of these professionals are baby boomers who were born at the right time. Here again, although the masculine characters are seen as wealthy, professionally successful university professors who are enjoying sexual freedom, the female characters are either part-time lecturers, readers, or a spouse who is cheated on by her beloved husband. As in the previous cases, the easy-living masculine characters in *Le déclin de l'empire américain* cannot be seen as heroes, mainly because they do not deserve their wealth and success, made at the expense of partners who were, one way or another, excluded from the elite. Even in Arcand's latest film, *L'âge des ténèbres* (2007), the main character, Jean-Marc, sometimes dreams that he is a hero, a noble cavalier from the Middle Ages, instead of being a boring bureaucrat rejected by the woman he loves.

Recent films produced in Québec reconfirm the impossibility of creating a Québécois hero, such as *La grande séduction* (2003), which tells the story of a naïve doctor who moves to a remote region in northeastern Québec for work; he realizes that his friends and his girlfriend have lied to him about themselves. This comedy directed by Jean-François Pouliot from a script written by Ken Scott will get a triple remake in 2012: in English Canada, France, and Italy.

This overview of the representation of men in Québec cinema would not be complete without the inclusion of the recent feature film titled *Polytechnique* (2009), directed by Denis Villeneuve. It is based on an actual event that occurred at Montréal's École polytechnique, in which a man killed 14 young women in front of their classmates after screaming his contempt for women and before committing suicide. This horrible hate crime against women, committed simply because they were women, was a national trauma in Canada; it also illustrated in a brutal and spectacular way what sociologist Anthony Synnott calls 'the stereotypes of women as victims and men as villains', and contributed to confirming what Synnott calls 'the angelization of women and the demonization of men' during the 1990s (2009: 77). Villeneuve's film is very impressive; it was named Best Canadian Feature of 2009 by the Toronto Film Critics Association (CBC, 2010), followed by the Rogers Best Canadian Film Award.

Conclusion

There are not many heroes in Québec's culture; but is there a typical masculine identity in Québec? The few examples presented in this chapter show that there is obviously a Québecois culture, with its typical language and a set of influences that are different from anywhere else in North America, mainly because the Québécois consume culture and the media in French and perceive cultures from abroad (movies, popular music, or television programs) as being foreign, that is, from the outside. Regarding the audiovisual culture made in Québec for the big and small screens, there are main characters who are not heroes (in the 'heroic' sense of the term) but who remain well-known by their audiences, are easy to recognize, and in some cases have received the status of 'cultural icon' (like Séraphin half a century ago).

One should not conclude that the Québécois are not capable of creating national heroes or typical characters that receive unanimous praise from the population. A story of an authentic Québécois hero made into a movie would be *Maurice Richard* (2005), directed by Charles Binamé, starring Roy Dupuis. Such heroes exist in reality (including many hockey players from the Montreal Canadiens), and the Québécois have their own 'star system' that is not limited to global figures like Céline Dion. For example, one should look at cherished characters such as Émilie Bordeleau and Ovila Pronovost (played by Roy Dupuis, a praised model of virility) in *Les filles de Caleb*, a television series directed by Jean Beaudin and taken from a best-selling novel by Arlette Cousture. We should rather question the masculine heroic model, which in fact exists only in Hollywood movies and in almost no other country. As a contrast, the films made by Canadian directors such as David Cronenberg, Atom Egoyan, and Guy Madden do not depict heroes of any kind. The Québécois film tradition, which owes a lot to the documentary and '*cinéma direct*' genres, is based rather on realism. Audiences in Québec are used to seeing natural, realistic characters, either masculine or feminine, in 'their' homemade stories. Sometimes weaknesses and shortcomings make characters more human. But being weak does not always mean being feeble or a villain. Very often, masculine characters who are not heroes are 'the bad guys', and over-generalization can come along too easily. To summarize, the specificity of Québec masculinities within Canada is not just an oddity or a regional case; it clearly reconfirms the unique, distinct society that constitutes the Québécois nation.

Discussion Questions

1. Do you think that the Québécois culture, that is, its movies, music, TV shows, and way of life, are different from elsewhere in Canada? Support your answer with examples.
2. With regard to the first question, how are masculinities similar or different between Québécois and other Canadian communities?
3. As a group, are the Québécois similar or different from French Canadians living in Canadian provinces outside Québec (such as Ontario or New Brunswick)? Support your answer with examples.

4. Do you believe there are sometimes prejudices against the Québécois in the Canadian public discourse, for example, in some daily newspapers or on some local radio stations?
5. Have you ever seen a TV show or movie produced in Montréal or Québec? If so, what similarities or differences did you notice as compared to other Canadian productions? If not, why is it easier to watch or buy a DVD/Blu-Ray from Hollywood instead of one from Canada or Québec? Why aren't TV stations from Québec available in many Canadian cities, even though one can access so many networks from the United States?
6. Do you believe that many Québécois consider themselves as a 'distinct society' because they feel they are 'distinctive', 'distinguished', special, or even better than Anglophones? Support your answer with specific examples.
7. From what you know, do you consider that the music of Céline Dion is typical of Canadian or Québécois culture? Did you know that this singer has also recorded many albums in French?
8. Why do you think most Québécois are bilingual, whereas most Anglophones do not understand French? Would Canada be a better place if all Canadian citizens spoke both English and French?

Recommended Websites

National Film Board of Canada (NFB): www. nfb.ca

Société Radio-Canada: www.radio-canada.ca/ television

Les Archives de Radio-Canada: www.archives. radio-canada.ca

CBC, 'Toronto Film Critics Name *Polytechnique* Top Canadian Feature', 13

January 2010, Canadian Press: www. cbc.ca/arts/film/story/2010/01/12/ polytechnique-film012.html

Valerie Bourdeau, 'How to Tell If You're from Quebec': www.zompist.com/quebec.html

International Association of Quebec Studies: www.aieq.qc.ca/frame_aieq_en.html

References

Annandale, E. 2010. 'Health Status and Gender', in W. Cockerham, ed., *The New Blackwell Companion of Medical Sociology*. Oxford: Wiley-Blackwell.

Baillargeon, J.-P., ed. 1986. *Les pratiques culturelles des Québécois: Une autre image de nous-mêmes*. Québec: Institut québécois de recherche sur la culture.

Bertrand, J. 1981. *Moi Tarzan, toi Jane*. Longueuil: Inédi Raffin.

Cameron, D., and R. Simeon, eds. 2009. *Language Matters: How Canadian Voluntary Associations Manage*

French and English. Vancouver: University of British Columbia Press.

CBC. 2010. 'Toronto Film Critics Name *Polytechnique* Top Canadian Feature', *Canadian Press*, 13 Jan., www.cbc. ca/arts/film/story/2010/01/12/polytechnique-film012. html.

Dassylva, M. 1981. 'Moi Tarzan, toi Jane' (interview with Janette Bertrand), *La Presse*, 18 April, C-1.

Faurschou, G., S. Mookerjea, and I. Szeman, eds. 2009. 'Introduction', in *Between Empires: A Canadian*

Cultural Studies Reader. Durham, NC: Duke University Press.

Forth, C.E., and B. Taithe, eds. 2007. *French Masculinities: History, Culture and Politics*. Basingstoke, UK: Palgrave.

Gaudreault-DesBiens, J.-F. 2007. *Les solitudes du bijuridisme au Canada: Essai sur les rapports de pouvoir entre les traditions juridiques et la résilience des atavismes identitaires*. Montréal: Thémis.

Kimmel, M., and A. Aronson, eds. 2004. *Men and Masculinities: A Social, Cultural, and Historical Encyclopedia*. Santa Barbara, CA: ABC-CLIO Press.

Laberge, Y. 2010. 'Je ne savais pas qu'il était Canadien', Paper presented at Colloque international 'Les Canadiens aux États-Unis: Culture, économie et société', Université de Montréal, 13 May.

——— and M. Smith. 2004. 'Film', in M.D. Smith, ed., *Encyclopedia of Rape*. Santa Barbara, CA: Greenwood Press.

MacLennan, H. 1945. *Two Solitudes*. New York: Duell, Sloan & Pearce.

'Mon Oncle Antoine' in Wise, W., ed., 2001. *Take One's Essential Guide to Canadian Film*. Toronto: University of Toronto Press.

'My Uncle Antoine' in Pratley, G., 2003. *A Century of Canadian Cinema. Gerald Pratley's Feature Film Guide. 1900 to the Present*. Toronto: Lynx Images.

Raboy, M. 1990. *Missed Opportunities: The Story of Canada's Broadcasting Policy*. Montréal and Kingston: McGill-Queen's University Press.

Sauvageau, F., ed. 1999. *Variations sur l'influence culturelle américaine*. Sainte-Foy, QC: Presses de l'Université Laval.

Synnott, A. 2009. *Re-thinking Men: Heroes, Villains and Victims*. Farnham, UK: Ashgate.

Tremblay, M. 1990. *Les vues animées*, Montréal: Leméac.

In thinking about what to include in this text, it was striking to contemplate popular notions of the Canadian Forces versus the US military establishment. The popular notions that internationally Canada serves in peacekeeping whereas the United States conducts policing are overly simplistic depictions of their respective military roles and dispositions. Interestingly, these stereotypes are analogous to ideas about feminine versus masculine roles more generally. So, in regards to Canada, what is the historical context in which military identity has developed, and how are masculinities constructed within and because of this?

In this chapter, McGaughey provides insights about the historical and contemporary phenomena at play in military identity in Canada. In particular, she argues that since the eighteenth century, Canadian military masculinities have been informed and influenced by British and, later, American images of war and warriors. The title, 'Fighting in the Shadow', describes both the internal cultural dilemmas within military circles in Canada and the insecurities and tensions they face vis-à-vis the US military. Readers with little background in military history or culture are likely to benefit a great deal from this compelling angle from which to view masculinities in Canada. As you read the chapter, consider how personal and developmental as well as broader community aspects resonate with the way in which Canadian military identity has unfolded.

Fighting in the Shadow: American and British Cultural Influences on Canadian Military Manhood[1]

Jane McGaughey

In 1757, two years before his death on the Plains of Abraham, then Colonel James Wolfe (1768) wrote his *Instructions for Young Officers*. In two pages, he summarized the qualities most desired in an effective British serving officer. 'When a young gentleman betakes himself to the profession of arms,' he wrote,

> he should seriously reflect upon the nature and duties of the way of life he has entered into, and consider, that is it not as the generality of people vainly imagine, learning a little of the exercise, saluting gracefully, firing his platoon in his turn, mounting a few guards (carefully

enough) and finally, exposing his person bravely in the day of battle; which will deservedly, and in the opinion of judges, acquire him the character of a good officer: no, he must learn chearfully [*sic*] to obey his superiors, and that their orders and his own be punctually executed. . . . A young officer should never think he does too much.

For Wolfe, one of the most legendary names in both British and Canadian military history, bravery and skill needed to be coupled with obedience, command, and an infinite capacity to serve the cause. These were traditional expectations for British officers, valued from the time of Hastings and Agincourt to the Falklands.

Two hundred and fifty years after Wolfe's death, the Canadian Forces, heirs of the traditions and loyalties of his British troops in Quebec, were enjoying a renaissance of popularity and public prestige. Michael Valpy (2009) noted:

> Not much more than a decade ago, Canada's armed forces were all but invisible, out of sight in remote bases and discreetly dressed in civilian clothes in the cities. Now they march around Ottawa's streets in combat gear. They have become the heroes of middle Canada, celebrated at sporting events, remythologized as the new icons of nationalism.

After the scandals of the 'Somalia Affair' and the disbandment of the Airborne Regiment, it was good again to be a soldier in Canada. The traditional manly ideals of bravery, blood sacrifice, and serving in uniform once more were elements that defined the Canadian military, this time in the twenty-first century.

Canada's participation in the War on Terror through the mission in Afghanistan marks the remilitarization of society in a manner not seen since the World Wars, with modern twists that couple the overseas conflict with cultural patriotism. On Fridays Canadians are encouraged to wear red to show support for the troops. Movie theatres air adventurous commercials before the film starts that encourage young Canadians to think of the military as a desirable career choice. *Hockey Night in Canada's* ever-popular 'Coach's Corner' segment has become a mainstay of patriotic support for our men and women in uniform, with Don Cherry paying tribute to the fallen at the end of nearly every show. The most watched night of television in the country has become a monument to military service. Perhaps the best-known instances of this renewed appreciation for the armed

forces are the grassroots tributes to the fallen on overpasses between Canadian Forces Base Trenton and the morgue in Toronto, where autopsies are performed on soldiers killed in Afghanistan. As the hearses make their way down the road, crowds of mourners wave flags and salute the latest names added to the Book of Remembrance in the Peace Tower on Parliament Hill. While Highway 416 leading into Ottawa has been known as the 'Veteran's Memorial Highway' since 1999, when it opened, 2007 saw the stretch of Highway 401 between Trenton and Toronto renamed the 'Highway of Heroes' (Juergensen, 2007) in response to popular demand.

So what is it that we are celebrating in the achievements and sacrifices of men and women serving in Afghanistan? How do their triumphs and defeats compare to the legacy of Canadians in uniform since Confederation? Canada has always debated its military episodes, resulting in conscription crises, divisions between French and English Canada, and the ever-present fear of becoming 'too American' in choosing violence over diplomacy. The Canadian experience of warfare in the twentieth century is in many ways a metaphor for the competition and perceived insecurities embedded in the formation of masculine identities. We fear both emulating and antagonizing the 'other'. Defining ourselves in opposition to demonstrations of British and American military machismo has been a national pastime predating Confederation. As for impressions of our own martial manhood, enduring the double burden of inheriting British military traditions and living next to the leviathan of American military prowess has arguably eradicated (Granatstein, 1998; 2002) some of the awareness of Canada's military heritage.

Fighting in the shadow of two of the world's great military powers has affected our collective images of courage, aggression, moral righteousness, and the role of the warrior in modern society. Who were we before the Highway of Heroes? An examination of Canadian military manliness over the past century can help to contextualize the country's current embrace of our men in uniform. Allan D. English (2004) contends that the concept of military culture is important because it clarifies differences between the branches of the armed services and various approaches to combat, leadership, and technology, and why some units perform differently in roughly the same conditions. In this light, it follows that an analysis of American and British influences on Canadian military culture through the lens of masculine stereotypes and imagery can illuminate society's shifting conceptualizations of Canadian soldiers and the cultural-political importance given to representations of martial manliness throughout the twentieth century.

I

It is somewhat of a truism to state that there is an intrinsic connection between men and military service. As R. Connell (2000) has stated, the millions of members serving in uniform around the globe are overwhelmingly men, particularly within command positions. Enemy targets are also predominately male and men predominate in warlike conduct in other areas of life, such as body-contact sports, the business world, and industrial labour. As always, language is of utmost importance in historical analyses of gender. John Tosh (2005) provides strong justification for labelling 'manliness' as a term that 'belongs to another era', namely the nineteenth century, with its concern about physical prowess, romantic chivalry, and proper comportment in all-male society. However, in describing national militaries, institutions that have strong roots in nineteenth-century values and patterns of organization, I believe that using the term 'manliness' is a valid linguistic choice in characterizing popular impressions of men in uniform. Similarly, associating masculinity with the nation pre-dates our postmodern era, with male and female stereotypes used as symbols of strength, weakness,

and pride to foster feelings of patriotism. The association of masculine virtue with soldiering and a martial lifestyle can be a source of great national strength and power during a military conflict. In describing the Great War as a masculine event, George L. Mosse (1996) proposes that the image of the warrior in the trenches provided a 'climax' to the modern concept of manliness. The conflict of 1914 to 1918 accentuated certain aspects of manhood, such as determination, hardiness, and perseverance, which were prized in peacetime but attained a richer status within a military context. With the Great War standing as one of the high-water marks of Canada's becoming visible to the rest of the world as something more than a British colony, its importance in solidifying a Canadian ideal of soldiering was invaluable.

Not surprisingly, correlations between gender and militarization have often been accorded only to men throughout the history of warfare, with female combatants standing as rare exceptions to the rule. Mary K. Meyer (2000) has suggested that full citizenship within a patriarchal state is reserved for men, whose blood sacrifice as citizen-soldiers and warriors is privileged and rewarded by society. While this is certainly true of conflicts in the twentieth century, the Canadian military has seemed to envelop its female soldiers quite easily in the broader language of masculine warfare, such as when General Walter Natynczyk (Valpy, 2009), the Chief of Defence Staff for the Canadian Forces, described Leading Seaman Stephanie Russell as 'a strong woman warrior'. Women first served in the Canadian military as nurses during the North-West Rebellion of 1885, while the final barrier to equal service, prohibiting women from serving on submarines, was removed in 2001. Although equal on paper to male soldiers at the dawn of the new century, Canada's women in arms quickly became part of the ancient blood-sacrifice myth within heroism. After becoming the first Canadian female combat officer to be killed in combat, in 2006, Captain

Nichola Goddard was posthumously awarded the Sacrifice Medal and the Meritorious Service Medal (Blatchford, 2006), given for outstanding actions that bring benefit and honour to the nation. Having women in the military does not seem to have changed the appearance of the Canadian Forces; after nearly 30 years of acceptance as military officers, female soldiers have been accorded the same honours as their male counterparts and have been subsumed, superficially at least, into the culture and language of armed service. Female influences on representations of Canadian military manhood are highly important but are not the central issue in the following argument. What has had more influence on our collective masculine imagery of Canadians in uniform is the legacy of our associations with British and American militarization and also the depictions of Canadian manliness in battle written by generations of historians and commentators.

II

The Canadian military has long been caught between images of Great Britain and the United States. As Desmond Morton argues, close identification with the British and the Americans has 'sometimes attenuated military identification with Canada itself' (1987: 637–8). Although the British paradigm of military valour held sway until the Second World War, the 'Americanization of the armed forces since the 1950s, in equipment, tactical doctrine, and even appearance, may reflect Canada's own transfer from the British to the American empire.' In this, Canadian men in uniform assume the position of the 'other' in the formation of militarized masculinities, appearing secondary to nations with greater military prestige and having to define themselves in relation to the stronger power.

This stance is not new; if anything, Canadians have negatively defined themselves as 'not American' since the time of the War of 1812, if not before. The very definition of a Canadian is a fluid entity informed by historical episodes and loyalties. French Canadians after 1763, United Empire Loyalists after 1776, and immigrants across the centuries have come to Canada and acculturated themselves by noting the things they are not: not American, not British, not militaristic, and not aggressive. This negative self-definition has deep roots, creating a 'self-conscious aura of the secondary and the derivative and a spirit of envy and insecurity, especially vis-à-vis the United States' (Black, 1995: 101). During the Second World War, it was argued that the British would be alarmed by the 'Americanization of the senior Dominion', but that, compared to Americans, Canadians were both less impulsive and 'far less given to violence' (McCormac, 1940: 147–55). Even during the grip of global conflict, Canadians were defined as being susceptible to overt influence but unable to mirror such masculine elements as aggression and decisiveness. While Canada focused on social welfare and economic development through much of the twentieth century (Morton, 1987), America grew into 'an unchallengeable military supremacy' on the continent.

When Canadians did serve in foreign wars, official historians greatly affected how the general public valued the men's participation. Tim Cook's *Clio's Warriors: Canadian Historians and the Writing of the World Wars* looks in depth at how such historians as C.P. Stacey, George Stanley, and S.F. Wise shaped the popular narrative of Canadian victory and failure on the battlefield. He rightly points out that warfare is 'almost completely dominated by issues of gender as an almost exclusive masculine activity, yet there is no dialogue between historians of gender and the military' (2006: 250). In narrowly defining the applicability of military history, many of its chroniclers in twentieth-century Canada used traditional gendered language that casts Canada's military men as either triumphant heroes or untested failures, repeating assertions by British and American commentators that Canadians were the 'poor cousins' (Cook, 2004: 996) of their more skilled counterparts on the battlefield.

This label of being lesser than other soldiers involves the issue of marginalized masculinities. Marginalization (Connell, 1995) involves relations between dominant and subordinated classes or ethnic groups. Marginalization also includes authorization and support of the more dominant image of masculinity by those who fall outside its boundaries. Within the realm of Canadian martial manliness, this meant that any validation of British or, later, American soldiering by Canadian troops as an ideal to emulate automatically set up their own concerns about inferiority and competing national standards of manhood demonstrated under fire. The British tradition of a military life that stresses duty, honour, and national service was taken up by the United States Army in the latter half of the twentieth century with its 'Be All You Can Be' attitude. Both nations have left concrete impressions on how Western societies imagine and organize their own military institutions. Caught between these two military superpowers through the boundaries of history and geography, Canada's self-perceived status as the 'poor cousin' of more well-established and idealized armed forces marginalized the possibilities for valuing battlefield heroics and manly behaviour before any shots had been fired.

Canadian historiography's love affair with the concept of failure has not enhanced depictions of the nation in a martial context. As Seymour Lipset once argued, Canada 'must justify its *raison d'être* by emphasizing the virtues of being separate from the United States' (1965: 64). In this, the language of Canadian historiography, perhaps unintentionally, has promoted notions of masculine marginalization and inferiority by citing the nation's failings, both on and off the battlefield. Donald Creighton's damnation of Canada's future in 'The Decline and Fall of the Empire of the St Lawrence' stated that the country had become 'a military satellite of the American Republic' (1969: 22–3)

with the 1940 Ogdensburg Agreement, decolonized by 'the irresistible penetrative power of American economic and military imperialism', and that Canadians were 'held back from any determined action on their own behalf both by their own fears and inhibitions and by the bluffs and threats of Americans and their government'. Northrop Frye similarly concluded that it was 'not much wonder if Canada developed with the bewilderment of a neglected child, preoccupied with trying to define its own identity, alternately bumptious and diffident about its own achievements' (1976: 338–9). Michael Bliss (2006) made his own departing salvo in 'Has Canada Failed?', an article that highlighted our secondary place in the global war on terror (Valpy, 2006) and the 'ineffective bit role' Canada had played in helping to defeat Communism.

III

It wasn't always like this. At the turn of the twentieth century, following the massive involvement of Canadian volunteers in the South African War, positive views of the military and militarization grew in society, particularly among Canadians with strong loyalties to the British Empire. Although the presence of threatened militarism during and after the American Civil War had been an impetus for Canadian Confederation in 1867 (Valpy, 2009), Sir John A. Macdonald had been contemptuous of a full-time Canadian military in the nineteenth century. Morton (2007) has argued that pacifism was 'an old and respected tradition' in Canada, dating from the time when Lieutenant-Governor John Simcoe exempted Mennonites and Dunkers from militia service in Upper Canada, and was enhanced by immigrants in the late nineteenth century seeking a refuge from conscription policies in Tsarist Russia and the Habsburg Empire.

However, the imperial arms race at the turn of the century and Canada's role, both in South Africa and in creating the Canadian Navy out of the aftermath of the Naval Bill Crisis of 1910, shifted some attitudes. In the era of the degeneracy crisis, the creation of the Boy Scouts by Lord Baden-Powell, and the macho presidency of Teddy Roosevelt, Canadians (Morton, 2007) who believed in 'patriotism, discipline, subordination, and order' put their energies into cadet training and the establishment of a Canadian militia under the auspices of Colonel Sam Hughes. Named as the minister of militia in 1911, Hughes was a blunt militarist, anti-Catholic Orangeman and veteran of the South African War. *The Busy Man's Magazine*, founded by Lt.-Col. John Bayne Maclean, characterized Hughes (Anonymous, 1912) as Canada's 'First Warrior', the 'real stuff that soldiers are made of', who 'breakfasts on a French-Canadian every morning, and has a Roman Catholic for lunch.' In particular, the magazine highlighted Hughes's efficient cadet work, drilling thousands of boys during the summer months. 'The Colonel will be popular with the cadet boys,' the article predicted, as 'he knows boys and he loves them. He has the boy heart.' This capacity to be simultaneously a firm instructor and a free spirit apparently made Hughes a model of military masculinity for Canada's young men. Hughes himself remarked that joining the militia was a moral duty for Canadian boys, as

> the ranks of crime are not recruited from the boys who wear the uniform—from the soldiers. . . . The cadet corps of the country is doing a splendid work, and the day is going by fast when people oppose their sons entering the service. They are fast learning that the militia uplifts the morals of the country.

In a 1913 speech given in Napanee, Ontario, Hughes emphasized the need to train Canadian youth in aspects of soldiering in order to make them

> self-controlled, erect, decent and patriotic . . . instead of growing up as under

present conditions of no control, into young ruffians or young gadabouts; to ensure peace by national preparedness for war; to make the military camps and drill halls throughout Canada clean, wholesome, sober and attractive to boys and young men (Morton, 2007: 128).

The superficial militarization of Canadian society in the years immediately preceding the Great War was not geared only toward young boys. Hughes noted (Anonymous, 1912) that 'Canada has a million and a half of men capable of bearing arms. Give me a million such men capable of hitting the bull's eye . . . and no foe will ever dare to cross the boundary into the Dominion.' In the Edwardian era, North America seemed to fill a quasi-exotic role within the British Empire, where men fulfilled childhood dreams of adventure by becoming explorers, hunters, trappers, and members of the North-West Mounted Police, like the famous Sam Steele during the Klondike Gold Rush. Robert Stead's (1956) poem 'The Squad of One' heralded the 'all-round kind of man' created by the North-West Mounted Police, romantically declaring that a Canadian constable was 'A man who can finish whatever he starts, and no matter how it began; / A man who can wrestle a drunken bum, or break up a range stampede — / Such are the men of the Mounted Police, and such are the men they breed.' In *Scouting for Boys*, Lord Baden-Powell characterized the constables as 'peace-scouts', naming them 'men accustomed to live on their own resources, taking their lives in their hands, brave and loyal to their employers, chivalrous and helpful to each other, unselfish and reliable; MEN, in fact, of the best type' (1908: 13, 300). However, even in this most imperial of manuals outlining military masculinity, Canadians, unlike their colonial counterparts in Australia, South Africa, and India, did not merit a separate section in Baden-Powell's history of the British Empire, but were omitted completely in favour of his history of colonial America and the exploits of Captain John Smith. Instances of American heroic histories superseding representations of Canada's men in arms thus occurred long before the United States entered either world war.

Despite the possibilities of heroic legend stemming from colonial warfare at home, best symbolized by the involvement of the North-West Mounted Police and the Royal Canadian Regiment in defeating Louis Riel in the North-West Rebellion of 1885, the advent of the twentieth century and Canadian soldiers' exploits in the South African War focused the country's sights on fighting for Canada while in foreign lands. In a rather caustic analysis, Morton states that South Africa had taught 'a warlike people how they could fight while remaining as essentially unmilitary as ever. They could go overseas' (1987: 633). This belief quickly became fact with the outbreak of the Great War, surrendering representations of Canadian soldiers and their actions to global opinion, American and British influence, and the judgment of historians for the rest of the century.

The Great War made Canada a nation. The Canadian Corps (Cook, 2006) was a legendary fighting force, regarded as the 'shock troops that were thrown into the bloodiest campaigns to deliver victory.' General Sir Arthur Currie (Canadian War Museum, 1919), commander of the Canadian Corps, proudly described his men as the 'hardest-hitting force' in the Empire. Between 1914 and 1918, soldiers were the dominant representation of masculinity in Western societies. The power associated with this supremacy helped to legitimize violence as a means of achieving cultural immortality on both an individual and a collective level among men in uniform. Connell (1995) has argued that national military forces 'show an organization effort to produce and make hegemonic a narrowly defined masculinity' that will make its participants emblematic of a national ideal of manliness. To this day, the Canadian shock troops of the Great War remain the watershed of modern military manliness in Canadian society, through their participation in the war

that heralded Canada's presence on the world stage and the individual acts of heroism that demonstrated the quality of Canadian bravery. At a time when America remained an isolationist country, avoiding international conflict as a matter of government policy, four Canadians were awarded the Victoria Cross for their actions at Vimy Ridge, perhaps the most exalted battle in Canadian history. Private William Johnstone Milne, Private John George Pattison, Lance Sergeant Ellis Wellwood Sifton, and Captain Thain Wendell MacDowell all were cited for their conspicuous bravery and devotion to duty while under attack. Only Captain MacDowell survived the war, underscoring the link between blood sacrifice on the battlefield and the nation's attainment of greatness.

Benedict Anderson (1983) sees the nation as an invented political society based on horizontal comradeship and fraternalism for which men would both kill and sacrifice. This notion of a sacrificial brotherhood introduces masculinity into the question of 'nation'. The link between nationalism and gender often has involved the use of male and female stereotypes of strength, weakness, and pride to foster feelings of patriotism. Nations have been culturally represented by female figures such as Eire, Britannia, Columbia, and Marianne. Masculinity and nationalism, meanwhile, have most often merged in the realm of militarization and warfare. The association of masculine virtue with soldiering and a martial lifestyle was a source of national strength and power during the era of the Great War, with romanticized violence encouraging cultural constructions of heroism, duty, and loyalty.

The claim that Canada achieved nationhood during the Great War has been argued by generations of Canadian historians, including Donald Creighton, Desmond Morton, and Tim Cook, although with certain caveats. Creighton (1969) argued that, in many respects, the First World War was 'the great divide in Canadian history', marking a time of cultural and economic expansion that was quickly lost in the postwar years. Cook (2006) declares that, although Confederation occurred in 1867, Canada was truly forged in the Great War, but also notes that the sacrifice of the conflict 'nearly destroyed the country' so that the 'colony-to-nation' myth heralded by previous generations of historians has to be tempered by acknowledging that the Conscription Crisis of 1917 was perhaps the worst blow to French–English relations in the twentieth century. Desmond Morton has, perhaps, the most interesting perspective on the importance of the Great War in Canadian military history. In the first edition of *A Military History of Canada* in 1985, Morton heralded Vimy Ridge as a triumph that showed the 'apprenticeship was over; the master work was complete' (2007: 144–5). He continued that Vimy was 'a nation-building experience' which, for some, symbolized Canada's war of independence against colonialism 'even if it was fought at Britain's side.' In his article 'Defending the Indefensible: Some Historical Perspectives on Canadian Defence, 1867–1987', Morton added a tone of division to his previous analysis, writing that if 'a sense of nationhood was born at Vimy in 1917, others remember that year for the Conscription Crisis, a scar so deep that Canadians can still feel it on their body politic' (1987: 635). However, his greatest about-face regarding Vimy Ridge came in November 2008, when he argued in the *Globe and Mail* (Morton, 2008) that Canadians should remember November 11 of 1871 rather than 1918 as our moment of independence, as the moment when British troops west of Halifax left Canada. Americans celebrate their liberation against Britain on the Fourth of July, and, Morton argues:

> Canadians are now being told by their government and its friends that we achieved the same joyous state on a snowy April 9, 1917, when four Canadian divisions advanced to capture Vimy Ridge at a cost of about 10,000 dead and wounded—enough to bring

on a nationally divisive crisis as the English-Canadian majority tried to conscript the French-speaking majority for a war Quebec had never embraced. This may be Stephen Harper's version of history, learned in the schools of Ontario. But that would be selling ourselves short. In fact, we have been on our own, at least militarily, since another Nov. 11— in 1871, to be precise. It was on that day when the 60th Rifles (Royal American) left Quebec's Citadelle, marched to the docks, boarded HMS *Orontes* and sailed for England. Forever.

Morton underlines that Canadians mourn our 60,000 dead in the Great War on Remembrance Day, but we forget those not included in that monolithic statistic, the 'savagely mutilated in mind or body' and their impoverished families because, ultimately, the Great War was a divisive and devastating event rather than a moment of heroic legend or mythic proto-nationalism. Morton does not criticize individual soldiers or their singular acts of bravery that no doubt truly merited awards and national renown; rather he castigates the political machinery around military remembrance, whose narrow focus oversimplifies the complexities of war into a series of important names and dates devoid of content, context, or contemporary relevance.

So what do these opinions mean in determining the role of Canadian military masculinities in the Great War? Obviously, the image of the Canadian soldier in the trenches remains one of the most potent representations of the military in Canadian society, remembered on the National War Memorial in Ottawa, the repatriation ceremony of the Unknown Soldier in May 2000, Canada Post's televised 'Heritage Minutes', the annual recitations of John McCrae's 'In Flanders Fields', and the war cemeteries visited by thousands of Canadians each year in France and Belgium. Criticism of the individual soldier was a rare activity, thereby preserving his singular role as a standard of manliness to be emulated by future generations; instead, contemporary and historical criticism grew around the institution of the military itself, its political manipulation and its effectiveness in battle as a representation of the nation. This was never more apparent than in the most contentious of Canadian military missions: the raid against Nazi-occupied France at Dieppe in August 1942.

IV

Dieppe is Canada's Gallipoli. Code-named 'Operation Jubilee', it is one of the most controversial episodes in the country's history, producing feelings of frustration, shame, betrayal, and failure. The planned attack was catastrophic (Balzer, 2006; Morton 2007), with 3,367 casualties out of the 5,000 Canadian troops involved. Alongside the Canadians (*Hamilton Spectator*, 1950) were British Commandos, some 50 American Rangers and a few Free French troops. Landing at Puys, the Royal Canadian Regiment was caught between the cliff and the sea and duly mown down. On the beach in front of Dieppe, the main force faced heavy gunfire, and the few groups of men who did enter the town were able to achieve very little. The use of tanks on the pebbled beach was futile. At Pourville, the South Saskatchewan Regiment and the Winnipeg Camerons were able to penetrate inland against relatively light opposition, but they were unable to reach their objectives and suffered massive casualties during the necessary withdrawal. Most of those captured spent the next three years of the war in captivity. By any measure, Dieppe was a tragic and disastrous event for both the Canadian military and the country.

In comparing the First and Second World Wars, essentially a contrast between Vimy Ridge and Dieppe, Creighton notes that although casualty rates were higher in 1914 to 1918, the nation as a whole was more profoundly affected by the war against Nazi Germany. 'The Second World War marked a fresh beginning in the Canadian experience,' he wrote, as the entire nation 'changed its direction and its pace. The next eighteen years brought an equally important alteration in its character' (1976: 37). This next phase in the search for Canadian identity included new paranoia and insecurity that, because of Dieppe, Canadian soldiers had not lived up to the standards of victory set in 1917. Of course, this was not what had been expected before the Canadian troops went into battle in August 1942. The previous May, the *Globe and Mail* had described the training Canadian soldiers received alongside the British Commandos. J.V. McAree (1942) recorded that commandos made 'a strong appeal to the hero-worshipping instinct' as 'they are all . . . potentially V.C. men.' 'We saw the other day,' he added, 'that Canadians are receiving commando training. None should take to it more readily.' In a similar vein, the *Hamilton Spectator* quoted Quentin Reynolds (1942), the war correspondent at *Colliers' Weekly*, that '"Canadians fight like Russians. There is no higher praise." Those two sentences are worth more to Canada in the eyes of their neighbours than the output of a regiment of press agents.' Homosocial interaction—the relations among men in all-male societies, organizations, and institutions—often could include instances of both peer pressure and currying favour. Impressing one's peers was important for men, on both an individual and a collective level. Reynolds's statement that 'Canadians fight like Russians' put the country's armed forces on par with a known military power and, according to the *Hamilton Spectator*, such accolades could only increase Canada's prestige in the eyes of its neighbour and, within such an impression, highlight the comparative manly quality of our troops.

The reality of 'Operation Jubilee' was, obviously, very different from what had been expected. War correspondents had an incomplete knowledge of the events (Balzer, 2006) and, partly because of censorship laws during the

war, emphasized 'heroic human-interest stories' in place of sombre casualty lists. Stories
of men's individual acts of bravery, including
those of Victoria Cross winners Lt.-Col. Charles
Merritt and the Reverend Lt.-Col. John Foote
were the initial focus for news reports from the
beaches. The *London Gazette* (1942) recorded
that Merritt won the Victoria Cross for 'matchless gallantry and inspiring leadership', while
the same newspaper noted that Foote (*London
Gazette*, 1946) 'personally saved many lives by
his efforts and his example inspired all around
him. Those who observed him state that the
calmness of this heroic officer as he walked
about, collecting the wounded on the fire-
swept beach, will never be forgotten.'

This journalistic tactic was encouraged by
the military authorities (Library and Archives
of Canada, 1942), as noted in a memorandum
for the Jubilee Communiqué Meeting, in the
files of the First Canadian Army, which stated
that, in case the planned raid was unsuccessful,

> We cannot avoid stating the general
> composition of the force, since the
> enemy will know it and make capital
> of our losses and of any failure of the
> first effort of Canadian and U.S. troops.
> Therefore, in the event of much failure,
> the communiqué must then stress the
> success of the operation as an essential
> test in the employment of substantial
> forces and heavy equipment. We then
> lay extremely heavy stress on stories of
> personal heroism—through interviews,
> broadcasts, etcetera—in order to focus
> public attention on BRAVERY rather than
> OBJECTIVES NOT ATTAINED.

Not only were the authorities at Combined
Operations Headquarters, including Lord
Louis Mountbatten and Canadian General
Andrew McNaughton, using stories of warrior
manliness to detract from the casualty rate and
failure of the mission, appealing to traditional
romantic war reporting in order to obfuscate

unpleasant realities about Dieppe, but they also
believed that the enemy would make much of
the Canadians' failure in battle.

When news of Dieppe first became public, Canadians were not immediately associated with the raid. In an ironic twist of fate,
the British Commandos and American Rangers
received the majority of initial press coverage.
It was not until 8 September 1942, nearly three
weeks after the battle, that Winston Churchill
clarified the central role Canadian troops had
played at Dieppe. Speaking in the House of
Commons (Hansard, 1942), he announced:

> It is a mistake to speak or write of this
> as 'a Commando raid,' although some
> Commando troops distinguished them-
> selves remarkably in it. The military
> credit for this most gallant affair goes to
> the Canadian troops, who formed five-
> sixths of the assaulting force. . . . The
> raid must be considered as a reconnais-
> sance in force. It was a hard, savage clash
> such as are likely to become increasingly
> numerous as the War deepens. . . . I,
> personally, regarded the Dieppe assault,
> to which I gave my sanction, as an in-
> dispensable preliminary to full-scale
> operations.

Before Churchill gave Canadians the credit and the responsibility for Dieppe (Balzer,
2006), C.P. Stacey had noted the American
emphasis on the participation of the US
Rangers and the overall lack of recognition
given to Canada. Creighton (1976: 76) recalls that the British and American troops
shared the credit when Dieppe was seen as
a success. He chides the British newspapers
for not knowing better, that they 'lavished
such quantities of praise on the navy, the RAF
and the Commandos that there was hardly
any space to acknowledge the mere presence
of the Second Canadian Division.' Despite
having trained with the Commandos and
being known in the American press for their

fighting abilities, Canadian troops once again came third behind British and American soldiers in terms of immediate association with battle and the soldiering lifestyle. This lack of heroic glory became all the more difficult to amend in the face of damning reports from the German troops regarding Canadian prowess under fire.

German intelligence reports (Stacey, 1944) stressed that 'The Second Canadian Division had lain for quite some time in the south of England, most of the time in camps. . . . Canadians on the whole fought badly and surrendered afterwards in swarms.' When news of the Nazis' poor evaluation of Canadian military prowess became public after the war (*Hamilton Spectator*, 1946), *Maclean's* warned its readers that 'there may be Canadians whose pride is touched—or who feel their reputations are tarnished—by what the Germans have recorded.' In the immediate aftermath of the raid, stories of singular Canadian courage were swiftly overshadowed by feelings of despair and failure. The *Globe and Mail* (1942a) reported that 'Dieppe, the name that thrilled the nation with high hopes scant days ago, has brought deep gloom to hundreds of Canadian homes. . . . That gloom will be slow to lift. No brilliance of valour in the field, no tale of sacrificial courage is quite enough to speed its passing.' While the *Globe* was one of the harshest critics of Mackenzie King's Liberal government, the *Ottawa Journal* also began to doubt the veracity of official stories about Dieppe. 'Can we be expected to know the truth,' it asked, 'and act upon it if those who are leaders keep the facts from us and try to feed us on sugar-coated stories?' (Balzer, 2006: 421). The *Regina Leader-Post* was also critical of any journalistic tendency to 'soften the blow, to minimize the losses, and accentuate the "glory" part of Dieppe.' Nearly a month after the raid, the *Globe and Mail* (1942b) began to question the Canadian force's effectiveness overseas, noting that it considered it unwise for Canada to 'expand her overseas force from a corps to an

army.' In April the next year, the *Globe* (1943) declared, 'Put aside the heroism of the men of Dieppe, and that action ranks as a fiasco of the first order; a tragedy of military blundering without parallel in this war.'

By the spring of 1943, the word most associated with Dieppe was 'failure', used in both the press and the House of Commons, particularly during debates between Dr H.A. Bruce, the Progressive Conservative MP for Toronto Parkdale, and Colonel James Ralston, the government's minister of national defence. Ralston consistently denied that Dieppe or the fall of Hong Kong in 1941 had been 'tragic mistakes'. Contrary to this (Cragg, 1943), Dr Bruce stated that operations had failed because of 'incompetent leadership in the High Command.' For the men at Dieppe, he added, 'Their ability, courage and tenacity were never doubted. There has never been any criticism of the men; on the contrary there has been nothing but the highest praise. One might with equal justice criticize the men who took part in the Charge of the Light Brigade.' Lord Keyes (Barclay, 1943), Mountbatten's predecessor as Director of Combined Operations in Britain, wrote:

> This generation was taught afresh at Dieppe the lessons which were indelibly impressed on the memory of all who witnessed at Gallipoli on April 25, 1915, the heroic but unsuccessful struggle and costly efforts to capture in daylight a much less heavily defended beach than that of Dieppe. . . . But the loss of over 3,000 Canadians with all their tanks was a heavy price to pay for the experience which, we are told, was gained in this ill-conceived and ill-fated enterprise.

On both sides of the ocean, Dieppe was associated with failure, inept command, and the shades of slaughter felt by the ANZAC troops at Gallipoli nearly 30 years before. C.P. Stacey had, in fact, cited Gallipoli as a precedent for the outcome at Dieppe in his official history for the Canadian Military (Balzer, 2006), but Combined Operations removed the reference to avoid 'damning comparisons'. Only in December of 1944 did a representative of the Liberal government acknowledge that Dieppe had been a mistake. When James G. Gardiner, minister of agriculture, announced that Dieppe had occurred 'just to prove we were not yet ready for a second front' to the Soviet Union, the *Globe and Mail* (1944) immediately added that it was 'a terrible admission to have to make that the operation was undertaken, not on sound military advice, but under public pressure. For this a noble band of young men was sacrificed; for this the Government has extolled its own virtues. It was a cruel thing to do.' The heroism of individual Canadian men in uniform, those like Foote and Merritt and the thousands of others who attacked the beaches, was never in question by the Canadian press; however, it was easy for them to lay aside those actions and to accuse the Canadian military and government as institutions symbolizing ineptness, failure, and the fatal bungling of operations.

The question of who was to blame for Dieppe's failure continued long after the war, debated among military authorities and generations of historians (Balzer, 2006; Mountbatten, 1974; Villa, 1990; Ziegler, 1986). What is of interest here, however, is how Dieppe's legacy affected the masculine nature of Canada's military prestige in the Second World War. The traditional vocabulary of warrior manliness from the Victorian era still existed when describing the individual soldiers, terms such as 'matchless gallantry', 'noble band', 'sacrifice', and 'heroism', but such romantic language rang hollow and was not what the public or the press fixated on; instead, Dieppe created a sense of impotence and betrayal that dampened the previous imagery of Canadian soldiers as the invincible shock troops who had proved victorious when all other countries had failed. Even C.P. Stacey's lauded official histories (Cook, 2006) have been 'often used by other historians to justify claims that the Canadians were

among the weakest fighting forces in Europe'. Now Canadians were lacklustre and ineffective, first failing to garner the largest headlines when it was thought that Dieppe was a triumph, then carrying the weight of responsibility when the raid proved to be a disaster. Lieutenant J.E.R. Wood, MC (*Globe and Mail*, 1947), formerly of the Royal Canadian Engineers and a prisoner of war taken at Dieppe, told the Empire Club of Toronto that the main reason for Dieppe's heavy casualties was 'the inexperience of the Canadians'. Even former members of the Canadian Army could not avoid associating Dieppe with failure, a feature that emasculated the troops en masse and complicated representations of manhood in the Canadian military for years to come.

If the historiography of Dieppe is one of controversy, then it is also one of controversial descriptions regarding the manliness of the Canadian troops, combining Victorian romantic rhetoric of brave warriors with tales of inexperience, failed objectives, and Canadians captured and in chains (Mountbatten, 1974). Lord Mountbatten ultimately regarded Dieppe as a success in that it was an invaluable mine of information for the eventual D-Day landings in 1944, an opinion shared by General Crerar, commander-in-chief of the Canadian Army overseas, Colonel C.P. Stacey, the official historian for the Canadian Army, and numerous future academics (*Globe and Mail*, 1945; *Toronto Daily Star*, 1948; *Hamilton Spectator*, 1948; Morton, 2007). Mountbatten himself seems to have retained much of his warrior's reputation after Dieppe. While Canadian newspapers (Bryce, 1942; Daniell, 1942) had noted the admiral's playboy reputation, 'daring courage', and chiselled good looks prior to August 1942, he was still held in high regard by many of his former subordinates up until his death. Killed by an Irish Republican Army bomb while onboard his boat in 1979, he had often visited with Dieppe survivors on his tours of Canada. Brig.-Gen. Forbes West (*Globe and Mail*, 1979), who was part of the Dieppe raid, believed that

Mountbatten had been 'the greatest soldier of World War II'. Lt.-Col. John Foote, winner of the Victoria Cross at Dieppe, added that he was 'a great admirer of [Mountbatten's] and he was very popular with the men'. Criticism of Mountbatten's culpability in the August 1942 episode seems to be confined largely to academics such as Brian Loring Villa (1990), who argued that 'Canadian troops had been used' at Dieppe. However accurate this sentiment may be, the association of Canadian troops en masse with terms such as 'failure', 'surrender', 'inexperience', 'weakness', and 'being used' all added to a public representation of Canada and Canadian soldiers as the 'other' in the Allied cause, a country less proficient at arms than Britain or America and, thereby, a military unit less immersed in the masculine world of warfare and conflict.

One of the more interesting footnotes to the Dieppe saga came in 1997 with a Bell Telephone commercial (Bell Canada, 1997). A young man backpacking through Europe calls his grandfather. Expecting stories of amorous conquests in Paris, the grandfather is shocked to hear that his grandson is, in fact, at Dieppe. As bagpipes play in the background, the camera pans to photos of the grandfather during World War II. The grandson then adds, 'I guess—I guess I'm calling to say "thanks", Grandpa.' Fighting back tears, the grandfather thanks the grandson for phoning. Apart from the obvious sentimental value of the commercial, the one-minute television spot also highlighted the tremendous importance Canadians continued to place on Dieppe as a site of national and martial identity. Rather than choosing to film on location at Juno Beach in Normandy, the site of Canada's victorious advance during the D-Day landings in 1944, a choice was made to film at Dieppe, a place haunted by memories of Canadian casualties. The nation's romance with moments of failure continues as the grandson thanks his grandfather for being at that specific battle. The emotional journey of the grandfather is also of note: beginning with joy and

hinted sexual nostalgia, before moving to surprise, shock, and, finally, tearful emotion. A young man is showing interest in the country's and his family's military heritage—not a young woman, interestingly, as though the backpacking odyssey for Canadians remained, at heart, a masculine adventure dating back to the time of the Grand Tour. Beyond this obvious reminder for young Canadians to honour their elders, the commercial also showed the emotional price of war, with the grandfather humbled by his memories of friendship and a lost battle rather than overtly associating his time in uniform with triumph or masculine pride. This was not a commercial emphasizing 'Be All You Can Be'. The fact that a mere 60 seconds of material could hold so many facets of Canadian martial manhood underscored the continuing complexity of war memories and identity in Canada and the sombre, almost reverential, tone that the single word 'Dieppe' could evoke.

In his final analysis of the Second World War, Creighton underscored that Canadian efforts had a secondary aim beyond defeating the enemy—to make a contribution that gained 'recognition for Canada as a separate and distinct Allied partner' (1976: 83), an ambition that was not successful. Instead, Canada remained within the British and American spheres of influence, with their potent notions of heroism and manliness informing our own, if not superseding the idea of Canadian martial masculinity entirely. To make an international impact that defined our men in arms, perhaps Canada, as a peaceful nation that fought its wars overseas, was better suited to keeping the peace than making war.

V

Peacekeeping was, without a doubt, a Canadian idea. The brainchild of Lester Pearson during the Suez Crisis of 1956, peacekeeping became synonymous with Canadian troops serving abroad for the next 45 years. As an ancient archetype, peace is a feminine notion, embodied by the Greek goddess Eirene and the Roman goddess Pax, as opposed to the brutal aggression and blood sport of Ares/Mars, the god of war. Conrad Black (1995) has proposed that our habitual need to define our identity, both within the country and without, may have contributed to the nation's 'flair' for the job, with Canadians providing nearly one-tenth of the United Nations' peacekeepers. Morton believes that Canadian support for institutions such as the UN and the Commonwealth are less a stance about collective global security than an avenue 'to escape suffocation in the bilateral alliance with the United States' (1987: 636). If peacekeeping is just a ruse to solidify Canadians' self-definitions of being 'not American', it has been rather successful. The popular 'Joe Canadian' beer commercial (Molson, 2000) used polite jingoism as a platform for selling not only alcohol but also an idea of Canadians at the dawn of a new century. Dressed in the uber-Canadian uniform of jeans and a plaid flannel shirt, 'Joe' epitomized the casual male Canadian: courteous, competitive (about hockey, at least), and full of comparative definitions between Canada and the United States, including the pointed reference 'I believe in peacekeeping, not policing.' 'The Rant', as it became known in the media, was a nod to the acceptable form of militarization for Canadian men (and women) in the twenty-first century, one which upheld Canadian moralistic values about the importance of pacifism while also creating a courageous reputation for Canadians in uniform.

However, there was a dark side to the legacy of Canadian peacekeeping and military involvement which stands as a counterpoint to all the heroic accolades Canadian soldiers have earned since the Great War. Although Canadians had been welcomed as keepers of the peace in Sinai, Cyprus, the Golan Heights, and Bosnia, the consequences of the 'Somalia Affair' dealt a severe blow to the international standing of Canadian men in uniform. The Airborne Regiment was formed in 1968, originating from two parachute battalions of the Second World War. It had served as a peacekeeping unit on numerous tours in Cyprus during the 1970s and 1980s and was deployed into Somalia in late 1992 as part of the overarching US-led mission 'Operation Restore Hope', a peace*making* intervention, according to Chapter 7 of the UN Charter. The Airborne Regiment (Morton, 2007) was known as a 'tough' and 'aggressive' force that soon had to settle in for months of heat and boredom in a land where the rule of law was non-existent. At night on 16 March 1993, Shidane Abukar Arone was captured on the military camp. Some soldiers tortured and killed him while taking photographs of the event. The crime and its subsequent attempted cover-up (Valpy, 2009) became known as The 'Somalia Affair'. According to news reports during the public inquiry (Farnsworth, 1994), Arone was blindfolded and tied up, then 'punched in the jaw, kicked with heavy military boots, struck with a baton, burned on the soles of his feet with a cigarillo and smashed in the shins with a metal bar.' Nine soldiers faced charges ranging from second-degree murder to negligence of duty. The main culprit, Master Corporal Clayton Matchee, attempted to hang himself after his arrest and suffered enough brain damage that he was deemed unfit to stand trial. Private Kyle Brown was found guilty of manslaughter and torture, dismissed from the army, and sentenced to five years in prison.

The reputation of the Airborne was further damaged by the revelation in March 1995 of the regiment's gruesome hazing rituals. A video of a 1992 hazing at the regiment's base in Petawawa, Ontario, showed drunken soldiers eating vomit and excrement (Farnsworth, 1995) and dragging 'a black trooper around on a leash with the legend "I love the KKK" written on the soldier's back.' The killing of Arone and these new revelations doomed the Airborne Regiment; it was disbanded by Defence Minister David Collenette in 1995. As the *New York Times* reported, the regiment 'once regarded as Canada's version of the Green Berets of the United States Army, had lost the confidence of Canadians' (Farnsworth, 1995: A7). The title of the Somalia Commission's findings, *Dishonoured Legacy*, aptly summarized the public shame attached to the Canadian military in the 1990s.

Aggression has been a lauded quality of the warrior mystique since antiquity; savagery, however, has no place in the list of gallant attributes. To the Western tradition of heroism, savagery and cruelty are anathema, examples of the 'other' at work on the battlefield. In Ancient Greece, the culture that gave the West its initial definitions of the heroic, the words for courage and manliness were the same: *andréia*. On a figurative level, the *andréia* of the Airborne Regiment disappeared when their actions became less than honourable. They became separate from the traditional Western (and thereby Canadian) examples of acceptable conduct in a warrior. Morally, their actions shamed the nation; historically, they were an unappetizing aberration from what Canadian soldiering had symbolized in previous decades and centuries; culturally, they made a familiar institution foreign. Instead of merely punishing a would-be thief and initiating recruits through demeaning ritual, the guilty members of the Airborne Regiment emasculated the Canadian Forces.

An article in the *New York Times* (DePalma, 1997: A13) questioned Canada's relationship with its 40-year history of peacekeeping and the appropriateness of using armies trained for war in the role of keeping the peace. It highlighted Prime Minister Jean Chrétien's phrase alluding to peacekeepers as 'Boy Scouts with guns', a complicated metaphor based on youth organizations, boys' culture, and assumptions of cleanliness and order mixed with violence. Retired general Lewis W. Mackenzie noted in the same article that, in Canada, 'Peacekeeping became an end unto itself and then we started to lose the warrior ethic. Soldiers became hesitant, asking themselves "Do I fire? Don't I fire?"' What kind of men were in Canada's military?

Were they the drunken, immature sadists of the Airborne videos and torture photographs, or were Canadian men in uniform meant to be something smarter, cleaner, and more impressive, harkening back to a different age? In a similar vein, to what extent were Canadians' controversial actions in Somalia emblematic of the nation itself or a violent display of the perceived Americanization within the forces since the end of World War II?

One of the more obvious possible Americanizations of Canadian military manhood came in the late spring of 2000, when Canada commemorated the national Tomb of the Unknown Soldier. The ceremony was presided over by Governor General Adrienne Clarkson and Prime Minister Jean Chrétien in front of a crowd of more than 20,000 people in downtown Ottawa (Corbett, 2000). Until then, Canadians paid their respects in Westminster Abbey to the Unknown Warrior, a soldier exhumed from the Western Front and buried among kings as a symbol of all the British and dominion servicemen who had died in the Great War. In distancing Canada from its imperial ties, however, did this solemn event evoke an American influence over Canadian military culture? Professor Richard Toporoski's 'Better dead in France than buried in Ottawa' (2000: A15) letter to the editor pointed out that the phrase 'Tomb of the Unknown Soldier' is an American expression based on a lauded grave at Arlington Cemetery. Furthermore, Toporoski emphasized that, as Newfoundland was not a part of Canada during either World War, the Canadian soldier buried in Ottawa truly was an unknown. 'They can reflect,' he wrote, 'that there is at least a small possibility that the soldier buried in the ancient church in Westminster might be a Newfoundlander. It is certain that the soldier buried in the traffic island in Ottawa is not.'

Toporoski is right in that 'Unknown Soldier' is a term more affiliated with American military remembrance than 'Unknown Warrior', and he is also thoroughly correct in noting that

Canada's honoured soldier could not possibly have been from Newfoundland. However, in an ironic twist, the *Oxford Dictionary of National Biography* (Stearn, 2004) disputes the possibility that the Unknown Warrior is any soldier from the New Army or the dominions, negating the possibility of Newfoundland's soldier as the unknown hero twice over. Furthermore, Britain's cenotaph in Whitehall is also part of a traffic island, like Canada's national war memorial, emphasizing the need to make war remembrance part of everyday activity, not something closeted away for most of the year. Perhaps the Government of Canada was making a more nationalistic or Americanized gesture in wanting to re-entomb a Canadian soldier in Ottawa as opposed to London, but in commemorating those who have fallen in battle, it is nearly impossible not to imitate some other nation's funereal rites. The Unknown Soldier in Ottawa is a British tradition wrapped in American language surrounded by Canadian rituals of remembrance. The tomb praises and sanctifies our national virtues: sacrifice, duty, courage, and, perhaps unavoidably, a controversy of definition and meaning in the public sphere. Re-buried under a flag he would not recognize—and perhaps not even like—the Canadian soldier from France is, ultimately, as unknowable as he is unknown. That, ultimately, is the conundrum at the heart of Canadian military manhood and its Anglo-American influences—it is everything and nothing, heralded one moment and denigrated the next, a site of change, debate, great feeling, and fleeting definition.

VI

Then came September 11, 2001, and the War on Terror. The *Toronto Star* noted that Canadians could 'take pride in having been among the very first, along with the British, to stand with Americans in their dark hours of loss' (*Toronto Star*, 2001: A26) and that Prime Minister Jean Chrétien's decision to send

Princess Patricia's Canadian Light Infantry to Afghanistan was 'just the latest evidence of Ottawa's clarity of purpose and strength of resolve'. No longer could Canada be accused of being 'soft' on terror. Militarism, however, remained an American vice. Despite our involvement in Afghanistan and the slow rehabilitation of the Canadian armed forces since the scandals of the 1990s, the Canadian public were not about to morph into militaristic warhawks. A line had to be drawn, and its creation ushered in new debates about the perceived weakness of Canadian military might.

The great break with American militarism came in March 2003 with Jean Chrétien's announcement that Canada would not participate in the Iraq war. It was met with cheers by Liberals and disapproval from the Conservative opposition (Sallot, 2003). Chrétien (DePalma, 1996) had once argued that 'Canada may not be a superpower but we are a nation that speaks on the international scene with great moral authority'. Now that sense of moral authority and, perhaps, superiority dictated that Canada would participate in the global War on Terror, but within Afghanistan only. Chrétien's statement did not materialize from nowhere: Stockwell Day (O'Neil, 2001), the former Canadian Alliance leader, had likened the prime minister to Neville Chamberlain, the British prime minister who tried to appease Hitler in the late 1930s and who, by many, was seen as a symbol of weakness and moral turpitude. The political opposition wanted to portray the prime minister as a cowardly figure, detached from popular opinion and unsuited to lead in a time of growing military uncertainty.

When the announcement came of Canada's non-participation in Iraq, it received a standing ovation from Liberals in the House of Commons, angry disappointment from the government of President George W. Bush, and questions about the quality of the Canadian armed services. Greg Weston of the *Toronto Sun* wrote that it was no secret that Canada has virtually no military might left to contribute to any kind of force anywhere. Existing peace-keeping commitments around the world are already straining Canada's military resources to the limits in both man-power and equipment. . . . This is def-initely no one's finest hour (2003: 15).

Coming after years of scandal and little positive media exposure, Canada's refusal to fight in Iraq appeared to be an admission of weakness to some, most notably CBC hockey commentator Don Cherry. On the 'Coach's Corner' segment of *Hockey Night in Canada* that aired four days after the government's decision to stay out of Iraq (*Kingston Whig-Standard*, 2003), Cherry famously chided the government for its 'lack of support for our American friends'. Sporting a star-spangled tie, Cherry declared, 'I hate to see them go it alone. We have a country that comes to our rescue, and we're just riding their coattails.' To Cherry, Canada was betraying the memory of the shock troops—soldiers and veterans he annually praised on episodes of Coach's Corner close to Remembrance Day—by refusing to fall in with its traditional allies. We were not brothers-in-arms but shirkers unworthy of our past heroic legacies. The troops were noble, but those in charge of sending them into battle were, in Cherry's estimation, lesser men.

While the press and media figures debated the relative machismo of Chrétien's decision not to fight alongside Britain and America in Iraq (Sallot, 2003), the prime minister distinguished Iraq from the War on Terror: 'Terrorism is in Afghanistan,' Chrétien said re-peatedly. As the number of Canadian casualties in Afghanistan grew, that statement became impossible to ignore. Something happened in the time between the 2005 announcement that Canada would take NATO responsibility for Kandahar province and the renaming of part of Highway 401 as the 'Highway of Heroes' in 2007. The militarization of Canadian society became acceptable to many Canadians. They might disagree with the mission in Afghanistan and want the troops to come home, but the soldiers themselves were increasingly held up as examples of beloved Canadian virtues and values: courage, duty, tenacity, valour, freedom, and fighting for peace.

Rick Hillier, the Chief of Defence Staff from 2005 to 2008, played a highly import-ant role in resanctifying the Canadian military tradition. According to the *Globe and Mail*'s Michael Valpy (2009), Hillier 'has been—and remains—an indefatigable apostle of Canada's military as warriors', yet also an officer who de-nies that this rebranding of Canadian soldiers is an Americanization of our troops. Hillier's media presence and genuine popularity across the country demonstrated the power one man could have in single-handedly rehabilitating a force left in metaphoric tatters by scandal and budget cuts. He and his successor, Walt Natynczyk, have emphasized the inclusiveness of the masculine warrior ideal (*The Economist*, 2008): gay soldiers marched in uniform for the first time at the 2008 Toronto Gay Pride Parade and also set up a recruiting booth at the event. Women have been accepted at the Royal Military College since 1980 and gays and lesbians have served openly in the Canadian Forces for nearly 20 years. The 'manhood' of the Canadian military is a microcosm of Canada's metaphoric Cultural Mosaic, encom-passing all of its soldiers in its vocabulary of armed service and *andréia*.

So, what does Canadian military manhood look like now? Traditional romantic language and associations remain part of the manly characteristics of military service. Canadians were at the forefront of NATO attacks against the Taliban (Wingrove, 2010), forming 'the tip of the spear' in Kandahar. The year 2010 marked the centenary of the Canadian Navy: a force that was once referred to by Stephen Leacock as a 'tin-pot navy' (Morton, 2007) was honoured by nearly two hundred separate events throughout the year, including conferences, balls, parades, a royal visit, and numerous material and public commemorations. Meanwhile, Canada's new immigration guide (Government of Canada, 2009) stresses the importance of the nation's military history and suggests that service in the Canadian Forces is 'a noble way to contribute to Canada and an excellent career choice'. Bearing arms has been a central attribute of manhood since feudal times, when manliness was qualified by skill in combat and chivalric bearing. Tosh has argued that the romantic chivalry Victorian men associated with warfare actually detached them from a military lifestyle, displacing 'valour and danger into a safe haven of agreeable fantasy' (2005: 65). Although this may have been the fashion at the time of Canadian Confederation, the dominion Sir John A. Macdonald helped to create no longer supports that kind of nineteenth-century thinking. While Canada as a country may prefer peace and democracy to war and terror, the country considers the institution of the military and the warrior culture it creates to be valuable, effective, and long-lasting. It is 'noble' again to wear the uniform of a Canadian soldier. The fact that few eyes blink at the notion that men and women can wear that uniform and equally represent the overarching warrior ethos and masculine attributes of military service is, if anything, the most Canadian part of our armed forces.

To say that the service and sacrifices in Afghanistan somehow erase the dishonour and iniquities of the 'Somalia Affair' is an oversimplification, as is using a masculine inferiority/superiority complex to explain the Anglicization and Americanization of Canadian military men since 1867. The British connection is unavoidable: it is part of our history through imperial and Commonwealth ties, providing an occasionally contentious legacy, but one that also has provided substance, affiliation, and historicity to Canadian men and women passing through the Triumphal Arch at the Royal Military College in Kingston, Ontario. The American influence on military manliness, as in all other realms of Canadian identity crises, has been both pervasive and immediate, awakening insecurities of

the 'other' and raising questions of our armed forces' contribution in a world where war itself tends to escape concrete definition. The elephant of American militarism casts a large shadow on its neighbours and friends. That nation's bold military aggression and action since 1941 has redrawn the power dynamics of global politics, and it is true that, as a middle power, Canada has at times been involved in American-led activities such as NORAD purely because of geographic circumstance rather than military consensus.

That said, Canadian military masculinity is not an American sideshow, nor is it a colonial bastardization of British tradition. General Wolfe's principle that a military man can never do too much has found new meaning in Canada some 250 years after his death at Quebec. Canada retains its martial links to Britain in many respects: the commander-in-chief of the armed forces is the governor general, the Queen's representative in Canada; the Prince of Wales, the Duke of York, the Princess Royal, the Earl of Wessex, Princess Alexandra, and other members of the royal family hold positions of colonels-in-chief for various Canadian regiments; military dress uniforms are lobster-back red; and the official march for the Canadian Navy is 'Heart of Oak', a song associated with the Royal Navy since the mid-eighteenth century. And yet we are increasingly detached from the sphere of British influence, despite the wishes of Donald Creighton. While representations of British officers informed Canadian ideals of the same up to and including World War II, the United Kingdom's direct influence on images of Canadian military manhood have notably weakened in the past 50 years. The British are now allies in the field, not standards of heroism our soldiers need to emulate.

Americana, on the other hand, is increasingly evident. Future historians of torture may mention My Lai, the 'Somalia Affair', and Abu Ghraib in the same sentence, citing them as demonstrations of battlefield apathy, misplaced fraternal anger, and aggressive cruelty (Connell, 2000) that have only enhanced the age-old link between masculinity and violence. To what extent is America linked to images of violence in the Canadian popular imagination? This is a question that demands a much more in-depth and contextualized analysis, but one which also could provide more concrete evidence about the extent of Americanized military culture north of the border. Our martial relationship with America has been both friendly and fraught in recent years. We are different from both the colonial 'motherland' and from our 'big brother' to the south. Rick Hillier is not General MacArthur. Afghanistan is not Vietnam—not yet, at any rate. Canada is not Britain or America. Our country's martial masculinity has been informed historically by both, but not defined by either.

The Highway of Heroes declares that the Canadian shock troops are back. Canada made the moral decision to fight in Afghanistan, not Iraq, and that, for some, vindicates our presence in Kandahar and honours our troops.

When they fall in battle, the nation mourns, and Remembrance Day has and will have new meaning for an entire generation. The Canadian public, often on its own initiative, wears red on Fridays, honours its soldiers, and keeps the home fires burning, not for peacekeepers, but for *warriors*. Canadian military manhood is not a gendered term separating men from women, but a system of language that imparts courage, valour, and a sense of communal service through aggressive action, regardless of an individual's sex. Its Canadianness lies in its universality of gendered applicability as opposed to a narrow definition of sex roles based on expectations of behaviour or physical strength and size. While the war in Afghanistan continues—while the shock troops enjoy their reincarnation—the accepted militarization of Canadian society can prosper. But, having embraced the military realities of the new century and the warrior manliness of old, what will happen when the boys and girls come home?

Discussion Questions

1. The author argues that Canadian historiography has a 'love affair with failure'. Do you agree or disagree? Support your answer with specific examples. How does this idea affect historical depictions of Canada's soldiers?
2. How have images of military masculinity changed through Canada's involvement in Afghanistan?
3. How strong is the influence American militarism has had on Canadian representations of heroism and manliness?
4. Is Canada a militaristic country? Why or why not?
5. In what ways have women been embraced as equals in the Canadian Forces? Is this acceptance superficial or will it last?
6. Which country has had a more lasting influence on the Canadian Forces—Britain or America? Why is this?
7. Is peacekeeping a masculine or feminine occupation?
8. Why is war so strongly connected to masculinity?

Recommended Websites

Canadian War Museum: www.warmuseum.ca

The Canadian Forces: www.forces.gc.ca

Juno Beach Centre: www.junobeach.org

Veterans Affairs Canada: www.vac-acc.gc.ca

Note

1. The author wishes to express her appreciation and thanks to Professor Gail Bederman and Professor Mark Noll and the Canadian History class at the University of Notre Dame for their insightful comments and assistance in bringing this chapter to fruition.

References

Anderson, B. 1983. *Imagined Communities: Reflections on the Origin and Spread of Nationalism*. London: Verso.

Busy Men's Magazine. 1912. 'In the Public Eye. A Character Sketch: Colonel Sam Hughes', 2 Feb.

Baden-Powell, R. 1908/2005. *Scouting for Boys*. Oxford: Oxford University Press.

Balzer, T. 2006. 'In Case the Raid is Unsuccessful . . .': Selling Dieppe to Canadians', *Canadian Historical Review*, 87, 3: 409–30.

Barclay, F. 1943. 'Dieppe Held Expensive Experiment', *Globe and Mail*, 6 July.

Bell Canada. 1997. 'Dieppe', http://wn.com/Dieppe_Bell_Commercial, accessed 10 Feb. 2011.

Black, C. 1995. 'Canada's Continuing Identity Crisis', *Foreign Affairs*, 74, 2: 99–115.

Blatchford, C. 2006. 'Losing the PR War at Home and Abroad', *Globe and Mail*, 30 Oct.

Bliss, M. 2006. 'Has Canada Failed?', *Literary Review of Canada*, 14, 2: 3–6.

Bryce, P. 1942. 'Lord Louis Mountbatten Commander of Commandos', *Toronto Daily Star*, 28 Aug.

Canada. 2009. *Discover Canada: The Rights and Responsibilities of Citizenship*. Ottawa: Minister of Public Works and Government Services.

Canadian War Museum. 1919. Fonds of General Sir Arthur Currie. MCG: Textual Records. 58A 1 61.4. Letter from Currie to M.H. Dobie., 9 Feb.

Connell, R. 1995. *Masculinities*, 2d ed. Cambridge, UK: Polity Press.

———. 2000. *The Men and the Boys*. Berkeley: University of California Press.

Cook, T. 2004. 'Review: Terry Copp, *Fields of Fire: The Canadians in Normandy* (2003)', *International Journal*, 59, 4: 994–6.

———. 2006. *Clio's Warriors: Canadian Historians and the Writing of the World Wars*. Vancouver: University of British Columbia Press.

Corbett, R. 2000. 'Canada's Lost Son "Lost No More": Thousands Pay Tribute to Unknown Soldier', *Ottawa Citizen*, 29 May, A1.

Cragg, K. 1943. 'Canada's Battle Honours "Two Tragic Failures," Dr Bruce Tells House', *Globe and Mail*, 26 May.

Creighton, D.G. 1969. 'The Decline and Fall of the Empire of the St. Lawrence', *Historical Papers/ Communications historiques*, 4, 1: 14–25.

———. 1976. *The Forked Road: Canada, 1939–1957*. Toronto: McClelland & Stewart.

Daniell, R. 1942. 'Tough Cousin of King George Trains Commandos and Is as Hard as They Are', *Globe and Mail*, 6 May.

DePalma, A. 1996. 'Canada Likes the Peacekeeper's Mantle', *New York Times*, 17 Nov., E3.

———. 1997. 'Canada Ponders Its Peacekeeper Role: Warriors or Watchdogs?', *New York Times*, 13 April, A13.

The Economist. 2008. 'Canada's Military: Hockey Sticks and Helicopters', 388 (8590), 26 July.

English, A. 2004. *Understanding Military Culture: A Canadian Perspective*. Montreal and Kingston: McGill-Queen's University Press.

Farnsworth, C. 1994. 'Torture by Army Peacekeepers in Somalia Shocks Canada', *New York Times*, 27 Nov., 14.

———. 1995. 'Canada Ends Top Regiment after Charges', *New York Times*, Jan. 25, A7.

Frye, N. 1976. 'Conclusion', in C.F. Klinck, ed., *Literary History of Canada: Canadian Literature in English*, 2d ed., vol. 2. Toronto: University of Toronto Press.

Globe and Mail, The. 1942a. 'Men of Dieppe', 24 Aug.

———. 1942b. 'The Misery of Dieppe', 16 Sept.

———. 1943. 'Why Sugar the Pill?', 27 April.

———. 1944. 'Mr Gardiner's Admission', 12 Dec.

————. 1945. 'Crerar Pictures Dieppe as Glorious Failure', 7 Nov.

————. 1947. 'Success, Failure Seen in Dieppe', 7 Feb.

————. 1979. 'Earl Took Part in Planning of the Dieppe Raid', 28 Aug., 2.

Granatstein, J.L. 1998. *Who Killed Canadian History?* Toronto: HarperCollins.

————. 2002. *Canada's Army: Waging War and Keeping the Peace.* Toronto: University of Toronto Press.

Hamilton Spectator. 1946. 'Dieppe Aftermath', 27 Feb.

————. 1948. 'Secret of Victory Given', 28 Aug.

————. 1950. 'Churchill Calls Dieppe "Mine of Experience"', 30 Oct.

Hansard. 1942. *House of Commons Debates*, vol. 383, col. 84, 8 Sept.

Juergensen, M. 2007. 'Portion of 401 to Become "Highway of Heroes"', *Globe and Mail*, 24 Aug.

Kingston Whig-Standard. 2003. 'Cherry Rips Habs' Fans for Booing U.S. Anthem', 24 March, 19.

Library and Archives of Canada. 1942. Memorandum for Jubilee Communiqué Meeting. Operation Jubilee papers. File 59-1-0 INT.215 C1 (D360), vol. 10708, RG 24.

Lipset, S. 1965. 'Revolution and Counter Revolution: The United States and Canada', in T. Ford, ed., *The Revolutionary Theme in Contemporary America.* Lexington: University of Kentucky Press.

London Gazette. 1942. 'Supplement', No. 35729, 2 Oct., 4323–4.

————. 1946. 'Supplement', No. 37466, 14 Feb., 941.

McAree, J.V. 1942. 'British Commandos Trained Like Athletes', *Globe and Mail*, 7 May.

McCormac, J. 1940. *Canada: America's Problem.* New York: Viking Press.

Meyer, M. 2000. 'Ulster's Red Hand: Gender, Identity and Sectarian Conflict in Northern Ireland', in S. Ranchod-Nilsson and M.A. Trétreault, eds., *Women, States and Nationalism: At Home in the Nation?* London: Routledge.

Molson Canadian. 2000. 'The Rant', /www.thai-software.com/Doug/IAmCanadian.html, accessed 10 Feb. 2011.

Morton, D. 1987. 'Defending the Indefensible: Some Historical Perspectives on Canadian Defence, 1867–1987', *International Journal*, 42, 4: 627–44.

————. 2007. *A Military History of Canada*, 5th ed. Toronto: McClelland & Stewart.

————. 2008. 'Yes, Think of Nov. 11—But 1871, Not 1918', *Globe and Mail*, 11 Nov.

Mosse, G. 1996. *The Image of Man: The Creation of Modern Masculinity.* Oxford: Oxford University Press.

Mountbatten, L., 1st Earl Mountbatten of Burma. 1974. 'Operation Jubilee: The Place of the Dieppe Raid in History', *Journal of the Royal United Services Institute for Defence Studies*, 119, 1: 25–30.

O'Neil, P. 2001. 'Canada Should Back Iraq Attack: Stockwell Day Accuses Chrétien of Being Like Neville Chamberlain', *Ottawa Citizen*, 22 Dec., A4.

Reynolds, Q. 1942. 'Actions Such as Dieppe Will Serve to Publicize Canada Best in America', *Hamilton Spectator*, 27 Aug.

Sallot, J. 2003. 'Canada Parts Ways with U.S. Neighbour', *Globe and Mail*, 18 March, A10.

Stacey, C.P. 1944. Headquarters, LXXXI Army Corps HQ, 22 August 1942, Intelligence Station, 'Intelligence Report on British Landing at Dieppe on 19 Aug 42', Canadian Military Headquarters Report No. 116, 'Operation "Jubilee" The Raid on Dieppe, 19 Aug 1942, Additional Information from German Sources', Department of National Defence, 10 May.

Stead, R. 1956. 'The Squad of One', in J.L. Gill and L.H. Newell, eds., *Invitation to Poetry: An Anthology for Junior Students.* Toronto: Macmillan.

Stearn, R. 2004. 'Unknown Warrior, The (d. 1914?)', in H.C.G. Matthew and B. Harrison, eds., *Oxford Dictionary of National Biography.* Oxford: Oxford University Press, www.oxforddnb.com/view/article/77079, accessed 16 March 2010.

Toporoski, R. 2000. 'Better Dead in France Than Buried in Ottawa', *Globe and Mail*, 8 June, A15.

Toronto Daily Star. 1948. 'Official Historian's Verdict about the Dieppe Raid', 4 May.

Toronto Star. 2001. 'Canada Pulls Its Weight in War on Terror', 16 Nov., A26.

Tosh, J. 2005. *Manliness and Masculinities in Nineteenth-Century Britain: Essays on Gender, Family and Empire.* Harlow, UK: Pearson Longman.

Valpy, M. 2006. 'Is the National Dream Over?', *Globe and Mail*, 11 March.

————. 2009. 'Canada's Military: Invisible No More', *Globe and Mail*, 20 Nov.

Villa, B. 1990. 'Mountbatten, the British Chiefs of Staff, and Approval of the Dieppe Raid', *Journal of Military History*, 54, 2: 201–26.

Weston, G. 2003. 'We, the Unwilling; Evasive PM Keeps Us out of Muddled War', *Toronto Sun*, 18 March, 15.

Wingrove, J. 2010. 'Canadians to Be "Tip of the Spear" in Kandahar', *Globe and Mail*, 17 Feb., A1.

Wolfe, J. 1768. *Instructions for Young Officers.* London: J. Millan.

Ziegler, P. 1986. *Mountbatten: The Official Biography.* London: Smithmark.

This section of the text has focused on themes that congeal a sense of what 'Canadian' means as an adjective, as well as its relationship with masculinities. From historical moments to popular culture and literature to the role of certain geographic and institutional locations such as Quebec and the military, we are looking for ways to identify whether and how there may be a Canadian understanding of masculinities.

Throughout our history human beings have come together, or been pulled apart, over matters relating to sport and competition. This can be relatively easily considered in gendered terms. When thinking about Canadian sports, hockey is almost certainly first to come to mind. In this chapter, Bridel and Clark begin with a desire to dig deeper, considering how lesser-known sports contribute meaning to Canada and to masculinities. They soon determine that Canada—both as a place and as an identity—is inextricably linked with hockey, and particularly men's ice hockey; in turn, these are linked with the construction of both nation and masculinities. In short, digging deeper doesn't reveal what they thought they would find about other sports' roles, but rather that the roots of hockey are deeper even than assumed.

Through historical and contemporary examples, this chapter synthesizes the developmental and cultural ideas explored throughout previous chapters. As well, it sets a foundation for Part III, which deals directly with the complexities of intersectional identities such as race, sexual orientation, and indigeneity by describing the dynamics and language associated with their construction and lived experiences.

If Canada Is a 'Team', Do We All Get Playing Time? Considering Sport, Sporting Masculinity, and Canadian National Identity

William Bridel and Martyn Clark

A Sikh man wearing a turban and a Canadian hockey sweater said it best. . . . 'I knew we had the players. What I didn't know was that we had the team.' We had the team. Not just in hockey, curling or speed skating. The team he was talking about was Canada. The country itself felt like a team (Ignatieff, 2010).

The gold medal game [in hockey] was a civic event—hockey is the thread that sews together the patches of Canada's cultural quilt—that begged to be shared among those of the maple leaf persuasion (Farber, 2010a).

The concept of nation escapes simple definition, in particular given the blurring of national boundaries in a time of significant globalization. Benedict Anderson contends that nations are in fact 'imagined' political communities (Anderson, 1991: 6). When you think about it, most members of a nation will never know one another and yet understand each other to be part of a shared national community. The imagined links between members of a nation are constructed through the shared histories and mythologies we tell about ourselves that come to be accepted as truths about the nation and its people. The construction of 'nation' and 'national identity', therefore, is a process. Importantly, the process is never complete, never static, and never uncontested. While many social institutions contribute to 'nation-building', our interest in this chapter is in the role that sport and sporting masculinity play in this process in the Canadian context.[1]

Sport has often been positioned as a way to develop individual and group identities through both participation and consumption. Ideas of nation, nationalism, and national identity have also been connected to sport, sporting events, and sporting figures (Cronin and Mayall, 1998: 2). Sport sociologist Alan Bairner has suggested that 'except in times of war, seldom is the communion between members of the nation, who might otherwise be classed as total strangers, as strongly felt as during major international [sporting] events' (2001: 17). Sport, it is argued, allows for the possibility of symbolic binding of the people of a nation, be it through the hosting of an international sporting event such as the Olympic Games or the celebration of an athlete or team's victory against rival teams from other countries. In brief, sport and sporting figures simultaneously shape and reflect dominant ideas of the nation. However, some sports and sporting figures, such as men's ice hockey and its 'star' players in Canada, for example, are often more connected to ideas of national identity than others.

Our initial intentions for this chapter did not include a focus on hockey because, to put it simply, we wanted to give less popular sports a space, and alternative sporting figures a voice, within the Canadian sporting landscape. But in trying to think about the particular role that sport and sporting masculinity plays in the construction of Canadian identity, we kept coming back to hockey and, in particular, men's ice hockey.[2] Though there are other sports and sporting figures in Canada, there is no question that hockey has been and remains dominant in mediated representations of sport, corporate marketing, and (some) people's everyday lives. And, importantly, it continues to be implicitly connected to Canadian society in largely celebratory ways. But what does this mean for Canadians who may play (and even excel at) other sports at the grassroots level or higher? What does this say about Canadians who (like one of the authors) do not have any real attachment or relationship to hockey? And most importantly, what does this say about Canada when ideas of Canadian national identity have been and remain so connected to hockey?

In a sense, we are beginning our chapter with what we intend as our conclusion. While many Canadians participate in and consume other sports on a daily basis, and may excel at them in international competition, the dominant representations of sport and sporting figures connect hockey and the men who play it to ideas of Canadian national identity. This contributes to a very specific idea of national identity—'Canadianness'—that is gendered and raced.[3] Therefore, in this chapter we contend that sport in Canada helps construct a national identity that is masculine and white as well as heterosexual and able-bodied.

In order to make this argument, we draw from the work of others in the academy who have previously considered the relationship of sport (in particular) and Canadian athletes to the production of national identity. We also turn a critical lens to mediated representations of sport and sporting figures both inside and outside of hockey at the 2010 Winter Olympic Games, given the overwhelming popularity of the Games and the dominant discursive constructions of the Games and its athletes in relation to nation-building. In order to explore these representations we draw on what scholars refer to as *critical discourse analysis*.[4] In particular, our analysis follows in the traditions established in Birrell and McDonald's critical inquiries into sport and their attestation that sports celebrities can be read as texts and that these readings 'offer unique points of access to the constitutive meanings and power relations of the larger worlds we inhabit' (2000: 3). Our analysis is further supported by texts that interrogate the ways in which Canadian identity is raced and gendered (and, thus, exclusionary).

In order to make the connection between sport, masculinity, and the nation clearer, we discuss the historical connection between hockey and ideas of Canadianness. We will show how this connection was fortified through media coverage of the 2010 Winter Olympic Games, coverage that privileged men's ice hockey and its male stars such as Sidney Crosby. We also consider how the stories of non-hockey-playing athletes such as Alexandre Bilodeau and Jon Montgomery—both of whom won gold medals at the 2010 Games—were filtered through hockey narratives and what this might mean. Finally, in order to emphasize that while men's ice hockey (and the form of masculinity it reproduces) is firmly and troublingly connected to Canadianness, mediated representations of male athletes (namely Simon Whitfield and Ben Johnson) show how even when hockey is not a part of the story, sporting figures are still used to produce particular ideas of Canadianness. Each idea in its own way is inextricably linked to the production of whiteness as the centre or 'norm' of Canadian identity, a norm that is mostly hidden by the ideology of multiculturalism.

Whiteness and Multiculturalism: Key Ideas

Similar to other scholars who have turned to interrogations of the production of whiteness through sport, our chapter is about the production of whiteness within the Canadian context.[5] It is therefore important before going any further to explain what we mean by the term 'whiteness'. We adopt the perspective that

racialized identities are the result of social formations, meaning that ideas of race can shift, alter, and be understood in multiple ways; race is not a static category. While 'race' is often constructed as any skin colour other than white, we work with the understanding that 'white' is also a socially constructed racialized identity. When it is not seen as such, whiteness is established as the invisible norm to which all other racialized identities are contrasted and subordinated. Within this chapter, we unpack constructions of whiteness and 'how it converges with other social categories that modify and fortify white privilege' (Levine-Rasky, 2002: 18). In the Canadian context, whiteness and white privilege are hidden by official multiculturalism and dominant discursive constructions of Canada as a nation of pluralities.

It is important to understand that many criticisms have been levelled at both the ideology and structural manifestations of multiculturalism since it was first introduced as an idea in the early 1970s and then formally institutionalized in the 1988 Multicultural Act. Many scholars, politicians, and community leaders have argued that the ideology behind multiculturalism does not play out in lived experience. On the surface, multiculturalism seemingly promotes a heterogeneous Canadian identity; however, what many argue is that, contrarily, it essentializes identities within an 'us/them' binary. The 'us' in this case represents white Anglophones and the 'them' is everyone else. Stated another way, multiculturalism, rather than creating a pluralist or multiracial national identity as it proposes, instead reifies a white Anglophone identity as the core or centre of Canadianness. When the core of Canadianness is white, English, and European, all other racial identities become constructed as 'other' or as 'visible minorities'. A visible minority can exist only if there is an 'invisible majority' to which it is contrasted and defined.[6]

Recognizing that, as Birrell and McDonald posit, 'the power lines of race, class, gender, and sexuality (and age, nationality, ability, religion, etc.) do not work independently and thus cannot be understood in isolation from one another' (Birrell and McDonald, 2000: 4), whiteness is not represented by all English/European subjects, but rather there is a very specific idea constituting the core or centre of Canadian identity. This idea is white, heterosexual, male, middle-class, Anglophone, and able-bodied and has been, as scholars have argued, represented through different archetypes and allegorical figures throughout Canada's short history. This contradicts the ideals of multiculturalism by reifying or rearticulating a very particular form of whiteness (and, more specifically, white masculinity) at the centre of a Canadian identity.[7] Undoubtedly these are all complex—but critically important—ideas. We hope to make them more clear by showing how sport and the dominant representations of sporting figures more specifically contribute to the production of white masculinity at the centre of Canadianness, beginning with a discussion about hockey and the particular form of masculinity reproduced in the sport.

Past to Present: Challenging Hockey's 'Natural' Link to the Nation

The hosting of the 2010 Winter Olympic Games in Vancouver, British Columbia, and the medal-winning performances of Canadian athletes there produced a heightened sense of national pride. Remarking on this, Liberal leader Michael Ignatieff declared Canada in its entirety a 'team'. It wasn't just the Canadian athletes winning Olympic medals; it seemed to be the entire nation's win. But while Canadian athletes won 26 medals, 14 of which were gold (setting a new record for most gold medals won in a single Winter Games), Sidney Crosby's overtime goal that clinched victory for the Canadian men's ice hockey team seemed to mean more than any other moment at the Olympic Games. His goal, and the team's win, has become the stuff of legend, already being referred to in popular discourse as a defining

moment in Canadian history. This is just the most recent representation of hockey's tie to the nation, a tie that is anything but natural, though it is often presented as such.

Sport historian Michael Robidoux contends that ice hockey has been one expression of nationalism that has remained constant since Canadian Confederation but is not, as so often presented, a 'natural' Canadian cultural resource that emerged from out of Canada's wintry environment (see Chapter 7 in this text). Rather, hockey is a socially and culturally constructed phenomenon that follows broader social and cultural trends (Gruneau and Whitson, 1993). We will not give an exhaustive history of hockey here, as others have gone a long way toward accomplishing this.[8] However, key aspects of that history shed light on hockey's connection to the Canadian nation today.

Hockey's popularity in Canada began in the mid- to late nineteenth century precisely because of the type of masculinity displayed within it and how it was seen by many as a truly Canadian game. At this time organized sport was largely understood as a means of social control and conditioning (Jarvie and Maguire, 1994: 109) that helped foster the 'manly virtues' deemed necessary for a strong national community.[9] Institutionalized sports in the British colonies such as cricket served to reproduce a Victorian social order in which young men learned to be 'gentlemen' (Robidoux, 2002: 212). The indigenous game of baggatway (later renamed lacrosse) was Canada's first truly popular game because it was different from British sport. Baggatway allowed white colonists—first French-Canadian men and later other white men—the opportunity to display a violent and aggressive form of masculinity practised by First Nations men that seemed to speak to the lived experience of settler colonial life in northern North America. An emergent Canadian ruling class looking to forge a 'truly Canadian national identity' that was different from Britain and the United States advocated for baggatway/lacrosse's national adoption because of the rough and tough masculinity displayed in the sport that set it apart from more gentlemanly sports.

In an effort to solidify baggatway as a dominant part of Canadian sport culture, individuals in power modernized it, stripping the sport of its indigenous roots by renaming it lacrosse and creating formal rules and restrictions on play. As part of this modernization, only those who were considered 'amateurs' (in this context, gentlemen) were allowed to play, forcing men from various other ethnic and class backgrounds to look elsewhere for sport. According to Robidoux, this opened the door for sporting enthusiasts to embrace other uniquely Canadian sports such as hockey (Robidoux, 2002: 218). While lacrosse became exclusive, hockey—a sport that provided the same violent, aggressive, and masculine type of play desired by Canadian nationalists—was more accessible to the masses. So while we often think of hockey as a natural part of Canadian history, it in fact emerged out of a very specific sociocultural context and for very specific reasons. As lacrosse's popularity waned because of the restrictions placed on participation, hockey's popularity grew.

By the 1920s, hockey had emerged as the most popular sport in Canada. At the same time that Canadian society was becoming more industrial, urban, and commercial, hockey was becoming more professional and being sold to Canadians by businessmen who controlled the professional game, seeking to profit from it. By the end of the 1930s, millions of English and French Canadians were tuning their radios to National Hockey League (NHL) games on CBC's *Hockey Night in Canada* (HNIC), leading scholars to suggest that 'never before had so many Canadians in all corners of the country engaged in the same cultural experience at the same time' (Gruneau and Whitson, 1993: 101). By the 1950s HNIC radio broadcasts had become well established as a Canadian national ritual, and despite there being only two Canadian teams— the Montreal Canadiens and the Toronto Maple Leafs—the NHL was unquestionably the most dominant hockey league in Canada. The move of HNIC to television in 1952 allowed the NHL and new hockey stars such as Maurice Richard, Gordie Howe, Bobby Hull, and Bobby Orr to gain popularity. This all helped to cultivate even larger Canadian audiences, a trend continuing into the 1970s, a time of significant cultural, political, and economic change in Canada.

The 1960s and 1970s were two decades fraught with challenges to the idea of a singular Canadian national identity; feminist and sexual liberation movements, threats of Quebec separatism, and the emergence of the ideology of multiculturalism all contributed to questions of Canadianness at the time. Despite these struggles in the broader social context, hockey became a particularly Canadian institution that continued to symbolically join Canadians together (Gruneau and Whitson, 1993: 276–7). In short, hockey was used to help Canadians imagine themselves as part of a shared national community. This is evidenced through the Canadian victory over the Soviet Union in the 1972 Summit Series.

The 1972 Summit Series pitted Canadian-born NHL players against men from the Soviet Union in an eight-game series that was constructed in the Canadian media as a Cold War battle between East and West. This fostered an 'us versus them' dynamic in which Canadians were encouraged to cheer for Canada's representatives. As popular writers and academics alike have noted, the Summit Series gained mythic stature as a major cultural rather than just sporting moment.[10]

Millions of Canadians, children and adults alike, watched the games in person or on television. However, more than just cheering on Canada in an East versus West scenario, Canadians also cheered for a very particular style of play. As Michael Robidoux points out, in order to win, the Canadian team resorted to physically assaulting the arguably more skilled Soviet squad and literally fought their way to victory (Robidoux, 2002: 212). Thus, the Summit Series cemented the 'Canadian style' of hockey as violent and aggressive at the same time as it was heroic and chivalrous. The Canadian players were constructed as heroes not only for the victory but also for quite literally 'beating' their Soviet competitors.

The Summit Series went a long way toward connecting a violent and aggressive style of hockey to Canadian culture. Several events of the 1980s and 1990s revealed the significance of this connection even further. As one example, in 1988 NHL superstar Wayne Gretzky, arguably the best-known Canadian athlete of all time, was traded from the Edmonton Oilers to the Los Angeles Kings. Gretzky's trade was understood less as a trade and more as a cultural blow, a symptom of the broader Americanization of Canadian culture at the time (Jackson, 1998). Fear of Americanization was further exacerbated in the early to mid-1990s, when two Canadian NHL franchises, the Winnipeg Jets and the Quebec Nordiques, were sold to American business interests and replanted in US cities while several other Canadian teams struggled to survive. On the international stage, the national hockey teams, comprising NHL players, did not win two major tournaments that the 'country' expected them to: the 1996 World Cup of Hockey and the 1998 Winter Olympic Games. This all incited fear that Canada was losing its grip on hockey (*our* game!) and not only led to concerns expressed around water coolers in offices all over the country and in the media, but also sparked a Hockey Canada conference that proposed to try to find ways to reassert Canada's dominance in the sport at the international level.

Thus, when the Canadian men's ice hockey team won the gold medal at the 2002 Winter Olympics in Salt Lake City, it provided (supposedly) all of Canada a chance to celebrate *our* victory in *our* game, a celebration that (perhaps not surprisingly) took on much different meaning than the gold medal win of the Canadian women's ice hockey team at the same Games. Sport sociologist Mary Louise Adams

has suggested that 'although the [Canadian] women's victory [in Salt Lake City] was certainly seen to be sweet, it was celebrated in much the same way as victories in speed skating or skiing. It was not portrayed, as the men's victory would be, as confirmation of the "hockeyness" of this country or as a boost to national morale' (2006: 72). Even at the 2006 Games, when the Canadian women won hockey gold (again!) and the men finished a dismal seventh, the women's victory was in no way given the same level of recognition or prestige in the Canadian media; rather it was constructed along the same lines as the other non-hockey medals won, similar to the way it was written about in 2002.

However, nothing matches the epic nature of the 2010 Games and the quest for men's ice hockey gold. While significant amounts of money were allocated to Canadian medal hopefuls through the Own the Podium program, with the goal of winning the most medals of any nation, no gold medal seemed to count nearly as much as men's hockey gold. And so when the Canadian team qualified for the gold medal game against the United States, the stage was set for a major national drama to unfold.

No event at the Olympics came close to attaining the same amount of national attention as the men's final game. An estimated 20 million Canadians tuned in to at least some part of the broadcast on CTV, while 16.6 million Canadians watched Crosby slip the puck past US goaltender Ryan Miller (Dojc, 2010: 19). This was more than twice the number of viewers who watched the Canadian women win gold and constituted the largest audience in Canadian television history to that point in time. Immediately following the 'fairytale ending', swarms of Canadians spilled out into city streets dressed in red and white, waving Canadian flags in celebration of *Canada's* triumph. It is interesting, to say the least, that sport, and especially men's ice hockey, elicits such a strong nationalistic response across the country. This clearly displays the close relationship that exists between sport and its cast of hetero-normative, white, able-bodied, male characters, such as Crosby, with the nation and Canadianness.

Crosby, it follows, came to represent Canada's overall success at the Olympics; his image was plastered over magazine covers, newspapers, the television, and the Internet during and after the Games. Crosby is white, able-bodied, and heterosexual (we don't know otherwise), and, although he rarely fights, he plays a hard-nosed, aggressive style of the game that is said to be 'Canadian'. In what is very much taken for granted (and therefore problematic), Crosby comes to represent another manifestation of the particular type of sporting masculinity that is connected to notions of Canadianness. He easily represents Canadian identity in contemporary times because he symbolizes the (invisible) white masculine centre of Canadianness that is reproduced in men's ice hockey. And when a *Sports Illustrated* article following the 2010 Games claimed, 'The gold medal game was a civic event—hockey is the thread that sews together the patches of Canada's cultural quilt,' it seems common sense (Farber, 2010b: 36). However, if hockey is the thread that holds life in Canada together, then, as Adams deduces, and as we have attempted to articulate here, life in Canada is decidedly 'white and masculine' (Adams, 2006: 71).

And herein lies the significant problem of the continued connection of men's ice hockey to Canadianness. Though Canada is often constructed as a nation that allows for a range of masculine (and feminine) possibilities, a contextually privileged or hegemonic form of masculinity always emerges to which other masculinities and femininities are subordinate. The hegemonic or dominant form of masculinity typically associated with sport is one in whole or in part that promotes, expects, celebrates, and reveres aggression, violence, power, brute strength, and the physical domination of one's opponents. It is a masculinity that seems to promote a 'win at any cost' mentality and it

is a form of masculinity in which one's body might be used as a weapon of sorts—regardless of the outcome to one's well-being. It is a masculinity that is largely unemotional and one that is constructed in opposition to traditional conceptualizations of dominant femininity, and one that, as such, has remained atop the gender hierarchy.[11]

Within the Canadian context it is all of these things while also simultaneously demanding graciousness, civility, and humility. In short, Canadians seem to like their male athletes to be tough, competitive, and dominant on the field of play while at the same time gracious in victory and defeat, polite and civil beyond the sport barriers, perhaps best exemplified by Wayne Gretzky in the eighties and nineties and Sidney Crosby today. It is a very particular, exclusionary form of white masculinity that—admittedly—not every white male hockey player in the country performs. However, it is the largely dominant form of masculinity reproduced within the sport of hockey.

Academic investigations of ice hockey have shown that the NHL continues to showcase aggressive forms of masculinity, most obviously in on-ice fighting. For example, Sarah Gee has examined the contemporary mythological hockey 'warrior' character represented in the NHL's 2005–6 'Inside the Warrior' advertising campaign, arguing that the NHL continues to promote and reinforce a form of hegemonic masculinity that closely articulates with the masculinist underpinnings of sport and its status as a male preserve (2009: 578). Similarly, Kristi Allain demonstrates how peripheral NHL media such as Don Cherry of 'Coach's Corner' on HNIC reinforce violent masculine stereotypes. She notes that the widely popular Cherry is 'openly hostile to those who want to diminish expressions of hegemonic masculinity, including fighting, within the game' (2008: 472). Ultimately, Allain argues that mass cultural representations of hockey work alongside the structure of the game and its players' own performances of masculinity to create a desirable masculine practice within Canadian junior hockey, suggesting the ways in which representations of elite or professional levels of sport may play out in lived experience at other levels of the game. Furthermore, the reproduction of a very particular type of masculinity within and through men's ice hockey (the game and mediated representations) influences greatly who gets to play, how the game is played, how it is represented in popular discourse, and what this means for those who perform other types of masculinities and femininities. It also, oddly, seems to influence representations of athletes who gain success in other sports besides hockey.

Non-Hockey-Playing Athletes and the Reproduction of Canadianness

There are other popular sports besides hockey that Canadians participate in and/or consume on a regular basis. Soccer, for example, has the largest number of participants of any sport. Curling is a popular spectator sport. Skate Canada is the largest figure-skating organization in the world, boasting an annual membership of approximately 200,000. Softball, golf, football, rugby, swimming, gymnastics, skiing of all sorts, and myriad other sporting activities all hold a place in the Canadian sportscape. Though there are multiple sporting opportunities available to Canadians, none holds the prestige of hockey. Perhaps Gamal Abdel-Shehid articulated this best: 'There are other "important" Canadian sports, such as rowing, lacrosse, and curling. But these are second in popularity to hockey. There is, if you will, a third place (space?) of sports (basketball, track and field, boxing) in Canada' (2005: 98). The marginalization of these sports works to reify hegemonic forms of masculinity within hockey, thereby subordinating other forms of masculinities and femininities. Despite this marginalization, certain Canadian sporting figures excelling in these more peripheral sports are often still represented in ways that also reify a version of Canadian identity that asserts white

masculinity as its core. This includes the representations of certain athletes as 'All-Canadian' while discursively stripping others of their Canadian citizenship (a point to which we will return). It also includes the use of, strangely, hockey as a filter through which to construct narratives of non-hockey-playing athletes.

A Freestyle Skiing Gentleman and a Skeleton Daredevil: New Canadian Identities?

Journalist Andrew Coyne proposed that a new Canadian identity was displayed at the 2010 Winter Olympics based on the ideas of winning at all costs, national pride, and being boastful about it while perhaps maintaining a little bit of generosity and compassion. Rather than using Crosby or any other male hockey player to symbolize the new, 'cocky' Canadian identity, he proposes that it is represented best by two other Olympic gold medal winners: '[freestyle skier Alexandre] Bilodeau, with his manifest decency and humility, whose first thought on winning was of his disabled brother, [and skeleton athlete Jon] Montgomery, the muscle-flexing, beer-swilling skeleton dare-devil, who only took up the sport as a way to get to the Olympics' (2010: 187). Though constructing the two athletes as quite different, Coyne suggests that there is in fact no contradiction between the two and that the new Canadian identity is all of these things: 'we can hold fast to those traditional Canadian virtues of compassion, generosity, and fairness, and still be aggressive, ambitious, and competitive as all get out' (ibid.). While constructing two non-hockey-playing athletes as personifications of Canadianness might appear on the surface to challenge what we have argued thus far is a problematic connection between hockey, masculinity, and the production of whiteness at the centre of Canadian identity, the ways in which Bilodeau and Montgomery were constructed in the majority of the mainstream media instead reify the connection, given the rather odd usage of hockey as a filter through which to tell their stories.

Alexandre Bilodeau took on a special symbolic role at the 2010 Winter Olympic Games mainly because he was the first Canadian athlete to win an Olympic gold medal on Canadian soil. On 14 February, he finished first in men's moguls at the Cypress Mountain venue, 'delivering a piece of history to the 2010 Canadian Olympic Team and to all Canadians' (Canadian Olympic Committee, 2010). The *Globe and Mail* stated that Bilodeau was 'Canada's newest hero' and that his victory was 'shared by an entire nation' (Blatchford, 2010). Michael Chambers, outgoing president of the Canadian Olympic Committee, likened it to Paul Henderson's goal in the 1972 Summit Series (MacQueen, 2010). In a Vancouver2010 news release following his victory, a humble Bilodeau tried to put the hype about his gold medal into perspective by stating that 'the first gold medal is not worth more than the last' (Anonymous, 2010). The last gold medal won at the 2010 Games was in hockey, and Bilodeau's supposedly inadvertent comment gained much media attention with great speculation about his intention behind the statement: 'There will be many Canadian golds, [Bilodeau] predicted, and the first is worth no more than the last. By that he meant all golds. But just maybe the kid who quit hockey was also hoping the last would be won with sticks and a puck. It would be a sweet moment to reflect on the life-changing sacrifice he made for his brother and his family, and all that work and wonder that brought him to the mountaintop' (MacQueen, 2010: 83).

In all of this it is suggested that Bilodeau wished for gold in men's hockey because, as is made abundantly clear, he was a hockey player first and a freestyle skier second. Beyond the reference to the 'sacrifice he made' by giving up hockey, it is also noted that his father was a 'skilled' major junior hockey player. Furthermore, we are told that Bilodeau might well have continued playing hockey, a sport he was 'passionate about as a young boy', but that hockey excluded his brother, who has severe cerebral palsy. Bilodeau's mother urged him to

take up skiing, a sport his brother could access. Though he won gold in freestyle skiing, hockey factored heavily into media representations of Bilodeau in much the same way as it did in the stories of Jon Riley Montgomery.

Five days after Bilodeau won his event, Montgomery won gold in men's skeleton, a dangerous sport in which men and women slide head-first down an icy track at speeds of more than 135 kilometres an hour. Montgomery became more than another Olympic gold medallist when, captured by camera crews, he marched down Vancouver city streets 'chugging' a pitcher of beer in celebration of his win. It was an image that solidified him as a beer-drinking, crazy partier—a sort of 'hardcore' Canadian athlete. However, his construction as hardcore seemed to have less to do with his participation in skeleton and more to do with his name. Montgomery's name was 'derived from a pair of tough-as-nails NHL players'—Stan Jonathon and Terry O'Reilly—who were former teammates on the 'big, bad Boston Bruins' (Longley, 2010). *Maclean's* also focused on Montgomery's name, referring to his two namesakes as 'the two most ruthless pugilists in the NHL.' The article goes further to explicate his connection to hockey: 'Jon himself grew up playing hockey. A proud Canadian, he wears his patriotism less on his sleeve than over his heart, where he had a maple leaf tattooed as a teenager' (McIntosh, 2010: 118). Hockey, it seems, is never far away from stories of Montgomery, as yet another article suggests Montgomery's victory could in some way be attributed to former NHL player, Theo Fleury, who Montgomery stated was one of his heroes and who had led him to believe that if you 'wanted anything you needed to hang tough' (Starkman and McGran, 2010).

Both Bilodeau and Montgomery were constructed as Canadian heroes and icons both for their victories and for their behaviours following (despite the fact that their post-win reactions were quite different). While each seemed to represent a different type of 'Canadianness' (i.e., Bilodeau as the humble and polite citizen and Montgomery as the beer-drinking, partying, exuberant, and 'cocky' citizen), their stories, we contend, reaffirmed ideas of Canadianness that are tied to white masculinity. Though both athletes were constructed as representing a 'new type of Canadian identity', it really was the same old thing, in particular when hockey imagery became such a key part of the narratives created about them.

The use of hockey is not unusual in the constructions of white male athletes participating and succeeding in sports that seem to require or promote less dominant forms of sporting masculinity. For example, academics interested in the production of gender and sexuality within the sport of figure skating have suggested that often male figure skaters are represented in the media as having ties to hockey. Without ever stating as much, this connection works to masculinize the stars of a sport which is often (at least in North America) positioned as being mostly a sport for girls.[12] In other words, when hockey is used in narratives about sporting figures, a very particular form of white masculinity works to shape our understandings of these figures as well as our understanding of national identity, given the ideological relationship of sport to the nation. That said, and in keeping with our earlier assertion that this is not a paper exclusively about men's ice hockey, there are other ways in which white masculinity is reified as the centre of Canadian identity without having to mention ice hockey at all. And so here we move outside the hockey rink (for sure this time!) and consider what others in the academy have argued with respect to the production of whiteness and national identity through sport.

A Triathlete and a Sprinter: On the Reification of White Masculinity as Canadianness

On 16 September 2000, Simon Whitfield produced a spectacular burst of speed in the last kilometre of the inaugural Olympic triathlon, surging into the lead. He went on to win the race, securing his place in both Canadian and Olympic history. Not only was this the first time the sport of triathlon had been held at the Olympic Games but Whitfield's win was the first by a Canadian athlete at the event. Headlines proclaimed him 'Canada's golden boy' (Young, 2000: 1). The fact that the 25-year-old triathlete had not been considered a legitimate medal contender by most, in addition to the 'come from behind' nature of his win (he began the run portion of the race in 25th place), only furthered the excitement of and attention to his victory. As Neil Stevens of the Canadian Press wrote: 'Whitfield had been so far behind during the first two segments that, in retrospect, his win has to go down as one of the most amazing feats in Canadian sports history' (2000). Following his victory, Whitfield became an instant star of the Canadian team (he was selected to carry the Canadian flag into the closing ceremonies), the Canadian media, and sponsors.[13] The relevance of Whitfield's victory to this chapter is in the ways in which he was constructed by the Canadian sport media following his gold medal performance. His victory, and the way he handled himself following, reproduced certain qualities connected to Canadianness that did not rely on hockey and yet that reified the white masculinity at its centre nevertheless.

In an in-depth analysis of the media representations of Whitfield, Simon Darnell and Robert Sparks suggest that he was constructed overwhelmingly as a Canadian national hero, demonstrating characteristics of what is often considered ideally Canadian: overcoming adversity and being gracious in the face of victory (read: polite!). Furthermore, Whitfield was said to 'embody the kind of wholesomeness, honesty and self-effacing character that typify the "boy next door" and that have long been the hallmark of Canadian heroes' (Darnell and Sparks, 2005: 358). He was, in every way, the 'all-Canadian golden boy'. The only difference between Whitfield and the more recent representations of Bilodeau and Montgomery is that there was far less reliance on hockey to create his story.[14]

The representations of Whitfield—the tri-athlete who brought pride to Canada through his victory at the 2000 (and his silver medal at the 2008) Olympic Games—not only further cement the idea that sport continues to contribute to notions of Canadian identity but, importantly, that this identity continues to be linked to white masculinity without ever having to say so. That is how whiteness operates; it is the unspoken, 'invisible', normalized centre to which all other citizens are contrasted. This is particularly evident in the construction of Whitfield as the 'all-Canadian boy', as this speaks to the ways in which Canadian identity is most often tied to whiteness without ever saying as much. That is, despite the supposed multicultural context of contemporary Canadian society (and thus, what should be contested meanings of citizenship and national identity), the representations of Whitfield (as just one example) are 'shaped by a tacitly racist conception of a "Canadian" as someone who is white and middle class with Anglo-centric sensibilities' (Darnell and Sparks, 2005: 373). In quite a different way (but with the same end result), narratives created around sprinter Ben Johnson only further solidify normalized notions of Canadianness with white masculinity.

Ben Johnson, a world champion and world record holder at one point in time, became a Canadian icon when he won the gold medal in the 100-metre event at the 1988 Olympic Games in Seoul, Korea. However, after he tested positive for performance-enhancing drugs, his title was stripped by the International Olympic Committee and his gold medal taken away. Prior to the announcement of his failed drug test, the Canadian media had represented Johnson as a hero and a success story. Following the decision that ended in the loss of his (and Canada's) gold medal, Johnson was very specifically constructed as a failure and a villain, and—ultimately—was discursively stripped of his Canadian citizenship. The fact that he was an immigrant from Jamaica became the primary way in which his identity was constructed.

Not subtly, once Johnson's failed drug test was made public, there was a 'progression in the representation of Ben Johnson from one of a "Canadian hero" in victory to one of a "Jamaican" after disqualification' (Abdel-Shehid, 2005: 73). Steve Jackson similarly contends that, save for the period of time when Johnson's racial identity was temporarily displaced by the label of 'Canadian' (a period of time that coincided with his reign as world champion), 'the media almost always represented Ben Johnson through signifiers that defined him as the "racial other"'. In other words, when successful, Johnson was labelled unquestionably Canadian, a prime example of the progressive immigration policies and opportunities for immigrants in Canada, seen to correspond with multiculturalism. However, once his athletic success was no more (i.e., when he lost the title of both Olympic champion and 'world's fastest man') Johnson was similarly discursively stripped of his citizenship.

In his excellent and important text *Who Da Man? Black Masculinities and Sporting Cultures*, Gamal Abdel-Shehid (2005) exposes the problematic nature of sporting cultures and nations more generally, arguing that both aspire to the production of sameness and homogeneity, thereby effectively erasing social differences (i.e., race).[15] He does this by interrogating not only the representations of Ben Johnson following the 1988 Olympics but also other Black athletes such as Olympic wrestling champion Daniel Igali, the Toronto Raptors, and Black quarterbacks playing in the Canadian Football League. The constructions of these athletes and Black athletic masculinities in Canada work to produce what Abdel-Shehid refers to as the 'whitening' of the Canadian nation. In an effort to create the illusion of a clean, pure, racism-free nation, Johnson—upon the failure of the drug test—immediately becomes non-Canadian, thus distancing him from the nation itself and notions of Canadianness (2005: 73).

Even though it may seem rather obvious to make this point, it is nevertheless an important one to reiterate and hang on to at this point: masculinity is not a monolith. Forms of masculinity differ over time, between cultures, and even within specific cultures; masculinity is contextual. That said, not all forms of masculinity are equal. The representations of Ben Johnson before, during, and after the 1988 Olympic Games, and the ways in which Black athletic masculinity has been represented in the Canadian sport media more generally, are part of a larger and troubling issue related to the management of racialized subjects in sport, in particular given the relationship of sport to the nation. Rather than providing an opportunity for alternative performances of identity, sport cultures instead work to promote sameness, homogeneity, and conformity through the disciplining of certain bodies in (sometimes contradictory) ways that reflect dominant cultural norms of idealized behaviours.[16] Bodies that disrupt this sameness within such homologous cultures or spaces are often punished or disavowed. The 'repressive nature of sporting cultures and nationalism result[s] in the need for social difference to be constantly managed. Those marked as "different" are encouraged or rather expected to, assimilate or fit in to the existing frameworks of team or nation' (Abdel-Shehid, 2005: 4). This framework, we suggest, is very much connected to dominant forms of white masculinity. And this is where the mediated representations of Bilodeau, Montgomery, Whitfield, and Johnson (as examples) converge.

Yasmin Jiwani has argued that while sports boast 'meritocracy [they] remain deeply gendered, sexualized, and racialized' (2008: 12). The representations of Bilodeau, Montgomery, and Whitfield, along with the misrepresentations of Johnson and other Black athletes, further reify a very particular form of white masculinity at the centre of Canadian identity. In other words, the ways in which the Canadian media constructed these four Olympic gold medalists between 1988 and 2010 speaks to the ways in which sporting 'heroes' are framed

as symbolic representations of a very particular form of 'Canadianness'. At no point in the narratives about Bilodeau, Montgomery, and Whitfield was it implicitly stated that they were white, able-bodied, heterosexual men, which works to reify a problematic representation of normative Canadian identity as white without ever saying as much. As Dyer (1997: 1) notes in articulating the importance and necessity of bringing whiteness to the forefront of discussions of race, 'as long as race is something only applied to non-White people, as long as White people are not racially seen and named, they/we function as a human norm. Other people are raced, we are just people.' Thus, it is the *not* naming of white as a racial identity that allows whiteness to remain the norm and standard that, without conscious deconstruction, goes unnoticed.

In sum, at the same time that the core white masculine identity of Canadianness is reinforced through the mediated representations of Bilodeau, Montgomery, and Whitfield and the taken-for-grantedness that the core Canadian identity is white and masculine, the narratives created around Ben Johnson and the way in which he moves from Canadian hero to non-Canadian villain only further reinforce whiteness as the central point of Canadianness, by symbolically distancing Johnson (as just one example) from the nation itself. His is one story in a long and troubling history of misrepresentations of other racialized subjects in the Canadian media. This all sheds even greater light on the ways in which white masculinity reasserts itself continuously and vigorously into notions of Canadianness in multiple ways and from all directions.

Sport and the Production of Canadianness: Concluding Remarks

Using sport as a focus by which to explore the production of Canadianness and the ways in which national identity, as we have argued following others, is raced and gendered, we hope that it has become clearer that notions of Canadianness have been and continue to be tied to dominant notions of white masculinity. We have used three different—yet related— ideas to support this claim.

First, turning to a brief history of hockey and the ways in which it has been connected to the nation more generally reveals that there is, in fact, nothing natural about the links between hockey and Canada. The point here is that it could really have been any sport that contributed to notions of Canadianness, but hockey—because of its rough, aggressive, and violent form of play—was cultivated specifically as a 'truly Canadian sport'. This continues today. The importance given to the men's gold medal in ice hockey at the 2010 Winter Olympic Games by the media and Canadian political and sport leaders and the excitement and national pride the game seemed to generate amongst Canadians (evidenced by the huge television viewership and the celebrations in streets, bars, and homes that followed) both speak to the way hockey is woven into ideas of Canadianness. It is difficult to imagine that a gold medal in curling, figure skating, gymnastics, or swimming would generate such an enthusiastic, nationwide response. Furthermore, the representation of Sidney Crosby as the 'star of the Games' overall—over athletes in other sports who also won gold medals—works to further engrain the importance given to men's ice hockey and those who play it.

Second, the use of hockey as a filter through which to construct narratives of non-hockey-playing athletes (Bilodeau and Montgomery as the two most recent exemplars) speaks to the ways in which hockey's history and mythologies work to construct athletes in very particular ways that reassert white masculinity at the centre of Canadianness. These Olympic 'heroes' became representative of the nation itself not only through their victories but also because of their ties to hockey.

Lastly, white masculinity and the privilege that goes along with it are not only tied to hockey—that is an important point. As imperative as it is to continue to be critical of the dominant representations of hockey—and here we re-emphasize that it is men's ice hockey that we are speaking about—and the type of masculinity reproduced through representations of the sport and its players as 'truly Canadian', it is equally critical to note that other sports also work to reify white masculinity. We cannot simply say that more peripheral sports allow for alternative performances of masculinities and femininities and, therefore, challenge dominant notions of Canadianness. While this may be true to a point, there is still, as evidenced by the representations of Whitfield and Johnson, a conceptualization of the nation that is gendered and raced. Sport both contributes to and reflects this conceptualization in the larger context.

The population of Canada is becoming more diverse, yet white masculinity continues to be asserted as the unnamed, unmarked, hegemonic centre of Canadian identity—paradoxically and problematically excluding most Canadians. That is not to say that the white masculine centre of Canadianness is not contested. Not every Canadian is the same and very few Canadians 'fit' with this symbolic representation of Canadianness. However, perhaps Gamal Abdel-Shehid articulated it best when he wrote that Canadian athletes (and here we would extend the sentiment to Canadians in general) who differ in some way from this symbolic ideal are constructed as a 'threat to our Canadianness instead of reaffirming [or redefining] our Canadianness' (2005: 98–9). Rather than promoting and celebrating diversity and plurality—as multiculturalism purports to do—there seems instead to be a continued connection being made to ideas of Canadianness that are troubling insofar as they contribute to the 'us/them' binary and very particular ideas of who in fact is 'Canadian'. Canadians may be able to buy tickets to the game, but only a few get to sit on the bench. Even fewer get to become Canadian heroes.

Discussion Questions

1. How did hockey become the dominant sport in Canada? Is hockey natural to Canadian culture?
2. According to the authors, how does hockey reproduce white masculinity? Why might this be problematic?
3. Explain the authors' view on how the reproduction of white masculinity as the dominant or core Canadian identity works to marginalize Canadians who are not white men? Do you have an alternative view to this idea? If so, describe your position and examples to support it.
4. How and why is Sidney Crosby seen as a "true" Canadian? Is this problematic? Why or why not?
5. How was hockey used to signify the "Canadianness" of Alexandre Bilodeau and Jon Montgomery? Was the media's use of hockey to tell their stories necessary? Why or why not?
6. How did Ben Johnson's public image/identity change after he was stripped of his gold medal for steroid use? Why do you think this happened?
7. Can you think of different or 'alternative' sports that challenge dominant ideas of 'Canadianness'?
8. How might sport be used to challenge the reproduction of white masculinity as the core Canadian identity?

Recommended Websites

Canadian Association for the Advancement of Women and Sport and Physical Activity: www.caaws.ca

Whiteness Studies. Deconstructing (the) Race: https://pantherfile.uwm.edu/gjay/www/Whiteness/index.html

Notes

1. We would like to thank Brendan Irish and Lauren McNicol for reviewing our text in its early stages. Their feedback was valuable and helped inform the final version of this chapter.
2. Please note that we use 'men's ice hockey' and 'hockey' interchangeably in this chapter, not with the intention of reifying dominant discursive constructions that qualify all other types of hockey (e.g., women's ice hockey, men's field hockey, sledge hockey, etc.) while assuming 'hockey' with no qualifier is men's ice hockey, but rather for stylistic purposes. Unless otherwise specifically stated, 'hockey', then, refers to men's ice hockey.
3. Here we work with the same understanding as scholars who have suggested that Canadian national identity—despite official multiculturalism—is raced and gendered. See, in particular, F. Henry and C. Taylor, *Discourses of Domination: Racial Bias in the Canadian English-Language Press* (Toronto: University of Toronto Press, 2002); E. Mackey, *The House of Difference: Cultural Politics and National Identity in Canada* (Toronto: University of Toronto Press, 2002); and S. Razack, *Looking White People in the Eye: Gender, Race and Culture in Courtrooms and Classrooms* (Toronto: University of Toronto Press, 2001).

4. We understand that critical discourse analysis, as a methodological approach, seeks to uncover the ways in which texts both shape and reflect power relations. For further discussion see, in particular, Norman Fairclough's *Discourse and Social Change* (Cambridge: Polity Press, 1992).

5. A special edition of the *Sociology of Sport Journal*, 22 (September 2005) was dedicated to interrogating the production of whiteness through sport. Each essay in that issue contributes to an understanding of the way whiteness is produced in various sporting and 'national' contexts. See also T.A. Walton and T.M. Butryn, 'Policing the Race: U.S. Men's Distance Running and the Crisis of Whiteness', *Sociology of Sport Journal*, 23 (2006): 1.

6. The creation of the category of 'visible minority' through multiculturalism and the implications of such categorization are fleshed out further in these important works: H. Bannerji, 'On the Dark Side of the Nation: Politics of Multiculturalism and the State of "Canada"', *Journal of Canadian Studies*, 31, 3 (1996); Mackey's *House of Difference*; and P. Wood and L. Gilbert, 'Multiculturalism in Canada: Accidental Discourse, Alternative Vision, Urban Practice', *International Journal of Urban and Regional Research*, 293 (2005). The important point to recognize is that the ideology of multiculturalism does not play out in lived experience as intended. In order for multiculturalism to 'work', these scholars all argue that there has to necessarily be a centre or core identity from which all 'other' identities are problematically constructed.

7. Despite the diversity of peoples in Canada, it has been argued that English-Canadian cultural identity (the dominant identity outside of Quebec) has been primarily based on British civility, which helped to construct a white masculine national identity. See, in particular, D. Coleman's *White Civility: The Literary Project of English Canada* (Toronto: University of Toronto Press, 2006) and Mackey's *House of Difference*.

8. See, in particular, Gruneau and Whitson, 1993; C. Howell, *Blood, Sweat and Cheers: Sport and the Making of Modern Canada* (Toronto: University of Toronto Press, 2001); A.C. Holman, *Canada's Game: Hockey and Identity* (Montreal and Kingston: McGill-Queen's University Press, 2009); B. Kidd, *The Struggle for Canadian Sport* (Toronto: University of Toronto Press, 1996); and M. Robidoux, 'Imagining a Canadian Identity through Sport: A Historical Interpretation of Lacrosse and Hockey', *Journal of American Folklore*, 115 (2002): 209.

9. For more in-depth discussion about this relationship, see Howell, *Blood, Sweat and Cheers*, and G. Bederman, *Manliness and Civilization: A Cultural History of Gender and Race in the United States, 1880–1917* (Chicago: University of Chicago Press, 1995).

10. Popular accounts, such as K. Dryden and R. MacGregor's *Home Game: Hockey and Life in Canada* (Toronto: McClelland and Stewart, 1989), are rather uncritical of the relationship of hockey to Canadian identity and, thus, see the 1972 Summit Series in a different way from academics, who have been more critical. In particular, see Gruneau and Whitson, 1993, and Robidoux, 2002.

11. Many academics interested in interrogating sporting spaces and the reproduction of masculinities have used R.W. Connell's theoretical concept of 'hegemonic masculinity', discussed in *Masculinities*, 2d ed. (Berkeley: University of California Press, 2005).

12. For excellent discussions on the efforts made by the media and figure-skating officials to masculinize male figure skaters, see M.L. Adams, 'To Be an Ordinary Hero: Male Figure Skaters and the Ideology of Gender', *Avante*, 3, 3 (1997): 93; and M.L. Adams, 'Separating the Men from the Girls: Constructing Gender Difference in Figure Skating', paper given at the 1998 conference of the North American Society for the Sociology of Sport. See also E. Kestenbaum's *Culture on Ice: Figure Skating and Cultural Meaning* (Middletown, CT: Wesleyan University Press, 2003), Chapters 8 and 9 in particular.

13. Whitfield also won a silver medal at the 2008 Summer Olympic Games in Beijing, China. Similar to the media representations of Whitfield following his gold medal performance in Sydney, in 2008 he was once again constructed as a Canadian hero—along with teammate Colin Jenkins. His second-place finish was very much due to the efforts of Jenkins, who acted as a 'domestique' on the cycling portion of the event in order to keep Whitfield in medal contention. Whitfield was constructed as 'gutsy' while Jenkins was highlighted for being willing to sacrifice his own race for the good of Whitfield and Canada as a whole.

14. Though not a major point in the media representations of Whitfield, it is interesting to note that in some of the media coverage around his victory in the 2000 Olympic Games triathlon he was noted to be a huge fan of the country of Canada—a statement in which hockey figured quite prominently. It was also noted that Whitfield had himself been a hockey player, in a church youth hockey league when he was much, much younger.

15. For full reviews of Abdel-Shehid's text, see W. Bridel's 'Considering Gender in Canadian Sport and Physical Activity', *International Journal of Canadian Studies*, 35 (2007): 179, and S. King's 'Who Da Man? Black Masculinities and Sport Culture Book Review', *New Dawn: Journal of Black Canadian Studies*, 1 (2005): 99.

16. For excellent discussions on the way sport is seen to manage non-white male athletes within

norms of 'white masculinity', see G. Abdel-Shehid, *Who Da Man?*; G. Hughes, 'Managing Black Guys: Representation, Corporate Culture, and the NBA', *Sociology of Sport Journal*, 21 (2004): 163; and

Y. Jiwani, 'Sports as a Civilizing Mission: Zinedine Zidane and the Infamous Head-Butt', *Canadian Journal of Cultural Studies*, 19 (2008): 11.

References

Abdel-Shehid, G. 2005. *Who Da Man? Black Masculinities and Sporting Cultures*. Toronto: Canadian Scholars' Press.

Adams, M.L. 2006. 'The Game of Whose Lives? Gender, Race, and Entitlement in Canada's "National" Game', in R. Gruneau and D. Whitson, eds., *Artificial Ice: Hockey Culture and Commerce*. Toronto: Broadview Press.

Allain, K.A. 2008. 'Real Fast and Tough: The Construction of Canadian Hockey Masculinity', *Sociology of Sport Journal*, 25, 4: 472.

Anderson, B. 1991. *Imagined Communities: Reflections on the Origin and Spread of Nationalism*. London: Verso.

Bairner, A. 2001. *Sport, Nationalism, and Globalization: European and North American Perspectives*. Albany: State University of New York.

Birrell, S., and M.G. McDonald. 2000. 'Reading Sport, Articulating Power Lines: An Introduction', in S. Birrell and M.G. McDonald, *Reading Sport: Critical Essays on Power and Representation*. Boston: Northeastern University Press.

Blatchford, C. 2010. 'Gold Comes Home', *Globe and Mail*, 15 Feb., accessed 15 Feb. 2010.

Canadian Olympic Committee. 2010. 'Bilodeau Rocks Cypress and Skies to Take Gold', 14 Feb., www.olympic.ca/en/news/bilodeau-rocks-cypress-and-skies-take-gold/, accessed 15 Feb. 2010.

Coyne, A. 2010. 'Canada Reborn', *Maclean's*, 15 March.

Cronin, M., and D. Mayall. 1998. 'Sport and Ethnicity: Some Introductory Remarks', in M. Cronin and D. Mayall, eds., *Sporting Nationalisms: Identity, Ethnicity, Immigration, and Assimilation*. London: Frank Cass Publishers.

Darnell, S., and R. Sparks. 2005. 'Inside the Promotional Vortex: Canadian Media Construction of Sydney Olympic Triathlete Simon Whitfield', *International Review for the Sociology of Sport*, 40: 358.

Dojc, M. 2010. 'After the Gold Rush: When Canadians Woke Up and Felt the Patriotism Pumping', *Chill*, 19 (March/April).

Dyer, R. 1997. *White: Essays on Race and Culture*. New York: Routledge.

Farber, M. 2010a. 'Canada Obsessed', *Sports Illustrated*, 8 Feb., http://sportsillustrated.cnn.com/vault/article/magazine/MAG1165562.index.htm, accessed 6 April 2010.

———. 2010b. 'Canada's Day', *Sports Illustrated*, 8 March.

Gee, S. 2009. 'Mediating Sport, Myth, and Masculinity: The National Hockey League's "Inside the Warrior" Advertising Campaign', *Sociology of Sport Journal*, 26, 4: 578.

Gruneau, R., and D. Whitson. 1993. *Hockey Night in Canada: Sport, Identities, and Cultural Politics*. Toronto: Garamond Press.

Ignatieff, M. 2010. 'With These Games, Canada Has Made a Statement to Itself', *Globe and Mail*, 28 Feb., www.theglobeandmail.com/news/opinions/with-these-games-canada-has-made-a-statement-to-itself/article1484540/, accessed 5 April 2010.

Jackson, S. 1998. 'A Twist of Race: Ben Johnson and the Canadian Crisis of Racial and National Identity', *Sociology of Sport Journal*, 15, 1.

Jarvie, G., and J. Maguire. 1994. *Sport and Leisure in Social Thought*. London: Routledge.

Jiwani, Y. 2008. 'Sports as a Civilizing Mission: Zinedine Zidane and the Infamous Head-Butt', *TOPIA: Canadian Journal of Cultural Studies*, 19: 11–33.

Levine-Rasky, C. 2002. *Working through Whiteness: International Perspectives*. Albany: State University of New York Press.

Longley, R. 2010. 'Gold-Medal Champ Hard-Core Canadian', *Toronto Sun*, 20 Feb., www.torontosun.com/sports/vancouver2010/news/2010/02/20/12964396.html, accessed 21 Feb. 2010.

MacQueen, K. 2010. 'Hearts of Gold', *Maclean's*, 15 March.

McIntosh, J. 2010. 'Get This Man a Beer: How Jon Montgomery went from Prairie-Boy Auctioneer to Canada's Most Loveable Hero', *Maclean's*, 15 March.

Robidoux, M.A. 2002. 'Imagining a Canadian Identity through Sport: A Historical Interpretation of Lacrosse and Hockey', *Journal of American Folklore*, 115, 456: 209–25.

Starkman, R., and K. McGran. 2010. 'Canada's Jon Montgomery Slides into Gold', *Toronto Star*, 20 Feb., http://olympics.thestar.com/2010/article-Print/768725#, accessed 21 Feb. 2010.

Stevens, N. 2000. 'Canadian Triathlete Whitfield Charms after Winning Olympic Gold', Canadian Press, 17 Sept.

Vancouver2010. 'Canada (Freestyle): Canada Hails

"Alexandre the Great"', *Vancouver2010 News Release*, 15 Feb., www.vancouver2010.com/olympic- news /n/news/ afp-news/canada-(freestyle)--canada-hails-alexandre-the-great_278598Ut.html, accessed 15 Feb. 2010.

Young, C. 2000. 'Canada's Golden Boy: Canadian Wins Inaugural Men's Triathlon', *Toronto Star*, 17 Sept., Sports Section, 1.

PART III

Borders and Crossings
Canadian Intersectional Masculinities

CHAPTER 12

Parts I and II of the text have explored the overall construction of masculinities in terms of individual identities and then broader cultural contexts. In this section, we turn attention to how masculinities intersect with other dimensions of identity. Such analysis can offer robust possibilities for understanding multiple social phenomena at once. This is not unlike the value of studying chemical interactions, in that we can understand more about one chemical's composition by observing how it interacts with another, and in turn how they might produce a new substance altogether. In this way, the chapters in this section offer opportunities to learn about masculinities—both generally and in particular—by examining how gender and other characteristics commingle within an individual or community.

Earlier chapters also introduced sometimes contentious topics relating to power, privilege, oppression, and marginalization. For instance, Chapter 11, relating to hockey, discussed how white masculinities enjoy privilege and dominance in part derived from invisibility, among other factors, and how naming the situation destabilizes that arrangement. Part III goes further, giving voice to particular constructions and experiences of masculinities as they manifest across multiple identities, and calling out examples of hegemonic dominance and their concomitant oppression.

We begin with questions of religion. In this chapter, Dube speaks about how the espoused multiculturalism in Canada obscures the dominance of Christianity, both its overt practices and its pervasive influences generally and in terms of masculinities. It is important to understand that this is not an indictment of Christianity per se, but rather of how its various practices are implicated in the production of masculinities and broader questions of sociocultural identity in Canada. Understanding Christianity will also benefit in that the author compares and contrasts multiple expressions of it, such that it too can be used in the plural form, Christianities.

Masculinit(y)ies and Religion(s) in Canada

Siphiwe I. Dube

This chapter explores the representations of hegemonic Christian masculinities in Canada, with a view to similarities and differences across the Protestant and Catholic traditions. Furthermore, the chapter discusses very briefly how non-majority religious traditions can begin to navigate the messages of hegemonic masculinit(y)ies, especially in light of their own constructions of masculinit(y)ies.

Regarding Religions and Masculinit(y)ies

This chapter deals with two fertile areas of scholarly interest in their own respective right, namely, religion(s) and masculinit(y)ies. The concepts of religion(s) and masculinit(y)ies raise significant problems when attempts at defining either are made, let alone the difficulty of defining the two together. In particular, the concepts pose two problems: First, what exactly is either of these things called religion(s) or masculinit(y)ies, and how does one begin to quantify them? Second, if we accept at the outset that both concepts entail a plurality that transcends current discursive boundaries, is it possible to say anything at all about either religion(s) or masculinit(y)ies without being misunderstood or essentializing them? Furthermore, another core question that the chapter addresses is this: given both the positive and critical development in scholarship on gender studies and religious studies in Canada, why has it taken so long for scholars of religion(s) in particular to explore and trouble the notion of masculinit(y)ies? Even though not all these questions are addressed in detail within this chapter, it is very significant to keep them in mind as constituting part of the general framework of the chapter's analysis.

To contextualize further, this chapter takes it as given that we should talk about masculinities, rather than masculinity, and religions, rather than religion. This is not to make any definitive ontological claims about either of the singular appellations, but rather to highlight the specific and strategic way that these concepts are employed in this chapter, because such a strategy has specific ramifications for the approaches I take in addressing the intersection of the two themes in the context of Canada. Consequently, while there is a great deal to attend to regarding this topic, the chapter will limit itself to what it deems to be three issues of significance concerning the intersectionality of religion(s) and masculinit(y)ies in the Canadian context: first, a general introduction to the theme of religion(s) and masculinit(y)ies; second, an exploration of the prevalent theme(s) in the intersection of religion(s) and masculinit(y)ies in Canada; and third, the problem(s) raised by the specificity of a Canadian context for this topic, especially in a context where, as this chapter argues, scholarship (both academic and non-academic) has

to look beyond the hegemonic Christian focus that has been prevalent so far.

Definitions

In a chapter examining religion and gender, Pamela Dickey Young writes, 'it is not self-evident how religion ought to be defined. Even the scholarly notion of specific religious traditions is a particularly Westernized notion that grows out of a Christian-informed imperialistic view that often classifies religions in categories that best fit Christianity and only more tenuously fit other traditions' (2005: 509). This notwithstanding, there is utility in holding some general concept of religion(s) such that we are not left just grasping at straws. To that end I concur with Dickey Young's strategic definition that 'religions provide symbol systems, that is, particular ways to understand and portray what is thought to be ultimate' (ibid.: 510). Furthermore, while this sense of 'ultimate concern' has historically been practised in communal settings, most recently various religious practitioners have tended to individualize their religious meanings. For the purposes of this chapter, however, the emphasis will be on the communal and institutional aspects of religion(s) even while acknowledging that this is not representative of 'the gamut of both communal and individual belief and practice' (ibid.) that falls under this category.

The related problem of definition attends the category of masculinit(y)ies as well. For the purposes of this chapter, it is significant to evaluate ways in which scholars have dealt with this problem, even if rather limitedly. For example, in a provocative article titled 'Three Arguments for the Elimination of Masculinity', Seth Mirsky argues that there is an unchallenged, or assumed, category of 'masculinity' in much of contemporary men's studies. In particular, Mirsky says: 'by this I mean the tendency of men's studies analyses to treat the category of masculinity as coextensive with the category of men's lives. Within such a framework, individual men and groups of men can always be understood to be exhibiting, expressing, or struggling with *some* version of masculinity, be it "hegemonic" or otherwise' (1996: 30). The approach of men's studies identified by Mirsky is in contrast to the way in which women's studies, as a directly analogical case in point, is not 'characterized by its practitioners as "the study of femininities"' (ibid.: 29). In other words, women's studies scholars do not take femininit(y)ies as a given 'fact' of women's essence; they take the opposite approach. The discipline of women's studies problematizes the concepts of both sex and gender as constructed and interreliant, whereby the performance of sex and gender roles identified with appellations such as *woman*, *feminine*, and *female* has been shown to rely on discursively naturalized conceptions of these terms.

The important point to draw from both this last point and Mirsky is that critical men's studies is not a study of maleness as given biological sex; otherwise this would mean that one only has to be 'male' to be 'masculine'. However, as feminist theorists such as Judith Butler, Mary Daly, and Simone de Beauvoir have demonstrated, we have to take the deconstruction of 'natural' gender and sex beyond simply the notion of social construction, and take seriously the view toward sex and gender performance as the ground of such identities. This is because without this recognition or allowance we might fail to 'usefully understand masculinity as a thoroughly contingent category which is politically implicated in the patriarchal structuring of the gender order' (Mirsky, 1996: 31). It will be important to keep Mirsky's warning in mind as we explore some of the ways in which the categories 'men', 'masculinit(y)ies', and 'religion(s)' intersect in the Canadian context. For the most part, as we shall see, the scholarship that touches on this topic in Canada has so far not heeded this warning very much.

Gender and Feminisms

If one were to take a quick look over course syllabi in departments of religious studies across Canada, one would find a variety of courses dealing with the topic of 'women and religion'. Of course the content of the courses themselves varies with regards to how they approach the topic, but there is no doubt as to the need for such courses. The need is premised on the observation that since women have been the 'other' in, and of, traditionally institutionalized religions and the academic study of religion(s), there is a necessary epistemological and ontological corrective to this unfair representation. In other words, there is recognition that a particular focus on women and the constructions of 'femininity' within the general discourses called 'religions' is necessary and requires an application of various tools of investigation such as anthropology, history, sociology, and theology, in both very critical and creative ways. This corrective history of feminism in Canada is a relatively short one thus far, and even as we speak, women's studies departments across Canada are still under continuous threat of institutional abandonment. Therefore, there remains a critical need, also ethical, to preserve what feminist studies have to contribute to analyses of society, especially the importance of how 'gender' as a lens through which to proffer critique is still a significant general category of analysis that deserves and requires specialized discourses within the academy. In other words, it is not as if granting the right to vote to 'women' has removed the need for critical analysis of the insidiousness of gender discrimination.

To the end that this last observation holds true, it lends support to the two strategic reasons given later for framing this chapter through an analysis of the relationship between women's studies, feminisms, and religion(s) in talking about religion(s) and masculinit(y)ies. First, it is to point to the 'fact' that the study of men and masculinit(y)ies owes its origins as a self-reflexive enterprise (both historic-ally and conceptually) to feminisms, feminist theories, feminist activists, and feminist aca-demics. Feminist theorists, both academic and non-academic, have sustained a long struggle against the ways in which knowledge, and its application, has been specifically gendered to privilege 'men'. In its various guises, femin-ism has long pointed out that the man's voice has traditionally assumed a stance of objectiv-ity and impartiality that supposedly belongs to all humans, but also has authority precisely because it represents the category of 'men's ex-periences' as paradigmatic for all human be-ings. However, with the advent of the decon-struction of the categories of 'sex' and 'gender' by scholars of feminisms since the 1960s, mostly in departments of women's studies and by activist women's groups in various locations of these projects in the 'West', there has been a sustained undermining of the supposed all-encompassing nature of 'men's experiences' as representing all human experiences.

In order to demonstrate what is regarded as the social construction of gender, femin-ist scholars and activists have had to construct very distinct notions of what it means to be a 'woman' in a world defined mostly in terms of gender construction according to men's ways of knowing (epistemology) and being (ontology) in the world. As Victor Seidler notes, 'feminism deeply challenged the ways that men are and the ways that men relate. It drew attention to the power men sustained in their relationships with women and showed that what liberalism conceived of as a relationship of equality [. . .] was in reality a relationship of power and sub-ordination' (1994: 96). To that end, since femin-ist scholars and activists saw themselves largely as correcting long-standing misconceptions about 'women', the experiences of 'men' as also gendered did not play a significant role in the early phases of understanding gender as socially constructed.[1]

Second, highlighting the relationship be-tween women's studies, feminisms, and religion(s) in considering religion(s) and masculinit(y)ties also points to another 'fact': namely, that the examination of the relationship between religion(s) and masculinit(y)ties in aca-demia has an even shorter history than that of masculinit(y)ies and/or men's studies period.[2] However, in the years following 9/11 we have observed a spike of interest in the topic of reli-gion and masculinities. One way of reading this rise in interest, and a sinister one, is that most of these studies are interested mostly in masculinity as an assertion of male aggression through a cul-tural medium that seems to naturally promote violence, namely religion. Such a reading be-comes especially sinister in light of observation that many of the studies examining religion(s) and masculinit(y)ies have focused on religious traditions such as Hinduism, Islam, and Sikhism as the violent religions par excellence—a clear throwback to Orientalism.

Another way, however, and a positive one, is to see the impact of this interest as demonstration that there is a need to reflect on masculinit(y)ies and religion(s) within the broader context of the intersections of studies in gender and studies in religion(s). Furthermore, such an interest need not be read as a cry by men to reassert their significance, even though this is an important caveat to keep in mind in light of the history of skewed gender dynamics within the practi-ces of various religious traditions and academic research. In other words, having made the rec-ognition that gender is a construct and that we perform our gender identities, it is important then to move into the next phase of evaluating how this performance affects individual men and women, without having to freeze all men or all women into categories of either oppres-sors or victims respectively and without agentic say into such constructions.

This observation becomes especially sig-nificant in light of another observation: that religions are usually thought of as providing a different and higher-order view of reality, thus demanding complete submission in ways that become understood as beyond change (or at least difficult to change). To this end, it is not only that religions relegate women to a status of subordination, but also that religions demand that men act in ways that affirm their roles as superior to women. By masking their masculinit(y)ies in religious rhetoric, then, men have consistently reflected on this gendered experience not as men but only as the generic human, and this has had the effect of perpetuating the subsuming of women's religious experiences under men's religious experiences. Where such reflection has occurred, at least in the Canadian context, it has assumed essentialist categories of both men and masculinit(y)ies, as the next section demonstrates.

Before proceeding further, however, it is imperative to explore another caveat regarding the ways in which this chapter engages with the categories 'men' and 'masculinit(y)ies'. One thing that contemporary feminist studies have been demonstrating, especially in sexuality and trans studies, is that the idea of masculinit(y)ies doesn't have to be linked to 'men' at all. This idea is expressed in many ways, but the most obvious is that 'women' can re-present masculine identities and qualities as well, through performance of masculine empowerment and/or internalizing sexist ideas, for example.[3] Also, trans studies scholars have done work on how trans identities and drag performances (two very different things, of course) have challenged the idea that concepts of masculinit(y)ies have to be linked to a body (male or female) at all. They argue that other ways of thinking about masculinit(y)ies have to do with discourses of masculinist languages that appear in militarism, nationalism, sexual violence, and war.[4] These deconstructive constructions push further the thinking on 'masculine' and 'men' as gendered categories that are not simply natural. In such languages/narratives, bodies and men don't have to be in the picture at all (even though men have come to symbolize and are propagating these languages/ narratives). While this chapter does focus on masculinit(y)ies in religion(s) as specifically

men's and male experiences, it is still important to point out that there are other ways of understanding, as well as problematizing, masculinit(y)ies.

Studies in Men and Masculinities and Men's Studies in Religion

In 1999 Cecilia Morgan argued that 'at present, little scholarly research has been undertaken on masculinity and institutional politics in either international or Canadian history' (1999: 12). Although her observation has since been challenged within the general international arena (given the surge in publications on masculinity and masculinities across the globe), the situation in Canada remains somewhat the same; hence the need for the current text. Furthermore, as Morgan notes, 'this absence is curious because, after all, political institutions were exclusively male throughout the nineteenth century' (ibid.). That is to say, one would expect that we should have a better understanding of men and masculinit(y)ies, since traditional epistemological paradigms have purported to represent generic humanity while actually developing models of knowing that privileged men. However, it should be noted that despite the clear central role attributed to men in both academia and religious institutions, there's been a general failure to produce consistent reflection on the privilege associated with the masculine construction of religious discourses until only recently.

To put it in other words, historically most religions around the world have been male-identified despite the fact that women have always been part of organized or institutional religions—at least if we take religious texts, hagiographies, and official documents as credible evidence of women's presence in institutional religion. Therefore, the dearth of male-centred reflection on masculinit(y)ies in religious contexts is surprising, especially if we also accept that masculinity (as a social construct) has always been equated with being 'biologically' male. As Lynne Marks notes with reference to her study of church discipline records in Upper Canada, 'religious and secular ideologies had much in common: male dominance was accepted by both, as was a gendered division of labour and, to some extent, a gendered division of leisure' (1999: 48). However, we should recall Mirsky's warning that we should not equate men with masculinity without clear reflection, or take masculinity as a given fact, by dint of which we should not be surprised, then, by the lack of self-reflexivity on how masculine identity as gendered is problematic in similar ways as the assumption of 'femininity'.

Consequently, we can restate one of the questions posed earlier regarding the status of men and reflection on masculinit(y)ies: 'Why has it taken so long for men to explore their masculinity?' (Seidler, 1994: 109). The question can be rephrased in light of the other concern of this chapter to read as follows: why has it taken so long for religious men to explore and trouble their masculinit(y)ies? Seidler's response to the first question is that the workings of hegemonic masculinity have remained invisible, especially within modernity, where 'dominant men have learned to speak in the impartial voice of reason' (ibid.). The argument that men have not reflected on their gendered identity as much as women have, as a result of questions and challenges raised by (and through) feminisms, feminist scholars, and feminist activists, is important for religion partly because this is one sector of human cultural construction that has sustained and perpetrated (and still does to a large extent) a significant amount of gender discrimination against both women and those men who yield less power within the institutions of religions. This is true for all so-called major 'world religions', also a problematic term. Consequently, the challenges wrought by feminists have also had a particularly significant and felt impact on religious traditions, since religions can no longer address questions of ultimate concern without dealing with the gendered impact of that concern. In other words, religions can no longer be granted special status, whether implicitly or explicitly, in terms of how much they can be challenged without losing their 'essences', as well as how much they can and should change to accommodate the changing nature of human experience. This privilege has long been under attack, and men's studies in religion has also taken it on in an attempt to unmask the androcentricity of religious traditions as well as the academic discourses on said religious traditions.

As a case in point regarding this last observation, Björn Krondorfer and Philip Culbertson argue in their exposition 'Men's Studies in Religion' that 'the compelling simplification that this new field is constituted by "men writing about religion" is misleading because it does not recognize that the sphere of the sacred has been traditionally male-centered and male-dominated. In many religions, religious norms and male experiences are indistinguishable, making men the beneficiaries of religiously sanctioned hierarchies' (2005: 5862). Put differently, clear distinctions need to be made between the academic study of men in religion, on the one hand, and the socially accepted forms of male religiosity on the other hand, represented, for example, by men's spiritual movements such as the mythopoetic movement or the Promise Keepers. Whereas the latter tend to essentialize the notion of 'masculinity' by appealing to biological arguments regarding differences between men and women, the former takes the approach that men are culturally constructed, and gendered, and perform contradictory roles because of constantly changing ideologies of masculinit(y)ies. As Stephen Boyd, Merle Longwood, and Mark Muesse argue, men's studies in religion analyze and understand 'the role of religion in supporting or resisting unstable masculine identities' (1996: 286).[5] To that end, men's studies in religion is entering a stage of self-reflexivity about the gendered nature of religious discourse that has long been engaged with by feminisms and their theorists.

Given the above shift, it should be clear that men's studies in religion can encompass a variety of topics and issues, thus making it difficult to define exactly what it is that scholars interested in these studies do. However, Krondorfer and Culbertson provide us with a working definition of what men's studies in religion entail. They note:

> these studies may examine male religious authority, analyze societal attitudes toward men, or study religious practices that enforce gender norms. They may probe theologies that justify patriarchal hierarchies or investigate men's participation in religiously sanctified oppression. They may also suggest alternative devotional and spiritual practices for men and reenvision men's roles as caregivers in both the profane and sacred realms (2005: 5862).

In other words, men's studies in religion do not only problematize or merely describe the relationship between men and religion(s), or masculinit(y)ies and religion(s), they also attempt to offer insights into how men might come to understand their roles as religious beings in gendered societies. As far as the current project is concerned, it addresses mostly the descriptive part of what Krondorfer and Culbertson define as the concerns of men's studies in religion, by tracing some of the genealogy of the relationship between religion(s) and masculinit(y)ies in Canadian history.

Within the field of the academic study of religion(s) in North America, we can map the specific ways in which scholars have come to address the intersection of religion(s) and masculinit(y)ies. In particular, it can be noted that, in response to the impact of both secular and religious feminist discourses, critical men's studies, and the ascendancy of the discourse of gay men's issues in religion, the general analysis of men's issues in religion has become a recognized area of concern within the large

North American–based scholarly association of the American Academy of Religion (AAR). As Krondorfer and Culbertson note, 'finally, in the 1990s men's studies in religion emerged as a field in its own right at the AAR' (ibid.).

Boyd affirms the same point elsewhere, noting:

> The Men's Studies in Religion Program Unit was organized in 1990 in order to apply the critical perspectives of the inter-disciplinary area of the new, or anti-sexist, men's studies to the study of religion. . . . However, while a growing number of AAR program units studied men's spiritual and religious lives, very few of these groups supported a sustained inquiry into what religious beliefs and practices entail for men as men. MSRG was begun to provide a forum for investigating both: how men's gender identities shape the religions men create and practice and how religions construct and shape men's gender identities (1999: 265).

In the context of the United States this initiative has led to the publication of various books directly addressing religion and men in the United States, focused *mostly* on analyzing the historical impact of the tradition of 'muscular Christianity' in both Catholic and Protestant churches.[6] Canada,[7] on the other hand, does not boast a similar publication record, as evinced by works that focus on both religion and spirituality.[8] As a result, it behooves us to investigate the status of the topic of men, masculinit(y)ies, and religion(s) in Canada even if this is only another small brick laid in a complex and multifaceted structure.

Religion(s) and Studies in Men and Masculinit(y)ies in Canada

As part of the complex North American reality, one might suppose that Canada is culturally and religiously similar to the United States. While that is generally true, Canada's historical evolution differs in significant ways. One of the first things we can note for the purposes of this chapter is that in the context of Canada there are two elements at work/play regarding masculinit(y)ies and religion(s) (specifically Christianity): namely, a focus of this discourse on Christianity before the 1960s, and the location of much of this scholarship within work on family in general. However, before we get into the implications of these foci, it is necessary to contextualize the Canadian religious situation for the purposes of our investigation. In particular, what should be of interest is the observation that a significant amount of scholarship on religion in Canada has centred or centres on Christianity, even though variedly understood. Despite the claim that Canada is a multireligious country, the discourse on religion(s) and masculinit(y)ies is a far cry from this claim.

Paul Bramadat argues, for example, that, 'any even casual assessment of the existing academic writing about religion in Canada will demonstrate that scholars have focused almost exclusively on the place of Christianity in Canadian history and society' (2005: 3). Robert Choquette supports this argument further by noting that 'until World War II, Canada was a visibly Christian country in just about every respect, the only exceptions being handfuls of members of other faith communities, Jews, Amerindians, and Muslims for example' (2004: 377). From a historical perspective, it can be argued that this Christian focus makes sense, especially given that even in the 2001 census a vast majority of Canadians (72 per cent) continued to identify with Christianity. Nonetheless, one has to keep in mind the limitations of the census in being able to reflect the gamut of levels of identification attached to the religious tradition called (and experience of) Christianity. The above claim notwithstanding, the important point is that scholarship on religion in Canada has privileged Christianity.

Whether scholars have been right to do so is now more questionable, especially given the history of the assimilation projects of missionary movements and the industrial residential schools in Canada. In other words, the 'fact' that Christianity was or is dominant in Canada is not a good reason for privileging research on this religious tradition—especially if we are to take the idea of multiculturalism seriously. Consequently, in the context of Canada, the argument of lack of reflection by religious men in particular about their 'gendered' experience of religions, as well as the gendered nature of their religious traditions, has the added demand of addressing the imperial history that has come to define Canada as a modern nation-state. Indeed, the two-pronged impact of empire and religion has had a marked effect on the kind of scholarship that has dealt with masculinit(y)ies and religion(s) in Canada.

Moreover, given the Christian dominance in men's studies in religion in general,[9] as well as the historical dominance of Christianity in studies of religion(s) in Canada, it is no surprise that much of the scholarship on religion(s) and masculinit(y)ies in Canada has tended to focus on the period prior to World War II, since that period represents the heyday of the idea of Canada as a Christian 'dominion'. Cecilia Morgan notes the same focus in her book on religion and politics in Upper Canada. She argues that 'work on masculinity in this country has generally been pioneered by labour and working-class historians, who have examined the meanings of masculinity as relational. . . . Much of this work, though, like that in Canadian women's history, examines masculinity in the late-nineteenth- or twentieth-century contexts' (1996: 12)—or, if further, only as far as the 1960s (Roussel, 2003).

The idea that studies in religion(s) and masculinit(y)ies in general tend to focus on Christianity can be noted in the work of Sean Gill as well. Gill, who in answer to a question regarding the impact of critical perspectives on religion by studies on men and masculinities, makes a case for the prevalence of studies on Christianity by arguing:

> Early studies in this area were dominated by the paradigm of "muscular Christianity", and concentrated on the means by which Christian theology and praxis both in the evangelical home, and in the usually Broad or High Church public school, helped to create and sustain a model of masculinity which placed a premium upon physical and sporting prowess as well as sexual and emotional continence (2005: 207–8).

Although arguing in the context of the scholarship on Victorian England, Gill's argument is echoed in the 'new colonies' of New England and Upper Canada. As Clifford Putney argues in his book on manhood and sports in America between 1880 and 1920, 'Muscular Christians were active not only in America but also England, where the term "muscular Christianity" arose in the 1850s' (2001: 1) to describe a specific form of Christian manliness. In addition, if we recall Choquette's and Bramadat's observations earlier that the Christian-centredness of scholarship on religion(s) in Canada has reflected mostly a pre-1960s Canada, the following examples should further illustrate the claim regarding the focus on Christianity, along with the second one regarding the examination of religion(s) and masculinit(y)ies as appearing mostly under research concerned with familial studies in Canada.

Of particular interest for Canada is the work of Jean-François Roussel (2003). Even though addressing Quebec's Catholic 'masculinity' in the period leading up to and during the Quiet Revolution (1960s), Roussel makes an observation that has implications for the wider Canadian context regarding the relationship between Christian 'men and religion' prior to the 1960s, especially his observations regarding 'Muscular Christianity'. Roussel notes:

> According to religious literature, men seemed less interested in rites and religion. Ministers regularly recommended men to be faithful to sacraments and prayers and to be responsible for their children's immortal souls. Some recall the important role of the father in the family prayer and spirituality. Despite all this, men were distant from spiritual life. They considered piety an emotional activity, good for women and children but not for them. That perception was even reinforced by the re-action of clergymen, as well as by the Leagues of the Sacred Heart, the same movement with the mandate to reach families through men (2003: 150).

What's of particular interest from Roussel's observation for the purposes of the current argument, is that it highlights the significance of the family in defining masculinit(y)ies through recommendations for active fatherhood and responsible husbandhood.

In addition, as part of a larger concern about Christianity as an 'effeminate' religion in Canada, the 'muscular Christianity' movements and the 'Men and Religion Forward' movement produced literature and discourses whose purpose was to rethink the relationship between 'manhood' or 'masculinity' and Christianity, where both identity markers were constructed in singular terms but, more important in Canada, in social terms directly privileging the family. What's more, this was a concern that affected both Catholic and Protestant Christianity in Canada. Patricia Dirks (2002), for example, examines the discourse on 'masculinity' within Protestant denominations (between 1900 and 1920) and demonstrates how the revitalization of the Sunday School movement and the Young Men's Christian Association (YMCA) exemplify the persistence of an obsession with the difficulty of encouraging men to attend church specifically in relation to women, as husbands or sons.

Elsewhere, Krondorfer and Culbertson argue along similar lines to Roussel regarding 'muscular Christianity' and the 'Men and Religion Forward' movement. They note:

Christian men's movements arose in the nineteenth and twentieth centuries in the Western world out of the panic that women were moving into the sphere of the sacred and were taking over religious institutions. The first such development in the first half of the nineteenth century was known as Muscular Christianity. It was followed by the Freethought movement (1880–1920), which characterized Christian churches as feminized, numerically dominated by women, and therefore weak, sentimental, and irrational. The third development, the Men and Religion Forward movement (from about World War I through to the 1950s), coined the slogan 'More Men for Religion, More Religion for Men' (2005: 5862).

Although the context for Canada has marked differences from other 'Western' countries in terms of how the ideology of Christian men reclaiming religion has worked, it is clear that Protestant Canada in particular, nonetheless, participated extensively in aspects of the larger ideology of the movement and the historical moment associated with muscular Christianity.

As a result, much of the scholarship dealing with religion(s) and masculinit(y)ies in Canada has been informed by this paradigm to some extent, a paradigm that disregards the presence of other men with different religious traditions from Christianity. The implications of this myopia for the wider context of studies in men and masculinit(y)ies is that even a recent text on gender in Canada (Nelson, 2010: 101–3) that addresses 'men, masculinities, and spirituality' deals only with the mythopoetic men's movement and the Promise Keepers—movements informed by a Christian-centred ideology. Both

these movements, although recent, form part of the larger concern within studies of men, masculinit(y)ies, and religion(s) in Canada that has focused on addressing the problem of lack of interest in religion amongst men, a problem informed by a particularly Christian concern of pre-1960s Canada.

Turning to the second trend in the scholarship on religion(s) and masculinit(y)ies, as already alluded to, the Canadian context reveals an emphasis on familial studies as the location of studies on religion(s) and masculinit(y)ies. Morgan, for example, argues that in the context of late-eighteenth- to mid-nineteenth-century Canada 'masculinity was constructed within the home as well as on the hustings or in the workplace. Fathers, sons, and, to a lesser degree, husbands were the subject of a great deal of religious and secular discourse concerning their spiritual and moral obligations' (1996: 7). Moreover, as Roussel notes in the context of Quebec, 'whatever movement one looks at, there is an overriding conviction: the kind of man that you are is defined by the way that you assume your responsibilities in the context of your social location: as spouse, father, Christian, citizen, worker, or, one may add, clergyman' (2003: 149). In other words, Canadian religious groups and leaders during the late eighteenth century onwards have 'placed great importance on the family and familial relationships' (Morgan, 1996: 102).

Nancy Christie also affirms this point in the introduction to her collection of essays on family, gender, and community in Canada between 1760 and 1969. In particular, in describing a set of essays in this book, she notes 'the degree to which the familial model of society testified to by clergymen was to a remarkable degree shared by the Christian populace' (2002: 11). In sum, the arguments proffered by Christie, Morgan, and Roussel go far in affirming one of the main observations regarding masculinit(y)ies and Christianity in the Canadian context, namely, the significance of the family. That is to say, while dealing with very different parts of Canada and time periods, Christie, Morgan, and Roussel affirm the significance of the family, and in particular the importance placed on the roles of father and husband as emblematic of masculine identity within Christian groups in Canada.

To reiterate, the emphasis on family has meant that scholarship on men and/or masculinit(y)ies and religion(s) in Canada has been subsumed under the analysis of how religious discourses regarding men seem concerned with how to make men responsible fathers or with moulding boys into responsible men of the family. In particular, as Christie argues,

> The role of the Christian household was directed to creating a viable 'civil society' by rescuing single men from their selfish preoccupations and turning them into 'steady, energetic, and useful citizen[s]'. This ideal of 'highest manhood' depended most affirmedly upon the man's 'conjugal role' as paterfamilias. . . . Late-nineteenth-century pamphlets on Christian domesticity were thus perorations on a single theme: the regulation of male behaviour, which hinged upon the dual recognition of individual ambition and family duties (ibid.: 16–17).

In other words, general discourse on the Christian domesticity of men within Canada has tended to hinge upon the dual recognition of both the pursuit of individual ambition (as per the discourse of muscular Christianity) and the fulfillment of family duties. Furthermore, the emphasis on affective qualities in the descriptions of manliness of Christian Canada, in contrast to the counterpart rugged masculinity of either the hegemonic English or American muscular Christianity tradition, produces a distinctly relational idea of Canadian hegemonic masculinity. In this sense, the hegemonic masculinit(y)ies privileged in Canadian Christianity, both Catholic and Protestant, can be said to hold an in-between status,

between affirming certain aspects of muscular Christianity such as the emphasis on individual development on the one hand and those of relational masculinit(y)ies on the other, such as the emphasis on familial roles.

Morgan notes, for example, in the context of Methodist itinerant ministers travelling in Upper Canada: 'The kind of rugged manliness of a Ryan or a Connor [both preachers on the early Methodist circuits] was also mingled with an emotional sensibility that in any other context might have been viewed as effeminate. As preachers, men like the Reverend John Dempster, who travelled the Bridgewater circuit in 1819, were expected to rouse the emotions of others and to display their own' (1996: 117). However, such expression of emotions was not only a privilege afforded ministers, as the above citation might suggest. Pursuant to her argument cited above, Christie argues that 'fathers were instructed to develop their "feminine" qualities and to express their emotions in an affectionate manner to their spouses and children, while sons were enjoined to recognize early that "life is a struggle of individuals", so they could competently earn a good wage and secure an independent existence for themselves and their families' (2002: 17). This is a trend that can also be observed beyond the confines of Victorian Upper Canada (addressed by both Morgan and Christie), into mid-twentieth-century Quebec.

Roussel notes, for example, that the manly virtues that are glorified and pursued by the 'muscular Christianity' and the 'Men and Religion Forward' movements remained almost absent from Catholic discourse in French Canada of that time (2003: 149). Accordingly,

> the 'Habitant' was then the main French-Canadian model of manliness. . . . The spirituality of the Habitant was defined by elements such as the family, work, and the land as a source of nurture and giver of God's gifts. This spirituality had a communal dimension, manifested particularly through hospitality (especially

toward [male] vagabonds), as well as volunteering on a regular or intermittent basis to ensure the well-being of everyone in the parish (ibid.: 150).

Significantly, while notions of nurture and hospitality have been understood as traditional feminine virtues, their appearance in discourse of religious masculinit(y)ies is illuminating for signifying a different discourse of masculinit(y)ies in Canadian Christianity at least.

Consequently, the argument that much of the concern of Christianity in Canada has been informed by an obsession about bringing men back to the church has to be re-evaluated on the basis of the observation that there have been two discourses at play informing this obsession— 'muscular Christianity' on the one hand and a 'relational' masculinity discourse on the other. The latter has tended to emphasize responsibility to the family, where the family is conceptualized in broader terms than simply the nuclear family. The work of Patricia Dirks and Kenneth Draper is important for this observation. In particular, as Christie notes (drawing from Draper) with regards to the post-1880 era in Canada, 'because the churches saw as their principal social task the proper formation of male citizens within liberal social order, they embarked on a new trajectory which, in the twentieth century, witnessed the elaboration of social Christianity and the erection of a panoply of religious organizations functioning beyond the purview of the church congregation, all directed to propping up the stability of the family' (2002: 114–5). In other words, the literature on Christian domesticity hinged upon the dual recognition of individual ambition and family duties noted earlier.

Furthermore, as Draper himself argues, despite the fact that the 'rhetoric of home had little place in the strategies of male-dominated organizations' (2002: 275) such as the YMCA, they encouraged the presence of family members, during conversion meetings, for example. That is to say, 'while the rhetorics of the redemptive

home and the redeeming choice were widely divergent, they supported each other. Women used the authority of their relational networks to bring their households to revival meetings in order to force or inspire a choice, particularly among their young men' (ibid.: 284). Patricia Dirks also supports the argument that the focus of the relationship between masculinit(y)ies and religion(s) in Canada has been informed by the familial context. She notes, for example, that 'Church criticisms of early-twentieth century parents were clearly tied in with attempts to redefine Christian masculinity for the modern age' (2002: 291).

Dirks further argues that this concern with linking Christianity and masculinit(y)ies was rooted in the 'widespread social dislocation of the early 1900s', when the message being disseminated was that 'good fathers were well-rounded individuals who devoted time and energy to fulfilling their essential and unique duties, upon which the religious health of their families, and ultimately their churches and the nation, depended' (ibid.: 292). To that end, since men had to be convinced that they had an important role to fulfil, there was a need to balance the notion of muscular Christian principles on the one hand, premised as they were on an individual man making individual autonomous choices (hence the success of organizations such as the YMCA), and, on the other hand the notion of parental responsibility, which emphasized a relational approach to being 'manly'.

These interdependent constructions of masculinit(y)ies can be observed further in two comments made by Dirks. On the one hand, the message of the YMCA was very clear: 'unless Christian men maximized their physical, mental, and social strengths, their religious development would go to waste. Religion, in other words, was not for sissies; only the strong could hope to attain Christian manhood' (ibid.: 302). On the other hand, there was an emphasis on fatherhood and on fathers building up the relationship with their 'boys': 'devoting time and effort to parenting and home life established one's masculinity. It was courageous men who "ma[d]e friends of [their] boys and honestly and self-sacrificingly tr[ied] to play a friend's true part toward them'" (ibid.: 307). What's of significance to note from the comments above is that in response to muscular Christianity's construction of religion as effeminate, hence deterring men from the church pews, there is an emphasis on religion as a demanding exercise fit only for the strong-willed. Canadian Christianity, in other words, is a 'manly' religion, but that manliness is more akin to Roussel's definition of Quebec Catholic masculinity as that of the figure of the habitant than it is to the manliness of traditional muscular Christianity.

The above notwithstanding, it is important to point out that location of the study of masculinit(y)ies in familial studies in Canada, including the subsequent discourse of relationality, is fundamentally tied to men's sexuality, in particular heterosexuality. In the descriptions of men's roles in Canadian Christianity, the men are centrally identified by their roles as husbands (marital relations) and fathers (reproductive relations). Marriage and fatherhood are the material evidence that these men have achieved 'masculinity' 'manhood'. Furthermore, sex and gender are seen as the same thing and fundamentally heterosexual. So to be a real man, one has to be masculine; one becomes masculine through 'proper' gendered behaviours, activities, and relations with women. This noted reference to the underlying heterosexual nature of both the religious tradition under scrutiny and the bias of scholars who study masculinit(y)ies exposes how the studies of 'men in religion'—as new and progressive as they are—still take heterosexual relations as a given. That is, 'relation' and 'familial' are unspoken heteronormative categories.

What Significance the Difference in the Dominion?

Clearly a problem arises with representing particular and hegemonic constructions of religious masculinit(y)ies as archetypes for the broader and widely variegated religious traditions that comprise the Canadian landscape. As Paul Bramadat argues in his introduction to the co-edited book *Religion and Ethnicity in Canada*, 'Historical "meta-narratives" such as the traditional sociological account of religion in Canada, tend to obscure certain changes underway in our society. Non-Christians (and for the most part, even "ethnic" Christians) do not really appear in traditional story' (2005: 5). This is a story that tends to make the dominance of Christianity in Canada seem normal and natural. To that end, a question arises regarding the purchase of the model of the relationship between religion(s) and masculinit(y)ies in Canada proffered in this chapter, especially given that between 1991 and 2001, as per the 2001 census, we have seen a decrease in numbers within most Christian denominations, while membership in (and identification with) Muslim, Hindu, Buddhist, and Sikh traditions has increased dramatically. In other words, unlike Christianity's experience of masculinity being a crisis of bringing men back into the churches, other religious communities in Canada do not seem to fall into this model. However, since there has been an accepted dominant focus on Christianity within academic scholarship in Canada, we are not yet in the position to make concrete claims regarding either the purchase of the model that has been examined in this chapter or claims regarding the status and perception of masculinit(y)ies in other religious traditions.

Part of the problem is that the 'religious and ethnic intra-communal diversity' (ibid.: 13) one finds in each of the religious traditions found in Canada foregrounds the difficulty of thinking about both masculinit(y)ies and religion(s) in Canada. To put it in the form of a question, is it the case that concepts of masculinit(y)ies engaged in by religious communities other than those already found in Canada are redeployed in a uniquely Canadian way, or is the case that concepts are merely relocated *in toto*? If we accept that both religion(s) and masculinit(y)ies are in a state of constant flux, and that any attempt at group studies or individual studies has to negotiate this variety very well, the best conclusion we can make without painstaking ethnographic evidence is that there has to be some negotiation that takes places between different concepts of masculinit(y)ies, especially in light of the argument that 'the forms of Islam, Buddhism, Judaism, Sikhism, Chinese religion, and Hinduism that one finds in Canada are very much the products of complex processes of negotiation' (ibid.: 13–14).

Furthermore, we can expect that since all religious traditions do not emerge out of nowhere, nor do they currently exist in a vacuum, there will inevitably be some continuities with the orthodox constructions of masculinit(y)ies in the newer terrains. However, such orthodox understanding, construction, or engagement is already in negotiation with the hegemonic understanding of the relationship between Christianit(y)ies and masculinit(y)ies already found in the Canadian context. This argument is not meant to signify anything other than that renegotiation is already the relationship that frames 'otherness'—where the 'others' in this context are the religious traditions that claim behaviours, beliefs, doctrines, histories, ideologies, liturgies, practices, and authenticities other than those defined as Christian.

Where such renegotiation has occurred it seems to have been framed negatively vis-à-vis the hegemonic discourses, where the masculinit(y)ies of other religious traditions have been seen as violent and an affront to the 'civilized' Canadian (Christian) one(s).[10] In particular, two examples come into focus: questions and debates in Canada around turbans and kirpans among Sikhs as public identifiers of a specific masculine identity, and debates surrounding Muslim groups and individuals who are regarded as intransigent. In both situations the activities of a minority are presented and reinterpreted in the public sphere in ways that reflect on the whole religious tradition with very little acknowledgement of variety or

historical contextualization. Paying particular attention to the Sikh context, it can be noted that regardless of 'the presence of sophisticated Sikh women and men at all levels of Canadian society, who are capable of reflecting with similar eloquence on the complex intersection of belief, ethnicity, and culture, researchers have found that South Asians as a group suffer from the consequences of many prejudices in mainstream Canada' (Mahmood, 2005: 53). In particular, as Cynthia K. Mahmood notes further in light of the work of Norman Buchignani and Doreen Marie Indra (1989), 'Sikhs are intimately connected with terrorism and alleged security and immigration problems that have been associated with this community since the 1980s' (ibid.). Such perceptions, and the isolationist response they elicit, have helped create an image of Sikh Canadians as a chauvinistic group that will not easily fit in.

The aforementioned perceptions are not aided by Canadian media representations of Sikhism as a monolithic and insular immigrant religion bent on maintaining old traditions that don't meld well with Canadian liberalism, despite the fact that Sikhs have been in Canada since 1904. The focused reporting on stories that are sensational regarding the kirpan and the turban is a telling bias toward a specific form of representation that privileges one view of a multifaceted tradition.[11] In this monolithic narrative, the experiences of mostly Sikh Khalsa males, because of the turbans they wear, are marked as signalling difference, but not just for themselves. Religious markers such as the turban shape not just the performance of gendered identities; they also define the manner in which the practitioners of the religion are perceived as being able to integrate into the hegemonic religious culture of Canada. As Geetanjali Singh Chanda and Staci Ford (2009: 1) note, 'Religious identifications such as the turban that bear the moral burden of older value systems and notions of masculinity and femininity collide with changing survival systems, and women and men may have to negotiate different moral compasses.' In the case of Canada such negotiation of the moral compass in terms of masculinit(y)ies and religion(s) has pitched a supposedly sanitized Christian masculinity against a violent Sikh masculinity.

With particular reference to the model of the relationship between religion(s) and masculinit(y)ies presented in this chapter, we can note a predominantly divergent negotiation of Sikh masculinit(y)ies with the hegemonic Christian one(s). Specifically, it is worth noting how the colonialist dubbing of Sikhs as a 'martial race' by the British is carried on into scholarship that examines Sikh identity in Canada. For example, in her chapter on Sikhs in Canada in a collection of essays on religion and ethnicity in Canada, Cynthia Keppley Mahmood makes some interesting remarks regarding Sikh identity:

> Sikh history is replete with stories of persecution, sacrifice, and military valour, which Sikhs do not see as inconsistent with the spiritual serenity at the heart of the tradition. When the British arrived in the region of Punjab, the Sikh empire of Maharaja Ranjit Singh was at its height, and the notion that Sikh military might, Sikh tradition, and Punjabi culture were somehow congruent became established in colonialist thinking. Sikhs were dubbed a 'martial race' by the British, unifying religion and biology in that peculiar brew that would become lethal in many parts of the post-colonial world (2005: 55).

Mahmood's observation affirms that media representations of Sikh identity as hypermasculine, referred to earlier, and therefore equating the male practitioners of this religion with a non-relational masculinity, have a longer history. Moreover, while Mahmood is critical of the British construction of Sikh identity as a martial race, she also praises the Sikh history

of military valour. The effect of such a contradictory representation is that it inadvertently continues the stereotype it criticizes.

Furthermore, such a limited construction of Sikh identity, premised on a narrow definition of Sikhs as turban-wearing men also known as Khalsa (and the privileging of the turban as the *sine qua non* of Sikh 'manhood'), further perpetuates the idea that to be masculine in this religious tradition is to be violent. This characterization masks the violence that is inherent in the discourse on masculinit(y)ies and religion(s) in general, and especially Christianity, by making it seem that it is the non-Christian traditions in Canada that don't fit into the liberal model rather than mapping out how Christianity in Canada has participated in this violent discourse as well. In other words, one of the observations raised by the specificity of examining the relationship between religion(s) and masculinit(y)ies in the Canadian context is a challenge that scholarship, both academic and non-academic, has to look beyond the hegemonic Christian focus that has been prevalent so far, granted that this chapter has provided only one clear example as counterdiscourse to the normative narrative presented earlier. This call for diversity of scholarship is nothing new per se, but it bears repeating if only for the sake of pointing out that the claim to diversity in the public sphere in Canada requires more intentional work on the part of everyone.

Conclusion

As noted throughout this chapter, Canada's religious composition is very diverse (even within Christianity), and thus the preponderant focus on Christianity in this area of study is now very much questionable. However, since there is not yet much work available on other religious tradition's histories of masculinit(y)ies in Canada, the chapter has also fallen into the trap of privileging the 'Christianities' narrative as the 'Canadian' narrative. That being said, in presenting this narrative, the author has insisted on acknowledging that this is only one perspective amongst many, where even within the rubric of 'Christianity' there exist many 'Christianities' in Canada. While the chapter has shown to some extent that there are some distinctions amongst the various Christian denominations in their construction of masculinit(y)ies, for the most part these have been presented as generally similar. In other words, the chapter has presented ideas about both religion(s) and masculinit(y)ies that are somewhat reductive. Such reductionism has been attended to through an emphasis on observations of diversity throughout, and an acknowledgement of the effects of limited resources on this specific topic, which has meant an overreliance on select scholarship.

Clearly more work needs to be done on the topic of the intersection of the histories of masculinit(y)ies and religion(s) in Canada, in both the archaeological (or genealogical) and eschatological sense of such histories. This demand for more work is especially urgent if scholars are serious about upholding the demands of multiculturalism and interdisciplinarity, both of which have serious implications for how the work of scholars of religion(s) and gender(s) in Canada affects the larger religious and non-religious communities. Moreover, given that 'gender' has often been a signifier of relationships of power, it is imperative that warnings against effacing the advances made by feminists of all ilks in unmasking the assiduous nature of patriarch(y)ies not be taken at all lightly. This is part of what men's studies in masculinit(y)ies in general, and masculinit(y)ies and religion(s) specifically, need to achieve: a self-reflexive critique of masculine performance within the various religious discourses where such masculine performance might be given to the idea of itself as given, natural, and unchanging.

Discussion Questions

1. What are some of the advantages and disadvantages of emphasizing the communal and institutional aspects of religion(s) over individual expressions?
2. What other positive reasons can you think of in defence of the need to reflect on masculinit(y)ies and religion(s) within the broader context of the intersections of studies in gender(s) and studies in religion(s) in Canada?
3. The chapter offers its own reasons for why it has taken so long for religious men to explore and trouble their masculinit(y)ies in Canada; what is your evaluation of these reasons?
4. The chapter makes a distinction between the academic study of men in religion and normative male religiosity—what is this distinction, and why is it important?
5. One of the observations highlighted in the chapter regarding the study of religion(s) in Canada is that a significant amount of scholarship on religion in Canada has centred (and still centres) on Christianity, even though the term is variedly understood. According to the chapter, and from your own observations, what problems are posed by this limitation in particular regard to the idea of masculinity?
6. The author argues that the larger concern within studies of men, masculinit(y)ies, and religion(s) in Canada has focused on addressing the problem of lack of interest in religion amongst men, a problem informed by a particularly Christian concern of

pre-1960s Canada. Do you think that this is still a prevalent problem today for any of the religious traditions practised in Canada, including Christianity?

7. The author argues that the emphasis on family within scholarship examining men and/or masculinit(y)ies and religion(s) in Canada reveals a distinctly relational idea of Canadian hegemonic masculinity that stands in contrast to the counterpart 'rugged masculinity' in either England or America. What does the author mean by this idea of relational masculinity in Canada?

8. One of the significant questions raised by the chapter is this: is it the case that concepts of masculinit(y)ies engaged with by religious communities other than those already found in Canada are redeployed in a uniquely Canadian way, or is the case that concepts of masculinit(y)ies are merely relocated *in toto*?

Recommended Websites

Journal of Men, Masculinities and Spirituality: www.jmmsweb.org

Men and Masculinities: www.sagepub.com/ journals/Journal200971?siteId=sage-us&prodTypes=any&q=masculinities

Promise Keepers Canada: www.promise keepers.ca/content/index

Religion and Gender: www.religionandgender. org

'Why Men Hate Church': www.cbn.com/ spirituallife/ChurchAndMinistry/ menhatingchurch.aspx

Notes

1. Indeed, Seidler is not the only one to make this observation. See, e.g., J. Beynon, *Masculinities and Culture* (Buckingham, UK: Open University Press, 2002); H. Brod and M. Kaufman, eds., *Theorizing Masculinities* (Thousand Oaks, CA: Sage, 1994); N. Christie, *Households of Faith: Family, Gender, and Community in Canada, 1760–1969* (Montreal and Kingston: McGill-Queen's University Press, 2002); M.S. Kimmel and M.A. Messner, eds., *Men's Lives*, 6th ed. (Boston and New York: Pearson Allyn & Bacon, 2004); U. King, ed., *Religion and Gender* (Oxford: Blackwell, 1995); K. McPherson, C. Morgan, and N.M. Forestell, eds., *Gendered Pasts: Historical Essays in Femininity and Masculinity in Canada* (Oxford: Oxford University Press, 1999); P.F. Murphy, ed., *Feminism and Masculinities* (Oxford: Oxford University Press, 2004).

2. See, e.g., S. Boyd, W.M. Longwood, and M.W. Muesse, eds., *Redeeming Men: Religion and Masculinities* (Louisville, KY: Westminster John Knox Press, 1996); M. Ghoussoub and E. Sinclair-Webb, eds., *Imagined Masculinities: Male Identity and Culture in the Modern Middle East* (London: Saqi Books,

2000); B. Krondorfer, ed., *Men's Bodies, Men's Gods: Male Identities in a (Post-)Christian Culture* (New York: New York University Press, 1996); C. Morgan, *Public Men and Virtuous Women: The Gendered Languages of Religion and Politics in Upper Canada, 1791–1850* (Toronto: University of Toronto Press, 1996); L. Ouzgane, ed., *Islamic Masculinities* (London: Zed Books, 2006).

3. See, e.g., J. Halberstam, *Female Masculinity* (Durham, NC: Duke University Press, 1998); B.J. Noble, *Masculinities Without Men? Female Masculinity in Twentieth-Century Fictions* (Vancouver: University of British Columbia Press, 2004); B.J. Noble, *Sons of the Movement: FtM's Risking Incoherence in a Post-Queer Cultural Landscape* (Toronto: Women's Press, 2006).

4. See, e.g., C.J. Pascoe, *Dude, You're a Fag: Masculinity and Sexuality in High School* (Berkeley: University of California Press, 2007), for a chapter on masculinity in girls; S. Stryker and S. Whittle, eds., *The Transgender Studies Reader* (New York: Routledge, 2006).

5. See also S. Boyd, 'Domination as Punishment:

Men's Studies and Religion', *Men's Studies Review* (Spring 1990): 1–9.

6. See S.B. Boyd, ibid.; S.B. Boyd, *The Men We Long to Be: Beyond Domination to a New Christian Understanding of Manhood* (San Francisco: HarperCollins, 1995); S.B. Boyd, W.M. Longwood, and M.W. Muesse, eds., *Redeeming Men: Religion and Masculinities* (Louisville, KY: Westminster John Knox Press, 1996); V. Burrus, *Begotten Not Made: Conceiving Manhood in Late Antiquity* (Stanford, CA: Stanford University Press, 2000); D.S. Claussen, *The Promise Keepers: Essays on Masculinity and Christianity* (Jefferson, NC: McFarland, 2000); P. Culbertson, *New Adam: The Future of Male Spirituality* (Minneapolis, MN: Augsburg Fortress Publishers, 1992); P. Culbertson, *The Spirituality of Men: Sixteen Christians Write about Their Faith* (Minneapolis, MN: Augsburg Fortress Publishers, 2002); D. Hall, ed., *Muscular Christianity: Embodying the Victorian Age* (Cambridge, UK: Cambridge University Press, 1994); M. Kuefler, *Manly Eunuch: Masculinity, Gender Ambiguity, and Christian Ideology in Late Antiquity* (Chicago: Chicago University Press, 2001); Charles Lippy, 'Miles to Go: Promise Keepers in Historical and Cultural Context', *Soundings*, 80, 2/3 (Summer/Fall 1997): 289–304.

7. It has to be emphasized that for the most part this is in reference to Anglophone Canada, since the scope of this chapter touches only very slightly on the Francophone context.

8. See, e.g., S.B. Boyd, W.M. Longwood, and M.W. Muesse, eds, *Redeeming Men: Religion and Masculinities* (Louisville, KY: Westminster John Knox Press, 1996); D.C. James, *What Are They Saying about Mas-culine Spirituality?* (New York: Paulist Press, 1996); E. Magnuson, *Changing Men, Transforming Culture: Inside the Men's Movement* (Boulder, CO: Paradigm, 2007); C. Putney, *Muscular Christianity: Manhood and Sports in Protestant America, 1880–1920* (Cambridge, MA: Harvard University Press, 2001).

9. See M.J. Clark, 'Teaching Men's Studies in Religion at an All-Women's College', *Journal of Men's Studies*, 9, 2 (2001): 267–98.

10. See, e.g., a recent article in *Maclean's* by John Geddes, 'What Canadians Think of Sikhs, Jews, Christians, Muslims . . .', www2.macleans. ca/2009/04/28/what-canadians-think-of-sikhs-jews-christians-muslims/. On the basis of analysis of an online poll conducted by Angus Reid Strategies from 14 April 2009 to 15 April 2009, Geddes notes, 'Islam and Sikhism face the highest hurdles when it comes to persuading many Canadians they are not inherently violent faiths. The problem varies across regions. By far the highest percentage who viewed Islam as encouraging violence was found in Quebec, 57 per cent. Sikh doctrine is mostly likely to be viewed as violent in the province where about half of Canadian Sikhs live: 30 per cent of British Columbians said they think Sikhism encourages violence.'

11. See T. Milewski, CBC News, 'Symbolism and Suits: Sikh Extremism Enters Mainstream Canadian Politics', www.cbc.ca/news/background/sikh-politics-canada/index.html, 8 June 2007; CBC News Online, 'Timeline: The Quebec Kirpan Case', www.cbc.ca/news/background/kirpan/, 2 March 2006.

References

Beynon, J. 2002. *Masculinities and Culture*. Buckingham, UK: Open University Press.

Boyd, S.B. 1990. 'Domination as Punishment: Men's Studies and Religion', *Men's Studies Review* (Spring): 1–9.

———. 1995. *The Men We Long to Be: Beyond Domination to a New Christian Understanding of Manhood*. San Francisco: HarperCollins.

———. 1999. 'Trajectories in Men's Studies in Religion: Theories, Methodologies, and Issues', *Journal of Men's Studies*, 7, 2: 265.

———, W.M. Longwood, and M.W. Muesse, eds. 1996. *Redeeming Men: Religion and Masculinities*. Louisville, KY: Westminster John Knox Press.

Bramadat, P. 2005. 'Beyond Christian Canada: Religion and Ethnicity in a Multicultural Society', in P. Bramadat and D. Seljak, eds, *Religion and Ethnicity in Canada*. Toronto: Pearson-Longman.

Brod, H., and M. Kaufman, eds. 1994. *Theorizing Masculinities*. Thousand Oaks, CA: Sage.

Buchignani, N., and M.D. Indra. 1989. 'Key Issues in Canadian-Sikh Ethnic and Race Relations: Implications for the Study of the Sikh Diaspora', in G. Barrier and V. Dusenberry, eds, *The Sikh Diaspora: Migration and the Experience beyond Punjab*. Delhi: Chanakya.

Burrus, V. 2000. *Begotten Not Made: Conceiving Manhood in Late Antiquity*. Stanford, CA: Stanford University Press.

CBC News Online. 2006. 'Timeline: The Quebec Kirpan Case', 2 March, www.cbc.ca/news/background/kirpan/.

Chanda, G.S., and S. Ford. 2009. 'Sikh Masculinity, Religion, and Diaspora in Shauna Singh Baldwin's *English Lessons and Other Stories*', *Men and Masculinities*, 5 Feb., 462–82.

Choquette, R. 2004. *Canada's Religions: An Historical Introduction*. Ottawa: University of Ottawa Press.

Christie, N. 2002. *Households of Faith: Family, Gender, and Community in Canada, 1760–1969*. Montreal and Kingston: McGill-Queen's University Press.

Clark, M.J. 2001. 'Teaching Men's Studies in Religion at an All-Women's College', *Journal of Men's Studies*, 9, 2: 267–98.

Claussen, D.S. 2000. *The Promise Keepers: Essays on Masculinity and Christianity*. Jefferson, NC: McFarland & Co.

Culbertson, P. 1992. *New Adam: The Future of Male Spirituality*. Minneapolis, MN: Augsburg Fortress Publishers.

———. 2002. *The Spirituality of Men: Sixteen Christians Write about Their Faith*. Minneapolis, MN: Augsburg Fortress Publishers.

Dickey Young, P. 2005. 'Religion', in P. Essed, D.T. Goldberg, and A. Kobayashi, eds, *A Companion to Gender Studies*. Oxford: Blackwell.

Dirks, P. 2002. 'Reinventing Christian Masculinity and Fatherhood: The Canadian/Protestant Experience, 1900–1920', in N. Christie, *Households of Faith: Family, Gender, and Community in Canada, 1760–1969*. Montreal and Kingston: McGill-Queen's University Press.

Draper, K.L. 2002. 'Redemptive Homes—Redeeming Choices: Saving the Social in Late-Victorian London, Ontario', in N. Christie, *Households of Faith: Family, Gender, and Community in Canada, 1760–1969*. Montreal and Kingston: McGill-Queen's University Press.

Geddes, J. 2000. 'What Canadians Think of Sikhs, Jews, Christians, Muslims . . .' *Maclean's*. www2.macleans .ca/2009/04/28/what-canadians-think-of-sikhs-jews-christians-muslims/.

Ghoussoub, M., and E. Sinclair-Webb, eds. 2000. *Imagined Masculinities: Male Identity and Culture in the Modern Middle East*. London: Saqi Books.

Gill, S. 2005. 'Why Difference Matters: Lesbian and Gay Perspectives on Religion and Gender', in U. King and T. Beattie, eds, *Gender, Religion and Diversity: Cross-Cultural Perspectives*. London: Continuum.

Halberstam, J. 1998. *Female Masculinity*. Durham, NC: Duke University Press.

Hall, D., ed. 1994. *Muscular Christianity: Embodying the Victorian Age*. Cambridge, UK: Cambridge University Press.

James, D.C. 1996. *What Are They Saying about Masculine Spirituality?* New York: Paulist Press.

Kimmel, M.S., and M.A. Messner, eds. 2004. *Men's Lives*, 6th ed. Boston and New York: Pearson Allyn & Bacon.

King, U., ed. 1995. *Religion and Gender*. Oxford: Blackwell.

Krondorfer, B., ed. 1996. *Men's Bodies, Men's Gods: Male Identities in a (Post-)Christian Culture*. New York: New York University Press.

——— and P. Culbertson. 2005. 'Men's Studies in

Religion', in L. Jones, ed., *Encyclopedia of Religion*, 2d ed., vol. 9. Detroit: Macmillan Reference USA.

Kuefler, M. 2001. *Manly Eunuch: Masculinity, Gender Ambiguity, and Christian Ideology in Late Antiquity*. Chicago: University of Chicago Press.

Lippy, C. 1997. 'Miles to Go: Promise Keepers in Historical and Cultural Context', *Soundings*, 80, 2/3 (Summer/Fall): 289–304.

Magnuson, E. 2007. *Changing Men, Transforming Culture: Inside the Men's Movement*. Boulder, CO: Paradigm.

Mahmood, C.K. 2005. 'Sikhs in Canada: Identity and Commitment', in P. Bramadat and D. Seljak, *Religion and Ethnicity in Canada*. Toronto: Pearson-Longman.

Marks, L. 1999. 'No Double Standards?: Leisure, Sex, and Sin in Upper Canadian Church Discipline Records, 1800–1860', in K. McPherson et al., eds, *Gendered Pasts: Historical Essays in Femininity and Masculinity in Canada*. Oxford: Oxford University Press.

McPherson, K., C. Morgan, and N.M. Forestell, eds. 1999. *Gendered Pasts: Historical Essays in Femininity and Masculinity in Canada*. Oxford: Oxford University Press.

Milewski, T. 2007. 'Symbolism and Suits: Sikh Extremism Enters Mainstream Canadian Politics', *CBC News*, 8 June, www.cbc.ca/news/background/sikh-politics-canada/index.html.

Mirsky, S. 1996. 'Three Arguments for the Elimination of Masculinity', in B. Krondorfer, ed., *Men's Bodies, Men's Gods: Male Identities in a (Post-)Christian Culture*. New York: New York University Press.

Morgan, C. 1996. *Public Men and Virtuous Women: The Gendered Languages of Religion and Politics in Upper Canada, 1791–1850*. Toronto: University of Toronto Press.

———. 1999. '"When Bad Men Conspire, Good Men Must Unite!": Gender and Political Discourses in Upper Canada, 1820s–1830s', in K. McPherson, C. Morgan, and N.M. Forestell, eds, *Gendered Pasts: Historical Essays in Femininity and Masculinity in Canada*. Oxford: Oxford University Press.

Murphy, P.F., ed. 2004. *Feminism and Masculinities*. Oxford: Oxford University Press.

Nelson, A. 2010. *Gender in Canada*, 4th ed. Toronto: Pearson.

Noble, J.B. 2004. *Masculinities Without Men? Female Masculinity in Twentieth-Century Fictions*. Vancouver: University of British Columbia Press.

———. 2006. *Sons of the Movement: FtM's Risking Incoherence in a Post-Queer Cultural Landscape*. Toronto: Women's Press.

Ouzgane, L., ed. 2006. *Islamic Masculinities*. London: Zed Books.

Pugh, D. 1983. *Sons of Liberty: The Masculine Mind in Nineteenth-Century America*. Westport, CT: Greenwood Press.

Putney, C. 2001. *Muscular Christianity: Manhood and Sports in Protestant America, 1880–1920*. Cambridge, MA: Harvard University Press.

Razack, S.H. 2004. *Dark Threats and White Knights: The Somalia Affair, Peacekeeping, and the New Imperialism*. Toronto: University of Toronto Press.

Roussel, J.-F. 2003. 'Roman Catholic Religious Discourse about Manhood in Quebec: From 1900 to the Quiet Revolution (1960–1980)', *Journal of Men's Studies*, 11, 2: 145–55.

———— and C. Downs. 2007. 'Epistemological Perspectives on Concepts of Gender and Masculinity/Masculinities', *Journal of Men's Studies*, 15, 2: 178–97.

Seidler, V.J. 1994. *Unreasonable Men: Masculinity and Social Theory*. London: Routledge.

CHAPTER 13

In this chapter, Kwan-Lafond begins by discussing the construction of race and racial identity as a precursor to analyzing its intersections with masculinities. She is interested in approaching her subject from an anti-racist perspective. This is an important qualifier, in that one's perspective can have different consequences for the subject studied. In this instance, race is an idea rather than a biological fact. The ways in which a population co-shapes ideas of race also situate these ideas in terms of power relations. An anti-racist perspective is interested in critically interrogating and dismantling these processes rather than deferring to and rigidifying them.

The author revisits some of the concepts we examined earlier (e.g., hegemony and whiteness) but expands upon and extends them for a deeper understanding of the socio-cultural dynamics of race and gender that have a profound influence on human experiences within Canadian society (among other places). She invites the reader to reflect upon often hidden, touchy, uncomfortable, or even contentious issues of race grappled with in a multicultural Canada. In the second part of the chapter, two particular examples of intersections are considered: Asian and Black masculinities. Once again, compelling personal narratives are an important contribution to understanding consequences of socially constructed ideas of race and gender. Kwan-Lafond offers keen insights into the imposition of racial ideas on masculinities—racialization—and how the respective experiences in the two communities help us to consider a socially just future for Canada.

Racialized Masculinities in Canada

Danielle Kwan-Lafond

This chapter examines racialized masculinities within the context of a multicultural Canada. We must begin with the idea that, although neither race nor gender exist in any firm biological sense, both still persist today as ideas that are widely shared and influential in our society: one's race and one's gender still have profound impacts on one's life experiences, even though we might argue that Canada is less overtly racist and less sexist today than it has been in the past, and that ideas about gender roles and racial stereotypes have changed over time. This chapter is written from an anti-racism standpoint, meaning that the ultimate goal is social change in favour of social justice,

not just an academic exercise. One of the most famous quotes about race comes from Black scholar W.E.B. Du Bois, who in 1903 wrote, 'the problem of the Twentieth Century is the problem of the color-line' (1995: v). In the twenty-first century, despite long-standing efforts to create more equal societies, such as official multiculturalism in Canada and the American civil rights movement, there is still resistance to anti-racist education; systemic and institutionalized racism are still a reality in Canada.

Canada provides an important context to understanding how race and racism work, because of the implementation of a multicultural policy that celebrates diversity and encourages interaction between and among different ethnocultural groups. This chapter is premised on the now nearly universal understanding of race (in the social sciences) as a non-scientific, non-biological social construct (or idea) that has a great impact on how people interact with different forms of power, authority, and privilege. In Canada, overt racism is rare in most places, yet institutionalized (or systemic) racism still persists (Omi and Winant, 1993).

In this chapter we begin by reviewing some of the key concepts needed to understand racialized masculinities: race and racialization, whiteness, racism and multiculturalism in Canada, and anti-racism. Then we will briefly summarize the concepts of masculinities and racialized masculinities in order to examine two specific examples of how some masculinities are racialized in Canada: Asian masculinities and Black masculinities.

What Is 'Race'?

In the social sciences and humanities, it is nearly universally accepted that the term 'race' does not represent a biologically sound, a naturally occurring, or a genetic human trait. Certainly, there is a genealogy that each person has inherited, representing a history of people's adaptations to living conditions in a specific geographic location, or of their partnering choices and their migrations across the planet. But research has shown that there is more diversity and variation within ethnic groups than between them. This means that, scientifically speaking, there is no such thing as 'race': people's differences or similarities may be related to their genetics and heredity, or to their upbringing, or to sociocultural norms and values, but not to their 'race'. Therefore, people are not smarter, taller, fatter, funnier, or more inclined to be good at music, sports, or leadership simply because they are from a certain racial group. The traditional ideas that we have in Western societies about race are changing,

and we can see this as multicultural cities grow and as social interactions and community ties between people from different backgrounds become a normal part of everyday life.

A contemporary example of how notions of racial categories are changing can be found in diverse cities such as Toronto, where multiracial people are becoming more and more common.[1] Mixed unions (marriages or common-law relationships between people from a visible minority and a non-visible minority, or between visible minorities from different ethnocultural backgrounds) are on the rise: in 2006, mixed unions made up 3.9 per cent of Canadian couples, up from 3.1 per cent in 2001 and 2.6 per cent in 1991 (Statistics Canada, 2006). Multiracial identities challenge how we think about racial categories, because they do not fit ideas of a single racial group and their experiences expose the shifting and contextual processes of racialization that all people of colour experience (Lafond, 2009).

Terms such as 'race', 'racism', 'racialization', 'ethnicity', and 'culture' are already complicated ideas, each stepping somewhat on the toes of the others; 'mixed race' further muddles these terms, challenging our understandings of the categories of difference implied by race and ethnicity. To be sure, these are terms that even sociologists use inconsistently: both 'race' and 'ethnicity' imply notions of a common biological or genealogical heritage and of a shared group history. In general, the concept of race usually refers more to skin colour and phenotype (e.g., facial features or hair type), while 'ethnicity' refers more specifically to linguistic or religious practice or to other cultural features that are shared within a group. For example, in Canada, the dominant group of people who colonized the lands was racially white, but those people came from separate ethnic groups: the French and the English (and later others). Each had a different language, culture, and religious tradition. Among Canada's First Nations, there are many ethnic groups with different languages and traditions.

Stereotypes, prejudice, and discrimination can be based on ideas about either race or ethnicity, or both. These racial or ethnic stereotypes can also intersect with gender, with other aspects of social identity, such as social class, or with sexual orientation. This chapter discusses how men from different racial groups experience the intersections between race and gender. We will explore why, for example, 'Asian' men and 'Black' men have different experiences and understandings of their identities in Canada.

The popularly held ideas in our society about what kinds of people make up a race are constantly shifting; we can trace varying interpretations of its meaning through different cultures and historical periods. Most social scientists now agree that race has historically referred to the *meanings assigned* to various physical and phenotypic traits, such as eye colour, hair type, skin tone, nose shape, etc. (Gandy, 1998; Hier, 2007; Martin-Alcoff, 2007; Tate, 1997; Thompson, 2007). The important point is that their meanings (whether positive or negative) are socially assigned, as opposed to being rooted in some objective biological property of human beings. Precisely because meaning is a social, not biological, phenomenon, the assigned meanings and assumptions tied to different 'races' are not fixed: they are always changing, shifting, and being renegotiated. In other words, being 'raced', or racialized, is an active process. It happens through conversations, images, and ideas put forth in the media, through literature and history, and through many other avenues in our culture. For the most part, dominant ideas are reinforced, but new ideas and new expressions of identities are always being forged. Multiracial people are one example, but all racial groups have fluid and shifting ideas about them that change over time and place.

The idea that race has no biological significance has taken hold in popular culture as well as within academia. In fact, some have stretched this point, arguing that because race is not real, racism must not be real either. Related to the argument that race is not 'real' are arguments that people can be 'colour-blind', and that those of us who 'see' race are reinforcing it, and thus responsible for the continued effects of racism. Race remains one of the most salient aspects of identity formation and of social organization, not just in Canadian society but also across the globe (Omi and Winant, 1993). As anti-racism scholar George Dei (2007) cautions, denial of race can be dangerous, for it can lead to a failure to acknowledge racism. At the same time, we need to remember that while race matters, it is neither permanent nor a scientific fact. Being and becoming 'raced' is a social process, and this process is called *racialization*.

What Is 'Racialization'?

If race has no biological significance and the ideas that we have about race are made and reinforced through our culture (socially created), then 'racialization' is the process by which meaning is assigned to phenotypical features, skin colour, or other social signifiers of race in order to categorize a person in a specific racial category. Hier (2007) points out that groups of human beings have been assigning meaning to social signifiers of difference since long before the language of race came into common usage. He traces the use of the term 'race' (in Europe) as a tool to classify groups of humans back to the sixteenth century. Hier adds that the process of racialization involves not only assigning meaning to otherwise irrelevant physical characteristics but also the 'additional stipulation that socially constructed collectivities (not races) are understood in terms of, or perceived as, real or imagined ancestral groups' (2007: 28). Race, he says, is a specific discourse that is relatively recent, whereas racialization is the 'dialectical social process' of using physical features to group people along real or imagined ancestral lines.

In other words, the process of 'othering' people based on perceived differences is not new; what is more recent is our use of the term 'race' and all the complex assigned meaning we call up with it. Omi and Winant (1993) also point to the importance of studying the 'socially constructed status of the concept of race', or what they call the *process of racial formation* (racialization). Martin-Alcoff states, 'I will take race to be the very real aspect of social identity, one that is marked on the body through learned perceptual practices of visual categorization, with significant sociological and political effects as well as a psychological impact on self-formation' (2007: 173).

Racialization occurs when we take differences that we can see on bodies (skin colour, hair, etc.) and assign meanings to those traits that are falsely thought of as rooted in biology: straight hair means the person is smarter; darker skin means that people are better suited for physical labour; people with lighter skin are better dancers, etc. Hier (2007) says that when sociocultural signifiers (language, religion, clothing, etc.) are used (instead of physical traits) to group people into categories that supposedly share inherent characteristics, this is the process of *ethnicization*. Social scientists use the term 'racialization', or 'racialized identities', to remind us that we are socially conditioned to observe differences in people, to group people according to those differences, and to hold beliefs about what those differences mean. The approach to race and racialization taken here can be called a *social constructionist* approach—as Satzewich states, 'social constructionism challenges biological and essentialist understandings of race and race difference. . . . What constitutes race and race difference, as well as the creation, application, and maintenance of racial labels and group boundaries, then, are matters of social definition, claims-making activities, and differential power relations' (2007: 68).

Whiteness

In any discussion of race and racialization, it is important to note that for white people, racialization happens differently, because they are the culturally dominant (or hegemonic) group in our society. Although there can be

discriminatory beliefs and behaviours against non-white racialized communities by other non-whites, the global restructuring of world resources in the nineteenth and twentieth centuries along white European ideological lines puts whiteness at the centre of any critical examination of racialization, for it is Western thought that still informs our ideas about race and racism. Further, racialized people are rapidly increasing in numbers in North American and European cities, in part because people from all over the world are migrating to these places to escape the inequality, lack of opportunity, and oppression in their countries of origin, much of which was caused by unfavourable interactions with powerful (white) nations or with international organizations serving the interests of powerful (white) nations. Except perhaps in the most isolated communities, whiteness is globally recognized as a privileged signifier of difference (Leonardo, 2002). Omi and Winant speak about the global context of race, stating that the 'territorial reach of racial hegemony is now global' (1993: 8). In other words, white dominance transcends national boundaries (Leonardo, 2002), even in places where white people may not be the numerical majority of the population.

In studies of race and identities, whiteness should not be thought of as a culture or a race in the scientific sense, but rather as a social concept (Leonardo, 2002), just as the race of any other group is a social concept (as discussed earlier in the chapter). As a social concept, the racial category of whiteness changes over time. We can see this if we look at the experiences of the Irish around 1800 in America, or Jews in the first half of the twentieth century. Both of the following examples remind us of how social class and race are profoundly linked.

Large numbers of early Irish immigrants initially arrived in the Americas in the 1800s, fleeing famine in Ireland. In Europe, they were oppressed by the British (Protestants), who banned Catholic holidays and the Irish language (Leonardo, 2002). When they arrived in the Americas, Irish people found themselves in the position of having to compete with Blacks for labouring jobs, and both groups were exploited by whites (although, unlike Blacks, the Irish were never enslaved). At this point, the Irish were considered a race of people who were different in character from 'whites'. Had the Irish aligned themselves with Blacks (an example of solidarity based on their similar social class positions), it would have threatened white supremacy in the United States, but this did not happen. Instead, the Irish increasingly came to align themselves with white bourgeois power, and they 'embrace[d] whiteness as a path to social mobility and economic independence' (2002: 42).

As Satzewich explains,

In the nineteenth century . . . the Irish were regarded as racial others whose presence constituted a significant threat to American democracy. The Irish, however, underwent a remarkable transformation during the course of the nineteenth century. They were able to renegotiate their externally imposed racial otherness, assert a white identity, and come to be accepted as members of the 'white race'. Having been accepted as white, they turned around and became some of the most vigorous defenders of whiteness. In many cases, their defence of a newly acquired whiteness put them at the forefront of hostilities and conflicts with black people (2007: 68).

For the Irish, social class and aspirations for upward mobility created a context in which it was advantageous for them to try to gain entry into the category of whiteness. Several generations later, no Irish person in North America would be considered non-white, but it is important to recall that this was not always the case.

A second example can be found in the way that some Jewish identities have come to be included in the category of whiteness, when only some 60 years ago, Jews were widely regarded in Europe and elsewhere as an inferior and threatening race that needed to be eliminated in the name of preserving white power. The Jewish example is perhaps one of the most useful for exposing how uncertain and flexible categories of race can be. Who exactly falls into the category of 'white' is something that clearly changes over time and place; but what doesn't always change is the idea that races do exist, and that we can tell something about people if we know what race they are. As Kaye/Kantowitz's text *The Colors of Jews* (2007) highlights, Jewish people are multi-ethnic and multilingual, and there are many communities of Jews who are people of colour (e.g., the Hebrew Israelites in the United States, Arab Jews in the Middle East, Ethiopian Jews in Africa, and mixed-race Jews around the world), so it is a mistake to assume that if someone is Jewish, he/she will look white (or Ashkenazi). Jewish ethnicities (languages, cultures, religious practices) are multiple (Kaye/Kantowitz, 2007) but in North America, the largest group of Jews came from Europe, and today these people are considered racially white. The 'othering' of Jewish people today tends to focus on ethnic differences from dominant white culture rather than on so-called racial differences between Jews and non-Jews. In her book *How Jews Became White Folks and What That Says about Race in America*, Karen Brodkin links class mobility with the 'whitening' of American Jews (1998). This is another example that helps us to see that race is a sociopolitical category that is intimately linked to power relations, and that it is not a self-evident category bound to physical characteristics (Levine-Rasky, 2008).

Classroom discussions of whiteness and white privilege often invoke white guilt: the idea that white people are personally responsible for white privilege and white domination, and that white people are inherently racist. This is not useful; it reduces whites to the inevitable enemies of people of colour, and does not allow for whites to take up action-oriented strategies like anti-racism. White people need to acknowledge the complexities of how their racialized white identities intersect with power and privilege, while also understanding that while they may benefit from the status quo, the systemic and institutionalized valuing of whiteness over non-whiteness is not due to their individual actions.

Although whites should critically examine the privileges that whiteness has accrued them over the past few generations (and beyond), the important work is in linking these privileges to larger social structures. There is a difference between whiteness, white culture, and white people (Leonardo, 2002). We need to focus on critiques of whiteness as an organizing principle (like any other 'race') that cuts across social class, gender, and other aspects of social identity. Not all white people are equally privileged, and not all people of colour are oppressed in the same way. However, white dominance means that the nation-state and its major institutions, values, and practices are rooted in Western European thought, and that this thought tradition is responsible for colonization and the devaluing of non-Western thought. Further, centuries of exploitive interactions between groups, regions, and nations has resulted in a profoundly unequal distribution of wealth and power, one which continues to reinforce social hierarchy and which long outlives the ideas that originally attempted to rationalize them. Western thought values individualism, so perhaps this helps explain why white people can 'get stuck' in white guilt. On the other hand, it is also easy to blame racism and continued disadvantage on the historical wrongs done by those of past generations, without linking these histories with the significant social barriers that people, such as Aboriginal people in Canada, still face today.

Canadian scholar Cecil Foster (2007) presents a way to think about whiteness that goes beyond appearance or skin tone; he suggests that both Blackness and whiteness are categories that change over time, but that there are certain key features that can help us think about how these categories are created. He proposes 'reading' Blackness and whiteness according to

(a) appearance (i.e., skin tone and other physical features—Foster calls this 'the somatic');
(b) status (access to wealth, power, entitlement, influence, ownership);
(c) culture (shared or common cultural expression); and
(d) ideals (common myths, theories of the world, shared philosophies).

Further, Foster says that 'idealized Blackness and whiteness are what is "given" to us by culture out of our myths and moral education' (2007: 96). To say that we socially construct ideas of race is to understand that we are each implicated in how racial categories are formed, without any of us having the power to unilaterally direct how these ideas are carried forward.

Racism and Multiculturalism in Canada

My 2009 study of racialized men who live in Toronto found that many were troubled by the discontinuities between the ideology of multiculturalism and the realities of racism in Canada. As Levine-Rasky (2008) and others (Bannerji, 2000) point out, there are tensions between the official Canadian Multiculturalism Act as enshrined in the Constitution, on the one hand, which promotes liberal-democratic values such as equality and fairness, and the persistence of discrimination, intolerance, and racism in Canada on the other. Kobayashi (1993) and Bannerji (2000) illustrate how multicultural policy in Canada has been uninterested in political goals such as achieving social justice or taking an anti-racist stand. Any discussion of multiculturalism in Canada takes on the challenge of dealing with many different understandings and opinions of official policy.

As well, there is a range of meanings associated with the related concepts of diversity and racism, and each comes with its own politically charged discourse.

As scholars Carr and Lund put it, 'Power does have a colour in Canada, despite official multiculturalism, making our nation appear superficially to be a harmonious society in which anyone can be successful with the right attitude and effort' (2007: 3). Even though Canadians value multiculturalism, and most Canadians would not condone overt racist behaviour or speech, there is ample evidence that systemic racism is a reality in Canada. However, systemic discrimination is often invisible and hard to document (Caouette and Taylor, 2007).

Racism is about the beliefs and practices that are used to privilege some and oppress others. Racial inequality is maintained through ideologies (ideas) that rationalize, legitimize, and sustain the unequal distribution of resources among different racial groups. One of these powerful ideologies is 'meritocracy'—the idea that whatever privileges, be they job opportunities, wealth, or education, we have acquired in life were merited (earned) and are therefore deserved. This idea goes hand in hand with the idea that certain groups' lack of success in society is due to their individual failings or cultural inadequacies (Caouette and Taylor, 2007).

The most persistent criticism raised about multiculturalism is that, despite its being a very prominent Canadian value, racism continues to persist. In my interviews with mixed-race men in Toronto in 2009, participants and I discussed multiculturalism in Canada. First, it should be noted that I draw a distinction between 'official multiculturalism', which is made up of organized events, policies, festivals, and curricula, and what Walcott (2003b) refers to as 'everyday multiculturalism' or 'popular multiculturalism': the daily interactions that take place in cities like Toronto, where people are engaging in a crossing of cultural barriers, cultural translation, and remaking themselves in relation to the other people and institutions in their lives.

Over the course of the interviews I conducted, it became clear that when the participants talked about multiculturalism, they were often using it as a descriptor of their social realities in Toronto rather than discussing policy. They spoke about their schools, neighbourhoods, their peer groups, and the public in Toronto as being 'multicultural', and they often paired this with discussions of how racism still exists, especially outside Toronto (Lafond, 2009). The important point is that multiculturalism in Canada creates a particular sociopolitical context within which identities are formed; yet ideas about race and systemic disadvantage still persist, and this creates a point of tension between multicultural ideas and the lived experiences of many who are disadvantaged.

In terms of understanding the existence of non-overt (covert or hidden) forms of racism, Henry and Tator (1994) discuss what they refer to as 'aversive racism' or, similarly, 'symbolic racism'. When describing 'aversive racists', Henry and Tator state: '[S]uch individuals are prejudiced but do not act out their beliefs in actual discriminatory behaviour. Some aversive racists avoid contact with Blacks and other minorities but when contact is unavoidable, they assume a demeanour of formal politeness' (1994: 5).

These authors also refer to the set of attitudes and other behaviours that go along with aversive racism as 'symbolic racism'—actions that are justified using criteria that are non-racial but that work to maintain the status quo, and that may also contribute to negative views about particular groups. An example of symbolic racism could be people organizing to protest against progressive social policies that are meant to bring about social justice, such as affirmative action policies. Some whites may take part in symbolic acts such as picketing because they believe that affirmative action goes against the principles of fairness and equality, not because they have an overt desire to maintain inequality and the status quo. Their largely symbolic act, which seemingly has nothing to do with race per se, can end up contributing to and reinforcing the societal view among the dominant group that Blacks are making unreasonable demands (Henry and Tator, 1994).

Henry and Tator's work on the ideology of racism offers an additional concept, closely related to aversive/symbolic racism, that they say is especially useful for considering the Canadian case. The authors say the following about racism in Canada, which they term 'democratic racism':

> White Canadians tend to dismiss easily the accumulated body of evidence documenting racial prejudice and differential treatment. . . . There is a deep attachment to the assumption that in a democratic society individuals are rewarded solely on the basis of their individual merit and that no one group is singled out for discrimination . . . .'Democratic racism' refers to an ideology which permits and sustains the ability to justify maintaining two apparently conflicting values. . . . One set of values consists of a commitment to a democratic society motivated by egalitarian values of fairness, justice and equality. Conflicting with these liberal values are attitudes and behaviours which include negative feelings about people of colour and which carry the potential for differential treatment or discrimination against them (1994: 2–3).

Also written in 1994, Charles Taylor's often-referenced essay titled 'The Politics of Recognition' links the foundations of multiculturalism with what he calls the 'politics of equal respect' (Taylor et al., 1994: 68), based in liberal humanist thought. As Minelle Mahtani, a mixed-race scholar who has looked at the links between multiculturalism in Canada and multiracial women's identities, states, 'Multicultural policy, where ethnic identities are celebrated as a backdrop for Canadian identity, often ensures that forms of institutionalized racism are rendered invisible' (2002: 475).

Despite its contradictions, multiculturalism's strong influence in Canadian society has helped provide people from many different backgrounds with a solid foundation upon which to build Canadian identities, yet we will see how racism and discrimination also play an influential role in how some men construct their sense of masculinity within this often conflictual context.

Anti-racism

> When looking through an anti-racist lens, I am able to see how skin color, shade, texture of hair and shape of eyes influence the opportunities we have in life, the rights we enjoy, the access we have to resources and the representation and respect we receive. . . . I can see how the ways in which we have organized our lives and our institutions, around race and other identities, have brought us to our present positions (Lee, 2006: 404).

Anti-racism is helpful for understanding racialized masculinities. Anti-racist thought places race at the centre of human experience, understands that though it is not a biological phenomenon, it remains a key marker of identity because it has powerful social effects. It is an appropriate tool for looking at racialized people's experiences because it advocates that the goal and purpose of such work, ultimately, is social change in favour of those who are disadvantaged. Critical analyses require a very nuanced personal understanding of racism, multiculturalism, and racial identity. As Mohanty states, 'resistance lies in self-conscious engagement with dominant, normative discourses and representations and in the active creation of oppositional analytic and cultural spaces' (1990: 185). George Dei's scholarly work has served as a guide in anti-racist theory, which he describes as 'an action-oriented strategy for institutional, systemic change to address racism and the interlocking systems of social oppression' (2000: 25).

Anti-racist scholars such as Omi and Winant (1993) point to the continuing significance of race, despite its ever-changing categories and conceptualizations. Their focus is helpful for thinking about racialization experiences because they draw attention to the relational character of racial identity and to the fact that it is created through a constantly changing social and global context of race processes. Their analyses help to explain why, despite the fact that many people of colour do not live in majority-white communities, they are still influenced by a system that values whiteness over non-whiteness.

Despite the lack of scientific or biological evidence for the existence of race, anti-racism allows for race to be placed solidly at the centre of the discussion (Dei, 2000). Haney-Lopez states: 'Race is neither an essence nor an illusion, but rather an ongoing, contradictory, self-reinforcing, plastic process subject to the macro forces of social and political struggle and the micro effects of daily decisions' (1995: 165).

Haney-Lopez (1995) is an anti-racist scholar who is also influenced by his experience of being mixed race: he describes that he and his brother, who are of mixed Latino and white American descent, have different racial identities. He highlights the importance of the relational way that races are constructed; that is, there is no 'Black' without 'white'. Race is socially constructed, and different races are constructed in relation to other races.

Other anti-racist scholars, such as Mohanty (1990) and Dixson and Rousseau (2005), remind us that another important part of anti-racism scholarship is about giving voice to those who have historically been denied a place in the literature.

What Is Masculinity?

Perhaps the most influential scholar on the topic of masculinities is R.W. Connell (2005), who states that biological determinism and social constructionism, or the simple acceptance that both play a role, are not adequate for understanding the complex processes involved in the construction of masculinities. As Connell states, '[Masculinity] is simultaneously a place in gender relations, the practices through which men and women engage that place in gender, and the effects of these practices in bodily experience, personality and culture' (2005: 71).

According to Connell, what it means to be a man or a woman in society is tied up in how one enacts a general set of expectations related to one's sex. As Schippers (2007) explains, there are certain bodily features, certain behaviours, and certain personality traits that together provide enough information to create categories of 'male' and 'female' that people are classified into. As with race, here again the language we use pre-dates (and in many cases is inadequate in evoking) contemporary biological and sociological understandings of the true diversity of human bodies and experiences.

One of the key ideas is that masculinities are caught up in gender relations. In Connell's work, 'any one masculinity, as a configuration of practice, is simultaneously positioned in a number of structures of relationship, which may be following different historical trajectories. Accordingly masculinity, like femininity, is always liable to internal contradiction and historical disruption' (2005: 73). 'Gender relations' refers to masculinity and femininity—these relations are historical and situational. Like categories of race, gender relations are not always the same within a culture or society, and masculine and feminine ideals are culturally dependent (they are different from one culture to another). Connell explains that gender relations are part of larger social structures, and that gender shapes how social practices happen. These practices are more than individual 'masculine' or 'feminine' acts; they relate to, and help define and reproduce, particular ideas about gender within social structures.

Connell focuses on four main 'practices and relations' that are involved in making and remaking our notions of masculinities. In order to understand racialized masculinities, the two most relevant, and the focus here, are hegemony and marginalization. However, Connell's other two practices and relations involved in the maintenance of masculinity, subordination and complicity, are also important.

Subordination refers to the idea that within gender relations, there are dominant (those considered 'normal' or successful in their achievement of masculinity) kinds of men and subordinate groups of men. The most obvious example is how homosexual masculinities are oppressed by hegemonic heterosexual masculinities: gay men are discriminated against, excluded from parts of society, or legally oppressed or criminalized (as in anti-sodomy laws or laws against gay marriage). *Complicity* is the notion that even though few individual men actually fit all of the ideas bound up in hegemonic masculinity, the majority of men benefit from the way gender relations continue to operate, with women as a whole subordinate to men. Therefore, individual men do not have to personally dominate their wives or behave in ultramasculine ways; still, the overall structure of gender relations (which includes men's relation to women, as well as relations between groups of men or women) makes it such that 'not many men actually meet the normative standard' but 'the majority of men gain from its hegemony' (Connell, 2005: 79).

Hegemony 'refers to the cultural dynamic by which a group claims and sustains a leading position in social life' (Connell, 2005: 77). This means that some kinds of masculinity are 'culturally exalted', meaning that they are accepted, celebrated, and considered to be success examples of manhood, while other kinds of masculinities are devalued, disallowed, punished, discouraged, or considered inferior (which is often equated with womanliness or femininity).

Connell accounts for other aspects of men's social identities, namely race and class, by looking at *marginalization*, or 'the relations between the masculinities in dominant and subordinated classes' (2005: 80). This allows Connell to

analyze how, for example, Black male athletes can be held up as stars and can be wealthy and successful, yet this does not accrue benefits to Black men as a (subordinate) group in general. In the discussion of Black masculinities in Canada that follows, we will see how the aspiration to be an athletic star is deeply ingrained as part of the subculture of Black Canadian youth in Toronto (James, 2003), but that success in sport does not change the overall dominant/subordinate relations between groups of men.

Connell and Messerschmidt (2005) also pay close attention to the geography of masculinities, or how performances or expectations of masculinities change in different settings. The authors point to the importance of local, regional, and global geographies, and they say that they are all related to one another, because each requires a different construction of masculinity. On this point, Farough noted that in his study, white men felt 'white', or racialized, in mostly Black settings; this shows 'how such seemingly mundane acts of moving across physical space highlight the context-specific ways white men must periodically confront being interpreted as privileged, as their identity is transformed from "non-racial" to "racial"' (2004: 241). Farough calls the lack of awareness of a racialized self, such as that experienced by mainstream white men in majority-white settings, 'sovereign individuality'.

The questions that Connell (2005) and Connell and Messerschmidt (2005) raise about hegemonic masculinities lead to discussions about the relations of power between and among different masculinities. These questions complement the questions that anti-racist scholars ask about the construction of racialized identities: what are the relationships of alliance, domination and subordination, inclusion and exclusion, and intimidation that occur between identities? Connell asks this from a gender politics point of view, but my interviews with racialized men in 2009 showed that they have a collapsed construction of gender where race is ever-present. In other words, they relate their gender to their race and vice versa, and it is not useful (or possible) for them to talk about how their gender impacts their lives without taking their race into account. Many social scientists write about how race, class, gender, sexual orientation, and other aspects of one's social identity are experienced as a whole (the intersectionalist model, with overlapping systems of oppression) (Crenshaw, 1989; Davis, 2008), and not as individual or separate identities. It is worth noting that while the men seemed unable to separate gender from race, they did talk about race without naming gender (Lafond, 2009).

What Do We Mean by Racialized Masculinities?

The idea that masculinities are racialized means that one's race (along with other aspects of social identity) influences ideas about what it is to be 'a man'. In other words, to be 'a man' is to have your ideas about 'manliness' change depending on how your race is socially constructed. What kinds of men or women are more likely to be associated with the image of a doctor? A thief? A drug dealer? A university professor? A math whiz? A violin prodigy? A computer genius? A basketball star? These kinds of stereotypes are both race-based and gender-based, and when we talk about racialized masculinities, we infer that both race *and* gender affect performances and expectations of masculinity.

As Connell (2005) points out, there is a traditional stand-in for the hegemonic man (white, middle-class, rational, etc.), but this is not the only idea of manhood that exists in society. There are also many other kinds of masculinities; these are the 'marginalized' or 'subordinate' forms of masculinity. So for a gay man, an Asian man, or a gay Asian man, this does not necessarily mean that he is not recognized in society as a 'man', but that the kind of 'manliness' (masculinity) that is expected for him, or valued by him, may be different from the hegemonic norm, and is influenced by ideas about how he can (or should) behave as a man

from a specific social subcategory. Racialized masculinities are, according to Connell, an example of marginalized masculinities.

Black Masculinities in Canada

Discussions of Blackness in Canada should begin by acknowledging that while many Black people share some common experiences with anti-Black racism, there is great diversity among communities of Blacks in Canada; each has a different historical relationship with Canada, and different social realities. Some groups, such as the Scotians, have been in Canada for eight or more generations, and they constitute an important and sizeable community in Nova Scotia. In this community overall, 91 per cent of Blacks are Canadian-born, versus 40 per cent of Blacks who are Canadian-born in Toronto (James and Lloyd, 2006). At the same time, Walcott reminds us that we should not place different Black communities (in this case, urban and rural) in Canada in opposition to one another, for this would fail to account for the 'diaspora connectedness' that Black communities do share (Walcott, 2003a). So, while this discussion applies to how Black men in Canada are racialized, it is important to recognize that these patterns of racialization, and the way Black masculinities are constructed by others, change depending on social class, status in Canada (immigrant or Canadian-born), country of origin, and many other factors. Although not all Black men experience the same degree of stereotyping or discrimination, I suggest that all Black men in Canada live in relation to hegemonic masculinities, and that they must find ways to resist or respond to the way Black masculinities are constructed. As Archer and Yamashita (2003) propose, masculinities are racialized, but not in simple, homogeneous, unchanging, or consistent ways. In their study of minority ethnic boys in inner-city London, England, they found that masculinities were 'culturally entangled', meaning that they represent a constantly changing or mixing of identity constructions. So, while the

Black boys in their study were clearly aware of how Black masculinities were constructed, their own notions of masculinities 'combine traces of various social, historical, geographical and cultural elements, and indicate the shifting nature of masculinities' (2003: 120). These authors also point out that there are differences in how Caribbean masculinities and African masculinities are ethnicized, and that class, migration, and cultural practice are integrally connected. Connell points to the importance of bodies, reminding us that in our society 'the physical sense of maleness and femaleness is central to the cultural interpretation of gender' (2005: 52). For racialized men, bodies, especially physical appearance, skin tone, and phenotype, are central to their lived experiences. I suggest that while there are important social, political, or economic differences among Blacks in Canada, most Black men share, as Connell puts it, a 'bodily experience [that] is often central in the memories of our own lives, and thus in our understanding of who and what we are' (2005: 53).

Perhaps the most pervasive image of Black male bodies in our society is in professional sport. While it is true that many of these images come from the United States, James (2003) postulates that young Black men in Toronto identify with their African-American counterparts because, even within multicultural Canada, people have difficulty imagining Blackness as part of Canada. Therefore, these young men look south of the border for identification with a subculture of professional Black athletics. Ferber (2007) provides a historical overview of depictions of Black men in the United States, and she examines how they have been constructed as a threat to whites while also being accepted into roles as servants or entertainers of whites. This seems like a contradiction, but recall that race and masculinities are always being constructed in relation to other social dynamics, and that these contradictions can indeed exist. Similarly, Ferber points to what seems like another contradiction: 'white audience members' worship of Black male athletes

may seem a positive embrace of diversity', but 'the mainstream media spectacle of sport does nothing to encourage an interrogation of white supremacy and racism' (2007: 12). Ferber states that 'both Black men and women have been reduced to their physical bodies' (2007: 15) but that racism has shifted its focus from the biological to the cultural. Under 'cultural racism', racialized peoples' lack of success is seen as 'the product of their lack of effort, loose family organization, or inappropriate values' (Bonilla-Silva and Embrick, 2005: 40). Canadian scholars also discuss so-called colour-blindness as a problematic feature of Canadian racism within multiculturalism. So while stereotypes about Black bodies were in the past attributed to supposed biological traits in people, now they are attributed to deficiencies in 'Black culture'. As Ferber points out, the images of Black athletes are not so different from older stereotypes about the animal nature of Blacks, which emphasize strength, aggressiveness, and sexual prowess. In fact, the sheer number of images of Black male athletes presented in the media, versus the number of representations of Black men in other roles, may in fact reinforce the myth that Blacks are naturally good at sports. Although many Black men obviously do excel at sports, the problem is that their accomplishments get attributed to their natural abilities, while whites' accomplishments are instead attributed to their moral character, intelligence, preparedness, etc. 'Thus', writes Ferber, 'the success of Black men in sports is entirely consistent with White supremacist ideology' (2007: 20).

The racialized men I interviewed in 2009 who identified as Black also talked about the criminalization of young Black men in Toronto, and that this was a stereotype they had to contend with on a regular basis. In our conversations about race and racialization experiences, the topic of gender did not enter the conversation unless I brought it up. In other words, when the participants think about racism, they are not necessarily relating it to being male; they are focused on the racialized part of their identities. The absence of any mention of gender is not surprising: race is very salient and can many times become the central aspect of focus in one's identity, especially when racism and discrimination enter the picture. Further, as men embedded in gender relations, they are part of the dominant gender, and thus do not have to think about their gendered selves to the degree that women do, because the male gender is the 'norm'. What I want to call attention to here is that when gender was raised as the focal point of the discussion, the participants' responses to questions about gender or masculinity still focused on race. Here is one example, from my interview with Isaac, who is mixed Jamaican/white:

Interviewer: How do you think about gender, male or female-ness . . . do you think it's an important part of your life, or of your identity?
Isaac: Well, being a Black guy, even though I'm light, is really different. I was lucky—I had really great role models, Black people, that I always knew, so I didn't take in all of the negative self-concept stuff that I know lots of Black people have to deal with. I think it just comes from everywhere—the media, and like people have some pretty bad stereotypes about Black guys, so it can be hard to get away from that.

Here is another participant, a university student in his twenties, who identifies as Black. In these comments, he is discussing his relationship with his girlfriend, Linh, who is Asian, and her family:

Dante: They [Linh's family] had never met me before, but they heard that I was half Black, and they automatically assumed that I was like [pause] like the majority of young Black guys from Scarborough. Which I'm not. I'm not even from Scarborough. So . . . they own

a [small business], and they dealt with a lot of . . . the darker . . . or the more negative stereotypes . . . of Black people you could say, and so I guess they had a . . . painted a picture of Black people . . . and assumed that that's what I was. I mean, they didn't take into account the fact that I'm a student, I have a job, and I don't sell drugs, and I don't fall into those stereotypes for the most part.

Dante does not want to be disrespectful of Linh's family, but he admits that they hold negative stereotypes about Black men, and that this was reinforced through their experiences in Scarborough. In the Greater Toronto Area (GTA), Scarborough is often perceived as having higher crime rates than the rest of Toronto, when in fact the crime rate there is lower than in other parts of the city, according to police chief Bill Blair in 2008 (Milley, 2008). However, there were a number of high-profile incidents involving gang-related violence, and media across Canada began running stories characterizing Scarborough as crime-ridden and unsafe (Gillmor, 2007). The issue of gang violence in Toronto is racialized, where the term 'gang' implies non-white males. It is unclear by his statements whether Dante is implying that Linh's family had actually had negative interactions with Black men and that their discriminatory beliefs were based in some kind of personal experience that was then generalized and socially reinforced, but he clearly links negative stereotypes about Black men to the geographic context of Scarborough.

Dante is aware of the perception by Linh's family that because he is a Black male and he lives in Scarborough, he is more likely to be involved in crime. He says that he is not like 'the majority of young Black guys from Scarborough', which perhaps implies that he himself has internalized some of these beliefs about young Black men. He makes it clear that he is employed and a student, and that he does not fit these stereotypes. Next, he explains how he dealt with Linh's brother, who is a head figure in the family:

Dante: He's the one who really instigated the thing of like 'my sister is not going to be dating a Black guy', so [pause] . . . it's not like they said 'Don't come to our house', but I'm like, if I do go to your house, I don't want to have to like fight your brother in his house. I'm not going to disrespect your house, so I'm just not going to go at all.

Dante described how he stayed away from Linh's house for many months, but that slowly, as he and her family got to know each other more, they began to accept him despite his Blackness. Dante did not feel that being part white was of any importance or of any benefit in this situation: he was racialized as Black, and when Linh's family, especially her brother, finally accepted him, it was because he was 'an exception' to the stereotypes about young Black men in Scarborough. Over time, they learned about his work and study habits and saw that he was not involved in crime or in activities they disapproved of, and they got to know him personally.

Dante: Now it's all okay, everyone gets along, and they know that I'm not one of 'those guys', I'm all right, you know. I don't worry about it, I'm just glad it all worked out.

Linh's family racialized Dante as Black, and when the two first began dating, he experienced discrimination based on being a Black male from Scarborough. In his interview, Dante was unable to discuss what his experience of being 'male' was like except when he related it to being a Black male. Through his Blackness, Dante has experienced discrimination, and he relates this to being seen as both Black *and* male. His masculinity as a Black man is racialized, and these two aspects of his identity are equally important in shaping how others treat him.

Another participant, Damien, who is mixed Black and Brown (Indian Hindu background) from Trinidad, answered as follows when I asked him about the significance of his gender:

Damien: I don't know what it's like to be a female, so it's hard to say what my gender means to me. I guess, you know, there's a lot of stereotypes and beliefs that Black men are a certain way, and in Toronto, like I find if you dress a certain way, people will assume that you're a drug dealer or that you're poor, that you live in the ghetto. You know, my dad always says 'Black men are an endangered species'. Like, it's easier to fall into that if you're Black, because people expect that, and so I think some guys just give in, because if people are just going to assume anyways, then you might as well give them what they want. Also it makes us mad, Black people, so it's easier to end up an angry person. But I think my way of making up for it is like, I'm always afraid that people are like, thinking the worst of me, so I try to be extra nice, to show that like, I'm not like that. Like I work with kids a lot, and I think it's important to role model for them that we're not all gangsters, that that's just the media.

Damien first notes that he does not know what it is like to be female, and so, comparatively, he is unable to say what it means to be male. He then begins to tell me about the difficulties of being Black and male. He points to the low expectations and stereotypes people have about Black men, and he points out that this can contribute to anger and to Black men's internalizing these discriminatory and negative beliefs, which may increase the chances that someone will turn to violence and crime. Damien states that he is worried that people will perceive him negatively and that he makes efforts to be extra nice in order to avoid being treated with prejudice. Damien's mannerisms were very gentle, he spoke with a very calm voice, and he smiled a lot when we were speaking. Part of Damien's performance of his racialized masculinity—his gentle demeanour—might be a kind of racial performance that, as a response to racial stereotypes, is deliberately aimed at countering negative assumptions about Black men.

Tator and Henry (2006) write that discussions about racial profiling in Canada are often focused on recent events, which would suggest the idea that racially biased policing is a new phenomenon in Canada. Contrary to this, the authors point out that Black Canadians have a long history of marginalization, and that racism in law enforcement is nothing new. The long history of criminalization of racialized people contributes to the idea that there is a link between racial background and crime. Their book provides ample evidence that there are significant disparities in the way that Blacks and other racialized groups in Toronto are treated by law enforcement, and that this is not exclusive to Canada. When crime rates are linked to race or culture, other aspects of social and political life become invisible: what are the links between racism, resistance, wealth and resource distribution, and crime? How are these and other important questions obscured when the focus of the questions we ask is shared by biased and discriminatory discourse? Black men are racialized according to stereotypes about Black culture and Black bodies, and these stereotypes shift according to context. It is important to recognize that gender and race are inseparable when it comes to how identities are read and responded to in society.

Asian Masculinities in Canada

Like Black masculinities, Asian masculinities in Canada share a similar history and set of stereotypes with the United States, because the two countries have similar historical and contemporary relationships with Asians. 'Both nations . . . vilified, feminized, and pathologized Asian masculinity in popular and legal discourses and so disciplined, regulated, and punished Asian North Americans' (Pon, 2000: 142). For example, both countries brought Chinese men over around the turn of the twentieth century to build the railroads, both countries disenfranchised Asians until the 1940s, and both interned people of Japanese descent in World War II (Pon, 2000; Wei, 1993). My own ancestors were among the earliest groups of men who came to Canada from Toisan (in Guangdong, China) but because of exclusionary laws and head tax policies were excluded from staying in Canada. Members of my family came back to Canada much later, in the 1970s. In the early twentieth century, the 'yellow peril' stereotype was used to racialize Asians as 'yellow', and this helped reinforce the idea that they were best suited for certain kinds of work, that they should live in 'Chinatowns' (segregated communities away from whites), and that racial mixing between Asian men (for most early immigrants were men whose wives and families did not immigrate) and white women was dangerous (Pon, 2000). 'Unlike stereotypical images of black males as physically powerful, Chinese men were typically imagined as small, effeminate and weak in relation to the bodies and masculinities of white men' (Millington et al., 2008: 198). As we have seen, seemingly contradictory stereotypes can exist at the same time: while Asian men were racialized as being better suited for hard labour, they were also emasculated. Millington and colleagues point out that Chinese men's identities in Vancouver during the late 1800s and early 1900s were limited because they were not allowed to bring their families to Canada, and so could not fulfil the masculine roles of fathers and husbands. These authors also provide evidence that racialized masculinities play an important role in how young Asian men in Vancouver schools engage in sport. They found that young men often formed teams that were racially homo-geneous (made up of young men from similar ethnoracial backgrounds), and that 'traditional stereotypes of Chinese masculinities as passive and effeminate remain engrained in the school culture of BC' (2008: 205). Wang (2000) found that Chinese-Canadian young men value non-athletic pursuits, that they participate in fewer competitive sport activities than young white men do, and that they identify a strong work ethic as a central marker of manhood.

In my interview with Manuel, who is in his early twenties and of Chinese and Dutch ancestry, he discusses how expectations of his behaviour toward women in clubs changes, de-pending on whether people think he is Asian or not:

> *Interviewer*: What about your gender? How do you think it affects your every-day life?
> *Manuel*: Hmm. I don't really think about it. I guess, though, it limits the dating scene for me. I'm young, I've only had a couple of girlfriends, but like, I no-tice that white girls, and Black girls too, actually, don't really look at me. Mostly only Asian girls, or sometimes brown girls, want to date Asian guys. Depends, though—not everyone sees me as Asian, so it depends.
> *Interviewer*: How would it change things if they see you as Asian versus not Asian?
> *Manuel*: Uh, well, I don't know. I don't know how people see me, but I just know that like, I feel like I have more negative stereotypes about me if I'm Asian, versus, like if they think I'm a Spanish guy, then . . . I don't know. Like I think if I talked to a white girl in like a club or something, she would say I was Spanish, just because she wouldn't think a Chinese guy would talk to her. And if race comes up, well . . . maybe if she learns I'm not Spanish and I'm Asian, she would be like, 'oh'. I don't know if it

would change things, but I think if they know up front, it makes a difference.

Manuel's comments illustrate how men of different racial backgrounds are differently constructed: he says that by simply approach-ing a white girl in a club, he is more likely to be constructed as Spanish (or Latino), because there is a perception that Asian men would not approach a white girl, whereas Spanish/Latino men would. This is evidence of the continued pervasiveness of the stereotype that Asian men are less sexually powerful than other men.

In contrast to the diminished construction of Asian men when it comes to masculinity, Asians as a group are now often characterized as the 'model minority', and some researchers have even revisited the idea that Asians might be genetically more intelligent than non-Asians (Leonardo, 2002). Recall that earlier examples from the Irish and Jewish experiences show that upward mobility in social class often helps groups to shed negative racial stereotypes, and this is true for Asians in Canada as well. More recent immigrants from Asian countries have been wealthier, and some people have even suggested that Asians are 'honorary whites', or that the category of whiteness is changing to include Asians in some contexts (Zhou, 2004). In addition to being limiting and reductionist, the main problem remains that, whether or not Asian men are stereotyped as what could be framed as 'positive' (the 'model minority' dis-course), this creates a hierarchy of desirability of immigrants based on race, and that so-called positive stereotypes (such as Asian intelligence) are still being linked to race. If Asian men are excluded from expressing their masculinity through sport, then the ways that they live out masculine lives will necessarily focus on some-thing else—in this case, on academic pursuits, which in turn reinforces the stereotype of the 'whiz kid' Asian. We must begin to recognize that there are complex dynamics that influence how social identities are shaped, and that we cannot simply ascribe a group's tendencies to their race or culture; this seriously limits the scope of our analysis and cuts us off from more accurate (albeit, more complicated) analyses of gender, race, class, sexual orientation, status, and other socially defined characteristics that shape our lives. Further, if we cannot see the whole picture, with all its discontinuities, then our attempts to change social dynamics will be only partially informed and more easily countered.

Conclusion

Masculinities are complex identities, and other social factors may play a strong, if not central, role in shaping them on an individual and societal level. Race is a salient feature of our lives, particularly in shaping access to power, wealth, and privilege. The Canadian context is interesting and unique: on the one hand, Canada is shaped by relatively well-entrenched multicultural policies, and their corresponding values are a proud part of Canadian identities; Canada also has a unique history of immigration and several large, multiethnic cities; on the other hand, Canada has persistent inequality and pervasive systemic racism. Understanding how these social constructions shape, enable, or limit our lives, interactions, and institutions, will allow us to engage in the positive task of renegotiating and reshaping our own personal biases and institutional rigidities, to promote practices and policies that truly reflect social justice and shared democratic values.

Discussion Questions

1. How is the concept of 'race' similar to or different from the concept of 'racialization'?
2. Discuss how 'whiteness' as a category has changed over time for some groups.
3. What are some of the contradictory aspects of Canadian multiculturalism?
4. Explain Connell's notions of subordinate and dominant masculinities.
5. What is colour-blindness, and how does it relate to how some men experience racism or racialization?
6. Discuss how gender and racialization impact some Asian men and some Black men differently. What are the similarities or differences?
7. Discuss whether and how Canadian multiculturalism helps minimize racism and discrimination.
8. How do you think about 'everyday multiculturalism' versus 'official multiculturalism'?
9. How are notions of masculinity related to the concept of gender relations?
10. Is hegemonic masculinity a racialized category? Why or why not?

Recommended Websites

The Men's Bibliography: http://mensbiblio.xyonline.net

Masc Magazine: www.mascmag.com

Note

1. I use the terms 'mixed race' and 'multiracial' interchangeably to refer to individuals whose two biological parents are considered to be from two different ethnoracial groups. For further discussion of the difficulties and ambiguities of this definition, please see Lafond (2009).

References

Archer, L., and H. Yamashita. 2003. 'The Rising Inner-City Masculinities: "Race", Class, Gender and Education', *Gender and Education*, 15, 2: 115–32.

Bannerji, H. 2000. *The Dark Side of the Nation: Essays on Multiculturalism, Nationalism and Gender*. Toronto: Canadian Scholars' Press.

Bonilla-Silva, E., and D. Embrick. 2005. 'The (White) Color of Color Blindness in Twenty-First-Century Amerika', in W.E. Ross and V. Ooka Pang, eds., *Race, Ethnicity, and Education*, vol. 4: *Colorblind Racism: Racism/Anti-racist Action*. New York: Praeger.

Brodkin, K. 1998. *How Jews Became White Folks and What That Says about Race in America*. New Brunswick, NJ: Rutgers University Press.

Caouette, J., and D. Taylor. 2007. '"Don't Blame Me for What My Ancestors Did": Understanding the Impact of Collective White Guilt', in P.R. Carr and D.E. Lund, eds., *The Great White North? Exploring Whiteness, Privilege and Identity in Education*. Rotterdam: Sense Publishers.

Carr, P.R., and D.E. Lund. 2009. 'The Unspoken Color of Diversity: Whiteness, Privilege, and Critical Engagement in Education,' in S. Steinberg, ed., *Diversity and Multiculturalism: A Reader*. New York: Peter Lang.

Connell, R.W. 2005. *Masculinities*. Berkeley: University of California Press.

———— and J.W. Messerschmidt. 2005. 'Hegemonic Masculinity: Rethinking the Concept', *Gender and Society*, 19, 6: 829–59.

Crenshaw, K. 1989. 'Mapping the Margins: Intersectionality, Identity Politics, and Violence against Women of Color', *Stanford Law Review*, 43, 6: 1241–99.

Davis, K. 2008. 'Intersectionality as Buzzword: A Sociology of Science Perspective on What Makes a Feminist Theory Successful', *Feminist Theory*, 9, 1: 67–85.

Dei, G.J.S. 2000. 'Towards an Anti-racism Discursive Framework', in A. Calliste and G.J.S. Dei, eds, *Power, Knowledge and Anti-racism Education: A Critical Reader*. Halifax: Fernwood.

Dixson, A.D. and Rousseau, C.K. 2005. 'And We Are Still Not Saved: Critical Race Theory in Education Ten Years Later.' *Race, Ethnicity and Education*, 8, 1: 7–28.

Du Bois, W.E.B. 1995. *The Souls of Black Folk*, 100th anniversary ed. New York: Penguin.

————. 2007. 'Speaking Race: Silence, Salience, and the Politics of Anti-racist Scholarship', in S.P. Hier and B.S. Bolaria, eds, *Race and Racism in 21st-Century Canada: Continuity, Complexity and Change*. Peterborough, ON: Broadview Press.

Farough, S. 2004. 'The Social Geographies of White Masculinities', *Critical Sociology*, 30, 2: 241–64.

Ferber, A.L. 2007. 'The Construction of Black Masculinity: White Supremacy Now and Then', *Journal of Sport and Social Issues*, 31, 1: 11–24.

Foster, C. 2007. 'Blackness and Goodness: Frameworks of Study', in C. Foster, *Blackness and Modernity: The Colour of Humanity and the Quest for Freedom*. Montreal and Kingston: McGill-Queen's University Press.

Gandy, O.H.J. 1998. 'The Social Construction of Race', in O.H.J. Gandy, ed., *Communication and Race: A Structural Perspective*. London: Arnold.

Gillmor, D. 2007. 'The Scarborough Curse', *Toronto Life* (Dec.), www.torontolife.com/features/scarborough-curse/?pageno=2.

Haney-Lopez, I. 1995. 'The Social Construction of Race', in R. Delgato, ed., *Critical Race Theory: The Cutting Edge*. Philadelphia: Temple University Press.

Henry, F., and C. Tator. 1994. 'The Ideology of Racism: Democratic Rracism', *Canadian Ethnic Studies/Etudes ethniques au Canada*, 26, 2: 1–10.

Hier, S.P. 2007. 'Studying Race and Racism in 21st-Century Canada', in S.P. Hier and B.S. Bolaria, eds, *Race and Racism in 21st-Century Canada: Continuity, Complexity and Change*. Peterborough, ON: Broadview Press.

James, C.E. 2003. 'Schooling, Basketball and U.S. Scholarship Aspirations of Canadian Student Athletes', *Race Ethnicity and Education*, 6, 2: 123–44.

———— and B. Lloyd. 2006. 'Differentiating the "Other"/Disaggregating "Black": On the Diversity of African

Canadian Communities', in D. Zinga, ed., *Navigating Multiculturalism, Negotiating Change*. Newcastle, UK: Cambridge Scholars Press.

Kaye/Kantowitz, M. 2007. *The Colors of Jews: Racial Politics and Radical Diasporism*. Bloomington: Indiana University Press.

Kobayashi, A. 1993. 'Multiculturalism: A Canadian Institution', in J. Duncan and D. Ley, eds, *Place/Culture/Representation*. London: Routledge.

Lafond, D. 2009. 'Multiracial Men in Toronto: Identities, Masculinities and Multiculturalism', MEd thesis (Ontario Institute for Studies in Education, University of Toronto).

Lee, E. 2006. 'Looking through an Anti-racist Lens', in E. Lee, D. Menkhart, and M. Okazawa-Rey, eds, *Beyond Heroes and Holidays: A Practical Guide to K–12 Anti-racist, Multicultural Education and Staff Development*. Washington, DC: Teaching for Change.

Leonardo, Z. 2002. 'The Souls of White Folk: Critical Pedagogy, Whiteness Studies, and Globalization Discourse', *Race, Ethnicity and Education*, 5, 1: 29–50.

Levine-Rasky, C. 2008. 'White Privilege: Jewish Women's Writing and the Instability of Categories', *Journal of Modern Jewish Studies*, 7, 1: 51–66.

Mahtani, M. 2002. 'Interrogating the Hyphen-Nation: Canadian Multicultural Policy and "Mixed Race" Identities', *Social Identities*, 8, 1: 67–90.

Martin-Alcoff, L. 2007. 'Comparative Race, Comparative Racisms', in J. Garcia, ed., *Race or Ethnicity? On Black and Latino Identity*. Ithaca, NY: Cornell University Press.

Milan, A., and B. Hamm. 2004. *Mixed Unions*. Statistics Canada, *Canadian Social Trends*, Catalogue No. 11-008, Summer.

Milley, D. 2008. 'Police Brings Message of Safety to 42 Division Meeting', 16 April, www.insidetoronto.com/article/55706--police-bring-message-of-safety-to-42-division-meeting.

Millington, B., P. Vertinsky, E. Boyle, and B. Wilson. 2008. 'Making Chinese-Canadian Masculinities in Vancouver's Physical Education Curriculum', *Sport, Education and Society*, 13, 2: 195–214.

Mohanty, C.T. 1990. 'On Race and Voice: Challenges for Liberal Education in the 90s', *Cultural Critique*, 14: 179–208.

Omi, M., and H. Winant. 1993. 'On the Theoretical Concept of Race', in C. McCarthy and W. Crichlow, eds., *Race, Identity and Representation in Education*. New York: Routledge.

Pon, G. 2000. 'The Art of War or the Wedding Banquet? Asian Canadians, Masculinity and Antiracism Education', *Canadian Journal of Education*, 25, 2: 139.

Satzewich, V. 2007. 'Whiteness Studies: Race, Diversity, and the New Essentialism', in S.P. Hier and B.S. Bolaria, eds, *Race and Racism in 21st-Century Canada: Continuity, Complexity and Change*. Peterborough, ON: Broadview Press.

Schippers, M. 2007. 'Recovering the Feminine Other: Masculinity, Femininity, and Gender Hegemony', *Theory and Society*, 36: 85–102.

Statistics Canada. 2008. 'Canada's Ethnocultural Mosaic, 2006 Census', Catalogue no. 97-562-X. Ottawa: Minister of Industry.

Tate, W.F. 1997. 'Critical Race Theory and Education: History, Theory and Implications', *Review of Research in Education*, 22: 191–243.

Tator, C., and F. Henry. 2006. 'The Culture of Policing', in C. Tator, ed., *Racial Profiling in Canada: Challenging the Myth of 'A Few Bad Apples'*. Toronto: University of Toronto Press.

Taylor, C., K.A. Appiah, J. Habermas, S.C. Rockefeller, M. Walzer, and S. Wolf. 1994. *Multiculturalism: Examining the Politics of Recognition*. Princeton, NJ: Princeton University Press.

Thompson, D. 2007. 'The (Mono)-racial Contract: Mixed-Race Implications', MA thesis (University of Toronto).

Walcott, R. 2003a. *Black Like Who? Writing Black Canada*. Toronto: Insomniac Press.

———. 2003b. 'What Is the Future of Multiculturalism? Ask the Experts'. http://aries.oise.utoronto.ca/experts/october2003/rwalcott300.mov, accessed 2 Dec. 2008.

Wang, A. 2000. 'Asian and White Boys' Competing Discourses about Masculinity: Implications for Secondary Education', *Canadian Journal of Education*, 25, 2: 113–25.

Wei, W. 1993. *The Asian American Movement*. Philadelphia: Temple University Press.

Zhou, M. 2004. 'Are Asian Americans Becoming "Whites"?' *Contexts*, 3, 1: 29–37.

CHAPTER 14

One of the most complex and contentious aspects of the Canadian story relates to the impact of colonial development of Canada on indigenous communities, and their associated tensions and struggles both historically and presently. In this chapter, Sam McKegney highlights the dispossession of indigenous traditional roles relating to gender and masculinities. He begins with a critical self-consciousness necessary to recognize the wide diversity of indigenous cultures, and thus to avoid collapsing a myriad of gender expressions into one simplistic view. Indeed, there are hundreds of indigenous communities and nations, and they do not necessarily hold common views on gender. This is important, because popular cultural depictions remove dimension from this reality.

McKegney especially explores cultures within the Iroquois Confederacy, historically and currently, to illustrate the richness of ideas about masculinities. He also interrogates the imposition of assimilative policies, media stereotypes, and other oppressive phenomena, and their consequences. Readers will also benefit from the author's transparency in speaking about how he approaches the subject as a non-indigenous scholar, offering important lessons to those interested in engaging in study of cultures other than one's own. There are important ethical implications for such work, and the humility and reverence offered by the author help to provide useful guidance for social relations and research.

Warriors, Healers, Lovers, and Leaders: Colonial Impositions on Indigenous Male Roles and Responsibilities

Sam McKegney

Before gendering can be understood, it must be conclusively disentangled from this European category of 'sex' and placed where it belongs, under the Haudenosaunee heading of 'balance' . . .

—Barbara Alice Mann[1]

Of the Indigenous peoples of Turtle Island,[2] Mohawk activist Sakej Ward declares, 'We are a warrior race.' However, according to Ward, the colonial process through which European peoples came to dominate most of North America has obscured this truth, encouraging many Indigenous peoples to deny traditional identities and mistakenly 'think of themselves as colonized subjects of Canada'. 'We try to bring back roles and responsibilities,' Ward laments, 'but we always fail to bring back the traditional role that encompasses half of our people: the male population' (Alfred, 2005: 67). Colonization by Europeans has exiled hundreds of thousands of Indigenous individuals from sacred landscapes inhabited by their nations from time immemorial; at the same time, colonization has alienated many from tribal-specific roles and responsibilities. This double removal—from physical landscapes and from senses of social cohesion and purpose—has engendered significant crises of identity for many contemporary Indigenous individuals, particularly, as Ward notes, men. Métis writer Kim Anderson contends that while 'many Native women have been able to continue their traditional responsibilities of creation and nurturing . . . many men's responsibilities have been greatly obscured by the colonial process. It is more difficult for men than it is for women to define their responsibilities in the contemporary setting and reclaim their dignity and sense of purpose' (2000: 239). Non-Indigenous scholar Timothy Sweet agrees, arguing that 'if femininity was altered [by colonialism], so was masculinity. Thus [the] project of "recovering the feminine"' in Indigenous communities must, for Sweet, 'be complemented by an endeavour to recover the masculine in order to attain a full understanding of gender in . . . tribal societies' (1993: 475).

The rudimentary question with which the investigations of this chapter must begin, therefore, is 'What is Indigenous masculinity?' In other words, what is the 'masculine' that Sweet seeks to 'recover'? What is the 'traditional role' that Ward endeavours to 'bring back'? This core question, however, is inadequate, crippled by a generalizing impulse that presupposes gender congruity among diverse Indigenous populations. 'What is Indigenous masculinity?' implies that maleness means the same thing, or at least similar things, for Indigenous nations throughout North, Central, and South America, as well as Africa, Australia, New Zealand, and elsewhere. Well, what about 'Indigenous Canadian masculinity'? Without even addressing the arbitrary imposition of national borders on the pre-existing Indigenous nations of Turtle Island (several of which straddle the 49th parallel between Canada and the United States) or the enforcement of Eurocentric notions of land ownership on Indigenous persons who may or may not self-identify as 'Canadian', 'Indigenous Canadian masculinity' as a category lumps together the unique traditions and worldviews of hundreds of Indigenous nations from the T'lingit, Nuu'chah'nulth, and Haisla on the Pacific coast to the Mi'kmaq, Penobscot, and Naskapi on the Atlantic coast to the Inuvialuit, Gwich'in, and Igloolik Inuit on the Arctic coast to the Iroquois, Anishinabe, and Blackfoot in between. If the question were narrowed to a tribal-specific designation such as 'Cree masculinity', the problem of generalization would endure: are we referring to the Woodland Cree of Lac La Ronge or the Swampy Cree of Red Earth or the Plains Cree of Peepeekisis? Each of these communities has its own linguistic idioms, its own oral and written histories, its own traditional songs and stories, its own customs and social systems.

As a result, this chapter makes no attempt to authoritatively define 'Indigenous masculinity'. Indigenous masculinity has not meant and cannot mean something once and for always, for all Indigenous nations, for all groups within a single Indigenous nation, or even for individuals over time. Cherokee-Greek author Thomas King critiques the problematic tendency in Indigenous studies

> to imagine that there is a racial denominator which full-bloods raised in cities, half-bloods raised on farms, quarter-bloods raised on reservations, Indians adopted and raised by white families, Indians who speak their tribal language, Indians who speak only English, traditionally educated Indians, university-trained Indians, Indians with little education, and the like all share. We know, of course, that there is not. We know that this is a romantic, mystical, and in many instances, a self-serving notion that the sheer number of cultural groups in North America, the variety of native languages, and the varied conditions of the various tribes should immediately belie (1990: x–xi).

The desire to consolidate various aspects of living, breathing Indigenous societies beneath an essentialist banner of 'Indian' betrays a colonial approach to non-European cultures that treats as 'authentic' only those characteristics associated with imagined pre-contact purity, thereby denying Indigenous societies the capacity to adapt, grow, and evolve without forfeiting their distinct identities. As Sioux intellectual Vine Deloria, Jr, argues, 'Unlike many other . . . traditions, tribal [traditions] . . . have not been authoritatively set "once and for always." Truth is in the ever-changing experiences of the community. For the traditional Indian to fail to appreciate this aspect of his heritage is the saddest of heresies. It means the Indian has unwittingly fallen into the trap of Western religion, which seeks to freeze history in an unchanging and authoritative past' (Warrior, 1995: 84). What King and Deloria make clear is the danger of both geographical and temporal generalizations. So just as this chapter must resist conceptualizations of Indigenous masculinity in the singular, so too must it resist the presumption that tribal-specific Indigenous masculinities remain stable and unchanging over time (or the valuation that they are deficient should they fail to do so). In other words, this chapter treats tradition as an ongoing, dynamic series of actions and relations rather than as a definable artefact; it sees tradition as a verb rather than a noun.

A final reason for my reluctance to define Indigenous masculinity comes from my status as a settler scholar. I use the term 'settler' to acknowledge that, as a non-Indigenous person, my presence on Turtle Island depends on the often violent history of colonial expansion from which I have, in many ways, benefited *and* to acknowledge that my land 'ownership' in Canada and my Canadian citizenship constitute a form of 'settlement' on Indigenous lands that is not somehow separate from colonial history. Even if a definition of Indigenous masculinity were possible—and, as suggested above, I don't believe it is—it needs to come from Indigenous sources. As this chapter will demonstrate, tremendous damage has been wrought in Indigenous communities by non-Indigenous authority over definitions of

Indigenous identity;[3] the last thing Indigenous communities need is another privileged non-Indigenous scholar presumptively proclaiming who they are. As a settler scholar, I can understand Indigenous identities in only abstract and intellectual ways through what I have observed, read, and been told; my understandings cannot be conditioned by the weight of lived experience. Furthermore, 'as a non-Native critic [of Indigenous studies] I simply do not stand to inherit the adverse social and political consequences of my critical work' (McKegney, 2007: 38–9), and this places ethical limitations on what I can and should address. Building from the work of Cherokee scholar Jace Weaver, I strive in this chapter toward the critical position of a non-Indigenous ally of Indigenous sovereignty movements,[4] and I expect to be held accountable for the arguments found herein by Indigenous readers for whom the issues of the chapter are neither abstract nor theoretical but are rather the terrain of daily existence.

In this chapter, therefore, I do not intend to postulate 'authentic' Indigenous masculinity but rather to explore how colonial processes have intervened in traditional Indigenous gender relations. In particular, I will examine how governmental experiments in social engineering from residential schools to the Indian Act have conspired with popular cultural images of Indigenous manhood in literature, film, and other media to alienate many Indigenous men from tribal-specific roles and responsibilities. I will argue that this process has contributed to considerable social problems in many Indigenous communities and underlies the urgent need to 'recover the masculine' voiced by Sweet earlier in this chapter.[5] Aware of the dangers of generalization, I will focus my discussion on male roles and responsibilities among the nations of the Iroquois Confederacy as represented in two seminal texts by Iroquoian authors: *Iroquoian Women: The Gantowisas* (2000) by Seneca scholar Barbara Alice Mann and *And Grandma Said . . . Iroquois Teachings as Passed Down through the*

Oral Tradition (2008) by Mohawk elder Tom Porter (Sakokweniónkwas). My analysis will thus build from a foundation of Iroquoian self-representation that will discourage my own speculation on definitive Iroquoian identities.

I have chosen to root my discussion in the knowledge traditions of the Iroquois Confederacy for several reasons. First, the lands on which I live and work are considered by many to be traditional Iroquois territory, and I believe it is a responsibility of settler scholars of Indigenous issues to produce intellectual work of value to the nations whose lands they occupy.[6] Second, the exchange of power along gender lines among the Iroquois, at various levels of governance and social relations, is particularly striking (with matrilineal clan-based social systems and consensus-based political decision-making, processes adjudicated by female clan mothers and exercised by male sachems or chiefs). Third, the image of the Mohawk warrior—the Mohawk being a member nation of the Iroquois Confederacy—has come to symbolize Indigenous hypermasculinity in popular Canadian consciousness and has gained considerable (albeit problematic) symbolic currency in both Indigenous and non-Indigenous circles.

I will begin by using Mann's depiction of the Iroquois creation story to introduce some ideas about traditional Iroquoian gender relations, with particular emphasis on male roles and responsibilities. Then I will illustrate how specific colonial interventions—from residential schooling to the Indian Act to capitalist consumerism—have sought to fundamentally alter those roles and responsibilities, thereby problematizing the place of men in Iroquoian communities. I will then consider how popular cultural images of Indigenous men, which rely on hypermasculine stereotyping, alienate Indigenous men further from what Mann and Porter discuss as traditional Iroquoian notions of maleness. I will conclude by examining the way Porter employs the Iroquois ritual of condolence in his oral telling of the Aionwahta tale to guide listeners

toward traditional expressions of healthy, non-dominative Iroquoian maleness attuned to the complexities of the contemporary moment.

From a Rib or from the Sky? Some Thoughts on Creation Stories and Gender Relations

Non-Indigenous literary scholar J. Edward Chamberlin notes in his book *If This Is Your Land, Where Are Your Stories?* that 'we all have stories that hold us in thrall and hold others at bay. What we share is the practice of believing, which we become adept at very early in our lives; and it is this practice that generates the power of stories' (2004: 2). Although evident all around us, the power of stories finds perhaps its most potent expression in creation narratives, which inform the relationships of believers with each other and with the worlds they inhabit. Creation stories are full of cultural signs and signifiers that point listeners or readers toward meaning and cultural value, and they tend to speak volumes about gender relations.

I begin this section by comparing Mann's Iroquois creation story of Sky Woman with the Old Testament creation story of Genesis from the King James Bible. In doing so, I don't mean to suggest an unbridgeable gap between the spiritual systems implicated in either narrative. Nor do I wish to imply that Mann's telling represents the beliefs of all Iroquoian people or that the latter represents the beliefs of all North Americans of European descent—many Indigenous people don't consider themselves spiritually traditional; many non-Indigenous Canadians don't consider themselves Christian; and many Indigenous and non-Indigenous people bring these spiritual traditions together in dynamic and mutually generative ways. Rather, I want to consider the gendered consequences of specific differences in the ways the two creation stories imagine the world. In particular, I will argue that the Iroquois creation story, as envisioned by Mann, informs how gender roles are interwoven into the complex fabric of traditional Iroquois governance, producing ideas of manhood that are considerably different than those envisaged in Genesis.[7]

Mann introduces her critical study of Iroquois womanhood with the following telling of 'Woman Falling from the Sky':

'Look!' cried Eagle, in some consternation. 'A woman is falling from the sky!'

Heron and Loon craned their necks up to see the falling woman. There she was, all right, crashing down at a quick pace.

'What sort of creature is that?' Loon asked Heron. 'She has no feathers or flippers. I don't think she can live on the water.'

Heron glanced down to the water world below, and then back up at the flailing woman, tumbling down, down, down, arms and legs akimbo.

'It does look as if she'll drown,' Heron agreed. 'We had better help her.'

With that, Heron and Loon flew close together, the feathers of their wings interlocking to form a feathery cushion. Positioning themselves just below the Woman Falling from the Sky, they scooped her up midair, breaking her free fall. She seemed very frightened.

After a few hours, Heron began to complain. 'This one is heavy. My wings are tired. We have to set her down somewhere.'

Loon cast his eye about for a place to deposit her but saw none. 'Uh oh,' he muttered. 'Now we've done it. There's nowhere to put her.' Ruefully, Heron agreed.

Soaring above them, Eagle spotted Grandfather Turtle,[8] that Great Snapping Turtle, swimming through the waters of the watery planet. He called down, 'The Woman Fallen from the Sky needs somewhere to stay, but there is no dry land for her. What shall we do?'

Grandfather Turtle mused on that for a while. He did not like to think too quickly. 'We must hold a council to see what is to be done,' he said at last, causing a moccasin to be sent around, announcing a quick council of all the swimmers and flyers.

Muskrat, that jittery fellow, arrived first; then came Beaver, Toad, and Otter, all marvelling greatly at the strange, unfloatable creature now lying on the feathers of Loon and Heron. When the Elder Spirits of all the swimmers and flyers had arrived, Grandfather Turtle began. 'Shall we save this Woman Fallen from the Sky?' he asked. The others considered this great question for a long time.

'We'll have to feed her,' Beaver pointed out.

'I can do that,' Bass volunteered.

'Then you've got no sense,' Beaver retorted. The others laughed.

Eventually, however, the Elder Spirits agreed to sustain that Sky Woman because, if she were allowed to be dropped into the water to drown, her death might injure Earth.

'I've been thinking,' said Grandfather Turtle, 'if we're going to keep her, we'll have to create dry land for her to live on. I will carry that island on my carapace forever, but one of you must dive for the dirt.'

'It's a long way down to the bottom of the ocean,' Otter observed disconsolately. Others murmured their assent.

After a long time during which they all gazed into the oceanic depths, Muskrat finally said, 'I'll go.' With that, she dived, swimming down into those waters, down till she thought her chest would burst, down to the very bottom of the sea. There, she scooped up a mouthful of dirt, turned, and raced for the top. Sadly, she was more eager than able.

The swimmers floated about Grandfather Turtle, awaiting the return of Muskrat. They were scanning the waves for her, when several cried out at once, 'We see her! She's there!' only to watch, stunned, as the limp body of Muskrat bobbed about on the surface, her mouth still smeared with the dirt she had so valiantly tried to bring up. Silence lapped across the waves, and a damper closed down around the former zeal of the council. It was a long time before Otter moved forward, quietly offering to try next.

Down he dived with greater force than Muskrat had possessed, all the way down in a heroic splurge of energy. Rubbing a large dab of sea floor dirt on his nose, he thrust himself back up, but, halfway there, his strength began to fail him. He realized that he had piled up more dirt than he could carry. As he tried to shake some of it off his nose, he lost his bearings, mistakenly going deeper into the water instead of higher. Otter drowned too.

After these two failures, enthusiasm for the earth-forming venture ebbed low, so that most of the animals looked away when the call came around for a third volunteer. At last, Beaver, who had always had a good opinion of himself, swam forward. 'I'm very strong, and good at creating,' he said. 'I'll go.'

Now Beaver dived his best dive, going farther down than he had ever gone before, struggling to get his bulk to the sea floor. He lunged now with all his might, but he could not quite touch the bottom with either his paws or his nose. About to give up, he flapped his tail in frustration, serendipitously scooping up dirt as it hit the sea floor. Excited, and thinking of the honours due him upon success, that vain Beaver hurried to the surface, breaking through with an open mouth and glittering eyes. 'I've got it! I've got it!' he gasped. The others quickly helped him smear that little bit of dirt across the back of Grandfather Turtle, creating Turtle Island—North America—while Loon and Heron gently set Sky Woman down upon her new home (Barbara Alice Mann, 2000: 1–2).

The Iroquois creation story begins with an image of collision or convergence, of the coming together of unlike things. In contrast to the creation story of Genesis—in which the universe is formed through a series of divisions when a single creative force, in the figure of a male God, separates light from the darkness, heaven from the earth, and land from the waters—Turtle Island is created through the collaboration of several figures who come together creatively to deal with the crisis of the Woman Falling from the Sky's introduction into the water world. As opposed to division, the Iroquois creation story stresses unification, as symbolized by the wings of Heron and Loon 'interlocking to form a feathery cushion' to support the Woman fallen from the Sky World, thereby signalling the dynamic fusion of disparate worlds. Here several creatures work collectively to solve the problem of Sky Woman's inability to survive in a landless environment. Heron and Loon unite to catch her, the council of swimmers and flyers convenes to establish an appropriate course of action, Grandfather Turtle offers his carapace for the land on which Sky Woman will live but requires Beaver to collect the necessary morsel of earth from the sea floor, and the council works as one to help Beaver 'smear that little bit of dirt across the back of Grandfather Turtle, creating Turtle Island'. The act of creation for the Iroquois is essentially collaborative, requiring several parties who are undifferentiated in terms of their capacity to engender positive change. Whereas the creation story of Genesis restricts the formation of the universe to a specific temporal period (from 'the beginning' to 'the seventh day') and attributes the creative act to a single cosmic force (the God figure), the Iroquois narrative imagines creation to both precede and follow Sky Woman's story (as suggested by the existence of both the Water and Sky Worlds prior to Sky Woman's arrival and by the ongoing acts of creation suggested by the birth of Sky Woman's children after Mann's version of the creation story closes) and to emerge from a plethora of sources (from Grandfather Turtle to Beaver to the council to Sky Woman herself).

The balance of creative power throughout the Iroquois creation story signals an important difference from Genesis. The primary active force throughout Genesis remains the God figure—again envisioned in the masculine—while the rest of creation either is acted upon or achieves only surrogate agency beneath the overarching authority of the God figure; man's power over the beasts by virtue of his being forged in the God figure's image (*Holy Bible*, 2000: 1:27) is an example of the latter. The Iroquois creation story has no such power structure. Although Grandfather Turtle has the authority to call together the council of flyers and swimmers, he cannot make decisions on the council's behalf or produce Turtle Island without the assistance of other creatures. The Iroquois creation story gestures toward the importance of balance within structures of power, while Genesis gestures toward the importance of hierarchical authority, each of which has ideological implications for relationships within human societies and between humans and the natural world. Genesis weaves hierarchy into the creation process through the disparate valuing of the halves into which the universe is divided. For example, as 'Heaven' is divided from the 'Earth', Heaven is conceived theologically to be the superior of the two. Similarly, as 'Day' is divided from 'Night', the former is afforded greater value, as evidenced by the description of the 'great lights' by which each is governed: 'the *greater* light to rule the day, and the *lesser* light to rule the night' (1:16). Not only do the adjectives 'greater' and 'lesser' imply a hierarchical relationship between

sun and moon, but the fact that they are configured as *ruling* the day and night suggests the pervasive influence of authority as a regulating force in Genesis as a whole.

The role of hierarchy is illustrated even more powerfully in Genesis by humankind's proclaimed relationship to the natural world: '[A]nd God said unto [man and woman], Be fruitful, and multiply, and replenish the earth, and subdue it: and have dominion over the fish of the sea, and over the fowl of the air, and over every living thing that moveth upon the earth' (1:28). The duty of humankind, in this configuration, is to forcibly bring the natural world under human control, as suggested in the term 'subdue', which requires a radically different valuation of the natural than is implied through Sky Woman's grateful reverence for the fecund and expanding natural world upon Grandfather Turtle's back. Furthermore, the relationship between the human and animal realms of existence in the Iroquois creation story is predicated on consensus and balance that is radically dissimilar to the 'dominion' enjoyed by humankind in Genesis. While the term 'dominion' asserts human rule over 'fish', 'fowl', and 'every [non-human] living thing . . . upon the earth', the animal and human worlds in the Iroquois creation story are entirely integral. In fact, the survival of the human world depends on the active decision-making of empowered anthropomorphic flyers and swimmers. In this manner, while Genesis seems to suggest that humankind must conquer and control the natural world of plants and animals, 'Woman Falling from the Sky' seems to suggest the importance of kinship relations among humans, plants, and animals, with no element of creation ruling over any other.

The comparison I am drawing here between the hierarchical division privileged in Genesis and the egalitarian unification privileged in the Iroquois creation story forms some of the ideological backdrop to the discussions of gender with which this chapter is concerned. If we extend the principle of hierarchical division to gender relations in Genesis, the male is placed in authority over the female because the female is depicted as being derived from the male—'And she shall be called Woman, because she was taken out of Man' (2:22)—and because the male is presented as sharing affinity with the masculine God figure—'So God created man in his *own* image, in the image of God created he him' (1:26). The power dynamic in the Iroquois creation story is quite different, as the first human is decidedly female and the creative power that in Genesis is isolated in the God figure is shared for Mann among male and female characters. Sky Woman, as the first human, is also an active agent in the creation of Turtle Island along with Grandfather Turtle, Beaver, and the other council members.

In his discussion of the tale of Sky Woman, Mohawk elder Tom Porter notes that as the dirt was smeared on the back of Grandfather Turtle, Sky Woman

> started a kind of sideways shuffle walk in a circle. . . . And as she started to move she started chanting the language of Karonhià:ke [the Sky World]. . . . And as she went around there, the miracle of birth began. And the granules of dirt began to multiply and grow. Instead of a little speckle, it had become a pile. And as she continued to sing or to chant that song, it began to multiply even more. And not only that, but the turtle began to grow bigger in accordance with the growth of that dirt. And as she continued to go around in an even-bigger circle, the turtle grew and grew. . . . That was the miracle of birth (2008: 52–3).

Porter's use of the term 'birth' to describe the emergence of Turtle Island clearly resonates with the power to 'give birth', which is claimed solely by women; the connection here is rendered more fertile, in Porter's discussion, by the fact that Sky Woman is pregnant at the time of her descent from the sky. In this way, the Iroquois creation story celebrates female creative power; however, it does not do so to the exclusion of male creative power, as illustrated by the roles of Grandfather Turtle and Beaver in Turtle Island's creation.[9]

The association of Sky Woman with the 'birth' of Turtle Island also informs the vital association of women with agriculture in traditional Iroquois societies. In describing the gendered nature of traditional existence, Mann argues that '[t]he forest, home of the hunt, was the natural half [of creation] belonging to men, just as the field was the natural half belonging to women' (2000: 103). However, unlike Eurocentric conceptions of agriculture as a masculine quest to order and render 'productive' the chaos of nature—in the words of Genesis, to 'replenish the earth, and subdue it' (1:28)—Iroquois gendering of the agricultural space relates to 'the extraordinary power inherent in women as the bearers of life' (Denis, 1993: 28). As such, traditional Iroquoian relationships with agriculture do not involve authority, domination, and control, but rather nurturing and creative collaboration—women farmers striving like Sky Woman to help the earth grow rather than aiming to conquer it.

In her study, Mann describes the process of 'gendering' as 'the most crucial commonplace of the Iroquoian universe' (2000: 64). Yet, as the comparison above is meant to suggest, the existence of 'two . . . genders' does not 'inevitably impl[y] antagonism' in Iroquois worldviews (2000: 63). Rather than relying on the hierarchical binaries so crucial to Genesis—Heaven/Earth, day/night, human/animal, male/female—Mann argues that the Iroquois principle of 'twinship' recognizes and even celebrates difference while mobilizing that difference positively within kinship networks based on balance and complementarity:

> As a reflection of [the] twinship principle, the genders are seen as simultaneously independent, yet interdependent, each gender one-half of the paired, human

whole. A pure expression of Iroquoian thought, the relationship between men and women in Haudenosaunee[10] culture developed from the bedrock of principles [of] . . . reciprocity, balance, cooperation, mutuality, and the joyful coming-together of two to create one self-perpetuating whole (2000: 90).

Traditional Iroquois societies do not deny gender difference, according to Mann, but they take great care to ensure freedom from domination for both men and women.[11] Mann calls the relationship between the genders in traditional Iroquois societies '[e]qual and complementary, interdependent yet individual', arguing that

the genders fall into natural halves that parallel one another, socially, politically, economically, and religiously. Neither gender interferes with the other's allotted half of existence. Each half is left to operate as it sees fit, so long as the ultimate outcome of activity forms a beneficial whole. In short, women do women's things, while men do men's things, together yet apart in their complementary spaces of the female-field and the male-forest. Thus, women farm, and men hunt, but, in the final analysis, all the people are fed (2000: 97–8).

Such gender balance is further illustrated by the roles of men and women within traditional Iroquois systems of governance. At the time of initial sustained contact with Europeans, the Iroquois Confederacy consisted of five nations, including the elder sibling nations of the Mohawk (the Keepers of the Eastern Door), the Seneca (the Keepers of the Western Door), and the Onondaga (the Keepers of the Council Fire), and the younger sibling nations of the Oneida and the Cayuga; the Tuscarora became part of the Confederacy after expansion by the United States left them landless, bringing the political union of Iroquois nations to six.

The Confederacy binds the nations together through intricate kinship systems of clan-based social organization, subject to a democratic constitution known as the Great Law of Peace. The political structures of the Confederacy ensure not only that all nations and all clans within nations are represented at the Grand Council Fire, but also that women and men are mutually engaged in political decision-making. Non-Indigenous historian J. R. Miller writes:

Simply put, the Iroquois developed complex and sophisticated institutions of government because their social circumstances [as large populations concentrated in semi-permanent agrarian villages] required that they have mechanisms for regulating relations among large numbers of people normally resident in one location. . . . [T]he women of their communities had prominent political roles. For example, clan mothers were responsible for selecting a new chief, and deciding to make war or peace also fell within their jurisdiction. Iroquoians were matrilineal and matrilocal peoples, meaning that they traced kinship through the mother's family, and when a man married he relocated to the longhouse of his bride's family. Much of the prominence of Iroquois women's public role seems to have stemmed from their contribution in agriculture. In short, farming was women's work, with the result that women controlled the food supply and thereby gained great influence (Miller, 2004: 57).

Although we should be cautious of some of the causal implications of Miller's analysis (insofar as he views the Iroquois political structure and the role of women in Iroquois society as primarily products of 'social circumstances' rather than ideological priorities), his introduction to Iroquois governance illustrates its emphasis on gender balance. For instance, while the male sachem or chief speaks on behalf of his clan at the nation's council and, along with the sachems of the other clans, on behalf of his nation at the Grand Council Fire, he carries no coercive authority over the people and can be removed from his position by the clan mother if he does not voice the people's will, as established through prior consensus. The authority of the male sachem, therefore, is radically different from the authority of a prime minister or president and especially from that of a monarch.

The role of the sachem involves profound responsibility rather than heightened power and influence. His only means of instigating action is through the persuasiveness of his rhetoric; he cannot compel his clan to do anything but is, rather, subject to the clan's collective will. It is unsurprising, therefore, that as Porter notes, it is 'forbidden to *seek* leadership' (2008: 338) among traditional Iroquois because such a pursuit betrays a desire for power that is anathema to the freedom from coercion so central to Iroquois worldviews. According to Porter, the Mohawk word for sachem is 'Roiá:nehr and it means *he's good*. And the [word for clan mother] is Iakoiá:nehr, *she's good*. And the law is called Kaianere'kó:wa, *the great good*. That's the Constitution. So compared to that, the word "Chief" sounds degrading' (2008: 340). The role of the male leader, the sachem, is always balanced by the role of the female leader, the clan mother. Mann describes the role of the clan mother through the Iroquoian term *gantowisas*, meaning

> political woman, faithkeeping woman, mediating woman; leader, counsellor, judge. *Gantowisas* indicates mother, grandmother, and even the Mother of Nations. . . . In the first decades of the twentieth century . . . Cayuga Chief *Deskaheh* (1873–1925) . . . defined *gantowisas* as a mature woman acting in her official capacity. Her official capacity was public in every way. Her duties were

frankly political, economic, judicial, and shamanic. *Gantowisas*, then, means indispensable Woman' (2000: 16).

As indicated by Miller, Porter, and Mann, clan mothers are central to traditional Iroquois structures of governance as primary overseers of the authority of male sachems, as the holders of women's councils, as key figures of consensus-building within the clan or nation, and as the arbiters of war and peace. Yet even the authority of clan mothers is tempered by checks and balances. According to Porter, the clan mother only 'initiates' the central processes of governance and the selection of leaders; she does not dictate decisions. 'All she does,' he explains, 'is she's the voice of the people of that clan' (2008: 340).

The central role of women in traditional Iroquois governance as well as the matrilineal nature of kinship delineation, the political emphases on non-interference and consensus decision-making,[12] and the cultural emphasis on balance signalled by the coming together of Sky Woman, Grandfather Turtle, and the swimmers and flyers in the creation story all have profound implications for traditional male roles and responsibilities among the Iroquois.[13] Certainly, as Mann argues, at the time of initial European settlement, '[t]he forest, home of the hunt, was the natural half [of creation] belonging to men' (2000: 103) and therefore balanced the agricultural and domestic domain of the field that was the purview of Iroquois women,. And as non-Indigenous historian Matthew Denis posits, traditional male 'identity and status' thus 'stemmed from . . . actions in masculine zones beyond the clearings, where they achieved note through hunting, diplomacy, or warfare' (1993: 28). However, the cultural meanings of 'hunting, diplomacy, [and] warfare' need to be interrogated before the relationship between masculine 'identity' in traditional Iroquois societies and male roles and responsibilities can be adequately considered.

For example, Eurocentric conflations of hunting with masculine virility and the conquering of the effeminized 'wild' animal must be weighed against the interweaving of hunting and agriculture in Iroquois society, wherein '[w]omen's planting assesses the strength of men's hunting', according to Mann (2000: 98), and presumably compensates for its inadequacies. Similarly, Denis's idea of 'achiev[ing] note' through diplomacy must be radically disentangled from Western individualist notions of personal political advancement. The male sachem among traditional Iroquois speaks not on his own behalf but rather on behalf of his clan, whose views have been arrived at through consensus. The male role in such diplomacy is intimately interwoven with and dependent upon the female role. Lastly, according to Kanien'kehaka scholar Taiaiake Alfred, the traditional Iroquoian word for warrior is *rotiskenhrakete*, which literally means 'carrying the burden of peace'. Alfred explains, 'The word is made up of *roti*, connoting "he"; *sken* in relation to *skennen*, or "peace"; and *hrakete*, which is a suffix that combines the connotations of a burden and carrying' (2005: 78). Given the imperative of peace and the authorizing influence of clan mothers, who determine when to make peace and when to go to war, the male role of warrior for traditional Iroquois seems to rest upon neither dominance nor violent power, but rather aspires toward the protection and support of the community.

Each of the categories for assessing Iroquois masculinity identified by Denis is thus not a means of distinguishing traditional Iroquois males from the group but rather of integrating them into the clan, nation, and Confederacy in non-dominative ways. The danger, of course, comes as the social systems that support and are supported by such traditional roles and responsibilities are decimated through colonial interventions and Denis's three categories become contaminated by Eurocentric individualism and gender hierarchies. The next section of the chapter will explore the effects of specific

institutions of the Euro-Canadian government on traditional Iroquois masculinities.

Colonialism and the Imposition of Patriarchy: Some Thoughts on Alienation from Culturally Specific Roles and Responsibilities

As colonial expansion continued throughout the eighteenth and nineteenth centuries, several factors conspired to alter traditional male roles and responsibilities among the Iroquois, including the diplomatic upheaval caused by colonial warfare, the decimation of animal populations caused by settler encroachment, and the aggressive missionary work of several Christian denominations. In this section I will look at the impact of three specific colonial interventions in Iroquois communities to consider how these potentially intervened in traditional gender relations, displacing some characteristics of male roles and responsibilities introduced above. I will briefly examine in turn the impact of the Indian Act, the residential school system, and the introduction of capitalist economics in Iroquois communities.

The Indian Act of 1876 brought together and formalized all previous legislation by the British Crown and the newly inaugurated government of the Dominion of Canada pertaining to Indigenous peoples. This vast and often confusing document, which has been added to and amended considerably over the past 130-plus years, has two primary functions: first, to categorize and define Indigenous identity, and second, to legislate a political system for controlling Indigenous nations in a manner that ensures their subordination to the Canadian state. Each of these functions has considerable implications for Indigenous gender relations. Certainly until 1985 and in many ways after,[14] these goals of the Act constituted a two-pronged attack on gender balance in Indigenous communities by seeking to silence the political voices of Indigenous women and imposing patriarchal systems of identification on often matrilineal and matrilocal nations such as those of the Iroquois Confederacy. Aimed at the very heart of Indigenous nationhood—the defining of group membership and the organization of structures of governance—this legislation produced wide-ranging effects within and beyond Indigenous communities. As Mi'kmaq scholar Bonita Lawrence argues in 'Gender, Race, and the Regulation of Native Identity in Canada and the United States: An Overview', the 'overarching nature [of the Indian Act] as a discourse of classification, regulation, and control . . . has indelibly ordered how Native people think of things "Indian"' (2003: 3–4).

Among the most significant aspects of national sovereignty is a group's autonomy to determine its own membership, and prior to the Indian Act most Indigenous nations did so according to kinship ties, integration into the community, and consensus; Mohawks were deemed Mohawks because of their kinship commitments to others within the Mohawk nation and the broader Iroquois Confederacy and because they were recognized as such by their communities. This process had nothing to do with racialized conceptions of 'Indian blood'. Yet, with the Indian Act, the Canadian government began to determine who would legally be perceived as Indigenous through the category of 'status Indian', which would be based, among other things, on blood quantum. In the Act for the Gradual Enfranchisement of Indians of 1869, which would become a key element of the Indian Act seven years later, the denial of community membership to individuals based on blood quantum was introduced in relation to economic entitlement. Section IV states, 'In the division among members of any tribe, band, or body of Indians, of any annuity money, interest money or rents, no person of less than one fourth Indian blood . . . shall be deemed entitled to share' (INAC, 1869). This section, in effect, economically exiled those of less than one-quarter Indigenous ancestry from their Indigenous nation, irrespective of the community's will. Such legislated banishment

became even more striking along gender lines. Section VI reads:

> Provided always that any Indian woman marrying any other than an Indian, shall cease to be an Indian within the meaning of this Act, nor shall the children issue of such marriage be considered as Indians within the meaning of this Act; Provided also, that any Indian woman marrying an Indian of any other tribe, band or body to which she formerly belonged, and become a member of the tribe, band or body of which her husband is a member, and the children, issue of this marriage, shall belong to their father's tribe only (INAC, 1869).

Through this section, the Act directly attacks the matrilineal clan-based system of the Iroquois (and other Indigenous nations), placing under erasure centuries of gender balance and supplanting it with Eurocentric patriarchy. Notice that I refer to the imposed system as patriarchal rather than patrilineal. In traditional Iroquois kinship systems, a man retains his clan-based identity when he marries, bringing the knowledge traditions of his heritage with him as he moves into the longhouse of his wife's relations. In the system enforced by the Indian Act, a woman's cultural identity disappears in the eyes of the government upon her marriage outside the group; in the tradition of European patriarchy, her identity is reconceived as subordinate to and dependent on that of her husband. The Indian Act thus strikes a blow at the heart of Iroquois social systems by displacing women from positions of power in the home and recasting them as dependent, first on fathers, then on husbands, as well as in the broader community, by denying the significance of women's heritage formerly affirmed through the matrilineal tracing of ancestry.

The assault on gender balance in Iroquois and other Indigenous nations further extended to forcible denial of women's voices in the political arena. Blatantly denying the validity of the three-tiered system of consensus-based governance employed by the nations of the Iroquois Confederacy for centuries, the Indian Act instituted a band council system of quasi-democratic governance under the umbrella of Indian Affairs that fundamentally disenfranchised the female half of the Iroquois population. Section X of the 'gradual disenfranchisement act' declares that

> [t]he Governor may order that the Chiefs of any tribe, band, or body of Indians shall be elected by the male members of each Indian Settlement of the full age of twenty-one years at such time and place, and in such manner, as the Superintendent General of Indian Affairs may direct, and they shall in such case be elected for a period of three years, unless deposed by the Governor for dishonesty, intemperance, or immorality (INAC, 1869).

Not only is this section appallingly undemocratic in the unchecked powers it affords both the superintendent general of Indian Affairs and the governor—the latter of whom could depose any Indigenous leader aggressive to Indian Affairs policies, based on such subjective categories as 'intemperance' and 'immorality'—but it also erases the central role of women in Iroquois political life, leaving only men to vote for and to become leaders. Far from the interwoven web of checks and balances in which clan mothers and sachems worked collaboratively to discern and act upon the will of the people through extensive consultation and compromise, this imposed system was fundamentally incapable of achieving consensus insofar as half the population was entirely left out of decision-making.

The effects of these two facets of the Indian Act have been protracted and profound for the Iroquois and other Indigenous nations. Women have been forced to suffer the compound oppression of racist discrimination from outside the community combined with the injection of patriarchy and misogyny into the community itself (which isn't to say that the Indian Act overturned centuries of gender balance in one fell swoop, but rather to recognize that pressure from the government to tip the scales of gender relations away from balance into hierarchy offered opportunities for some Iroquois men to dominate spouses and children to compensate for their own disempowerment in other facets of their lives). While the Indian Act's assault on Indigenous women is heinous and troubling, its manipulation of gender balance must simultaneously be construed as an assault on Indigenous men. Male power, under the Act, ceased to flow from the dynamic relationship between the genders signified by twinship and complementarity, but rather had to be seized from the other half of gendered society, the women, and exercised to their exclusion.

The gender hierarchies introduced through the Indian Act were further enforced through the residential school system, which functioned in Canada from the 1870s to the 1980s and sought to undermine the linguistic, cultural, and political coherence of Indigenous nations by removing Indigenous children from their communities and educating them in a Eurocentric manner. The motivation here was expressly genocidal insofar as the government sought to render Indigenous nations unviable entities, by engineering their children to identify as Canadian rather than as members of their tribal communities. Inaugural prime minister John A. Macdonald explained in 1887, 'The great aim of our legislation has been to do away with the tribal system and assimilate the Indian people in all respects with the inhabitants of the Dominion as speedily as they are fit for the change' (Ennamorato, 1998: 72). Minister of Indian Affairs Duncan Campbell Scott famously affirmed this objective in 1920, arguing, 'I want to get rid of the Indian problem. . . . Our objective is to continue until there is not a single Indian in Canada that has not been absorbed into the body politic, and there is no Indian question, and no Indian Department' (Milloy 1999: 46). As I have written elsewhere, 'Despite the manifold failings of the residential school system, the vigour with which the goal of separating children from their cultural, spiritual, and linguistic heritages was pursued ensured that most of the children would experience a profound sense of disconnection from family, culture, and community upon re-entering Aboriginal society' (McKegney, 2007: 28). Nowhere has this sense of disconnection been more pervasive than in the area of gender relations.

One way of destroying Indigenous cultures was to deny the validity of gender balance and to replace it with a hierarchical gender binary that would privilege males while relegating females to positions of subservience. The residential school system enforced this task, often quite brutally. The religious orders that ran the schools impressed upon students that the domination of women by men was divinely sanctioned and natural, that the physical body was filthy and degenerate, and that sexuality and desire were inherently sinful, all of which engendered crises of identity among Indigenous children who had generally come from communities that valued gender equality, viewed the human body as essentially good, and construed desire as among the most natural elements of human experience. Inuvialuit writer Anthony Apakark Thrasher recalls, 'We were told [at residential school] not to play with the girls, because that would . . . be a sin. I thought that was strange, because I had played with girls before I came to school. Now they were telling me I shouldn't touch them' (1976: 14). Métis author Maria Campbell writes in her seminal autobiography *Halfbreed* that 'the [non-Native] system that fucked me up fucked our men even worse. The Missionaries had impressed upon us the feeling that women were a source of evil' (1982: 144). I argue in *Magic Weapons* that

[t]he results of this onslaught are now widely documented: Native children divorced from their traditional Native cultures, while at the same time refused entry into prosperous white Canada because of inferior educational practices and racism, and occupying a liminal space characterized by disillusion, identity crisis, and despair. The legacy of this genocidal atrocity ripples throughout Native Canada, its fingerprints on the domestic violence, poverty, alcoholism, drug abuse, and suicide rates that continue in many Native communities (2007: 28).

Both the residential school system and the Indian Act have functioned under the banner of the capitalist system, seeking to tear Indigenous individuals from extended kinship systems committed to the sharing of communal resources and to refashion them as capitalist consumers. In effect, the matrilineal kinship system of the Iroquois was violently suppressed by the Canadian government in order to disentangle vital communal connections and replace them with discrete nuclear family units. What Cherokee scholar Daniel Heath Justice calls 'the tribal web of kinship rights and responsibilities that link the People, the land, and the cosmos together in an ongoing and dynamic system of mutually affecting relationships' (2007: 151) was rent asunder and reformulated as an expansive grid of mini gendered hierarchies. Lawrence recognizes the profoundly detrimental impact of these political, pedagogical, and economic impositions on Indigenous societies. She argues that 'a central aspect of the colonization process has been the development of systems of classification and regulation of Native identity. These systems forcibly supplanted traditional Indigenous ways of anchoring relationships among individuals, their communities, and the land—erasing knowledge of self, culture, and history in the process.' The rupture Lawrence identifies is further 'facilitated' in her view 'by the images of Native people that exist within the colonizing culture; images that have been crucial to the colonization process and that at the same time represent the concrete residue of its history. These racist images assist in normalizing government regulation of Native identity even as they are central to creating its categories' (2003: 24). It is to these images—or 'simulations'—that I will now turn.

Masculindians—Some Thoughts on Euro–North American Simulations of Indigenous Masculinity

In her influential study of Indigenous feminisms titled *I Am Woman*, Stoh:lo writer Lee Maracle argues that 'the result of being colonized is the internalization of the need to remain invisible. The colonizers erase you, not easily, but with shame and brutality. Eventually you want to stay that way' (1996: 8). According to Chickasaw legal scholar James (Sakej) Youngblood Henderson, this forceful erasure creates for contemporary Indigenous people a

> realization of their invisibility [that] is similar to looking into a still lake and not seeing their images. They become alien in their own eyes, unable to recognize themselves in the reflections and shadows of the world. As their grandparents and parents were stripped of their wealth and dignity, this realization strips Aboriginal [people] of their heritage and identity. It gives them an awareness of their annihilation (2000: 59).

The systematic decimation of traditional Indigenous social systems and the suppression of traditional roles and responsibilities has indeed created significant crises of identity for many Indigenous people; however, these crises, created by erasure and absence, are also exacerbated by images of Indigeneity simulated by popular culture that actually *stand in* for Indigenous presence. Popular North American

culture is saturated with stereotypical images of Indigenous people created and controlled by non-Indigenous people for the benefit of the non-Indigenous majority. As Audre Lorde puts it succinctly in the Black American context, 'it is axiomatic that if we do not define ourselves for ourselves, we will be defined by others—for their use and to our detriment' (Jackson, 2006: 133). Such external control over definitions and image production has led Mohawk scholar Patricia Monture-Angus to suggest that 'growing up "Indian" in this country is very much about not having the power to define yourself or your own reality. It is being denied the right to say, "I am!"—instead finding yourself saying, "I am not!"' (1995: 3).

In his article '"I Guess Your Warrior Look Doesn't Work Every Time": Challenging Indian Masculinity in the Cinema', non-Indigenous scholar Brian Klopotek argues convincingly that '[f]or at least the last century, hypermasculinity has been one of the foremost attributes of the Indian world that whites have imagined. With squaws and princesses usually playing secondary roles, Indian tribes are populated predominantly by noble or ignoble savages, wise old chiefs, and cunning warriors. These imagined Indian nations comprise an impossibly masculine race' (2001: 251). In tandem with the colonial move to suppress the political power of Indigenous women comes the representational move to *re-present* Indigenous cultures as overtly and hyperbolically masculine in non-Indigenous art, literature, film, and media. Representations of Indigenous men in each of these fields have tended to remain within the restrictive triangulation of 'noble savage', 'bloodthirsty warrior', and 'drunken absentee', each deeply invested in the trope of the vanishing Indian that would naturalize the demise of Indigenous nations and deny the validity of the Indigenous feminine. I offer the following diagram—which I entitle 'Masculindians' in order to foreground its constructedness and therefore its inability to represent the real lived experience of Indigenous individuals and nations—as an interpretive tool:

Figure 14.1   Masculindians

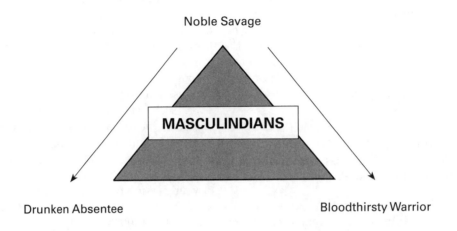

The 'noble savage' is positioned atop the diagram because it represents what non-Indigenous North American society has romanticized as the most admirable features of Indigenous cultures: rugged autonomy, physical bravery, and spiritual connection with nature—all elements of imagined masculinity that non-Indigenous North Americans have worried are missing from their own increasingly urban middle-class lifestyles over the past hundred years or so. As I will discuss in a moment, however, the noble savage is imagined as unable to survive in industrializing North America, so this pushes imagined male Indigenous characters toward one of the other points on the triangle, which represent alternative pathways of degeneration. The 'bloodthirsty warrior' is the embodiment of hypermasculine fury untempered by the spiritual dignity, restraint, and stoic endurance of the noble savage. In a continuum in which the noble savage represents the height of a desirable 'natural' masculinity uncontaminated by industrialization, the bloodthirsty warrior moves dangerously beyond the ideal toward an extreme of masculine violence unmoored by reason or morality. The 'drunken absentee' represents degeneration in the other direction. Unable to

retain the dignity of the noble savage in the face of colonial oppression, the drunken absentee stereotype becomes immobilized and powerless, struggling not against a colonial enemy (like the bloodthirsty warrior) but against himself and his community through domestic violence, parental absenteeism, and the potential suicide of alcoholism and drug abuse. In their article 'White Men, Red Masks', David Anthony Tyeeme Clark and Joanne Nagel grapple with the political and ideological purpose of hypermasculine representations in literary Westerns. They argue that literary Westerns seek to recreate what they call 'hegemonic masculinity' among non-Indigenous North Americans through the depiction of 'endless struggles with Indian supermen before they were, in the minds of the conquerors, overpowered, tamed, imprisoned, and thus emasculated, on reservations' (2001: 116). The noble savage and the bloodthirsty warrior represent the *before* image in this scenario and the drunken absentee represents the *after*.

As suggested earlier, the unrelentingly dignified, brave, and stoic noble savage signifies for mainstream audiences the pinnacle of Indigenous social development. The noble savage is generally a chief or medicine man who commands the respect of his people. He is attuned to the natural world and deeply invested in the spiritual traditions of his people. In literary and filmic representations, the noble savage remains an advocate of his people's worldview despite the onslaught of European 'civilization', while befriending (and often sacrificing himself for) a well-meaning European who has become an honorary member of the community. The noble savage is almost always portrayed as a tragic figure, as silent, solitary, and humourless. The latter features are demonstrated strikingly in the portraiture of British-American painter George Catlin, who travelled throughout the United States and Canada in the early and mid-nineteenth century to document what he believed to be 'vanishing' Indigenous cultures. Catlin focused his artwork largely on male leaders of Indigenous nations garbed in traditional regalia. Although immensely popular in their time, Catlin's paintings presented a limited idea of the Indigenous masculine by segregating male leaders from the context of their communities and rendering them in the style of European monarchs; thus, paintings of Indian chiefs or sachems became interpreted by non-Indigenous audiences as representing a form of coercive male authority akin to monarchy that bore scant resemblance to actual tribal nations. Catlin's portraits, therefore, simulated a model of Indigenous leadership with little relation to the reality of consensus-based systems of Indigenous governance, at the same time that they denied the principle of twinship between the masculine and the feminine.

The noble savage in art, as in literature and film, is meant to be respected and admired, but ultimately to be grieved because of his inevitable demise. The noble savage constitutes an anachronism because his attachment to a tribal worldview and lifestyle is portrayed as admirable but doomed—according to those like Catlin who do the representing—in the face of European expansion. For example, in the films *Dances with Wolves* (1990), *Black Robe* (1991), and *The Last of the Mohicans* (1992),

audiences are encouraged to sympathize with the characters of Kicking Bird, Chomina, and Chingachgook, respectively—all of whom display several characteristics of the noble savage stereotype—yet each of these characters ultimately (and inescapably) has faded away by the film's conclusion; he bears no possibility for imagined persistence beyond the film's final credits. *Dances with Wolves* concludes with Kicking Bird, played by Oneida actor Graham Greene, retreating to the 'winter hunting grounds' against the advancing American cavalry. Here the 'winter' image carries with it the none-too-subtle implication that the Lakota Sioux culture for which Kicking Bird has become the film's figurehead is at the end of its existence, fading into the hills like the characters themselves. If cultural demise is at all in question, the film ends with an epilogue declaring that thirteen years later '[t]he great horse culture of the plains was gone and the American frontier was soon to pass into history' (Costner, 1990). In *Black Robe*, Montagnais leader Chomina, played by Mohawk actor August Schellenberg, ultimately dies from wounds inflicted upon him by his tribe's enemies, the Iroquois. Having heretofore refused baptism from the film's protagonist, Father Laforgue, Chomina is depicted as returning to the dream world of his people as he dies, symbolically carrying their spiritual ways with him. The demise of Chomina's spiritual system is reinforced in the film through Laforgue's eventual baptism of the entire tribe of Huron he journeys to convert. *The Last of the Mohicans*, adapted from the novel by James Fenimore Cooper, signals by its very title the extinction of an Indigenous culture. In the film, as in the novel, the final 'Mohican' is the noble and brave Chingachgook, played by Lakota activist Russell Means. In the monologue with which the film concludes, Chingachgook not only declares himself the last of his people, a race that will die with him, but also frames this as part of the inevitable demise of all Indigenous peoples:

The frontier moves with the sun, pushes the Red Man of these wilderness forests in front of it until one day there will be nowhere left. Then our race will be no more or be not us. . . . The frontier place is for people like my white son and his woman and their children. And one day there will be no more frontier (Mann: 1992).

Significantly, the Mohican elder envisions a possible future for the film's European protagonists, but not for his people or any other Indigenous nation, noting, as if to provide consolation, 'But once . . . we were here' (Mann, 1992).

The remaining two points on the masculindians diagram illustrate potential responses to the inevitable demise imagined for the noble savage. The bloodthirsty warrior constitutes a hypermasculine reaction to the assimilative march of colonization, and the drunken absentee represents resignation to the demise of a people wherein the Indigenous man becomes participant in his own destruction through the narcosis of drugs and alcohol. In each of the three films mentioned above, the noble savage is placed opposite a bloodthirsty warrior figure. In *Black Robe* the role of the bloodthirsty warrior stereotype is filled by an Iroquois war chief who, after delighting in the torture of Father Laforgue and his two male companions, cuts off Laforgue's finger and slices the throat of Chomina's young son with neither sympathy nor remorse. The role of the bloodthirsty warrior is played in each of the other two films by Cherokee actor Wes Studi. The nameless character played by Studi in *Dances with Wolves* is referred to in the film's credits simply as 'the toughest Pawnee'. The nemesis of Kicking Bird's Lakota band, he charges forward against overwhelming odds and meets his death defiantly, fist raised and shouting. Here the rage of the toughest Pawnee guarantees his eventual death. Studi's role as Magua in *The Last of the Mohicans* portrays the irrational hypermasculine violence

of the bloodthirsty warrior even more blatantly. A figure consumed by anger, Magua has dedicated his entire existence to extracting revenge against his enemy, Colonel Munro. When asked by the French marquis, with whom he is allied, why he loathes the English colonel so intensely, he responds with the declaration, 'Magua will eat his heart' (Mann, 1992). Speaking of himself in the third person, Magua is so fixated on vengeance that he cannot even put into words the reason for his anger; he collapses back upon the violent act of revenge itself, thereby removing it from any meaningful context and obscuring its causal function. Magua is thus symbolic of a dangerous masculine virility that non-Indigenous North American society imagines within Indigenous cultures, but a masculinity that cannot be channelled into productive actions through 'civilized' logic; he is thus doomed to perpetuate cycles of violence until he too is killed.

The furious moment of defiant self-sacrifice imagined for the bloodthirsty warrior seems paired in popular consciousness with the protracted self-destruction of the drunken absentee, who is depicted as so wounded by unavoidable cultural loss that he segregates himself from family and community by drinking himself to death. Rather than perishing in resistance like the bloodthirsty warrior, this stereotype internalizes and is immobilized by the pain of his nation's cultural erasure. He thus performs the sapping of the strength of the noble savage and functions as evidence for the colonial hypothesis that the glorious elements of Indigenous cultural traditions have become contaminated and therefore have been lost. These three stereotypical images— which I must again stress are the products of biased Euro–North American images rather than representations of Indigenous realities past or present—therefore serve a variety of purposes for colonial powers. When I asked Kanien'kehaka scholar Taiaiake Alfred in an interview about the function of these images of the Indigenous masculine, he clarified that all of those stereotypes were instrumental to someone else's agenda. . . . So for the violence of conquest you needed a violent opponent so you kind of created this image of the Native as violent warrior . . . but there's no living with it, because it's not meant to be lived with; it's meant to be killed, every single time. They're images to be slain by the white conqueror (personal interview, 2005).

The stereotypes of masculindians serve to justify colonial expansion and act as evidence for colonialism's success. The bloodthirsty warrior, although perhaps admirable in his fearlessness and compelling in his hypermasculine violence, provides what Alfred calls the foil for colonial conquest; he's the perfect enemy who, in defeat, solidifies the masculinity of his conqueror.

According to non-Indigenous critic Elizabeth Cromley, 'The manhood of the Indian' in white representations 'was attached to their ruthless violence, so when readers imagined Indians as actors in these stories, they saw men, physically courageous and bold, yet unable to channel their masculinity into "civilized" and productive acts' (1996: 269), which leads to what Michael T. Wilson identifies as the 'central white criticism of Indian "nature": Indians' alleged lack of masculine self-control' (2005: 132). Through literature, art, film, and media, non-Indigenous audiences could thus consume the supposedly 'virile' and 'natural' Indigenous masculinity of bloodthirsty warriors but then perfect that masculinity through the 'civilizing' force of interpretive restraint. In this delineation, the drunken absentee serves as evidence that the hypermasculine violence of the bloodthirsty warrior has been subdued and contained by colonial expansion and that the noble savage—so admired and romanticized in non-Indigenous literature, film, and art—has become an anachronism. Thus, while the decimation of Indigenous societies is portrayed as somewhat tragic within this system of stereotyped

images—insofar as the loss of the noble savage is to be lamented—the non-Indigenous self-image is exonerated of complicity because it is all presented as inevitable; it seems as if it could have happened no other way.

Although these stereotyped images are simulations created by non-Indigenous people to serve colonial agendas, they bear genuine consequences for Indigenous men and Indigenous communities because they saturate popular culture. In a contemporary context in which many Iroquois and other Indigenous men have been systematically alienated from traditional male roles and responsibilities and are profoundly disempowered by ongoing racism and by economic and political disenfranchisement, the images of Indigenous hypermasculinity from popular culture become potentially attractive to Indigenous men in terms of the power they display. As Alfred suggests, 'the image of . . . the absentee, the drunk, the tough guy, the warrior . . . [can seem] good for the man . . . in the short term' (personal interview, 2005). This is because they offer relief from often untenable social conditions as well as a sense of masculine agency that colonization has rendered difficult for many Indigenous men to attain in other ways. Recognizing the hunger for autonomy in many Indigenous communities in the wake of colonial incursions, Chippewa scholar Gail Guthrie Valaskakis notes how 'the images of . . . Indians' produced by and for popular North American culture have been 'appropriated by Indians themselves' (2005: 38). Focusing on the 'monolithic representations of Indian militants' in the media during incidents of Indigenous resistance, Valaskakis notes how the trope of the 'military masculine' (2005: 39)—which, I would argue, bears a direct lineage from the stereotype of the bloodthirsty warrior—becomes attractive to 'young warriors . . . [who] reappropriat[e] the media's monolithic, military representation of the bandana-masked, khaki-clad, gun-toting warrior and the western Plains warrior from which it has evolved' (2005: 60).

These images of Indigenous masculinity remain, however, products of a non-Indigenous imagination. They flirt with what Rupert Ross, Clare Brant, and others have theorized as the 'ethic of non-interference' privileged in many Indigenous worldviews, but they significantly recast that independence through an individualist paradigm that is forcibly removed from the context of kinship and community. These images promote seductive stereotypes of Indigenous masculinity that are problematic because they seek power through domination and violence rather than through communal responsibility and twinship with the feminine. Alfred argues that

> the way to confront [these stereotypes] and to defeat [them] and to recover something meaningful for Natives is to put the image of the Native male back into its proper context, which is in the family. And so if the image of the Native male is defined in the context of . . . responsibilities to the family—to the parents, to the spouse, to the children (or nephews, nieces, or whatever, or even just youth in general)—if you put the person back into their proper context there are responsibilities that come with that, as opposed to just serving the one responsibility, which is as the foil for white conquest in North America (personal interview, 2005).

What Alfred is calling for here, it seems, is the need to imagine Indigenous masculine power as persisting through kinship ties and communal responsibilities rather than through the individual performance of Indigenous hypermasculinity in emulation of the colonial image-making machine. The burden, strain, and joy of community are imperative, in Alfred's vision, for the nurturing of non-dominative Indigenous male roles and responsibilities that don't fall into the traps of Eurocentric individualism and patriarchy and therefore have the capacity to support the continuance and healing of Indigenous communities.

Condolence and the Burden of Peace— Some Thoughts on Iroquois Models for Indigenous Male Renewal

This chapter began with calls from Sakej Ward to 'bring back' the 'traditional role' of Indigenous men and from Timothy Sweet to 'recover the masculine' in 'tribal societies'. Although it is impossible to define traditional Indigenous masculinity in the singular, the Iroquois creation story of 'Woman Falling from the Sky' presented earlier does posit some plausible characteristics of traditional male roles and responsibilities within *a specific* Indigenous cultural community, as represented by community member Barbara Alice Mann. In Mann's telling, such characteristics for the Iroquois include (a) the valuing of gender balance, complementarity, and twinship; (b) the conception of identity as being achieved through integration into, rather than individualistic separation from, the community; and (c) the understanding of personal power as persisting solely within the context of responsibility. Iroquois masculinity, in Mann's narrative, is expressed through commitment to the well-being of the group rather than through the exercise of an independent male will. These values undergird the care taken to ensure gender balance within the sophisticated traditional governance structures of the Iroquois Confederacy. However, as I've attempted to show, those governance structures have come under ruthless attack from the Canadian government through assimilative systems such as the Indian Act and residential schooling, while the worldview those structures express and uphold has been similarly assaulted by representations of Indigenous hypermasculinity in mainstream art, literature, and film. These two prongs of colonial intervention in Indigenous gender relations have alienated many Iroquois and other Indigenous men from traditional roles and responsibilities, leaving various forms of devastation in their wake.

And yet the ideas and values placed under erasure by colonial forces are not gone. Traditional male roles and responsibilities have not disappeared, just as the traditional governance systems of the Iroquois Confederacy continue to function, at times in alliance but often in conflict with the band council system imposed by the Canadian government through the Indian Act. I conclude this chapter with Mohawk elder Tom Porter's version of the tale of Aionwahta, because it is both contemporary and traditional. Transcribed from oral teachings and published in 2008, Porter's tale is also both oral and written. It is both sacred story and critical gloss. It tells a story of loss and yet declares resoundingly the human capacity to recover and heal. And as such, it has a great deal to say about how gender crises inflicted by colonialism can be confronted and challenged and how traditional roles and responsibilities can be self-consciously inhabited in the present moment.

Porter tells the following tale of 'a man who lived in Onondaga':

They call this man Hiawatha in English. In my language we call him Aionwahta.
. . .

And also in Onondaga, there was this man who was evil, or like a witchcraft-man. He had the ability to turn his body into a deer or into an owl or into a wolf. Some people call that a shape-changer or something like that. . . . He had great medicine, but he used it in an evil kind of way.

This witchcraft-man, this evil man, used to look at Aionwahta's wife. And he fell in love with her. He wanted to take her away from Aionwahta. So he would make advances to her, but she would always turn the other way. He would talk to her, to try to lure her to be his girlfriend. But she was married to another

man, so she wouldn't look at him. She wouldn't answer him or even acknowledge him . . .

After a while, because that witch-guy could not take her with his medicine, he began to make a medicine to do away with her . . . 'Because if I can't have her, nobody's gonna have her.' That's what he thought. So he began to poison her life until she got sick.

Aionwahta, the husband, tried to find medicine to help her, but nothing he made could fix her. She got sicker and sicker. The medicine didn't have enough power. It wouldn't work. And so this evil man eventually . . . took the life of Aionwahta's wife.

She died.

Aionwahta was very, very sad because he had lost his wife whom he loved very much. When they buried his wife, he was lonesome. But even though he was sad, he had seven daughters yet to take care of, see. So he was able to have some hope.

But it didn't stop there.

The evil man began to also make advances to his older daughter. Because he could not have the wife, he wanted the daughter. She also ignored him and rejected him, and so he began to make medicine on this second person, the oldest daughter. And she started to get sick. And the father tried to help her by fixing medicine. But no matter what he did, he couldn't help her. Every day she got sicker and sicker, until she died too.

Now Aionwahta was not just sad from his wife dying; he was three, four times sadder because now his older daughter had died too, just a short time later. And then the next one: he tried to chase the next daughter. And he kept doing that until all the daughters were killed.

He killed all the daughters 'cause none of them wanted him.

And so Aionwahta became . . . hopeless because his whole sacred family had all been killed, taken away from him. . . . He said, 'I'm just gonna walk to the end of the world. And I don't care what happens to me. I've got nothing to live for. Nothing, no hope.' And so Aionwahta walked, aimlessly, in no particular direction. He just walked . . .

He came to a small lake . . . covered from shore to shore with a blanket of geese and ducks, water birds . . . [and] just went straight into the water. He didn't care if he drowned. He was gonna walk right through. But when he started to walk, all the ducks and geese, they jumped and flew up. And as they flew up, all the water stuck in their feathers. They almost drained that lake, the birds did. That's how many were in there . . .

As he walked [across the lake bed] . . . he noticed something on the ground. It was a white, bright thing. And he picked it up. It was a quahog shell. . . . The shells are cylindrical. They're white, and they're purple. And he found those in the lake.

He didn't know what they were for. But he took some sinew that he had and he began to string them together as he found them. And so they formed different variations of white and purple. And when he would finish one, here's what he'd say. 'With this string I made from this wampum that I found, if there is somebody in the world that is as sad and tearful, as full of grief as I am, with nothing to live for . . . I would go see them. And I would take from the very beautiful blue sky a pure eagle feather. And I would wipe the dust of death from the sad one's ears, so that he could hear the children talk and sing and laugh again. So that he could hear his children and nephews when they speak to him. That's what I would do with this wampum if

I knew somebody who was as sad as I am. I would console them by taking the death from their ears.'

And then he picked some more up and he strung them. And he said, 'If there was somebody as sad as I am, walking this earth, I would take, from the very beautiful clear blue sky, a soft little deer skin that's like white cotton. And I would wipe the tears from his eyes. I would use that cloth to wipe the tears, the pain of lonesomeness away from him. So he can see again the beauty of our Mother Earth and the beauty of his children and nephews and nieces. So he can see life again. That's what I would do, if there was somebody as sad as I am, to lose their whole family that they love.'

Then as he continued to walk, he found some more of those same beads on the ground. And he strung them up. 'With this wampum,' he said, 'if there was somebody in this world who was as sad as I am, with heaviness upon them, what I would do is I would take from the very beautiful blue sky, a medicine water and I would offer it to him. So when he drank it, it would dislodge the grief and the sadness, about the loved ones who died in his family. That way he could eat again and the food would taste good. And that way he could speak without a stutter to his loved ones, the ones that remain on earth. And so I would say to him, 'From the very beautiful blue sky, I give you a glass of water so that you will be refreshed. And you can live again and you can speak, and you can eat again and be nourished.' And that's what I would do, if there was somebody who was in as much grief as I am' . . .

And so he kept walking towards the east . . . [and] when that Aionwahta got over to the Mohawk country, the Peacemaker was waiting for him . . .

. . . [T]he Peacemaker stood up. He

took [his own] wampum [from years earlier] and he said, 'My brother, my cousin, I see you are so sad and your mind is so heavy. Your eyes are filled with tears. Your ears are filled with the dust of death. You can't hear.' And so he went through the strings of wampum, which were the same as the other ones that Aionwahta made, before they met.

And the Peacemaker began to condole him and do everything that Aionwahta said he would do for somebody. . . . And together they travelled all over to the nations that were warring, to bring them peace . . . (Tom Porter [Sakokweniónkwas], 2008: 293–7).

When I teach this story in undergraduate classes, students never fail to point out Porter's omission of what happens to the 'evil man'. If the story of Aionwahta were a Hollywood film, the 'witchcraft-man' would surely be punished; in fact, this would likely be reserved for the climax and would occur in dramatic fashion. Yet Porter's story speaks nothing of vengeance toward the killer of Aionwahta's wife and daughters. In fact, Porter implies that what happens to the killer is largely beside the point, which signals significant culturally specific implications of the tale that I want to connect to this chapter's discussion of gender. Despite the extremity of the wrong perpetrated against his family, Aionwahta's manhood is not upheld through violent retaliation of any kind. The story implies that violent retribution would ring hollow, serving only to placate an irrational individual hunger on the part of Aionwahta; it would not put a community that had been thrown into disorder by violence back into balance. Rather, Aionwahta reasserts his manhood by absorbing his own needs and desires in the needs of the broader community, which is why he imagines what he will do when he meets one as grief-stricken as himself and why he eventually dedicates his life to spreading the Peacemaker's message of peace. His own

healing cannot take place in isolation but rather must occur within the context of restoring balance to the broader community. Although in a way emasculated by grief, Aionwahta recovers his masculine power by dedicating himself to others' healing, finding his own voice by seeking ways of encouraging others to speak. In this way, Aionwahta's masculinity is expressed not through violent reaction but rather through proactive gestures of kinship responsibility. The shift in Porter's tale from being immobilized by one's own grief to becoming an activist advocate for the healing of others has fertile implications for those alienated from traditional roles and responsibilities by colonial impositions. Whereas the colonial image-making machine seems to desire Indigenous men to deal with the trauma of their disenfranchisement either through individualist attempts to seize power over others or through voluntary narcosis, here Porter's tale refuses indulgence in individualist violence as a viable pathway to empowerment. Aionwahta's healing is entirely contingent on his commitment to the healing of others, which he demonstrates by 'wip[ing] the dust of death' from their ears, 'wip[ing] the tears' from their eyes, and 'dislodg[ing] the grief' from their throats. Each of these acts removes a symbolic obstruction that prevents the individual from recognizing his or her place within the kinship network that extends from the 'nephews and nieces' to 'Mother Earth'. By facilitating such recognition, Aionwahta enables the individual, who can 'eat again', to 'be nourished' at the same time that he reawakens that individual's agency, allowing her or him to once again 'speak' and therefore 'live'. Mann speaks in *Iroquois Women: The Gantowisas* about 'the urgent need to revive ancient knowledge, not to retreat from the present into a romance of the past, but to shore up the present with the strength of memory, the agility of cultural wisdom' (2000: 4). Here Porter employs 'ancient knowledge' through the traditional tale of Aionwahta to speak directly to the concerns of a present in which many Iroquois men have been alienated from traditional roles and responsibilities through colonial violence. The story of Aionwahta, however, doesn't advocate a violent reaction to that history or a turn toward what Alfred calls 'individualistic and materialistic definitions of freedom and happiness', but rather focuses on retrieving clarity of vision 'by embedding individual lives in the shared identities and experiences of collective existences' (2005: 187).

Discussion Questions

1. In the service of accountability and awareness, consider on which Indigenous nation's (or nations') traditional lands you have encountered this chapter. If you have read this for a class, on which tribal territory is your institution of higher learning located? If you've read this for your own interest, on which tribal nation's traditional lands did you grow up? Once you've uncovered this information, perform research into the traditional gender roles and responsibilities for that nation. Are they similar to or different from those of the Iroquois Confederacy?
2. Why are creation stories important, even within countries such as Canada that self-define as secular societies?
3. Consider the images of Indigenous masculinity that you have encountered in popular culture. Have these been created, framed, and disseminated by Indigenous or non-Indigenous entities (or both)? What assumptions about Indigenous men do these images rely upon? And what are the consequences of such representations?
4. Investigate media portrayals of Indigenous acts of resistance during the Vancouver Olympics in 2010, at the Ardoch blockade of exploratory uranium drilling in 2007, at the Six Nations land reclamation in Caledonia in 2006, at the Grassy Narrows blockades of logging roads during the previous few decades, or at the Kanehsatake resistance near Oka, Quebec, in 1990. Do mainstream media portrayals rely on colonial stereotypes of the bloodthirsty warrior and the noble savage? Are they similar to or different from the filmic representations of Indigeneity that are discussed in this chapter?
5. What are the similarities and differences between the traditional governance structure of the Iroquois Confederacy, as delineated in this chapter, and Euro-Canadian systems of governance both at the time of first sustained interhemispheric contact and today?
6. What checks and balances are in place within Iroquoian social and political systems to ensure that there is no domination of the society by any individual, party, group, or gender?
7. What do you imagine the effects of the Iroquoian stipulation against individuals seeking particular political roles would be in terms of communal well-being? Could this be implemented in different societies, and, if so, would it be a good thing? What if only those who were chosen by their communities and not simply those who decided themselves to run for office could hold political roles in Canadian society?
8. Read examples of contemporary literature by Indigenous Canadian authors such as Richard Van Camp (Dogrib), Gregory Scofield (Métis), Eden Robinson (Haisla),

Joanne Arnott (Métis), Neal McLeod (Cree), Armand Garnet Ruffo (Anishinabe), and others. How do their representations of Indigenous men support or depart from some of the paradigms put forth in this chapter? What political work is being done by their representations of Indigenous masculinities?

Recommended Websites

Assembly of First Nations: www.afn.ca

Native Women's Association of Canada: www.mwac.ca

Native Youth Sexual Health Network: www.nativeyouthsexualhealth.com/index.html

Indian Residential Schools Truth and Reconciliation Commission: www.trc-cvr.ca/index_e.html

Kahnawake Longhouse of the Haudenosaunee: www.kahnawakelonghouse.com/index.php

Kanatsiohareke Mohawk Community, with spiritual leader Tom Porter: www.mohawkcommunity.com

Iroquois Confederacy (through the Iroquois Museum website): www.iroquoismuseum.org/ve3.htm

Native Wiki: www.nativewiki.org/Main_Page

Native Seek: www.nativeseek.com

Native Traditions Search: www.angelfire.com/ak/anakee/nativesearch.html

Two Spirit Cherokee poet, scholar, and activist Qwo-Li Driskill: http://dragonflyrising.wearetheones.info

Notes

1. I wish to thank Barbara Alice Mann and Tom Porter (Sakokweniónkwas) for their generous permission to reprint lengthy sections from their work. I encourage readers to seek out *Iroquoian Women: The Gantowisas* and *And Grandma Said . . . Iroquois Teachings as Passed Down through the Oral Tradition* for elaboration of Iroquoian teachings that this chapter only scratches the surface of.

   I also wish to thank Rick Monture and Barbara Mann for providing insightful feedback on this chapter and guiding me in significant and positive directions; the limitations of the chapter remain my own.

   And I wish to thank the Iroquoian friends and acquaintances from whom I've learned over the past several years, including Janice Brant, Paul Carl, Audra Simpson, Paul DePasquale, Daniel David Moses, and Taiaiake Alfred.

2. North America is referred to by many Indigenous peoples as 'Turtle Island', the land resting on Grandmother Turtle's back. In his telling of the Iroquois creation story, Mohawk elder Tom Porter describes how dirt is rubbed upon Grandmother Turtle's back, causing her to get 'bigger and bigger until it became what they call Turtle Island. That's why the Lakota, the Blackfoot, the Mohawks, most all of the original people, when they refer to the earth, call it *Turtle Island*' (Porter, 2008: 53).

3. Such definitions include governmental categorizations pertaining to 'Indian status', anthropological recordings of 'authentic' cultural materials, and popular cultural representations such as the 'noble savage'.

4. In *Magic Weapons*, I elaborate the position of the non-Indigenous ally as follows:

   'To respect the creative work of Native writers, the intellectual work of Native critics, and the activist work of Native community members, one must engage—listen, learn, dialogue, and debate. The critical posture I endeavour to occupy as a non-Native critic of Native literatures, therefore, is that of the ally. Weaver states:

We need simpatico and knowledgeable Amer-
European critical allies. . . . We *want* non-Natives
to read, engage, and study Native literature. The
survival of Native authors, if not Native people
in general, depends on it. But we do not need
modern literary colonizers. We only ask that non-
Natives who study and write about Native peoples
do so with respect and a sense of responsibility
to Native community (Weaver, Womack, and
Warrior, 2006: 11).

'An ally, in my understanding, is one who acknowledges the limits of her or his knowledge, but
neither cowers beneath those limits nor uses them
as a crutch. She or he recognizes the responsibility
to gain knowledge about the cultures and communities whose artistic creations she or he analyzes
before entering the critical fray and offering public
interpretations. She or he privileges the work of
Native scholars, writers, and community members—not as a political gesture, but as a sincere attempt to produce the most effective criticism—yet
she or he does not accept their work uncritically;
she or he recognizes that healthy scepticism and
critical debate are signs of engagement and respect,
not dismissal. Further, she or he appreciates that
multilayered and ultimately valid understandings
of cultures, communities, and histories can never
emerge solely from book research, and that the
ongoing vitality of Indigenous communities must
serve to augment and correct what Jana Sequoya
calls "the alienated forms of archive material"
(1993: 458). Most importantly, the non-Native ally
acts out of a sense of responsibility to Indigenous
communities in general and most pointedly to
those whose creative work is under analysis. Cherokee author, academic, and activist Daniel Heath
Justice argues that "to be a thoughtful participant
in the decolonization of Indigenous peoples is to
necessarily enter into an ethical relationship that
requires respect, attentiveness, intellectual rigor,
and no small amount of moral courage" (2007: 9).
Allied critical endeavours, it seems to me, aspire to
such participation.' (McKegney, 2007: 56–7)

5.   However, I must reiterate that tradition is neither
static nor confined to the past; tradition endures in
contemporary iterations as much as in pre-contact
lifeways.

6.   The territory on which Kingston, Ontario, rests is
claimed jointly by Iroquoian nations (such as the
Mohawks of the Bay of Quinte, currently settled
on the Tyendinaga Reserve, 60 kilometres west
of Kingston) and Algonquin nations (such as the
Ardoch Algonquin First Nation, currently located
in a variety of settlements including Bob's Lake and
Sharbot Lake between 60 and 70 kilometres north
of Kingston). The Mohawks of the Bay of Quinte
are considered by many to be western relations of
the Iroquois of Hochelaga, the immense Iroquoian

settlement upon which Montreal was constructed.
Kingston rests on the northern shore of what is
commonly called Lake Ontario between present-
day Montreal and Tyendinaga.

7.   I am using previously published versions of both
creation stories (by Iroquois and Christian sources)
to avoid co-optation and appropriation. I'm
neither Iroquois nor Christian; I wish to respect
those for whom these stories are sacred, and I
do not intend in this section to deny their sacred
power. I am, however, reading them critically as
analyzable texts in order to chart traditional forms
of Iroquois masculinity and to consider how the
colonial imposition of Christianity in Iroquois
communities caused male roles and responsibilities
to shift. Therefore, I am examining these creation
stories to unearth some of their many possible
ideological implications, not to supply definitive
interpretations.

8.   As in many missionary accounts of the Iroquois
creation story, Mann here refers to the great turtle
who would become the foundation of the earth
as male—'Grandfather Turtle'. However, as Mann
clarified in an email conversation with me, this
is a misrepresentation of the Iroquoian view of
the earth as essentially female. Mann considers
'Grand*father*' to be a colonial manipulation of the
original 'Grand*mother* Turtle', thereby rendering
the creation story more in line with patriarchal
European traditions; at the time of the publication
of *Iroquoian Women* she was unable to combat this
pressure but now asserts that the use of the male
turtle is inaccurate. Tom Porter's 'Thanksgiving
Address' is helpful here in clarifying the feminine
spirit of creation embedded in the earth. When
the earth was formed, according to Porter, 'the
Creator said that [it] is gonna be a woman. And
not just any woman, she's gonna be the mother of
all women. Or *all* life forms. And she will have the
power to give life to the trees and the birds, to the
bears, to the deer, to the humans. That's why she's
exceptional. . . . And that's our Mother, the Earth'
(2008: 11). Grandfather Turtle in this telling can
therefore be usefully thought of rather as Grandmother Turtle.

9.   Although, as referenced in Note 8, the Turtle on
whose back Turtle Island develops in most Iroquoian traditions is gendered female to correspond
with the principle of Mother Earth.

10. 'Haudenosaunee' is a term of self-definition for the
Iroquois.

11. According to Mann, traditional Iroquoian understandings of maleness and femaleness are not
biologically determined. For example, although
'judges were all women', Mann suggests that 'this
did not mean that men needed not apply. . . . It
just meant that, before a man could be appointed
dispute mediator, he had first to have been "made a

woman," that is, to have had the ceremonial status of *gantowisas* conferred upon him. Thereafter, he was a "woman" for the purposes of that position. (By the same token, a woman might be made a "man," for instance, to take up the appointment of warrior)' (2000: 123).

12. The traditional system of governance for the Iroquois seeks balance through 'consultation and compromise' (Miller, 2004: 59). It avoids combative partisanship in efforts toward adaptive consensus at the level of the clan, the nation, and the Confederacy. As Miller suggests, the decisions of the Confederacy have 'to be unanimous. Lengthy periods of speech-making and consultation [are] required to reach a decision with which all the nations of the League [feel] they [can] live' (2004: 59). In this way, the Iroquois struggle to ensure that, in the words of Rupert Ross, 'the process of arriving at . . . decision[s] [is] communal' (2006: 27). According to Miller, such emphasis on consensus-building 'perfectly reflect[s] the value system of Aboriginal societies, which [place] a premium on

mutual support, generosity, and non-interference in the affairs of others' (2004: 60-1).

13. I wish to stress again here that I do not intend to define precisely what traditional male roles and responsibilities are and have been for all Iroquois, but rather to consider some elements of traditional male roles and responsibilities as represented in significant Iroquois sources and to analyze how those elements have been troubled by colonial interventions.

14. In 1985 the federal government passed Bill C-31 with the intention of amending the discriminatory sections of the Indian Act pertaining to gender. According to Mi'kmaq scholar Bonita Lawrence, 'As a result of the bill, approximately 100,000 Native women and their children have received Indian status. However, although Bill C-31 officially brought the Indian Act into compliance with international human rights standards, it has still managed to maintain divisions among Native people along the basis of gender and blood quantum, largely through not addressing past injustices' (2003: 13).

References

Alfred, T. 1999. *Peace, Power, Righteousness: An Indigenous Manifesto*. Don Mills, ON: Oxford University Press.

———. 2005. *Wasáse: Indigenous Pathways of Action and Freedom*. Toronto: Broadview Press.

———. 2007. Personal interview. Victoria, BC. 23 April.

Anderson, K. 2000. *A Recognition of Being: Reconstructing Native Womanhood*. Toronto: Second Story Press.

Beresford, B., (Director) and B. Moore (Writer). 1991. *Black Robe*. Alliance Atlantic.

Campbell, M. 1982. *Halfbreed*. Lincoln: University of Nebraska Press.

Chamberlin, J.E. 2004. *If This Is Your Land, Where Are Your Stories?* Toronto: Random House, Vintage Canada Edition.

Clark, D.A.T., and J. Nagel. 2001. 'White Men, Red Masks: Appropriations of "Indian" Manhood in Imagined Wests', in M. Basso, L. McCall, and D. Garceau, eds., *Across the Great Divide: Cultures of Manhood in the American West*. New York: Routledge.

Costner, K., (Director) and M. Blake (Writer). 1990. *Dances with Wolves*.

Cromley, E. 1996. 'Masculine/Indian', *Winterthur Portfolio*, 31, 4 (Winter): 265–80.

Denis, M. 1993. *Cultivating a Landscape of Peace: Iroquois-European Encounters in Seventeenth-Century America*. Ithaca, NY: Cornell University Press.

Ennamorato, J. 1998. *Sing the Brave Song*. Schomberg, ON: Raven Press.

Henderson, J. (Sakej) Youngblood. 2000. 'Postcolonial Ghost Dancing: Diagnosing European Colonialism', in M. Battiste, ed., *Reclaiming Indigenous Voices and Vision*. Toronto: University of British Columbia Press.

Holy Bible, Containing the Old and New Testaments, King James Version. 1999. New York: American Bible Society.

Indian and Northern Affairs Canada (INAC). 1869. 'An Act for the gradual enfranchisement of Indians, the better management of Indian affairs, and to extend the provisions of the Act 31st Victoria, Chapter 42' (assented to 22 June, 1869). Ottawa: Government of Canada, www.ainc-inac.gc.ca/ai/arp/ls/pubs/a69c6/a69c6-eng.pdf, accessed 4 April 2010.

Jackson, R.L., II. 2006. *Scripting the Black Masculine Body: Identity, Discourse, and Racial Politics in Popular Media*. New York: State University of New York Press.

Justice, D.H. 2006. *Our Fire Survives the Storm: A Cherokee Literary History*. Minneapolis: University of Minnesota Press.

———. 2007. '"Go Away, Water!" Kinship Criticism and the Decolonization Imperative', in C.S. Womack, D.H. Justice, and C.B. Teuton, eds., *Reasoning Together: The Native Critics Collective*. Norman: University of Oklahoma Press, 2007.

King, T., ed. 1990. *All My Relations: An Anthology of Contemporary Canadian Native Fiction*. Toronto: McClelland & Stewart.

Klopotek, B. 2001. '"I Guess Your Warrior Look Doesn't

Work Every Time": Challenging Indian Masculinity in the Cinema', in M. Basso, L. McCall, and D. Garceau, eds., *Across the Great Divide: Cultures of Manhood in the American West*. New York: Routledge.

Lawrence, B. 2003. 'Gender, Race, and Regulation of Native Identity in Canada and the United States: An Overview', *Hypatia: A Journal of Feminist Philosophy*, 18, 2: 3–25.

Mann, B.A. 2000. *Iroquoian Women: The Gantowisas*. New York: Peter Lang.

———. 2010. Email to the author, 28 June.

Mann, M. (Director). 1992. *The Last of the Mohicans*. Based on the novel by J.F. Cooper. Adaptation by J.L. Balderston.

Maracle, L. 1999. *I Am Woman: A Native Perspective on Sociology and Feminism*. Vancouver: Press Gang.

McKegney, S. 2007. *Magic Weapons: Aboriginal Writers Remaking Community after Residential School*. Winnipeg: University of Manitoba Press.

Miller, J.R. 2004. *Lethal Legacy: Current Native Controversies in Canada*. Toronto: McClelland & Stewart.

Milloy, J.S. 1999. *'A National Crime': The Canadian Government and the Residential School System, 1879 to 1986*. Winnipeg: University of Manitoba Press.

Monture-Angus, P. 1995. *Thunder in My Soul: A Mohawk Woman Speaks*. Halifax: Fernwood.

Porter, T. (Sakokweniónkwas). 2008. *And Grandma Said . . . Iroquois Teachings as Passed Down through the Oral Tradition*. Transcribed by L. Forrester. Bloomington, IL: Xlibris Corporation.

Ross, R. 2006. *Dancing with a Ghost: Exploring Aboriginal Reality*. Toronto: Penguin.

Sequoya, J. 1993. 'How(!) Is an Indian? A Contest of Stories', in A. Krupat, ed., *New Voices in Native American Literary Criticism*. Washington, DC: Smithsonian Institute Press.

Sweet, T. 1993. 'Masculinity and Self-Performance in the Life of Black Hawk', *American Literature*, 65, 3: 475–99.

Thrasher, A.A. 1976. *Thrasher . . . Skid Row Eskimo*, ed. G. Deagle and A. Mettrick. Toronto: Griffin House.

Valaskakis, G.G. 2005. *Indian Country: Essays on Contemporary Native Culture*. Waterloo, ON: Wilfrid Laurier University Press.

Warrior, R.A. 1995. *Tribal Secrets: Recovering American Indian Intellectual Traditions*. Minneapolis: University of Minnesota Press.

Weaver, J., C.S. Womack, and R. Warrior. 2006. *American Indian Literary Nationalism*. Albuquerque: University of New Mexico Press.

Wilson, M.T. 2005. '"Saturnalia of Blood": Masculine Self-Control and American Indians in the Frontier Novel', *Studies in American Fiction*, 33, 2: 131–47.

CHAPTER 15

In this text we have been exploring how gender identities are subjected to binary ideas of masculine and feminine, in an attempt to unpack these into pluralistic alternatives. This chapter introduces the term 'queering' as a verb, articulating a process in which we go further and blur and bend ideas and ideals of gender and sexual identity. There is a great deal of value to this idea for the purpose of freeing individuals and communities from more confining scripts imposed on us individually and collectively.

In this chapter, James McNinch confronts a history of subtle, overt, and sometimes violent tactics in Canadian society aimed at securing a particular gendered social order. People who do not conform, whether outwardly or within their inner beliefs and feelings, often face significant experiences of fear, isolation, and harm. Masculinity is something that one must prove, whether through physical or sexual prowess (as defined collectively) or a constant exercise in persuasion. Refusal or failure to conform has a set of consequences that vary across communities but in any case interfere with our ability and need to be authentic, open, and in relation to other human beings.

McNinch offers us his personal experiences of these dynamics, observations made over time, and scholarly connections to social and historical issues. He points to specific examples of policies, incidents, and viewpoints implicated in the policing of gender and sexual rules. As you read this chapter, think about your own development and whether the descriptions and examples resonate with your observations and experiences. Questions about how gender and sexual orientation are connected, or not, become important in understanding the idea of queering identity.

Dualistic gender and sexual boundaries, such as rigid distinctions between male and female and heterosexual and homosexual, impose unrealistic and often unattainable standards of behaviour on all of us. This is not to suggest that these dynamics affect everyone equally. On the contrary, many gay and lesbian people—or those perceived to be so—have been subjected to physical and emotional harm, and to increased incidence of suicide and depression as a result. McNinch is proposing a liberatory agenda in which all of us can be our true selves, and in which our varying feelings and expressions over time are part and parcel of natural human diversity.

Que(e)rying Canadian Manhood:
Gay Masculinity in the Twenty-First Century
James McNinch

You see, there are still people who view bully-
ing as a rite of passage, a necessary evil, a
phase young people go through before the
laws of propriety begin applying to them.
Children and young teens are expected to
torment each other. The only question is what
determines whether you're the attacker or
the attacked. In my hometown, it came down
to this: you can't be a man until you defend
yourself. And the word that should incite you
to violence in your own defence is 'Faggot'. If
that word didn't send you flying into a rage,
then chances are, you were one.

> —D. Hagen, 'Growing Up Outside the Gender
> Construct', in J. McNinch and J.M. Cronin, eds.,
> *I Could Not Speak My Heart: Education and Social*
> *Justice for Gay and Lesbian Youth* (Regina: CPRC
> Press, 2004), 20.

'He said we would change the world. Gays.
   Homos.'
'And we have haven't we?'
Wally smiles weakly. 'I suppose we have.'
Equal rights, TV shows, civil unions, even
   honest-to-goodness marriage in some
   places. Ned might be dead [of AIDS] . . .
   but still, we did it. We changed the world.
'I wouldn't ever be straight,' Dee's saying,
   'even if it meant things would be easier for
   me. I know that much anyway'.

> —W.J. Mann, *All American Boy* (New York:
> Kensington Books, 2005), 231–2.

As an openly gay middle-aged and well-educated
Canadian white man, I find it seductive to
think that a sense of my own maleness and the
embodiment of my own masculinity have been
accepted in Canada, not just under the law, but
by society at large in the everyday.

Contemporary examples of non-heterosexual males flourishing in fields of entertainment, sports, and politics abound, and this
chapter will make reference to some of them.
Unfortunately, Canadian society still ascribes
sexual-minority identity and behaviour as a
'lifestyle choice'—as if sexual orientation were
a preference akin to deciding to be a vegetar-
ian or buying a hybrid cross-over vehicle (trans
or bi?). Yet we also know that 'coming out' as
a non-heterosexual male is still fraught with
great trauma: suicide rates of gay youth continue unfortunately to confirm this. The pressure to be a heterosexual male, that is, a 'real
man', persists in Canada. The so-called choice
not to be heterosexual is not a preference but a
brave act of self-inscription.

This chapter argues that the pressures inherent in a field as contested as masculinity in
general, and Canadian masculinity in particular, do real damage to individuals seeking to
break the binaries surrounding the construction of 'real' men and 'authentic' masculinity.
The potential for such damage continues. In
Ontario in 2010 a furor erupted over suggested changes to the sex education curriculum that would allow children to learn words
such as *penis* and *testicle* and *vagina* in grade
one. Sexual orientation was to be included in
a list of individual differences in grade three,
as were discussions of masturbation, gays and
lesbians, and safe sex in grade seven. Faced
with strong opposition from a variety of conservative and religious forces that argued these
changes were inappropriate and served merely
to advance, among other things, a 'gay agenda', the government shelved the changes and
called for further consultation with the public ('Sex-Ed Change Needs Rethink', 2010).
This is the context in which discussions of

Canadian masculinity occur. In a culture saturated with sex, many still argue that education about sex is inappropriate. Sexual difference is even more taboo.

However, this chapter also suggests that the que(e)rying of Canadian manhood implies that traditional understandings of what it means to be masculine (and, by default, feminine) have been challenged over the past 40 years. Manhood, as a gender position and a sexual construct, has always been highly problematic. This chapter suggests that a number of contemporary social phenomena—queer identity, queer love, queer sex, and queer marriage—have contributed to the erosion of rigid binaries and stereotypes that have imprisoned all men, regardless of their sexual orientation.

Framing the Discussion

To better frame this discussion, I would ask each of you reading this chapter to position yourself in connection to a complex and difficult issue: the sexual abuse of boys and young men by coaches, teachers, and priests.

(1) In this land of ice and snow, male hockey players who were seduced by and engaged in sex with their male coaches are seen as abused victims because their identity as 'real' men has been compromised by such illicit liaisons. Graham James, a junior hockey coach who had sex with his young players, including former NHL players Sheldon Kennedy and Theoren Fleury, was granted a pardon by his parole board at the end of his time in prison in 2007 (Cosh, 2010). When this became public in 2010, the public outrage and the official stance of the government that this pardon was a travesty of justice, and that the law governing pardons for sexual offenders must be changed, reflected Canadian society's common-sense presumption not only that individual young men have been damaged by such contaminated relationships, but also that the very essence of Canadian masculinity had been sullied by these covert sexual liaisons.

A queer reading of Graham James's situation, however, suggests that 'it takes two to tango'. Adolescents' sexuality is needy and ambivalent, and replete with its own power dynamics and duplicity in relation to peers and coaches. We know that hockey schools and other same-sex institutions, such as prisons, breed same-sex liaisons, often called 'situational sex'. The real issues are the abuse of power by men in positions of authority over youth, and the willingness of junior hockey players craving success in the NHL and pushed by ambitious parents to, under such duress, do anything, including engaging in sexual acts with their coach to succeed. To what exactly do such young men aspire? They want to 'make it', which means embodying the epitome of Canadian masculinity: becoming a player in the NHL.

A former university student of mine, a Métis man in his early thirties and an award-winning high school teacher and basketball and football coach working with inner-city Aboriginal youth for the past decade, has been charged with six sexual offences involving one 14- and two 16-year-old adolescents ('Regina Teacher Charged with Sex Offences', 2010). In the roles of teacher and coach all men are in a vulnerable position. Some research shows that men are reluctant to enter the teaching profession for fear that, in doing their job, allegations of sexual impropriety may brand them forever as 'perverts' (Harris, 2009). There are no details in this particular case, but the point is that such allegations sometimes stem from deeply conflicted and contradictory impulses and motives related to the construction of masculinity.

As my partner, Michael, has reminded me, as a closeted young teenager in small-town Saskatchewan in the seventies, he would have been only too willing to jump into David Hasselhoff's *Knight Rider* smart car or jump up behind Erik Estrada on his motorcycle in the television series *C*H*I*P*S* and leave his closeted and suicidal life behind. Assuming a simplistic binary of adult perpetrator and youthful victim serves to confirm and maintain the status quo relating to definitions of heterosexual masculinity. The truth of same-sex desire between youth and adults is much more complex and disrupts simple notions that link masculinity only with heterosexuality.

(2) Just as confusing and complicated is the conflation in the Catholic Church of sexual abuse with homosexuality; it has suggested, if only to distance itself from the issue, that there is a deep psychological connection between homosexuality and child molestation (Clowes and Sonnier, 2005). Given such an argument, the 'perversion' of Catholic priests exploiting boys is seen as a direct assault on real, that is, authentic and appropriate, definitions of patriarchy. That the Catholic Church has tried to deal with this problem internally rather than regarding it as a public criminal offence is part of the embedded patriarchy of the Church itself. The Catholic Church's assumptions about the relationship between its priests and its laity have been seriously undermined by revelations of cover-ups of youth–priest liaisons in countries around the world. One prevalent argument is that the Catholic Church's insistence on celibacy and its denial of primal sexual urges has led to this travesty. The logic here is that if priests were allowed to marry heterosexually, then such issues would disappear. What does this argument imply about sexual attraction, orientation, and circumstantial same-sex relationships? There are many examples of Catholic priests leaving the church to marry women. We also know that the prevalence of sexual molestation of children is lower in so-called gay populations than it is in the heterosexual population (Herek, 2006).

But do not such revelations also call into question the nature of masculinity itself and the role that sex plays in such a construct? What if we thought of men who hold power, such as hockey coaches or teachers or priests, as innately seductive to young sexualized men? Would this change our understanding of masculinity? Isn't the performance of masculinity embodied in sexual molestation the same

when a male high school teacher molests one of his female students or a CFL official accosts his 15-year-old babysitter? The difference is that in heterosexual cases, masculinity may be deemed to have 'made a mistake' or 'failed' or 'been compromised', but the actions do not call into question the very notion of masculinity itself. Eric Tillman, a former Saskatchewan Rough Riders general manager, claimed that stress and booze and pills accounted for his sexually charged behaviour. Alcohol has been a standard excuse in sexual assault cases and one that is often accepted sympathetically by the courts (McNinch, 2008; 2010). Following Tillman's tearful apology, prosecutors said they were not opposed to a discharge in the case, and 'the girl's parents said they were not opposed to Tillman's continuing his employment with the football club' ('Riders GM Pleads Guilty', 2010). This paints a picture and privileges the idea of a heterosexual man's being able to excuse an excess of booze- and drug-induced sexual behaviour as being completely 'natural', given heterosexual desire. This same privilege is not accorded to same-sex relationships involving adults and minors.

In a heterosexual construct we are not asked by the media to feel shame, but rather to extend sympathy and understanding to a man who has crossed sexual and ethical boundaries. Is this a double standard? Eric Tillman's judgment may be brought into question by his actions. Similarly, the homoerotic behaviour of three white men in their twenties involved in the sexual assault of a 12-year-old Aboriginal girl may be interrogated, but their masculinity is never questioned because of the heterosexual nature of the crime (McNinch, 2010). The masculinity of coaches and teachers and priests in situations involving same-sex controversies, however, is interpreted as 'gay' and therefore 'suspect and sick'. I would argue that such a double standard serves to privilege and preserve our notions of heterosexual masculinity.

I hope that these extreme examples of illegal sexual relationships have helped you, as reader, to position yourself in this highly contested field. Idealistically, a que(e)rying of Canadian manhood might be regarded as part of a liberationist agenda, freeing all of us from the narrow constraints of sexual and gender binaries. Others, however, will argue that as Canadian society becomes softer and 'more gay' it signals the demise of an important part of our Canadian identity: the hegemonic male supposedly in charge and in control of himself and others. This chapter suggests that a broader understanding of masculinity, which includes GLBTTQ identities, will serve to save Canadian masculinity from itself.

Just One of the Guys

Homosocial behaviour is referred to by the British as 'laddishness'. This is the phenomenon of men preferring the company of men rather than women (but who remain their sexual and often marital partners). The lighter side of homosociality translates into heterosexual men developing close friendships and spending lots of time together. In North America 'a night out with your buddies' specifically excludes females. The darker side of homosociability is misogyny—the expressed loathing of the opposite sex. Men crudely refer to women as sexual objects. From a queer perspective, this contempt for the opposite sex seems to be part of a bizarre love/hate binary of heterosexual desire. Being one of the lads situates one's masculinity in an all-male environment that is non-judgmental and sympathetic to the travails of being a 'man': breadwinner, husband, and father. Consolation for embodying such a domestic and thus de-masculinizing role is found through drinks at the local pub with your mates. This show of masculinity has traditionally been considered quintessentially heterosexual. However, the need for same-sex company can also be seen as socially adjudicated and repressed homoerotic desire (McNinch, 2008). Men, regardless of their sexual orientation can be flattered, assuaged, and 'pumped'

by the support, the gaze, and the sublimated desire of other men. Homosocial behaviour is premised on both sides of the Atlantic by an implicit romantic idea that there once was a time, in some mythic golden past, when 'men and women occupied established gender roles in a stable social system in which men's roles were prime and men had power and control' (Haywood and Mac an Ghaill, 2003: 6).

What About the Boys?

Such an understanding of heterosexual relations leads to lamentations about boys failing school and schools failing boys and questioning why more than 60 per cent of the university population are women. This 'what about the boys' discourse contains a concern that boys are in danger of 'turning' gay, and isn't this proof of a failure of masculinity itself? Other examples of dysfunctional masculinity include the absent father who doesn't provide affection or child support, the violent hockey fan who beats up cab drivers, and the disengaged and underachieving male who finds himself still living at home at the age of 28, and in his lack of ambition takes solace in smoking dope and playing video games with his buddies. The reality that some men are attracted sexually to other men is lumped into this construct of failed masculinities. This argument is promulgated by upholders of traditional patriarchy who suggest that a crisis of masculinity is upon us. This argument often starts illogically by excusing the father and blaming the working mother for putting her children in the hands of daycare 'strangers', which leads to detachment and de-masculinization of her sons. Such implicit common-sense knowledge of what contributes to boys being boys and what masculinity and femininity 'really' are continues unabated in our society, despite all the progress made by feminists and queer activists over the past 50 years. The so-called crisis of masculinity reflects society's concern with change. The concept of identity itself is conflicted, fragmented, and dislocated, and it depends on context (Gill, 2007): 'Identity is only in crisis when something regarded as fixed, coherent, and stable is displaced by doubt and uncertainty' (Haywood and Mac an Ghaill, 2003: 28.)

The Problem with Hormones

The so-called crisis in masculinity in turn means we have to come to terms with the common-sense assumption that it is easier to be(come) a girl than it is to be(come) a boy (Pleck, 1983). Women do have the babies, so that seems 'natural'; men ejaculate, inseminate, and then fall asleep and snore, and this too is deemed biologically natural. Any definition of a gay man is premised by the idea that his masculinity is formed through a failure to engage in this kind of behaviour. However, expectations of strength, power, and sexual competence for male roles might be broadened if we understand that such traditional attributes can be applied to homosexual as well as to heterosexual men.

Rather than conceiving of same-sex desire as exposing a gap between traditional ideal roles and lived experiences and as proof of 'failure' for boys and men, we might rather critique the traditional ideal roles themselves. This is already happening as heterosexual men marry women with more education and income than them, and then take paternity leave and become stay-at-home dads rather than primary income-earners. These men prove that their power and sexual competence are not limited by traditional male roles. I can attest that I feel more competent in these roles in a same-sex relationship than I did in a failing heterosexual one. Does this help to break down the homo/hetero male/female masculine/feminine male/female binaries we are discussing?

Another commonplace discourse that needs to be confronted is how society looks at 'failed' masculinity as 'proof' of masculinity itself. An excess of testosterone is blamed as the 'natural' cause of everything from bullying, gangs, and sexual assault to violence in hockey and other contact sports, and to boys refusing and excusing themselves from female-dominated institutions such as schools. This argument suggests that such 'failure' is because men's 'natural' need for such things as competition and hierarchies has somehow been thwarted. Not surprisingly, such essentialist arguments also infer that some men must lack sufficient testosterone, and they link this with constructivist notions of failure caused by a lack of appropriate male role models and the influence of dominant mothers to create effeminate boys.

Whether Canadian masculinity is a construction or an essence, the question very baldly might be, If we don't have a problem with heterosexual men who cook and clean and look after baby, why do we have trouble with men who like to have sex with other men? In a more academic way we can ask, Has official legal and governmental (as well as unofficial social and personal) 'sanctification' of gay relations in this country served to disaggregate the overinflated and overgeneralized concept of patriarchy and masculine identity? Haywood and Mac an Ghaill (2003: 9) ask, 'Is it the relationship between social [and power] structures that determine how gender [and sexual] relationships are lived out?'

One of the reasons that the so-called gay liberation movement is indebted to the feminist movement is related to the 'ideology of [re]production' (Hearn, 1987: 98). In the same way that 50 years ago the birth control pill gave power to women by separating their reproductive role from their sexual identity, so too the gay liberation movement separated sexual conduct from the patriarchal view of men's role in the reproduction of the species. What does this mean in the everyday? It should mean that this separation will allow for multiple performances of masculine sexuality, orientation, and identity.

Gay Masculinity

One of the aims of this chapter is not only to suggest that gay men have altered our understanding of Canadian masculinity, but also to show that in fact gay men embody masculinities in multiple ways. Brian Pronger has argued that 'male homosexuality is a violation of masculinity. . . . Because it gnaws at masculinity, it weakens the gender order. But because masculinity is at the heart of homoerotic desire, homosexuality is essentially a paradox in the myth of gender' (1990: 20).

In part this means understanding how much society has changed since the iconic Stonewall riots in New York in 1969, when gay and trans-gendered individuals fought their arrest as 'perverts' who engaged in bathhouse sex. The decriminalizing of homosexuality in Canada in the same year led, through activism, to gay choirs, gay sports leagues and gay Olympics, summer camps for queer kids, parliamentary lobbying, fundamental changes in legislation, rulings by the Supreme Court, gay marriage, gay parenting, and gay adoption, and to a celebration of same-sex relationships and sexuality as signs of health and vigour, not disease or degeneration. In 40 years, all of this has become part of a new social norm. Homosexuality was classified as a mental disorder by the American Psychiatric Association until it was declassified in 1973. Although the landscape has changed, has this changed our understanding of Canadian masculinity?

Some argue that, 'acting on dissident identities', gay men have caused 'a transformation of intimate life: relationships between and among men that have challenged and ultimately changed understandings of masculinities' (Haywood and Mac an Ghaill, 2003: 138). Weeks (1977) explained almost 35 years ago that gay identity politics and collectives gave 'a sense of rebirth—a reinvention of masculinity beyond pathology, regulatory forces—criminalization, medicalization'. Plummer (1981) argues that struggles to legitimize gay identities provide 'concrete' evidence that masculinity is not something one is born with or an inherent possession but rather is 'an active process of achievement, performance and enactment'.

Portraits of the Canadian Gay Man: Nothing Is Straightforward

It may be useful to offer some sketches of men who embody traditional performances of masculinity but whose identities also destabilize that construct. Their identities remind us that sexual identity, orientation, and behaviour constitute a complex intersection of individual differences. Nothing is simple; everything is complicated; and much is compromised, including traditional constructs of Canadian masculinity.

Let's start with some children. My partner, for example, first played doctor and nurse with a little girl when he was five but immediately ran off to play doctor and doctor with his male friend, with whom he continued to have a sexual relationship until their early teens. Then there is Nate, a 10-year-old boy whom even his parents (my friends) refer to as their 'gay son'. Last Easter he ran up to me to show off his 'perfectly purple' shirt and matching tie for the tuxedo-style suit he had chosen to wear to church. I ache for Jesse, a kid now entering the trauma of grade seven, who loves to sing and dance and has long hair, and who screamed at his mother, 'Why didn't you let me start school as a girl like I wanted to?' The mother of 14-year-old Richie worries about his age-inappropriate behaviour. I notice that he smokes, but the real problem is that he regards himself as the 'fiancé' of a 23-year-old man. Such sexual- and gender-variant behaviours, which were once masked, are becoming more open and more common. Is this coming out at an earlier age a sign that maleness has become more complex? Has this coming out compromised Canadian masculinity itself?

Adrian is a good-looking young Aboriginal man in his late twenties. He works shifts in a steel mill and with a landscaping firm on the weekends, climbing high in the air to trim trees. He is flattered by the attention of a group of older gay men. His own narcissism encourages these men, and he is charming and not quite as naïve as he pretends to be. He has already failed in a relationship with a woman, which situates him as something of a victim, but he professes and acts on his responsibility for the child who was the product of this brief union. His need is for flattery and attention, perhaps as a substitute for love or intimacy. He finds in the company of gay men a position of power because of his physical beauty and his goodness. How does that define Canadian masculinity in 2011?

Let me introduce you to Jeff. Now in his thirties, he too is physically fit and attractive; he is gifted mechanically and works in construction even though he has a university degree, because he 'didn't know what to do with it'. This indecision relates to his coming out as a gay man during his undergraduate years. He began to explore his same-sex desire through the Internet, in a closeted relationship with an older man who has over the years turned abusive and controlling. As he pulls into the A&W in the small Saskatchewan town where he lives and works, the high school girl at the drivethrough says to Jeff, 'I heard you're gay. That isn't true, is it?' Like all gay men at every intersection of their complicated lives, Jeff must make a decision to be out or not. At this particular point Jeff chooses to say, 'Yeah, I'm gay, but what does that have to do with me ordering an effing Papa Burger!' How does Jeff define Canadian masculinity?

Cliff, now in his forties, is a high school teacher. For students and parents alike he defines the hip and engaging young professional. To look at him, one would assume that Cliff is straight—he's big, athletic, strong, and good-looking. He once sported blond dreadlocks, but fashion and thinning hair led him to shave his head. Cliff had many sexual liaisons with women in the school division he taught in, but he also has a sexual attraction to young men. Is it a coincident that he gravitated to coaching basketball, which involvies many road trips? Cliff is a man torn apart by guilt that sends him sliding into depression. This once handsome athletic man has been plagued by injuries, both physical and psychological, because he faces the threat of harassment and degradation for

the kind of erotic encounters he can only wish for.

Another friend of mine, Jason, spent a summer on a combine at his uncle's farm thinking about his conflicted sexual orientation, and decided that instead of coming out as a gay man, he would marry the aggressive Asian woman who was pursuing him. For a 'love that dares not speak its name', here's another snapshot of Canadian masculinity.

In contrast, Russell and Brian are men who have professed their love for one another for many years and are married. One of them is a minister in the United Church. They adopted two boys relatively 'easily' because both were 'special needs' children. This same-sex couple describe themselves as embodying nontraditional definitions of masculinity and are indeed proud to do so. Their goal of building pride and leadership and resiliency skills in queer youth reflects their commitment to changing the definition of masculinity in Canada. This summer a female United Church minister is officiating at a same-sex wedding in my garden. Friends and family, including two daughters from a previous marriage of one of the men, have arranged for all that a marriage ceremony entails. Do not these same-sex couples, married by church and state, represent a new face of Canadian masculinity?

Homophobia and a Little History

Narrow definitions of masculinity are still constructed through homophobia as the last acceptable prejudice in our society. Judith Timson has noted:

> Comedian and telethon host Jerry Lewis has just publicly apologized for using the word fag, and actor Isaiah Washington may have been kicked off the hit television show *Grey's Anatomy* for the same reason, but make no mistake: despite gay pride, legal victories and *Will and Grace*, homophobia—the

irrational hatred and fear of homosexuals and what they do—is alive and well (*Globe and Mail*, 8 September 2007: F7).

Timson added 'especially in the United States', which inspires the question, How different are we in Canada and how much do the American media inform our views of homosexuality? To what extent does homophobia in American society contribute to the construction of Canadian masculinity? *Archie* comics now have a gay character, Kevin Keller. An executive with the company says the introduction of the 'strapping blonde gay man' is about 'keeping the world of Archie Comics current and inclusive' ('Archie Comics Unveils Gay Character', 2010). In Canada this may simply mean finally acknowledging a reality we already live.

The year 2009 marked the 40th anniversary of the decriminalization of homosexuality in Canada, in a bill brought forward in 1969 by then justice minister Pierre Trudeau. His son Justin commemorated the occasion in Ottawa with EGALE, a national lobby group dedicated to advancing sexual-minority rights in Canada. What has happened over those 40 years? In 1977 Quebec became the first jurisdiction in the world to prohibit discrimination based on sexual orientation. In 1995, based on a case brought forward by a same-sex couple seeking pension benefits (*Egan vs Canada*), the Supreme Court of Canada ruled that sexual orientation should be read into Section 15 of the Canadian Charter of Rights and Freedoms, the section that applies protection against all discrimination to laws currently in effect. In 2000 the Supreme Court ruled (in a case of *Little Sisters Book Store vs Canada*) that queer publications, even those deemed pornographic, are protected by the freedom of speech and expression clauses of the Canadian Charter. In 2002 the Northwest Territories added both sexual orientation and gender identity to protection under its Human Rights Act. In 2005 the House of Commons and Senate passed Bill C-38, the Civil Marriage Act, formally legalizing same-sex marriage in

Canada. Such legislation followed similar bills in the Netherlands (2001) and Belgium (2003). Spain (2005), South Africa (2006), and Norway and Sweden (2009) have followed since, and six US states now allow same-sex marriage, although there is considerable pushback in some jurisdictions, such as California ('Forty Years Later . . .', 2009; *Globe and Mail*, 'Trials of the Decade', 26 December 2009: F5).

Canada's relatively progressive position on same-sex rights and relationships needs to be put in a world context. The recent work of Evangelical American Christians in Africa prompted a Ugandan politician to introduce a bill that would make homosexual acts punishable by death. Such difference illuminates the Canadian context, where homosexuality is regarded, at least legally, as normative. Discourse in Uganda conflates masculinity with heterosexuality, and it follows that 'the gay movement is an evil institution' whose goal is 'to defeat the marriage-based society and replace it with a culture of sexual promiscuity' where 'homosexual men sodomize teenage boys' ('How an Anti-gay Rally Pitted Uganda against the West', 2010). The same newspaper article quotes Stosh Mugisha, a female gay rights activist who was raped by a farmhand who wanted to 'cure her of her attraction to girls'. Mugisha claims she was impregnated and infected with HIV. Presumably the farmhand was acting on a colonial and Christian understanding of what masculinity needs to embody in twenty-first-century Uganda.

Similar horror stories emanate from non-Christian countries as well, notably fundamentalist countries such as Iran. In September 2007, to shouts of derision at Columbia University, the Iranian president denied that there were any gays in Iran. 'In Iran we don't have homosexuals like in your country . . . I don't know who has told you that we have it' ('Ahmadinejad Claims Iran Has No Gays', 2007). Such blatant dissembling, in the face of documented tortures, lynchings, and public executions of hundreds of individuals accused of homosexuality, helps us to appreciate that at least in Canada no one is regarded as a criminal in the eyes of the state simply for being gay. They may, however, still be regarded as less than masculine.

Although such toxic environments as Iran and Uganda are literally half a world away, I would be remiss not to note the violence of heterosexual men inflicted upon women, many of them Aboriginal, and upon gay men in this country. Brutal rapes and gay bashing by straight men are phenomena that define the fringes of masculinity. I have made the point elsewhere that the homoerotic bonding of straight men as they engage in such sexual violence queers their own identity. 'Gang bangs' and gang bashings bond men in their fear and loathing of the 'other', as a feeble but violent way of shoring up their own sense of themselves (see Janoff, 2005, and McNinch, 2008). It's like the guy in the muscle car who speeds through the neighbourhood with much screeching of tires. As a straight woman remarked, '[H]e's just overcompensating for his tiny penis.' While this may be an exaggeration, such overt displays of 'muscle' are a thin veneer masquerading as masculinity when they really demonstrate the fear of a lack of this elusive essence.

As I am editing these words, a story breaks of a group of male youths in Edmonton who attacked a group of self-identified lesbians. The assault is described as a 'hate crime' by the group. One of the women was kicked unconscious and suffered a crushed left eye socket and facial nerve damage. We learn that the investigating police officer did not file a report of the incident. The victim is quoted as saying, 'I think in this day and age, we've become complacent and passive about educating the young to accept people's differences. . . . Everyone's under the assumption that we're past all that, but it's right here. It's happening to people that you know, that I know and love, all the time' (Rusnell, 2010). A few weeks later, Judge Grove of the BC Supreme Court handed down a ruling on the 2008 beating by a young man of two men who were holding hands in the gay village in Vancouver. 'One of the men was knocked unconscious and suffered a concussion and broken jaw for daring to challenge the bullies who called him and his boyfriend faggots.' The judge's determination that the beating constituted a hate crime gives gay activists hope that this precedent will affect other rulings in similar cases. The judge noted, 'It's hard to imagine that something as innocent as two men holding hands could cause such a visceral, vicious, unprovoked, and cowardly assault. . . . In Canada, people are free to live their lives as they choose, regardless of sexual preference' ('Hatred Motivated Attack on Gay Man', 2010). But the plaintiff might ask, 'If I can't beat up fags' how can I define my masculinity?'

Essences and Constructions

Even Judge Grove, however, in using the word 'preference' as if sexual orientation were a lifestyle choice, conflates and confuses the notions of gender and sexuality. He is not alone in this regard. Margaret Somerville is a Canadian ethicist who argues that, grounded in heterosexuality, 'real' masculinity is essential to the survival of the species. She critiques same-sex marriage and defends patriarchy and the male's role in traditional marriage. She has argued that 'same-sex marriage opens up the possibility of polygamy because it detaches marriage from the biological reality of the basic procreative relationship between one man and one woman'. Somerville (2007) concludes that the 'traditional' definition of marriage is now open to any and all interpretations. What Somerville conveniently forgets is that, historically, marriage has been an institution designed to amass and preserve property and to ensure its safe passage to the next generation. As a kind of 'extreme patriarchy' in many cultures, polygamy has been one of the only means of sustaining familial status and power. Somerville should also acknowledge that women in polygamous relationships are never equal to each other or to their husband. In contrast, same-sex marriage upholds the idea of reciprocity between two equals, and indeed is premised by the European and relatively recent notions of 'romantic love' being a better reason for union than the preservation of power and privilege.

In Canadian society today, sexual relationships (hetero or homo, in or out of marriage) are patterned largely by serial monogamy and serial affairs because we are steeped in romantic notions of love: of finding the right person to be the object of our sexual desire. Polygamy may affront us not because it isn't 'natural' but because it doesn't adhere to our romantic ideals. There is no need for Somerville to blame same-sex unions, as a now legislated deviation from her preferred biological norm, for creating a 'slippery slope'. Many heterosexual couples cannot or choose not to have children, and many non-heterosexual individuals and couples wish to be parents. Their insistence on the right to do so through various technologies and interventions blurs Somerville's notion that one man and one woman constitute the 'basic procreative relationship'. Within different historical, social, and cultural contexts, both polygenic and same-sex relationships have existed longer than so-called traditional heterosexual unions. We may not like to think of marriage as an economic union, but many would argue that marriage is just that, regardless of the numbers or the sexual orientation of those involved. According to her own logic, Somerville should, in refuting same-sex unions, be embracing polygamy as a kind of über-hetero marriage in which traditional masculinity is subservient to the procreating and raising of children as its primary raison d'être. There are now many examples of same-sex married or common-law partners who are embroiled in costly adversarial litigation relating to the end of the romantic and sexual relationship and determining who owes what to whom. Many would ask, what kind of liberation is that?

At the other end of the sexual and political spectrum from Somerville is queer artist and activist Sky Gilbert, who asserts, 'When being gay is the same as being straight, I quit' (2009). Gilbert's point is that being gay in Canada has become too bourgeois: 'Monogamy, respectability and good citizenship is not the world I signed onto when I filled out my gay card.' Gilbert suggests that 'gay' now means being acceptable to the straight community and being gay has lost its frisson as a critique of heterosexual masculinity. He rightly points to 'the contradictions of postmodern culture', where middle-class white men enjoy unparalleled privileges as gay members of Canadian society, and yet for every one who has been so assimilated there are others who remain closeted or end up 'drowning themselves in suicidal drugs and unsafe sex'. Similarly, Kenji Yoshino (2005) talks about the 'irresistible banality of same-sex marriage' as an antidote to the difficult lives of many gay men: 'We need comedy more than tragedy and happy endings [like marriage] like everybody else.' Gilbert (2009) laments the assimilation of 'boring' gay couples into the mainstream of Canadian society and the loss of a gay world that challenged the provincialism and parochialism of our society by engaging in gender-bending displays of blatantly non-heterosexual activity. Commentators accuse him of getting old, of being worse than homophobes, of regretting that he has become passé because his sexual orientation is no longer seen by the majority of Canadians as a revolutionary or even rebellious subject position. But does this discourse also not question what we have or have not defined as 'straight' masculinity? Gilbert has decided that he's not gay—he's ESP—an 'effeminate sexual person', advocating for sexual promiscuity and gender play. This lament of a gay persona is also implicitly a lament for the binaries of gay and straight that once bound us.

In a more academic way Jen Gilbert makes a similar point. She argues that Derrida's theory of hospitality helps us to appreciate the limitations of Canada's same-sex marriage laws. 'When the ideal of hospitality is articulated in the juridical and legislative domain as accommodation, an affirmation of [the variations of] how people choose to live in relation to one another is lost' (2006: 29). In other words, Derrida's idea of 'perfectability' is compromised because only the standard of 'marriage' as a relationship between individuals is privileged, leaving many non-traditional relationships beyond the pale.

On the other hand, as someone who teaches courses on sexual and gender identity and schooling, I would argue that the significance of Bill C-38 is to remove, despite various moral and religious objections, any critical distinction between homosexual and heterosexual relationships. If the state can sanctify same-sex marriage, then other public institutions, including schools, must also accept same-sex relationships. This is a fundamental shift in Canadian discourse on sex and gender. But the question remains, what impact does this have on our more traditional understandings of masculinity?

One of the greatest challenges to these traditions comes from transgendered and transsexual individuals. As Jen Gilbert writes, the trans phenomenon 'reminds [us] that gender is work, and not just for those who make a transition'. The challenge for masculinity is to 'welcome what is most foreign within the self' (2006: 32). Our culture and our laws may have led us to understand masculinity in a new way. On the other hand, being sexually attracted to someone of the same sex or reassigning one's gender has simply reinforced, perhaps, our notions of binaries and of what is 'normal'.

It's a Drag, Man

The exaggerated performativity of drag also challenges us to examine the binaries of masculinity and femininity. Whether it is football team members donning cheap wigs and ugly pleated skirts and shoving balloons down their jerseys for a laugh, the exotic creatures of Mardi Gras, or the lip-synching queens in gay clubs, drag is an emulation, affirmation, send-up, and put-down of femininity. Such performances

provide gay men with a way of affirming their own masculinity: 'gay men define masculinity as not being (like) a drag queen' (Moore, 2004: 111). Unlike the deliberate theatricality of drag, cross-dressing has become central to the identity construction of transgendered individuals who wish to dress, act, and 'pass' as members of the opposite sex. Some feminists have condemned drag as a pastiche that is inherently insulting to females. Many gay men profess to 'hate' drag queens because they are so 'faggy'. Such a stance bolsters their sense of masculinity and gender performance. Drag queens themselves often draw attention to their manhood by grabbing their crotch and complaining about the tape and tucks and adjusting their false boobs with great exaggeration. In his understanding of gender performance, noted drag queen RuPaul (1996) remarked that 'we are born naked; after that everything is drag'.

But drag can also be 'straight', or, more accurately, 'acting straight' can be a form of drag for gay men. There are gay men who 'like many of us have a preference for "straight acting" men—men that have very few effeminate traits but still like to *get down* with other men' (see 'About Us', http://straightacting.com); the Straight Acting.com website insists this is simply a 'preference' of some gay men for 'butch' rather than 'fem' presentations of sexuality. This discourse blurs the binary of 'top and bottom' applied to same-sex intercourse. If both men are apparently 'straight' (acting), then heterosexual notions of dominant and passive roles in sex are replaced by something akin to mutual desire. An online quiz can be used to determine supposedly just how straight-acting one appears. Another website offers heterosexual pornography for homosexuals (Straight Guys for Gay Guys, http://tour.sg4ge.com). The reality of 'hard', that is, straight-looking/acting gays, often in multipartner sexual liaisons, questions a traditional understanding of manhood that links tough masculinities only with heterosexuality. In a chat forum this 'tough guy' attitude is succinctly captured by

one blogger who writes, 'Romance is for puss-
ies. Let's go change a tire or scratch each others'
balls or something' ('Hanging Out', 2010). So if
straight-acting *is* gay, then maybe Sky Gilbert is
right and it's time to flee definitions of gayness
that are so dependent on the performance of
straight masculinity.

Conflicted Spaces

Inherent tensions remain in constructions of
masculinity in the Canadian context, a land of
the 'severely normal', as Ralph Klein, one-time
premier of Alberta, defined the Christian Right
(Filax, 2006). Despite many significant human
rights advances for GLBTTQ people, much work
remains in order to better embrace inclusivity, which in turn requires a broadening of our
understanding of masculinity. Research shows
that the physical and psychosocial isolation of
sexual- and gender-minority individuals struggling with complex questions of sexual identity
is a major factor leading to alienation, quitting
school, and most extremely to depression, substance abuse, self-abuse, and suicide (Filax,
2006; Gibson, 1989; Khayatt, 1994; McNinch,
2004). Despite the Internet's ability to connect
isolated individuals around the world, sexual-
minority and gender-variant individuals living
in rural and small-town Canada who hear and
read about queer life in big cities can only imagine and envy the luxurious freedom and support such spaces can provide.

Initiatives such as Gay–Straight Alliances
in high schools (Wells, 2006), as well as re-
siliency-building initiatives such as Camp
fYrefly (Grace and Wells, 2007), encourage
young people to be more than just advocates
for themselves and their friends. It helps to
situate such activism in the larger context of
social justice and anti-oppressive education
(Kumashiro, 2004). In other words, redefining masculinity is a much bigger process than
providing 'social support' to individuals who
don't or won't or can't ascribe to the so-called
norms of masculine behaviour. Resistance and

advocacy groups in society that champion the
'other' have educational and political purposes.
This radical agenda challenges masculinity by
expanding society's comfort zone beyond relatively narrow constructs such as 'straight/gay'
or 'gay/lesbian' and extends a hand to those
who struggle and/or self-identify with labels
that include 'bisexual', 'transgender', 'transsexual', 'two-spirit', and 'queer'.

In 2008, a high school Gay–Straight Alliance
in Regina used 'found narratives' from *I Could
Not Speak My Heart* (McNinch and Cronin,
2004) for a regional high school drama competition; these were first-person anecdotes from
sexual- and gender-minority youth. Peter, one
of the actors, a young gay man, told the drama
teacher (and GSA advisor) that his involvement
in the production was important but painful because his parents did not support what he was
doing, had made a point of not attending the
performance, and would not pay for his music
lessons if he participated. Josh, a drama student
and member of the high school football team,
played the role of a gay boy being bullied. Josh
found this role to be challenging, particularly in
relation to his football-playing peers, but said to
his mother, 'Well, I guess if Heath Ledger can
do it [in *Brokeback Mountain*], so can I.' A vice-
principal recently told me that one straight high
school student who thought his school was celebrating Pink Shirt Day (an anti-bullying event
in March) was harassed all day for wearing pink
and therefore being 'one of them', was smashed
into a locker, and was offered 10 dollars to 'give
me a blow job, faggot'. Unfortunately, everyone
working in high schools across Canada has stories like these to share.

The Body as a Project

How gay men embody their masculinity helps
us understand gender and attitudes toward it
as a social construction that is learned. Men
can do so without ascribing to the extreme image of the steroid-enhanced bodybuilder for
whom his built body becomes, complete with

swollen blood vessels, a representation of the engorged erect penis. Other physical types or performances abound: 'bears' (older, bigger, hairy men, or at least ordinary-looking men who profess not to pay much attention to their looks) and their opposite, 'twinkies' (young, slender gay men obsessed with their looks and grooming). Somewhere in the middle of this continuum of masculine performance, epitomized by middle-aged men with goatees and chest hair on the one hand and hairless, nearly anorexic 'boy toys' on the other, are the former *Designer Guys* Steve Sabados and Chris Hyndman. With their mainstream CBC afternoon television show, this openly gay couple 'offer fun advice and decor, fashion, food, and relationships tips' (*Steven and Chris*, 2010). Constructions of the metrosexual and of male 'manscaping' and 'makeovers' are part of this continuum. The marketing of male 'beauty' products, and attempts to invigorate the fashion of manhood more specifically, has been described as the commodification of a gay influence on masculinity and an encouragement of the narcissism at the core of many performances of masculinity, both straight and gay (Allen, 2006). The launch of a perfume for men insists that the scent is 'designed to leave a man feeling empowered and ready to take on life's challenges with unshakable confidence'. Despite the contradiction between the text and the accompanying picture of a very pretty half-naked man, sales will be made by appealing to 'masculine physical and mental strength' ('Force of Nature', 2010).

Imagine, reader, traditional performances of masculinity embodied by the hockey player or the biker, the woodsman, the rancher, or the hot-car dude. Now infuse these images with the viscerality of same-sex desire. Iconic images of masculinity can be shattered or at least altered by understanding that these men are not always attracted to women. In fact, in their extreme definitions of 'maleness', such queer men find themselves attracted to their own image of masculinity—others like themselves.

The fashion a decade ago among gay men for checked lumberjack shirts over white T-shirts was a carefully studied and replicated parody of straightness that was seen as erotic because it wasn't 'effeminate'. I am manly and I am attracted to others equally manly, but our desire is for ourselves and for others like ourselves.

Despite significant social and legal advances in the rights of gay men in Canada, the chatter and doubt about what it means to be a 'real man' continues. An anonymous columnist in the *Globe and Mail*, lampooning the television program *Battle of the Blades*, suggests Toller Cranston and Sean Avery would make a great duo. This is funny because it pairs a now openly gay, very 'artistic', and tie-dyed figure skater from the seventies with a current NHL hockey player who has been adored and ridiculed in the media because he professes an interest in fashion and design, but who as a hockey player fights on the ice and off with his fists and his mouth. Avery acknowledges that he likes to dress up, liked to play with dolls, and has lots of gay friends. Known as 'the most hated man in hockey' by his peers, this Canadian player with the New York Rangers is an agitator with an attitude who did an internship as an editor with *Vogue*, a hunk and a hitter who loves Armani and wears scarves and paints his fingernails black. Is this the new look of Canadian masculinity in the twenty-first century (Paumgarten, 2008)?

Many examples, once they have retired, of 'straight'-acting or 'passing' men who turn out to be gay exist in the world of sport. In Canada, Mark Tewksbury, an Olympic gold medallist swimmer at the 1992 Barcelona games, is one of Canada's most famous. In 1999 he told his story: having fallen in love with the high school quarterback, he was labelled a fag and took solace in swimming and contemplated suicide. It took him many years to realize that his homosexuality and his public image as a national sports hero need not be mutually exclusive and could be reconciled in his own reclaimed and heroic definition of Canadian masculine identity. This coming-out process continues. The 2010 Olympics in Vancouver featured for the first time 'Pride Houses' at both Whistler and in downtown Vancouver, designated as welcoming spaces for gay and lesbian athletes, coaches, fans, and allies. Tewksbury was the official host of numerous events at the Pride Houses, which were sponsored by high-profile corporate sponsors including hotels, airlines, and car and beer companies, as well as community-based organizations (www.pride-house.ca). In 2010 at the Olympics, Canadian society embraced sexual difference as a new norm.

It's a Sporting Life

In late 2009, Brian Burke, president and general manager of the Toronto Maple Leafs and a man known for advocating violent approaches to the game of hockey, came out as the father of his gay son, Brendan, a student manager with a University of Ohio hockey team. The media frenzy that followed focused on the support that Burke extended to his son, whom he described as a 'leader and visionary' (Cox, 2009). How could such a 'tough guy' as Brian Burke support homosexuality? Burke the elder went so far as to say, 'I judge people on their talent . . . not their lifestyle, not their choices.' When asked if professional hockey was prepared for an openly gay player, Burke made it clear that 'the Toronto Maple Leafs are ready' ('Brian and Brendan Burke', 2009). Cynical bloggers were quick to note that the dismal performance of the Toronto Maple Leaf hockey team could only be helped by an infusion of gay players.

The tragic death of Brendan in a car accident in February 2010 revived the gay issue in the media. The hockey world presented a united front of solidarity in support of the gay kid who was killed and in support of the father who had stood beside him (Dellapina, 2010). Many would argue that definitions of Canadian masculinity were fundamentally changed by these events. The binary between macho and fag was forever blurred. The love of a father for his gay son served to override simplistic notions of masculinity.

Some would see this shift at the personal and human level as more important than any law or policy. When the Sidney Crosbys of this world can be openly gay, we will know that basic assumptions about Canadian masculinity will have changed fundamentally, because understandings of sexual orientation will be disengaged from gender constructions of what it means to be a 'real' man. This in turn demonstrates the need for an understanding of plurality and multiple identities. Beyond binaries, issues are complex, complicated, and full of ambiguity. One sports blogger pointed out, 'You should never assume a singularity to anyone's personality.' The former vice-president of the United States, arch-conservative Republican Dick Cheney, for example, is 'still an ass-hole' even though his daughter Mary is gay and he is in favour of gay rights ('Out of Left Field', 2010).

Is It Just about the Sequins?

However, the quarrelling isn't over; Canadian masculinity is still a highly contested project. The 2010 Olympics men's figure skating championship became another forum to discuss representations of masculinity. We're still worried, it seems, about sequins. Skate Canada, the governing body for figure skating in Canada, in 2009 initiated discussions to 'de-gay' figure skating by 'injecting some masculinity to draw in the hockey crowd' ('Canada Heads Effort to "De-Gay" Figure Skating', 2009). Elvis Stojko, a Canadian Olympic medallist figure skater, joined the debate by criticizing men's Olympic skating programs for not being macho enough in challenging the complexity and difficulty of required jumps. Stojko declared that he would prefer to be associated with a 'real' sport like hockey and not the 'sequined world' (and implicitly the faggy or femininized world) of men's figure skating. Stojko emphasized that the binary between feminine and masculine should be explicit and

It has nothing to do with your sexual preference [sic]. . . . It's all about what men's skating is—power and strength. Whether he's gay or straight, it doesn't matter. . . . If you're very lyrical and you're really feminine and soft, well, that's not men's skating. . . . Men's skating is power, strength, masculinity, focus, clarity of movement, interpretation of music (Buffery, 2009).

Queerly enough, many homosexual men would agree with him if they are attracted to that particular performance of masculinity.

Despite the tautology that masculinity is by definition what is not feminine, Stojko's target at the 2010 Olympics was US figure skater Johnny Weir, who, while coy about his sexual orientation, reminded us that our sexual partners should be a matter of personal intimacy and not public gossip. Weir is 'out' with his decision to design his own (cut away and sequinned) performance outfits and hopes to become a designer of his own line of clothing (Beker, 2010). Does this debate advance our understanding of Canadian masculinity or simply retrench the binaries by insisting that the 'faggy' elements of figure skating detract from an appropriate projection of masculinity? Commentators on the Quebec French-language version of TSN were forced to offer an apology of sorts after questioning the manhood of the lipstick-wearing Weir. Does such political correctness advance the cause of multiple masculinities or just drive the allegiance to macho hetero-masculinity underground? International Skating Union consultant Ted Barton defended Weir by arguing that skating 'doesn't discriminate based on sexuality'. Chris Rudge, president of the Canadian Olympic Committee, added, '[T]his kid is doing his own thing, and he has the right to interpret movement however he wants' (Sager, 2010).

This discourse occurred while the National Hockey League was trying (or not) to come to terms with excessive violence in hockey that has led to serious concussions and related brain injuries, which calls into question the contribution of violent 'play' to our understanding of 'real men' in Canadian society. As parents of hockey-playing boys (and girls) withdraw their children from hockey and enrol them in soccer, they are redefining the performance of gender for their children. And this is not without pushback from the hockey establishment. *Hockey Night in Canada* commentators Mike Milbury and Don Cherry described the move in the NHL to ban fighting as the 'pansification' of the game (Houston, 2009).

We also have to remember that definitions of gender and 'sexually appropriate behaviour' exist on a continuum between fluid rather than fixed definitions of masculinity and femininity. Pictures of the Canadian women's hockey team drinking beer and smoking cigars in celebration of their Olympic gold medal were flashed around the world. Immediately questions of appropriateness and propriety were raised as well as the issue of 'double standards'. Why did females adopt traditional male artefacts of success to celebrate their victory? If definitions of what women can or cannot 'do' change, then just as easily what men are 'allowed' to do can change. If women can play hockey and drink beer and smoke cigars, then surely men who figure skate can wear sequins.

The CTV series *Battle of the Blades* proved popular in Canada in the fall of 2009. This television program paired Canadian female figure skaters with retired, overweight, straight male hockey players, such as Tie Domi, who tried to be graceful and then admitted how difficult it was. Some would argue that this show, while apparently trivial, was another defining moment for Canadian masculinity: macho hockey players were engaged in the athleticism and elegance of figure skating, trying to ballroom dance on ice—and the audience loved it. I would argue that these guys helped to 'bend' gender by proving that 'real' (i.e., straight) men can engage in a highly suspect activity like figure skating and as a result broaden our understanding of what behaviours constitute masculinity in Canada, regardless of sexual orientation.

Crisis? What Crisis?

If this chapter does anything, then, it will help to destabilize fixed notions of masculinity: 'A hegemony of masculinity is established by the domination of one [form or performance] of masculinity over another' (Haywood and Mac an Ghaill, 2003: 9). Hegemony has been challenged, for example, by the complicated and contradictory 'Don't ask, don't tell' policy (regarding sexual orientation) for the US military promoted by former president Bill Clinton. In the first part of this century this policy was seen as a way of respecting individual soldiers' rights while not making gay rights an official policy of the American military. Yet in 2010 some American military leaders suggested that this accommodation, particularly in other countries such as Canada and the Netherlands, compromised the military mission in Afghanistan (Nurwisah, 2010). Contrast that with the reality in Canada: in 1992 sexual orientation as a reason for not being in the military was struck from the books. Today, same-sex partners in the Canadian Forces and the RCMP enjoy all the benefits, such as sick leave, maternity and paternity leave, and pensions, as their heterosexual comrades. Is the Canadian military less 'masculine' because it is less closeted than its American counterpart about same-sex relationships? If that were the case, then the argument would follow that 'straight' masculinity must be dependent, in the American context, on keeping homosexuality and same-sex relationships closeted.

The Internet is another arena where issues of sexuality and masculinity are scrutinized. In virtual realities such as *Second Life* and *Dragon Age Origins*, a role-playing video game, sexual identity can be 'forged' in the sense that a player can pretend to be whomever he wants to be. Anecdotally, I know that straight men take this

virtual reality as an opportunity to 'play' at being gay, vicariously exploring what it means to be the object of desire of another man. Some might argue that such a 'queering' of masculinity is merely fabricated, but I see this as a way for men to flirt with same-sex relationships without any of the physical or psychological dangers of real-life encounters at gay clubs or public washrooms. Queer life online can be simultaneously completely open and completely closeted. Does such 'play' compromise Canadian masculinity? I would suggest that this Internet exploration is more open and honest than any of the desperate booze- or drug-induced fondling that most men experience in high school or college as they experiment with expressions of sexual desire with their buddies.

Constructions of my identity and your identity are determined not just by who we think we are but also by the judicial, parliamentary, and educational systems that make the rules by which, and the context in which, we live. This identity continues to be contested. For example, the question of whether marriage commissioners in Saskatchewan, who are paid by the province, should have the right not to marry same-sex couples is part of this public policy debate (Pacholik, 2010). Another example is still before the courts in Alberta. It starts with an evangelical pastor in 2002 writing about 'the wicked homosexual machine'. A gay rights advocate took him to court for spreading hate against gays. But an Alberta court deemed that while these arguments were 'jarring, offensive, bewildering, puerile, nonsensical, and insulting', they were not 'hateful or extreme'. Once again the issue of freedom of speech and religion comes up against community standards. Mr Boisson, the pastor, had written that the gay agenda taught that it was okay for two men to kiss and accused gay activists of 'spreading their psychological disease' and likened people who support gays to pedophiles, drug dealers, and pimps (Brean, 2010).

The so-called crisis of masculinity referred to in other chapters of this book is a reflection of a wider crisis of late and post-modernity. Once-fixed concepts of identity are now conflicted, fragmented, and dislocated. We appreciate that identity is not only fluid but also completely dependent on context (cf. DiPiero, 2002, and the concept of heterosexual panic and hysteria). How culture, in beer commercials, for example, represents masculinity has always been dependent on gender 'markers'— usually of such things as whiteness and social class. This is how we understand that Canadian masculinity is an issue ultimately of the ideology of social representation. How each man 'measures up' to those representations is not about the individual; it is about the relationship of each of us to the constructs of power in our society. The gay couple in Malawi sentenced to 14 years in jail for 'unnatural acts and gross indecency' for holding an engagement party understand that only too well (York, 2010).

Social Change: Gay Marriage and Normativity

Scott Brison, the first openly gay and legally married member of the Liberal caucus, jokes that in his small hometown in Nova Scotia with a population of two hundred, a gay pride parade occurs whenever he and his partner walk together to the corner store. He went on, in his address to the 13th annual Breaking the Silence on Sexual and Gender Difference Conference (Saskatoon, 5 March 2010), to deprecate his own role in changing the culture of Canadian society. He reminded us that it is ordinary Canadians, in both rural and urban Canada, who have accepted new definitions of masculinity, ever since Trudeau in 1969 said that the state had no place in the bedrooms of the nation. Brison defers to others who preceded him, such as former NDP representative Svend Robinson, the first openly gay Member of Parliament, for paving the way to a world that accepts him and his same-sex marital partner.

Public figures such as Brison lend support to sexual- and gender-minority youth across Canada who hunger for connections beyond the narrowness and prejudice of their immediate family, school, and community. Brison also argues, in light of our ability to embrace this kind of diversity in Canada, that we have a leadership role to play on the world's stage, helping other countries to understand that accommodating same-sex relationships does not mean that definitions of masculinity are compromised. On the contrary: that Canadian masculinity is able to embrace 'the homosexual other' gives Canadian masculinity a more expansive, more generous, and more humane face. Such generosity provides a new definition, Scott Brison would argue, of Canadian masculinity (Brison, 2010).

I met the other day with a local Lutheran pastor with whom I work to organize Camp fYrefly, a residential summer camp to promote self-esteem and resiliency in queer kids who have been damaged by their experience of being different in small towns and on reserves across Saskatchewan. This is important work, funded by individuals who have experienced exclusion from the broad assumptions of hetero-normativity in Canada. Pastor Carla is worried about events in her own ministry. A married couple announced they are leaving her Lutheran congregation because they are unhappy with her 'pro-gay' stance. Such controversy in the highly contested field of faith and belief systems is not surprising. However, the couple, who happen to be first-generation immigrants of Chinese ancestry, have been contributing more than twenty thousand dollars a year to the operating budget of this church. Money doesn't talk, it swears, said Bob Dylan years ago. The church is now scrambling to put its finances in order and yet remain true to its belief in inclusivity and celebration of diversity, including LGBTTQ issues. Invited recently to a rural Lutheran high school, Pastor Carla was told by the high school counsellor that gays and lesbians are the devil's work.

Social change, as we have seen, then, does not happen without conflict and pushback.

A telling example from the political arena occurred in 2010, when Conservative Citizenship and Immigration Minister Jason Kenney blocked any reference to gay rights in a new study guide for immigrants applying for Canadian citizenship. Civil servants responsible for representing Canada to new Canadians had urged that the guide include sections noting that homosexuality was decriminalized in 1969, that the Charter of Rights and Freedoms forbids discrimination based on sexual orientation, and that same-sex marriage was legalized nationally in 2005. That this information has been omitted in the half-million copies of the new guide means that the government chooses not to send a positive message to the thousands of immigrants seeking shelter in a nation where homosexuality and same-sex relations are not only tolerated but also enshrined in law (*Globe and Mail*, 3 March 2010: A2). This omission provides little solace for prospective immigrants from countries such as Iran or Uganda where laws prohibiting and punishing homosexuality can lead to death. From this example, should we understand that traditional definitions of sexual identity and heteronormative masculinity are still being privileged in Canadian society? At the very least, wouldn't it be important for immigrants to know that sexual orientation and same-sex relationships are understood in quite a different way in this country than perhaps in their country of origin? Wouldn't such information help them to become better-informed citizens of Canada?

People Keep Changing, and So Do the Binaries

I meet with a fellow member of an arts organization over a glass of wine. John and I have adjacent lockers at the YMCA, where we are both fitness volunteers. He first asks if he can make a donation to Camp fYrefly because he knows how important it is for youth to come to terms with their sexual and gender identity. But, he says,

the real reason I want to talk to you is to tell you that as a 58-year-old man and after 35 years of marriage and raising two now adult children, I am coming out of the closet as a gay man. I have been living a double life for more than a decade and the hypocrisy is eating me up. I have known since I was a little kid that I have been sexually attracted to members of my own sex, but I have been in denial because if I was ever identified as gay, then my masculinity would be suspect. I now know that Canadian society has moved so quickly and is so positive about all of this, that I finally understand that my masculinity need not be compromised by my sexual attraction to men. In fact, this attraction actually makes me feel more masculine. I am a man and I love men.

Isn't John's admission a real definition of courageous masculinity? Forget for a moment the 'down-low' duplicity of his sexual relations with both in and out gay men just like him. Protected by law, the marriage of two gay men has become, it could be argued, a much lesser act of bravery than declaring that as a man your sexual attraction is to men and not to women, as John has done.

The concept of hero implies its opposite: the archetype of failure—unsuccessful at love or fortune—to which both homo- and hetero-mythologies ascribe. Archetypes of the spurned lover and the wounded hero have parallels in the straight and gay worlds. For both hetero- and homosexual men, the issue of shame and guilt, simply for being a man and by definition *lacking something* in relation to others, hinges in a neo-Freudian sense on a fear of psychological castration, that is, a fear of lack of power and control, particularly in relation to sexual, racial, gendered, and class-based issues (DiPiero, 2002; Lacan, 1977). So gay and straight men have that in common too. From this perspective such 'lack' defines the elusive essence of maleness, regardless of the particular object of any man's sexual desire.

In conclusion, this chapter has argued that the realities of gay life, enhanced by the laws in Canada, have allowed us to understand Canadian manhood not as uniform hegemony but as a 'fluidity of male behaviours' (Brittan, 1989: 2) and a 'plurality of masculinities' (Haywood and Mac an Ghaill, 2003: 20). One of the aims of this chapter has been not only to suggest that gay men have altered our understanding of Canadian masculinity, but also to show that in fact gay men embody masculinities in multiple ways. A sense of crisis regarding the performance of Canadian masculinity is tied to the rapid rate of social change over the past 40 years. Canadian masculinity has been bifurcated by narrow understandings of patriarchy. Elements of popular culture and social policy have begun to erode those binaries. This has served to liberate all men, regardless of their sexual orientation, from the 'prison of masculinity' (Baldwin, 1985/1954: 105). Masculinity and sexual orientation will always be contested fields. This chapter has attempted to disrupt the idea that masculinity is a rational and biological concept embedded in the natural order of things. It takes a real man to admit to being gay. Queer is just another form of masculinity.

Discussion Questions

1. We all experience some sense of difference and otherness in relation to the world around us. Can you remember a time from your childhood when you noticed that you were 'different' from others or that others were different from you? Do you now regard this difference as trivial or significant? Explain.
2. What memory is invoked in you by the phrase 'sex education'? Describe the situation and your reaction to it. Put into your own words the difference between your sex and your gender. Provide an example of the difference between your sexual orientation and your sexual behaviour.
3. This chapter asks you to position yourself in relation to the issue of sexual molestation. Examples of priests, a teacher, and a football general manager were used by means of illustration. Why do many people say this abuse is an issue of power and not of sex?
4. In this chapter there is a reference to 'the love that dares not speak its name'. Do a Google search to find out who said this and in what historical context.
5. In the nature vs nurture debate, how much do you think biology controls your destiny? How much does biology determine your sexuality? If a 'gay gene' is ever discovered, what might be some positive and negative consequences?
6. This chapter provides a number of examples of so-called failed masculinity. How many of them can you remember? Can you provide one of your own? Describe the 'norm' against which such failures are implicitly or explicitly measured?
7. Jen Gilbert is quoted as saying 'gender is work'. RuPaul says, 'We are born naked; after that everything is drag.' What do these writers mean and what are some implications for you and your peers?

8. Why do you think that so many people still refer to homosexual behaviour as a 'life-style choice'? If you self-identify as a heterosexual (that is, someone who is sexually attracted to the opposite sex), what is it about your sexuality that you have chosen?

9. Several other countries besides Canada are referred to in this chapter that have different attitudes and laws regarding homosexuality. Choose any country in the world and find out what their official and unofficial attitudes and sanctions are to same-sex relations.

10. The author concludes that heterosexual masculinity and homosexual masculinity share many of the same attributes. Indeed they may be more similar than they are different. What are these basic similarities? Explain why you agree or disagree with the author's point of view.

Recommended Websites

Bullying Canada: www.bullyingcanada.ca

Montreal Gazette: www.montrealgazette.com/news/Bullying+affects+gays+health+Study/4216993/story.html

Truth Wins Out: www.truthwinsout.org/blog/2010/11/12582

Queer Legal Resources: www.qrd.org/qrd/www/legal

Glow, the Queer and Questioning Community Centre: http://knowyourglow.ca/links

Gay–Straight Alliance Network: http://gsanetwork.org

The Feminist Blog Project: http://feministblogproject.blogspot.com/2009/12/queer-feminism-lgbt-blogs.html

Canadian Gay and Lesbian Chamber of Commerce: www.cglcc.ca

References

Allen, D.W. 2006. 'Making over Masculinity', *Genders Online*, www.genders.org/g44/g44_allen.html, accessed 25 March 2010.

'Ahmadinejad Claims Iran Has No Gays'. 2007. http://PinkNews.co.uk, 27 Sept., accessed 14 Dec. 2009.

'Archie Comics Unveils Gay Character'. 2010. http://today.msnbc.msn.com/id/36739351/ns/today-today_books/, 23 April.

Baldwin, J. 1985/1954. 'The Male Prison', in *The Price of the Ticket: Collected Non-fiction, 1948–1985*. New York: St. Martin's Press.

Beker, J. 2010. 'Olympian Johnny Weir Skates a Fine Line', *Globe and Mail*, 26 Feb., L5.

Brean, J. 2010. 'Judges Grapple with Canada's Legal Test for Hatred', *National Post*, 9 April, and *National Post*, 5 Dec. 2009, A7.

'Brian and Brendan Burke'. 2009. http://tsn.ca/story/print/?id=2999904, 25 Nov., accessed 11 Feb. 2010.

Brison, S. 2010. 'Not Easy Growing Up Gay in Small-Town Canada', *Globe and Mail*, 12 Feb., L4.

Brittan, A. 1989. *Masculinity and Power*. Oxford: Basil Blackwell.

Buffery, S. 2009. 'Elvis Stojko: If You're Very Lyrical . . . and Soft, Well That's NOT Men's Skating', 3 May, http://torontosun.com, accessed 1 Feb. 2010.

'Canada Heads Effort to "De-Gay" Figure Skating'. 2009, 13 May. http://slapupsidethehead.com, accessed 1 Feb. 2010.

Clowes, B., and D. Sonnier. 2005. 'Child Molestation by Homosexuals and Heterosexuals', http://catholic-culture.org/culture/library/view.cfm?recnum=6506, accessed 22 April 2010.

Cosh, C. 2010. 'Pardon Him?' www.macleans.ca, 13 April.

Cox, B. 2009. 'A Son's Secret, Brian Burke's Love', *Toronto Star*, 25 Nov.

Dellapina, J. 2010. 'Grieving Burke Arrives in Vancouver Ready to Lead', www.nhl.com, 15 Feb.

DiPiero, T. 2002. *White Men Aren't*. Durham, NC: Duke University Press.

Filax, G. 2006. *Queer Youth in the Province of the 'Severely Normal'*. Vancouver: University of British Columbia Press.

'Force of Nature'. 2010. *National Post*, 1 May, WP10.

'Forty Years Later . . .' 2009. *InfoEGALE: A Newsletter for EGALE Canada* (Summer): 1–2.

Gibson, P. 1989. *Report of the Secretary's Task Force on Youth Suicide*, vol. 3, *Gay Male and Lesbian Youth Suicide*. Washington, DC: US Department of Health and Human Services.

Gilbert, J. 2006. '"Let Us Say Yes to Who or What Turns Up": Education as Hospitality', *Journal of the Canadian Association of Curriculum Studies*, 4, 1: 25–34.

Gilbert, S. 2009. 'If That's What It Means to Be Gay, I Quit', *Globe and Mail*, 1 Dec.

Gill, R. 2007. *Gender and the Media*. Cambridge, UK: Polity Press.

Grace, A., and K. Wells. 2007. 'Everyone Performs, Everyone Has a Place: Camp fYrefly an Arts-Informed, Community-Based Education Work and Inquiry', in D. Clover and J. Stalker, eds., *The Arts and Social Justice: Re-crafting Adult Education and Community Cultural Leadership*. Leicester, UK: National Institute of Adult Continuing Education.

Hagen, D. 2004. 'Growing Up Outside the Gender Construct', in J. McNinch and J.M. Cronin, eds., *I Could Not Speak My Heart: Education and Social Justice for Gay and Lesbian Youth*. Regina: CPRC Press.

'Hanging Out (aka Is This a Date?)'. 2010. http://realjock.com/gayforums/862390, 19 March.

Halberstam, J. 2005. 'Shame and White Gay Masculinity', *Social Text* (Fall/Winter): 219–34.

Harris, S. 2009. 'Paedophile Fears Are Driving Male Teachers from Primary Schools', *The Free Library*, 25 Sept., http://thefreelibrary.com/(News)-a0208427072, accessed 11 April 2010.

'Hatred Motivated Attack on Gay Man'. 2010. *Globe and Mail*, 1 May, A12.

Haywood, C., and M. Mac an Ghaill. 2003. *Men and Masculinities: Theory, Research and Social Practice*. Buckingham, UK: Open University Press.

Hearn, J. 1987. *The Gender of Oppression*. Brighton, UK: Wheatsheaf Books.

Herek, G. 2006. 'Scapegoating Sexual Minorities', http://beyondhomophobia.com/blog/category/myths-stereo-types, accessed 8 April 2010.

Houston, W. 2009. 'Gay Rights Group Outraged by CBC's Use of Pansification', *Globe and Mail*, 28 Jan.

'How an Anti-gay Rally Pitted Uganda against the West'. 2010. *Globe and Mail*, 4 Jan., A9.

Janoff, D. 2005. *Pink Blood: Homophobic Violence in Canada*. Toronto: University of Toronto Press.

Khayatt, D. 1994. 'Surviving School as a Lesbian Student', *Gender and Education*, 6: 47–62.

Kivel, P. 1998. *Men's Work: How to Stop the Violence That Tears Our Lives Apart*. New York: Ballantine.

Kumashiro, K. 2004. *Against Common Sense: Teaching and Learning toward Social Justice*. New York: Routledge and Falmer.

Lacan, J. 1977. *Ecrits*. Trans. A. Sheridan. New York: Norton.

Mann, W.J. 2005. *All American Boy*. New York: Kensington Books.

McNinch, J. 2004. 'Playing by the Rules: Building a Rationale to Offer a Course on Schooling and Sexual Identities in a Faculty of Education', in J. McNinch and M. Cronin, eds., *I Could Not Speak My Heart: Education and Social Justice for Gay and Lesbian Youth*. Regina: CPRC Press.

———. 2007. 'Queering Seduction: Eros and the Erotic in the Construction of Gay Teacher Identity', *Journal of Men's Studies*, 15, 2: 197–215.

———. 2008. 'Queer Eye on Straight Youth: Homoerotics and Racial Violence in the Narrative Discourse of White Settler Masculinity', *Journal of LGBT Youth*, 5, 2: 87–107.

———. 2010. 'I Thought Pocahontas Was a Movie: Using Critical Discourse Analysis to Understand Race and Sex as Social Constructs', in C. Schick and J. McNinch, eds., *'I Thought Pocahontas Was a Movie': Perspectives on Race/Culture Binaries in Education and Service Professions*. Regina: CPRC Press.

Moore, P. 2004. *Beyond Shame: Reclaiming the Abandoned History of Radical Gay Sexuality*. Boston: Beacon Press.

Nurwisah, R. 2010. 'Retired US General Blames Gay Dutch Soldiers', *National Post*, 19 March.

'Opposite Sex Marriage'. 2009. *Globe and Mail*, 26 Dec., F5.

'Out of Left Field'. 2010. http://neatesager.blogspot.com/2009/11/what-some-reaction-to-brendan-burke.html, 14 Jan.

Pacholik, B. 2010. 'Many Want Say in Regina's Fight', *Regina Leader Post*, 15 Jan., accessed 23 March 2010.

Paumgarten, N. 2008. 'Puckhead', *New Yorker*, 28 April.

Pleck, J.H. 1983. *The Myth of Masculinity*. Cambridge, MA: MIT Press.

Plummer, K., ed. 1981. *The Making of the Modern Homosexual*. London: Hutchinson.

Pridehouse.ca/. 2010. 26 Feb.

Pronger, B. 1990. *The Arena of Masculinity: Sports, Homosexuality and the Meaning of Sex*. London: Gay Men's Press.

'Regina Teacher Charged with Sex Offenses'. 2010. http://cbc.ca/canada/saskatchewan/story/2010/04/14/sk-teacher-charges-1004.html, 14 April.

'Riders GM Pleads Guilty to Sexual Assault'. 2010. http://
    nationalpost.com/related/topics/index.html?subject
    =Eric+Tillman&type=Person, 5 Jan., accessed 6 Jan.
    2010.

RuPaul. 1996. *Letting It All Hang Out*. New York: Hyperion
    Books.

Rusnell, C. 2010. 'Lesbian Victim of Assault Says It
    Was a Hate Crime', http://cbc.ca/canada/edmonton/
    story/2010/04/21, 22 April.

Sager, N. 2010. 'Canadian Commentators Fail to Cool It
    with Johnny Weir Jokes', 20 Feb., http://sports.yahoo.
    com, accessed 20 Feb. 2010.

'Sex-Ed Change Needs Rethink'. 2010. http://cbc.ca/can-
    ada/toronto/story/2010/04/22/sex-ed.html, 22 April.

Sedgwick, E. Kosofsky. 1995. 'Shame and Performativity',
    in D. McWhirter, ed., *Henry James's New York Edition
    Prefaces*. Stanford, CA: Stanford University Press.

Somerville, M. 2007. 'If Same-Sex Marriage, Why Not
    Polygamy?', *Globe and Mail*, 11 Aug.

Steven and Chris. 2010. www.cbc.ca/stevenandchris,
    21 March.

Straight Acting.com 2010. 'About Us.' http://straight-
    acting.com, 20 March.

Timson, J. 'Lisps, Limp Wrists and the Last Refuge of the
    Bigot', *Globe and Mail*, 8 Sept. 2007, F7

Weeks, J. 1977. *Coming Out: Homosexual Politics in Britain
    from the Nineteenth Century to the Present*. London:
    Quartet Books.

Wells, K. 2006. *The Gay–Straight Student Alliance
    Handbook: A Comprehensive Resource for Canadian
    K–12 Teachers, Administrators, and School Counsellors*.
    Ottawa: Canadian Teachers' Federation.

York, G. 2010. 'Malawi Gay Couple Face 14 Years', *Globe
    and Mail*, 19 May, A4.

Yoshino, K. 2005. 'How Opponents of Gay Marriage
    Will Be Bored into Submission', *Village Voice*, http://
    villagevoice.com/2005-06-14/people/the-irresistible-
    banality-of-same-sex-marriage, 4 April.

CHAPTER 16

O ne of the central goals of this text is to consider whether and how there may exist a Canadian form of masculinity, or perhaps a series of masculinities. One key approach to determining this is to examine the experiences of men who migrate to and re-settle in Canada. This chapter discusses experiences faced by men as they acclimate to Canadian life.

Men and masculinities are often defined by questions of eminence, such as in the realm of work and economic productivity. As such, one key conflict faced by immigrant men is an experience of deskilling, whereby their credentials and type of work are defined one way in their home country and potentially differently (and with more onerous credentialling requirements or lower relative market value) in Canada. This is exacerbated by under- or unemployment. As well, family structures and the roles and rights of men, women, and children vary across countries and regions. Important debates about the rightness or wrongness of these varying paradigms, along with perceived and real differences, contribute to confusion, isolation, and conflict amongst a diverse range of gender identities.

Chapter 14 explored a range of masculinities represented in indigenous cultures that by definition pre-date colonization, and that continue to contend with the consequences even as they seek to preserve and assert their agency. This chapter will help to identify specific cultural elements of colonial modern Canadian masculinities by pointing to the intersections with immigrant ones. In each of these constellations we find stories of struggle and conflict that have substantial implications for individuals, communities, and Canada more generally.

Negotiating Migration, Destabilizing Masculine Identities

Gillian Creese

Nearly one in five residents of Canada, or more than six million people, are immigrants who report more than two hundred different countries of birth (Statistics Canada, 2007: 7–9). Immigration contributes to the cultural, ethnic, and racialized diversity of the population in numerous ways, including the production of multiple, often contested, gendered identities. This chapter explores how processes of migration to Canada can undermine immigrant men's sense of masculinity through common experiences of deskilling, underemployment, and new expectations about parenting and gender relations between spouses.[1] Drawing on research with migrants in metro Vancouver who came from diverse countries in sub-Saharan Africa, this chapter explores how and why men's identities as fathers and husbands, and their conceptions of masculinity, are destabilized in the Canadian context, and the multiple ways they negotiate new expectations in Canada.

African Immigrants, Racialization, and Masculinity

Gendered identities and practices are enacted within social and cultural contexts that vary across time and space. Men learn, adapt, resist, and redefine what it means to be masculine in the context of hegemonic conceptions of gender embedded in the cultural and historical milieus in which they live. Learning how to be a 'proper' son, brother, nephew, uncle, husband, father, or grandfather occurs through observing those around us and absorbing tacit lessons about broader gender relations and gender hierarchies. Masculinity is never static or monolithic; within a given cultural, spatial, and historical context, differences of class, ethnicity, racialization, age, and sexuality remain critical axes of power (Abdel-Shehid, 2005; Connell and Messerschmidt, 2005; Kimmel and Messner, 2007). Hegemonic meanings and practices of masculinity are invariably enacted by those who are located in privileged class positions, from dominant ethnic and racialized groups, middle-aged or older (depending on cultural context), and publicly aligned with heterosexuality (Connell, 2005; 1995; Connell and Messerschmidt, 2005). Most men who migrate to Canada from countries in sub-Saharan Africa experience a loss of privilege on some of these indices in comparison to their pre-migration lives. Migrants encounter different definitions and practices of masculinity that clash with cultural expectations, and they must negotiate new terrain to attain status as 'good men'. Some of the challenges African immigrants face, such as underemployment and downward class mobility, are common to most immigrants in Canada; other challenges are linked more specifically to processes of racialization and to competing cultural expectations that have particular meanings for those from sub-Saharan Africa.

Although peoples of African origin have lived in Canada since the seventeenth century, by the nineteenth century immigration policies had curtailed migration directly from Africa.

Significant migration from Africa only began to occur in the 1980s, and it constituted just over 10 per cent of all newcomers between 2001 and 2006 (Konadu-Agyemang and Takyi, 2006; Statistics Canada, 2007: 11). African immigrants form a 'new African diaspora' that is distinctive from other Canadians who have African descent but have never lived in the African continent (Konadu-Agyemang, Takyi, and Arthur, 2006). Although a relatively new diaspora, migrants from sub-Saharan Africa enter a 'social imaginary' in Canada where they 'are already constructed, imagined, and positioned' through hegemonic discourses of Blackness and practices of white privilege (Ibrahim, 1999: 253). Before coming to Canada, they 'had little need to explore the larger African identity and never knew they were Black' (Okeke-Iherjirika and Spitzer, 2005: 221). Once here, new subjectivities of 'Blackness' and 'Africanness', layered through existing national and ethnic identities, form in relation to contested notions of 'Canadianness' (Creese, 2011). Common-sense assumptions about 'Canadianness' are embedded in a white 'imagined community' that has historically been central to Canadian nation-building (Bannerji, 2000; Li, 2003; Mackey, 2002; Thobani, 2007).

Images of Black masculinity in North America are also refracted through narratives of 'African American pathology' that dominate American popular culture, in which Black men are simultaneously portrayed as 'weak' (unable or unwilling to support their families) and as prone to violence and criminality (Collins, 2005).[2] Popular forms of cultural resistance by African-American artists in hip-hop and rap music and videos contribute to these discourses of Black masculinity through glorification of street gangs and misogyny. Though these discourses have nothing to do with traditional notions of masculinity in African countries, they constitute, along with one-dimensional representations of sports stars, almost the only daily images of Black masculinity in North American popular culture, and they have a considerable impact on how African-Canadian youth 'learn to be Black' in Canada (Ibrahim, 1999; Kelly, 1998; 2004). For migrants from sub-Saharan Africa, these discourses about Black masculinity shape their racialized experiences in Canada and challenge models of how to be 'good men'.

Against the largely pejorative images of Black men prevalent in North American popular culture, most men in this research shared a more nostalgic conception of masculinity in their images of the 'ideal' heterosexual family in Africa. Across a range of African countries, in both matrilineal and patrilineal kinship systems, this 'ideal family' rests on perceptions of 'essential gender differences' between boys and girls, a sharp gender division of labour in households, masculine authority, respect for elders, and a nexus of extended families (Arthur, 2000; Matsuoka and Sorenson, 2001; Mianda, 2004). Migration to Canada destabilizes these assumptions about gender differences, gender relations within families, the division of labour in households, and spheres of male authority in ways that many men found difficult to negotiate.

The following discussion of migration and masculinity draws on a case study of African immigrants living in the metro Vancouver area. The study is based on interviews with 30 men and 31 women racialized as Black who migrated from 21 countries in sub-Saharan Africa.[3] There are no large concentrations of migrants from specific African nations living in Vancouver. The 'new African diaspora' as a whole is very small, constituting less than 1 per cent of the metro Vancouver population, living in a diverse multicultural metropolis in which 4 in 10 residents are immigrants, 4 in 10 identify as people of colour, and yet all people racialized as Black comprise less than 1 per cent of the population (Statistics Canada, 2006 Census; Statistics Canada, 2007; 2008). The specifics of place figure centrally in the re-creation of community and identity, and a common theme in interviews was to reference the

emergence of a local 'African community' (rather than local Somalian or Ghanaian communities, for example) (Creese, 2011). Masculine identities, expressed largely through reflections on paid work, spousal relations, and parenting in Canada, were saturated with expectations located in a pan-African discourse of the importance of authority and deference based on gender, age, and social class.

Class and Masculinity

Canadian immigration policy is designed to recruit immigrants who are highly educated and hence in privileged class locations in societies of the global South. However, once in Canada, immigrants routinely find they are unable to convert their previous education into expected jobs and incomes. A large body of research documents the growing wage gap between immigrant and non-immigrant Canadians (Aydemir and Skuterud, 2004; Frenette and Morissette, 2005; Picot and Sweetman, 2005) and racialized wage differences among immigrants and among the Canadian-born that disadvantage people of colour (Galabuzi, 2006; Pendakur and Pendakur, 2004; Tran, 2004). Barriers created by employers' demands for Canadian education and Canadian experience, compounded by the routine denigration of African English accents, constitute a systematic process of deskilling that results in downward class and occupational mobility for African immigrants in Canada (Creese, 2010; Creese and Wiebe, forthcoming).

Two-thirds of research participants had been in Canada for at least five years, and one-third for more than a decade, but their locations in the Canadian labour market remained marginal. Most were very highly educated: two-thirds had a university degree and another 16 per cent had a college or technical diploma, for a total of 83 per cent with post-secondary education. Most had received their post-secondary education prior to migration, but one-third pursued additional education after settling in

Canada.[4] In spite of these educational qualifications, downward mobility was the norm. Over half (53 per cent) of the men were employed in professional and managerial jobs in Africa; in Canada only 10 per cent were so employed. In contrast, only 3 per cent were employed in blue-collar labour in Africa; in Canada 55 per cent of African men worked in manual labour. Overall, 77 per cent of men had experienced downward occupational mobility; 18 per cent stayed at roughly the same occupation level; and only one man with a Canadian graduate degree experienced upward career mobility. Those who stayed at the same level can be divided into two groups: a few were in low-skilled jobs both in Africa and in Canada, and others completed Canadian graduate degrees in order to re-enter their previous professional fields.

With 'foreign' credentials and experience unrecognized, most African men found employment in unskilled blue-collar labour. These jobs were often short-term, part-time, and low wage, with frequent bouts of unemployment. Such jobs were routinely described as 'survival jobs' by research participants, providing little more than meagre financial rewards and making it difficult to support a family and build a promising future (Creese and Wiebe, forthcoming). For example, Furaha, an unemployed Sudanese veterinarian, described going from 'one job to another . . . trying to collect some money' (Interview M44). A Malawian with a post-graduate degree from an eastern European university, Culibali explained that 'despite my education, I was sweeping just to earn a living' (Interview M36). Banda was an accountant from Mozambique working as a security guard, forced 'to do any type of job in order to survive' (Interview M60). And Mimi, a politician in his country of origin, described himself as 'a simple worker. The one I am doing now is just to survive' (Interview M59). Yalala, who worked 'odd jobs' but had a degree in business administration and was once CEO of a large company, reflected on the stark contrast between his employment opportunities in Nigeria and Canada:

Yalala: The type of job we get here is the type in Nigeria you get people to come and do for you. You even beg them and give them free food and drink before they can do it for you. Those are the type of jobs we are getting, so that one is completely out of proportion. You don't get the job that require your qualification here; you just work to pay rent and to survive (Interview M45).

Before migration, almost all African men in this study enjoyed middle- or upper-class lives and experienced the trappings of middle-class masculinity that brought status and respect: high educational attainment, responsible and respected jobs, and relative affluence. All this was stripped away as they were deskilled in the Canadian labour market, undermining their ability to accomplish middle-class masculine expectations through high status or personally rewarding careers, or the ability to provide expected financial resources for their families. Poverty and its associated hardships were one significant effect of deskilling. The scarcity of financial resources, and the need to support one's family in whatever ways possible, in turn made it difficult for most men to chart a different course by reinvesting in additional Canadian education to improve their job prospects. Thus, even after a decade in Canada, most research participants were stuck in precarious low-wage employment with little hope of betterment.

Loss of social status and, with it, a respected place in the broader community were equally important outcomes of deskilling. Men whose identities were embedded in middle-class privilege in Africa found themselves thrust toward the bottom of the social structure in ways that, as Yalala pointed out, they had previously believed were reserved for the most ill-educated and poorest of their countrymen. With restricted opportunities in the labour market and low social status attached to their work in Canada, and in the context of pejorative discourses of

Black masculinity that further undermined African men's social standing in the wider society, most sought reaffirmation of identities through idealized notions of husbands and fathers in African family systems. These conceptions of masculinity were embedded in traditions of respect for elders and the unquestioned authority of husbands and fathers. When these too were challenged, some men redefined new forms of masculinity that better fit Canadian realities, while others sought ways to recreate idealized African traditions within Canada.

Redefining Gender Relations

Research on gender relations among the new African diaspora in North America suggests that gender is destabilized in complex ways. For example, Arthur's study of African immigrants in the United States concludes that gender relations are a source of considerable tension but are 'generally more egalitarian [in the United States] than it would be in Africa' (2000: 119). Matsuoka and Sorenson's study of Eritreans, Ethiopians, and Oromos in Toronto found the household was 'a gendered location for negotiating identity' (2001: 142). New anxieties, as well as new freedom from the gaze of in-laws, resulted from the loss of extended family or traditional community support, creating new models of femininity that threatened male control. Mianda's (2004) study of African immigrant women in Toronto and Montreal, and Donkor's (2005) study of Ghanaian women in Toronto, also emphasized how migration challenges gender norms with the intensification of domestic tasks leading to redistribution of domestic work in some households and increased conflict in others. And Manuh's study of Ghanaians in Toronto concluded that women identify Canada as a site of increased rights and domestic equality, while men see Ghana as the preferred space, where relations with women 'flowed in a stable, predictable order' (2003: 153).

Redefining gendered identities and practices in the new African diaspora in Vancouver was an uneven and multifaceted process embedded simultaneously in dislocations of class and culture and in new material realities and institutional contexts. Prior to migrating, family life in Africa was buffered by middle-class affluence, extended kin networks that played central roles in socializing offspring and providing childcare and other domestic support, and familiar cultural and institutional practices that shored up masculine authority. The transition to Canada meant the loss of extended kin nearby and isolation in the conjugal family unit. For most research participants, low incomes also limited their ability to purchase domestic support and childcare. In addition, unfamiliar cultural and institutional practices emphasized the individual rights of family members, in particular women and children, in ways that challenged male authority.

Migration greatly intensified women's domestic work. Like other Canadians, two-income earners are the norm in dual-parent households from sub-Saharan Africa, so women in this study were also employed, mostly in low-wage white-collar jobs. In itself women working for pay did not destabilize African notions of masculinity; women in this study were just as likely to work for pay in their countries of origin before coming to Canada.[5] However, the precarious nature of much employment could undermine notions of a dominant male breadwinner at times when wives might be the only breadwinner, or over time as more women than men attained Canadian educational qualifications that enhanced their job prospects relative to their spouses.[6]

Equally important, as exhausted women tired of doing all the childcare and domestic work on top of their paid jobs, men faced significant pressures to take on some of these responsibilities. An unbalanced gender division of labour is common in most Canadian households, with a recent Statistics Canada study reporting that in dual-earner households with children, women performed 1.6 additional hours of domestic work each day compared to male partners (2006: 37). African women in this study faced an even sharper gender division of labour, as well as a larger volume of work linked to processes of settlement. Immigrant women are typically the central emotional supporters, cultural transmitters, and chief mediators of unfamiliar institutional practices, for example, negotiating their children's schooling, health care needs for family members, and unfamiliar routines for shopping (Creese, Dyck, and McLaren, 2009; Das Gupta, 1995).

Pressures to renegotiate the gender division of labour in the household also implied redefining masculine and feminine identities so that women could forgo some responsibilities and still be respectable women and good wives, and men could take on some 'women's work' and still be good husbands and respectable men. The absence of extended family in Vancouver, lamented on many fronts, was acknowledged as key to redefining gender relations. Conjugal families were now constituted in private spaces outside the watchful eyes of extended kin, who tend to police gender conformity. For many women, this ability to redefine the gender division of labour was central to feelings of greater freedom. As Bara explained,

Bara: You know from the communities of, where I was born, when you are a married woman, especially married woman, the expectations are almost constricting or restraining. And there are things you cannot do because you are married, because of your in-laws here. You have to respect that but in a constraining way, not in a way liberating that you do that from your heart, or you don't do that from your heart out of the conviction or something. I get to experience what it is not to be expected to wash dishes if I cannot because of time or any other commitment. My husband will really almost raise his voice to say 'No, I am going to wash dishes.' He's going to wash dishes in other words, let me not worry

about that and many other pressures that women in our society back in Africa come across. Those pressures really are not there (Interview F30).

This was not an uncomplicated revisioning of being a 'good wife'. Some women questioned whether they would be criticized back home for being negligent wives who did not provide enough care for their husbands. And although renegotiating domestic tasks occurred in some households, women retained the overall responsibility of caring for their families, especially their children, which remained central to identities as wives and mothers. Arguably, easing some of the domestic workload could even make women better able to care for their families in other ways and so reaffirm their status as 'good' wife and mother.

Redefining masculinity such that men might routinely engage in some 'women's work' in the household, and indeed, over time, redefining domestic labour as ungendered work to be shared, was a more challenging matter. The privilege of not having to perform domestic tasks and to have others take care of you is a cultural expectation enjoyed by many men in many parts of the world, including Canada. Men from sub-Saharan Africa in this study had pressing reasons to hold on to this tradition of masculine privilege, but they also had good reasons to choose to redefine masculine identities in more equitable ways. The pressures to redefine masculinity were clear: the intensification of domestic labour in two-income families, without financial or community/kin resources to offset the workload, led to increased marital conflict. On the other hand, reasons to hold on to masculine privilege were also compelling: most men from sub-Saharan Africa had already lost their previous middle-class status in the workplace and in the broader society, leaving the home front the only place most could try to reclaim masculine authority.

Renegotiating gender relations in Canada implied shifting power within the family in ways that advantaged women. Not surprisingly, the majority of men in this study expressed considerable resistance to renegotiating power, be it sharing domestic labour or decreasing their direct authority over wives and children. Increased family conflict and the threat of divorce were one result of these tensions, an outcome many men attributed to women 'abandoning African traditions' in favour of Western views on marriage and gender relations. Portais and Kivete expressed this fairly common point of view:

> *Portais:* They want to adapt into the system of life of where they are and sometimes they forget their tradition. Just like, they forget the roles and that they must do their duties according. Sometimes they demand to do because they are now in Canada. . . . I find mostly women here, our spouses when we come here, most of them at the end of the day, our marriages doesn't last longer (Interview M34).
>
> *Kivete:* Back home if I shout the wife keeps quiet. She listens to what I say. But here, no. And it is going to worse. There are some, I have learnt there are so many marriages get divorce. They divorce. The wife says 'no'. Because they know, here they say women have their rights. So some women, they take their advantage (Interview M50).

As discussed more later in this chapter, attempts to transplant unchanged gendered practices from Africa to Canada not only critiqued women's redefinition of gender relations, including demands that their husbands adopt new forms of masculinity, it also targeted what was perceived as problematic discourses of individual rights and Canadian legal institutions that many men believed undermine family stability in Canada.

Although many African men sought to hold on to pre-migration conceptions of masculinity,

some men redefined themselves and took pride in their new-found expertise in domestic tasks. These men framed successful adaptation to life in Canada through new models of masculinity and femininity, re-visioning marriage as a partnership with a more flexible division of labour.

> *Mokili:* Spousal roles have changed and you have to do a lot of things that is expected of a husband here as opposed to things expected of husbands in Africa. I have adopted duties that I would not have adopted and I have relinquished duties that I should not have relinquished, but all that are because I came here a long time ago. And I got exposed to education that allowed me to adapt quickly and change (Interview M33).
>
> *Kalumbi:* Yeah, back home you can employ a housegirl. You can employ a cleaner. Here you cannot because you don't have, it cost too much. Yeah it cost too much. So here you have to do even the cleaning you know. So that is another thing that has changed when you come to this country. There is no job that you say that is job for a woman. If it means washing dishes, you wash them. So that also is a change since we came to Canada (Interview M32).

These men talked about performing a wide range of domestic tasks in Canada that they had never done before, such as cooking, cleaning, and childcare. How much work was redistributed varied in individual families, and many households in this study experienced little change. Those households that transformed the gendered division of domestic labour reaped unexpected rewards. New forms of masculinity not only redefined domestic work but also led to closer bonds between husbands and wives and fathers and children.

Redefining African masculinity was not linked only to performing new household chores; it was also connected to increased inter-dependence within conjugal households. Inter-dependence grew out of husbands' daily sharing of domestic labour and fathers' daily involvement in children's activities. For example, Kazi observed that more intensive relationships of fathers and offspring were produced through the different forms of parenting expected in Canada. In part this was a product of heightened perceptions of danger that made him a more vigilant father in Vancouver. In part it was linked to closer relationships with his children that came from paying more attention to what they did:

> *Kazi:* With children I am positive, is positive side. And I make more attention to them now than before, yeah. Because there are many, many things here. There are many TV channels maybe not for children. There are sexual abuses, many sexual abuses. There are drugs. There are many things, so I have to pay more attention to them than before (Interview M46).

Similarly, Kalumbi pointed out the importance of active parenting to help children navigate the local school system, a pressing concern since academic failure could have lifelong consequences for offspring:

> *Kalumbi:* If you are not careful you can lose your kids immediately if you're not educated on how the culture here is. Especially if you come with young children and you think that you will treat them the way you were doing in Africa. You are not helping them on homework. You are not being protective of them. You will either lose them academically, socially you will lose them, or they can even be at risk (Interview M32).

Thus greater levels of individual parental (rather than community) responsibility for children involved redefining expectations for 'good' mothers and fathers that brought new stresses and additional work and promised closer bonds with their children.

This reorientation of masculine identities focused on men's place within the conjugal family in Canada rather than men's place in broader kin and community networks in Africa. This transition was also facilitated by the absence of the kinds of public spaces for male collective leisure that many participants identified in Africa. Kasunga, for example, pointed out that in his native Nigeria, men had many opportunities to socialize without their wives and offspring. In Vancouver he was not part of a similar community of men that could divert his attention. Moreover, there were fewer inexpensive leisure venues to occupy his time away from his family. While many men lamented this loss of public space for male bonding, Kasunga also identified positive aspects:

> *Kasunga:* As spouse interacting more with your wife, there is a more culturality here. There are certain reasons here why you spent most of your time with your family and with your wife more at home here. . . . Having that kind of inclusiveness in the family brings a good family bonding of, as a spouse with your wife, as a father to your children, and then with a unified force. [*Mambo:* And some closeness?] Closeness, ok. Like back home, if a man is coming back from work, you serve your dinner. Dinner is served, you are going out from one meeting to another to meet your colleagues for one reason or the other. Other family issues take up your time. But here there is less place to go (Interview M38).

Some women in this research also pointed out that less access to leisure and male sociability, as well as more limited financial resources, enhanced husbands' marital fidelity in Canada, further strengthening bonds between spouses.

Parenting and Challenges to Authority

Conceptions about appropriate parenting are central to heterosexual gender identities. Migration can pose fundamental challenges to culturally bounded ideals of mothering and fathering as the ground shifts on which men and women learned appropriate parenting practices. Expectations about child-rearing may be harder to implement or at odds with new realities. New generational conflicts over appropriate behaviour emerge and are mediated through unfamiliar sets of institutional and cultural norms. Hence African men and women in this study experienced considerable dissonance between their experiences of parenting in Africa and the new circumstances encountered in Canada.

As noted above, the 'traditional' division of labour identified in African countries placed most responsibility for daily childrearing on mothers and extended female kin. Although many African men in Vancouver were more involved with child-rearing after migration, women continued to have primary responsibility. The context of migration posed fundamental challenges to conceptions of 'good' mothering and fathering practices. These pressures were particularly problematic for men because being a good father was so closely linked to authority over offspring, and this authority was fundamentally challenged in Canada. In contrast, pressures to adjust mothering practices, while significant, did not threaten women's overall sense of good mothering, which was defined less by authority and more by providing care and support for their children. Unlike men, women could redefine parenting strategies without undermining culturally embedded concepts of femininity and mothering. For men, new parenting strategies required fundamentally rethinking the core of masculinity as well.

African models of family revolve around extended kin, with the twin values of respect and obedience toward elders, particularly older men. Children are socialized to pay particular attention to the authority of fathers and uncles, as well as others in positions of authority. Migration to Canada disrupts the immediacy of extended family influences and authority in the socialization of children, and also undermines the unquestioned authority of fathers. As Twagira notes,

> *Twagira:* As Africans when you are a father in the family, you are like a big boss. You are having your way to say, when you say something in your family, everyone from mom, from kids, they understand dad has said this. But here it is not the case. . . . In Africa we are the chief of the family. Here, mom and kids they are the chief (Interview M55).

The decline of male authority is not so much linked to the shift from extended to conjugal family structures, though this plays some role in diminishing community authority over children, as it is a result of the distinct cultural and institutional context encountered in Canada.

The public school system in Canada constitutes a critical institution that helps to redefine relations within immigrant families. Schools teach much more than the formal curriculum of literacy, numeracy, and knowledge of diverse subjects. Schools also teach about Canadian values and norms in ways that are both implicit and explicit. One might argue that this is as it should be: in a context where immigrant children constitute a majority of pupils, as they do in metro Vancouver, teaching about life in Canada is surely an important component of the curriculum. However, we need to recognize the tensions created for groups whose values and norms are not represented or indeed may be actively undermined by the 'hidden curriculum'.

The hidden curriculum in Canadian schools reinforces values of individualism, personal freedom, equality, and self-expression (Henry et al., 1995).[7] In particular, it teaches models of interaction between children and adults that stress equality and individualism more than respect, deference, and authority. These sets of cultural norms are reinforced by other institutions, such as social services and family and criminal law, that produce a discourse of individual 'rights' and protections that police families. African-Canadian youngsters are more strongly influenced by the local culture than those who migrate as adults.[8] For African youth in North America these influences typically include immersion in African-American forms of popular culture such as hip-hop and rap music that revel in tropes of hypermasculine anti-establishment (Arthur, 2000; Ibrahim, 1999). In addition, socialization in the Canadian school system includes significant 'peer pressure to be cool' that can be overwhelming for adolescents (Matsuoka and Sorenson, 2001).

Not surprisingly, these influences combined to produce behaviour in children that often clashed with their parents' expectations. Most African men and women were very critical of their Canadian-raised offspring's behaviour when they failed to show appropriate respect or deference to their parents. Parents complained that their children sought too much independence, asserted their own opinions, talked back rather than listened to them, called adults by their first names, defied their instructions, and, for sons in particular, wore clothing associated with street gangs and disrespect for authority, which was common in rap and hip-hop videos. In short, parents complained that their children behaved like many other Canadian youngsters, in the process discarding African traditions in favour of less desirable elements of Canadian culture.

Parenting African-Canadian offspring involved clashes over culturally bounded expectations about behaviour and ongoing struggles over power and authority. For fathers, challenges to parental authority were yet another blow to pre-migration conceptions of masculinity and threatened a central basis upon which men had built their identities. Many men in this study responded to this challenge by trying

even harder to recreate African masculine identities in Vancouver, stressing the need to inculcate 'African traditions' of respect and authority as the only effective parenting strategy. These fathers argued that the discourse of individual rights encountered in schools and popular culture helped usurp their authority as fathers and thereby prevented proper rearing of offspring:

Fadela: In Africa we have the authority of the parents. The parents have the rights to educate the children, of course in a good way. But here the parents don't have the total dominion, total rights on the children. The children have also their own rights. So there is a kind of conflict between the authority of the parents and the children (Interview M37).

Bangila: What I don't like about families here is the fact that parents have been stripped of their rights, to right their kids. So taking those rights. And the shift is going from the parents to the kids. Now you have all these kids who have the freedom to do bad things and not the freedom to do good things for their parents (Interview M41).

The rights discourse explicitly taught in Vancouver public schools includes the rights of children vis-à-vis their parents. Schoolchildren are taught to dial the emergency code 911 if they are in any danger, including threat of physical assault by a parent. This is critical information all children need to have, but it became apparent in research interviews that threats to call 911 were a way for children to effectively undercut parental authority in general, not only in contexts of potential physical violence. This threat, combined with well-founded fear of coercive state scrutiny of African immigrant families, further tilted power relations between immigrant parents and children. Research participants, especially men, commonly asserted that proper disciplining of children was impossible in Canada:

Furaha: That is why, when you say study and you have to go to bed early because you have to go to school tomorrow. And they want to play Internet and then they say, 'If you say that I will call you 911.' Yeah, that is really different with us over there (Interview M44).

Kivete: You cannot discipline your child here. You discipline your child here, you enter into big trouble (Interview M50).

Many fathers argued that the rights discourse in schools and elsewhere thereby undermined their ability to pass African cultural values on to their children. Paradoxically, as Solola points out, a strong foundation in African values, rather than more individual freedom, could be the very thing needed to help youngsters navigate the perils of adolescence in Canada.

Solola: In the name of freedom I think we destroy, you know, attitudes. You know we destroy attitudes in children so that, that is why you find a lot of, you know, a lot of young people dropping out of school, taking the drugs (Interview M39).

Both men and women in this research believed their sons were particularly at risk of being 'lost' in Canada due to pervasive influences of African-American popular culture, peer pressure, the paucity of strong Black male role models, racism in the wider society, and rejection of their parents' teachings about appropriate models of masculinity. Hence both fathers' and sons' affirmation of 'proper' masculinity was seen to be in jeopardy.

Many African men in this research sought to reassert pre-migration conceptions of masculinity even in the face of significant domestic conflict between spouses (over the division of domestic labour) and between parents and children (over authority). Most men retained a strong orientation to their countries and communities of birth, where their status as 'good'

men remained unchallenged and may even have been enhanced through migration. Financial remittances were made to family in Africa, proving immigrant men's roles as extended family providers. Some research participants built houses in their home communities, either for relatives (usually parents) or for themselves in anticipation of retiring there at some point in the future. Still others raised money for schools and other development programs in their local communities, and hence retained an acknowledged political role in their communities of birth. A few research participants also sent their children to live with relatives in Africa for a period of time in an effort to more effectively instill African cultural values and tie the next generation more closely to their extended families. Many men also talked about organizing to build an African cultural centre in metro Vancouver that was envisioned as a space to better inculcate youth in the traditions and values of Africa. These were all important ways in which African men reaffirmed traditional notions of masculine identity in Vancouver that had been challenged in the process of migration.

A smaller number of men, and most of the women who participated in this research, sought instead to redefine masculinity by reorienting their gaze from Africa to Canada. Men's position in relation to extended kin and community 'back home' become less important for framing identity, and the immediate conjugal family and material context in Vancouver became central. These men tried to adapt to different institutional norms and practices by redefining household arrangements (such as sharing some domestic work) and adopting new child-rearing practices in the Canadian context. Hence some men and most of the women in this research identified new strategies to mediate cultural and generational clashes. These strategies included doing more things collectively as a family, striving for better lines of communication, actively monitoring homework, granting their children more autonomy in decision-making, and accepting (even if somewhat reluctantly) that youngsters raised in Canada can learn African cultural values and develop different models of masculinity and femininity relevant for the Canadian context.

Courouma, for example, observed that 'it is not possible to be here now for a couple of years and not have experienced changes in the way you deal with the children' (Interview M48). Unlike men who saw declining parental authority as failure as a father, Courouma believed that new forms of parenting were required under new circumstances. Definitions of 'good' parenting in Canada meant being more flexible, adopting a more child-centred focus, and identifying what would help children flourish in Canada in the long term. As one of the women in this project put it, 'I want to know, how am I going to raise him in this Canadian life? I don't want to change my culture, but at the same time there are things here in Canada that I have to fit in along with raising my son' (Silata, Interview F22). For the new African diaspora in Vancouver, as for many other immigrant parents, developing strategies that will accomplish both these goals can be challenging, all the more so when new parenting practices require rethinking the very essence of masculine identities.

Conclusion: Masculinity and Migration

Migration is a gendered process with different outcomes for men and women (Curran et al., 2006; Donato et al., 2006; Itzigsohn and Giorguli-Saucedo, 2005; Jones, 2008; Mahler and Pessar, 2006). Even women and men coming from the same cultural, racialized, and class backgrounds will face diverse circumstances in Canada as they enter a differently gendered labour market and civil society. It should come as no surprise, then, that increased conflict over appropriate gender relations is a common outcome of migration experiences. Gender relations, hierarchies, discourses, and identities are embedded in material, institutional,

cultural, and historical contexts; when these contexts change, pressures increase to redefine normative meanings of masculinity and femininity. New tensions also develop between generations, further unsettling gendered identities and practices.

This case study illustrates how masculinity among migrants from diverse countries in sub-Saharan Africa is profoundly unsettled through migration to Canada. The combination of downward class and occupational mobility, with its loss of economic resources and social status, is compounded by immersion in a 'social imaginary' in which pejorative discourses of Black masculinity further diminish social standing. In this context, most men in this research looked to the family as the only site in which they could recoup some of the authority and privilege previously enjoyed by well-educated, middle-class men in their countries of origin.

However, migration fundamentally affects gender relations within families as well, with different consequences for men and women. Without extended kin or the financial means to hire domestic help, the intensification of domestic labour and different forms of parenting required to successfully navigate institutions in Canadian civil society produced increased burdens on women. In turn, women pressured husbands to redefine the domestic division of labour. In doing so, women simultaneously redefined practices and discourses of femininity and masculinity. New institutional contexts, including the hidden curriculum of liberal individualist philosophy in schools and rights discourses in Canadian family and criminal law, further diminished the unquestioned authority of fathers.

Some African immigrant men renegotiated their masculine identities to accommodate and even celebrate taking on new domestic tasks in the household and adopting more hands-on parenting. These men discussed how they learned to accept more individual freedom of choice among offspring and, in essence, redefined marriage as a partnership in similar ways we heard from women in our research. For the majority of men we interviewed, however, migration to Canada so profoundly undermined their financial stability, class and social status, and masculine authority that they sought to reassert pre-migration conceptions of masculinity at home and maintained a stronger orientation to their countries of origin as critical touchstones to their value as 'good' men. Without mechanisms to integrate highly educated middle-class immigrants into more equitable positions in the Canadian labour market, significant challenges to masculine identities will remain central to migration experiences.

This process of destabilizing masculinity is linked less to specific cultural differences between Canada and other societies than to the difficulty of attaining economic or alternative forms of status and authority in Canada that are central to definitions of masculinity. Hence the process described here is not unique to those from countries in sub-Saharan Africa; instead, we should anticipate struggles to redefine gendered and generational identities and relations among recent immigrant families from diverse origins, as long as most experience significant and prolonged downward class and occupational mobility in Canada.

Discussion Questions

1. Think about migration experiences in your own family, or that of someone you know well. How did migration to Canada change their lives? Identify and explain different consequences for fathers and sons than for mothers and daughters.
2. Why does migration from one country to another lead to changes in gender roles within families? How do changing roles within the family affect ideas about masculinity and femininity?
3. Think about characteristics identified with 'performing' masculinity attached to different occupations, for example, factory workers compared to medical doctors. What do you think the consequences are for personal identity when a medical doctor in Uganda becomes a factory worker in Toronto?
4. Why is paid work so important for self-esteem and social status? Is it still more important for men, or is it equally important for women today?
5. What expectations have you grown up with about how to be a father? Are your expectations different than your parents' expectations? Are they different than your expectations about being a mother? Explain these differences.
6. How do different cultural expectations among groups in Canada shape ideas about how to be a good man? Is culture more or less important than differences of social class for defining models of masculinity?

Recommended Websites

Metropolis Canada: http://canada.metropolis.net

Metropolis BC: http://riim.metropolis.net

Statistics Canada: www.statcan.gc.ca/start-debut-eng.html

Canadian Census: www12.statcan.ca/census-recensement/index-eng.cfm

Notes

1. My thanks to all those who agreed to be interviewed for this study; to Edith Kambere and Mambo Masinda for their work as collaborators and research assistants on this project; to Brandy Wiebe for coding the interviews and helping to interpret patterns of 'survival employment'; and to the Social Sciences and Humanities Research Council for funding this research.

2. Collins points out that if African-American men are perceived as simultaneously too weak and too violent, women are characterized as too strong (domineering) and too promiscuous. In both cases the historical and contemporary contexts of slavery, institutionalized poverty, and ongoing racism are ignored.

3. Participants originated from 10 Commonwealth countries (Ghana, Kenya, Malawi, Nigeria, Sierra Leone, South Africa, Swaziland, Uganda, Zambia, and Zimbabwe), 7 countries in *la francophonie* (Burundi, Congo-Brazzaville, Democratic Republic of Congo, Guinea-Conakry, Rwanda, Senegal, and Togo), as well as Cape Verde, Ethiopia, Mozambique, and Sudan.

4. Ten per cent attained a Canadian bachelor's or master's degree, 17 per cent attained a Canadian college or technical diploma, and 7 per cent took additional university courses in Canada.

5. Most women in this study were also employed before migration, since they too were middle-class and relatively well educated (though not as highly educated as the men). However, prior to migration they had family and/or inexpensive paid domestic support to perform most of the domestic work in their households. Such support was unavailable in Vancouver.

6. Women were more disadvantaged in the labour market initially since, in a gendered labour market, they could get neither the blue-collar work men found (since few women are hired into these occupations) nor the lower-skilled white-collar jobs that are largely staffed by other women in Canada (because their English-language skills were unrecognized). The latter jobs typically required Canadian experience and a strong preference for local accents. As a result, two-thirds of women in this study pursued further education in Canada as a way to access the labour market and, in the long run, their employment prospects were somewhat better than their male counterparts (see Creese, 2011).

7. As Henry et al. (1995) demonstrate, Canadian schools also reinforce Eurocentrism and white middle-class privilege, influences that can have significant effects on African-Canadian youngsters.

8. Participants in this research identified as 'African' and 'African immigrant' but very seldom as 'Canadian' or 'African-Canadian'. In contrast, their children are more likely to adopt a dual identity as 'African-Canadians'. Hence the term 'African-Canadian' is used here only in reference to the children of research participants.

References

Abdel-Shehid, G. 2005. *Who Da Man? Black Masculinities and Sporting Cultures*. Toronto: Canadian Scholars' Press.

Arthur, J. 2000. *Invisible Sojourners: African Immigrant Diaspora in the United States*. Westport, CT: Praeger.

Aydemir, A., and M. Skuterud. 2004. 'Explaining the Deteriorating Entry Earnings of Canada's Immigrant Cohorts: 1966–2000', Statistics Canada Analytical Studies Branch Research Paper Series, Catalogue no. 11F0019MIE, No. 225, May 2004.

Bannerji, H. 2000. *The Dark Side of the Nation: Essays on Multiculturalism, Nationalism and Gender.* Toronto: Canadian Scholars' Press.

Collins, P. Hill. 2005. *Black Sexual Politics: African Americans, Gender, and the New Racism*. New York: Routledge.

Connell, R.W. 1995. *Masculinities*. Berkeley: University of California Press.

———. 2005. 'Change Among the Gatekeepers: Men, Masculinities, and Gender Equality in the Global Arena', *Signs: Journal of Women in Culture and Society*, 30, 31: 1801–25.

——— and J. Messerschmidt. 2005. 'Hegemonic Masculinity: Rethinking the Concept', *Gender and Society*, 19, 6: 829–59.

Creese, G. 2010. 'Erasing English Language Competency: African Migrants in Vancouver, Canada', *Journal of International Migration and Integration*, 11, 3: 295–313.

———. 2011. *The New African Diaspora in Vancouver: Migration, Exclusion and Belonging*. Toronto: University of Toronto Press.

———, I. Dyck, and A.T. McLaren. 2009. 'Gender, Generation and the "Immigrant family": Negotiating Migration Processes', in B. Fox, ed., *Family Patterns, Gender Relations*, 3d ed. Don Mills, ON: Oxford University Press.

———— and B. Wiebe. Forthcoming. 'Survival Employment: Gender and Deskilling among African Immigrants in Canada', *International Migration*.

Curran, S., S. Shafer, K. Donato, and F. Garip. 2006. 'Mapping Gender and Migration in Sociological Scholarship: Is It Segregation or Integration?', *International Migration Review*, 40, 1: 199–223.

Das Gupta, T. 1995. 'Families of Native Peoples, Immigrants, and People of Colour', in N. Mandell and A. Duffy, eds, *Canadian Families: Diversity, Conflict and Change*. Toronto: Harcourt Brace.

Donato, K., D. Gabaccia, J. Holdaway, M. Manalansan, and P. Pessar. 2006. 'A Glass Half Full? Gender in Migration Studies', *International Migration Review*, 40, 1: 3–26.

Donkor, M. 2005. 'Marching to the Tune: Colonization, Globalization, Immigration, and the Ghanaian Diaspora', *Africa Today*, 52, 1: 27–44.

Frenette, M., and R. Morissette. 2005. 'Will They Ever Converge? Earnings of Immigrant and Canadian-Born Workers over the Last Two Decades', *International Migration Review*, 39, 1: 228–58.

Galabuzi, G.-E. 2006. *Canada's Economic Apartheid: The Social Exclusion of Racialized Groups in the New Century*. Toronto: Canadian Scholars' Press.

Henry, F., C. Tator, W. Mattis, and T. Rees. 1995. *The Colour of Democrarcy: Racism in Canadian Society*. Toronto: Harcourt, Brace.

Ibrahim, A. 1999. 'Becoming Black: Rap and Hip-Hop, Race, Gender, Identity, and the Politics of ESL Learning', *TESOL Quarterly*, 33, 3: 349–69.

Itzigsohn, J., and S. Giorguli-Saucedo. 2005. 'Incorporation, Transnationalism, and Gender: Immigrant Incorporation and Transnational Participation as Gendered Process', *International Migration Review*, 39, 4: 895–920.

Jones, A. 2008. 'A Silent But Mighty River: The Costs of Women's Economic Migration', *Signs: Journal of Women in Culture and Society*, 33, 4: 761–9.

Kelly, J. 1998. *Under the Gaze: Learning to Be Black in White Society*. Halifax: Fernwood.

————. 2004. *Borrowed Identities*. New York: Peter Lang.

Kimmel, M., and M. Messner, eds. 2007. *Men's Lives*, 7th ed. Boston: Pearson Educational.

Konadu-Agyemang, K., and B. Takyi. 2006. 'An Overview of African Immigration to U.S. and Canada', in K. Konadu-Agyemang, B. Takyi, and J. Arthur, eds, *The New African Diaspora in North America*. Lanham, MD: Lexington Books.

———— and J. Arthur, eds. 2006. *The New African Diaspora in North America*. Lanham, MD: Lexington Books.

Li, P. 2003. *Destination Canada: Immigration Debates and Issues*. Don Mills, ON: Oxford University Press.

Mackey, E. 2002. *The House of Difference: Cultural Politics and National Identity in Canada*. Toronto: University of Toronto Press.

Mahler, S., and P. Pessar. 2006. 'Gender Matters: Ethnographers Bring Gender from the Periphery toward the Core of Migration Studies', *International Migration Review*, 40, 1: 27–63.

Manuh, T. 2003. '"Efie" or the Meanings of "Home" among Female and Male Ghanaian Migrants in Toronto, Canada and Returned Migrants to Ghana', in K. Koser, ed., *New African Diasporas*. London: Routledge.

Matsuoka, A., and J. Sorenson. 2001. *Ghosts and Shadows: Construction of Identity and Community in an African Diaspora*. Toronto: University of Toronto Press.

Mianda, G. 2004. 'Sisterhood versus Discrimination: Being a Black African Francophone Immigrant Woman in Montreal and Toronto', in M. Epp, F. Iacovetta, and F. Swyripa, eds, *Sisters or Strangers? Immigrant, Ethnic, and Racialized Women in Canadian History*. Toronto: University of Toronto Press.

Okeke-Iherjirika, P., and D. Spitzer. 2005. 'In Search of Identity: Intergenerational Experiences of African Youth in a Canadian Context', in W. Tettey and K. Puplampu, eds, *The African Diaspora in Canada: Negotiating Identity and Belonging*. Calgary: University of Calgary Press.

Pendukar, K., and R. Pendakur. 2004. 'Colour My World: Has the Majority–Minority Earnings Gap Changed Over Time?', Vancouver Centre of Excellence Research on Immigration and Integration in the Metropolis, Working Paper Series, No. 04-11, May 2004.

Picot, G., and A. Sweetman. 2005. 'The Deteriorating Economic Welfare of immigrants and Possible Causes: Update 2005', Statistics Canada Analytical Studies Branch Research Paper Series, Catalogue no. 11F0019MIE, No. 262, June 2005.

Statistics Canada. 2006. *General Social Survey on Time Use: Overview of the Time Use of Canadians, 2005*. July. Ottawa: Minister of Industry.

————. 2006 Census. 'Community Profiles', www12. statcan.ca/census-recensement/2006/dp-pd/ prof/92-591/index.cfm?Lang=E; 'Special Interest Profiles', www.statcan.gc.ca/bsolc/olc-cel/olc-cel? catno=97-564-XCB&lang=eng.

————. 2007. 'Immigration in Canada: A Portrait of the Foreign-Born Population, 2006 Census'. Dec. Catalogue no. 97-557-XIE.

————. 2008. 'Canada's Ethnocultural Mosaic, 2006 Census'. Catalogue no. 97-562-X. April.

Thobani, S. 2007. *Exalted Subjects: Studies in the Making of Race and Nation in Canada*. Toronto: University of Toronto Press.

Tran, K. 2004. 'Visible Minorities in the Labour Force: 20 Years of Change', *Canadian Social Trends*, 73, (Summer): 7–11.

Conclusion

Is There a Canadian Masculinity?

Jason A. Laker

As this is the last chapter of the text, it seems fitting to take stock of whether and to what extent the purpose of the text has been fulfilled. Its title, *Canadian Perspectives on Men and Masculinities*, implies at least three things. First, it suggests there is a perspective—or set of perspectives—that could substantively be described as Canadian. Second, the particular viewpoints are on the subject of men. And finally, there is no singular masculinity, but rather a cluster of masculinities in human lived experiences, and by extension there may be a set of them occurring uniquely in Canada. I confess that I am not sure whether these assertions are true or if they are, whether they can be 'proven' empirically. Having acknowledged this, I have come to believe that they are true and consequential, and I will explain why. But I will say from the outset that I have caveats which will probably lead my ultimate answer to really be 'well . . . kinda sorta . . .' In turn, I invite you to come to your own conclusions and determine whether you should act on them.

In my teaching, it is important to me to build students' capacities to utilize the conceptual and theoretical tools developed in the discipline in which we are situated. I use the metaphor of eyeglasses in order to affirm the notion that theories and models can be lenses through which to examine text, media, and lived phenomena. Generally, I ask students whether they are familiar with games and contests in which participants hold a game piece behind a coloured plastic film that allows them to view hidden messages that are clues or that tell them if/what they have won in the game. Another example would be 3-D glasses, which obviously allow the viewer to see elements of a picture sticking out from the background. In this way, I think theories and models allow us to temporarily bring certain elements to the front and push others to the back. The value of this is that the items are often switching their usual positions and thus are more clearly visible for direct study or understanding. It is also important to me not to insist that students adopt a position, whether politically or otherwise. This does not suggest that I or the other authors in this text do not have positions on the issues. Indeed we do, and many of these are passionately held. Given the interdisciplinary nature of this collection of chapters, I was struck by the consensus among them about many of these issues. Part of the explanation of course is that they were invited or self-selected into the work. But I would argue that this does not fully explain the ways and extent to which there is agreement about what may be Canadian, what masculinities are, how we make meaning of them, what the consequences are or may be, and what to do about it.

In order to explain further and to deal with the big questions of this book and chapter, I need to use another analogy. Please bear with me if you find this silly, but in any case most people will have heard of or participated in conversations that deal with the possible existence of Bigfoot, extraterrestrial beings, or the Loch Ness monster. Of course, there is a continuum of beliefs about them. Some believe not only that one or another of them exists but that they have had a direct encounter. Others believe the whole thing is a hoax or delusional. In between are people who say they don't know, don't care, and/or that the truth is inconsequential in any case. There is also variation in terms of willingness to engage in discussions about them regardless of their personal beliefs. Some find it fun or interesting to think about these questions and some find it annoying or even counterproductive—that raising them as topics legitimizes them, and this shouldn't happen. Some believe it is critically important to talk about them while others believe just as strongly that they shouldn't be discussed, perhaps because they can be scary, uncomfortable, or hurtful for themselves or others. I have found all of this to be true of gender as well, especially in terms of men and masculinities. To some extent, I have also found this to be true of discussing Canadian identity as such. Because people have beliefs and experiences across positions, the topics are politically loaded and could be rife with conflict. It has been my observation that definitions of masculinity and Canadian identity exist along a bell curve, which suggests not only a diverse range of descriptions, but also that certain ones enjoy wider consensus and as such are more powerful. Often they are mythologized or given sacred or romantic status, which I would argue makes them even more forceful, and as such it becomes more transgressive to question or not support or adhere to them. It is this characteristic that I believe is at the root of most conflict around the issues, and which can interfere with potentially valuable critical reflection and needed change. This multiplicity of beliefs is linked to their concomitant diversity of lived experiences. That is, some people find the more common definitions of 'masculinity' or 'Canadian' to exclude or marginalize them, and this is experienced in diminishing ways or even violently so. Chapters in this text have described occurrences of rigid collective enforcement of socially constructed dominant definitions. In short, there can be and often are real consequences to differences in beliefs, and particularly to differences in ways of acting on those beliefs.

One of the great difficulties, and yet for me one of the most interesting aspects, of developing this text is that Canadian and masculine identities share another thing in common. Namely, they are both defined very often by what they aren't instead of what they are. In the case of Canadian identity, I am referring to the discourses around its being 'not American'. In the case of masculinity, I am referring to the discourses around its being 'not feminine'. These phenomena have been discussed in more detail elsewhere in this text. For the purposes of this chapter I will speak more to what they are or might be rather than the converse.

To do this, I return to the earlier analogy about Bigfoot, extraterrestrials, and the Loch Ness monster. Whether they exist or not, suffice it to say that they are simultaneously ubiquitous and elusive. Rumours, insinuations, and references are made to them in many quarters, but unequivocal assertions that they have been seen are fairly rare. Those rare moments tend to be captured in grainy photos instead of high-resolution images and are subject to reactions of dismissal out of hand; technical critique; attack on the character, motives, or sanity of the claimant; or minimization (e.g., you are making a bigger issue out of this than warranted), which utilizes social awkwardness and rebuke to discipline the speaker into silence. The critical reactions can be matter-of-fact, assertive, or even aggressive or violent. When I talk with my students about social identities, especially with regard to masculinities, I pose a fundamental question to keep in mind as they do their own analysis: who or what is served by this? In the case of 'Canadian' or 'masculine', who or what is served by the prevailing ideas about them? And this is connected in part to another question: who or what is harmed by this?

Like you, the reader, I have been weighing the assertions made by the authors in this text along with my own experiences, observations, and study. My conclusion is that there is a global hegemonic masculinity that is socially constructed and reproduced systematically, in large and/or loud ways as well as through mundane and/or virtually invisible ones. Authors in this text and elsewhere have used the term 'patriarchy' to denote this phenomenon. I find hegemonic masculinity to be like a chameleon, generally maintaining its fundamental form but fitting snugly into most any location by changing its appearance or staying very still in order to elude sight. I observe 'Canadian' as an ethnicity of sorts, a congealed critical mass of predominately shared ideas about place and culture. Both are contested and negotiable, and indeed the idea of hegemony includes the naturalization and internalizing of definitions within and between people even as it expands and contracts through negotiation. I would further argue that those whose identities and/or expressions of identities are further away from the centre—the middle of the bell curve—are often more easily able to glimpse them directly. This isn't to suggest that they would assuredly notice. After all, it is hegemony's naturalization and internalization that maintain compliance amongst even those who are harmed by it. As well, this is not to say that those who are close to the centre can't ever see it. Some may see it quite well but might possibly enjoy the benefits too much to contemplate changing it.

So in my view it's not so much that there is a 'Canadian masculinity' per se, but rather that the two are intersectional identities. The locations described in this book—families, faiths, media, literature, among others—are the places where snapshots have been taken and displayed for you as a way of asserting and describing ways in which the metaphorical chameleon of masculinity operates in Canada, and how dominant ideas about Canada provide a hospitable environment for it.

Serendipity

On 17 July 2010 I was relaxing at my kitchen table reading the *Kingston Whig-Standard*, the local newspaper. This text was far from my mind, displaced by such pressing concerns as ensuring my coffee had the proper amounts of milk, sugar, and heat to allow me to remain seated and enjoy this weekend ritual. As I was browsing, I came upon a particularly nice photo of Queen Elizabeth II, holding a bouquet of flowers, smiling, and waving a white-gloved hand. The caption indicated the photo was taken upon her arrival in Winnipeg for a visit to the Forks earlier in the month, and directed the reader to the opinion piece below, in which Senator Hugh Segal wrote 'that the Queen's visit reminds us all about the roots of civility deepened by Canada having evolved our democracy with the Crown.'

As a relative newcomer to Canada, and as someone born and raised in the United States, I have always found the monarchy generally and the Queen and her family particularly interesting simply as cultural phenomena. I never developed any opinion about the relative pros and cons of the arrangement, nor did I aspire to, since I felt that it wasn't my place. Rather, I had been drawn to documentary stories about their history and lives with a face-value appreciation for an interesting collection of people and situations and their influence on Britain and other Commonwealth nations such as Canada. This said, I was struck by the caption as well as the opinion piece's headline, 'Progress Depends on Civility' (Segal, 2010). The article begins with the sentence 'The successful visit of Her Majesty reminds us that the ultimate centre of Canadian patriotism is surrounded by concentric circles of immense power.'

The subject of power can become quite fraught and provocative when considered in relation to identity, particularly when this is done critically, as the authors in this text have done. Indeed, several of the authors have been subjected to fierce public criticism in the media and the blogosphere for their work in this regard, and the publication of this text could activate more of the same. Senator Segal's column connects identity and power, but in a manner that enjoys wide favour. In the United States, the phrase, 'motherhood and apple pie' is used to describe certain topics and approaches to them. As an adjective, the expression refers to issues about which there is broad consensus that they are fundamental, universal, and unimpeachable. While the monarchy may not completely enjoy such a position, Her Majesty tends to personally. But in Canada even this is eclipsed by the notion of politeness, or in this case civility. Canada is defined internally and globally in such terms, and the senator claims and celebrates this when he says, 'The great intangible core at the centre of these powerful circles of virtue and decency is civility and the central belief that for all our modest inadequacies, disagreements, and weaknesses, the way our immense strengths interplay with the unique qualities and sensibilities of Canada and Canadians produces a brand and depth of civility unique in countless measures to Canada.' It is interesting that the article begins by noting circles of 'immense power' and this later morphs into 'powerful circles of virtue and decency', thus conflating particular forms of power with righteousness and securing it by insisting that patriotism, Canadian identity, and civility (e.g., tolerance and respectfulness) are inextricably linked. As such, anyone with objections—especially strenuously expressed ones—is at risk of being marginalized or excluded from Canadian identity, or at least kept at a distance by being suspect in this regard.

This is Canadian hegemony, complete with its unimpeachable centre and social policing of who's in and who's out by those closest to or who benefit most from its 'intangible' core. In this way, it shares a great deal with the hegemony of masculinity discussed in this text. Moreover, they share a social class dimension, serving as additional glue securing their position. Consider the term 'civility', which conjures up a refinement resulting from breeding. If America's politics are characterized by confrontation and aggression, Canada's are defined by genteel discourse, parliamentary procedure, and of course, monarchy and the Crown. What could be classier than that?

And so it became even more interesting to me that on the very same page was a lengthy letter to the editor denouncing a plan by Prime Minister Harper to sell off some federally held properties—lighthouses in particular—as part of his efforts to balance the budget (Miedema, 2010). In her letter, the writer poses the question, 'What could be more iconically Canadian than a lighthouse?' She describes how Canada possesses 68.5 per cent of the world's coastlines to amplify the relationship between lighthouses and Canada's maritime history. Having developed this connection, she says the plan is 'nothing short of selling off Granny's jewels to balance the family budget'. Here again, I do not take a position on lighthouses, but I am struck by the analogy she uses because of its implicit assumption that readers appreciate the sacredness of the objects about which she is concerned, that they resonate with the wealth and identity associated with the idea of family jewels, and thus will hold similar umbrage at the idea of even considering parting with them, even if it is to balance the budget. The consequence would be, in her words, 'No more breathtaking vistas. No more spectacular sunsets. No more wiling away a lazy summer afternoon lulled by the crescendo of cascading waves crashing on the rocks.' Since I do not personally own any jewels, nor have I the means or interest to experience the moments she describes, it is perhaps easier for me to wonder who exactly she is talking about. The recurring phenomena of ostensibly self-evident assertions in discourses of identity serve to weave a net so intricate that those interested in untangling them barely know where to begin.

This mystifying dynamic serves a purpose. To the extent that we are confused, afraid, and/or in conflict, we are not collectively interrogating and dismantling the metaphorical and actual structures that exclude, confine, and suffocate. The ultimate project in this regard is to recast Canadian and masculine identities in such a manner that the espoused values of inclusion and agency are fully realized.

The current arrangement is long-standing, but arguably unsustainable. The ways in which hegemonic forms of Canadian and masculine identities are socially constructed are much like pyramid schemes, continuously recruiting with the promise of big dividends in exchange for enrolling additional participants. People receive enticing benefits and exclusive deals in greater or lesser proportions based on their sales records. One needs only to keep the faith, to walk the walk, talk the talk, and not ask too many questions. Of course, not everyone is invited into the program, and many end up hurt or disappointed, but as long as enough people are receiving benefits and/or afraid of alternative possibilities, things are slow to change.

The authors have pointed to ways in which certain communities and people are affected by hegemonic identities, and how certain people benefit from them. It is common in such critical dialogues for readers to feel uncomfortable or even defensive as they wonder if we are asserting that Canada, Canadians, men, and/or masculinity are 'bad.' Before answering that, let me offer that this question is more complex than its face value suggests. As described earlier in this chapter and others in the text, the raising of critical questions is a violation of social convention. As such it is disruptive and tends to elicit discomfort and, often, anger. Behind anger is fear.

What is the fear about? It seems to me there are two overarching themes in this fear. For those who benefit from the hegemonic models of masculinity, Canadian identity, and/or other dimensions of identity, the fear is about loss of position and privilege. This may not be a conscious dynamic, since privilege can be and often is invisible, especially to those benefiting from it. For those who experience the hegemonic ideas and dynamics as suffocating, marginalizing, and/or violent, the fear is around whether there will be even more consequences for challenging the status quo, even if they are not personally doing it. In this case, the individuals and groups who have been oppressed

in the equation may experience disproportionate reprisal for being implicated in real or perceived ways in disruption and challenge.

I would suggest that social interactions that are compliant with hegemonic ideas, even if they can be harmful, are nonetheless efficient because of their familiarity. So, for instance, interpersonal dynamics which place men in dominant roles and women in subordinate ones can become habit for all parties concerned, creating a cost not only for sustaining them, but also for interrogating and changing them. To use another analogy, swimming upstream in a river takes more energy than does going with the flow. In the same analogy, those for whom hegemonic ideas are oppressive are taking the brunt of jagged rocks along the way, whereas those in the most privileged roles are floating along in a boat, well protected from harm's way.

Let's return to the fundamental question posed early in this chapter, 'Who or what is served by this?' When someone who raises a critical question is asked in turn whether he or she saying—in this case—that men or Canadian identity is bad, the problem is that this question redirects the focus from the object of critique (hegemonic masculinity or Canadian identity) back on the speaker, making that person suspect for raising the questions. This is a form of discipline that can consequently reify the hegemony through distraction and by delegitimizing the individuals raising the questions and their right to ask. This serves to protect the system of patriarchy and, by extension, the power derived from it. Systems are not people, but people must collude to sustain that system, and it is embedded with both rewards and consequences—carrots and sticks—to ensure that enough people keep it going.

The authors have talked about themes in masculine role construction that foster and sustain male dominance and rigidity of identity, and about themes in Canadian identity that enforce certain definitions of it. This is not the same thing as claiming that men, or Canadians for that matter, are inherently bad, or even that individual ones who enact the themes are necessarily doing a bad thing or harming anyone. Indeed, it is entirely possible and at times the case that good things are happening as a result. The proposal here is to make it safe and desirable for there to be questions raised, negotiations undertaken, concessions made, and flexibility ensured, so that more and maybe all can enjoy the dividends, and that no person or group consumes the lion's share of these benefits.

As more and different people come to Canada and the diversity of people already here becomes more visible and involved, it will be increasingly difficult to secure an inflexible hegemonic norm of national identity. The fundamental tensions between accommodation and assimilation will become more problematic and rancorous, threatening the ability to remain a nation defined by its politeness and civility (assuming that is seen as a desirable thing to maintain), and which has not yet fully realized its espoused belief in multiculturalism and inclusion. Similarly, as more and more men experience the liberation associated with expressing the full palette of human expression; are more connected to and take better care of their physical and mental health; and develop more authentic relationships with each other and with women, there will be fewer willing to maintain an archaic model of masculinity.

To be sure, both hegemonies are alive and enjoying a critical mass of stakeholder-beneficiaries who receive sufficient if not significant advantages, whether consciously or not. Hegemony is highly adaptive, as the chameleon analogy discussed earlier explained. Even things that appear to be progress can in fact be part and parcel. For instance, the proliferation of men's grooming products is supposedly illustrative of a new permission to nurture ourselves. I would argue otherwise, in that in addition to the obvious and enormous profit motive, it strengthens the imposition of superficial and unattainable beauty standards on everyone, and reinforces binary ideas of men and women, all of which have had colossal costs. Using a bit of moisturizer doesn't sound like evidence of a dangerous conspiracy, and in and of itself it isn't. But this is just the type of glimpse captured in the grainy photo I discussed earlier. The cosmetic item is not the monster but rather its footprint. You are invited to make a cast, document the sighting, confer with your peers, join the debate, and ultimately take an active role in deciding what role is right for you to play in determining the present state and future direction of masculinities, and of Canada.

References

Miedema, Y. 2010. 'Harper's Canada Apparently Doesn't Include Lighthouses', *Kingston Whig-Standard* (Kingston, Ontario), July 17, 5.

Segal, H. 2010. 'Progress Depends on Civility', *Kingston Whig-Standard* (Kingston, Ontario), 17 July, 5.

Suggestions for Further Reading

Abdel-Shehid, G. 2005. *Who Da Man?: Black Masculinities and Sporting Cultures.* Toronto: Canadian Scholars' Press.

Creese, G. 1999. *Contracting Masculinity: Gender, Class, and Race in a White-Collar Union, 1944–1994.* Toronto: University of Toronto Press.

Crichlow, W. 2004. *Buller Men and Batty Bwoys: Hidden Men in Toronto and Halifax Black Communities.* Toronto: University of Toronto Press.

Deslauriers, J.M., G. Tremblay, S. Genest-Dufault, D. Blanchette, and J.Y. Desgagnés. 2010. *Regards sur les homes et les masculinities: Comprende et intervener.* Quebec: Presses de l'Université Laval.

Dorais, M. 2008. *Ça arrive aussi aux garcons.* Montreal: Typo.

Doucet, A. 2006. *Do Men Mother?: Fathering, Care, and Domestic Responsibility.* Toronto: University of Toronto Press.

Dubeau, D., A. Devault, and G. Forget. 2009. *La paternité au XXIe siècle.* Quebec: Presses de l'Université Laval.

Dummitt, C. 2008. *Manly Modern: Masculinity in Postwar Canada.* Vancouver: University of British Columbia Press.

Forestell, N.M., K. McPherson, and C. Morgan. 2003. *Gendered Pasts: Historical Essays in Femininity and Masculinity in Canada.* Toronto: University of Toronto Press.

Hazan, M. 2010. *Le masculin.* Montreal: Québecor.

Kimmel, M.S., A. Aronson, and A. Kaler. 2011. *The Gendered Society Reader*, Cdn ed. Toronto: Oxford University Press.

Laker, J., and T. Davis. 2011. *Masculinities in Higher Education: Theoretical and Practical Considerations.* New York: Routledge.

Nonnekes, P. 2008. *Northern Love: An Exploration of Canadian Masculinity.* Edmonton: Athabasca University Press.

Robidoux, M. 2001. *Men at Play: A Working Understanding of Professional Hockey.* Montreal and Kingston: McGill-Queen's University Press.

Index

141; Irish and, 226; literature and, 97–8; masculinities and, 194–5, 232–6, 293–4; racism and, 135; *see also* masculinities, race and

Black Robe, 257, 258
Blainey, Justine, 5
Bliss, Michael, 167
blood quantum, 252
'bloodthirsty warrior', 255-60
Bly, Robert, 134
body: anxieties about, 38; gay masculinities and, 281–3; identity and, 15–16, 32–51; 'lived', 36, 45; masculine identity and, 32–51; as 'representation', 36–8, 45
body dysmorphic disorder, 38
Boily, Lisette, 98–9
Boisson, S., 285
Bonhomme, J.J., 34
Bourdieu, Pierre, 39, 45
bourgeoisie: masculinity and, 116–19
Bournival, Emily, *xvi*, 32–51
Boyd, S., et al., 207, 208
'boy panic/crisis', 8, 9; *see also* crisis of masculinity theory
boys: sexual abuse and, 271–3; *see also* children; youth
brain: gender and, 9–10
Bramadat, Paul, 209, 210, 214
Brant, Clare, 260
Brault, Michel, 158
Bridel, William, and Martyn Clark, *xvii*, 184–200
Bridges, T.S., 77
Brison, Scott, 286
Brittan, A., 21
Brodkin, Karen, 226
Brown, Kyle, 176
Brownmiller, Susan, 77
Bruce, H.A., 173
Buchignani, N., and D.M. Indra, 215
Buckler, Ernest, 94
bullying, 60–1, 270
Buma, Michael P., 94, 95, 107
Bunch, Ted, 75
Burke, Brian and Brendan, 283
Burstyn, V., 120
Bush, George W., 178
Butler, Judith, 103, 104, 127
Byers, Michele, 141

Calasanti, T., and N. King, 38
Camilleri, Anna, 102
Camp fYrefly, 281, 286, 287
Campbell, Colin, 7
Campbell, Maria, 254
Canada: Asian masculinities in, 236–8; Black masculinities in, 232–6; colonial, 116–19, 187–8; demographics of, 53; gay masculinities in, 275, 277, 281, 285, 286–7; identity and sport in, 184–200; immigration and, 292–4; 'leading men' in, 114–25;

masculinities in, 92–200, 307–12; men's narratives and, 59–64; as 'poor cousin', 166–7; racialized masculinities in, 222–3; racism in, 227–9; religion and masculinities in, 206–17; US and, 166, 180, 308
Canadian Corps, 169
Canadian Forces, 163, 180; *see also* military
Canadian National Survey of Woman Abuse in University/College Dating (CNS), 70, 81–2
Canadian Navy, 167, 179–80
'Canadianness': immigrants and, 293
Canadian Poetry Press, 98
cancer, prostate, 35
capitalism: Indigenous peoples and, 251, 254; masculinity and, 117
Cappon, Daniel, 8
Carle, Gilles, 158
Carr, P.R., and D.E. Lund, 228
Catholic Church, 210; sexual abuse and, 272; *see also* Christianity
Catlin, George, 257
Cayuga, 249, 250
censorship: *Degrassi* and, 141; pornography and, 83
Centre for Educational Research and Innovation, 9–10
Chamberlain, Neville, 178
Chamberlin, J. Edward, 244
Chambers, Michael, 192
Chanda, G.S., and Staci Ford, 215–16
Chariandy, David, 98
Charlesworth, S.J., 44
Charter of Rights and Freedoms, 277, 287
Cheney, Dick and Mary, 283
Cherry, Don, 6–7, 137–8, 164, 179, 190
chief (sachem), Indigenous, 249–51, 253, 257
children: bullying and, 60–1; forced labour and, 63; gay masculinities and, 270, 275; immigrants and, 299–303; Indigenous, 253–4; sexual abuse and, 271–3
Choquette, Robert, 209, 210
Chouinard, Normand, 159
Chrétien, Jean, 177, 178
'Christianities', 216–17
Christianity: Canada and, 209–10, 211; definition of religion and, 203; masculinities and, 202, 213–14, 216–17; muscular, 96–7, 208, 210, 211, 212–13
Christie, Nancy, 211–12
chromosomes, 127
Churchill, Winston, 172
civility, Canadian, 309–10
Civil Marriage Act, 277
clan mothers, 249–50
Clark, D.A.T., and J. Nagel, 256
Clarke, George Elliott, 95, 97–8, 99
class: Canadian masculinity and, 116–19; immigrants and, 293, 294–6; men's health and, 33–5, 39, 41–6
Clean Hotel Initiative, 83
Clements, Marie, 99, 100–1

Pollack, W.S., 19, 24–5
Pollock, Sharon, 99–100
polygamy, 278–9
Polytechnique, 159–60
Pon, G., 236
Poor Boy's Game, 136
popular culture: immigrants and, 293–4, 301, 302; Indigenous stereotypes and, 255–60; masculinities and, 128–39, 141–4
pornography, 80–5; educational use of, 82–3
Porter, Tom, 244, 248, 250, 261–4
Porter, Tony, 74–5
post-traumatic stress disorder, 62
power: civility and, 309–10; masculine relations of, 115–16, 121–4; men and women and, 14; naturalization of, 119
'Pride Houses', 283
prison experiment, 63
procreation: marriage and, 278–9
Promise Keepers, 207, 211
Pronger, Brian, 275
prorogation, 79
Protestantism, 210, 211
psychoanalytic theory, 13, 14, 18; help-seeking and, 57, 61
psychology: masculine identity and, 14
puberty, 19–20
Putney, Clifford, 210

Quebec: celebrities in, 155; discrimination in, 277; influences on culture in, 156; masculinities in, 13, 151–62; men's health in, 35–6, 41–5; religion in, 210, 212–13; suicide prevention in, 25
Quebec Nordiques, 189
Quebec Social and Health Survey, 22
'Queer CanLit', 102
'queering', 269; *see also* masculinities, queer

Raboy, M., 154
race: definition of, 223–7; masculinities and, 97–102, 105, 222–40; 'mixed', 223; sport and, 194–5; whiteness and, 186, 195
racialization, 222, 224–5; African immigrants and, 293–4; crime and, 233, 236; whiteness and, 225, 226–7
racial profiling, 236
racism: aversive, 228; cultural, 233; culture and, 135, 141; democratic, 229; diversity and, 228; gendered, 131; ideology of, 229; Indigenous peoples and, 131, 255, 259; multiculturalism and, 227–32, 238; pornography and, 80; race and, 224; symbolic, 228; systemic, 223; whiteness and, 225, 226–7; woman abuse and, 73
Radio-Canada, 154
Rak, Julie, 137–8
Ralston, James, 173

rape, 70–1, 73; film depiction of, 157–8; *see also* sexual abuse/assault
Raphael, Denis, 46
Rashid, Ian Iqbal, 98
Razak, S., 62
religion: definitions of, 203; dominance and gender and, 205–6; effeminate, 212; gay masculinities and, 285; male-identified, 206–7; masculinities and, 202–21; non-Christian, 214–16; women and, 204–6; *see also* Christianity; muscular Christianity; specific groups
Renzetti, C.M., 71
Report on the State of Public Health in Canada, 33
residential schools, 251, 253–4
responsibilities: masculine identity and, 25; self-, 41; traditional Indigenous, 241–2, 243, 251–5, 260
Rettberg, Jill Walker, 79–80
Reynolds, Quentin, 171
Rhéaume, Manon, 144
Richardson, John, 94
Rick Mercer Report, 60–1
Riel, Louis, 138–9, 169
rights: immigrant families and, 301–2
risk factors: health and gender and, 33, 40
risk-taking: health and, 40, 43
Roberts, Strother, 101
Robertson, S., et al., 35
Robidoux, Michael A., 114–25, 141, 187, 188
Robinson, Svend, 286
Roeg, Nicolas, 158
roles: traditional Indigenous, 241–2, 243, 251–5, 260; virtual, 285; *see also* gender roles
Ross, Rupert, 260
Ross, Sinclair, 102
rotiskenhrakete, 251
Roussel, Jean-François, 210, 211, 212–13
Roy, V., 14
Royal Canadian Regiment, 169, 171
Rudge, Chris, 284
RuPaul, 280
Russell, D.E.H., 82
Russell, Stephanie, 165
Russia, 38; *see also* Soviet Union
Rwanda, 61–2

Sabo, D., 40
sachem, 250, 251, 257
'salutogenic approach', 25
Samedi de rire, 159
Sanday, P.R., 81
Saskatchewan, 285
Satzewich, V., 225, 226
Sax, Leonard, 9
Sayer, A., 45
Scarborough, ON, 234–5